T0220777

Lecture Notes in Computer Science 12129

More information about this subseries at http://www.springer.com/series/7411

Chryssis Georgiou · Rupak Majumdar (Eds.)

Networked Systems

8th International Conference, NETYS 2020
Marrakech, Morocco, June 3–5, 2020
Proceedings

 Springer

Editors
Chryssis Georgiou
University of Cyprus
Nicosia, Cyprus

Rupak Majumdar
Max Planck Institute for Software Systems
Kaiserslautern, Germany

ISSN 0302-9743   ISSN 1611-3349   (electronic)
Lecture Notes in Computer Science
ISBN 978-3-030-67086-3   ISBN 978-3-030-67087-0   (eBook)
https://doi.org/10.1007/978-3-030-67087-0

LNCS Sublibrary: SL5 – Computer Communication Networks and Telecommunications

This Springer imprint is published by the registered company Springer Nature Switzerland AG
The registered company address is: Gewerbestrasse 11, 6330 Cham, Switzerland

Preface

This volume contains the papers presented at the 8th edition of the International Conference on NETworked sYStems (NETYS 2020). The conference was originally scheduled to be held in Marrakech, Morocco, between June 3 and 5, 2020. However, it moved to a fully virtual mode due to the Covid-19 pandemic.

The aim of the NETYS series of conferences is to bring together researchers and engineers from both the theory and practice of distributed and networked systems. The scope of the conference covers all aspects related to the design and the development of these systems, including, but not restricted to, concurrent and distributed algorithms, parallel/concurrent/distributed programming, multi-core architectures, formal verification, distributed databases, cloud systems, networks, security, formal verification, etc.

The Program Committee of NETYS 2020 included 38 researchers working in 16 different countries. There were 46 papers submitted to the conference, 38 as full papers, and 8 as short papers. The Program Committee selected 18 contributions out of the 38 full paper submissions for regular presentations at the conference (which represents an acceptance rate of 47%) as well as 4 extended abstracts for short presentations. Every submitted paper was read and evaluated by at least three members of the Program Committee. The committee was assisted by 14 external reviewers.

The program also included invited lectures, again hosted virtually, by C. Aiswarya, Chennai Mathematical Institute (India), Antonio Fernández Anta, IMDEA Networks Institute (Spain), Constantin Enea, University of Paris (France), Maria Potop-Butucaru, Sorbonne University (France), and Nitin Vaidya, Georgetown University (USA). In addition, C. Aiswarya, Antonio Fernández Anta and Maria Potop-Butucaru contributed invited papers.

The videos of all invited and contributed presentations can be viewed at: https://www.youtube.com/channel/UC3Y0phGAVVV_MyFbntZa0Ug/videos.

The program committee also selected a Best Paper and a Best Student Paper. The Best Paper was awarded to Quentin Bramas, Stéphane Devismes, and Pascal Lafourcade for their paper *Infinite Grid Exploration by Disoriented Robots*. The Best Student Paper was awarded to Carole Delporte-Gallet, Hugues Fauconnier, and Mouna Safir for their paper *Byzantine k-Set Agreement*. The author Mouna Safir was a full-time student at the time of the submission.

We are grateful to all members of the Program and Organizing Committees, to all referees for their cooperation, and to Springer for their professional support during the production phase of the proceedings. Finally, we would like to thank the sponsoring institutions without whom NETYS 2020 could not have been a reality. We are also thankful to all authors of submitted papers and to all participants of the conference.

Their interest in this conference and contributions to the discipline are greatly appreciated.

August 2020

Chryssis Georgiou
Rupak Majumdar

Organization

General Chair

Mohammed Erradi   ENSIAS, Mohammed V University in Rabat, Morocco

General Vice-chairs

Ahmed Bouajjani   University of Paris, France
Rachid Guerraoui   EPFL, Switzerland

Program Chairs

Chryssis Georgiou   University of Cyprus, Cyprus
Rupak Majumdar   Max Planck Institute for Software Systems, Germany

Program Committee

M. Faouzi Atig	Uppsala University, Sweden
Slimane Bah	EMI, Mohammed V University, Morocco
Yahya Benkaouz	FS, Mohammed V University, Morocco
Ismail Berrada	SMBAU, Morocco
Annnette Bieniusa	TU Kaiserslautern, Germany
Ahmed Bouajjani	University of Paris, France
Costas Busch	LSU, USA
Ioannis Chatzigiannakis	Sapienza University of Rome, Italy
Yu-Fang Chen	Academia Sinica, Taiwan
Evgenia Christoforou	University of Cyprus, Cyprus
Loris D'Antoni	University of Wisconsin-Madison, USA
Carole Delporte	University of Paris, France
Ankush Desai	Amazon, USA
Amr El Abbadi	UCSB, USA
Pierre Ganty	IMDEA Software Institute, Spain
Seth Gilbert	NUS, Singapore
Vincent Gramoli	University of Sydney, Australia
Radu Grosu	Vienna University of Technology, Austria
Aarti Gupta	Princeton University, USA
Mohamed Jmaiel	University of Sfax, Tunisia
Mohammed-Amine Koulali	ENSA d'Oujda, Morocco
Jan Kretinsky	Technical University of Munich, Germany
S. Krishna	IIT Bombay, India
Fabian Kuhn	University of Freiburg, Germany
Miguel Matos	INESC-ID & IST, University of Lisbon, Portugal

Miguel Mosteiro	Pace University, USA
Calvin Newport	Georgetown University, USA
Nicolas Nicolaou	Algolysis Ltd., Cyprus
Guevara Noubir	Northeastern University, USA
Andreas Podelski	University of Freiburg, Germany
Maria Potop-Butucaru	Sorbonne University, France
Azalea Raad	Imperial College London, UK
Michel Raynal	IRISA, Université de Rennes 1, France
Indranil Saha	IIT Kanpur, India
Elad M. Schiller	Chalmers University of Technology, Sweden
Thomas Wies	NYU, USA

Organizing Committee

Khadija Bakkouch	IRFC, Rabat, Morocco
Yahya Benkaouz	FS, Mohammed V University, Rabat, Morocco
Abdellah Boulouz	FS, Ibn Zohr University, Agadir, Morocco
Rachid Guerdaoui	Mohammed VI Polytechnic University, Ben Guerir, Morocco
Mustaf Hedabou	ENSA Safi, Cadi Ayyad University, Marrakech, Morocco
Zahi Jarir	FS, Cadi Ayyad University, Marrakech, Morocco
Abdellatif Kobbane	ENSIAS, Mohammed V University, Rabat, Morocco
Mohammed Ouzzif	EST, Hassan II University, Casablanca, Morocco

Students Committee

Hind Boukhairate	University Mohammed VI Polytechnic, Benguerir
Mohammed Lechiakh	University Mohammed VI Polytechnic, Benguerir
Rachid Zennou	ENSIAS, Mohammed V University, Rabat

Additional Reviewers

Ishtiyaque Ahmad
Mohammad Javad Amiri
Miëtek Bak
Abtin Bateni
Ignacio Cascudo
Lotfi Chaari
Samuel Drews

Earlence Fernandes
Sujaya Maiyya
Sebgui Marouane
Stefanie Mühlberger
Kausik Subramanian
Josef Tkadlec
Mouna Torjmen

Sponsors

MOHAMMED VI Polytechnic University

OCP Group

Springer

King Abdullah
University of Science
and Technology

Auto Hall

Fondation Hassan II

thinline

Université Mohammed
V de Rabat

ENSIAS

Association
Alkhawarizmi de Génie
Informatique

Abstracts

Reasoning About Concurrent Data Types

Constantin Enea

IRIF, University of Paris

Abstract. Modern software is typically built with specialized concurrent objects, which encapsulate shared-memory accesses or message-passing protocols into higher-level abstract data types. These objects are designed to behave according to certain consistency criteria like linearizability, eventual or causal consistency. In this talk, I will give an overview of recent results concerning formal reasoning about concurrent objects, from efficient testing algorithms to algorithmic verification methods. These results give rise to alternative specification frameworks to characterize the intended behaviors of such objects, which complement the existing generic formalizations of linearizability and weak consistency.

Security and Privacy for Distributed Optimization and Learning

Nitin Vaidya

Georgetown University

Abstract. Consider a network of agents wherein each agent has a private cost function. In the context of distributed machine learning, the private cost function of an agent may represent the "loss function" corresponding to the agent's local data. The objective here is to identify parameters that minimize the total cost over all the agents. In machine learning for classification, the cost function is designed such that minimizing the cost function should result in model parameters that achieve higher accuracy of classification. Similar problems arise in the context of other applications as well, including swarm robotics.

Our work addresses privacy and security of distributed optimization with applications to machine learning. In privacy-preserving machine learning, the goal is to optimize the model parameters correctly while preserving the privacy of each agent's local data. In security, the goal is to identify the model parameters correctly while tolerating adversarial agents that may be supplying incorrect information. When a large number of agents participate in distributed optimization, security compromise of some of the agents becomes increasingly likely. The talk will provide intuition behind the design and correctness of the algorithms.

Contents

Invited Papers

On Network Topologies and the Decidability of Reachability Problem

C. Aiswarya[1,2]([envelope])[iD]

[1] Chennai Mathematical Institute, Chennai, India
aiswarya@cmi.ac.in
[2] CNRS IRL ReLaX, Chennai, India
https://www.cmi.ac.in/aiswarya

Abstract. We consider models of distributed systems where processes communicate by means of point-to-point (unbounded) channels. The processes have a finite set of control states whose dynamics is given by a finite state automaton. They may sometimes have auxiliary storage like stacks. They may sometimes have variables storing values from an unbounded data domain. The channels may have access policies, like first-in first-out (queue). The channel may be assumed to be reliable or unreliable (lossy channel). The channels may be allowed to transmit only messages coming from a finite set, or may be allowed to transmit elements from an infinite set. The processes and the channels may be arranged in particular topologies, for example like a tree or a star. We view a topology as a node and edge labelled directed graph, where nodes represent the processes, and the directed edges represents the channels between them. The node labels describe the features of each process, and the edge label represents the assumptions on the channel. We consider local control state reachability on a single process. That is, given a distributed system over a topology, and a specific control state of a specific process, is it possible to ever reach a configuration where the specific process is in the specific control state. This problem is in general undecidable. We present a quick survey of the decidability status of this problem across different topologies.

Keywords: Distributed systems · Network topology · Reachability

1 Introduction

Mathematical modelling of distributed systems and formal reasoning about its correctness have been a central topic of research in formal methods. We focus on a very small part of it and accumulate a few results in the form of a short survey.

We consider distributed systems which consist of finite state or pushdown processes. The processes communicate between each other by means of point-to-point channels. The channels may follow a first-in first-out policy for the messages in it, or simple follow no particular order for delivery. Further the channel

Supported by DST Inspire.

C. Georgiou and R. Majumdar (Eds.): NETYS 2020, LNCS 12129, pp. 3–10, 2021.
https://doi.org/10.1007/978-3-030-67087-0_1

may be reliable (perfect) or unreliable (lossy) where it may non-deterministically lose arbitrary messages. The processes may work either on a finite data domain such as boolean programs, and transmit messages from a finite set of messages. Or the processes may have variables to store and transmit values from an infinite domain, such as protocols involving storing and passing of process ids. These attributes describe the type of processes and channels in the system.

The network topology is a graph that describes how the processes and channels are arranged in the network. We look in the literature to understand how the network topology affects the decidability status of the (local) control state reachability problem. We do not give proofs or proof ideas in this quick survey, but only make statements and give references to where one can find details.

2   Distributed Systems, Topology, Reachability Problem

We consider physically distributed systems consisting of processes communicating via channels. This is a vague description, as it gives a lot of freedom for what the processes could be, what the channels could be, and how they could be arranged. We capture this notion by topology/architecture.

As alluded to earlier, a distributed system consists of processes Procs and channels Channels. The channels offer dedicated end-to-end message transmission between processes. Thus each channel $ch \in$ Channels have a unique process that can write into it (denoted writer(ch)) and a unique process that can read from it (denoted reader(ch)).

When the Data Domain is Finite. First we consider the situation when the data domain is finite. Each process $p \in$ Procs has a finite set of control states States(p), transitions Trans(p), and a specified initial control state inState(p). Since we are interested only in control state reachability and not in language theory, we will ignore the alphabet and final states. However the transitions may also have associated actions, which in our case may be sending a message to a channel or receiving a message from a channel. The messages come from a finite set Msgs of messages. A send action snd(m, ch) indicates sending of the message m to the channel ch. The set of send actions of process p will thus be SndActions(p) = {snd(m, ch) | $m \in$ Msgs, writer(ch) = p}. Similarly RcvActions(p) = {rcv(m, ch) | $m \in$ Msgs, reader(ch) = p}. Thus, the transitions of p are of the form ($state_1$, op, $state_2$) where op $\in$ SndActions(p) $\cup$ RcvActions(p) $\cup$ {nop} and $state_1, state_2 \in$ States(p).

In addition, if the process is pushdown (has a stack) then the associated actions could also be push operations PushActions(p) = {push(s) | $s \in$ StackAlph} or pop operations PopActions(p) = {pop(s) | $s \in$ StackAlph}. Here StackAlph is the finite set of stack symbols.

When the Data Domain is Infinite. Let Ddom be the infinite data domain equipped with just the equality relation on the elements. The processes with finite control states are provided with variables/registers to store the values coming from the infinite domain (sometimes called data). A process has only finitely many variables available for storage. Let $\mathsf{Variable}(p)$ be the set of variables available for the perusal of process p. The operations are enriched to allow data updates as well. The operation $v \leftarrow *$ overwrites the content of the variable v by a non-deterministic value. The operation $v \leftarrow u$ copies the content of u to v. The operations $\mathsf{assert}(v = u)$ and $\mathsf{assert}(v \neq u)$ acts like transition guards – the transition can be performed only if the assertion holds for the contents of the respective registers.

One can consider a model where processes are equipped to handle data as above, but the channels can only transmit messages coming from the finite set Msgs of messages. For the reachability problem, this model is essentially the previous finite state system, via an abstraction that keeps track of the equivalence relation on the variables. Similar is the case for pushdown processes equipped with data where stacks can store only objects coming from the finite set $\mathsf{StackAlph}$. Thus decidability status of reachability problem with these kinds of processes coincide with the finite state versions.

Interestingly, if we allow data values to be transmitted via channels and stored in stack, we have a different story. For this we enrich the send actions to send the value stored in a particular variable also in a message. Thus $\mathsf{SndActions}(p) = \{\mathsf{snd}(m, v, ch) \mid m \in \mathsf{Msgs}, v \in \mathsf{Variable}(p), \mathsf{writer}(ch) = p\}$. Naturally we want to store a received data value in a specific register. The operation $\mathsf{rcv}(m, v, ch)$ receives a message from channel ch whose finite part is m, and the data value received along is stored into variable v. Similarly the push an pop operations can also be enriched if the process is pushdown, so that the stacks store sequence of elements from $\mathsf{StackAlph} \times \mathsf{Ddom}$.

The Channel Nature. We consider three kinds of channels. The multiset channel (or a bag) just stores the messages in a bag. The FIFO channel stores it in a queue. A lossy FIFO may lose the messages arbitrarily while the retained messages still preserve the FIFO order. We do not consider lossy multisets for reasons mentioned in Remark 1 below.

Configuration Graph. We understand the semantics of the distributed system in terms of a configuration graph. A configuration assigns a state to each process, and a sequence of messages (resp. stack symbols) to each channel (resp. process stack). The initial configuration assigns the initial states to each process, and all channels and stacks are empty. An edge in the configuration graph indicates the effect of a transition in a process. The successor configuration is as expected from the transition. Sending a message will prepend the message to the beginning of the sequence on the respective channel. So does a push. A pop will remove it from the beginning of the sequence as stacks follow last-in first-out policy. For a multiset/bag channel, a receive removes an arbitrary message from the sequence. For a FIFO channel, the receive removes the message at the end of the sequence. For a lossy channel as well, the message is removed from the end. There are some additional edges in the configuration graph to model the lossy channel.

The sequence corresponding to a lossy channel may lose an arbitrary number of messages, shrinking the sequence into a subsequence.

For the processes handling data, the configuration in addition assigns a data value to each of its variable. The stack in this case is assigned a sequence of pairs of the form (stack symbol, data value). If a channel is between processes handling data then the channel is also assigned a sequence of pairs of messages and data values. The semantics of the channels is reflected according to its nature.

We say a configuration is reachable from another if it is reachable in the configuration graph defined above.

Network Topology. The topology or architecture of a distributed system is a node- and edge-labelled directed graph. The nodes of this graph are the processes, and the directed edges represent the channels. The node label comes from the set {FS, DATA, PD, DATAPD} and indicates, respectively, whether the process is simply a finite state machine, or a finite state machine with variables to handle data from infinite domain, or a pushdown machine over a finite data domain, or a pushdown machine over infinite data domain. The edge labels from the set {BAG, FIFO, LOSSY} indicates respectively whether the channel is an unordered set, a reliable queue, or a lossy queue. A topology is depicted in Fig. 1.

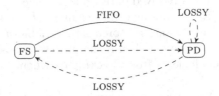

Fig. 1. A topology with two processes and four channels.

Reachability Problem. It takes as input a distributed system, a process p and a control state *target*. The reachability problem is to decide whether, starting from the initial configuration, it is possible to reach a configuration in which the process p is in the control state *target*.

3   Boundaries of Decidability

We focus on the decidability status of the reachability problem wrt. the topology. First of all we notice that the problem is undecidable in general. In fact the undecidability holds for the following restricted topologies. We provide brief explanations later, and give citations to the papers in the literature from which the main ideas for proving these results come from.

Theorem 1. *The reachability problem is undecidable as soon as the topology embeds any of the following.*

1. *A* FS *process with a* FIFO *self-loop [5].*
2. *Two* FS *processes with two* FIFO *channels between them (the direction of the* FIFO *channels does not matter [8, 9].*
3. *Two* PD *processes with a* FIFO *channel between them.*
4. *A* PD *process with a* LOSSY *channel self-loop.*
5. *A* DATA *process with a lossy channel self-loop [1].*
6. *Two* DATA *processes with two* LOSSY *channels (the direction of the channels does not matter) [1].*

Reachability of single FS process with a queue is undecidable [5]. One can use a perfect FIFO to store a Turing machine configuration. Using just the finite state control we can enqueue and dequeue to cyclically shift the channel contents, and at the same time update it to the next configuration. Two processes with FIFO channels between them in opposite directions can simulate a single process with a single queue: the second process just copies the contents from the incoming channel to the outgoing channel. Two processes with two queues between them in the same direction is also undecidable [8,9]. We can easily give a reduction from the Post's Correspondence Problem: The first process guesses a sequence of tiles and sends the top strings on one channel and the bottom strings on the other. Once it finishes the guessing it will send a special symbol to mark the end. The second process will receive from each channel in an interleaving manner checking that both channels deliver the same string until it receives the end marker from both, in which case it moves to the *target* state.

Two PD processes communicating via a FIFO channel can check the intersection-non-emptiness of context-free languages. One PD process non-deterministically generates a string in its language and transmits it over the FIFO channel as it is generated. The second process checks that the received string is in its language.

Pushdown processes with cycles of lossy channel are Turing powerful. One can use the a lossy channel instead of the perfect channel for simulating successive configurations of a Turing machine. We may require the Turing machine to finally erase the used tape cells from the right and accept on the first cell with a blank tape. In order to detect loss of messages, it will use the pushdown to count the number of currently active tape cells, according to the transitions. In the end if the pushdown is not empty it means that the channel has lost messages. It reaches the *target* state only if the stack is currently empty in addition to the Turing machine reaching a final state. Note that, this proof also works if we provide only a simple counter instead of the stack.

LOSSY channel with data can reliably encode two counter machines, and hence reachability is undecidable in this case too [1]. The idea is to use the data equality relations to induce a strict chain-like structure to the channel contents. This structure is broken by loss of messages, and once broken it can never be built back. The finite control with the help of variables can check if the structure is broken, and ignore such lossy runs. This ability to check loss of messages lets processes with a lossy channel and infinite data domain simulate perfect channels on finite data domain. This explains the last two undecidability results.

On the other hand we have a collection of decidability results as well.

Theorem 2. *The reachability problem is decidable for the following topologies.*

1. *If it has only* FS *or* DATA *processes and* BAG *channels [6, 12, 14, 16].*
2. *If it has only* FS *processes and* FIFO *channels, and the undirected topology does not have undirected cycles [9, 13]. Undirected topology treats the topology as an undirected graph by ignoring the direction in the edges.*
3. *If it has* FS *processes and* LOSSY *channels [2, 7].*
4. *If it has* PD *processes and* LOSSY *channels, and the undirected topology does not have cycles [4].*
5. *If it has only two* FS *processes and a* LOSSY *channel and a* FIFO *channel between them, both channels in the same direction [9].*
6. *If it has only* FS *processes, and topology can be decomposed into components, each of which is decidable, and the components are linked only by* LOSSY *channels [9].*
7. *If it has only* FS *processes, and if the topology can be fused along an essential edge (edge contraction) to result in a decidable topology, where an essential edge is a channel between different processes, and it is the only one between these in either direction [9].*

The first case of FS processes and BAG channels can be simulated easily by Petri nets or vector addition systems with states. Basically we provide a place for each (m, ch) pair. The number of tokens in that place indicates how many m-messages are present in channel ch. Our reachability problem corresponds to the coverability problem for Petri nets which is known to be decidable [6, 12, 16]. When these are DATA processes, it corresponds to Data nets—Petri nets with tokens carrying data. Coverability problem is decidable for Data nets [14].

The decidability of reachability problem in acyclic topologies containing only FS processes with FIFO channels was shown in [13] and also in [8, 9]. The decidability of LOSSY channel systems was shown in [2, 7]. Decidability of acyclic networks of pushdown processes communicating via LOSSY channels was shown in [4].

For different combinations of LOSSY and FIFO channels between FS processes, a complete picture of decidability status is given by Chambart and Schnoebelen in [9] (See also Chapter 5 of [8]). As per [9], a LOSSY channel and a FIFO channel between a pair of processes in the same direction is decidable. On the other hand if there are two LOSSY channels and one FIFO channel between a pair of processes in the same direction, it is undecidable. They give basic decidable and undecidable architectures consisting of only two FS processes. They also show that, a bigger topology consisting of components connected to each other via LOSSY channels, each component being a decidable topology, is again decidable. Also, if a bigger topology can be transformed into a smaller one by fusion along an essential channel (a channel that is not a loop which is the only channel between the writer and reader of this channel, independent of the direction) and if the smaller topology is decidable then so is the bigger. Chambart and Schnoebelen [9] even give a complete characterization of decidable topologies by means of fusion and splitting along lossy edges.

Remark 1. We do not consider lossy BAG channels. This is because the control states reachable by lossy BAG will exactly be the ones reached by perfect BAG channels, as we do not have emptiness check on channels. Already we have decidability for BAG channels, and this implies that the distributed systems with PD or DATA processes where the channels are any combination of perfect or lossy BAGs will have a decidable reachability problem.

4 Conclusions

Though this short survey captures several different models studied in the literature, it does not cover the vast area of distributed systems and all the decidability results pertaining to them. We have not considered other communicating paradigms such as broadcast or rendez-vous. We have not considered model checking problems, nor language theoretic problems. Even for the problem of reachability that we have considered, there is a plethora of work which achieves decidability by under- or over- approximation techniques. There are also unifying results which understand the behaviours of these systems as graphs and attribute the decidability to graph theoretic notions such as tree-width [15] or split-width [3,10,11].

References

1. Abdulla, P.A., Aiswarya, C., Atig, M.F.: Data communicating processes with unreliable channels. In: Proceedings of LICS 2016, pp. 166–175. ACM (2016)
2. Abdulla, P.A., Jonsson, B.: Verifying programs with unreliable channels. Inf. Comput. **127**(2), 91–101 (1996)
3. Aiswarya, C., Gastin, P., Narayan Kumar, K.: Verifying communicating multipushdown systems via split-width. In: Cassez, F., Raskin, J.-F. (eds.) ATVA 2014. LNCS, vol. 8837, pp. 1–17. Springer, Cham (2014). https://doi.org/10.1007/978-3-319-11936-6_1
4. Atig, M.F., Bouajjani, A., Touili, T.: On the reachability analysis of acyclic networks of pushdown systems. In: van Breugel, F., Chechik, M. (eds.) CONCUR 2008. LNCS, vol. 5201, pp. 356–371. Springer, Heidelberg (2008). https://doi.org/10.1007/978-3-540-85361-9_29
5. Brand, D., Zafiropulo, P.: On communicating finite-state machines. J. ACM **30**(2), 323–342 (1983)
6. Cardoza, E., Lipton, R., Meyer, A.R.: Exponential space complete problems for Petri nets and commutative semigroups (preliminary report). In: Proceedings of STOC, pp. 50–54. ACM (1976)
7. Cécé, G., Finkel, A., Iyer, S.P.: Unreliable channels are easier to verify than perfect channels. Inf. Comput. **124**(1), 20–31 (1996)
8. Chambart, P.: Du Problème de sous-mot de Post et de la complexité des canaux non fiables. Thèse de doctorat, Laboratoire Spécification et Vérification, ENS Cachan, France (2011). http://www.lsv.ens-cachan.fr/Publis/PAPERS/PDF/chambart-these11.pdf
9. Chambart, P., Schnoebelen, P.: Mixing lossy and perfect fifo channels. In: van Breugel, F., Chechik, M. (eds.) CONCUR 2008. LNCS, vol. 5201, pp. 340–355. Springer, Heidelberg (2008). https://doi.org/10.1007/978-3-540-85361-9_28

10. Cyriac, A.: Verification of communicating recursive programs via split-width. Ph.D. thesis, Laboratoire Spécification et Vérification, ENS Cachan, France (2014). http://www.lsv.ens-cachan.fr/Publis/PAPERS/PDF/cyriac-phd14.pdf

11. Cyriac, A., Gastin, P., Kumar, K.N.: MSO decidability of multi-pushdown systems via split-width. In: Koutny, M., Ulidowski, I. (eds.) CONCUR 2012. LNCS, vol. 7454, pp. 547–561. Springer, Heidelberg (2012). https://doi.org/10.1007/978-3-642-32940-1_38

12. Karp, R.M., Miller, R.E.: Parallel program schemata: a mathematical model for parallel computation. In: 8th Annual Symposium on Switching and Automata Theory (SWAT 1967), pp. 55–61 (1967)

13. La Torre, S., Madhusudan, P., Parlato, G.: Context-bounded analysis of concurrent queue systems. In: Ramakrishnan, C.R., Rehof, J. (eds.) TACAS 2008. LNCS, vol. 4963, pp. 299–314. Springer, Heidelberg (2008). https://doi.org/10.1007/978-3-540-78800-3_21

14. Lazić, R., Newcomb, T., Ouaknine, J., Roscoe, A.W., Worrell, J.: Nets with tokens which carry data. In: Kleijn, J., Yakovlev, A. (eds.) ICATPN 2007. LNCS, vol. 4546, pp. 301–320. Springer, Heidelberg (2007). https://doi.org/10.1007/978-3-540-73094-1_19

15. Madhusudan, P., Parlato, G.: The tree width of auxiliary storage. In: Ball, Th., Sagiv, M. (eds.) POPL 2011, pp. 283–294. ACM (2011)

16. Rackoff, C.: The covering and boundedness problems for vector addition systems. Theoret. Comput. Sci. 6(2), 223–231 (1978)

Hide Me: Enabling Location Privacy in Heterogeneous Vehicular Networks

Tobias Meuser[1,2], Oluwasegun Taiwo Ojo[2], Daniel Bischoff[1],
Antonio Fernández Anta[2(✉)], Ioannis Stavrakakis[3], and Ralf Steinmetz[1]

[1] Multimedia Communications Lab (KOM), Technische Universität Darmstadt,
Darmstadt, Germany
{tobias.meuser,daniel.bischoff,ralf.steinmetz}@KOM.tu-darmstadt.de
[2] IMDEA Networks Institute, Madrid, Spain
{oluwasegun.ojo,antonio.fernandez}@imdea.org
[3] National and Kapodistrian University of Athens, Athens, Greece
ioannis@di.uoa.gr

Abstract. In order to support location-based services, vehicles share their location with a server to receive relevant data. Revealing a vehicle's location compromises its privacy. One way to reduce this problem is obfuscating the vehicle's location by adding artificial noise. However, this increases the area where the true location of the vehicle may be. Hence, under limited available bandwidth, the server will provide fewer data relevant to the vehicle's true location, reducing the effectiveness of the location-based service. To compensate for this reduction, we allow that the data relevant to a vehicle is also shared through direct, ad hoc communication between neighboring vehicles. Through such Vehicle-to-Vehicle (V2V) cooperation, the impact of location obfuscation is mitigated. In this set up, and assuming that the data served may have different impact levels, we propose and study a game that determines the data subscription a vehicle should use, without explicit coordination among them. The aim is maximizing the expected impact of the data received, either directly from the server or via V2V. Our analysis and results show that the proposed V2V cooperation and derived strategy lead to significant performance increase compared to other uncoordinated approaches, and largely alleviates the impact of location obfuscation.

Keywords: Floating Car Data · Location-based services · Location privacy · V2V communication

1 Introduction

The vehicles of the future will be required to have increased awareness of their environment, in order to assist the driver or to support autonomous driving.

This work has been supported by the DFG within the CRC 1053 - MAKI (B1), the Spanish grant PID2019-109805RB-I00 (ECID), the Region of Madrid EdgeData-CM program (P2018/TCS-4499), and the NSF of China grant 61520106005.

C. Georgiou and R. Majumdar (Eds.): NETYS 2020, LNCS 12129, pp. 11–27, 2021.
https://doi.org/10.1007/978-3-030-67087-0_2

This awareness has typically been provided by sensors on the vehicles, which measure vital data about the environment of the vehicle. The data provided by these sensors is limited to the vehicle's immediate environment, due to the sensors' inherent physical limitations (e.g., their range). Nevertheless, information from locations away from a given vehicle may also be important to it (e.g., for traffic safety, route planning, or navigation). To make such information available to far away vehicles, passing vehicles may capture it through their own sensors, and communicate it to a server using an appropriate communication infrastructure such as a cellular network. Then, the vehicles desiring to receive such information indicate so to the server, and receive it via a similar infrastructure. By sharing their local perception of the environment via a cellular infrastructure, as described, vehicles can complement their local perception with distant data provided by other vehicles.

In order for vehicles to get this, so-called, Floating Car Data (FCD), they have to share their location with the server, which is usually assumed to be a trusted entity. The server selects the relevant FCD for the vehicles using their location, and distributes it accordingly. This continuous context and location exchange with a server is a risk to the privacy of the vehicles. Consequently, privacy-sensitive users either have to accept this risk, or turn off the option of receiving FCD. Clearly, users that disable the reception of FCD cannot benefit from location-based services and other services enabled by vehicular networks. It is therefore desirable to have a mechanism that allows the reception of FCD while preserving the location privacy of the user.

A technique that is often used to increase the privacy of a vehicle, is adding random noise to its true location (obfuscation). Hence, instead of providing the server with a position, the vehicle provides an area. (We will assume in the rest of the paper that this type of obfuscation to increase privacy is used.) A negative consequence of obfuscation is that the server cannot use the true location to deliver its best FCD to a vehicle, and may hence send it useless data. We assume that different data items may have different value (*impact level*) for a vehicle. A vehicle subscribes to some impact level, and the server provides to the vehicle all available data items with matching impact for the vehicle area. Since the available bandwidth is limited, vehicles using obfuscation end up receiving a smaller portion of data of a given impact that is useful to them. As a result, location-based services would be less effectively provided to privacy-concerned vehicles.

To alleviate this problem, and to increase the amount of location-relevant data provided to a vehicle, we propose that neighboring vehicles can exchange data through direct, ad hoc communication. That is, we assume Vehicle-to-Vehicle (V2V) cooperation for exchanging local relevant data. We assume that vehicles do not use location obfuscation with other neighboring vehicles, only with the server, and hence the messages exchanged via V2V are all relevant and useful. (Trying to hide a vehicle's location to a neighbor seems pointless, since the neighbor can "see" the vehicle with its local sensors.) Hence, through V2V cooperation, the negative impact of location obfuscation could be mitigated to some extent. The use of V2V cooperation has also been considered in [1] combined with vehicle clusters. As it will be discussed later and shown in the results, cluster-based approaches are complex and suffer from connectivity problems, which reduces their performance. For these reasons, in this work the V2V communication is not cluster-based but ad hoc through direct V2V exchanges.

Notice that, without any coordination, neighboring vehicles are expected to subscribe to the same high impact levels, which results in receiving overlapping sets of data. This reduces the potential benefit of V2V cooperation. To prevent that, we develop and study a game among the vehicles. This game drives vehicles to subscribe to certain impact levels, so that the aforementioned overlap is reduced. The design goal is to maximize the expected value of a utilization function as shaped by the participating (neighboring) vehicles as well. Our analysis and results show that the proposed V2V cooperation scheme and derived strategy lead to significant performance increase compared to non-cooperative approaches, while alleviating the impact on privacy of location-based services.

Related Work. Several techniques have been introduced in the literature to protect users' privacy in vehicular networks. Some of the common techniques include the use of pseudonyms [2–4], obfuscation [5,6], and the use of group communications [7–9]. The first technique involves users taking on other identities (pseudonyms) to dissociate their actual identity from their data [10]. The use of a single pseudonym is not very effective, and hence it is often required for users to change pseudonyms periodically, to maintain their level of privacy [11]. Such pseudonym changes are usually done in mix zones where drivers can switch pseudonyms [12]. These mix zones can be fixed [13] or specified dynamically [14]. However, the use of pseudonyms has been shown not to be effective against a global eavesdropper [15], and especially in environments with low car density like highways. Furthermore, the use of pseudonyms usually focuses on eavesdroppers monitoring V2V communications and involves having to deal with a trusted (or semi-trusted) server which coordinates the assignments of pseudonyms [8]. This still involves trusting a central server, which is a risk in the case that an adversary gets hold of such server. Our work focuses on the privacy of users in their communications with the central server.

Likewise, obfuscation has been extensively used in privacy protection in vehicular networks and location-based services. Obfuscation involves users providing (i) an inaccurate location, (ii) an imprecise region including their real location, or (iii) a vague description of their location [16]. To quantify the effectiveness of obfuscation, metrics like *k-anonimity*, which means that a user's shared location data makes it indistinguishable from $k - 1$ other users, have been introduced [17,18]. The imprecision added into the location of the user usually leads to users getting less relevant data and, thus, a decrease in efficiency. Our method mitigates against this decrease in performance by implicitly cooperating with other vehicles to get relevant updates through V2V communication.

Game-theory has been applied to modeling aspects of privacy, especially in mobile networks and location-based services [19,20], and in security and privacy assessment of vehicular networks [21]. Distinct from previous studies, our work focuses on privacy of users in their communications with the server considering the impact of the messages to the user. We adopt an obfuscation technique by reporting a region instead of their exact location, and mitigate against the resulting reduction in performance by implicitly coordination the vehicles through a game-theoretic approach, which maximizes the relevant data received by the vehicles.

Contributions. The contributions of this work are the following. First, we introduce privacy considerations in the management of FCD and reveal their impact on location-based services: given a fixed bandwidth availability, some data may not be forwarded to a vehicle due to location obfuscation. Second, in order to alleviate this problem, we propose that vehicles cooperate and forward relevant data to their neighboring vehicles, increasing in principle the data received by a vehicle beyond what is directly received from the server. An ad-hoc, direct V2V cooperation paradigm is employed instead of a cluster-based one, and we show the high performance deterioration of the latter in a real vehicular networking environment. Third, we develop and study of a game determining the strategies (in terms of probabilities that a vehicle is forwarded by the server data of a given impact level) that vehicles should follow, so that the expected utility is maximized. This is shown to lead to a diversification of the data received directly from the server by neighboring vehicles, and increases the effectiveness of V2V cooperation. Finally, the aforementioned contributions are supported through simulation evaluation.

Structure. The rest of the paper is as follows. In Sect. 2, we provide an overview of the system model considered, and describe the influence of location privacy on the network. In Sect. 3, we describe our proposed game theoretic approach for privacy sensitive communication. In Sect. 4, we evaluate the performance of our method. We conclude the paper in Sect. 5 with a discussion about our findings.

2 System Model

Definitions. We provide first an overview of the considered system model. We assume a context-aware vehicular network, in which a central server transmits context-sensitive messages to interested vehicles. In this network, time is assumed to be slotted (a typical slot length is 1 s). Every vehicle has a limited (average) bandwidth A (in bits per time slot) to receive these messages via a cellular network. This assigned bandwidth is generally low compared to the maximum (physically) available bandwidth, such that vehicles may exceed this bandwidth temporarily (as long as the average consumed bandwidth matches the predefined value). A message contains FCD as payload, as well as additional meta-information such as the source location, generation time, and type of FCD. In this work, we assume that FCD carry road-related information (e.g., accidents, traffic jams, traffic flow information) that can be useful for improving the driving behavior of the vehicles in proximity. Let $a(m)$ (in bits) denote the size of a message m, $s(m)$ the source location, $r(m)$ the radius of its dissemination area, and $\mu(m)$ its impact (which depends on the type of FCD: an accident has generally higher impact than traffic flow information). As our bandwidth is limited, the impact per utilized bandwidth is pivotal for our approach. Based on the message impact $\mu(m)$ and the dissemination radius $r(m)$, we divide messages in n_μ impact levels. For simplicity, we assume that every message m of impact level $i \in \{1, \ldots, n_\mu\}$ has the same dissemination radius $r(m) = r_i$ and impact $\mu(m) = \mu_i$. We assume that μ_i is the impact per bit assigned to impact level i. When convenient, we use $\mu_{n_\mu+1} = \infty$.

A vehicle can control the reception of messages from the server by expressing interest in certain *impact* levels and by providing a *representation of its location*. More specifically, a vehicle wants to receive a message m if (i) it has expressed interest in the corresponding impact level i of the message, and (ii) the vehicle's location is at most at distance r_i from the source $s(m)$ of the FCD. Let a_i denote the traffic load of messages of impact level i (in bits per time slot) expected for the vehicle if the provided location is accurate. A vehicle is either interested in an impact level or not, i.e., receives either all or no messages of this impact level. This interest can be changed dynamically at the beginning of every time slot.

Depending on the assumed privacy-sensitivity (referred to as privacy-level) $\phi \in \Phi$ of a vehicle v, the aforementioned *representation of the location* may be accurate or may be imprecise. We implement this imprecision by providing only a (circular) area in which the vehicle is certainly located (uniformly distributed), without actually revealing the exact location to the server. The privacy level ϕ chosen by the respective vehicle determines the radius r_ϕ of this area. That imprecise representation of the location increases the load of received messages due to the less accurate server-side filtering. To capture the additional bandwidth consumption, let $a_{\phi,i} \geq a_i$ denote the expected load (in bits) of messages of impact level i for a vehicle with privacy level ϕ.

The central server uses the announced interest of the vehicles to actively push new messages (i.e., messages containing yet unknown FCD.) via the cellular network to them. Since the available bandwidth is assumed to be limited, a vehicle aims to maximize the total impact of the received messages, which is achieved by dropping low-impact messages if the bandwidth is insufficient. To maximize that total impact of received messages, vehicles may cooperate to share bandwidth for the reception of messages; i.e., vehicles can locally broadcast messages, received via the cellular network, without additional costs to notify vehicles in their proximity. Thus, not every vehicle needs to receive all messages of its interest via the limited cellular bandwidth, as these messages might be provided by its neighbors.

Influence of Location Obfuscation. In the following, we provide an insight on the influence of privacy in our model. Each privacy level $\phi > 1$ adds a certain level of imprecision to the provided location, while $\phi = 1$ refers to no privacy-sensitivity. The privacy-sensitivity and, thus, location imprecision increases with ϕ and reduces the accuracy of the context-based message filtering at the server-side. Thus, a vehicle receives messages not relevant for its current context, while its share of relevant messages is reduced. This influences the number of received messages $n_{\phi,i}$ and their expected impact per bit $\mu_{\phi,i}$ for a privacy state ϕ and an impact level i. The number of messages received typically increases with increasing privacy level, while the expected impact per bit of a message decreases. We reflect this change for every impact level i by the *adaptation factor* $\rho_{\phi,i}$ as follows.

$$a_{\phi,i} = a_i \cdot \rho_{\phi,i} \quad \mu_{\phi,i} = \frac{\mu_i}{\rho_{\phi,i}} \tag{1}$$

$\rho_{\phi,i}$ depends on the context-sensitivity of the distributed messages for a vehicle of privacy level ϕ receiving messages with impact level i. For non-context-sensitive messages, $\rho_{\phi,i} = 1, \forall \phi \in \Phi$. For context-sensitive of messages, i.e., messages with a specific distribution-area with radius r_i, $\rho_{\phi,i} \geq 1, \forall \phi \in \Phi$. These statements are proven in Theorem 1.

Theorem 1. *The adaptation factor for a network with uniformly distributed messages is $\rho_{\phi,i} = \left(r_\phi/r_i + 1\right)^2$ for a circular geocast-area and a circular location-imprecision, where r_i is the radius of the geocast-area of the message of impact level i and r_ϕ is the radius of the location-imprecision area of privacy-level ϕ.*

Proof. Without location privacy, the vehicle receives all messages with a maximum distance of r_i to its current location. Thus, area of interest for the vehicle is $\pi \cdot r_i^2$. If the vehicle reduces the precision of its location by hiding inside an area of radius r_ϕ, the server will need to transmit all messages within a distance of $r_\phi + r_i$ from the center of the area to ensure that the vehicle receives all relevant messages. The size of this area is $\pi \cdot (r_\phi + r_i)^2$. This leads to $\rho_{\phi,i} = \left(r_\phi/r_i + 1\right)^2$.

3   Game-Theoretic Model for Privacy-Sensitive Communication

To enhance the performance of our impact-aware vehicular network, we employ a game-theoretic model with the aim to maximize the sum of impact of the received messages. Our innovative approach relies only on the number n_ϕ of vehicles of each privacy-level ϕ in proximity to find a mixed Nash-optimal solution for our developed game-theoretic model, i.e., vehicles receive messages with a certain probability. In our game, each actor (vehicle) aims to find the strategy (receive messages in a certain impact-range via the cellular network) that maximizes its utility (sum of impact values of all received messages, directly via cellular or from the neighbors) while sticking to cellular bandwidth constraints. This game is played periodically in every time slot to adjust the vehicles behavior to environmental changes, i.e. changes in the number of neighbors in proximity and changes in number of messages. Notice that vehicles are assumed to cooperate; thus, a vehicle might additionally receive messages directly by vehicles in proximity. The intuition behind this game model is that high-impact messages are generally prioritized, as their bandwidth usage is more efficient compared to low-impact messages. Thus, vehicles may rely on their neighbors to provide some high-impact messages to them, as a number of neighbors aims to receive these high-impact messages. These vehicles can then use a part of their available cellular bandwidth to receive low-impact messages and share these with their neighbors. The idea is similar to cooperative caching: Instead of storing all high-demand message at every local cache, some nodes fetch low-demand messages instead and satisfy the request of high-demand messages from nearby cooperative caches [22].

The vehicles are the only *actors* in this game; the server is not directly involved, but only determines the set of receivers of messages based on the strategies chosen by the vehicles. For this purpose, the vehicles share their strategy in the form of subscriptions with the server. The *strategy* is represented as a vector $\boldsymbol{p}_\phi$ with n_μ probability entries $p_{\phi,i}$ with $i \in \{1, \ldots, n_\mu\}$, and depends on the chosen privacy level ϕ_e of the vehicle. Each entry $p_{\phi,i}$ refers to the probability of the tagged vehicles to receive messages of the corresponding impact level. Additionally, $0 \le p_{\phi,i} \le 1, \forall p_{\phi,i} \in \boldsymbol{p}_\phi$. For the assignment of messages to an impact level, we use the impact μ_i. Note that μ_i does not depend on the privacy level ϕ. The privacy-dependent message impact $\mu_{\phi,i}$ is only used for the calculation of the utility of a vehicle. In the calculation, $\boldsymbol{p}_\phi$ needs to be chosen such that Eq. 2 holds, with $a_{\phi,i}$ being the expected number of bits in the received messages of impact level i and privacy level ϕ according to Eq. 1, and A being the usable bandwidth.

$$\sum_{i=1}^{n_\mu} a_{\phi,i} \cdot p_{\phi,i} \le A \qquad (2)$$

Notice that this differs from previous work, like [1], in which the vehicle is intended to receive all messages in the set $\{m | \mu_i \le \mu(m)\}$. The advantage of our new model is the additional flexibility provided by removing some of the message redundancy among neighboring vehicles, which improves the total impact of received messages (via cellular and direct neighbor forwarding) by each vehicle.

Each vehicle aims at maximizing its *utility*, which is defined in a way that captures the impact of the messages received. The utility used in this paper is defined in Eq. 3, and is based on the messages sent M_{snt}, the messages received M_{rcv}, and the impact $\mu(m)$ of every message m. $\mathbb{I}_{\{m \in M_{rcv}\}}$ is the indicator function of whether a message m has been received by the vehicle.

$$u = \sum_{m \in M_{snt}} \mu(m) \cdot a(m) \cdot \mathbb{I}_{\{m \in M_{rcv}\}} \qquad (3)$$

As the probability of a vehicle receiving a message depends on $\boldsymbol{p}_\phi$, we derive the expectation of the utility based on Eq. 3. For this purpose, we assume that the environment of each vehicle is similar, so that the strategies of two vehicles with the same privacy level are the same. Thus, the strategy of every privacy level can be calculated by every vehicle in proximity, which is the basis of our offloading approach. Thus, we only use the strategies $\boldsymbol{p}_\phi$ along with the number n_ϕ of vehicles for each privacy level ϕ to calculate the probability of receiving a message either via the cellular network or from one of the neighbors. The probability $p(\mu_i)$ to receive a message via any interface (cellular or V2V) with at impact level μ_i can be calculated as shown in Eq. 4. This formula assumes that there is no loss in the network, i.e., every transmitted messages is received by the intended receiver.

$$p(\mu_i) = 1 - \prod_{\phi \in \Phi}(1 - p_{\phi,i})^{n_\phi} \tag{4}$$

We use the probability $p(\mu_i)$ to receive a message to derive the expected utility $\overline{u}(\phi_e, \boldsymbol{p_1}, \dots, \boldsymbol{p_{|\Phi|}})$. This estimates the set of received messages M_{rcv} using the expected amount of sent messages a_i and the probability $p(\mu_i)$ to receive each message. The resulting expected utility for the tagged vehicle is shown in Eq. 5.

$$\overline{u}(\phi_e, \boldsymbol{p_1}, \dots, \boldsymbol{p_{|\Phi|}}) = \sum_{i=1}^{n_\mu} \mu_{\phi_e,i} \cdot a_{\phi_e,i} \cdot \left[1 - \prod_{\phi \in \Phi}(1 - p_{\phi,i})^{n_\phi}\right] \tag{5}$$

When clear from context, we refer to $\overline{u}(\phi_e, \boldsymbol{p_0}, \dots, \boldsymbol{p_{|\Phi|}})$ as $\overline{u}$ to increase readability. In the next section, we describe the process of deriving a utility-maximizing strategy for the described game. The advantage of determining the solution analytically is (i) the possibility to analyze and bound the effects of location privacy to the system, and (ii) the lower computational complexity compared to a non-linear solver.

3.1   Game-Theoretic Solution

We derive now the optimal strategy for a vehicle with privacy level ϕ_e, given that the privacy level and number of vehicles in each privacy level in its environment is known. For this purpose, we calculate the partial derivatives of the expected utility $\overline{u}$ with respect to the probabilities of the tagged vehicle $p_{\phi,i}$. However, it is important to consider the dependency between the probabilities $p_{\phi,i}, \forall \phi \in \Phi$, as Eq. 2 limits the possible values of $p_{\phi,i}$. (This approach would work similarly with any other probability $p_{\phi,i}|i \neq 1$.) We depict this dependency by expressing $p_{\phi,1}$ depending on the other probabilities $\{p_{\phi,i}|i > 1\}$ as shown in Eq. 6. Thus, $p_{\phi,1}$ depends on all other probabilities, i.e., the derivative of $p_{\phi,1}$ with respect to any probability $p_{\phi,i}$ is not always non-zero, which leads to our optimization problem.

$$p_{\phi,1} \leq \frac{A - \sum_{i=2}^{n_\mu} a_{\phi,i} \cdot p_{\phi,i}}{a_{\phi,1}} \tag{6}$$

While the inequality is sufficient to guarantee the bandwidth requirements, we will assume Eq. 6 to be an equation as higher values of $p_{\phi,1}$ cannot decrease the utility. As there is no dependency between any pair of probabilities $p_{\phi,i}$ and $p_{\phi,j}$ if $i \neq j \wedge i \neq 1 \wedge j \neq 1$, the derivative of the utility with respect to $p_{\phi,l}$ depends only on $p_{\phi,1}$ and $p_{\phi,l}$ for every $l > 1$ as shown in Eq. 7. Notice that $\mu_{\phi_e,i} \cdot a_{\phi_e,i} = \mu_i \cdot a_i$ according to Eq. 1. Additionally, we assume that $p_{\phi_e,l} \neq 0$.

We ensure that by considering the cases with $p_{\phi_e,l} = 0, \forall l \in \{1,\ldots,n_\mu\}$ separately as described in Sect. 3.2.

$$\frac{\partial \bar{u}}{\partial p_{\phi_e,l}} = \mu_l a_l n_{\phi_e} \cdot (1 - p_{\phi_e,l})^{n_{\phi_e}-1} \cdot P_l(\Phi \setminus \{\phi_e\})$$

$$+ \mu_1 a_1 \left(\frac{\partial p_{\phi_e,1}}{\partial p_{\phi_e,l}}\right) n_{\phi_e} \cdot (1 - p_{\phi_e,1})^{n_{\phi_e}-1} \cdot P_1(\Phi \setminus \{\phi_e\}) \quad (7)$$

with $P_j(\Phi) = \prod_{\phi \in \Phi}(1 - p_{\phi,j})^{n_\phi}$. Equation 1 displays the dependency of $p_{\phi_e,1}$ and $p_{\phi_e,l}$. Thus, the derivative of $p_{\phi_e,1}$ with respect to $p_{\phi_e,l}$ can be calculated according to Eq. 8.

$$\frac{\partial p_{\phi_e,1}}{\partial p_{\phi_e,l}} = -\frac{a_{\phi_e,l}}{a_{\phi_e,1}} \quad (8)$$

By setting the derivative of the utility to 0, we determine all possibly optimal solutions. This leads to Eq. 9 after some minor transformations. Notice that a_l and n_{ϕ_e}, are omitted as they are present on both sides of the equation.

$$\frac{\mu_l}{\mu_1} \cdot \left(\frac{1 - p_{\phi_e,l}}{1 - p_{\phi_e,1}}\right)^{n_{\phi_e}-1} \cdot P_l(\Phi \setminus \{\phi_e\}) = \frac{p_{\phi_e,l}}{p_{\phi_e,1}} \cdot P_1(\Phi \setminus \{\phi_e\}) \quad (9)$$

For a given impact level l, we divide the set of privacy levels Φ into $\Phi^+(l)$, which only contains privacy levels with $p_{\phi,l} > 0$, and $\Phi^-(l)$, which contains privacy levels with $p_{\phi,l} = 0$. This is necessary, as the derivative of the expected utility with respect to $p_{\phi,l}$ is always 0 if $p_{\phi,l} = 0$, thus, Eq. 9 does not hold. However, Eq. 9 still contains $p_{\phi,l}, \forall \phi \in \Phi^+(l)$ and $p_{\phi,1}, \forall \phi \in \Phi(l)$. We need to replace $p_{\phi,l}, \forall \phi \in \Phi^+(l) \setminus \phi_e$ to calculate $p_{\phi_e,l}$. We can calculate the $p_{\phi_e,l}$ using Eq. 10, according to Theorem 2.

Theorem 2. *For any probability $p_{\phi_e,l}, \forall \phi_e \in \Phi^+(l)$ with $n_{\phi_e} > 1$, we have that*

$$\frac{\mu_l}{\mu_1} \cdot \prod_{\phi \in \Phi^+(l) \setminus \{\phi_e\}} \left(\frac{p_{\phi_e,l} \cdot p_{\phi,1}}{p_{\phi,l} \cdot p_{\phi_e,1}}\right)^{n_\phi} \cdot \left(\frac{1 - p_{\phi_e,l}}{1 - p_{\phi_e,1}}\right)^{n^+(l)} = \left(\frac{p_{\phi_e,l}}{p_{\phi_e,1}}\right) \cdot P_1(\Phi^-(l)) \quad (10)$$

where $n^+(l) = \sum_{\phi \in \Phi^+(l)} n_\phi - 1$. Hence, $p_{\phi_e,l}$ depends only on $p_{\phi_e,1}$ and previously calculated probabilities.

Proof. We use full induction to prove the correctness of Eq. 10. For the basecase, we consider $\Phi = \{\phi_e\}$. Based on Eq. 9, we observe that $P_1(\Phi \setminus \phi_e) = 1$ and $P_l(\Phi \setminus \phi_e) = 1$, as Φ contains only ϕ_e. Additionally, $n^+(l) = n_{\phi_e} - 1$ for the same reason, which immediately leads to Eq. 10. For the induction step, we use $\Phi_+^+(l) \subseteq \Phi^+$ and $\Phi_-^+(l) \subseteq \Phi^+$ as auxiliary variables with $\phi \in \Phi_+^+(l) \oplus \Phi_-^+(l), \forall \phi \in \Phi^+(l)$, for which the index states if they have already been included in the calculation. Based on Eq. 9 and Eq. 10, we can derive Eq. 11 associated $\phi_e \in \Phi_-^+(l)$ as intermediate state of the calculation. Notice that $\phi_e \in \Phi_+^+$ by assumption. Additionally, the privacy levels in Φ^- are not considered on the left side of the equation, as $p_{\phi,l} = 0, \forall \phi \in \Phi^-$.

$$\frac{\mu_l}{\mu_1} \cdot \prod_{\phi \in \Phi_+^+(l)\backslash\{\phi_e\}} \left(\frac{\rho_{\phi_e,l}}{\rho_{\phi,l}}\right)^{n_\phi} \cdot \left(\frac{1-p_{\phi_e,l}}{1-p_{\phi_e,1}}\right)^{n_+^+(l)} \cdot P_l(\Phi_-^+ \backslash \{\phi_e\})$$

$$= \prod_{\phi \in \Phi_+^+(1)\backslash\{\phi_e\}} \left(\frac{\rho_{\phi_e,1}}{\rho_{\phi,1}}\right)^{n_\phi} \cdot \frac{\rho_{\phi_e,l}}{\rho_{\phi_e,1}} \cdot P_1(\{\Phi^-(l) \cup \Phi_-^+(l)\}) \quad (11)$$

with $n_+^+(l) = \sum_{\phi \in \Phi_+^+(l)} n_\phi - 1$.

We aim to include a privacy level ϕ_n into Φ_+^+. Thus, we solve Eq. 11 associated with ϕ_n for $p_{\phi_n,l}$ and insert it into Eq. 11 associated with all other $\phi_e \in \Phi_-^+(l)\backslash\phi_n$ to obtain Eq. 12.

$$\frac{\mu_l}{\mu_1} \cdot \prod_{\phi \in (\Phi_+^+(l)\cup\phi_n)\backslash\{\phi_e\}} \left(\frac{\rho_{\phi_e,l}}{\rho_{\phi,l}}\right)^{n_\phi} \cdot \left(\frac{1-p_{\phi_e,l}}{1-p_{\phi_e,1}}\right)^{n_+^+(l)+n_{\phi_n}} \cdot P_l(\Phi_-^+ \backslash \{\phi_n\})$$

$$= \prod_{\phi \in (\Phi_+^+(l)\cup\phi_n)\backslash\{\phi_e\}} \left(\frac{\rho_{\phi_e,1}}{\rho_{\phi,1}}\right)^{n_\phi} \cdot \frac{\rho_{\phi_e l}}{\rho_{\phi_e 1}} \cdot P_1(\{\Phi^-(l) \cup \Phi_-^+(l)\} \backslash \phi_n) \quad (12)$$

This equation is similar to our initial Eq. 11 if we set $\Phi_+^+ = \Phi_+^+ \cup \phi_n$ and $\Phi_-^+ = \Phi_-^+\backslash\phi_n$. Additionally, it is evident that Eq. 12 is equal to Eq. 10 if $\Phi_+^+ = \Phi^+$ and $\Phi_-^+ = \emptyset$. $\qquad\square$

Equation 10 still contains $p_{\phi_e,1}$ as an auxiliary variable. When replacing $p_{\phi_e,1}$ according to its definition in Eq. 6, we can derive the remaining variables $p_{\phi_e,i}, \forall i > 1$ only based on the other variables $p_{\phi_e,i}, \forall i > 1$. For that purpose, we introduce the variable Λ_l with $1 < l \leq n_\mu$ as defined in Eq. 14, which encapsulates the constant values and the dependency on other privacy levels ϕ for readability. Thus, we can transform Eq. 10 to Eq. 13 by taking the $n^+(l)$-th root and replacing $p_{\phi_e,1}$.

$$1 - p_{\phi_e,l} = \left[1 - \left(\frac{A}{a_{\phi_e,1}} - \sum_{i=2}^{n_\mu} \frac{a_{\phi_e,i} \cdot p_{\phi_e,i}}{a_{\phi_e,1}}\right)\right] \cdot \Lambda_l \quad (13)$$

with

$$\Lambda_i = \sqrt[n^+(i)]{\left(\frac{\mu_1}{\mu_i}\right) \cdot \left(\frac{\rho_{\phi_e,i}}{\rho_{\phi_e,1}}\right) \cdot \prod_{\phi \in \Phi^+(l)\backslash\{\phi_e\}} \left(\frac{\rho_{\phi,i} \cdot \rho_{\phi_e,1}}{\rho_{\phi,1} \cdot \rho_{\phi_e,i}}\right)^{n_\phi} \cdot \prod_{\phi \in \Phi^-(i)} (1-p_{\phi,1})^{n_\phi}}$$

$$(14)$$

The equation system described by Eq. 13 for all $2 \leq l \leq n_\mu$ cannot be solved without considering the dependency on the other privacy levels encapsulated in Λ_l. However, this dependency is hard to resolve except for some special cases, as it removes the linearity from Eq. 13. Thus, we assume that Λ_l is constant for

---

Algorithm 1: Determining the optimal strategy for all privacy-levels. **recal(...)** recalculates $p_{\phi_e,i}$ based on the current values of $p_{\phi,i}$. ϵ is the infinitesimal.

Result: $p_{\phi,i}, \forall \phi \in \Phi, i \in \{1, \ldots, n_\mu\}$

1 $p_{\phi,i} \leftarrow 0, \forall \phi \in \Phi, i \in \{1, \ldots, n_\mu\}$;

2 $c \leftarrow \infty$;

3 **for** $i \leftarrow 1; c > \epsilon; i \leftarrow (i \bmod |\Phi|) + 1$ **do**

4 $\quad$ temp$_j \leftarrow p_{i,j}, \forall j \in \{1, \ldots, n_\mu\}$;

5 $\quad$ recal($p_{i,j}$), $\forall j \in \{1, \ldots, n_\mu\}$;

6 $\quad$ $c \leftarrow \sum_{j=1}^{n_\mu} |$temp$_j - p_{i,j}|$;

7 **end**

8 **return** $p_{\phi,i}, \forall \phi \in \Phi, i \in \{1, \ldots, n_\mu\}$;

---

the calculation of $p_{\phi_e,l}, \forall l \in \{2, \ldots, n_\mu\}$. Thus, we can represent $p_{\phi_e,j} \neq 0$ as $p_{\phi_e,i} \neq 0$ by subtracting the representation of $p_{\phi_e,i}$ from the representation of $p_{\phi_e,j}$ according to Eq. 13 and obtain Eq. 15.

$$p_{\phi_e,i} = \Lambda_i \left(\frac{p_{\phi_e,j} - 1}{\Lambda_j} \right) + 1 \tag{15}$$

With this assumption, we can calculate every $p_{\phi_l,l}$ with Eq. 16, which can be derived from Eq. 13 and the representation of any $p_{\phi_e,i}$ as $p_{\phi_e,j}$ from Eq. 15. Notice, that $\Lambda_1 = 1$, as either $p_{\phi,1} = 0$ (then $1 - p_{\phi,1} = 1$ and disappears), or $p_{\phi,1} \neq 0$ (then $\phi \notin \Phi^-(1)$).

$$p_{\phi_e,l} = \frac{\left[A - \sum_{i=1 | i \neq l \wedge \phi_e \notin \Phi^-(i)}^{n_\mu} a_{\phi_e,i} \right] \Lambda_l}{\sum_{i=1 | i \neq l \wedge \phi_e \notin \Phi^-(i)}^{n_\mu} (a_{\phi_e,i} \cdot \Lambda_i)} + 1 \tag{16}$$

Based on Eq. 16, we can determine the strategies for each privacy level using Algorithm 1. This algorithm ensures that the initial error (induced by setting all probabilities to 0) converges, i.e., the initial error constantly reduces for each iteration of Algorithm 1. This algorithm converges immediately if there is no inter-dependency between the privacy levels, i.e., if there is no other privacy level $\phi_o \mid p_{\phi_o,i} = 0$. If there is an inter-dependency, it converges due to three factors: (i) In the calculation of $p_{\phi,1}$, all probabilities $p_{\phi,i}$ with $i > 1$ are utilized, thus, $p_{\phi,1}$ balances the error of the other probabilities. (ii) $p_{\phi,1}$ influences Λ_i of all privacy levels in $\Phi^-(i)$, but we can see that Λ_l in the nominator and Λ_i in the denominator partially cancel out the error of each other in Eq. 16. (iii) $\exists l, \phi \mid n_\phi < n^+(l)$, in which case the error in Λ_l gets reduced based on the errors of the other privacy levels.

3.2 Deriving the Utility-Optimal Strategy

In the previous section, we assumed that every probability under consideration is non-zero. To calculate the overall optimal strategy, we consider every possible combination of zero and non-zero probabilities of every privacy level, i.e., we consider every possible combination of $\Phi^+(l)$ and $\Phi^-(l)$. That is, the computational complexity of our approach is $\mathcal{O}(2^{|\Phi| \cdot n_\mu})$, i.e., is exponential with the number of privacy levels $|\Phi|$ and the number of impact levels n_μ. This exponential growth is justified by the separate consideration of zero probabilities, which leads to 2 tries per probability. While an exponential growth is generally bad, we need to remember the limited size of $|\Phi|$ and n_μ. As every single computation of probabilities is very fast, the total computation time of the probabilities remains comparably small (in our experiments, it stayed around 100 ms). In the calculation, we set the probabilities of all $p_{\phi,l} = 0 \mid \phi \in \Phi^-(l)$ and only calculate the remaining probabilities with our approach proposed in the previous section. The solution found has certain properties.

Optimality. For each possible set of $\Phi^+(j), \forall j \in \{1, \ldots, n_\mu\}$, the partial derivatives of the utility with respect to all probabilities are 0, i.e., are either local optima or saddle points. To prove that the found solutions are global optima, we need to ensure that there is no other optimum with a higher utility than the found solution. For this purpose, we investigate on the second derivative of the utility function.

$$\frac{\partial^2 \overline{u}}{\partial^2 p_{\phi_e,l}} = -\overline{\mu}_l \cdot \Psi_l - \overline{\mu}_1 \cdot \frac{a_l}{a_0} \cdot \left(-\frac{\rho_{\phi_e,l}}{\rho_{\phi_e,1}} \right)^2 \cdot \Psi_1 \qquad (17)$$

with $\Psi_j = a_l \cdot n_{\phi_e} \cdot (n_{\phi_e} - 1) \cdot (1 - p_{\phi_e,l})^{n_{\phi_e}-2} \cdot P_j (\phi \in \Phi \setminus \{\phi_e\})$.

As $\Psi_i, \overline{\mu}_i$, and a_i are non negative for all i, the second derivative of the utility with respect to any probability $p_{\phi_e,l}$ is always smaller or equal to 0. Thus, the expected utility presented in Eq. 5 is concave. This guarantees that the found solution maximizes the utility, but is not necessarily unique, i.e., there might be other solutions with similar utility.

Stability. The game solution found is a Nash equilibrium, as shown in the following theorem (the proof is omitted for space limitation).

Theorem 3. *The solution of our non-cooperative game shown in Eq. 16 is a Nash equilibrium, i.e., no vehicle has an incentive to deviate from the found solution.*

Observe that this equilibrium is only reached if every vehicle is aware that its neighbors follow the same strategy.

4 Evaluation

In this section, we evaluate the performance of our approach in a realistic vehicular network under varying environmental conditions. For this purpose, we utilize the vehicular extension of the Simonstrator framework [23] in conjunction with SUMO [24] to simulate a vehicular network in Cologne [25]. We compare our approach with state-of-the-art methods for cooperative communication in large-scale vehicular networks and non-cooperative uncoordinated approaches. In this large-scale vehicular network, messages are provided based on the current location of the vehicle (considering its privacy restrictions).

In our simulation, we generate messages randomly in an area of roughly $220 \times 220\,\mathrm{km}^2$, while the movement of vehicles and their networking is only simulated in an area of $2 \times 2\,\mathrm{km}^2$, to reduce the computational overhead. As all events with a possible influence to the network are simulated, we accurately model the message load in a large-scale vehicular network. Unless otherwise said, the bandwidth A is set to 10% of the total required bandwidth. We use messages of 4 impact levels $(1, 10, 100, 1000)$, with frequencies $(90\%, 9\%, 0.9\%, 0.1\%)$ and ranges $(10\,\mathrm{km}, 1\,\mathrm{km}, 100\,\mathrm{km}, 100\,\mathrm{km})$, respectively. The approaches that will be evaluated and compared are the following.

- *Game-Theoretic Privacy-Sensitive Cooperation (GTP)*. This is our approach proposed in Sect. 3, which relies on implicit coordination between vehicles.
- *No Cooperation (NC)*. The No-Cooperation (NC) approach does not consider cooperation between vehicles. Thus, vehicles using the *NC* approach receive similar messages as their neighbors, i.e., they do not share their messages.
- *Clustering with perfect failure detection (GK)*. Clustering is used as follows. A vehicle is chosen as cluster-head, which is the only one communicating directly with the server. The cluster-head distributes the received messages to the vehicles in proximity via V2V communication. In the *GK* approach we assume that the disconnection of the cluster-head (moving out of range) is immediately detected. GK is used as an (unrealistic) upper bound for the performance of our approach.
- *Clustering without perfect failure detection (CL)*. CL is similar to *GK*, with the exception that the detection of cluster-head disconnections is now imperfect. Thus, the vehicles need to wait for a timeout until they detect it and reorganize the cluster. This approach is more realistic than *GK*.

We use two metrics to evaluate the performance of our approach: the *achieved relative utility* and the *used bandwidth*. The *achieved relative utility* measures the performance of the network, i.e., how much data is provided to a vehicle in the network. This metric is between 0 and 1, where 1 states that the vehicle has received all the FCD that was sent and 0 states that the vehicle has received nothing. *Used bandwidth* captures whether the approach sticks to the average bandwidth limitation, i.e., if the side condition of the game is fulfilled.

We use box-plots and line-plots to visualize our results. In the box-plots, the boxes show the differences between vehicles inside of one simulation run. Next to each box, there is a line with a dot, visualizing the average value over all vehicles and simulation runs and the standard deviation of the average of all vehicles. In line-plot, the line displays the mean value for the vehicles in one simulation run.

Figure 1 depicts the performance of the approaches under different available bandwidths to each individual vehicle. It is evident that the performance of all approaches increases as the bandwidth increases, as depicted in Fig. 1a. For a full reception of all data available in the network via cellular, a bandwidth of roughly

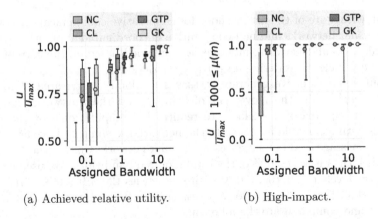

(a) Achieved relative utility.   (b) High-impact.

Fig. 1. Achieved relative bandwidth for different bandwidths (in messages/s).

100 messages per second is required. Even with a much smaller bandwidth of 10 messages per second, all approaches can achieve reasonable utility levels by prioritizing high-impact messages. It can be observed that our *GTP* approach outperforms the *CL* approach as well as the *NC* approach and has much smaller confidence intervals compared to the *CL* approach. Thus, our approach is more resilient and adaptive to different network conditions. Additionally, our approach is very close in performance to the *GK* approach. The same holds for a bandwidth of 1, while our approach decreases in performance for a bandwidth of 0.1. For a bandwidth of 0.1, our approach performs worse than the *CL* approach, as the redundant transmission of high-impact messages and the missing explicit coordination between vehicles decrease the performance of our *GTP* approach. This is also confirmed by Fig. 1b: For the high-impact messages, our approach performs well for both a bandwidth of 1 and 10, but struggles to receives the high-impact messages for a bandwidth of 0.1. That is, a bandwidth of 0.1 is not sufficient to receive the high-impact messages using only the available bandwidth of a single vehicle. Thus, the performance of our approach decreases below the performance of the *CL* approach, as the explicit coordination of vehicles in clustering approaches can handle low bandwidths well. Additionally, all approaches stick to the available bandwidth on average, while the bandwidth is temporarily exceeded by a subset of vehicles. This exceeding of bandwidth is justified by (i) the different number of available messages depending on the event location and (ii) the cooperative reception of messages by vehicles.

Figure 2 displays the influence of the share of privacy (fraction of privacy-sensitive vehicles) on our realistic vehicular network if the privacy-sensitive vehicles use an area of imprecision with radius 10 km. Figure 2a shows the behavior of the relative utility for all of the approaches. The *NC* approach decreases the most, as the privacy-sensitive vehicles have no possibility to compensate for their context imprecision. Additionally, our *GTP* approach constantly outperforms the *CL* approach and the *NC* approach independent of the level of privacy.

Most interestingly, the performance decrease of our *GTP* approach compared to the *GK* approach is not constant, it is lowest around 50% privacy. This can be justified by implicit coordination between privacy levels. This is also visible in Fig. 2b, which displays the relative utility of messages with an impact between 10 and 100. While the *NC* approach is not able to receive these messages at all, the utility of the other approaches decreases constantly. However, for our *GTP* approach, the utility remains constant for a very long duration, which leads to a comparably constant overall utility even for high privacy levels.

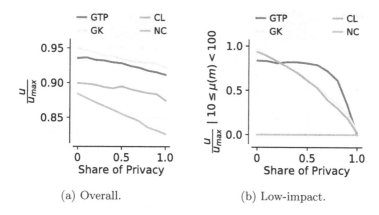

(a) Overall.   (b) Low-impact.

Fig. 2. Achieved relative utility for mixed environments.

5   Conclusion

In this paper we introduce privacy considerations in the management of FCD and have shown its impact on location-based services, since some data are not forwarded to a vehicle due to privacy considerations and the implemented location obfuscation. In order to alleviate this problem, we have introduced cooperation among vehicles so as to forward relevant data to their neighboring vehicles, enhancing in principle the data received by a vehicle only directly from the remote server. In this work, an ad-hoc, direct V2V cooperation paradigm is employed instead of a cluster-based one, also showing the high performance deterioration of the latter in a real vehicular networking environment. A major contribution of this work is the development and study of a game without coordination that determines the strategies (in terms of probabilities that a vehicle is forwarded by the server data of a given impact index) vehicles should follow, so that a properly defined utility is maximized; this is shown to lead to a diversification of the data received directly from the server by neighboring vehicles and increases the effectiveness of V2V cooperation.

In the evaluation, we analyzed the performance of our approach in a realistic vehicular network. Our results show the drastic performance increase compared to non-cooperative uncoordinated approaches, and the improvements over cluster-based approaches. Additionally, our approach performs almost similarly to a perfect clustering approach, which utilizes bandwidth optimally and detects disconnects immediately, but is not realizable in reality. When we analyze the performance of our approach for different privacy levels, we see that the performance remains constant for a long time.

References

1. Meuser, T., Bischoff, D., Richerzhagen, B., Steinmetz, R.: Cooperative offloading in context-aware networks: a game-theoretic approach. In: Proceedings of ACM International Conference on Distributed and Event-Based Systems (DEBS 2019). ACM (2019)
2. Golle, P., Greene, D., Staddon, J.: Detecting and correcting malicious data in VANETs. In: Proceedings of ACM International Workshop on Vehicular Ad Hoc Networks (VANET), VANET 2004, pp. 29–37. ACM, New York (2004)
3. Dötzer, F.: Privacy issues in vehicular ad hoc networks. In: Danezis, G., Martin, D. (eds.) PET 2005. LNCS, vol. 3856, pp. 197–209. Springer, Heidelberg (2006). https://doi.org/10.1007/11767831_13
4. Ying, B., Makrakis, D., Hou, Z.: Motivation for protecting selfish vehicles' location privacy in vehicular networks. IEEE Trans. Veh. Technol. **64**(12), 5631–5641 (2015)
5. Pan, X., Xu, J., Meng, X.: Protecting location privacy against location-dependent attacks in mobile services. IEEE Trans. Knowl. Data Eng. **24**(8), 1506–1519 (2012)
6. Ying, B., Nayak, A.: Social location privacy protection method in vehicular social networks. In: Proceedings of IEEE International Conference on Communications Workshops (ICC Workshops), pp. 1288–1292 (2017)
7. Wasef, A., Shen, X.S.: REP: location privacy for VANETs using random encryption periods. Mobile Netw. Appl. **15**(1), 172–185 (2010)
8. Sampigethaya, K., Huang, L., Li, M., Poovendran, R., Matsuura, K., Sezaki, K.: CARAVAN: providing location privacy for VANET. In: Embedded Security in Cars (ESCAR) (2005)
9. Liu, B., Zhou, W., Zhu, T., Gao, L., Luan, T.H., Zhou, H.: Silence is golden: enhancing privacy of location-based services by content broadcasting and active caching in wireless vehicular networks. IEEE Trans. Veh. Technol. **65**(12), 9942–9953 (2016)
10. Petit, J., Schaub, F., Feiri, M., Kargl, F.: Pseudonym schemes in vehicular networks: a survey. IEEE Commun. Surv. Tutor. **17**(1), 228–255 (2014)
11. Gerlach, M., Guttler, F.: Privacy in VANETs using changing pseudonyms - ideal and real. In: Proceedings of IEEE Vehicular Technology Conference (VTC-Spring), April 2007, pp. 2521–2525 (2007)
12. Palanisamy, B., Liu, L.: MobiMix: protecting location privacy with mix-zones over road networks. In: 2011 IEEE 27th International Conference on Data Engineering, pp. 494–505 (2011)
13. Freudiger, J., Raya, M., Félegyházi, M., Papadimitratos, P., Hubaux, J.-P.: Mix-zones for location privacy in vehicular networks. In: Proceedings of ACM Workshop on Wireless Networking for Intelligent Transportation Systems (WiN-ITS) (2007)

14. Ying, B., Makrakis, D., Mouftah, H.T.: Dynamic mix-zone for location privacy in vehicular networks. IEEE Commun. Lett. **17**(8), 1524–1527 (2013)
15. Wiedersheim, B., Ma, Z., Kargl, F., Papadimitratos, P.: Privacy in inter-vehicular networks: why simple pseudonym change is not enough. In: Proceedings of International Conference on Wireless On-Demand Network Systems and Services (WONS), pp. 176–183 (2010)
16. Duckham, M., Kulik, L.: Location privacy and location-aware computing. In: Dynamic and Mobile GIS, pp. 63–80. CRC Press (2006)
17. Gruteser, M., Grunwald, D.: Anonymous usage of location-based services through spatial and temporal cloaking. In: Proceedings of International Conference on Mobile Systems, Applications and Services (MobiSys), pp. 31–42. ACM, New York (2003)
18. Niu, B., Li, Q., Zhu, X., Cao, G., Li, H.: Achieving k-anonymity in privacy-aware location-based services. In: Proceedings of IEEE International Conference on Computer Communications (INFOCOM), pp. 754–762, April 2014
19. Liu, X., Liu, K., Guo, L., Li, X., Fang, Y.: A game-theoretic approach for achieving k-anonymity in location based services. In: Proceedings of IEEE International Conference on Computer Communications (INFOCOM), pp. 2985–2993 (2013)
20. Freudiger, J., Manshaei, M.H., Hubaux, J.-P., Parkes, D.C.: On non-cooperative location privacy: a game-theoretic analysis. In: Proceedings of the 16th ACM Conference on Computer and Communications Security, CCS 2009, pp. 324–337. ACM, New York (2009)
21. Du, S., Li, X., Du, J., Zhu, H.: An attack-and-defence game for security assessment in vehicular ad hoc networks. Peer-to-Peer Netw. Appl. **7**(3), 215–228 (2012). https://doi.org/10.1007/s12083-012-0127-9
22. Laoutaris, N., Telelis, O., Zissimopoulos, V., Stavrakakis, I.: Distributed selfish replication. IEEE Trans. Parallel Distrib. Syst. **17**(12), 1401–1413 (2006)
23. Meuser, T., Bischoff, D., Steinmetz, R., Richerzhagen, B.: Simulation platform for connected heterogeneous vehicles. In: Proceedings of International Conference on Vehicle Technology and Intelligent Transport Systems (VEHITS). SCITEPRESS, May 2019, pp. 412–419 (2019)
24. Lopez, P.A., et al.: Microscopic traffic simulation using SUMO. In: Proceedings of IEEE ITSC. IEEE (2018)
25. Uppoor, S., Fiore, M.: Large-scale urban vehicular mobility for networking research. In: Proceedings of IEEE Vehicular Networking Conference (VNC), pp. 62–69 (2011)

Blockchains and the Commons

Maria Potop-Butucaru[✉]

Sorbonne Universite, CNRS, LIP6, 75005 Paris, France
`maria.potop-butucaru@lip6.fr`

Abstract. Blockchain phenomena is similar to the last century gold rush. Blockchain technologies are publicized as being the technical solution for fully decentralizing activities that were for centuries centralized such as administration and banking. Therefore, prominent socio-economical actors all over the world are attracted and ready to invest in these technologies. Despite their large publicity, blockchains are far from being a technology ready to be used in critical economical applications and scientists multiply their effort in warning about the risks of using this technology before understanding and fully mastering it. That is, a blockchain technology evolves in a complex environment where rational and irrational behaviors are melted with faults and attacks. This position paper advocates that the theoretical foundations of blockchains should be a cross research between classical distributed systems, distributed cryptography, self-organized micro-economies, game theory and formal methods. We discuss in the following a set of open research directions interesting in this context.

Keywords: Blockchain · The commons · Open research directions

1 Introduction

Blockchain systems became today one of the most appealing area of research motivated mainly by the recent speculations on crypto-currencies such as Bitcoin [63] or Ethereum [76]. A blockchain is a distributed ledger that mimics the functioning of a classical traditional ledger (i.e. transparency and falsification-proof of documentation) in an untrusted environment where the computation is distributed. The set of participants in the system are not known and it varies during the execution. Moreover, each participant follows his own rules to maximize its welfare.

Blockchain systems maintain a continuously growing list of ordered blocks that include one or more transactions[1] that have been verified by the members of the system, called miners. Blocks are linked using cryptography and the order

---

[1] Transaction is used here as a generic name to be adapted to a broad class of use cases. For example, a transaction in Bitcoin [63] or Ethereum [76] can be a transfer of digital money or assets.

This position paper is based on the homonymous ERC Advanced submission [71]. It is assumed that the reader has some background knowledge on Blockchain technologies.

© Springer Nature Switzerland AG 2021
C. Georgiou and R. Majumdar (Eds.): NETYS 2020, LNCS 12129, pp. 28–44, 2021.
https://doi.org/10.1007/978-3-030-67087-0_3

of blocks in the blockchain is the result of a form of agreement among the system participants. Participants strongly agree only on a prefix of the blockchain; the suffix of the blockchain may be different from one participant to another.

Blockchain systems, beyond their incontestable assets such as decentralization, simple design and relative easy use, are not free of incidents and limitations. The most popular incident reported for Ethereum, for example, was the 60 million dollars ether theft which was possible by simply exploiting an error in the code and the lack of system specification.

A recent scientific analyse, [43], focus on several limitations of the most popular blockchain, Bitcoin, such as: weak security, low quality of services, storage limitations, low throughput and high cost and weak consistency.

Therefore, despite their large publicity blockchains are far from being a technology ready to be used in critical economical applications and scientists multiply their efforts in warning about the risks of using this technology before understanding and fully mastering it. Interestingly, many recent attempts to alarm on vulnerabilities of popular blockchains like Bitcoin are target of defenders brigading.

Nevertheless, once fully mastered, Blockchain systems will be the technical solution for fully decentralizing activities that were for centuries centralized such as, for example, administration or banking. The applications of tomorrow that potentially will be blockchainized are all different from each other. These applications may range from IoTs to notary passing by administration, banking or health. These applications have various consistency and quality of services requirements. Therefore, we advocate that there will not be only one blockchain but a family of modular blockchains that will have to offer various qualities of services and that will be eventually interconnected.

It should be noted that differently from classical distributed applications, some blockchains have a strong economical aspect, since participants should be constantly incited to participate to the system welfare by rewarding their contribution. This contribution is materialized either in the energy spent in solving cryptographic puzzles in order to generate blocks or in the bandwidth spent to route transactions and blocks. If participants massively leave the system then the system collapses, a phenomenon known in economy as the *tragedy of commons* [56,65,66]. In order to avoid this phenomenon, blockchains have to cross-over new distributed formally verified and proven algorithms with game theory tools and also government rules issued from self-organized micro-economies.

2   State of the Art

The birth of blockchains systems, as for the case of P2P systems in the early 2000, was in the non academic research. After the releasing of the most popular blockchains (e.g. Bitcoin [63] or Ethereum [76]) with a specific focus on economical transactions their huge potential for various other applications became evident.

Their popularity, transformed blockchains in a huge social experiment that confirmed the fact that blockchains can be a viable alternative for distributed systems of tomorrow. Starting with this point, the blockchain area started to became the focus of the academical research.

Interestingly, only recently distributed computing scientist started to investigate theoretical aspects of blockchains and several directions of research can be identified: blockchains based on *proof-of-work* and its alternatives such as *proof-of-stake*, *proof-of-space* or *proof-of-authority*, blockchains using as underlying building block the achievements in classical *practical Byzantine fault-tolerance* and finally *sortition* based blockchains.

The theoretical study of *proof-of-work* based blockchains has been pioneered by Garay et al. [51]. They decorticate the pseudo-code of Bitcoin and analyze its agreement aspects considering a synchronous round-based communication model. That is, messages sent in a round are assumed to arrive in the next round. This study has been extended by Pass et al. [68] to round based systems where messages sent in a round can be received later. The major criticisms for the *proof-of-work* approach are as follows: it is assumed that the honest miners hold a majority of the computational power, the generation of a block is energetically costly which yielded to the creation of mining pools and finally, the multiple blockchains that coexist in the system. Interestingly, the two alternatives for *proof-of-work* such as *proof-of-stake* (the power of block building is proportional to the amount of money they own in the system) or *proof-of-authority* (the power of block building is proportional to the amount of authority they own in the system) have not yet been fully analyzed from a theoretical point of view. The line of research that addresses the consensus in proof-of-stake based blockchains is pioneered by Daian et al. [44] that proposes a protocol for weakly synchronous networks. The execution of the protocol is organized in epochs. Similar to Bitcoin-NG [46] described below in each epoch a different committee is elected and inside the elected committee a leader will be chosen. The leader is allowed to extend the new blockchain. The protocol is validated via simulations and only partial proofs of correctness are provided.

In order to overcome the drawbacks of Bitcoin, [46] proposes a mix between proof-of-work blockchains and proof-of-work free blockchains referred as Bitcoin-NG. The idea is that the execution of the system is organized in epochs. In each epoch a leader elected via a proof-of-work mechanism will decide the order transactions that will be committed in the blockchain till the next epoch. Bitcoin-NG inherits the drawbacks of Bitcoin: costly proof-of-work process, forks, no guarantee that a leader in an epoch is unique, no guarantee that the leader do not change the history at will if the leader is corrupted.

Later, [58] initiates an alternative to the proof-of-work based blockchains, named Byzcoin. Their research build on top of *practical Byzantine fault-tolerance* [38] enhanced with a scalable collective signing process. The work in [58] is based on a leader-based consensus over a group of members chosen based on a proof-of-membership mechanism. As in Bitcoin, when a miner succeeds to mine a block it is included in the voting members set that excludes one member. This protocol also inherits some of the Bitcoin problems and vulnerabilities. Also Byzcoin voting core can be totally corrupted by a dynamic adversary. More recently,

SBFT [53] and Hyperledger Fabric [15] build also on top of [38]. In the same spirit, [42] proposes for the first time a leader-free algorithm to solve Consensus among participants in a consortium Blockchain where the specifications has been adapted to the Blockchain scenario. The same specification is then considered in DBFT [41], an evolution of the consensus algorithm in [42], in Tendermint Consensus algorithm [36]. In the same line of research SBFT [53] and Hot-Stuff [9] have been proposed recently.

In order to avoid some of the previously cited problems, Micali [62] introduced (further extended in [23,39]) the *sortition* based blockchains that completely replace the proof-of-work mechanism by sortition. These works focus again the agreement aspects of blockchains using probabilistic ingredients. More specifically, the set of nodes that are allowed to produce and validate blocks are randomly chosen and they change over the time. Interestingly, the study focuses only on synchronous round-based communication models which do not reflect the reality of blockchain technologies.

In another line of research, Pass *et al.* address in [69] one of the vulnerabilities of Bitcoin studied formally in Eyal and Sirer [47]. In [47] the authors prove that if the adversary controls a coalition of miners holding even a minority fraction of the computational power, this coalition can gain twice its share. Fruitchain proposed in [69] overcomes this problem by ensuring that no coalition controlling less than a majority of the computing power can gain more than a factor $1 + 3\delta$ by not respecting the protocol, where δ is a parameter of the protocol.

A full overview of the agreement protocols designed for blockchain systems can be found in [50].

Another interesting line of research has been opened by *Decker et al.* [45] which is related to the blockchains consistency. They propose PeerCensus system that targets to provide the linearizability of transactions. PeerCensus combines, similar to Byzcoin, the proof-of-work blockchain and the classical results in practical byzantine agreement fault tolerance. This line of research has been continued in [14,16,18,40].

All the above-mentioned studies leave a huge unexplored space in the theoretical distributed aspects of blockchains. Moreover, even though a strong effort has been recently dedicated to formalizing blockchain systems, it comes to evidence that blockchains still lack of formalization and theoretical understanding of their properties and their level of consistency face to *system asynchrony, churn and partitions, rational and irrational behaviors* and *multiple types of faults and attacks*. This important drawback limits drastically the integration of blockchains in industrial applications despite the huge interest of the main industrial actors in this technology. In the following we detail open research directions that may help in integrating blockchain solutions in practical applications.

3 Explore Novel Models of Reliability for Blockchains

Faults are studied in distributed systems for decades [19] and most of the time in isolation. Interestingly, faults and behaviors are defined in the distributed systems literature in a verbose mode which, in most of the cases leaves the place to the interpretation.

In a very popular paper, *Laprie et al.* [20] describe and classify the distributed system faults, errors and failures. Interestingly, Byzantine Altruistic and Rational model, a.k.a BAR [11] extends the model proposed in [20]. BAR model identifies three categories of processes: *altruistic*, those who follow a prescribed protocol; *rationals*, those who act in order to maximise their utility function; and *Byzantines*, those who may rationally deviate from a prescribed protocol. This later behavior can be seen as rational Byzantine behavior. In [8] the authors introduce the notion of robustness of a distributed system by introducing the notions of k-resiliency and t-immunity. In a k-resilient equilibrium there is no coalition of k players having an incentive to simultaneously change strategy to get a better outcome. On the other hand, the concept of t-immunity evaluates the risk of a set of t players to have a Byzantine behavior. It should be noted that the property of t-immunity is often impossible to be satisfied in practical systems [7].

In the context of blockchains, Micali *et al.* [39] advocate that blockchains should be tolerant to *churn* and to a very powerful *dynamic adversary*. Informally speaking, this adversary "can corrupt any user he wants, at any time; totally control and perfectly coordinate all corrupted users and schedule the delivery of messages". Moreover, Blockchains area brings a new direction of research by exposing *rational behavior* with effects similar to the irrational ones. This type of behavior is extensively studied in economics theories as for example the Elinor Ostrom work [56,65,66].

The hierarchy of *Laprie et al.* [20] extended with the BAR model or the (k,t)-robustness model covers complex faults experienced in blockchains such as dynamic adversaries, churn, transient faults, rational and irrational behaviors or combinations. Therefore, several research directions need to be explored in this context.

3.1 Blockchain Robustness to Dynamic Adversaries

The *dynamic adversary* that affects blockchains described by Micali in [39] has a Byzantine flavor and has similarities with Mobile Byzantine Adversaries studied in classical distributed systems. Intuitively, a mobile byzantine adversary can move agents from a process to another in order to deviate the process computation. When a process is infected by an adversarial agent, it behaves arbitrarily until the adversary decides to move the agent to another process. Most of the literature on Mobile Byzantine Adversaries [21,34,37,49,67,73,75] considered so far *synchronous round-based models*, and only between two consecutive rounds Byzantine agents are allowed to move from one process to another. Hence, the set of faulty processes at any given time has a bounded size, yet its membership may evolve from one round to the next. It is obvious that adversaries described so far by the classical distributed literature do not match Micali's description of dynamic adversary in blockchains. A challenge would be to explore Mobile Byzantine Adversaries decoupled from the synchronous communication of the system. However, this line of research still does not cover the dynamic adversary in blockchains and further research is needed in this direction.

Therefore, *the main challenge will be the formal specification of the robustness of blockchains face to dynamic adversaries.*

3.2 Robustness to Rationality and Irrationality

Common resources in blockchain systems can be seen at different levels. Participants gain a financial benefit from generating blocks. However, they bring to the system their energy. Moreover, the system itself uses participants as resources since functionalities of the system such as routing, overlay maintenance, mining or agreement, are totally dependent on the presence of the participants. The risk in these systems, as the one advertised recently for Bitcoin, is the fact that participants will leave the system and hence the system collapses. This phenomenon is known in economy as the *tragedy of commons*. Commons have similarities to the fair resource sharing in P2P networks where peers express rational behaviors. Each peer in a resource sharing system gains a certain benefit from using the system and pays a certain cost for participating to it. The incentives-based solutions proposed so far in P2P networks (e.g. [13]) are most of the time evaluated in an empirical model with no formalization. Also these solutions are not designed to cope with dynamic adversaries.

In order to avoid the *tragedy of commons* phenomenon in blockchains, new solutions have to be designed by combining self-organized micro-economies theories (in particular the work of Nobel Prize Elinor Ostrom) with on-the-shelf tools issued from mechanisms and game theories.

A first step would be to understand the effect of various behaviors on blockchain systems. From the game perspective point of view rationality in blockchains has been studies in [24] (for the case of Bitcoin protocol) or [74] (for the case of proof-of-stake protocols). Recently, in [12] the authors explore the robustness of Tendermint consensus core to rational and Byzantine behaviors. They analyze equilibrium interactions between Byzantine and rational committee members and derive conditions under which consensus properties are satisfied or not in equilibrium. However, the proposed framework is not general enough to be applied to other blockchain building blocks.

The challenge here will be to define a unified framework for specifying rational and irrational behaviors all together with mobility of faults and attacks and propose incentive rules tolerant to these behaviors.

One possible solution is first to extend the model proposed in [11] to the specificities of blockchain systems. In [11] the authors define a *Byzantine Altruistic Rational Tolerant* (BART) protocol that guarantees the specified set of safety and liveness properties in the presence of all rational deviations. A protocol is said to be *Incentive-Compatible Byzantine Fault Tolerant* (IC-BFT) if any rational user is incentivized to follow the prescribed protocol, also in presence of Byzantine users. Then, to make practical the model proposed in [8] by relaxing the requirements in terms of t-immunity. Then, propose combined rules resulted from various theories (games theory, mechanisms theory) that will be encoded in incentive rules.

4   Formal Abstractions for Blockchains Consistency

A large number of political, economical and social organisms invoke the possibility of blockchainize their activity. Obviously, the data that will be stored on the blockchain in each of these applications may have various levels of consistency: starting with very strong consistency for the case of banking or notary applications and finishing with weak consistency for applications such as IoTs. Identifying the exact requirements of consistency for representative applications in each class is a challenge in itself.

Studying the level of consistency provided by existing blockchains is related to the distributed shared register area. However, the similarity is moderated. A distributed register is a shared variable accessed by a set of processes through two operations, namely write() and read(). Informally, the write() operation updates the value stored in the shared variable while the read() obtains the value contained in the shared variable. The classical registers definitions [59] have been extended to the self-stabilizing area in [30]. This work considers that the system can be hit by arbitrary errors.

It should be noted that none of the above mentioned classical definitions captures the behavior of the popular blockchains such as Ethereum and Bitcoin. That is, values written in a classical register are potentially independent, and during the execution, the size of the register remains the same. In contrast, a new block cannot be written in the blockchain if it does not depend on the previous one, and successive writings in the blockchain increase its size. Also, differently from stabilizing registers, the prefix of the blockchain eventually converges, while no guarantees hold for the last created blocks.

The challenge here is to define new consistency abstractions that will capture the semantics of blockchains.

4.1   Defining New Consistency Abstractions for Blockchains

The first effort in specifying the properties of permissionless blockchain systems is due to Garay and Kiayias [51]. They characterized Bitcoin blockchain via its quality and its common prefix properties, i.e., they define an invariant that this protocol has to satisfy in order to verify with high probability an eventually consistent prefix. This line of work has been continued by [69]. In order to model the behavior of distributed ledgers at runtime, Girault et al. [52] present an implementation of the Monotonic Prefix Consistency (MPC) criterion and showed that no criterion stronger than MPC can be implemented in a partition-prone message-passing system. On the other hand, the proposed formalization does not propose weaker consistency semantics more suitable for proof-of-work blockchains as Bitcoin. In the same line of research, in [14], Anceaume et al. propose a new data type to formally model distributed ledgers and their behavior at runtime. They provide consistency criteria to capture the correct behavior of current blockchain proposals in a unified framework. In parallel and independently of [14], Anta et al. [17] propose a formalization of distributed ledgers modeled as an ordered list of records. The authors consider three consistency criteria: eventual consistency, sequential consistency and linearizability.

Providing a unified framework able to capture the specificity of blockchain systems is still an open problem.

Moreover, formalizing the definition of this class of blockchain consistency will help in further proving the correctness and formally verifying algorithms that implement them. The semantic of the consistency can be express in terms of events and partial orders to these events. Note that for the classical consistency criteria the recent work of Gotsman et al. [54] provided a rich formalism based on token systems. However, this formalism should be extended to the blockchain context.

4.2 Design and Formally Prove New Consistency Algorithms Tolerant to Complex Behaviors

It should be noted that existing effort for implementing consistency in blockchains (e.g. [23,51,62]) concentrate on solving the agreement (consensus) problem. However, it is already folklore that consensus is impossible to solve deterministically in asynchronous environments [48]. As pointed out in the state of the art section, implementing blockchain probabilistic consensus in asynchronous environments subject to dynamic faults is still an open problem. The deterministic implementation of registers (even with strong consistency guarantees) in various models characterized by the presence of multiple types of faults (crashes, byzantine, dynamic byzantine or transient) have been investigated in the past [30–32,35]. In blockchain systems, recent effort has been directed to both formalizing and implementing consistency criteria in systems prone to faults or Byzantine behaviors [14,16,18,40].

None of the above proposed solutions work with the severe model of blockchain adversary including rationality, irrationality, churns or partitions. Therefore, the implementation of blockchain objects with various consistency guarantees in a *asynchronous environment* with *dynamic models of adversary* when the *size of the network is unknown* is a real challenge that might be mitigated by combining the framework in [35] with abstractions such as *k-quorums* defined in [10] and *sortition* techniques or intersecting sets (i.e. the secure version of the classical distributed quorum systems).

5 Develop Correct-by-Construction Agreement Algorithms for Blockchains

The core of blockchains technologies is the agreement problem, studied in an environment where participants to the agreement may be controlled by a dynamic adversary. This form of agreement is known in distributed computing as Byzantine Agreement. Briefly stated, it requires that processors, some of which being potentially malicious, start the computation with an initial value and decide on the same value.

Byzantine Agreement, introduced by Lamport *et al.* [60], has been studied for decades in static distributed systems under different aspects (e.g., *possibility, complexity, cost*) in various models (from synchronous to asynchronous, from authenticated to anonymous) with different methodologies (deterministic or probabilistic).

5.1 Feasibility of Blockchain Agreement Face to Complex Faults and Behaviors

Garay et *al.* [51] and [62] pioneered the study of Byzantine Agreement in blockchains. However, their studies are restricted to only round-based synchronous systems.

In [29], the authors study deterministic Byzantine Agreement in environments where the set of nodes controlled by the adversary may change over time. Contrary to other approaches, the model considers that a process previously affected by the adversary may send messages (based on a corrupted state), it will behave correctly in the way it sends those messages: i.e., send messages according to the algorithm. This behavior is very similar to the way the adversary acts in blockchains systems. Interestingly, in order to implement Byzantine Agreement under the assumption of dynamic Byzantine adversary a system needs at least $5f + 1$ nodes while in the case of static Byzantine adversary only $3f + 1$ are sufficient, where f is the number of nodes controlled by the Byzantine. These studies leave a huge avenue to be explored. First, there is no extension of [29] to round-free environments. Second, in the same model of adversarial model there is no study related to feasibility of the agreement problem when the adversary movement is decoupled from the synchronous round of computation.

The above works do not implement agreement in asynchronous systems prone to dynamic adversary, rationality or churn.

An interesting challenge would be to explore the asynchronous probabilistic Byzantine agreement in systems prone to dynamic adversary and churn and where processes may have rational behaviors. One of possible solutions would be to considered the methodology proposed in [29] to round free churn exposed systems combined with *sortition* techniques and incentives rules issues from games and mechanisms theories.

5.2 New Abstractions for Blockchain Agreement

Agreement in blockchains has an *Approximate agreement* flavor since the agreement on blockchains should be guaranteed not on an exact value. In systems hit by Mobile Byzantine Adversaries (the closes to the blockchain dynamic adversary) [33] formalized the approximate agreement and prove lower bounds on problem solvability in various dynamic adversary models and further propose an optimal algorithm for approximate agreement in round based systems. The lower bounds range from $n > 3f + 1$ to $n > 6f + 1$ depending on the type of adversary.

The previous results do not cover the blockchain agreement for several reasons: blockchains are not round-based, the adversary is not bounded to the rounds change, the agreement value is not a real value but a prefix of an ever changing blockchain.

Formalizing the bockchain approximate agreement and then proposing solutions in asynchronous environments hit by a dynamic adversary and rationality is the scientific lock here.

6 Develop Correct-by-Construction Overlays and Routing Algorithms for Blockchains

Blockchain underlying overlays and the associate routing are totally unexplored from a theoretical point of view. However, the performances of blockchains technologies heavily depend on the performances of the underlying routing process. Recently, Lightning technologies [70] imposed themselves as a viable direction for improving the blockchains throughput. This technology builds on top of blockchains (e.g. Bitcoin) an overlay of secured channels opened by two parties involved in long term multi-transactions. This overlay is further used to route transactions. Although blockchain technologies make strong assumptions on their underlying overlays there is no academic research that focus on these overlays. The only prior research on the overlays topic has been developed in the context of dynamic networks such as P2P or wireless networks.

Another interesting point to be explored is the *liveness of the overlay* and more generally of the system. In blockchains the welfare of participants is a crucial factor. When participants desert the system in proof-of-work based blockchains the security of the system sinks, which yields to the global sink of the system. As mentioned previously, this phenomenon is known in economy as the *tragedy of commons*.

6.1 New Abstractions for Blockchain Overlays

Expanders theory proved recently its effectiveness for constructing overlays resilient to churn and partitions. The (node) expansion of an undirected graph is a characterization of the graph robustness. That is, graphs with good expansion are hard to be partitioned into a number of large connected components. In this sense, the expansion of a graph can be seen as a good evaluation of its resilience to faults and churn. However, the expansion of tree overlays is trivially $O(1/n)$ where n is the number of nodes in the tree overlay. This weakness to faults explains why tree overlays are not pervasive in real applications.

In [57], the authors measured the robustness of tree overlay networks by evaluating their *graph expansion* and proposed a logarithmic algorithm for the construction of a constant degree self* expander that improves the resilience to churn of P2P tree-overlays.

The existing works are not tolerant to dynamic adversaries which can disconnect the overlay before its stabilization. *The unexplored yet research direction concerns the construction of constant degree expenders tolerant to dynamic Byzantine behavior and multiple types of faults. A possible solution would be to extend the methodology in* [57] *with* sortition techniques.

6.2 New Formally Verified Routing Protocols for Blockchains

In order to increase the throughput in Bitcoin, the non academical research in blockchains proposed recently lightning routing networks [70]. Secured channels between two or more participants are opened on top of Bitcoin and transactions are routed on top of the virtual network formed by these channels. Routing in lightning networks has some similarities with routing in P2P or mobile wireless networks or delay tolerant networks. Flare [72], for example, which is one of the most prominent lightning routing was inspired by the wireless ZRP routing protocol.

Interestingly, there is no formal academic research on this topic so far and our preliminary studies show that Flare (and its derivates) present severe limitations such as weak resilience to churn or deadlocks. Moreover, none of these lightning routing protocols has been exposed to multiple types of faults, attacks or dynamic adversaries.

The most studied overlay for routing in classical distributed systems and networking theory is the minimum spanning tree (MST). Research on spanning trees tolerant to multiple faults has been conducted in [25–28]. None of the above cited algorithms is resilient to dynamic adversaries in conjunction with churn and attacks. The challenge here will be the design of new routing algorithms optimized for the context of lightning networks subject to multiple types of faults, attacks, rationality and dynamic adversaries.

7 Blockchains Interoperability

There are currently several operational systems for achieving interoperability between different blockchains such as Cosmos [2] or Polkadot [6]. These systems can be classified into two categories according to their decentralization level: systems that use a trusted third-party to validate transactions or systems that realize it directly between blockchains without the need of a trusted third-party.

In order to execute an exchange or a *swap* (i.e., a set of transactions between parties), transacting agents (i.e., blockchain users) are provided with a protocol to stick to. A protocol in this case consists of a specific sequence of instructions agents should perform to preserve the ACID properties [61] of the individual transactions or exchanges.

The first atomic swap solution has been proposed for Bitcoin by *Nolan* [64] making use of hash-time locked contracts enabling conditional assets transfers. *Decred* [3] implements Nolan's algorithm on UTXO-based premissionless. In [55] the authors generalize and prove correct *Nolan*'s scheme. Other projects such as

BartherDEX [5], part of the Komodo project [4], represents a cross-chain solution that matches orders and defines the swap protocol or *Blockchain.io* [1] implements atomic cross-chain swaps by combining centralized components (order matching) with decentralized ones (trade settlement and execution). These projects are not yet formally proved correct.

The academic research focuses on *hybrid* swap protocols, replacing decentralized commitment/locking schemes (hash-locks) with centralized ones, resulting more attractive and efficient. *AC3TW* and *AC3WN* [77] protocols propose atomic cross-chain swaps respectively with centralized and distributed trusted authorities (i.e. witnesses). It should be noted that different swap protocols differ essentially in the involved parties. The set of swap participants can be composed only of the asset owners (e.g., as in [55]) or by owners accompanied by a trusted third party (e.g., as in the AC3TW protocol [77]).

In [22], the authors propose a generic game theoretical framework that formalizes the swap problem and characterize equilibria of two representative recent protocols presented in [64] and [77] respectively. In the case of the protocol proposed in [64] and generalised in [55], following the protocol is the unique subgame perfect equilibrium (in dominant strategies), while in the case of the protocol proposed in [77], following the protocol is a Nash equilibrium.

These works open several research directions. Swap protocols and more generally blockchain intercommunication are not yet properly formalized and analyzed.

An important challenge in this area is to fully formalize the problem and analyze the robustness of protocols that implement it face to both rational and irrational behaviors, dynamic adversaries and attacks and coalitions.

8   Conclusions

Blockchains evolve in a very complex environment. Differently from the classical distributed systems, where faults are considered to appear in isolation and to affect the same node of the system during the whole computation, in blockchains environments faults do not follow the same pattern. Blockchains have to face in the same time classical pattens of faults such as crash faults, transient faults, Byzantine faults but also attacks, dynamic faults, churn and selfish or rational/irrational behaviors. Therefore, before addressing the algorithmic core of blockchains a fully characterization of the adversarial environment is necessary. Interestingly, faults and errors in most of the cases (even in classical distributed system) have only a verbose definition. When systems have to be released for industrial or critical economical use automatic verifications and mathematical proofs are necessary. Therefore, verbose definitions are not precise enough. In this paper we discuss five important challenges in this area. The first challenge is to explore and formalize blockchains robustness. The second challenge is to formally define universal abstractions for characterizing blockchains consistency. The third challenge is to provide new correct-by-construction abstractions for agreement in blockchains. The effectiveness of these building blocks will be insured by a formal verification and proof using formal methods tools. The fourth challenge is to develop optimized overlays and communication primitives for blockchains resilient to nodes churn, various attacks and adversary dynamic behaviors and target to avoid the partition or the sink of the system in a *tragedy of commons*. Finally, the formalization of blockchains interoperability is the fifth challenge.

References

1. Blockchain.io (Your gateway to the internet of value). https://blockchain.io/. Accessed 10 January 2020
2. Cosmos: A network of distributed ledgers. https://cosmos.network/cosmos-whitepaper.pdf. Accessed 10 January 2020
3. Decred cross-chain atomic swapping. https://github.com/decred/atomicswap. Accessed 10 January 2020
4. Komodo (Advanced blockchain technology, focused on freedom). https://docs.komodoplatform.com/whitepaper/introduction.html. Accessed 10 January 2020
5. Komodo barterdex. https://github.com/KomodoPlatform/BarterDEX. Accessed 10 January 2020
6. Polkadot: Vision for a heterogeneous multi-chain framework. https://polkadot.network/PolkaDotPaper.pdf. Accessed 10 January 2020
7. Abraham, I., Alvisi, L., Halpern, J.: Distributed computing meets game theory: combining insights from two fields. SIGACT News **42**, 69–76 (2011)
8. Abraham, I., Dolev, D., Gonen, R., Halpern, J.: Distributed computing meets game theory: robust mechanisms for rational secret sharing and multiparty computation. In: Proceedings of the Twenty-Fifth Annual ACM Symposium on Principles of Distributed Computing, PODC 2006, New York, NY, USA, pp. 53–62. Association for Computing Machinery (2006)
9. Abraham, I., Gueta, G., Malkhi, D.: Hot-stuff the linear, optimal-resilience, one-message BFT devil. CoRR https://arxiv.org/abs/1803.05069 (2018)
10. Aiyer, A.S., Alvisi, L., Bazzi, R.A.: Byzantine and multi-writer k-quorums. In: Proceedings of 20th International Symposium on Distributed Computing, DISC 2006, 18–20 September 2006, Stockholm, Sweden, pp. 443–458 (2006)
11. Aiyer, A.S., Alvisi, L., Clement, A., Dahlin, M., Martin, J.P., Porth, C.: BAR fault tolerance for cooperative services. In: SOSP 2005 (2005)
12. Amoussou-Guenou, Y., Biais, B., Potop-Butucaru, M., Tucci Piergiovanni, S.: Rationals vs byzantines in consensus-based blockchains. https://arxiv.org/abs/1902.07895 (2019). To appear AAMAS 2020
13. Anceaume, E., Gradinariu, M., Ravoaja, A.: Incentives for P2P fair resource sharing. In: Fifth IEEE International Conference on Peer-to-Peer Computing (P2P 2005), 31 August–2 September 2005, Konstanz, Germany, pp. 253–260 (2005)
14. Anceaume, E., Pozzo, A.D., Ludinard, R., Potop-Butucaru, M., Tucci Piergiovanni, S.: Blockchain abstract data type. In: Proceedings of the 31st ACM Symposium on Parallelism in Algorithms and Architectures (SPAA) (2019)
15. Androulaki, E., et al.: Hyperledger fabric: a distributed operating system for permissioned blockchains. In: Proceedings of the Thirteenth EuroSys Conference, EuroSys 2018, 23–26 April 2018, Porto, Portugal, pp. 30:1–30:15 (2018)
16. Anta, A.F., Georgiou, C., Nicolaou, N.C.: Atomic appends: selling cars and coordinating armies with multiple distributed ledgers. CoRR https://arxiv.org/abs/1812.08446 (2018)

17. Anta, A.F., Konwar, K., Georgiou, C., Nicolaou, N.: Formalizing and implementing distributed ledger objects. ACM SIGACT News **49**(2), 58–76 (2018)

18. Anta, A.F., Konwar, K.M., Georgiou, C., Nicolaou, N.C.: Formalizing and implementing distributed ledger objects. SIGACT News **49**(2), 58–76 (2018)

19. Attiya, H., Welch, J.: Distributed Computing: Fundamentals Simulations and Advanced Topics. Wiley, New York (2004)

20. Avizienis, A., Laprie, J.-C., Randell, B., Landwehr, C.: Basic concepts and taxonomy of dependable and secure computing. IEEE Trans. Dependable Secure Comput. **1**(1), 11–33 (2014)

21. Banu, N., Souissi, S., Izumi, T., Wada, K.: An improved byzantine agreement algorithm for synchronous systems with mobile faults. Int. J. Comput. Appl. **43**(22), 1–7 (2012)

22. Belotti, M., Moretti, S., Potop-Butucaru, M., Secci, S.: Game theoretical analysis of atomic cross-chain swaps. In: 40th IEEE International Conference on Distributed Computing Systems (ICDCS), Singapore, December 2020

23. Bentov, I., Pass, R., Shi, E.: The sleepy model of consensus. IACR Cryptol. ePrint Arch. **2016**, 918 (2016)

24. Biais, B., Bisière, C., Bouvard, M., Casamatta, C.: The blockchain folk theorem. Rev. Financ. Stud. **32**(5), 1662–1715 (2019)

25. Blin, L., Dolev, S., Potop-Butucaru, M.G., Rovedakis, S.: Fast self-stabilizing minimum spanning tree construction - using compact nearest common ancestor labeling scheme. In: Proceedings of 24th International Symposium on Distributed Computing, DISC 2010, 13–15 September 2010, Cambridge, MA, USA, pp. 480–494 (2010)

26. Blin, L., Potop-Butucaru, M., Rovedakis, S.: A super-stabilizing log(n)log(n)-approximation algorithm for dynamic Steiner trees. Theor. Comput. Sci. **500**, 90–112 (2013)

27. Blin, L., Potop-Butucaru, M., Rovedakis, S., Tixeuil, S.: A new self-stabilizing minimum spanning tree construction with loop-free property. Comput. J. **59**(2), 225–243 (2016)

28. Blin, L., Potop-Butucaru, M.G., Rovedakis, S.: Self-stabilizing minimum degree spanning tree within one from the optimal degree. J. Parallel Distrib. Comput. **71**(3), 438–449 (2011)

29. Bonnet, F., Défago, X., Nguyen, T.D., Potop-Butucaru, M.: Tight bound on mobile byzantine agreement. Theor. Comput. Sci. **609**, 361–373 (2016)

30. Bonomi, S., Dolev, S., Potop-Butucaru, M., Raynal, M.: Stabilizing server-based storage in byzantine asynchronous message-passing systems: extended abstract. In: Proceedings of the 2015 ACM Symposium on Principles of Distributed Computing, PODC 2015, 21–23 July 2015, Donostia-San Sebastián, Spain, pp. 471–479 (2015)

31. Bonomi, S., Potop-Butucaru, M., Tixeuil, S.: Stabilizing byzantine-fault tolerant storage. In: 2015 IEEE International Parallel and Distributed Processing Symposium, IPDPS 2015, 25–29 May 2015, Hyderabad, India, pp. 894–903 (2015)

32. Bonomi, S., Pozzo, A.D., Potop-Butucaru, M.: Tight self-stabilizing mobile byzantine-tolerant atomic register. In: Proceedings of the 17th International Conference on Distributed Computing and Networking, 4–7 January 2016, Singapore, pp. 6:1–6:10 (2016). To appear in TCS 2017

33. Bonomi, S., Pozzo, A.D., Potop-Butucaru, M., Tixeuil, S.: Approximate agreement under mobile byzantine faults. In: 36th IEEE International Conference on Distributed Computing Systems, ICDCS 2016, 27–30 June 2016, Nara, Japan, pp. 727–728 (2016)

34. Bonomi, S., Pozzo, A.D., Potop-Butucaru, M., Tixeuil, S.: Optimal mobile byzantine fault tolerant distributed storage: extended abstract. In: Proceedings of the 2016 ACM Symposium on Principles of Distributed Computing, PODC 2016, 25–28 July 2016, Chicago, IL, USA, pp. 269–278 (2016)
35. Bonomi, S., Pozzo, A.D., Potop-Butucaru, M., Tixeuil, S.: Self-stabilizing mobile byzantine-tolerant regular register with bounded timestamp. In: SRDS 2017, https://arxiv.org/abs/1609.02694 (2016)
36. Buchman, E., Kwon, J., Milosevic, Z.: The latest gossip on BFT consensus. arXiv preprint arXiv:1807.04938 (2018)
37. Buhrman, H., Garay, J.A., Hoepman, J.H.: Optimal resiliency against mobile faults. In: Proceedings of the 25th International Symposium on Fault-Tolerant Computing (FTCS 1995), pp. 83–88 (1995)
38. Castro, M., Liskov, B.: Practical byzantine fault tolerance and proactive recovery. ACM Trans. Comput. Syst. 20(4), 398–461 (2002)
39. Chen, J., Micali, S.: Algorand. arXiv preprint arXiv:1607.01341 (2017)
40. Cholvi, V., Anta, A.F., Georgiou, C., Nicolaou, N.C.: Brief announcement: implementing byzantine tolerant distributed ledger objects. In: Suomela, J. (ed.) 33rd International Symposium on Distributed Computing, DISC 2019, 14–18 October 2019, Budapest, Hungary, vol. 146 of LIPIcs, pp. 40:1–40:3. Schloss Dagstuhl - Leibniz-Zentrum für Informatik (2019)
41. Crain, T., Gramoli, V., Larrea, M., Raynal, M.: DBFT: Efficient byzantine consensus with a weak coordinator and its application to consortium blockchains. arXiv preprint arXiv:1702.03068 (2017)
42. Crain, T., Gramoli, V., Larrea, M., Raynal, M.: (Leader/Randomization/Signature)-free Byzantine Consensus for Consortium Blockchains. http://csrg.redbellyblockchain.io/doc/ConsensusRedBellyBlockchain.pdf (2017). Accessed 22 May 2018
43. Croman, K.: On scaling decentralized blockchains - (A position paper). In: Financial Cryptography and Data Security - FC 2016 International Workshops, BITCOIN, VOTING, and WAHC, Christ Church, Barbados, February 26, 2016, Revised Selected Papers, pp. 106–125 (2016)
44. Pass, D.R., Shi, E.: Snow white: provably secure proofs of stake. IACR Cryptol. ePrint Arch. 2016, 919 (2016)
45. Decker, C., Seidel, J., Wattenhofer, R.: Bitcoin meets strong consistency. In: Proceedings of the 17th International Conference on Distributed Computing and Networking Conference (ICDCN) (2016)
46. Eyal, I., Gencer, A.E., Sirer, E.G., Van Renesse, R.: Bitcoin-NG: a scalable blockchain protocol. In: 13th USENIX Symposium on Networked Systems Design and Implementation, NSDI 2016, 16–18 March 2016, Santa Clara, CA, USA, pp. 45–59 (2016)
47. Eyal, I., Sirer, E.G.: Majority is not enough: bitcoin mining is vulnerable. In: Christin, N., Safavi-Naini, R. (eds.) FC 2014. LNCS, vol. 8437, pp. 436–454. Springer, Heidelberg (2014). https://doi.org/10.1007/978-3-662-45472-5_28
48. Fischer, M.J., Lynch, N.A., Paterson, M.S.: Impossibility of distributed consensus with one faulty process. J. ACM (JACM) 32(2), 374–382 (1985)
49. Garay, J.A.: Reaching (and maintaining) agreement in the presence of mobile faults. In: Proceedings of the 8th International Workshop on Distributed Algorithms, vol. 857, pp. 253–264 (1994)
50. Garay, J.A., Kiayias, A.: SoK: a consensus taxonomy in the blockchain era. IACR Cryptol. ePrint Arch. 2018, 754 (2018)

51. Garay, J., Kiayias, A., Leonardos, N.: The bitcoin backbone protocol: analysis and applications. In: Oswald, E., Fischlin, M. (eds.) EUROCRYPT 2015. LNCS, vol. 9057, pp. 281–310. Springer, Heidelberg (2015). https://doi.org/10.1007/978-3-662-46803-6_10

52. Girault, A., Gössler, G., Guerraoui, R., Hamza, J., Seredinschi, D.-A.: Monotonic prefix consistency in distributed systems. In: Baier, C., Caires, L. (eds.) FORTE 2018. LNCS, vol. 10854, pp. 41–57. Springer, Cham (2018). https://doi.org/10.1007/978-3-319-92612-4_3

53. Golan-Gueta, G., et al.: SBFT: a scalable decentralized trust infrastructure for blockchains. CoRR https://arxiv.org/abs/1804.01626 (2018)

54. Gotsman, A., Yang, H., Ferreira, C., Najafzadeh, M., Shapiro, M.: 'Cause i'm strong enough: reasoning about consistency choices in distributed systems. In: Proceedings of the 43rd Annual ACM SIGPLAN-SIGACT Symposium on Principles of Programming Languages, POPL 2016, 20–22 January 2016, St. Petersburg, FL, USA, pp. 371–384 (2016)

55. Herlihy, M.: Atomic cross-chain swaps. In: Proceedings of the 2018 ACM Symposium on Principles of Distributed Computing, pp. 245–254. ACM (2018)

56. Hess, C., Ostrom, E.: Understanding knowledge as a commons. From theory to Practice (2007)

57. Izumi, T., Potop-Butucaru, M., Valero, M.: When expanders help self-healing distributed r-tree overlays. In: IEEE 12th International Symposium on Parallel and Distributed Computing, ISPDC 2013, 27–30 June 2013, Bucharest, Romania, pp. 143–150 (2013)

58. Kokoris-Kogias, E., Jovanovic, P., Gailly, N., Khoffi, I., Gasser, L., Ford, B.: Enhancing bitcoin security and performance with strong consistency via collective signing. In: Proceedings of the 25th USENIX Security Symposium (2016)

59. Lamport, L.: On inter-process communications, Part I: basic formalism and Part II: algorithms. Distrib. Comput. **1**(2), 77–101 (1986)

60. Lamport, L., Shostak, R., Pease, M.: The byzantine generals problem. ACM Trans. Prog. Lang. Syst. **4**(3), 382–401 (1982)

61. Lewis, P., Bernstein, A., Kifer, M.: Databases and Transaction Processing: An Application-Oriented Approach. Addison-Wesley Reading, Boston (2002)

62. Micali, S.: Algorand: the efficient and democratic ledger. arXiv preprint arXiv:1607.01341 (2016)

63. Nakamoto, S.: Bitcoin: a peer-to-peer electronic cash system (2008). https://bitcoin.org/bitcoin.pdf

64. Nolan, T.: Re: alt chains and atomic transfers. https://bitcointalk.org/index.php?topic=193281.msg2224949#msg2224949. Accessed 10 January 2020

65. Ostrom, E.: Governing the Commons. Cambridge University Press, Cambridge (2015)

66. Ostrom, E., Walker, J.: Trust and Reciprocity: Interdisciplinary Lessons for Experimental Research. Russell Sage Foundation, New York (2003)

67. Ostrovsky, R., Yung, M.: How to withstand mobile virus attacks (extended abstract). In: Proceedings of the 10th Annual ACM Symposium on Principles of Distributed Computing (PODC 1991), pp. 51–59 (1991)

68. Pass, R., Seeman, L., Shelat, A.: Analysis of the blockchain protocol in asynchronous networks. In: Coron, J.-S., Nielsen, J.B. (eds.) EUROCRYPT 2017. LNCS, vol. 10211, pp. 643–673. Springer, Cham (2017). https://doi.org/10.1007/978-3-319-56614-6_22

69. Pass, R., Shi, E.: Fruitchains: a fair blockchain. In: Proceedings of the ACM Symposium on Principles of Distributed Computing, PODC 2017, 25–27 July 2017, Washington, DC, USA, pp. 315–324 (2017)
70. Poon, J., Dryja, T.: The bitcoin lightning network (2016). https://lightning.network/lightning-network-paper.pdf
71. Potop-Butucaru, M.: Brace: Blockchains and the commons. submitted to ERC Advanced program (2017) Proposal ID : 788886 (Internal reference number: SEP-210446727) Call : ERC-2017-ADG Type of action : ERC-ADG Topic : ERC-2017-ADG. http://pagesperso.lip6.fr/Maria.Gradinariu/spip.php?article23
72. Prihodko, P., Zhigulin, S., Sahno, M., Ostrovskiy, A.: Flare: an approach to routing in lightning network white paper (2016)
73. Reischuk, R.: A new solution for the byzantine generals problem. Inf. Control **64**(1–3), 23–42 (1985)
74. Saleh, F.: Blockchain Without Waste: Proof-of-Stake. SSRN Scholarly Paper ID 3183935, Social Science Research Network, Rochester, NY, January 2019
75. Sasaki, T., Yamauchi, Y., Kijima, S., Yamashita, M.: Mobile byzantine agreement on arbitrary network. In: Baldoni, R., Nisse, N., van Steen, M. (eds.) OPODIS 2013. LNCS, vol. 8304, pp. 236–250. Springer, Cham (2013). https://doi.org/10.1007/978-3-319-03850-6_17
76. Wood, G.: Ethereum: a secure decentralised generalised transaction ledger. http://gavwood.com/Paper.pdf. Accessed 22 May 2018
77. Zakhary, V., Agrawal, D., Abbadi, A.: Atomic commitment across blockchains. Proc. VLDB Endow. (2020)

Regular Papers

On the State Reachability Problem
for Concurrent Programs Under Power

Parosh Aziz Abdulla[1], Mohamed Faouzi Atig[1(✉)], Ahmed Bouajjani[2],
Egor Derevenetc[3], Carl Leonardsson[1], and Roland Meyer[4]

[1] Uppsala University, Uppsala, Sweden
mohamed_faouzi.atig@it.uu.se
[2] IRIF, Université Paris Diderot, Paris, France
[3] Yandex.Technology GmbH, Berlin, Germany
[4] TU Braunschweig, Brunswick, Germany

Abstract. We consider the problem of safety verification, formalized as control-state reachability, for concurrent programs running on the Power architecture. Our main result shows that safety verification under Power is undecidable for programs with just two threads.

1 Introduction

For performance reasons, modern multi-processors may reorder memory access operations. This is due to complex buffering and cashing mechanisms that aim at improving responsiveness of memory queries (load operation), and at improving execution times by parallelizing operations and computation flows. Therefore, in general operations issued by processors may take time to be visible to other processors, they will not necessarily become visible to all processors at the same time, and they are not necessarily seen in the same order by the different processors (when they concern different addresses/variables). The only model where all operations are visible immediately to all processors is the Sequential Consistency (SC) [18] model that ensures so-called strong consistency, and which corresponds to the standard interleaving model where the program order between operations of a same processor is preserved. In fact, memory models corresponding to modern architectures are in general weaker than SC in the sense that they allow more behaviours. Many weak memory models have been considered such as TSO (Total Store Ordering) adopted in Intel x86 machines [15] for instance, POWER adopted in PowerPC machines [14], and ARMv7 [8]. While TSO allows the store-to-load relaxation of the program order that consists in letting loads overtake stores on different addresses/variables (due to the use of store buffers), POWER and ARMv7 models (that are quite similar, so we focus from now on POWER), are by far more complex, allowing much more relaxations, reordering all kinds of operations under some conditions. Indeed, POWER allows reordering between stores, and more importantly, it allows loads to be delayed past later loads, and even past later stores. Delaying loads corresponds actually to allowing speculation on the future of the execution: loads do not return values

C. Georgiou and R. Majumdar (Eds.): NETYS 2020, LNCS 12129, pp. 47–59, 2021.
https://doi.org/10.1007/978-3-030-67087-0_4

that are currently available, but values that will be stored later by some (other) processor. To avoid situations of circular causality between operations, reordering loads past other operations occurs only when the reordered operations are, roughly, control and data independent. On the other hand, in situations where synchronization is needed, requiring that some operations must be visible without delays, (various) fencing operations can be used by programmers in order to forbid reordering of some operations at some specific points in the program. A series of papers has addressed the issue of defining a formal model capturing the POWER semantics [4, 7, 19, 22]. We consider in this paper the model defined in [12, 22].

In general, the effects of all these relaxations on the executions of concurrent programs are extremely hard to apprehend. While most programmers can assume data-race-freeness which ensures that all behaviours are observationally equivalent to SC computations, this assumption does not fit all situations. Therefore, developing automatic verification approaches for concurrent programs under weak memory models is of paramount importance. This paper addresses the decidability and the complexity of verifying safety properties (or dually of verifying state reachability) under POWER. This problem is hard due to the high complexity and intricacy of the model. From the computational point of view, the formal model associated with POWER uses unbounded data structures for storing operations that are dispatched and executed later according to some specific rules. Therefore, decidability and complexity of the state reachability problem for this model is far from being trivial. Work investigating these issues for weak memory models are rare. In [9], Atig et al. addressed these issues for TSO and PSO (Partial Store Ordering), and subsequently they extended their result in [10] to a variety of abstract weak memory models where loads can be reordered past other operations. They have shown basically that the reachability problem is decidable for TSO and PSO, and even when additionally the load-to-load relaxation is allowed. Those results hold even for unbounded store buffers, i.e., when there is no a-priori bound on the distance between reordered operations in the original computation of the processor. On the other hand, they have shown that considering in addition the load-to-store relaxation (the obtained model is called RMO), leads to undecidability. However, the formal models considered in that work do not take into account dependencies between operations as in the case of POWER. So, these formal models are either not comparable with, or weaker (in the case of their RMO model) than the model of POWER considered here, and therefore the results established for them in [9, 10] do not apply directly to the case of POWER.

In this paper, we prove that the state reachability problem under POWER is undecidable in general. This result comes as a surprise, given that Power avoids the causality cycles [12] used in the undecidability proof for RMO [9]. The proof is technically involved and is based on a reduction from the reachability problem for *perfect FIFO channel machine (PCM)*. PCMs are known to be Turing-complete, even with only one channel [11]. Essentially, the simulation of PCM is due to allowing an unbounded number of speculating loads that can for instance be generated by a loop whose condition does not depend on the loads in its body.

1.1 Related Work

In the last few years, there were a number of works that propose approximate verification techniques for programs running under POWER (e.g., [3,5–7,13,20,21,23]). The work [5] extends the CBMC framework to programs running under different weak memory models including TSO and POWER using their axiomatic definitions [7] to detect potential cycles. The work in [6] combines partial orders with bounded model checking for the verification of programs running under various weak memory models including TSO and POWER. The works [3] and [2] develop stateless and bounded-context model checking techniques under POWER, respectively. More recently, the works [13] and [20] propose efficient SMT based bounded-model checking techniques for the verification of various weak memory models including TSO, POWER, and ARM.

The state reachability problem for programs running under the TSO memory model and causal consistency has been shown to be decidable in [9] and [17], respectively. This problem becomes undecidable for programs under the release-acquire semantics [1].

Finally, the paper [12] addresses the robustness problem for programs running under POWER, i.e., whether a program has the same (trace) semantics for both POWER and SC. This problem has been shown to be PSPACE-complete.

2 Programming Model

We give the syntax of concurrent programs and recall the semantics under POWER. We base our development on *automata* $A = (S, \Sigma, \Delta, s_0, F)$, where S is a set of states, Σ an alphabet, $\Delta \subseteq S \times (\Sigma \cup \{\varepsilon\}) \times S$ a set of transitions, $s_0 \in S$ an initial state, and $F \subseteq S$ a set of final states. We write $s_1 \xrightarrow{a} s_2$ if $(s_1, a, s_2) \in \Delta$ and generalize the relation to *computations* $\sigma \in \Sigma^*$ by existentially quantifying over the intermediary states. For $\sigma = a_1 \ldots a_n \in \Sigma^*$ we define the length to be $|\sigma| := n$ and access the ith letter with $\sigma(i) := a_i$. The automaton is *finite* if S and Σ are finite. It is *deterministic* if for every state s and every letter a there at most one state s' with $s \xrightarrow{a} s'$. Letters a and b *commute in state* s if for all $s' \in S$ we have $s \xrightarrow{a \cdot b} s'$ iff $s \xrightarrow{b \cdot a} s'$. The *language of* A consists of all computations that lead from the initial to a final state, $\mathcal{L}(A) := \{\sigma \in \Sigma^* \mid s_0 \xrightarrow{\sigma} s \in F\}$.

We use $[n]$ for the interval $[1, n]$. Given $f \colon X \to Y$, $x' \in X$, and $y' \in Y$, we define the updated function $f' = f[x' \hookleftarrow y']$ by $f'(x') := y'$ and $f'(x) := f(x)$ for $x \neq x'$.

2.1 Programs

A program $P = T_1 \ldots T_n$ is a finite sequence of threads, each carrying an identifier from TID $:= [n]$. *Threads* are given as automata $T_{tid} =$

$(Q_{tid}, \mathsf{CMD}, I_{tid}, q_0{}^{tid}, F_{tid})$ with $tid \in \mathsf{TID}$. We call these automata control-flow graphs, Q_{tid} the finite set of control states, and I_{tid} the *instructions*. The final states will be used to define safety verification as an emptiness problem.

Instructions are labeled by commands from the set CMD. It includes loads, stores, assignments, conditionals (assume), and three synchronization primitives:

$$\langle cmd \rangle ::= \langle reg \rangle \leftarrow \mathtt{mem}[\langle expr \rangle] \mid \mathtt{mem}[\langle expr \rangle] \leftarrow \langle expr \rangle$$
$$\mid \quad \langle reg \rangle \leftarrow \langle expr \rangle \mid \mathtt{assume}(\langle expr \rangle)$$
$$\mid \quad \mathtt{sync} \mid \mathtt{lwsync} \mid \mathtt{isync} \;.$$

Programs come with a finite domain $\mathsf{DOM} = \mathsf{ADR}$ that contains both the values and addresses, and we do not differentiate between the two. The domain is assumed to contain the value 0 and not to contain $\bot$. On $\mathsf{DOM} \cup \{\bot\}$, we have a set of (computable) functions FUN. We assume that these functions return $\bot$ iff any of the arguments is $\bot$. Besides the domain, let REG be a finite set of registers that take values from DOM. The set of expressions EXP is

$$\langle expr \rangle ::= \langle reg \rangle \mid \langle dom \rangle \mid \langle fun \rangle (\langle expr \rangle \dots \langle expr \rangle) \;.$$

To fix the terminology, when we refer to *loops* in a control-flow graph we mean loops that are simple in the sense that they do not repeat control states.

2.2 Power Semantics

The Power architecture supports program-order relaxations based on address, data, and control dependencies as well as non-store atomicity. The semantics of programs running on Power has been formalized in a series of papers [4,7,19,22] that bit by bit corrected mismatches between the model and the observable machine behavior until arriving at the by now considered stable [7]. We focus on this definition but give an operational presentation as in [12,22]. The state of a program running on a Power processor consists of the runtime states of the threads and the state of a storage subsystem.

The runtime state of a thread includes information about the instructions being executed by the thread. In order to start executing an instruction, the thread must *fetch* it. The thread can fetch any instruction whose source control state is equal to the destination state of the last fetched instruction. Then, the thread must perform any computation required by the semantics of this instruction. For example, for a load the thread must compute the address being accessed and read the value from this address into the target register. The last step of executing an instruction is *committing* it. Committing an instruction requires committing all its *dependencies*. For example, before committing a load the thread must commit all its *address dependencies*—the instructions which define the values of registers used in the address expression—and all *control dependencies*—the program-order-earlier (fetched earlier than the load) conditional instructions. Moreover, all loads and stores accessing the same address must be committed in the order in which they were fetched.

The storage subsystem keeps track, for each address, of the global ordering of stores to this address—the *coherence order*—and the last store to this address *propagated* to each thread. When a thread commits a store, this store is assigned a position in the coherence order which we identify by a rational number—the *coherence key*. The key must be greater than the coherence key of the last store to the same address propagated to this thread. The committed store is immediately propagated to its own thread. At some point later this store can be propagated to any other thread, as long as it is coherence order-later (has a greater coherence key) than the last store to the same address propagated to that thread. When a thread loads a value from a certain address, it gets the value written by the last store to this address propagated to this thread. A thread can also forward the value being written by a not yet committed store to a later load reading the same address. This situation is called an *early read*.

An important property of Power is that it maintains the illusion of sequential consistency for single-threaded programs. This means, reorderings on the thread level must not lead to situations where, e.g., a program-order-later load reads a coherence order-earlier store than the one read by a program-order-earlier load to the same address. In [22] these restrictions are enforced by the mechanism of restarting operations. We put these conditions into the requirements on final states of the running program instead.

Power provides three synchronization commands to enforce ordering among operations: sync, lwsync, and isync. We use the notation (lw)sync to mean a sync or an lwsync, and similar for (i)sync and (lw/i)sync. When an (lw)sync is committed, the *group-A set of stores* is captured. It consists of the last stores that were propagated to the thread performing the (lw)sync at the moment of commit. Once all group-A stores have been propagated to a thread, the (lw)sync can be propagated to this thread. We also say that the thread has *passed* the (lw)sync. If an (lw)sync has not yet been propagated to a thread, the thread *remains before* the (lw)sync. Once all threads have passed a sync, it is considered *acknowledged*.

Symmetrically, when a thread commits a store the *group-A set of (lw)syncs* is captured. It consists of all (lw)syncs that were propagated to the thread doing the store at the moment of commit. A store can be propagated to a thread only after all group-A (lw)syncs have been propagated to this thread.

An (lw)sync can be understood as a barrier that separates the group-A stores from the stores that have the (lw)sync in their group-A set of (lw)syncs. The semantics requires these barriers not to cross each other. Imagine four stores w_a followed by w'_a in the coherence order and w_b followed by w'_b on the addresses a and b, respectively. If one (lw)sync requires w'_b to be before w_a, then it cannot be the case that another (lw)sync requires the later w'_a to be before w_b. Such a cycle should also not occur transitively and is not restricted to the group-A stores. Instead, one keeps for each (lw)sync and each thread a snapshot of the last stores that were propagated to that thread at the moment when the (lw)sync is propagated to the thread. This *function of group-A stores* conservatively generalizes the set of group-A stores (held for the thread who committed the (lw)sync) to all threads.

Committing an (lw)sync requires all previous loads, stores, and (lw/i)syncs to be committed. Committing a load or a store requires all previous (lw/i)syncs to be committed and syncs to be acknowledged. Committing an isync requires all preceding loads and stores to have their addresses computed.

Finally, loading a value from memory or from an earlier store requires all previous (i)syncs to be committed and syncs to be acknowledged. In contrast, pending lwsyncs do not forbid speculative loads.

We turn to the formalization. It will be interesting to the reader familiar with the Power model. For a reader new to Power, we suggest to skip the details and get back to them when unsure about arguments given in the development. The semantics of program P on a Power processor is captured by the *Power automaton* $Z(P) := (S_Z, \mathsf{ACT}, \Delta_Z, s_{0Z}, F_Z)$.

Alphabet. The alphabet is the set of *actions*

$$\mathsf{ACT} := \mathsf{IID} \times \{\mathsf{f}, \mathsf{l}, \mathsf{c}, \mathsf{p}\} \times (\bigcup_{tid \in \mathsf{TID}} I_{tid} \cup \mathsf{IID} \cup \mathbb{Q} \cup \mathsf{TID}) .$$

Actions make visible the step (fetch, load, commit, propagate) performed during the execution of an instruction (instance). Instances of instructions are identified uniquely by an element from $\mathsf{IID} := \mathsf{TID} \times \mathbb{N}$. The natural number will be the index in the list of fetched instructions of the given thread. The identification scheme will guarantee that every action occurs at most once during a computation. For fetch actions, we also give the instruction being fetched. For load actions, we track the store that the load obtains its value from. For committed stores, we track the coherence index from $\mathbb{Q}$. Propagate actions moreover give the thread that a store or (lw)sync is propagated to. Fetch, load, and commit actions are said to be *local* because they do not interact with the storage subsystem.

States. A state $s_Z = (\mathsf{ts}, s_Y) \in S_Z$ of the Power automaton consists of the runtime thread states $\mathsf{ts} \colon \mathsf{TID} \to S_X$ and the storage subsystem state $s_Y \in S_Y$.

A runtime state $\mathsf{ts}(tid) = (\mathsf{fet}, \mathsf{com}, \mathsf{ld}) \in S_X$ of the thread $tid \in \mathsf{TID}$ includes a sequence of fetched instructions $\mathsf{fet} \in I_{tid}^*$ of length $|\mathsf{fet}| = n$, a set of indices of committed instructions $\mathsf{com} \subseteq [n]$, and a function $\mathsf{ld} \colon [n] \to \mathsf{IID} \cup \mathsf{INIT} \cup \{\bot\}$ giving the store read by a load and $\bot$ if the load has not yet received a value. The set $\mathsf{INIT} := \{\mathsf{init}_a \mid a \in \mathsf{ADR}\}$ contains, for each address, an initial store of value 0. If the state belongs to thread tid, we also apply fet, com, and ld to instruction ids of the form $iid = (tid, i)$ rather than natural numbers. For example, $\mathsf{fet}(iid) = \mathsf{fet}(i)$ returns the ith fetched instruction of thread tid. The initial state of a running thread is $s_{0X} := (\varepsilon, \emptyset, \lambda i.\bot)$.

A storage subsystem state $s_Y = (\mathsf{co}, \mathsf{p}, \mathsf{gast}, \mathsf{gasy}) \in S_Y$ contains the coherence order $\mathsf{co} \colon \mathsf{IID} \to \mathbb{Q}$ for stores, initially $\lambda iid.0$. The propagate function $\mathsf{p} \colon \mathsf{TID} \to \mathsf{ADR} \to \mathsf{IID} \cup \mathsf{INIT}$ maps thread tid and address a to the last store to a propagated to tid, initially $\lambda tid.\lambda a.\mathsf{init}_a$. The function of group-A stores $\mathsf{gast} \colon \mathsf{IID} \to \mathsf{TID} \to (\mathsf{ADR} \to \mathsf{IID} \cup \mathsf{INIT}) \cup \{\bot\}$ maps an (lw)sync iid, thread

tid, and address a to the last store to a that was propagated to tid at the moment when the (lw)sync is propagated to tid, initially $\lambda iid.\lambda tid.\perp$. The group-A (lw)syncs are given by $\mathsf{gasy}\colon \mathsf{IID} \to \mathbb{P}(\mathsf{IID})$, initially $\lambda iid.\emptyset$.

The initial state $Z(P)$ is $s_{0Z} := (\lambda tid.s_{0X}, s_{0Y})$ with s_{0Y} the initial state of the storage subsystem.

Note that a state $s_Z = (\mathsf{ts}, s_Y)$ does not contain the valuations of registers and addresses, nor does it declare any dependencies among instructions. We now define auxiliary functions that serve this purpose. Function $\mathsf{ev}(iid, e)$ returns the value of expression e in instruction iid, and $\perp$ when the value is undefined. Formally, $\mathsf{ev}(iid, e) := \mathsf{v}$ is computed as follows. If $e \in \mathsf{DOM}$, then $\mathsf{v} := e$. If $e = \mathsf{fun}(e_1 \ldots e_n)$, then $\mathsf{v} := \mathsf{fun}(\mathsf{ev}(iid, e_1) \ldots \mathsf{ev}(iid, e_n))$. Otherwise, $e = \mathsf{r} \in \mathsf{REG}$. We identify the last instruction iid' fetched before iid that is an assignment or a load to r. Formally, if $iid = (tid, i)$ then $iid' = (tid, i')$ where $i' \in [i-1]$ is the largest index so that $\mathsf{fet}(i')$ is of the required form. If there is no such instruction iid', we define $\mathsf{v} := 0$. If iid' is an assignment $\mathsf{r} \leftarrow e_\mathsf{v}$, then $\mathsf{v} := \mathsf{ev}(iid', e_\mathsf{v})$. If iid' is a load $\mathsf{r} \leftarrow \mathsf{mem}[e_\mathsf{a}]$, then $\mathsf{v} := \perp$ if $\mathsf{ld}(iid') = \perp$, and $\mathsf{v} := \mathsf{val}(\mathsf{ld}(iid'))$ otherwise. The definition of val is given in the next paragraph.

Function $\mathsf{adr}(iid)$ returns the value of the address argument in an instruction. If iid is a load $\mathsf{r} \leftarrow \mathsf{mem}[e_\mathsf{a}]$ or a store $\mathsf{mem}[e_\mathsf{a}] \leftarrow e_\mathsf{v}$, we set $\mathsf{adr}(iid) := \mathsf{ev}(iid, e_\mathsf{a})$. If there is no address argument, we use $\mathsf{adr}(iid) := \top$. We overload the function with $\mathsf{adr}(\mathsf{init}_\mathsf{a}) := \mathsf{a}$. Similarly, $\mathsf{val}(iid)$ returns the value of the value argument. If iid is a store $\mathsf{mem}[e_\mathsf{a}] \leftarrow e_\mathsf{v}$, an assignment $\mathsf{r} \leftarrow e_\mathsf{v}$, or a conditional $\mathsf{assume}(e_\mathsf{v})$, we set $\mathsf{val}(iid) := \mathsf{ev}(iid, e_\mathsf{v})$. Otherwise, $\mathsf{val}(iid) := \top$.

The functions $\mathsf{adep}(iid)$, $\mathsf{ddep}(iid)$, $\mathsf{cdep}(iid)$, applied to $iid = (tid, i)$, denote the ids of instructions in thread tid being address, data, and control dependencies of iid. The first two are defined recursively similar to ev. We define $\mathsf{cdep}(iid)$ to be the set $\{(tid, i') \mid i' \in [i-1] \text{ where } \mathsf{fet}(i') \text{ is a conditional}\}$.

The predicate $\mathsf{ack}(iid)$ checks whether a sync has been propagated to all threads. Formally, the predicate returns $\top$ if $\mathsf{gast}(iid, tid') \neq \perp$ for all tid', and $\perp$ otherwise.

Transitions. Consider state $s_Z = (\mathsf{ts}, s_Y)$ where thread tid is in state $\mathsf{ts}(tid) = (\mathsf{fet}, \mathsf{com}, \mathsf{ld})$. In the following, the instruction $iid := (tid, i)$ is always assumed to stem from this thread. The transition relation Δ_Z is the smallest relation defined by the rules below:

(T-F) Thread tid can fetch any instruction inst originating from its current control state in the control-flow graph. This state is q where (q', cmd, q) is the last instruction in fet. The transition appends inst to the list of fetched instructions:

$$(\mathsf{ts}, s_Y) \xrightarrow{((tid, |\mathsf{fet}|+1), \mathsf{f}, \mathsf{inst})} (\mathsf{ts}[tid \hookleftarrow (\mathsf{fet} \cdot \mathsf{inst}, \mathsf{com}, \mathsf{ld})], s_Y).$$

Note that the instruction id is the pair $(tid, |\mathsf{fet}| + 1)$.

(T-LDE) Let iid be a load that has not yet obtained its value, $\mathsf{ld}(iid) = \perp$, but whose address argument has been computed, $\mathsf{a} := \mathsf{adr}(iid) \neq \perp$. Let iid' be the last instruction fetched before iid that is a store to this address, $\mathsf{adr}(iid') = \mathsf{a}$. Assume the value of the store has been computed, $\mathsf{val}(iid') \neq \perp$, and iid' has not yet been committed, $iid' \notin \mathsf{com}$. Assume that all (i)syncs fetched before iid

have been committed and all syncs fetched before iid have been acknowledged. Formally, assume that for all $i' \in [i-1]$ the following holds. If $\mathsf{fet}(i')$ is an (i)sync then $i' \in \mathsf{com}$, and if $\mathsf{fet}(i')$ is a sync then $\mathsf{ack}(tid, i') = \top$. We now obtain the early-read transition

$$(\mathsf{ts}, s_Y) \xrightarrow{(iid,\mathsf{l},iid')} (\mathsf{ts}[tid \hookleftarrow (\mathsf{fet}, \mathsf{com}, \mathsf{ld}[iid \hookleftarrow iid'])], s_Y).$$

(T-LD)   Let iid be a load that has not yet obtained its value but whose address argument has been computed to be a. Let $iid' = \mathsf{p}(tid, \mathsf{a})$ be the last store to address a that has been propagated to thread tid. Moreover, assume that all previous (i)syncs have been committed and all previous syncs have been acknowledged. The load transition is

$$(\mathsf{ts}, s_Y) \xrightarrow{(iid,\mathsf{l},iid')} (\mathsf{ts}[tid \hookleftarrow (\mathsf{fet}, \mathsf{com}, \mathsf{ld}[iid \hookleftarrow iid'])], s_Y).$$

(T-C)   Assume iid has not yet been committed, $iid \notin \mathsf{com}$, and that it is not a store. Assume all dependencies have been committed, $\mathsf{adep}(iid) \cup \mathsf{ddep}(iid) \cup \mathsf{cdep}(iid) \subseteq \mathsf{com}$, and the address and value arguments have been computed, $\mathsf{a} := \mathsf{adr}(iid) \neq \bot$ and $\mathsf{v} := \mathsf{val}(iid) \neq \bot$. If there is an address argument, $\mathsf{a} \neq \top$, assume all previous instructions with address arguments have been committed, $\{i' \in [i-1] \mid \mathsf{adr}(tid, i') \in \{\mathsf{a}, \bot\}\} \subseteq \mathsf{com}$. In case iid is a conditional, assume it is satisfied, $\mathsf{v} \neq 0$. In case iid is a load, assume it has obtained its value, $\mathsf{ld}(iid) \neq \bot$. In case iid is a load or (lw/i)sync, assume all previous (lw/i)syncs have been committed, and all previous syncs have been acknowledged. In case iid is an (lw)sync, assume all previous iid' with address arguments have been committed, $\mathsf{adr}(iid') \neq \top$ implies $iid' \in \mathsf{com}$. In case iid is an isync, assume all previous instructions with address arguments have obtained their addresses. The transition is

$$(\mathsf{ts}, s_Y) \xrightarrow{(iid,\mathsf{c})} (\mathsf{ts}[tid \hookleftarrow (\mathsf{fet}, \mathsf{com} \cup \{iid\}, \mathsf{ld})], s_Y).$$

If iid is an (lw)sync, the transition is immediately followed by a **(T-PSY)** transition propagating the (lw)sync to thread tid.

(T-CST)   Assume all preconditions from the previous rule hold but iid is a store. Choose a coherence key $\mathsf{k} \in \mathbb{Q}$ such that there is no iid' with $\mathsf{co}(iid') = \mathsf{k}$. Then

$$(\mathsf{ts}, s_Y) \xrightarrow{(iid,\mathsf{c},\mathsf{k})} (\mathsf{ts}[tid \hookleftarrow (\mathsf{fet}, \mathsf{com} \cup \{iid\}, \mathsf{ld})], s'_Y)$$

with $s'_Y := (\mathsf{co}', \mathsf{p}, \mathsf{gast}, \mathsf{gasy}')$. We add the coherence key with $\mathsf{co}' := \mathsf{co}[iid \hookleftarrow \mathsf{k}]$ and record the group-A (lw)syncs with $\mathsf{gasy}' := \mathsf{gasy}[iid \hookleftarrow \{iid' \mid \mathsf{gast}(iid', tid) \neq \bot\}]$. The transition is immediately followed by a transition **(T-PST)** propagating the store to the thread tid where it was committed.

(T-PST)   To propagate a store iid that has been committed, let $\mathsf{a} := \mathsf{adr}(iid)$ be its address. Assume the last store to this address that has been propagated to thread tid' is older than iid, $\mathsf{co}(\mathsf{p}(tid', \mathsf{a})) < \mathsf{co}(iid)$. Assume all group-A (lw)syncs of iid have been propagated to tid'. Formally, $\mathsf{gast}(iid', tid') \neq \bot$ for all $iid' \in \mathsf{gasy}(iid)$. Then

$$(\mathsf{ts}, s_Y) \xrightarrow{(iid,\mathsf{p},tid')} (\mathsf{ts}, (\mathsf{co}, \mathsf{p}[(tid', \mathsf{a}) \hookleftarrow iid], \mathsf{gast}, \mathsf{gasy})).$$

(T-PSY) Let iid be an (lw)sync committed by thread tid and let tid' be a thread to which iid has not yet been propagated, $\mathsf{gast}(iid, tid') = \bot$. If $tid = tid'$, we have to capture the group-A stores of iid and there are no further preconditions. Otherwise, assume the stores currently propagated to tid' are more recent than the group-A stores of iid. Formally, $\mathsf{co}(w_\mathsf{a}) \leq \mathsf{co}(\mathsf{p}(tid', \mathsf{a}))$ for all $w_\mathsf{a} = \mathsf{gast}(iid, tid, \mathsf{a})$. Then

$$(\mathsf{ts}, s_Y) \xrightarrow{(iid,\mathsf{p},tid')} (\mathsf{ts}, (\mathsf{co}, \mathsf{p}, \mathsf{gast}', \mathsf{gasy}))$$

with $\mathsf{gast}' := \mathsf{gast}[(iid, tid') \hookleftarrow \mathsf{p}(tid')]$.

Action σ is *enabled in state* s_Z, if $s_Z \xrightarrow{\sigma} s_Z'$ for some s_Z'. Instruction iid is *ready to commit in* s_Z, if the commit action (iid, c) (for a store also the following propagate action) is enabled.

Final States. The set $F_Z \subseteq S_Z$ consists of all states with coherence order co and propagate map p so that for all threads with state $(\mathsf{fet}, \mathsf{com}, \mathsf{ld})$ the following holds:

(F-CO) Loads and stores agree with the coherence order. Let iid and iid' be loads of the same thread from the same address. If iid is fetched earlier, then it loads a coherence-earlier store, $\mathsf{co}(\mathsf{ld}(iid)) \leq \mathsf{co}(\mathsf{ld}(iid'))$. Similarly, if iid is an earlier store of the same thread to the same address, then $\mathsf{co}(iid) \leq \mathsf{co}(\mathsf{ld}(iid'))$.

(F-SY) The relation is acyclic that is formed as the union of the coherence order and the set of pairs (iid, iid') where iid has been propagated to the thread tid' before an (lw)sync, and tid' commits iid' after that (lw)sync. Formally, there is no sequence of store instructions $iid_0 \ldots iid_k$ with $iid_0 = iid_k$ so that for every $j \in [k]$ we have $\mathsf{co}(iid_{j-1}) \leq \mathsf{co}(iid_j)$ or there is an (lw)sync iid with $iid_{j-1} = \mathsf{gast}(iid, tid_j, \mathsf{adr}(iid_{j-1}))$ and $iid \in \mathsf{gasy}(iid_j)$, with tid_j the thread of iid_j.

(F-FIN) All instructions are committed, $\mathsf{com} = [1..|\mathsf{fet}|]$, and every thread tid is in its final state. More precisely, if the last fetched instruction is (q', cmd, q), then $q \in F_{tid}$. If the thread did not fetch any instructions, then $q_{0\,tid} \in F_{tid}$.

A key observation about the Power semantics is that in every state every action has at most one successor.

Lemma 1. $Z(P)$ *is deterministic.*

The lemma guarantees that every computation (which is a sequence of actions) gives rise to a unique sequence of states. Note that the lemma does not imply (and it is not true in general) that every state has only one successor.

The *safety verification problem under Power* is to check, given a program P, whether $\mathcal{L}(Z(P)) = \emptyset$. Note that, algorithmically, checking this emptiness amounts to finding a path from the initial to a final state. Under SC, safety verification is well-understood and PSPACE-complete [16]. Due to early-reads, single-threaded programs running on a Power processor appear to behave as if they were running under SC. Together, this yields a first observation.

Remark 1. For single-threaded programs, safety verification under Power is PSPACE-complete.

3   Undecidability

We prove that, in general, safety verification under Power is undecidable. The result came as a surprise to us, given that Power avoids the causality cycles [12] used in the undecidability proof for RMO [9].

Theorem 1. *Programs with at least two threads running under Power are Turing-complete.*

To obtain the result, we show how to mimic a *perfect FIFO channel machine (PCM)* by a program consisting of two threads and running under Power. PCMs are known to be Turing-complete, even with only one channel [11]. A PCM is a tuple $M = (S, C, \Sigma, \Delta, (s_0, cs_0))$, where S is a finite set of states, C is a finite set of channels, Σ is a finite set of messages, $\Delta \subseteq S \times (C \times \{?, !\} \times \Sigma) \times S$ is a set of transitions, and (s_0, cs_0) is an initial configuration. Configurations give the current state and the current channel content and are taken from $S \times \Sigma^{*C}$. The semantics is defined by the transition relation $\rightarrow$ among configurations, the smallest relation including

$$(s_1, cs) \rightarrow (s_2, cs[c \hookleftarrow cs(c) \cdot m]) \quad \text{if } (s_1, c!m, s_2) \in \Delta$$
$$(s_1, cs[c \hookleftarrow m \cdot cs(c)]) \rightarrow (s_2, cs) \quad \text{if } (s_1, c?m, s_2) \in \Delta .$$

Given a PCM M with one channel, we construct a program $P(M)$ whose behavior under Power mimics the semantics of the PCM. This program has two threads: T_{main} implements M using send and receive operations, T_{aux} is the thread implementing the perfect and unbounded FIFO channel.

We implement the channel using two variables x and y initially having the special value 0 which is not in the set of messages transmitted over the channel. Assume the value to be sent through the channel is stored in register r_{data}. We implement the send operation in T_{main} as follows:

$$q_1 \xrightarrow{r \leftarrow \mathsf{mem}[x]} q_2 \xrightarrow{\mathsf{assume}(r=0)} q_3 \xrightarrow{\mathsf{mem}[x] \leftarrow r_{\mathsf{data}}} q_4 .$$

This implementation blocks if sending fails.

Assume the value to be received from the channel must be written to register r_{data}. Then we implement the receive operation in T_{main} as follows:

$$q_1 \xrightarrow{r_{\mathsf{data}} \leftarrow \mathsf{mem}[y]} q_2 \xrightarrow{\mathsf{assume}(r_{\mathsf{data}} \neq 0)} q_3 \xrightarrow{\mathsf{mem}[y] \leftarrow 0} q_4 .$$

Similarly, the implementation blocks when the operation fails.

The auxiliary thread $T_{\mathsf{aux}} := (Q, \mathsf{CMD}, I, q_0, Q)$ copies x into y. The control states are $Q := \{q_0, \ldots, q_6\}$. The instructions I are the following:

$$q_0 \xrightarrow{r_{\mathsf{mask}} \leftarrow 1} q_1 \xrightarrow{r \leftarrow \mathtt{mem}[x]} q_2 \xrightarrow{r_{\mathsf{mask}} \leftarrow r_{\mathsf{mask}} \wedge (r \neq 0)} q_3 \xrightarrow{\mathtt{mem}[x] \leftarrow 0} q_4$$

$$q_4 \xrightarrow{r' \leftarrow \mathtt{mem}[y]} q_5 \xrightarrow{r_{\mathsf{mask}} \leftarrow r_{\mathsf{mask}} \wedge (r' = 0)} q_6 \xrightarrow{\mathtt{mem}[y] \leftarrow r \wedge r_{\mathsf{mask}}} q_1 \ .$$

Here, we assume $a \wedge 1 \equiv a$, $a \wedge 0 \equiv 0$, and comparisons to return 0 (false) and 1 (true).

The idea behind the construction is as follows. The send operation checks if T_{aux} has already processed the previously sent value (variable x contains 0). Only in this case the new value is written into x. The receive operation does the reverse, it reads the value from y, checks that this value is not 0 (i.e. was written by T_{aux}), and writes 0 to y to signal T_{aux} that a new value can be put there.

The thread T_{aux} executes a loop reading values from x and writing them to y. The thread uses register r_{mask} for remembering whether reading or writing a value did previously fail. After reading a value from x it checks that this value is not 0, i.e. some value was actually sent. If this is not the case, r_{mask} becomes 0. Next, the thread writes 0 to x, thus signalling that a new value can be sent. After that, the thread checks that y contains 0 (i.e. the previously written value was received). If not, again r_{mask} is set to 0. Finally, the thread writes either the value that was read (if $r_{\mathsf{mask}} = 1$) or 0 (if $r_{\mathsf{mask}} = 0$) to y. Accordingly, all subsequent receive operations will fail if T_{aux} at least once detected that x does not contain a value to be sent or y contains the previously copied value.

Note that the sequence of values loaded from x will be the same as the sequence of values written to y, as Power forbids reordering load operations from and store operations to the same address. This yields a FIFO channel. Moreover, the loads from and stores to y in T_{aux} can be delayed arbitrary long, which makes the delay between reading a new value from x and writing it back to y arbitrary large. This gives unboundedness of the channel. Finally, a value cannot be sent until it was read by T_{aux}. Similarly, a value cannot be written back by T_{aux} until the previous value was received by T_{main}. This makes the channel perfect.

Depending on scheduling, the channel implementation may fail. This is detected and the subsequent receive operations blocked. However, there always is a schedule in which no operation fails (except when one attempts to receive from an empty channel). Each send operation is immediately followed by the instructions $q_1 \ldots q_4$. Each receive operation is preceded by the instructions $q_4 \ldots q_1$ followed by actions that propagate the store to y to both threads.

4   Conclusion

In this paper, we have shown that the state reachability problem for programs running under the POWER memory model is undecidable. This result holds even for programs with just two threads. This undecidability result was not expected, given that Power avoids the causality cycles used in the undecidability proof for RMO [9]. As future work, we intend to identify interesting subclasses of programs for which the verification problem under the Power memory models is decidable. Such subclasses can be used as bases for defining scalable and efficient under-approximation techniques.

References

1. Abdulla, P.A., Arora, J., Atig, M.F., Krishna, S.N.: Verification of programs under the release-acquire semantics. In: McKinley, K.S., Fisher, K. (eds.) Proceedings of the 40th ACM SIGPLAN Conference on Programming Language Design and Implementation, PLDI 2019, 22–26 June 2019, Phoenix, AZ, USA, pp. 1117–1132. ACM (2019)
2. Abdulla, P.A., Atig, M.F., Bouajjani, A., Ngo, T.P.: Context-bounded analysis for POWER. In: Legay, A., Margaria, T. (eds.) TACAS 2017. LNCS, vol. 10206, pp. 56–74. Springer, Heidelberg (2017). https://doi.org/10.1007/978-3-662-54580-5_4
3. Abdulla, P.A., Atig, M.F., Jonsson, B., Leonardsson, C.: Stateless model checking for POWER. In: Chaudhuri, S., Farzan, A. (eds.) CAV 2016. LNCS, vol. 9780, pp. 134–156. Springer, Cham (2016). https://doi.org/10.1007/978-3-319-41540-6_8
4. Alglave, J.: A Shared Memory Poetics. Ph.D. Thesis, University Paris 7 (2010)
5. Alglave, J., Kroening, D., Nimal, V., Tautschnig, M.: Software verification for weak memory via program transformation. In: Felleisen, M., Gardner, P. (eds.) ESOP 2013. LNCS, vol. 7792, pp. 512–532. Springer, Heidelberg (2013). https://doi.org/10.1007/978-3-642-37036-6_28
6. Alglave, J., Kroening, D., Tautschnig, M.: Partial orders for efficient bounded model checking of concurrent software. In: Sharygina, N., Veith, H. (eds.) CAV 2013. LNCS, vol. 8044, pp. 141–157. Springer, Heidelberg (2013). https://doi.org/10.1007/978-3-642-39799-8_9
7. Alglave, J., Maranget, L., Tautschnig, M.: Herding cats: modelling, simulation, testing, and data mining for weak memory. ACM TOPLAS 36(2), 7:1–7:74 (2014)
8. ARM: ARM Architecture Reference Manual, ARMv7-A and ARMv7-R Edition (2014)
9. Atig, M.F., Bouajjani, A., Burckhardt, S., Musuvathi, M.: On the verification problem for weak memory models. In: POPL, pp. 7–18. ACM (2010)
10. Atig, M.F., Bouajjani, A., Burckhardt, S., Musuvathi, M.: What's decidable about weak memory models? In: Seidl, H. (ed.) ESOP 2012. LNCS, vol. 7211, pp. 26–46. Springer, Heidelberg (2012). https://doi.org/10.1007/978-3-642-28869-2_2
11. Brand, D., Zafiropulo, P.: On communicating finite-state machines. JACM 30(2), 323–342 (1983)
12. Derevenetc, E., Meyer, R.: Robustness against Power is PSpace-complete. In: Esparza, J., Fraigniaud, P., Husfeldt, T., Koutsoupias, E. (eds.) ICALP 2014. LNCS, vol. 8573, pp. 158–170. Springer, Heidelberg (2014). https://doi.org/10.1007/978-3-662-43951-7_14
13. Gavrilenko, N., Ponce-de-León, H., Furbach, F., Heljanko, K., Meyer, R.: BMC for weak memory models: relation analysis for compact SMT encodings. In: Dillig, I., Tasiran, S. (eds.) CAV 2019. LNCS, vol. 11561, pp. 355–365. Springer, Cham (2019). https://doi.org/10.1007/978-3-030-25540-4_19
14. IBM: Power ISA, Version 2.07 (2013)

15. Intel Corporation: Intel 64 and IA-32 Architectures Software Developers Manual (2012)
16. Kozen, D.: Lower bounds for natural proof systems. In: FOCS, pp. 254–266. IEEE (1977)
17. Lahav, O., Boker, U.: Decidable verification under a causally consistent shared memory. In: Proceedings of the 41th ACM SIGPLAN Conference on Programming Language Design and Implementation, PLDI 2020. ACM (2020)
18. Lamport, L.: How to make a multiprocessor computer that correctly executes multiprocess programs. IEEE Trans. Comput. **28**(9), 690–691 (1979)
19. Mador-Haim, S., et al.: An axiomatic memory model for POWER multiprocessors. In: Madhusudan, P., Seshia, S.A. (eds.) CAV 2012. LNCS, vol. 7358, pp. 495–512. Springer, Heidelberg (2012). https://doi.org/10.1007/978-3-642-31424-7_36
20. Ponce de León, H., Furbach, F., Heljanko, K., Meyer, R.: Portability analysis for weak memory models. PORTHOS: one tool for all models. In: SAS 2017, pp. 299–320 (2017)
21. Ponce de León, H., Furbach, F., Heljanko, K., Meyer, R.: BMC with memory models as modules. In: FMCAD 2018, pp. 1–9 (2018)
22. Sarkar, S., Sewell, P., Alglave, J., Maranget, L., Williams, D.: Understanding POWER multiprocessors. In: PLDI, pp. 175–186. ACM (2011)
23. Tomasco, E., Lam, T.N., Fischer, B., Torre, S.L., Parlato, G.: Embedding weak memory models within eager sequentialization, October 2016

On the Encoding and Solving of Partial Information Games

Yackolley Amoussou-Guenou[1,2(✉)], Souheib Baarir[1], Maria Potop-Butucaru[1], Nathalie Sznajder[1], Léo Tible[3], and Sébastien Tixeuil[1]

[1] LIP6, CNRS, Sorbonne Université, 75005 Paris, France
{yackolley.amoussou-guenou,souheib.baarir,maria.potop-butucaru,
nathalie.sznajder,sebastien.tixeuil}@lip6.fr
[2] CEA LIST, 91191 Gif-sur-Yvette, France
[3] IBISC, Univ Évry, Université Paris-Saclay, 91025 Evry, France

Abstract. In this paper we address partial information games restricted to memoryless strategies. Our contribution is threefold. First, we prove that for partial information games, deciding the existence of memoryless strategies is NP-complete, even for games with only reachability objectives. The second contribution of this paper is a SAT/SMT-based encoding of a partial information game altogether with the correctness proof of this encoding. Finally, we apply our methodology to automatically synthesize strategies for oblivious mobile robots. We prove that synthesizing memoryless strategies is equivalent to providing a distributed protocol for the robots. Interestingly, our work is the first that combines two-player games theory and SMT-solvers in the context of mobile robots with promising results and therefore it is highly valuable for distributed computing theory where a broad class of open problems are still to be investigated.

1 Introduction

Two-player games are a widely used and very natural framework for reactive systems, i.e. that maintain an ongoing interaction with an unknown and/or uncontrollable environment. It is intimately linked to model-checking of μ-calculus [18] and synthesis of reactive programs (see e.g. [9]). In classical two-player zero-sum games, two players play on a graph. One of the players tries to force the sequence of visited nodes to belong to a (generally ω-regular) subset of infinite paths, called the winning condition. Its opponent tries to prevent her to achieve her goal. When total information is assumed, each player has a perfect knowledge of the history of the play. In a more realistic model in regards to applications to automatic synthesis of programs for instance, the protagonist does not have access to all the information about the game. Indeed, in distributed systems,

---

This work has been done while Y. Amoussou-Guenou and L. Tible where affiliated LIP6. This work was supported in part by ANR project SAPPORO, ref. 2019-CE25-0005-1.

C. Georgiou and R. Majumdar (Eds.): NETYS 2020, LNCS 12129, pp. 60–76, 2021.
https://doi.org/10.1007/978-3-030-67087-0_5

each component may have an internal state that is unknown by other components. This requires to consider games of *partial information*, in which only a partial information on the play is disclosed to the players. The main question to solve regarding games in our context is the existence of a winning strategy for the player modeling the system. This is now well understood. We know that total information parity games enjoy the memoryless determinacy property [18] ensuring that in each game, one of the players has a winning strategy, and that a winning strategy exists if and only if there is a memoryless winning strategy, i.e. a strategy that depends only on the last visited node of the graph, and not on a history of the play. However, partial information games do not enjoy this property since the player may need memory to win the game. On the other hand, regarding tools implementations, the field of two-player games has not reached the maturity obtained in model-checkers area. For total information games, to the notable exception of `pgsolver` [23] that provides a platform of implementation for algorithms solving parity games, and `Uppaal-TiGa` [28] that solves in a very efficient way timed games (but restricted to reachability conditions), few implementations are available. SAT-implementations of restricted types of games have also been proposed [17], as well as a reduction of parity games to SAT [20]. As for partial information games, even less attempts have been made. To our knowledge, only `alpaga` [1] solves partial information games, but the explicit input format does not allow to solve real-life instances.

Motivated by a problem on swarms of mobile robots, we propose here an attempt to solve partial information games, when restricted to memoryless strategies.

Formal Methods for the Study of Networks of Robots. The study of networks of mobile oblivious robots was pioneered by Suzuki and Yamashita [27]. In their seminal work, robots are considered as points evolving *obliviously* in a 2D space (that is, robots cannot remember their past actions). Moreover, robots have no common chirality nor direction, and cannot explicitly communicate with each other. Moreover, robots are anonymous and execute the same algorithm to achieve their goal. Nevertheless, they embed visual sensors that enable sensing other robots positions.

Recently, the original model was extended to robots that move in a *discrete space*, modeled as a graph whose nodes represent possible robot locations, and edges denote the possibility for a robot to move from one location to another. The main problems that have been considered in the literature in this context are: *gathering* [21], where all robots must gather on the same location (not determined beforehand) and stop moving, *perpetual exploration* [7,12] where, robots must visit infinitely often a ring, and *exploration with stop* [19], in that case, robots must visit each node of the ring and eventually stops.

Designing correct algorithms for mobile robots evolving on graphs is notoriously difficult. The scarcity of information that is available to the robots yields many possible symmetries, and asynchrony of the robot actions triggers moves that may be due to obsolete observations. As a matter of fact, published protocols for mobile robots on graphs were recently found incorrect, as reported in model checking attempts to assess them [6,14,15].

In addition to finding bugs in the literature [6], *Model-Checking* was used to check formally the correctness of published algorithms [6,13,25]. However, the current models do not help in designing algorithms, only in assessing whether a tentative solution satisfies some properties. An approach based on *Formal Proof* has been introduced with the Pactole framework [3–5,10,11] using the Coq Proof assistant. Pactole enabled the certification of both positive [4,11] and negative results [3,10] for oblivious mobile robots. The framework is modular enough that it permits to handle discrete spaces [5]. The methodology enabled by Pactole forces the algorithm designer to write the algorithm along with its correctness proof, but still does not help her in the design process (aside from providing a binary assessment for the correctness of the provided proof).

By contrast, *Automatic synthesis* is a tempting option for relieving the mobile robot protocol designer. Indeed, Automatic synthesis aims to automatically produce algorithms that are correct by design, or, when no protocol can be synthesized, it inherently gives an impossibility proof. *Automatic program synthesis* for the problem of perpetual exclusive exploration in a discrete ring is due to Bonnet *et al.* [8] (the approach is however restricted to the class of protocols that are *unambiguous*, where a single robot may move at any time). The approach was refined by Millet *et al.* [22] for the problem of gathering in a discrete ring network using *synchronous* semantics (robots actions are synchronized).

Contributions. In the current paper, we propose a SAT-based encoding of two-player partial information games, when restricted to memoryless strategies. We also prove that this problem is NP-complete. Then we apply this result to automatic synthesis of mobile robot protocols. We significantly extend the work of Millet *et al.* [22] since we define and prove correct a general framework for automatic synthesis of mobile robot protocols, for any target problem, using the most general asynchronous semantics (*i.e.* no synchronization is assumed about robots actions). Our framework makes use of the results presented in the first part, since we need to look for memoryless strategies in a partial information game.

2   Preliminaries

We recall here few notations on 2-*player game with partial information*. A game on an arena is played by moving a token along a labeled transition system (the arena). Following previous work [16], the game is presented as follows. When the token is positioned on a state s of the arena, the player called the *protagonist* can chose the label a of one of its outgoing transitions. Then the *opponent* moves the token on a state s' such that (s, a, s') is a transition of the arena. The game continues in a turn-based fashion for infinitely many rounds. The winner is determined according to the winning condition, which depends on the sequence of states visited. In a game with partial information, the protagonist is not able to precisely observe the play to make a decision on where to move the token next. This is formalized by the notion of *observation*, which is a partition of the states of the arena in observation sets. Hence, the decision of the player is made solely according to the sequence of observations visited, and not the precise sequence of vertices.

Arena with Partial Information. A *game arena with partial information* $\mathcal{A} = (S, \Sigma, \delta, s_0, Obs)$ is a graph where S is a finite set of states, Σ is a finite alphabet labeling the edges, and $\delta \subseteq S \times \Sigma \times S$ is a finite set of labeled transitions, and s_0 is the initial state. The arena is total in the sense that, for any $s \in S$, $a \in \Sigma$, there exists $s' \in S$ such that $(s, a, s') \in \delta$. The set Obs is a partition of S in observations visible to the protagonist. For $s \in S$, we let $\mathbf{o}(s) \in Obs$ be the corresponding observation. We extend $\mathbf{o}$ to the sequence of states in the natural way. An arena can be finite or infinite. In this work, we only consider finite arenas.

Plays. A *play* π on the arena $\mathcal{A} = (S, \Sigma, \delta, s_0, Obs)$ is an infinite sequence $\pi = s_0 s_1 \cdots \in S^\omega$ such that for all $i \geq 0$, there exists $a_i \in \Sigma$ such that $(s_i, a_i, s_{i+1}) \in \delta$. The *history* of a play π is a finite prefix of π, noted $\pi[i] = s_0 s_1 \ldots s_i$, for $i \geq 0$.

Strategies, Consistent Plays. A *strategy* for a player is a function that determines the action to take according to what has been played. Formally, a strategy σ for the protagonist is given by $\sigma : S^+ \to \Sigma$. As we explained, in an arena with partial information, the protagonist does not have a full knowledge of the current play. This is formalized by the notion of *observation-based strategy*. A strategy σ is *observation-based* if, for all $\pi, \pi' \in S^+$ such that $\mathbf{o}(\pi) = \mathbf{o}(\pi')$, $\sigma(\pi) = \sigma(\pi')$. A strategy for the opponent is given by $\tau : S^+ \times \Sigma \to S$. Given two strategies for the players, σ and τ, we say that a play $\pi = s_0 s_1 \cdots \in S^\omega$ is (σ, τ)-*compatible* if for all $i \geq 0$, $\tau(\pi[i], \sigma(\pi[i])) = s_{i+1}$, where $\pi[i] = s_0 \cdots s_i$. We say that it is σ-*compatible* if there exists a strategy τ for the opponent such that π is (σ, τ)-compatible.

When σ depends only of the last visited state, σ is said to be a *memoryless* strategy. In that case, we may define σ simply as $\sigma : S \to \Sigma$. We highlight the fact that σ is a total function.

Winning Condition, Winning Strategy. A *winning condition* on an arena $\mathcal{A} = (S, \Sigma, \delta, s_0, Obs)$ is a set $\phi \subseteq S^\omega$. An observation-based strategy σ is *winning* for the protagonist in the game $G = (S, \Sigma, \delta, s_0, Obs, \phi)$ if any σ-compatible play $\pi \subseteq \phi$ (such a play is called a *winning play*). Observe that we do not require the strategy of the opponent to be observation-based.

When the observation set is the finest partition possible, i.e., for all $s, s' \in S$, if $\mathbf{o}(s) = \mathbf{o}(s')$, then $s = s'$, the game is of *total information*, and any strategy for the protagonist is observation-based.

We are interested in the following classical winning conditions:

- *Reachability* Given a subset $F \subseteq S$ of target states, the reachability winning condition is defined by **REACH**$(F) = \{\pi = s_0 s_1 \cdots \in S^\omega \mid s_i \in$

F for some $i \geq 0$}. The winning plays are then the plays where one target set has been reached.

- *Büchi* Given a subset $F \subseteq S$ of target states, the Büchi winning condition is given by $\mathbf{BUCHI}(F) = \{\pi = s_0 s_1 \cdots \in S^\omega \mid \mathit{Inf}(\pi) \cap F \neq \emptyset\}$. The winning plays are then those where at least one target state has been visited infinitely often.
- *co-Büchi* Given a subset $F \subseteq S$ of target states, the co-Büchi winning condition is given by $\mathbf{coBUCHI}(F) = \{\pi = s_0 s_1 \cdots \in S^\omega \mid \mathit{Inf}(\pi) \cap F = \emptyset\}$. The winning plays are then those where no target state has been visited infinitely often.
- *Parity* The parity winning condition requires the use of a *coloring function* $d : S \to [0, n]$ where $[0, n]$ is a set of colors. The parity winning condition is given by $\mathbf{Parity}(d) = \{\pi \mid \min\{d(s) \mid s \in \inf(\pi)\} \text{ is even}\}$. The winning plays are then those where the minimal color occurring infinitely often is even.

Observe that Büchi and co-Büchi winning conditions are special cases of parity winning conditions, and that a reachability game can be transformed into a Büchi (or a co-Büchi) game, hence into a parity game. Hence to establish general results on games it is enough to consider only parity games.

The following result is a well-known result, called the memoryless determinacy of parity games of *total information*.

Theorem 1 (*[18]*). *In any parity game of total information, either the protagonist or the opponent has a winning strategy. Moreover, any player has a winning strategy if and only if it has a memoryless winning strategy.*

This important result shows that it is then sufficient to consider only memoryless strategies to solve parity games.

However this does not hold true anymore when we consider the more general case of partial information games. The following result is also well-known [16].

Theorem 2. *There exist parity games of incomplete information where there exists a winning strategy for the protagonist, but no memoryless winning strategy.*

Parity games of partial information are then more difficult to solve, since their resolution implies a modification of the arena using a subset construction, hence an exponential blow-up [24].

From now on we explore resolution of games of partial information when one is only interested in memoryless strategies.

3   Resolution of Partial Information Games, with Memoryless Strategies

3.1   Complexity Results

In this subsection, we establish NP-completeness of the problem. In fact, we show that even for the simple case of reachability games, the problem is already NP-hard. Due to space limitations, the detailed proof of the following theorem can be found in [2].

Theorem 3. *Deciding the existence of a memoryless strategy for partial observation game with reachability objective is NP-complete.*

Proof (Sketch). We show NP-hardness by a reduction from 3-*SAT*. Let $\varphi = \bigwedge_{1 \leq i \leq k} c_i$ be a 3-*SAT* formula in conjunctive normal form over a set X of variables.

We define a reachability game $G_\varphi = (S, \Sigma, \delta, s_0, Obs, \phi)$. The set of states of the arena will include a state for each clause, and a state for each variable and negation of variable. Formally, $S = \{s_0\} \cup \{s_{c_i} \mid 1 \leq i \leq k\} \cup \{s_x, s_{\neg x} \mid x \in X\} \cup \{s_\top, s_\bot\}$. The game is supposed to go as follows. The opponent selects a clause that the protagonist must show valued to 1. To do so, the protagonist goes to a state s_ℓ with ℓ a literal (x or $\neg x$) appearing in the selected clause, which is supposed to be true. According to its actual valuation, the game goes to the winning state $s_\top$ or to the losing state $s_\bot$. We assume that for all $1 \leq i \leq k$, $c_i = \ell_{i,1} \vee \ell_{i,2} \vee \ell_{i,3}$, with $\ell_{i,j} \in \{x, \neg x \mid x \in X\}$. We define $\Sigma = \{0, 1, 2, 3\}$ and $\delta = \{(s_0, 0, s_{c_i}) \mid 1 \leq i \leq k\} \cup \{(s_{c_i}, j, s_{\ell_{i,j}}) \mid 1 \leq j \leq 3\} \cup \{(s_x, 1, s_\top), (s_x, 0, s_\bot), (s_{\neg x}, 0, s_\bot), (s_{\neg x}, 1, s_\top) \mid x \in X\} \cup \{(s_\top, 0, s_\top), (s_\bot, 0, s_\bot)\}$. Observe that non-determinism, hence choice of the opponent, appears only in the transitions from the initial state s_0. The opponent only choses the clause to prove to be true. The rest of the game is totally determined by the strategy of the protagonist. Finally, we define the observations. Each state has its own observation class, except for the literals: for all $x \in X$, $\mathbf{o}(s_x) = \mathbf{o}(s_{\neg x}) = \{s_x, s_{\neg x}\}$. For all state $s \in X \setminus \{s_x, s_{\neg x} \mid x \in X\}$, $\mathbf{o}(s) = \{s\}$. The objective of the game is $\phi = \mathbf{REACH}(\{s_\top\})$. Then the formula φ is satisfiable if and only if there is a memoryless observation-based strategy for the game G_φ.

The upper bound follows from the fact that once a memoryless strategy has been guessed, one can check its correctness by nspecting the arena reduced to the only transitions chosen by the strategy in polynomial time (by checking absence of a loosing cycle).

The problem is then *NP-complete*. □

Since any reachability game can be reduced to a parity game, the following result can be obtained.

Corollary 4. *Deciding the existence of a memoryless strategy for partial observation game with parity objective is NP-complete.*

Proof. NP-hardness of reachability games allows to conclude the NP-hardness of parity games. The upper bound relies on algorithmic on graphs: in the graph restricted to the edges allowed by the strategy that have been guessed, one needs to detect for each node if it belongs to a cycle with odd minimal parity. Then one must determine if one of these nodes is accessible from the initial state. This can be computed in polynomial time. □

3.2   Encoding a Partial Information Game as a SAT Problem

In this section, we show how to encode $G = (S, \Sigma, \delta, s_0, Obs, \phi)$ a partial information game in a propositional logic formula. Here, the winning condition ϕ can be either a reachability, a Büchi or a co-Büchi condition for a target set of states $F \subseteq S$. We give the proof for reachability games, but slight modifications of the constraint (4) allow to handle Büchi and co-Büchi conditions.

We encode the arena of the game by attributing a variable to each transition. Let $\mathcal{X} = \{\langle s_1, a, s_2 \rangle \mid (s_1, a, s_2) \in \delta\}$ be the corresponding set of variables. Valuation of a variable to 1 will mean that the corresponding transition is selected by the strategy.

Now we need to express the different constraints that characterize a strategy. First, the strategy chooses a label of a transition, not the estination state. Moreover, the decision of a player is made only according to observation, and cannot depend specifically on one state.

$$\bigwedge_{\substack{\langle s_1, a, s_2 \rangle, \langle s_1', a, s_2' \rangle \in \mathcal{X} \\ \text{s.t. } \mathbf{o}(s_1) = \mathbf{o}(s_1')}} (\langle s_1, a, s_2 \rangle \longleftrightarrow \langle s_1', a, s_2' \rangle) \tag{1}$$

Then, at each state, the strategy will choose a unique action:

$$\bigwedge_{\langle s_1, a, s_2 \rangle \in \mathcal{X}} \left(\left(\langle s_1, a, s_2 \rangle \longrightarrow \bigwedge_{\substack{\langle s_1, b, s_2' \rangle \in \mathcal{X}, \\ b \in \Sigma \setminus \{a\}}} \neg \langle s_1, b, s_2' \rangle \right) \wedge \right.$$
$$\left. \left(\neg \langle s_1, a, s_2 \rangle \longrightarrow \bigvee_{\substack{\langle s_1, b, s_2' \rangle \in \mathcal{X}, \\ b \in \Sigma \setminus \{a\}}} \langle s_1, b, s_2' \rangle \right) \right) \tag{2}$$

A valuation of these variables satisfying these constraints would hence describe a memoryless observation-based strategy. Now we add constraints to check that this strategy is winning.

To do so, we need to check that any play compatible with this strategy is winning. We then add boolean variables that will encode prefixes of plays compatible with the strategy, i.e. paths in the graph of the arena, *when restricted to edges selected by the strategy*. In the following we refer to this graph as the restricted arena.

- $\mathcal{P} = \{\langle s, s' \rangle \mid (s, s') \in S^2\}$. A variable $\langle s, s' \rangle \in \mathcal{P}$ encodes the existence of a path starting at s and ending with s'.
- $\mathcal{W} = \{\overline{\langle s, s' \rangle} \mid (s, s') \in S^2\}$. A variable $\overline{\langle s, s' \rangle} \in \mathcal{W}$ encode the fact that *all* paths starting at s and ending with s' visit a state from F (different from s).

Thus, the constraints characterizing valid prefixes are:

i) $\bigwedge_{\langle s_1, a, s_2 \rangle \in \mathcal{X}, \langle s_1, s_2 \rangle \in \mathcal{P}}(\langle s_1, a, s_2 \rangle \longrightarrow \langle s_1, s_2 \rangle)$. If the strategy allows a transition $(s_1, a, s_2) \in \delta$, then $\langle s_1, s_2 \rangle$ is a path in the restricted arena.

ii) $\bigwedge_{\langle s_1, s_2 \rangle \in \mathcal{P}, \langle s_2, a, s_3 \rangle \in \mathcal{X}}((\langle s_1, s_2 \rangle \wedge \langle s_2, a, s_3 \rangle) \longrightarrow \langle s_1, s_3 \rangle)$. A prefix $\langle s_1, s_2 \rangle$ is extended to $\langle s_1, s_3 \rangle$ if the strategy allows the transition $(s_2, a, s_3) \in \delta$.

iii) $\bigwedge_{\langle s_1, a, s_2 \rangle \in \mathcal{X}, s_2 \notin F} (\langle s_1, a, s_2 \rangle \longrightarrow \overline{\neg \langle s_1, s_2 \rangle})$. If the strategy allows a transition $(s_1, a, s_2) \in \delta$ where s_2 is not a target state then there is a path from s_1 to s_2 that does not visit any state from F.

iv) $\bigwedge_{\overline{\langle s_1, s_2 \rangle} \in \mathcal{W}, s_2 \notin F} (\overline{\langle s_1, s_2 \rangle} \longrightarrow$

$\bigwedge_{\langle s_3, b, s_2 \rangle \in \mathcal{X}, \overline{\langle s_1, s_3 \rangle} \in \mathcal{W}, s_3 \neq s_2} (\neg \langle s_3, b, s_2 \rangle \vee \overline{\langle s_1, s_3 \rangle}))$. If all the paths from s_1 to s_2 visit a state from F (different from s_1, while s_2 is not a target state, then it means that for every predecessor s_3 of s_2, all paths from s_1 to s_3 already visit a state from F.

The formula resulting of the conjunction of the previous constraints is noted (3).

It remains to show that the strategy is indeed winning, i.e., in the arena restricted to transitions allowed by the strategy, all the plays are winning. If this is not the case, then there exists a (infinite) play that never visits any set of F. Since the arena is finite, such a play necessarily contains a loop that does not visit a target state. The constraint expressing that the strategy is not winning is then: $\langle s_0, s \rangle \wedge \neg \overline{\langle s_0, s \rangle} \wedge \langle s, s \rangle \wedge \neg \overline{\langle s, s \rangle}$. So, to express that the strategy is winning, we just have to negate this formula and quantify over all variables of $\mathcal{P}$ and $\mathcal{W}$. We obtain:

$$\bigwedge_{\substack{\langle s_0, s \rangle, \langle s, s \rangle \in \mathcal{P}, \\ \overline{\langle s_0, s \rangle}, \overline{\langle s, s \rangle} \in \mathcal{W}}} (\neg \langle s_0, s \rangle \vee \overline{\langle s_0, s \rangle} \vee \neg \langle s, s \rangle \vee \overline{\langle s, s \rangle}) \tag{4}$$

The final formula encoding existence of a winning strategy is then the conjunction of all previous formulae:

$$\psi_G = (1) \wedge (2) \wedge (3) \wedge (4) \tag{5}$$

The detailed proof of the following theorem can be found in [2].

Theorem 5. $G = (S, \Sigma, \delta, s_0, Obs, \textbf{REACH}(F))$ *admits a memoryless winning strategy if and only if* ψ_G *is satisfiable.*

Proof (Sketch). Given a strategy σ on G, we define $\mathcal{A}_\sigma = (S, \Sigma, \delta_\sigma, s_0, Obs)$, where $\delta_\sigma = \{(s, a, s') \in \delta \mid \sigma(s) = a\}$ as the game arena restricted to the transitions allowed by the strategy σ.

Assume first that G admits a winning memoryless and observation-based strategy $\sigma : S \rightarrow \Sigma$. Then ψ_G is satisfied by the valuation $\nu_\sigma : (\mathcal{X} \cup \mathcal{P} \cup \mathcal{W}) \rightarrow \{0, 1\}$, defined as follows:

- for all $\langle s, a, s' \rangle \in \mathcal{X}$, $\nu_\sigma(\langle s, a, s' \rangle) = \begin{cases} 1 & \text{if} \sigma(s) = a. \\ 0 & \text{otherwise.} \end{cases}$

- for all $\langle s, s' \rangle \in \mathcal{P}$, $\nu_\sigma(\langle s, s' \rangle) = \begin{cases} 1 & \text{if there is play of } \mathcal{A}_\sigma \text{ with a prefix } s \ldots s'. \\ 0 & \text{otherwise.} \end{cases}$

$$- \text{ for all } \overline{\langle s,s'\rangle} \in \mathcal{W}, \nu_\sigma(\overline{\langle s,s'\rangle}) = \begin{cases} 1 & \text{if there is play of } \mathcal{A}_\sigma \text{ with a prefix } s\ldots s' \\ & \text{and all prefixes starting at } s \text{ and ending} \\ & \text{with } s' \text{ visit a state from } F \text{ different from } s. \\ 0 & \text{otherwise.} \end{cases}$$

It is then straightforward to check that $\nu_\sigma(\psi_G) = 1$.

Assume now that ψ_G is satisfiable and let $\nu : \mathcal{X} \cup \mathcal{P} \cup \mathcal{W} \to \{0,1\}$ such that $\nu(\psi_G) = 1$. We build a strategy $\sigma_\nu : S \to \Sigma$ as follows. For $s \in S$, let $a \in \Sigma$ and $s' \in S$ such that $\nu(\langle s, a, s' \rangle) = 1$ then $\sigma_\nu(s) = a$. Condition (2) ensures that σ_ν is well-defined. Moreover, if $s_1, s_1' \in S$ are such that $\mathbf{o}(s_1) = \mathbf{o}(s_1')$, then condition (1) ensures that, for all $a \in \Sigma$, $\nu(\langle s_1, a, s_2 \rangle) = \nu(\langle s_1', a, s_2' \rangle)$. Hence $\sigma_\nu(s_1) = \sigma_\nu(s_1')$ and σ_ν is observation-based.

To prove that σ_ν is winning, we rely on the following observation: in a game $G = (S, \Sigma, \delta, s_0, Obs, \mathbf{REACH}(F))$, if a strategy σ is not winning, then there exists a σ-compatible play $s_0 \cdots s \cdot \pi^\omega$, with $\pi = s_1 \cdots s_k$ for some $k \in \mathbb{N}$, and that play never visits a state from F. We can then prove that it is impossible to have such a play in $\mathcal{A}_\sigma$.   □

4   Application: Automatic Synthesis of Strategies for Swarms of Autonomous Oblivious Robots

In this section, we consider applying our methodology to formally study distributed algorithms that are designed for sets of mobile oblivious robots. Robots are mobile entities that evolve in a discrete space (here, a ring), When two robots are positioned on the same node, they form a *tower*. In this model, robots cannot remember their past actions (they are *oblivious*), have no common chirality nor direction, and cannot explicitly communicate with one another. However, they can sense their entire environment (using visual sensors). Moreover, robots are anonymous and execute the same deterministic algorithm to achieve their goal.

Each robot evolves following an internal cycle: it takes a snapshot of the ring, computes its next move, and then executes the movement it has computed. Several semantics for swarms of robots have been studied. In the fully synchronous semantics (FSYNC), all the robots evolve at the same time, completing an internal cycle simultaneously. In the semi-synchronous semantics (SSYNC), in each round, only a non-empty subset of the robots fulfills a complete cycle. Finally, in the asynchronous semantics (ASYNC), each robot completes its internal cycle at its own pace. The later semantics are considered the harder to design robot algorithms, since a robot may move based on obsolete observations.

In this section, we extend the work done by Millet *et al.* [22], where automatic synthesis of protocols of gathering in FSYNC and SSYNC semantics was considered. In the current paper, we first provide a general framework for automatic synthesis of mobile robot protocols, for any target problem, using the most general ASYNC semantics. Then, we use our propositional logic-based encoding to effectively solve the problem.

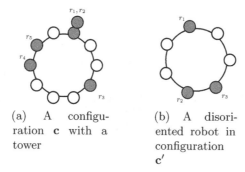

(a) A configu-
ration **c** with a
tower

(b) A disori-
ented robot in
configuration
c′

Fig. 1. Configurations of robots on a ring

4.1   Model for the Robots

We partly use notations defined in [26]. We consider a fixed number of $k > 0$ robots evolving on a ring of fixed size $n \geq k$. We denote by $\mathcal{R}$ the set of considered robots. Positions on the ring of size n are numbered $\{0, \ldots, n-1\}$.

Configurations and Robots Views. A *configuration* is a vector $\mathbf{c} \in [0, n-1]^k$ that gives the position of each robot on the ring at a given instance of time. We assume that positions are numbered in the clockwise direction. The set of all configurations is called $\mathcal{C}_{n,k}$, or simply $\mathcal{C}$ when n and k are clear from the context.

Decisions made by a robot are based on the snapshot it takes of the environment, called the *view* of that robot. We model it by the sequence of distances between neighboring robots on the ring, a distance of 0 means that the two consecutive robots share the same position on the ring. Formally, a view is then a tuple $\mathbf{V} = \langle d_1, \ldots, d_k \rangle$ such that $\Sigma_{i=0}^{n} d_i = n$. The set of all the views on a ring of size n with k robots is noted $\mathcal{V}$. Notice that two robots sharing the same position should have the same view. This might be problematic with our definition since when two robots share the same node, their distance is equal to 0, and this 0 is not at the same position in the tuple according to the concerned robot in the tower. To ensure this, we assume that the first distance in the tuple is always strictly greater than 0 (which is always possible by putting the first 0's at the end instead). In Fig. 1a is shown a configuration defined by $\mathbf{c}(r_1) = \mathbf{c}(r_2) = 0$, $\mathbf{c}(r_3) = 3$, $\mathbf{c}(r_4) = 7$ and $\mathbf{c}(r_5) = 8$. When looking in the clockwise direction, the view of robots r_1 and r_2 is given by the tuple $\mathbf{V} = \langle 3, 4, 1, 2, 0 \rangle$, and the view of robot r_3 is given by $\mathbf{V}' = \langle 4, 1, 2, 0, 3 \rangle$. Formally, for a view $\mathbf{V} = \langle d_1, \ldots, d_k \rangle$ giving the view of a robot starting in one direction, we write its view in the opposite direction $\overleftarrow{\mathbf{V}} = \langle d_j, \ldots, d_1, d_k, \ldots, d_{j-1} \rangle$, where $1 \leq j \leq k$ is the greatest index such that $d_j \neq 0$. In our example, it means that $\overleftarrow{\mathbf{V}} = \langle 2, 1, 4, 3, 0 \rangle$ and $\overleftarrow{\mathbf{V}'} = \langle 3, 0, 2, 1, 4 \rangle$.

Given a configuration $\mathbf{c} \in \mathcal{C}$ and a robot $i \in \mathcal{R}$, the view of robot i when looking in the clockwise direction, is given by $\mathbf{V_c}[i \to] = \langle d_i(i_1), d_i(i_2) - d_i(i_1), \ldots, n - d_i(i_{k-1}) \rangle$, where, for all $j \neq i$, $d_i(j) \in [1, n]$ is such that $(\mathbf{c}(i) + d_i(j)) \mod n = \mathbf{c}(j)$ and $i_1, \ldots, i_k$ are indexes pairwise distinct such that $0 < d_i(i_1) \leq d_i(i_2) \leq \cdots \leq d_i(i_{k-1})$. When robot i looks in the opposite direction, its view according to the configuration $\mathbf{c}$ is $\mathbf{V_c}[\leftarrow i] = \overleftarrow{\mathbf{V_c}[i \to]}$. Hence, in the configuration $\mathbf{c}$ pictured in Fig. 1a, $\mathbf{V_c}[r_1 \to] = \langle 3, 4, 1, 2, 0 \rangle$ and $\mathbf{V_c}[\leftarrow r_1] = \langle 2, 1, 4, 3, 0 \rangle$. Observe that in Fig. 1b, $\mathbf{V_{c'}}[r_1 \to] = \mathbf{V_{c'}}[\leftarrow r_1] = \langle 3, 1, 3 \rangle$. Robot r_1 is then said to be disoriented, since it has no way to distinguish one direction from the other. For a configuration $\mathbf{c}$, we let $\mathbf{Views}(\mathbf{c}) = \bigcup_{i \in \mathcal{R}} \{\mathbf{V_c}[i \to], \mathbf{V_c}[\leftarrow i]\}$ be the set of views of all the robots in this configuration.

Since robots are anonymous, given a configuration $\mathbf{c}$, the set of decisions taken by the robots based on their view in this configuration is invariant with respect to permutation of the robots or to any rotation of the ring. Since they have no chirality, a robot $i \in \mathcal{R}$ takes a decision solely based on $\langle \mathbf{V_c}[i \to], \mathbf{V_c}[\leftarrow i] \rangle$, hence the same decision is reached for any configuration symmetric to $\mathbf{c}$. Regarding decision taking, any two configurations that are obtained through symmetry or any rotation of the ring are equivalent. The notion of views captures handily this notion and we define the equivalence relation on configurations as follows.

Definition 6 (Equivalence Relation on Configurations). *Two configurations $\mathbf{c}$ and $\mathbf{c'} \in \mathcal{C}$ are equivalent if and only if $\mathbf{Views}(\mathbf{c}) = \mathbf{Views}(\mathbf{c'})$. We write then $\mathbf{c} \equiv \mathbf{c'}$. The equivalence class of $\mathbf{c}$ with respect to $\equiv$ is simply written $[\mathbf{c}]$.*

We now make some observations on the relations between configurations and views of the robots.

Let $\mathbf{V} \in \mathcal{V}$. We note $Config(\mathbf{V}) = \{\mathbf{c} \in \mathcal{C} \mid \mathbf{V} \in \mathbf{Views}(\mathbf{c})\}$.

Lemma 7. *Let $\mathbf{V} \in \mathcal{V}$, and $\mathbf{c}, \mathbf{c'} \in Config(\mathbf{V})$. Then $\mathbf{c} \equiv \mathbf{c'}$.*

We distinguish now some set of configurations that are useful in the remaining of the paper. Let $\mathbb{C}_\mathsf{T} = [\mathbf{c}]$ where $\mathbf{c}(i) = 0$ for all $i \in \mathcal{R}$ be the set of all the configurations where all the robots are gathered on the same position. For $i \in \mathcal{R}$ and $j \in [0, n-1]$, let $\mathsf{C}_i^j = \{\mathbf{c} \in \mathcal{C} \mid \mathbf{c}(i) = j)\}$ be the set of configurations where the robot i is on the position j of the ring, and we let $\mathsf{C}^j = \bigcup_{i \in \mathcal{R}} \mathsf{C}_i^j$ be the set of configurations where there is one robot on position j of the ring.

Protocols for the Robots. We are interested in modeling distributed protocols that govern the movements of the robots in a ring in order to achieve some predefined goal. Such protocols control each robot according to its local view. Robots being anonymous imply that two robots having the same view of the ring execute the same order. Having no common chirality implies that the protocol does not discriminate between the clockwise and the anti-clockwise view, hence gives symmetric move orders to robots in symmetric positions, and cannot decide where to move when the robot is disoriented, *i.e.* when both views are identical.

We denote by $\Delta = \{-1, 0, 1, ?\}$ the set of possible decisions given by the protocol, where 0 means that the robot will not move, -1 means an anticlockwise movement, 1 a clockwise movement and ? means that the robot moves but is disoriented, hence it has no control on the exact direction to take.

We review here some basic notations. For a function $f : A \to B$, we let $dom(f) = A$ its domain of definition, and for a subset $C \subseteq A$, we let $f_{|C} : C \to B$ the restriction of f on C, defined by $f_{|C}(c) = f(c)$ for all $c \in C$. We can now define the notion of decision function.

Definition 8. *Let $D : \mathcal{V} \to \Delta$ be a (partially defined) function. We say that D is a decision function if, for all $\mathbf{V} \in dom(D)$, (i) $\overleftarrow{\mathbf{V}} \in dom(V)$, (ii) if $\mathbf{V} = \overleftarrow{\mathbf{V}}$, then $D(\mathbf{V}) \in \{0, ?\}$, (iii) otherwise, $D(\mathbf{V}) \in \{-1, 0, 1\}$ and $D(\mathbf{V}) = (-1) \cdot D(\overleftarrow{\mathbf{V}})$.*
We denote by $\mathcal{D}$ the set of all decision functions.

A protocol $\mathfrak{P}$ for k robots on a ring of size n is simply a *total* decision function.

Executions. Recall that each robot behaves according to an internal cycle, alternating between a phase where it looks at its environment and computes its next move, and a phase where it actually moves. We model here the asynchronous semantics, where other robots can execute an unbounded number of actions between the two aforementioned phases.

Hence, to define the transition relation between two configurations, we need to enrich the notion of configuration with that of internal state of each robot, which determines the next action of a robot. The set of all possible internal states for the robots is $\mathcal{S} = \{-1, 0, 1, \mathbf{L}\}$, where -1 represents a move in the anti-clockwise direction, 0 not moving, 1 represents a move in the clockwise direction, and $\mathbf{L}$ represents the fact that the robot is ready to take a snapshot of its environment.

Let $\mathbf{s} \in \mathcal{S}^k$ be the vector of internal states of the robots. An *asynchronous configuration* is an element $(\mathbf{c}, \mathbf{s}) \in \mathcal{C} \times \mathcal{S}^k$. We say that $(\mathbf{c}, \mathbf{s}) \to_{\mathfrak{P}} (\mathbf{c}', \mathbf{s}')$ if and only if there exists a robot $i \in \mathcal{R}$ such that:

- $\mathbf{s}'(j) = \mathbf{s}(j)$ and $\mathbf{c}'(j) = \mathbf{c}(j)$ for all $j \neq i$,
- if $\mathbf{s}(i) = \mathbf{L}$ then $\mathbf{c}'(i) = \mathbf{c}(i)$ and $\mathbf{s}'(i) \in \{-1, 1\}$ if $\mathfrak{P}(\mathbf{V_c}[i \to]) =?$, and $\mathbf{s}'(i) = \mathfrak{P}(\mathbf{V_c}[i \to])$ otherwise. If $\mathbf{s}(i) \neq \mathbf{L}$ then $\mathbf{s}'(i) = \mathbf{L}$ and $\mathbf{c}'(i) = (\mathbf{c}(i) + \mathbf{s}(i))$ mod n.

Observe that given two asynchronous configurations $(\mathbf{c}, \mathbf{s})$ and $(\mathbf{c}', \mathbf{s}')$, two protocols $\mathfrak{P}$ and $\mathfrak{P}'$ such that $\mathfrak{P}_{|\mathbf{Views(c)}} = \mathfrak{P}'_{|\mathbf{Views(c)}}$, then $(\mathbf{c}, \mathbf{s}) \to_{\mathfrak{P}} (\mathbf{c}', \mathbf{s}')$ if and only if $(\mathbf{c}, \mathbf{s}) \to_{\mathfrak{P}'} (\mathbf{c}', \mathbf{s}')$.

Protocols for robots are meant to work starting from any initial configuration, or at least from a subset of possible initial configurations. The only requirement is that internal states of robots are set to $\mathbf{L}$ at the beginning of the execution. Hence, an initial asynchronous $\mathfrak{P}$-run is a (finite or infinite) sequence $\rho = (\mathbf{c}_0, \mathbf{s}_0)(\mathbf{c}_1, \mathbf{s}_1) \ldots$ such that: (1) $\mathbf{s}_0(i) = \mathbf{L}$ for all robot $i \in \mathcal{R}$, and (2) for all $0 \leq k < |\rho|$, $(\mathbf{c}_k, \mathbf{s}_k) \rightarrow_{\mathfrak{P}} (\mathbf{c}_{k+1}, \mathbf{s}_{k+1})$. For a robot $i \in \mathcal{R}$, we let $\mathbf{Act}_i(\rho) = |\{0 \leq k < |\rho| \mid \mathbf{s}_k(i) \neq \mathbf{L} \text{ and } \mathbf{s}_{k+1}(i) = \mathbf{L}\}|$ be the number of times this robot has been moved during the execution. A $\mathfrak{P}$-run is *fair* if, for all $i \in \mathcal{R}$, $\mathbf{Act}_i(\rho) = \omega$.

For a $\mathfrak{P}$-run ρ, the projection of ρ on the sequence of configurations is written $\pi_{\mathcal{C}}(\rho)$.

We can now define the synthesis problem under consideration in this work, where we are given an objective for the robots, describing the set of desirable runs.

Definition 9 (Synthesis Problem). *Given an objective $\Omega \subseteq \mathcal{C}^\omega$, decide wether there exists a protocol $\mathfrak{P}$ such that for all initial fair asynchronous $\mathfrak{P}$-run ρ, $\pi_{\mathcal{C}}(\rho) \subseteq \Omega$.*

Objectives. Classical objectives for the robots are gathering, perpetual exploration and exploration with stop. Formally, we call **GATHER** the synthesis problem where $\Omega = \{\mathbf{c}_1 \cdots \mathbf{c}_k \cdot \mathbf{c}_k^\omega \mid \text{for some } k \geq 1, \mathbf{c}_k \in \mathbb{C}_{\mathsf{T}}\}$, we call **EXPLORATION** the synthesis problem where $\Omega = \{\pi \in \mathcal{C}^\omega \mid \mathit{Inf}(\pi) \cap \mathsf{C}_i^j \neq \emptyset \text{ for all } i \in \mathcal{R} \text{ and } j \in [0, n-1]\}$ and **EXPLORATION-STOP** the synthesis problem where $\Omega = \{\mathbf{c}_1 \dots \mathbf{c}_k \cdot \mathbf{c}_k^\omega \mid \mathbf{c}_k \in \mathbb{C}_{\mathsf{T}}, \text{ and for all } j \in [0, n-1], \text{ there exists } 1 \leq \ell \leq k, \mathbf{c}_\ell \in \mathsf{C}^j\}$.

4.2   Definition of the Arena

We define now a partial information game $G_{n,k} = (S_{n,k}, \Sigma_{n,k}, \delta_{n,k}, s_0, \mathit{Obs}_{n,k}, \phi)$ that captures the asynchronous model for a set $\mathcal{R}$ of k robots evolving on a ring of size n. The protocol of the robots gives, according to the last view of the robot, the next move to do, taken from the set $\Delta = \{-1, 0, 1, ?\}$. The states of the arena are the possible distinct asynchronous configurations, enriched with a vector of bits $\mathsf{b} \in \{0, 1\}^k$ that keeps track of the various activated robots to ensure the fairness of the execution. We write $\mathbb{B} = \{0, 1\}^k$. Moreover, the initial configuration of the execution is chosen by the opponent. To ensure this, we add a special initial state, s_ι, that can access any possible initial configuration.

Hence the set of states $S_{n,k} = (\mathcal{C} \times \mathcal{S}^k \times \mathbb{B}) \uplus \{\iota\}$. Choosing a transition for the protocol means choosing a decision function for the possible views of the robots in a particular configuration $\mathbf{c}$. The labeling of the transitions is hence taken from $\Sigma_{n,k} = \mathcal{D} \uplus \{\varepsilon\}$, the set of all possible decision functions, along with a dummy label, ε, used only for the initial state. The protocol we look for is supposed to achieve the goal starting in any initial configuration. The transitions starting from the initial state of the arena (which is the special state ι) are all labelled by the same dummy action, and lead to any initial configuration. Formally, $\{(\iota, \varepsilon, (\mathbf{c}, \mathbf{s_L}, \mathbf{b}_0)) \mid \mathbf{c} \in \mathcal{C}\} \subseteq \delta_{n,k}$ with $\mathbf{s_L}(i) = \mathbf{L}$ for all $i \in \mathcal{R}$, $\mathbf{b}_0(i) = 0$ for all $i \in \mathcal{R}$.

Now, in any configuration, the protagonist choses the decision function corresponding to the decisions of the robots in this particular configuration, and the opponent chooses the resulting configuration. The opponent then decides which robot moves (the role of the scheduler), and, whenever a robot is disoriented where it actually moves. Formally, let $(\mathbf{c}, \mathbf{s}, \mathbf{b}) \in S_{n,k}$ be a state of the arena, and $f : \mathbf{Views}(\mathbf{c}) \to \Delta$ be a decision function. Let al.so $\overline{f} : \mathcal{V} \to \Delta$ be any protocol such that $\overline{f}_{|\mathbf{Views}(\mathbf{c})} = f$. Then, $((\mathbf{c}, \mathbf{s}, \mathbf{b}), f, (\mathbf{c}', \mathbf{s}', \mathbf{b}')) \in \delta_{n,k}$ iff $(\mathbf{c}, \mathbf{s}) \to_{\overline{f}} (\mathbf{c}', \mathbf{s}')$ and $\mathbf{b}'$ is defined as follows: let $\mathbf{b}'' \in \mathbb{B}$, such that $\mathbf{b}''(i) = \mathbf{b}(i)$ if $\mathbf{s}(i) = \mathbf{s}'(i)$, i.e. if the robot i has not been scheduled, and

$$
\mathbf{b}''(i) = \begin{cases} 1 & \text{if } \mathbf{s}(i) \neq \mathbf{L} \text{ and } \mathbf{s}'(i) = \mathbf{L} \\ \mathbf{b}(i) & \text{otherwise.} \end{cases}
$$

Then, $\mathbf{b}'$ is defined as follows. If $\mathbf{b}''(i) = 1$ for all $i \in \mathcal{R}$, then $\mathbf{b}'(i) = 0$ for all $i \in \mathcal{R}$, otherwise $\mathbf{b}' = \mathbf{b}''$. Hence, the bit $\mathbf{b}(i)$ is turned to 1 every time robot i has been scheduled to move. Once they all have been scheduled to move once, every bit is set to 1, and the entire vector is reset to 0. Finally we define the observation sets. Indeed, when the protocol is defined, it only takes into account the view of a robot, and it does not depend on the internal states of other robots, nor on the scheduling. Hence the strategy computed for the protagonist should only depend on the configuration. Moreover, as we have explained earlier, decisions of the robots are invariant to permutation of the robots, rotation of the ring or any symmetry transformation. The strategy then only depends on the equivalence class of the configuration. Formally we let $Obs_{n,k} = \{[\mathbf{c}] \mid \mathbf{c} \in \mathcal{C}\}$ and for any state $(\mathbf{c}, \mathbf{s}, \mathbf{b}) \in S_{n,k}$, $\mathbf{o}(\mathbf{c}, \mathbf{s}, \mathbf{b}) = [\mathbf{c}]$.

Given a set $\mathcal{R}$ of k robots evolving on a ring of size n, let $\phi \subseteq S_{n,k}^\omega$. Then, $\mathcal{A}_{n,k} = (S_{n,k}, \Sigma_{n,k}, \delta_{n,k}, s_0, Obs_{n,k})$ is the corresponding arena with partial information and $G_{n,k} = (S_{n,k}, \Sigma_{n,k}, \delta_{n,k}, s_0, Obs_{n,k}, \phi)$ is the two-player game with winning condition ϕ.

Proposition 10. *For GATHER, EXPLORATION or EXPLORATION-STOP, there exists a protocol for the robots if and only if there exists a memoryless winning strategy in $G_{n,k}$, with suitable winning condition (more precisely a combination of reachability, Büchi and co-Büchi condition).*

Definition 11. *Let $\mathcal{A}_{n,k}$ be an arena as described above, and $\mathfrak{P}$ a protocol for the robots. A play $s_0(\mathbf{c}_0, \mathbf{s}_0, \mathbf{b}_0)(\mathbf{c}_1, \mathbf{s}_1, \mathbf{b}_1) \ldots$ in $\mathcal{A}_{n,k}$ is equivalent to the initial asynchronous run $(\mathbf{c}_0, \mathbf{s}_0)(\mathbf{c}_1, \mathbf{s}_1) \ldots$.*

Moreover, observe that for any initial run $(\mathbf{c}_0, \mathbf{s}_0)(\mathbf{c}_1, \mathbf{s}_1) \ldots$, there exists a unique play $s_0(\mathbf{c}_0, \mathbf{s}_0, \mathbf{b}_0)(\mathbf{c}_1, \mathbf{s}_1, \mathbf{b}_1) \ldots$ in $G_{n,k}$ that is equivalent, since the sequence of $\mathbf{b}_i$ is entirely determined by the sequence of $\mathbf{c}_i$ and $\mathbf{s}_i$. In the following, we have two lemmas which prove the equivalence.

Lemma 12. *Let $\sigma : S_{n,k} \to \Sigma_{n,k}$ be an observation-based memoryless strategy on $G_{n,k}$. Then there exists a protocol $\mathfrak{P}^\sigma : \mathcal{V} \to \Delta$ such that any σ-compatible play is equivalent to an initial $\mathfrak{P}$-run, and any initial $\mathfrak{P}$-run is equivalent to a σ-compatible play.*

Lemma 13. *Let $\mathfrak{P} : \mathcal{V} \to \Delta$ be a protocol for k robots on a ring of size n. Then there exists an observation-based memoryless strategy $\sigma : S_{n,k} \to \Sigma_{n,k}$ such that any initial $\mathfrak{P}$-run is equivalent to a σ-compatible play of $G_{n,k}$ and any σ-compatible play is equivalent to an initial $\mathfrak{P}$-run.*

To conclude on the equivalence between solving the game for the robots and the synthesis problem defined in Sect. 4.1, it remains to state the following lemma.

Lemma 14. *Given ρ a run and π an equivalent play in the game, ρ is fair if and only if $\mathit{Inf}(\pi) \cap \{(\mathbf{c}, \mathbf{s}, \mathbf{b}) \mid \mathbf{b}(i) = 0 \text{ for all } i \in \mathcal{R}\} \neq \emptyset$.*

Proof (Proof of Proposition 10). In order to solve **GATHER**, we need to slightly modify the arena of $G_{n,k}$. Indeed, if the objective of the gathering resembles a reachability objective, it is also required that once robots are gathered, they do not leave their positions anymore, while in a reachability game, the play is won as soon as the objective is attained no matter what happens afterwards. In order to circumvent this problem, we modify $G_{n,k}$ as follows. For all $(\mathbf{c}, \mathbf{s}, \mathbf{b}) \in S_{n,k}$ such that $\mathbf{c} \in \mathbb{C}_T$, for all $(\mathbf{c}', \mathbf{s}', \mathbf{b}') \in S_{n,k}$, $((\mathbf{c}, \mathbf{s}, \mathbf{b}), f, (\mathbf{c}', \mathbf{s}', \mathbf{b}')) \in \delta$ if and only if $f(\mathbf{V}) = 0$ for all $\mathbf{V} \in \mathbf{Views}(\mathbf{c})$. The rest of the arena remains unchanged. We call this new game $G'_{n,k}$. Hence, this modification restricts the possibilities to decision functions that detect that a configuration where all the robots are gathered is reached, and commands not to move anymore. This does not change anything for Lemma 12, and it is easy to see that Lemma 13 could be adapted to the special protocols that command not to move while all the robots are gathered. We then let $T = \{(\mathbf{c}, \mathbf{s}, \mathbf{b}) \mid \mathbf{c} \in \mathbb{C}_T \text{ and } \mathbf{s}(i) \in \{\mathbf{L}, 0\} \text{ for all } i \in \mathcal{R}\}$. In the modified arena, any play $\pi = s_0 \cdot (\mathbf{c}_0, \mathbf{s}_0, \mathbf{b}_0)(\mathbf{c}_1, \mathbf{s}_1, \mathbf{b}_1) \cdots \in \mathbf{REACH}(T)$ is such that there exists $k \geq 0$, such that for all $\ell \geq k$, $(\mathbf{c}_\ell, \mathbf{s}_\ell, \mathbf{b}_\ell) \in T$. Indeed, let $k \geq 0$, such that $(\mathbf{c}_k, \mathbf{s}_k, \mathbf{b}_k) \in F$. Since we consider the modified arena, $((\mathbf{c}_k, \mathbf{s}_k, \mathbf{b}_k), f, (\mathbf{c}_{k+1}, \mathbf{s}_{k+1}, \mathbf{b}_{k+1})) \in \delta$ implies that $f(\mathbf{V}) = 0$ for all $\mathbf{V} \in \mathbf{Views}(\mathbf{c}_k)$. Hence, by definition, there exists $i \in \mathcal{R}$ such that $\mathbf{s}_k(i) \neq \mathbf{s}_{k+1}(i)$. If $\mathbf{s}_k(i) = \mathbf{L}$ then $\mathbf{s}_{k+1} = 0$ by definition of f and $\mathbf{c}_{k+1} = \mathbf{c}_k$; if $\mathbf{s}_k(i) = 0$ then $\mathbf{c}_{k+1} = \mathbf{c}_k$ and $\mathbf{s}_{k+1} = \mathbf{L}$. Then, $(\mathbf{c}_{k+1}, \mathbf{s}_{k+1}, \mathbf{b}_{k+1}) \in T$. We also need to consider unfair executions that should not be considered as loosing if they fail to reach T. Let $F = \{(\mathbf{c}, \mathbf{s}, \mathbf{b}) \mid \mathbf{b}(i) = 0 \text{ for all } i \in \mathcal{R}\}$, the set of configurations where the vector $\mathbf{b}$ has been reset to 0. □

With the general parity condition, one can also use $G_{n,k}$ (with slight suitable modifications) in order to solve **EXPLORATION** and **EXPLORATION-STOP**.

5   Conclusion

We studied the implementation of partial information zero-sum games with memoryless strategies. We proved that this problem is NP-complete and provided its SAT-based encoding. Furthermore, we used this framework to offer a solution to automatic synthesis of protocols for autonomous networks of mobile robots in the most generic settings (i.e. asynchronous). This encoding is then a generalization of the work presented in [22], where the encoding allowed only for the gathering problem in synchronous or semi-synchronous semantics.

This generalization is at the cost of an increasing of the size of the arena, as well as lifting the problem to parity games with partial information, hence making the problem more complex to solve, as we have seen earlier (NP-complete instead of linear time in the case of reachability games of total information studied in [22]). Results of Sect. 3.2 would allow us to solve this problem using a SAT-solver. Future work includes encoding this arena using a SMT-solver to effectively provide an implementation of the problem.

References

1. http://lit2.ulb.ac.be/alpaga/usermanual.html
2. Amoussou-Guenou, Y., Baarir, S., Potop-Butucaru, M., Sznajder, N., Tible, L., Tixeuil, S.: On the encoding and solving partial information games. Research report, LIP6, Sorbonne Université, CNRS, UMR 7606; LINCS; CEA Paris Saclay; Sorbonne Université (2018)
3. Auger, C., Bouzid, Z., Courtieu, P., Tixeuil, S., Urbain, X.: Certified impossibility results for byzantine-tolerant mobile robots. In: Higashino, T., Katayama, Y., Masuzawa, T., Potop-Butucaru, M., Yamashita, M. (eds.) SSS'13. LNCS, vol. 8255, pp. 178–190. Springer, Cham (2013). https://doi.org/10.1007/978-3-319-03089-0_13
4. Balabonski, T., Delga, A., Rieg, L., Tixeuil, S., Urbain, X.: Synchronous gathering without multiplicity detection: a certified algorithm. In: Bonakdarpour, B., Petit, F. (eds.) SSS'2016. Lecture Notes in Computer Science, vol. 10083, pp. 7–19. Springer, Cham (2016). https://doi.org/10.1007/978-3-319-49259-9_2
5. Balabonski, T., Pelle, R., Rieg, L., Tixeuil, S.: A foundational framework for certified impossibility results with mobile robots on graphs. Proc. ICDCN'18 **5**, 1–10 (2018). https://doi.org/10.1145/3154273.3154321
6. Bérard, B., Lafourcade, P., Millet, L., Potop-Butucaru, M., Thierry-Mieg, Y., Tixeuil, S.: Formal verification of mobile robot protocols. Distrib. Comput. **29**(6), 459–487 (2016)
7. Blin, L., Milani, A., Potop-Butucaru, M., Tixeuil, S.: Exclusive perpetual ring exploration without chirality. In: Lynch, N.A., Shvartsman, A.A. (eds.) Distributed Computing DISC 2010. Lecture Notes in Computer Science, vol. 6343, pp. 312–327. Springer, Berlin, Heidelberg (2010). https://doi.org/10.1007/978-3-642-15763-9_29
8. Bonnet, F., Défago, X., Petit, F., Potop-Butucaru, M., Tixeuil, S.: Discovering and assessing fine-grained metrics in robot networks protocols. In: SRDS Workshops 2014, pp. 50–59. IEEE Computer Society Press (2014)
9. Büchi, J.R., Landweber, L.H.: Solving sequential conditions by finite-state strategies. Trans. Am. Math. Soc. **138**, 295–311 (1969)
10. Courtieu, P., Rieg, L., Tixeuil, S., Urbain, X.: Impossibility of gathering, a certification. Inf. Process. Lett. **115**(3), 447–452 (2015)

11. Courtieu, P., Rieg, L., Tixeuil, S., Urbain, X.: Certified universal gathering in R^2 for oblivious mobile robots. In: Gavoille, C., Ilcinkas, D. (eds.) DISC 2016. Lecture Notes in Computer Science, vol. 9888, pp. 187–200. Springer, Berlin, Heidelberg (2016)

12. D'Angelo, G., Stefano, G.D., Navarra, A., Nisse, N., Suchan, K.: A unified approach for different tasks on rings in robot-based computing systems. In: Proceedings of IPDPSW'13, pp. 667–676. IEEE Press (2013)

13. Devismes, S., Lamani, A., Petit, F., Raymond, P., Tixeuil, S.: Optimal grid exploration by asynchronous oblivious robots. In: Richa, A.W., Scheideler, C. (eds.) SSS 2012. Lecture Notes in Computer Science, vol. 7596, pp. 64–76. Springer, Berlin, Heidelberg (2012). https://doi.org/10.1007/978-3-642-33536-5_7

14. Doan, H.T.T., Bonnet, F., Ogata, K.: Model checking of a mobile robots perpetual exploration algorithm. In: Liu, S., Duan, Z., Tian, C., Nagoya, F. (eds.) SOFL+MSVL 2016. Lecture Notes in Computer Science, vol. 10189, pp. 201–219. Springer, Cham (2016). https://doi.org/10.1007/978-3-319-57708-1_12

15. Doan, H.T.T., Bonnet, F., Ogata, K.: Model checking of robot gathering. In: Proceedings of OPODIS17, LIPIcs (2017)

16. Doyen, L., Raskin, J.-F.: Games with Imperfect Information: Theory and Algorithms, pp. 185–212. Cambridge University Press, Cambridge (2011)

17. Eén, N., Legg, A., Narodytska, N., Ryzhyk, L.: Sat-based strategy extraction in reachability games. In: Proceedings of AAAI', pp. 3738–3745. AAAI press (2015)

18. Emerson, E.A., Jutla, C.S.: Tree automata, mu-calculus and determinacy. In: Proceedings of FOCS'91, SFCS'91, pp. 368–377. IEEE Computer Society Press, Washington, DC, USA (1991)

19. Flocchini, P., Ilcinkas, D., Pelc, A., Santoro, N.: Computing without communicating: ring exploration by asynchronous oblivious robots. Algorithmica **65**(3), 562–583 (2013)

20. Heljanko, K., Keinänen, M., Lange, M., Niemelä, I.: Solving parity games by a reduction to SAT. J. Comput. System Sci. **78**(2), 430–440 (2012)

21. Kranakis, E., Krizanc, D., Markou, E.: The Mobile Agent Rendezvous Problem in the Ring. Synthesis Lectures on Distributed Computing Theory, 122 p. Morgan & Claypool Publishers, San Rafael (2010)

22. Millet, L., Potop-Butucaru, M., Sznajder, N., Tixeuil, S.: On the synthesis of mobile robots algorithms: the case of ring gathering. In: Felber, P., Garg, V. (eds.) SSS'2014. Lecture Notes in Computer Science, vol. 8756, pp. 237–252. Springer, Cham (2014). https://doi.org/10.1007/978-3-319-11764-5_17

23. https://github.com/tcsprojects/pgsolver

24. Reif, J.H.: The complexity of two-player games of incomplete information. J. Comput. Syst. Sci. **29**(2), 274–301 (1984)

25. Rubin, S., Zuleger, F., Murano, A., Aminof, B.: Verification of asynchronous mobile-robots in partially-known environments. In: Chen, Q., Torroni, P., Villata, S., Hsu, J., Omicini, A. (eds.) PRIMA 2015: Principles and Practice of Multi-Agent Systems PRIMA 2015. Lecture Notes in Computer Science, vol. 9387, pp. 185–200. Springer, Cham (2015). https://doi.org/10.1007/978-3-319-25524-8_12

26. Sangnier, A., Sznajder, N., Potop-Butucaru, M., Tixeuil, S.: Parameterized verification of algorithms for oblivious robots on a ring. In: Proceedings of FMCAD'17, pp. 212–219. IEEE Press (2017)

27. Suzuki, I., Yamashita, M.: Distributed anonymous mobile robots: formation of geometric patterns. SIAM J. Comput. **28**(4), 1347–1363 (1999)

28. http://people.cs.aau.dk/~adavid/tiga/

Efficient Concurrent Execution of Smart Contracts in Blockchains Using Object-Based Transactional Memory

Parwat Singh Anjana[1], Hagit Attiya[2], Sweta Kumari[2], Sathya Peri[1],
and Archit Somani[2(✉)]

[1] Department of Computer Science and Engineering, IIT Hyderabad, Sangareddy, India
cs17mtech11014@iith.ac.in, sathya_p@cse.iith.ac.in
[2] Department of Computer Science, Technion, Haifa, Israel
{hagit,sweta,archit}@cs.technion.ac.il

Abstract. Several popular blockchains such as Ethereum execute *complex transactions* through user-defined scripts. A block of the chain typically consists of multiple *smart contract transactions (SCTs)*. To append a block into the blockchain, a miner executes these SCTs. On receiving this block, other nodes act as *validators*, who re-execute these SCTs as part of the consensus protocol to validate the block. In Ethereum and other blockchains that support cryptocurrencies, a miner gets an incentive every time such a valid block is successfully added to the blockchain. When executing SCTs sequentially, miners and validators fail to harness the power of multiprocessing offered by the prevalence of multi-core processors, thus degrading throughput. By leveraging multiple threads to execute SCTs, we can achieve better efficiency and higher throughput. Recently, *Read-Write Software Transactional Memory Systems (RWSTMs)* were used for concurrent execution of SCTs. It is known that *Object-based STMs (OSTMs)*, using higher-level objects (such as hash-tables or lists), achieve better throughput as compared to RWSTMs. Even greater concurrency can be obtained using *Multi-Version OSTMs (MVOSTMs)*, which maintain multiple versions for each shared data item as opposed to *Single-Version OSTMs (SVOSTMs)*.

This paper proposes an efficient framework to execute SCTs concurrently based on object semantics, using *optimistic* SVOSTMs and MVOSTMs. In our framework, a multi-threaded miner constructs a *Block Graph (BG)*, capturing the *object-conflicts* relations between SCTs, and stores it in the block. Later, validators re-execute the same SCTs concurrently and deterministically relying on this BG.

A malicious miner can modify the BG to harm the blockchain, e.g., to cause *double spending*. To identify malicious miners, we propose *Smart Multi-threaded Validator (SMV)*. Experimental analysis shows that proposed multi-threaded miner and validator achieve significant performance gains over state-of-the-art SCT execution framework.

Keywords: Blockchain · Smart contract · Concurrency · Object-based Software Transactional Memory · Multi-version · Opacity · Conflict-opacity

© Springer Nature Switzerland AG 2021
C. Georgiou and R. Majumdar (Eds.): NETYS 2020, LNCS 12129, pp. 77–93, 2021.
https://doi.org/10.1007/978-3-030-67087-0_6

1   Introduction

Blockchains like Bitcoin [15] and Ethereum [2] have become very popular. Due to their usefulness, they are now considered for automating and securely storing user records such as land sale documents, vehicle, and insurance records. *Clients*, external users of the system, send requests to nodes to execute on the blockchain, as *smart contracts transactions (SCTs)*. An SCT is similar to the methods of a class in an object-oriented langugage, which encode business logic relating to the contract [4,8]. Listing 1 shows a smart contract function, transfer() of coin contract from Solidity [4]. It transfers the amount from sender to receiver if the sender has a sufficient balance.

Blocks are added to the blockchain by *block-creator* nodes also known as *miners*. A miner m packs several SCTs received from (possibly different) clients, to form a block B. Then, m executes the SCTs of the block sequentially to obtain the final state of the blockchain, which it stores in the block.

Listing 1: Transfer function

```
1   transfer(s_id, r_id, amt){
2     if(amt > bal[s_id])
3       throw;
4     bal[s_id] -= amt;
5     bal[r_id] += amt;
6   }
```

To maintain the chain structure, m adds the hash of the previous block to the new block B and proposes B to be added to the blockchain.

On receiving the block B, other nodes act as *validators* that execute a global consensus protocol to decide the order of B in the blockchain. As part of the consensus protocol, validators re-execute all the SCTs of B sequentially to obtain the final state of the blockchain, assuming that B will be added to the blockchain. If the computed final state matches the one stored in B by the miner m then B is accepted by the validators. In this case, the miner m gets an incentive for adding B to the blockchain (in Ethereum and other cryptocurrency-based blockchains). Otherwise, B is rejected, and m does not get any reward. This execution is known as *order-execute model* [5] adapted by Ethereum and several other blockchains such as Bitcoin [15], EOS [1].

Previous Work: Dickerson et al. [8] observed that both miner and validators can execute SCTs concurrently to exploit multi-core processors. They observed another interesting advantage of concurrent execution of SCTs in Ethereum, where only the miner receives an incentive for adding a valid block while all the validators execute the SCTs in the block. Given a choice, it is natural for a validator to pick a block that supports concurrent execution and hence obtain higher throughput.

Concurrent execution of SCTs poses a challenge. Consider a miner m that executes the SCTs in a block concurrently. Later, a validator v may re-execute same SCTs concurrently, in an order that may yield a different final state than given by m in B. In this case, v incorrectly rejects the valid block B proposed by m. We denote this as *False Block Rejection (FBR)*, noting that FBR may negate the benefits of concurrent execution.

Dickerson et al. [8] proposed a multi-threaded miner algorithm that is based on a *pessimistic Software Transactional Memory (STM)* and uses locks for synchronization between threads executing SCTs. STM [14,18] is a convenient concurrent programming interface for a programmer to access the shared memory using multiple threads. To avoid FBR, the miner identifies the *dependencies* between SCTs in the block while executing them by multiple threads. Two SCTs are *dependent* if they are *conflicting*, i.e., both of them access the same data item and at least one of them is a write. These dependencies among SCTs are recorded in the block as a *Block Graph (BG)*. Two SCTs that have a path in the BG are *dependent* on each other and cannot be executed concurrently. Later, a validator v relies on the BG to identify dependencies between the SCTs, and concurrently execute SCTs only if there is no path between them in the BG. In the course of the execution by v, the size of BG dynamically decreases and the dependencies change. Dickerson et al. [8] use a *fork-join* approach to execute the SCTs, where a master thread allocates independent SCTs to different slave threads to execute.

Anjana et al. [6] used an *optimistic* Read-Write STM (RWSTM), which identifies the conflicts between SCTs using timestamps. Those are used by miner threads to build the BG. A validator processes a block using the BG in a completely decentralized manner using multiple threads, unlike the centralized fork-join approach of [8]. Each validator thread identifies an independent SCTand executes it concurrently with other threads. The decentralized approach yields significant performances gain over fork-join.

Saraph and Herlihy [17] used a *speculative bin* approach to execute SCTs of Ethereum in parallel. A miner uses lock to store SCTs into two bins, *concurrent bin* stores non-conflicting SCTs while the *sequential bin* stores the remaining SCTs. If an SCT T_i requests a lock held by an another SCT T_j then T_i is rolled back and placed in the sequential bin. Otherwise, T_i is placed in the concurrent bin. To save the cost of rollback and retries of SCTs, they have used *static conflict prediction* which identifies conflicting SCTs before executing them speculatively. The multi-threaded validator in this approach executes all the SCTs of the concurrent bin concurrently and then executes the SCTs of the sequential bin sequentially. We call this the *Static Bin* approach.

Zhang and Zhang [20] proposed a pessimistic approach to execute SCTs concurrently in which the miner can use any concurrency control protocol while the validator uses *multi-version timestamp order*.

Exploiting Object-Based Semantics: Prior STM-based solutions of [6,20], rely on *read-write conflicts (rwconflicts)* for synchronization. In contrast, *object-based STMs (OSTMs)* track higher-level, more advanced conflicts between operations like insert, delete, lookup on a hash-table, enqueue/dequeue on queues, push/pop on the stack [11, 12, 16]. It has been shown that OSTMs provide greater concurrency than RWSTMs (see Fig. 1 in [7]). This is particularly important since Solidity [4], the language used for writing SCTs for Ethereum, extensively uses hash-tables. This indicates that a hash-table based OSTM is a natural candidate for concurrent execution of these SCTs.[1]

The pessimistic lock-based solution of [8] uses abstract locks on hash-table keys, exploiting the object semantics. In this paper, we want to exploit the object semantics of hash-tables using optimistic STMs to improve the performance obtained.

To capture the dependencies between the SCTs in a block, miner threads construct the BG concurrently and append it to the block. The dependencies between the transactions are given by the *object-conflicts (oconflicts)* (as opposed to rwconflicts) which ensure that the execution is correct, i.e., satisfies *conflict-opacity* [16]. It has been shown [11, 12, 16] that there are fewer oconflicts than rwconflicts. Since there are fewer oconflicts, the BG has fewer edges which in turn, allows validators to execute more SCTs concurrently. This also reduces the size of the BG leading to a smaller communication cost.

---

[1] For clarity, we denote smart contract transactions as SCTs and an STM transaction as a transaction in the paper.

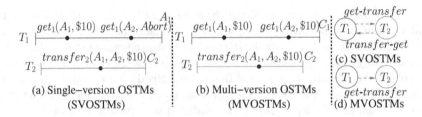

Fig. 1. (a) Transaction T_1 gets the balance of two accounts A_1 and A_2 (both initially \$10), while transaction T_2 transfers \$10 from A_1 to A_2 and T_1 aborts. Since, its conflict graph has a cycle (see (c)); (b) When T_1 and T_2 are executed by MVOSTM, T_1 can read the old versions of A_1 and A_2. This can be serialized, as shown in (d).

Multi-version object-based STMs (MVOSTMs) [13] maintain multiple versions for each shared data item (object) and provide greater concurrency relative to traditional *single-version OSTMs (SVOSTMs)*. Figure 1 illustrates the benefits of concurrent execution of SCTs using MVOSTM over SVOSTM. A BG based on MVOSTM will have fewer edges than an SVOSTM-based BG, and will further reduce the size of the BG. These advantages motivated us to use MVOSTMs for concurrent execution of SCTs by miners.

Concurrent executions of SCTs may cause inconsistent behaviors such as *infinite loops*, *divide by zero*, *crash failures*. Some of these behaviors, such as crash failures and infinite loops can be mitigated when SCTs are executed in a controlled environment, for example, the *Ethereum Virtual Machine (EVM)* [2]. However, not all environments can prevent all anomalies. The inconsistent executions can be prevented by ensuring that the executions produced by the STM system satisfy *opacity* [9] or one of its variants such as *co-opacity* [16]. Our MVOSTM satisfies opacity, while our SVOSTM satisfies co-opacity.

Handling a Malicious Miner: A drawback of the approaches mentioned above is that a malicious miner can make the final state of the blockchain be inconsistent. In the BG approach, the miner can send an incorrect BG, missing some edges. In the bin-based approach [17], the miner can place the conflicting transactions in the concurrent bin. This can result in inconsistent states in the blockchain due to *double spending*, e.g., when two concurrent transactions incorrectly transfer the same amount of money simultaneously from a source account to two different destination accounts. If a malicious miner does not add an edge between these two transactions in the BG [6] or puts them in the concurrent bin [17], then both SCTs can execute concurrently by validators. If a majority of validators accept the block containing these two transactions, then the state of the blockchain becomes inconsistent. We denote this problem as *edge missing BG (EMB)* for the BG approach [6] and *faulty bin (FBin)* for the bin-based approach [17]. In Sect. 4, we show the effect of malicious miners through experiments on the blockchain system.

To handle EMB and FBin errors, the validator must reject a block when edges are missing in the BG or when conflicting SCTs are in the concurrent bin, since their execution can lead to an inconsistent state. To detect this situation, validator threads monitor transactions performing conflicting access to the same data items while executing concurrently. In Sect. 3, we propose a *Smart Multi-threaded Validator (SMV)* which uses *counters* to detect this condition and rejects the corresponding blocks.

Dickerson et al. [8] suggest a lock-based solution to handle EMB errors. The miner generates and stores the lock profile required to execute the SCTs of a block along with the BG. The validator then records a trace of the locks each of its thread would have acquired, had it been executing speculatively independent of the BG. The validator would then compare the lock profiles it generated with the one provided by the miner present in the block. If the profiles are different then the block is rejected. This check is in addition to the check of the final state generated and the state in the block. This solution is effective in handling EMB errors caused by malicious miners. However, it is lock-based and cannot be used for preventing EMB issue in optimistic approaches such as [6]. The advantage of our SMV solution is that it works well with both optimistic and lock-based approaches.

Our Contributions: This paper develops an efficient framework to execute SCTs concurrently by a miner using an optimistic hash-table (both single and multi-version) OSTM. We use two methodologies to re-execute the SCTs concurrently by validators: the *fork-join approach* [8] and a *decentralized approach* [6]. To handle EMB and FBin errors, we propose a decentralized *smart multi-threaded validator*. To summarize:

- We introduce an efficient object-based framework for the concurrent execution of SCTs by miners (Sect. 3.2). We propose a way to execute SCTs efficiently using optimistic SVOSTM by the miner while ensuring *co-opacity* [16], a way to execute SCTs by the miner using optimistic MVOSTM [13] while satisfying *opacity* [9]
- We propose the concurrent execution of SCTs by validators using the BG provided by the miner to avoid FBR errors (Sect. 3.3), using either the fork-join or the decentralized approach.
- We propose a Smart Multi-threaded Validator to handle EMB and FBin errors caused by malicious miners (Sect. 3.4).
- Extensive simulations (Sect. 4) show that concurrent execution of SCTs by SVOSTM and MVOSTM miner provide an average speedup of $3.41\times$ and $3.91\times$ over serial miner, respectively. SVOSTM and MVOSTM based decentralized validator provide on average of $46.35\times$ and $48.45\times$ over serial validator, respectively.

2   System Model

As in [10,14], in each miner/validator there are n threads, $p_1, \ldots, p_n$ in a system that access shared data items (or objects/keys) in a completely asynchronous fashion. We assume that none of the threads/processes will crash or fail unexpectedly.

Events: A thread invokes the transactions and the transaction calls object-level methods that internally invoke read/write atomic events on the shared data items to communicate with other threads. Method invocations (or inv) and responses (or rsp) are also considered as events.

History: It is a sequence of invocations and responses of different transactional methods. We consider *sequential history* in which invocation on each transactional method follows the immediate matching response. We consider *well-formed* histories in which a new transaction does not begin until the invocation of previous transaction has not been committed or aborted.

Object-Based Software Transactional Memory (OSTM): OSTM exports higher-level methods: (1) STM_begin(): begins a transaction with unique id. (2) STM_lookup(k) (or $l(k)$): does a lookup on data item k from shared memory. (3) STM_insert(k, v) (or $i(k, v)$): inserts the value of data item k as v in its local log. (4) STM_delete(k) (or $d(k)$): deletes the data item k. (5) STM_tryC(): validates the transaction. After successful validation, the actual effects of *STM_insert()* and *STM_delete()* will be visible in the shared memory and transaction returns commit (C). Otherwise, it will return abort (A). We represent *STM_lookup()*, and *STM_delete()* as *return-value (rv)* methods because both methods return the value from hash-table. We represent *STM_insert()*, and *STM_delete()* as *update (upd)* methods as on successful *STM_tryC()* both methods update the shared memory. Methods *rv()* and *STM_tryC()* may return A. For a transaction T_i, we denote all the objects accessed by its $rv_i()$ and $upd_i()$ methods as $rvSet_i$ and $updSet_i$, respectively.

Listing 2 shows the concurrent execution of transfer() (from Listing 1 in the Sect. 1) using STM. On the invocation of transfer(), STM assigns the unique id using *STM_begin()* to each SCT (Line 8). Then, it reads the balance of the sender using *STM_lookup()* (Line 9) and validates it (Line 10). If the sender does not have a sufficient balance, then it *aborts* the SCT and throws an exception. Otherwise, it withdraws the amount from the sender account

Listing 2: Transfer function using STM

```
7   transfer(s_id, r_id, amt){
8     t_id = STM_begin();
9     s_bal = STM_lookup(s_id);
10    if(amt => s_bal) {
11      abort(t_id);
12      throw;
13    }
14    STM_delete(s_id, amt);
15    STM_insert(r_id, amt);
16    if(STM_tryC(t_id)!= SUCCESS)
17      goto Line 8;//Trans aborted
18  }
```

using *STM_delete()* (Line 14) and deposits the amount in the receiver account using *STM_insert()* (Line 15). With an optimistic STM, the effect of the *STM_delete()* and *STM_lookup()* will take place after successful validation of the SCT in *STM_tryC()* (Line 16). If validation is successful, then the SCT commits, and the amount is transferred from the sender to the receiver account. Otherwise, the SCT is aborted and re-execute from Line 8.

Valid and Legal History: If the successful $rv_j(k, v)$ (i.e., $v \neq A$) method of a transaction T_j *returns* the value from any of previously committed transaction T_i that has performed $upd()$ on key k with value v then such $rv_j(k, v)$ method is *valid*. If all the $rv()$ methods of history H are valid then H is valid history [16].

If the successful $rv_j(k, v)$ (i.e., $v \neq A$) method of a transaction T_j *returns* the value from previous closest committed transaction T_i that $k \in updSet_i$ (T_i can also be T_0) and updates the k with value v then such $rv_j(k, v)$ method is *legal*. If all the $rv()$ methods of history H are legal then H is legal history [16]. A legal history is also valid.

Two histories H and H' are *equivalent* if they have the same set of events. H and H' are *multi-version view equivalent* [19, Chap. 5] if they are valid and equivalent. H and H' are *view equivalent* [19, Chap. 3] if they are legal and equivalent. Additional definitions appear in [7].

3   Proposed Mechanism

This section describes the construction, data structures, and methods of concurrent BG, concurrent execution of SCTs by multi-threaded miner using optimistic object-based STMs, multi-threaded validator, and detection of a malicious miner.

3.1   The Block Graph

The multi-threaded miner executes the SCTs concurrently and stores their dependencies in a BG. Each committed transaction corresponding to an SCTis a vertex in the BG while edges capture the dependencies, based on the STM protocol. Multi-threaded miner uses SVOSTM or MVOSTM to execute the SCTs concurrently, using timestamps. The challenge here is to construct the BG concurrently without missing any dependencies. We modified SVOSTM and MVOSTM to capture *oconflicts* and *multi-version oconflicts* (*mvoconflicts*) in the BG.

SVOSTM-based miner maintains three types of edges based on oconflicts between the transactions. An edge $T_i \rightarrow T_j$ between two transaction is defined when: **(1)** $rv_i(k, v)$ - $STM\_tryC_j()$ *edge* : If $rv_i(k, v)$ on key k by T_i completed before $STM\_tryC_j()$ on k by a committed transaction T_j in history H such that T_i returns a value $v \neq \mathcal{A}$. Formally, $rv_i(k, v) <_H STM\_tryC_j()$, $k \in updSet(T_j)$ and $v \neq \mathcal{A}$; **(2)** $STM\_tryC_i()$ - $rv_j(k, v)$ *edge* : If $STM\_tryC_i()$ on k by a committed transaction T_i completed before $rv_j(k, v)$ on key k by T_j in history H such that T_j returns a value $v \neq \mathcal{A}$. Formally, $STM\_tryC_i() <_H rv_j(k, v)$, $k \in updSet(T_i)$ and $v \neq \mathcal{A}$; **(3)** $STM\_tryC_i()$ - $STM\_tryC_j()$ *edge* : If $STM\_tryC_i()$ on k by a committed transaction T_i completed before $STM\_tryC_j()$ on k by a committed transaction T_j in history H. Formally, $STM\_tryC_i() <_H STM\_tryC_j()$ and $(updSet(T_i) \cap updSet(T_j)) \neq \emptyset$).

MVOSTM-based miner maintains two types of edges based on *mvoconflicts* [13]. **(1)** *return value from (rvf) edge:* If $STM\_tryC_i()$ on k by a committed transaction T_i completed before $rv_j(k, v)$ on key k by T_j in history H such that T_j returns a value $v \neq \mathcal{A}$ then there exist an *rvf edge* from T_i to T_j, i.e., $T_i \rightarrow T_j$; **(2)** *multi-version (mv) edge:* consider a triplet, $STM\_tryC_i(), rv_m(k, v), STM\_tryC_j()$ in which $(updSet(T_i) \cap updSet(T_j) \cap rvSet(T_m)) \neq \emptyset$, (two committed transactions T_i and T_j update the key k with value v and u respectively) and $(u, v \neq \mathcal{A})$; then there are two types of *mv edge*: (a) if $STM\_tryC_i() <_H STM\_tryC_j()$ then there exist a *mv edge* from T_m to T_j. (b) if $STM\_tryC_j() <_H STM\_tryC_i()$ then there exist a *mv edge* from T_j to T_i.

Data Structure for the Block Graph: To maintain a block graph $BG(V, E)$, the set of vertices (or SCTs) V is stored as a vertex list and the set of edges (conflicts between SCTs) E is stored as an adjacency list. Two lock-free methods build the BG (see details in [7]): *addVertex()* adds a vertex and *addEdge()* adds an edge in BG. To execute the SCTs, validator threads use three methods: *globalSearch()* identifies an independent vertex with indegree 0 to execute it concurrently, *remExNode()* decrements the indegree of conflicting vertices and keeps it into thread local log if its indegree becomes 0, and *localSearch()* identifies the vertex with indegree 0 in thread local log to execute it concurrently.

Algorithm 1. Multi-threaded Miner(sctList[], STM): n threads concurrently execute the SCTs from sctList with STMs.

```
19: procedure Multi-threaded Miner (sctList[], STM)
20:     curInd = gIndex.get&Inc(); // Atomically read the index and increment it.
21:     while (curInd < sctList.length) do // Execute until all SCTs have not been executed
22:         curTrn = sctList[curInd]; // Get the current SCTto execute
23:         T_i = STM_begin(); // Begins a new transaction. Here i is unique id
24:         for all (curStep ∈ curTrn.scFun) do // scFun is a list of steps
25:             switch(curStep)
26:                 case lookup(k):
27:                     v ← STM_lookup(k); // Lookup data item k from a shared memory
28:                     if(v == A) then goto Line 23;end if break;
29:                 case insert(k, v): // Insert data item k into T_i local memory with value v
30:                     STM_insert(k, v); break;
31:                 case delete(k):
32:                     v ← STM_delete(k); // Actual deletion of data item k happens in STM_tryC()
33:                     if(v == A) then goto Line 23; end if break;
34:                 default: Execute the step normally // Any step apart from lookup, insert, delete
35:             endswitch
36:         end for
37:         v ← STM_tryC(); // Try to commit the transaction T_i
38:         if(v == A) then goto Line 23; end if
39:         addVertex(i); // Create vertex node for T_i with scFun
40:         BG(i, STMs); // Add the conflicts of T_i to block graph
41:         curInd = gIndex.get&Inc(); // Atomically read the index and increment it.
42:     end while
43:     build-block(); // Here the miner builds the block.
44: end procedure
```

3.2 Multi-threaded Miner

A miner m receives requests to execute SCTs from different clients. It forms a block with several SCTs (the precise number of SCTs depend on the blockchain), and executes these SCTs while executing the non-conflicting SCTs concurrently to obtain the final state of the blockchain. Identifying the non-conflicting SCTs statically is not straightforward because smart contracts are written in a turing-complete language [8] (e.g., Solidity [4] for Ethereum). We use optimistic STM to execute the SCTs concurrently as in [6] but adapted to object-based STMs on hash-tables to identify conflicts.

Algorithm 1 shows how SCTs are executed by an n-threaded miner. The input is an array of SCTs, $sctList$ and a object-based STM, (SVOSTM or MVOSTM), both supporting the BG methods described above. The multi-threaded miner uses a global index into the sctList $gIndex$ which is accessed by all the threads. A thread Th_x first reads the current value of $gIndex$ into a local value $curInd$ and increments $gIndex$ atomically (Line 20).

Having obtained the current index in $curInd$, Th_x gets the corresponding SCT, $curTrn$ from $sctList[]$ (Line 22), and begins a STM transaction corresponding to $curTrn$ (Line 23). For every hash-table insert, delete and lookup encountered while executing the scFun of $curTrn$, Th_x invokes the corresponding STM methods: $STM\_lookup()$, $STM\_insert()$, $STM\_delete()$, either on an SVOSTM or on an MVOSTM. Otherwise, it simply executes the step. If any of these steps fail, Th_x begins a new STM transaction (Line 23) and re-executes these steps.

Upon successful completion of transaction T_i, Th_x creates a vertex node for T_i in the block graph (Line 39). Then, Th_x obtains the transactions (SCTs) with which T_i is conflicting from the OSTM, and adds the corresponding edges to the BG (Line 40). Th_x then gets the index of the next SCTto execute (Line 41).

An important step here is how the underlying OSTMs (either SVOSTM or MVOSTM) maintain the conflicts among the transactions which is used by Th_x (see [7]). Both SVOSTM and the MVOSTM use timestamps to identify the conflicts.

Once all the SCTs of sctList have been executed successfully and the BG is constructed concurrently, it is stored in the proposed block. The miner then stores the final state of the blockchain (which is the state of all shared data items), resulting from the execution of SCTs of sctList in the block. The miner then computes the operations related to the blockchain. For Ethereum, this would constitute the hash of the previous block. Then the multi-threaded miner proposes a block which consists of all the SCTs, BG, final state of all the shared data items and hash of the previous block (Line 43). The block is then broadcast to all the other nodes in the blockchain.

We prove the next properties (see [7]):

Theorem 1. *The BG captures all the dependencies between the conflicting nodes.*

Theorem 2. *A history H_m generated by the multi-threaded miner with SVOSTM satisfies co-opacity.*

Theorem 3. *A history H_m generated by multi-threaded miner with MVOSTM satisfies opacity.*

3.3 Multi-threaded Validator

The validator re-executes the SCTs deterministically relying on the BG provided by the miner in the block. BG consists of dependency among the conflicting SCTs and restrict validator threads to execute them serially to avoid the FBR errors while non-conflicting SCTs execute concurrently to obtain greater throughput. The validator uses *globalSearch()*, *localSearch()*, and *remExNode()* methods of the BG library as described in Sect. 3.1.

After successful execution of the SCTs, validator threads compute the final state of the blockchain which is the state of all shared data items. If it matches the final state provided by the miner then the validator accepts the block. If a majority of the validators accept the block, then it is added to the blockchain. Detailed description and proofs of the next theorems appear in [7].

Theorem 4. *A history H_m generated by the multi-threaded miner with SVOSTM and a history H_v generated by a multi-threaded validator are view equivalent.*

Theorem 5. *A history H_m generated by the multi-threaded miner with MVOSTM and a history H_v generated by a multi-threaded validator are multi-version view equivalent.*

3.4 Detection of Malicious Miners by Smart Multi-threaded Validator (SMV)

We propose a technique to handle edge missing BG (EMB) and Faulty Bin (FBin) caused by the malicious miner as explained in Sect. 1. A malicious miner mm can remove some edges from the BG and set the final state in the block accordingly. A multi-threaded validator executes the SCTs concurrently relying on the BG provided by the mm and results the same final state. Hence, incorrectly accepts the block. Similarly, if a majority of the validators accept the block then the state of the blockchain becomes inconsistent. For example, due to double spending.

A similar inconsistency can be caused by a mm in bin-based approach: mm can maliciously add conflicting SCTs to the concurrent bin resulting in FBin error. This may cause a multi-threaded validator v to access shared data items concurrently leading to synchronization errors. To prevent this, an SMV checks to see if two concurrent threads end up accessing the same shared data item concurrently. If this situation is detected, then the miner is malicious.

Algorithm 2. SMV(scFun): Execute scFun with atomic global lookup/update counter.

45: **while** (scFun.steps.hasNext()) **do** //scFun is a list of steps
46:    curStep = scFun.steps.next(); //Get the next step to execute
47:    **switch** (curStep) **do**
48:       **case** lookup(k):
49:          **if** ($k.gUC == k.lUC_i$) **then** //Check for update counter (uc) value
50:             Atomically increment the global lookup counter, $k.gLC$;
51:             Increment $k.lLC_i$ by 1. //Maintain $k.lLC_i$ in transaction local log
52:             Lookup k from a shared memory;
53:          **else** return ⟨*Miner is malicious*⟩;
54:          **end if**
55:       **case** insert(k, v):
56:          **if** (($k.gLC == k.lLC_i$) && ($k.gUC == k.lUC_i$)) **then** //Check lookup/update counter value
57:             Atomically increment the global update counter, $k.gUC$;
58:             Increment $k.lUC_i$ by 1. //Maintain $k.lUC_i$ in transaction local log
59:             Insert k in shared memory with value v;
60:          **else** return ⟨*Miner is malicious*⟩;
61:          **end if**
62:       **case** delete(k):
63:          **if** (($k.gLC == k.lLC_i$) && ($k.gUC == k.lUC_i$)) **then** //Check lookup/update counter value
64:             Atomically increment the global update counter, $k.gUC$;
65:             Increment $k.lUC_i$ by 1. //Maintain $k.lUC_i$ in transaction local log
66:             Delete k in shared memory.
67:          **else** return ⟨*Miner is malicious*⟩;
68:          **end if**
69:       **case** default:
70:          curStep is not lookup, insert and delete;
71:          execute curStep;
72: **end while**
73: Atomically decrement the $k.gLC$ and $k.gUC$ corresponding to each shared data-item key k.

To identify such situations, an SMV uses *counters*, inspired by the *basic timestamp ordering (BTO)* protocol in databases [19, Chap. 4]. It tracks each global data item that can be accessed across multiple transactions by different threads. Specifically, the SMV maintains two global counters for each key of hash-table (shared data item) k (a) $k.gUC$ - global update counter (b) $k.gLC$ - global lookup counter. These, respectively, track the number of **updates** and **lookups** that are concurrently performed by different threads on k. Both counters are initially 0.

When an SMV thread Th_x is executing an SCT T_i it maintains two local variables corresponding to each global data item k which is accessible only by Th_x (c) $k.lUC_i$ - local update counter (d) $k.lLC_i$ - local lookup counter. These respectively keep track of number of updates and lookups performed by Th_x on k while executing T_i. These counters are initialized to 0 before the start of T_i.

Having described the counters, we will explain the SMV Algorithm 2 at a high level. Suppose the next step to be performed by Th_x is:

1. $lookup(k)$: Thread Th_x will check for equality of the global and local update counters, i.e., $(k.gUC == k.lUC_i)$ (Line 49). If they are not same then SMV will report the miner as malicious (Line 53). Otherwise, (i) Th_x will atomically increment $k.gLC$ (Line 50). (ii) Th_x will increment $k.lLC_i$ (Line 51). (iii) Perform the lookup on the key k from shared memory (Line 52).

2. $update(k, val)$: Here, Th_x wants to update (insert/delete) k with value val. So, Th_x will check for the equality of both global, local update and lookup counters, i.e., $(k.gUC == k.lUC_i)$ and $(k.gLC == k.lLC_i)$ (Line 56 or Line 63). If they are not same then SMV will report the miner as malicious (Line 60 or Line 67). Otherwise, (i) Th_x will atomically increment $k.gUC$ (Line 57 or Line 64). (ii) Th_x will increment $k.lUC_i$ (Line 58 or Line 65). (iii) Update key k with value val in the shared memory (Line 59 or Line 66).

Once T_i terminates, Th_x will atomically decrements $k.gUC, k.gLC$ by the value of $k.lUC_i, k.lLC_i$, respectively (Line 73). Then Th_x will reset $k.lUC_i, k.lLC_i$ to 0.

The reason for performing these steps and the correctness of the algorithm is as follows: if Th_x is performing a lookup on k then no other thread should be performing an update on k. Here, $k.gUC$ represents the number of updates to k currently executed by all the threads while $k.lUC_i$ represents the number of updates to k on behalf of T_i by Th_x. Thus the value of gUC should be same as lUC. Otherwise, some other thread is also concurrently performing the updates to k. Similarly, if Th_x is performing an update on k, then no other thread should be performing an update or lookup on k. This can be verified by checking if lLC, lUC are respectively same as gLC, gUC.

Theorem 6. *Smart Multi-threaded Validator rejects malicious blocks with BG that allow concurrent execution of dependent SCTs.*

The same SMV technique can be applied to identify the *faulty bin* error as explained in Sect. 1. See proof of Theorem 6 in [7].

4   Experimental Evaluation

This section demonstrates the performance gains by proposed multi-threaded miner and validator against state-of-the-art miners and validators. To evaluate our approach, we considered Ethereum smart contracts. The virtual environment of Ethereum, EVM, does not support multi-threading [2,8]. So, we converted the smart contracts of Ethereum as described in Solidity documentation [4] into C++ multi-threaded contracts similar to [6]. Then we integrated them into object-based STM framework (SVOSTM and MVOSTM) for concurrent execution of SCTs by the miner.

We chose a diverse set of smart contracts described in Solidity [4] as benchmarks to analyze the performance of our proposed approach as was done in [6,8]. The selected benchmark contracts are (1) *Coin*: a financial contract, (2) *Ballot*: an electronic voting contract, (3) *Simple Auction*: an auction contract, and (4) a *Mix* contract: combination of three contracts mentioned above in equal proportion in which block consists of multiple SCTs belonging to different smart contracts.

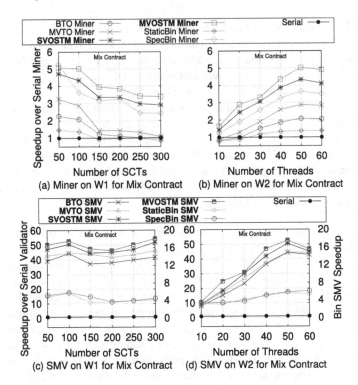

Fig. 2. Multi-threaded and SMVs Speedup over Serial Miner and Validator for Mix Contract on W1 and W2

We compared the proposed SVOSTM and MVOSTM miner with state-of-the-art multi-threaded: BTO [6], multi-version timestamp order (MVTO) [6], Speculative Bin (or SpecBin) [17], Static Bin (or StaticBin) [17], and Serial miner.[2] We could not compare our work with Dickerson et al. [8] as their source code is not available in public domain. We converted the code of StaticBin and SpecBin [17] from Java to C++ for comparing with our algorithms.

Concurrent execution of SCTs by the validator does not use any STM protocol; however it uses the BG provided by the multi-threaded miner, which does use STM. To identify malicious miners and prevent any malicious block from being added to the blockchain, we proposed Smart Multi-threaded Validator (SMV) for SVOSTM, MVOSTM as SVOSTM SMV, MVOSTM SMV. Additionally, we proposed SMV for state-of-the-art validators as BTO SMV, MVTO SMV, SpecBin SMV, and StaticBin SMV and analysed the performance.

Experimental Setup: The experimental system consists of two sockets, each comprised of 14 cores 2.60 GHz Intel (R) Xeon (R) CPU E5-2690, and each core supports 2 hardware threads. Thus the system supports a total of 56 hardware threads. The machine runs Ubuntu 16.04.2 LTS operating system and has 32GB RAM.

---

[2] Code is available in: https://github.com/PDCRL/ObjSC.

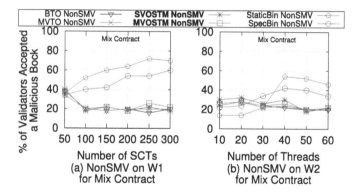

Fig. 3. % of average multi-threaded validator (NonSMV) accepted a malicious block for Mix Contract on W1 and W2

To analyze the performance, we evaluated the speedup achieved by each contract on two workloads. In the first workload (W1), the number of SCTs varied from 50 to 300 while the number of threads fixed is at 50. The maximum number of SCTs in a block of Ethereum is approximately 250 [3,8], but is growing over time. In the second workload (W2), the number of threads varied from 10 to 60, while the number of SCTs is fixed at 100. The average number of SCTs in a block of Ethereum is around 100 [3]. The hash-table size and shared data items are fixed to 30 and 500 respectively for both workloads. For accuracy, results are averaged over 26 runs in which the first run is discarded and considered as a warm-up run. The results of serial execution is treated as the baseline for evaluating the speedup. This section describes the detailed analysis for the Mix contract and analysis of Coin, Ballot and Simple Auction benchmark contracts are in [7].

Experimental Results: Fig. 2(a) and (b) show the speedup of MVOSTM, SVOSTM, MVTO, BTO, SpecBin, and StaticBin miner over serial miner for Mix contract on workloads W1 and W2, respectively.[1] The average speedup achieved by MVOSTM, SVOSTM, MVTO, BTO, SpecBin, and StaticBin miner over serial miner is $3.91\times$, $3.41\times$, $1.98\times$, $1.5\times$, $3.02\times$, and $1.12\times$, respectively.

As shown in Fig. 2(a), increasing the number of SCTs leads to high contention (because shared data items are fixed to 500). So the speedup of multi-threaded miner reduces. MVOSTM and SVOSTM miners outperform SpecBin miner because MVOSTM and SVOSTM miners use optimistic object-based STMs to execute SCTs concurrently and construct the BG whereas SpecBin uses locks to execute SCTs concurrently and constructs two bins using the pessimistic approach. SpecBin miner does not release the locks until the construction of the concurrent bin, which gives less concurrency. However, for the smaller numbers of SCTs in a block, SpecBin is slightly better than MVOSTM and SVOSTM miners, which can be observed in the Fig. 2(a) at 50 SCTs. MVOSTM and SVOSTM miners outperform MVTO and BTO miners because both of them are consider rwconflicts. It can also be observed that MVOSTM miner

---

[1] In the figures, legend items in bold.

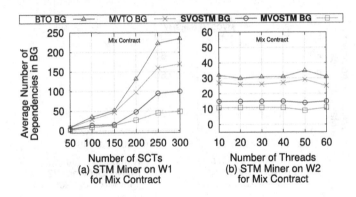

Fig. 4. Average Number of Dependencies in BG for Mix Contract on W1 and W2

outperforms all other STM miners as it has fewer conflicts, which gets reflected (see Fig. 4) as the least number of dependencies in the BG as compared to other STM miners. For the multi-version (MVOSTM and MVTO) miners, we did not limit the number of versions because the number of SCTs in a block is finite. The speedup by StaticBin miner is worse than serial miner for more than 100 SCTs because it takes time for *static conflict prediction* before executing SCTs.

Figure 2(b) shows that speedup achieved by multi-threaded miner increases while increasing the number of threads, limited by the number of hardware threads available on the underlying experimental setup. Since, our system has 56 logical threads, the speedup decreases beyond 56 threads. MVOSTM miner outperforms all other miners with similar reasoning, as explained for Fig. 2(a). Another observation is that when the number of threads is less, the serial miner dominates BTO and MVTO miner due to the overhead of the STM system.

The average number of dependencies in BG by all the STM miners presented in Fig. 4. It shows that BG constructed by the MVOSTM has the least number of edges for all the contracts on both workloads. However, there is no BG for bin-based approaches (both SpecBin and StaticBin). So, from the block size perspective, bin-based approaches are efficient. But the speedup of the validator obtained by the bin-based approaches is significantly lesser than STM validators.

Figure 2(c) and (d) show the speedup of Smart Multi-threaded Validators (SMVs) over serial validator on the workloads W1 and W2, respectively. The average speedup achieved by MVOSTM, SVOSTM, MVTO, BTO, SpecBin, and StaticBin decentralized SMVs are $48.45\times$, $46.35\times$, $43.89\times$, $41.44\times$, $5.39\times$, and $4.81\times$ over serial validator, respectively.

It can be observed that decentralized MVOSTM SMV is best among all other STM validators due to fewer dependencies in the BG. Though the block size is less in bin-based approaches as compared to STM based approaches due to the absence of BG, however, STM validators outperform bin-based validators because STM validators precisely determines the concurrent SCTs based on BG. In contrast, bin-based validator gives less concurrency using a lock-based pessimistic approach.

The speedup of SMV is significantly higher than multi-threaded miner because the miner has to execute the SCTs concurrently either using STMs (including the retries of aborted transactions) and constructs the BG or prepare two bins (concurrent and sequential bin using locks in SpecBin and static analysis in StaticBin). On the other hand, the validator executes the SCTs concurrently and deterministically relying on BG (without any retries) or bins provided by miner.

A malicious miner may cause either EMB or FBin errors in a block. Figure 3 illustrates the percentage of validators without SMV logic embedded, i.e., NonSMVs accepting a malicious block on workloads W1 and W2, respectively. Here, we considered 50 validators and ran the experiments for the Mix contract. The Fig. 3 shows that less than 50% of validators (except bin-based NonSMV) accept a malicious block. However, SpecBin and StaticBin NonSMVs show more than 50% acceptance of malicious blocks. Though, it is to be noted that the acceptance of even a single malicious block result in the blockchain going into inconsistent state.

To solve this problem, we developed a Smart Multi-threaded Validator (SMV), which identifies the malicious miner (described in Sect. 3.4). We prove that the SMV detects malicious block with the help of *counter* and rejects it. In fact all the validators shown in Fig. 2 (c) and (d) are SMV based. Another advantage of SMV is that once it detects a malicious miner during the concurrent execution of SCTs, it can immediately reject the block and need not execute the remaining SCTs in the block thus saving time.

To show the degree of parallelism, we consider *diameter* of BG which shows the longest path of the BG implies that a longest sequence of transactions to be executed sequentially. To observe the diameter of BG, we consider another workload W3 in which the number of shared data items varied from 100 to 600 while the number of threads, SCTs, and hash-table size is fixed to 50, 100, and 30, respectively. In Figure 5, Y1 axis shows the speedup achieved by SMV over serial and Y2 axis demonstrates the diameter of the BG in considered STMs. It shows that highest speedup achieved when diameter of the BG is least.

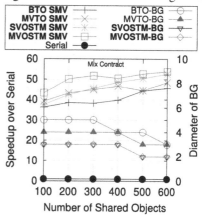

Fig. 5. Speedup of SMV over serial and Diameter of BG

We presents additional experiments that cover the average number of dependencies in the BG, additional space required to store the BG into the block, compared the time taken by the SMV and NonSMV, and speedup of fork-join validator for all the workloads in [7].

5   Conclusion and Future Directions

This paper presents an efficient framework for concurrent execution of smart contracts by miners and validators based on object semantics. In blockchains that follow order-execute model [5] such as Ethereum [2] and Bitcoin [15], SCTis executed in two different contexts: first by the multi-threaded miner to propose a block and later by the multi-threaded validator to verify the proposed block by the miner as part of the consensus. To avoid FBR errors, the miner on concurrent execution of SCTs capture the dependencies among them in the form of a BG as in [6,8]. The validator then re-executes the SCTs concurrently while respecting the dependencies recorded in the BG to avoid FBR errors.

The miner executes the SCTs concurrently using STMs that exploit the object semantics: SVOSTM and MVOSTM. The dependencies among the SCTs are collected during this execution and used by the miner threads to construct the BG concurrently. Due to the use of object semantics, the number of edges in the BG is smaller, which benefits both miners and validators by enabling them to execute SCTs quickly in a concurrent setting.

We also considered a malicious miner, which may proposes an incorrect BG that does not have all the edges, resulting in EMB error. To handle malicious miners we have proposed a SMV that can identify these errors and reject the corresponding blocks.

The proposed SVOSTM and MVOSTM miner achieve on average speedup of $3.41\times$ and $3.91\times$ over a serial miner, respectively. Proposed SVOSTM and MVOSTM decentralized validator outperform with an average speedup of $46.35\times$ and $48.45\times$ over serial validator, respectively, on Ethereum smart contracts.

There are several directions for future work. A malicious miner can intentionally append a BG in a block with additional edges for the purpose of delaying other miners. Preventing such a malicious miner from doing this would be an immediate future work. A natural question is whether the size of BG can become a significant overhead. Currently, the average number of SCTs in a block is ≈ 100 in Ethereum. So, storing the BG inside the block does not consume much space. The BG constructed by MVOSTMs has fewer dependencies as compared with state-of-the-art SCT execution as shown in Fig. 4. However, the number of SCTs in a block can increase over time and as a result storing the BG will consume more space. Hence, constructing storage optimal BG is an interesting challenge. Alternatively, it might be possible to concurrently execute SCTs correctly without incurring any extra storage overhead, and without compromising speedup. This opens up the question what the optimal storage required for achieving the best possible speedup.

Another interesting research direction is optimizing power consumption, since, multi-threading on the multi-core system consumes more power. Additional power is consumed by the multiple miner and validator threads to propose and validate the blocks concurrently. Hence, we would like to explore trade-off between harnessing the number of cores and power consumption.

Finally, since EVM [2] does not support multi-threading, it is not possible to test the proposed approach on Ethereum. So, another research direction is to design multi-threaded EVM. We plan to test our proposed approach on other blockchains such as Bitcoin [15], EOS [1] which follow the order-execute model and support multi-threading.

Acknowledgment. We are thankful to the anonymous reviewers for helpful suggestions. This research was supported by ISF grant 380/18, IMPRINT Project number 6918F funded by MHRD, and MEITY project number 4(20)/2019-ITEA.

References

1. EOS. https://eos.io/. Accessed 08 Mar 2020
2. Ethereum. http://github.com/ethereum. Acessed 08 Mar 2020
3. Ethereum Stats. https://etherscan.io. Accessed 08 Mar 2020
4. Solidity Documentation. https://solidity.readthedocs.io/. Accessed 08 Mar 2020
5. Androulaki, E., et al.: Hyperledger fabric: a distributed operating system for permissioned blockchains. EuroSys (2018)
6. Anjana, P.S., Kumari, S., Peri, S., Rathor, S., Somani, A.: An efficient framework for optimistic concurrent execution of smart contracts. In: PDP, pp. 83–92 (2019)
7. Anjana, P.S., Attiya, H., Kumari, S., Peri, S., Somani, A.: Achieving greater concurrency in execution of smart contracts using object semantics. CoRR ArXiv:1904.00358 (2019). http://arxiv.org/abs/1904.00358
8. Dickerson, T., Gazzillo, P., Herlihy, M., Koskinen, E.: Adding Concurrency to Smart Contracts, pp. 303–312. In: PODC. ACM, NY, USA, New York (2017)
9. Guerraoui, R., Kapalka, M.: On the correctness of transactional memory. In: PPoPP (2008)
10. Guerraoui, R., Kapalka, M.: Principles of Transactional Memory, Synthesis Lectures on Distributed Computing Theory (2010)
11. Hassan, A., Palmieri, R., Ravindran, B.: Optimistic Transactional Boosting, vol. 49, pp. 387–388. ACM, New York, NY, USA 2014)
12. Herlihy, M., Koskinen, E.: Transactional boosting: a methodology for highly-concurrent transactional objects. In: PPoPP (2008)
13. Juyal, C., Kulkarni, S., Kumari, S., Peri, S., Somani, A.: An innovative approach to achieve compositionality efficiently using multi-version object based transactional systems. In: Izumi, T., Kuznetsov, P. (eds.) SSS'2018, pp. 284–300. Springer, Cham (2018)
14. Kuznetsov, P., Peri, S.: Non-interference and local correctness in transactional memory. Theor. Comput. Sci. **688**, 103–116 (2017)
15. Nakamoto, S.: Bitcoin: a peer-to-peer electronic cash system (2009)
16. Peri, S., Singh, A., Somani, A.: Efficient means of achieving composability using transactional memory. In: NETYS (2018)
17. Saraph, V., Herlihy, M.: An empirical study of speculative concurrency in ethereum smart contracts. In: Tokenomics (2019)
18. Shavit, N., Touitou, D.: Software transactional memory. In: PODC (1995)
19. Weikum, G., Vossen, G.: Transactional Info Systems: Theory, Algorithms, and the Practice of Concurrency Control and Recovery (2002)
20. Zhang, A., Zhang, K.: Enabling concurrency on smart contracts using multiversion ordering. In: Web and Big Data (2018)

Exploring IoT Trickle-Based Dissemination Using Timed Model-Checking and Symbolic Execution

Boutheina Bannour[1]([✉]), Arnault Lapitre[1], and Pascale Le Gall[2]

[1] CEA LIST, Gif-sur-Yvette, France
{boutheina.bannour,arnault.lapitre}@cea.fr
[2] MICS Laboratory, University of Paris-Saclay, Gif-sur-Yvette, France
pascale.legall@centralesupelec.fr

Abstract. We focus on studying an IoT algorithm called Trickle using a formal model-based approach. The algorithm has an essential role in traffic regulation across distributed networks of wireless sensors which are part of IoT. The algorithm allows efficient dissemination of information such as critical applicative data, firmware upgrades or security fixes. In this paper, we develop timed asynchronous computational models for Trickle. We show how reachability properties can be assessed on such models using a combination of model-checking and symbolic execution implemented by the tools UPPAAL and DIVERSITY, respectively. Our experiments produce promising results on highlighting updated or outdated nodes situations during dissemination.

1 Introduction

Context. Sensors networks (WSN) play an essential role in the uptake of the Internet of Things (IoT) as they allow direct connection between the physical environment and the digital systems. They come with a reduced economical cost, and they can easily be deployed in inaccessible areas. WSN involve constrained-energy devices (sensors) which operate over long periods. The information dissemination across these networks is often subject to constraints to reduce the communication cost, with the objective not to exhaust the batteries of such nodes that are in general neither rechargeable nor replaceable after the deployment. Gossip paradigm has been recognized as being efficient in practice to control the communications of each node, roughly speaking: (i) every node try quickly to transmit new data, and (ii) in case of redundant data reception, the node reduces the transmissions frequency over time. The algorithm Trickle [23,25,27] is one of the most known: It comes as a standard library in TinyOS [24] and Contiki [16], two well-known firmware Operating Systems (OS) for WSN. The algorithm is involved in recently standardized WSN protocols namely the Multicast Protocol for Low Power and Lossy Networks (MPL) [17] and the IPv6 Routing Protocol for Low Power and Lossy Networks (RPL) [1]. There are many others like FireFly Gossip (FiGo) [8], Energy Efficient Gossiping (E-Gossip) [22], Multi Randomized Gossip-Consensus-based Sync (Multi RGCS) [29], and new ones continue to be proposed given the economic interest of WSN.

© Springer Nature Switzerland AG 2021
C. Georgiou and R. Majumdar (Eds.): NETYS 2020, LNCS 12129, pp. 94–111, 2021.
https://doi.org/10.1007/978-3-030-67087-0_7

Case Study: Trickle Dissemination. The goal of Trickle is to reach a stable global state of the network where all the nodes have the same up-to-date information. Each node applies a set of rules to control its transmissions as follows [27]:

- each node maintains a current interval I, a counter c and a broadcasting time t in interval $[I/2, I[$,
- global parameters to all nodes are k the redundancy constant, I_{min} (resp. I_{max}) the smallest (resp. largest) interval,
- each node applies the following rules:
    1. at the start of a new interval, the timer and counter c are reset and t is randomly set to a value in $[I/2, I[$,
    2. if a received message is consistent with the information the node holds, the counter c is incremented,
    3. when the timer reaches t and $c < k$, a message carrying the node information is transmitted to neighbours in broadcast,
    4. when the timer expires at I, the interval length is increased by setting I to $\min(2 \cdot I, I_{max})$ and a new interval starts,
    5. when a received message is inconsistent with the node information, then I is set to I_{min}, and a new interval starts. Otherwise, nothing happens.

Trickle uses "polite gossip" to exchange information with its network neighbours. It breaks time into dynamically adjustable intervals, and at a random point in each interval, it considers broadcasting the information it holds. If Trickle has already heard several other nodes gossip the same information in this interval, it politely stays quiet: "repeating what someone else has said is rude" [25].

Motivation and Related Work. As it may show from Trickle, popular gossip protocols are sophisticated and complex on the nature of applied control on node transmissions. For that reason, most of the validation effort of this class of protocols relies mainly on testbeds or simulations, and at a less extend on analytical methods, more exhaustive, yet they lack automation: among the latter, we can cite those developed for Trickle in [7,12,19,28,31]. On the other hand, formal methods and in particular model-checking [11] come with a high degree of automation. They consider computational models which, by its nature, delimit the perimeter of the analysis and the kind of properties to be verified. The survey [9] overviews many relevant works on applying formal methods on WSN protocols, including gossip-based protocols. The following papers [15,20,32–34]) have successfully applied model-checking on gossip protocols, among which [15,33,34] concern Trickle. The early work [15] proposed formal models for WSN based on classic process algebras. The work developed a simplified model of Trickle for illustration purposes, then translated into a network of Timed Automata (TA) [2] supported by the model-checker UPPAAL. In their model, Trickle intervals are not adjustable and are of fixed length, which restricts the coverage of performed analyses. More recently, authors in [33,34] have proposed model-checking techniques for WSN, and Trickle has been proposed for illustration as well. The work [34] provides formal semantics for a subset of NesC programs used to built TinyOS [24] applications; such semantics have been implemented in the model-checking framework PAT [26] which supports TA too. The work [33] focuses on combining probabilistic model checking provided by the tool PRISM [21] with automated debugging algorithms in order to find pathological typologies which cause some failure: typically in case of Trickle, it is about finding the topology pattern that prevents recent information from being spread. In both works [33,34], Trickle models have not been given. In this paper, we are interested in the distributed nature of WSN nodes [31], that is they are dephased by some duration because often they do not share a common zero as classically in distributed systems. Gossip protocols, Trickle included, do not have any assumption on nodes that should be synchronized. The control they provide on transmission instants is usually implemented by introducing some time randomness to benefit from desynchronized nodes. Besides, inline with such assumption, we consider asynchronous communications which can take time to deliver data, all previous works have not taken into account such desynchronized hypothesis.

Contribution and Paper Outline. We provide formal models for Trickle as Extended Timed Automata (XTA) in which data can be used to define computations, random updates, constraints on clocks and communication actions. A network of XTA can then be designed to form the overall Trickle topology of nodes. The network is endowed with operational semantics in which XTA communicate their data via unbounded queues. In this paper, we are interested in highlighting some situations of updated or outdated nodes using reachability properties under the desynchronized assumption. To assess such properties on XTA, which are more expressive than classical TA because they introduce data, we propose to combine model-checking [11] with symbolic execution [18]. The latter virtually executes models (or code) for symbolic input parameters rather than concrete values. Each execution path is associated with logical constraints on those input parameters computed at each execution step, the so-called Path Conditions (PC). PCs are a compact representation of classes of actual values for input parameters for executing those paths; they can be solved using SMT solvers such as CVC4 [6] or Z3 [13]. Symbolic execution can be applied on timed models (e.g., [4]).

Yet enumerating all execution paths to check a property of interest is combinatorial, this is an identified problem of the technique that we have experimented as well on some early work on Trickle [5,30]. The idea is then to apply model-checking first on XTA in which data is numeric and random updates are restricted to some values, yet clock constraints are handled as usual by zone-based abstraction implemented in UPPAAL using the efficient Difference Bounded Matrices data structure (DBM) [14]. In case the property is verified, the corresponding sequence of transitions of a solution is used to guide symbolic execution. We experiment with the combined techniques in UPPAAL and in the symbolic execution tool DIVERSITY [3]. The rest of the paper is organized as follows. Section 2 introduces the formal model of the network of XTA and its operational semantics. Section 3 proposes a Trickle model designed as a network of XTA. Section 4 introduces our approach of combining model-checking and symbolic execution to assess reachability properties and evaluates it on UPPAAL-DIVERSITY connection. Section 5 concludes the paper.

2 Network of Extended Timed Automata

The model of Timed automata [2] is a well-established formalism for modelling the timing behaviour of systems. This section defines syntax and semantics of an extension of timed automata introducing data updates, communication actions with data transmission, and non-trivial data-dependent time constraints. Those appear in functional specification of systems, as in the specification of Trickle in the introduction.

Data Domain. We use a universal data domain D to abstract all values of time variables, called clocks as usual, and other data variables. Data variables can be of any type, whereas clocks are typed in a time domain $T \subseteq D$ which is isomorphic to $\mathbb{Q}_+$, the set of positive rational numbers.

Data Valuations. For a set of data variables V, a data valuation is a type-preserving mapping $v : V \to D$. We canonically extend data valuation to usual arithmetical expressions defined over V, i.e., $v(e)$ is the value of e for the valuation v. We denote by D^V the set of all such valuations.

Data Formulae. The set $\mathcal{F}(V)$ of data formula f over V is either: an atomic formula of the form *true*, *false*, $e_1 = e_2$, $e_1 \prec e_2$, and $e_1 \succ e_2$ with $\prec \in \{<, \leq\}$ and $\succ \in \{>, \geq\}$: or built over those using usual connectives: conjunction ($\land$), disjunction ($\lor$), and negation ($\neg$).

Sequential Data Updates. We consider sequential updates defined as follows:

$$u ::= \text{skip} \mid x := e_1 \mid e_1 \prec : x :\prec e_2 \mid u_1; u_2 \mid \text{if}(f)\text{then}\{u_1\}\text{else}\{u_2\} \mid \text{repeat}(n)\{u_1\}$$

skip is the null update; $x := e_1$ assigns the variable x with a new value denoted by e_1; $e_1 \prec : x :\prec e_2$ assigns x with a new random value bounded from below by the value denoted by e_1, the value of x is also bounded from above by the value denoted by e_2. Moreover, updates can be built using usual control primitives: sequence (;), condition (if ... then ... else ...) or counted-loop (repeat(n)) allowing the repetition of the enclosed update n times.

The set of update functions $\mathcal{U}(V)$ is defined by functions $[\![u]\!]$ from D^V to $2^{(D^V)}$. The set of valuations $[\![u]\!](v) \in 2^{(D^V)}$ is defined on the form of u as follows[1]:

$$[\![\text{skip}]\!](v) = \{v\} \tag{1}$$

$$[\![x := e_1]\!](v) = \{v[x \to v(e_1)]\} \tag{2}$$

$$[\![e_1 \prec : x :\prec e_2]\!](v) = \{v[x \to y] | v(e_1) \prec y \prec v(e_2)\} \tag{3}$$

$$[\![u_1; u_2]\!](v) = \{v' \mid \exists v'' \in u_1(v), v' \in u_2(v'')\} \tag{4}$$

$$[\![\text{if}(f)\text{then}\{u_1\}\text{else}\{u_2\}]\!](v) = u_1(v) \quad v(f) \tag{5}$$

$$[\![\text{if}(f)\text{then}\{u_1\}\text{else}\{u_2\}]\!](v) = u_2(v) \quad \neg v(f) \tag{6}$$

$$[\![\text{repeat}(n)\{u_1\}]\!](v) = [\![u_1; \text{repeat}(n-1)\{u_1\}]\!](v) \quad n > 0 \tag{7}$$

$$[\![\text{repeat}(0)\{u_1\}]\!](v) = \{v\} \tag{8}$$

---

[1] Given a function $h : A \to B$, a subset $X \subset A$, the function $h' = h[x \to y, \; x \in X]$ is defined as follows: $h'(z) = y$ if $z \in X$ otherwise $h'(z) = h(z)$. In case X is a singleton of the form $\{x\}$, we denote $h' = h[x \to y]$ in short.

Clock Formulae. Given a set of clocks Cl disjointed from V ($Cl \cap V = \emptyset$), a clock valuation is a mapping $w : Cl \to T$. With previous notation, the set $\mathcal{G}(Cl, V)$ of clock formulas g over Cl and V is either an atomic formulas of the form $true$, $false$, $clk \prec e$ or $clk \succ e$ where e is an expression over V typed in time domain T; or a conjunction of those. The set of clock invariants $\mathcal{I}(Cl)$ is defined by conjunctions of formulas of the form $clk \prec e$. We define a universal valuation $v \oplus w : V \cup Cl \to D$ as the resulting valuation which coincide with v and w on V and Cl respectively. This valuation can be canonically extended to formulas as usual.

Communication Actions with Data. Given a set of interaction points, often called ports, P, the set of communication actions $\mathcal{C}(P, V)$ contains two kind elements: output actions of the form $p!e$ which denotes an emission on some port p of a piece of data corresponding to the current valuation of e; or input actions of the form $p?x$ which denotes a reception of a piece of data that is stored in the variable x. Moreover, we consider the special action ϵ which denotes the absence of communication action. The valuations of actions of the form $p!e$, $p?x$, and ϵ, are defined by $v(p!e) = p!v(e)$, $v(p?x) = p?v(x)$, and $v(\epsilon) = \epsilon$ respectively.

Extended Timed Automaton. An extended timed automaton (XTA in short) is a tuple $(L, l_0, V, Cl, P, Tr, Inv)$ where L is a finite set of locations, $l_0 \in L$ is the initial location, V is a set of variables, Cl is a set of clocks, P is a set of ports, $Tr \subseteq L \times \mathcal{F}(V) \times \mathcal{G}(Cl, V) \times (\mathcal{C}(P, V) \cup \{\epsilon\}) \times \mathcal{U}(V) \times 2^{Cl} \times L$ is a set of transitions, and $Inv : L \to \mathcal{I}(Cl)$ is a state invariant mapping.

For a transition $tr = (l, f, g, ca, u, R, l') \in Tr$, l and l' are respectively the source and target location of tr; f and g are respectively the data guard and time guard of tr, i.e., enabling conditions on data variables and clocks; ca is the communication action of tr; u is an update function through which data variables are updated when tr is executed; and $R \subseteq Cl$ is the set of clocks to be reset.

The semantics of an XTA is a labeled transition system where states s are triples (l, v, w) where l is a location, v and w are data and clock valuations respectively. The transition relation is defined as follows:

- delay transition: $(l, v, w) \xrightarrow{d} (l, v, w')$ where for all $clk \in Cl$, $w'(clk) = w(clk) + d$ with some $d \in T$ such that $v \oplus w' \models Inv(l)$
- action transition: $(l, v, w) \xrightarrow{a} (l', v', w')$ if and only if there exists a transition $(l, f, g, ca, u, R, l') \in Tr$:
  - $v \oplus w \models f \wedge g$,
  - $a = v(ca)$,
  - $v' \in \llbracket u \rrbracket(v)$,
  - $w' = w[clk \to 0, \ clk \in R]$.

In the following, we introduce a network of XTA which exchange data using broadcast communication.

A Network of Extended Timed Automata. A network of XTA denoted by $\mathcal{N} = ((\mathcal{A}_i)_{i \in \{1,...,n\}}, \mathcal{K})$ is defined as follows:

- $(\mathcal{A}_i)_{i \in \{1,\ldots,n\}}$ a family of XTA $\mathcal{A}_i = (L_i, l_0^i, V_i, Cl_i, P_i, Tr_i, Inv_i)$ which do not share variables and clocks, i.e., for all $i, j \leq n$ we have that $V_i \cap V_j = \emptyset$, $Cl_i \cap Cl_j = \emptyset$, and $P_i \cap P_j = \emptyset$,
- a total function $\mathcal{K} : P_\mathcal{N} \to 2^{P_\mathcal{N}}$ specifying connections between ports.

The set of all ports of $\mathcal{N}$ is denoted by $P_\mathcal{N} = \bigcup_{i \leq n} P_i$. Besides, the set of all variables (resp. clock variables) of $\mathcal{N}$ is denoted by $V_\mathcal{N} = \bigcup_{i \leq n} V_i$ (resp. $Cl_\mathcal{N} = \bigcup_{i \leq n} Cl_i$).

We make the hypothesis that latent data issued (potentially by different sources) and targeting some internal port in delivered on that port in the order they were sent, i.e., we will implement this using queues with a policy of first-in-first-out (fifo). In the following, we denote by the function $q : P_\mathcal{N} \to D^*$ the pending data in the network as being the content of queues associated with receiving ports.

The semantics of a network of XTA is a labeled transition system in which: states are tuples of the form $S = ((l_1, v_1, w_1), \ldots, (l_n, v_n, w_n), q)$ with initial states S_0 verify for all $i \leq n$, $l_i = l_0^i$; and transitions are defined as follows:

- delay transition:

$$((l_1, v_1, w_1), \ldots, (l_n, v_n, w_n), q) \xrightarrow{d} ((l_1, v_1, w_1'), \ldots, (l_n, v_n, w_n'), q)$$

iff for all $i \leq n$ there exists $(l_i, v_i, w_i) \xrightarrow{d} (l_i, v_i, w_i')$
- internal output transition:
$$((l_1, v_1, w_1), \ldots, (l_i, v_i, w_i), \ldots, (l_n, v_n, w_n), q) \xrightarrow{a}$$

$$((l_1, v_1, w_1), \ldots, (l_i', v_i', w_i'), \ldots, (l_n, v_n, w_n), q')$$

iff there exists $(l_i, v_i, w_i) \xrightarrow{a} (l_i', v_i', w_i')$ with $a = p!m$, q' is such that for all port p_1 either $p_1 \in \mathcal{K}(p)$ then $q'(p_1) = q(p_1).m$ otherwise $q'(p_1) = q(p_1)$,
- internal input transition:
$$((l_1, v_1, w_1), \ldots, (l_i, v_i, w_i), \ldots, (l_n, v_n, w_n), q) \xrightarrow{a}$$

$$((l_1, v_1, w_1), \ldots, (l_i', v_i', w_i'), \ldots, (l_n, v_n, w_n), q')$$

iff there exists $(l_i, v_i, w_i) \xrightarrow{a} (l_i', v_i', w_i')$ with $a = p?m$, $q(p)$ is not empty and is of the form $q(p) = m.q_1$, and q' is such that $q'(p) = q_1$ and for all $p_1 \neq p$ we have $q'(p_1) = q(p_1)$,
- silent or external action transition:
$$((l_1, v_1, w_1), \ldots, (l_i, v_i, w_i), \ldots, (l_n, v_n, w_n), q) \xrightarrow{a}$$

$$((l_1, v_1, w_1), \ldots, (l_i', v_i', w_i'), \ldots, (l_n, v_n, w_n), q)$$

iff there exists $(l_i, v_i, w_i) \xrightarrow{a} (l_i', v_i', w_i')$ with $a = \epsilon$ or $a = p!m$ (resp. $a = p?m$) such that $\mathcal{K}(p) = \emptyset$ (resp. for all p_1, $p \notin \mathcal{K}(p_1)$).

In a nutshell, the above definition shows that time advances in the same way for all clocks of XTA forming the network. Besides, an internal emission $p!m$ on a port p has the effect of filling all the fifo associated to the ports of $\mathcal{K}(p)$ and an internal reception $p?m$ on port p consumes the first message stored in its fifo.

When a silent action or an external action (reception or an emission) occurs on a port which is not connected to other XTA ports, it is executed with no effect on fifo queues, since it is assumed to be connected to some implicit environment.

A run of the network is derived from the labelled transition system as a path starting in an S_0 and alternating delay transitions and action transitions. The property we are interested in is the reachability of states S. A state S is reachable iff there exists a run in which S occurs. In practice, such states are those which satisfy some user-specified formula $\phi = f \wedge g$ on data and clocks.

Let us denote by tr-seq(r) the sequence of (syntactic) transitions in $\bigcup_{i \leq n} Tr_i$ covered by a run r. We recall that such sequence intertwines transitions of different automata composing the network based on induced fifo-communications causalities discussed above.

Two runs r_1 and r_2 are said to be *coverage equivalent* if and only if tr-seq(r_1) = tr-seq(r_2), i.e., they cover the same (syntactic) transitions sequence.

The equivalence classes characterized by this relation guide the symbolic execution to search for all runs of a given class (as a symbolic path together with its path condition). On the other hand, model-checking will be used to compute some representative runs of the class that satisfy a reachability property ϕ. In practice, from the latter, we extract the transition sequence that guides the exploration performed by the symbolic execution.

3   Trickle Models

Trickle Node Behavior. We propose the XTA $(L, Init, V, Cl, P, Tr, Inv)$ which specifies Trickle behaviour of each node in the network, the automaton is depicted in Fig. 1. The XTA has 5 locations.

$L = \{Init, Listen_1, Listen_2, Check_1, Check_2\}$ in which $Init$ is the initial location. The clocks set is a singleton $Cl = \{clk\}$ containing one clock used to implement the Trickle timer. The set of variables contains 5 variables $V = \{I, t, c, myv, rcv\}$: the former three variables I, t and c are Trickle variables which respectively represent the value of the current interval, the instant of transmission and the counter value (whereas I_{min}, I_{max}, k are Trickle constants). Without loss of generality, in this automaton, Trickle is used to maintain consistency of version number across the network, the variable myv stores the most recent version the node holds and rcv is used to store received versions from neighbors.

The automaton has 10 transitions composing the set Tr, that we will overview next together with meaning associated with state invariants defined by mapping Inv. A node can be started at any time; this is captured by state invariant $Inv(Init) : true$ in location l_0, which means that any duration can elapse in this location. The transition $Init \rightarrow Listen_1$ is fired to start the Trickle behaviour. It sets I to I_{min}, assigns counter c and clk with 0, and finally chooses a the transmission time $I/2 \leq: t :< I$ within the second-half of the interval current interval I. The state invariant $Inv(Listen_1) : clk \leq t$ constrain time elapsing to be bounded by t. When clk reaches t, there two possible behaviors: either the transmission

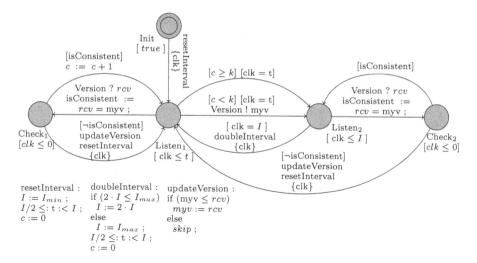

Fig. 1. An extended timed automaton (XTA) of a Trickle node behavior

occurs given $c < k$ is fulfilled (horizontal transition $Listen_1 \rightarrow Listen_2$ with action $Version?rcv$), otherwise the transmission is suppressed (curved transition $Listen_1 \rightarrow Listen_2$ with action ϵ). A first reception handling is defined by transition $Listen_1 \rightarrow Check_1$. Once started, the automaton satisfies the input enable less property: in every state ($Listen_1$ or $Listen_2$), it is possible to receive every input (action $Version?rcv$). Each time, a version is received, it is compared to the current version of the node: in case of consistency (same version $rcv = myv$), the counter c is incremented ($c := c + 1$), we recall that the latter counts redundant versions; otherwise (case of inconsistency) a new interval is started, and the node updated its version if it is older.

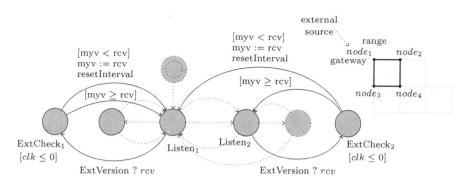

Fig. 2. Setting a network of XTA for a Trickle dissemination

State invariant $Inv(Listen_2) : clk \leq I$ constrains time elapsing to be at most of the value denoted by current interval length I. Subsequently, a new interval is started by doubling I (until I_{max}) and a new t is chosen as previous (transition $Listen_2 \rightarrow Listen_1$). Similar reception handling as in location $Listen_1$ is defined.

Network Modelling. A transmission can be associated with several receivers, which are exactly those situated within the broadcast range of the node, i.e., they are its neighbours. A typical Trickle topology contains some gateway node $node_1$ in Fig. 2, which can receive versions to be disseminated across the network from an external source. A network of XTA one per node can be naturally designed for such topology. Among those, XTA of gateway nodes are extended with extra transitions which allows the reception of new versions from the external source (transitions $Listen_1 \rightarrow ExtCheck_1$ and $Listen_2 \rightarrow ExtCheck_2$ with input $ExtVersion?myv$). The connections between XTA ports, defined by function $\mathcal{K}$, are inferred from topology connections: e.g., $\mathcal{K}(node_1.Version) = \{noed_2.Version, node_3.Version\}$ for the four-nodes topology depicted by the bidirectional graph in Fig. 2. Note that ports of gateway nodes are implicitly connected to external source and can receive any value.

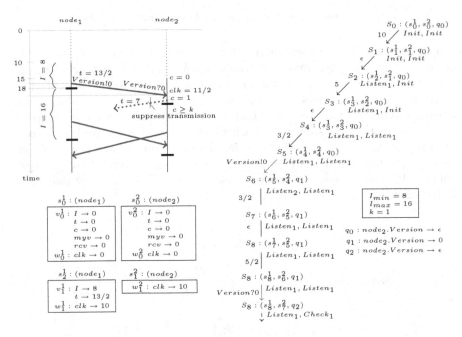

Fig. 3. A run of a two-nodes network of XTA.

Illustration of Network Runs. Figure 3 depicts a simple sequence diagram together with a run of a simple two-nodes network of XTA. The run shows that both nodes exchange a version of value 0, that they both initially hold (see data valuations in initial state S_0). As the redundancy constant k is set to 1, the receiver node gets its counter saturated, i.e., c reaches k. Therefore, it suppresses its transmission. This is a typical trickle behaviour which reduces the number of transmissions (gossip) when the neighbourhood is up-to-date.

4 Exploring Trickle with UPPAAL and DIVERSITY

UPPAAL Model. We have created a model in UPPAAL, which corresponds to the network of XTA presented in Sect. 3. The UPPAAL model has a very similar structure in terms of states and transitions. Locations $Check_1$ and $Check_2$ have been declared as *Committed* (marked with a "C") which means that time cannot elapse in this location as intended in the original model. Also, such locations have a higher priority to be taken than non-committed ones. This reduces interleaving between automata if the latter are not executing on their turn transitions from committed locations. To implement asynchronous communication actions, we have created c-like functions in UPPAAL which implement fifo operations on queues. Unlike XTA which uses unbounded queues, those are arrays of fixed parameter size QUEUE_SIZE.

In UPPAAL, clocks are only compared to integer expressions, and clock guards are essentially conjunctions. This does not allow the specification of guards of the form $clk \leq t$ where t can take any random value in the dense interval $[I/2, I[$. In XTA, those values are (isomorphic to) positive rationals ($\mathbb{Q}_+$). In Fig. 4, we propose a UPPAAL pattern so that values assigned with t are positive integers ($\mathbb{Z}_+$). This is compliant with the nature of clock constraints supported by UPPAAL, i.e., clocks in guards are bounded by integer expressions. On the other hand, UPPAAL provides a *select* statement $s : [L, U]$ on transition which selects a random value for an integer variable s within a specified integer interval. Interval bounds L and U are necessarily constants. It is equivalent to an update $L \leq: s :\leq U$ in XTA. The pattern

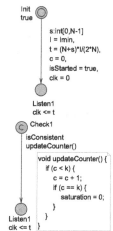

Fig. 4. UPPAAL transitions.

allows the selection of at most N values for t within the current interval $[I/2, I[$: first an integer s is selected in the interval $[0, N - 1]$, s is then used to assign t with a value denoted by the expression $e = (N + s) \cdot I/(2 \cdot N)$, however t is an integer variable, so t will be assigned exactly by the greatest integer less than or equal to the valuation of e. For instance, for $I = 8$ (resp. for $I = 16$) and $N = 4$, t can be assigned with the four integers 4, 5, 6 and 7 (resp. 8, 10, 12 and 14). The variable t can have an infinite number of possible values within the second half of I; the pattern allows exploring with UPPAAL just a few (at most N integers, we experiment with small values). But since we are interested in reachability, if a solution exists for those, the verification concludes.

Model Exploration in UPPAAL. The tool uses the notion of *zone* to represent the set of valuations of clocks symbolically. A zone is defined by the conjunction of difference constraints of the form $clk \prec s$ or $clk - clk' \prec s$ where s is an integer. The simulation graph in UPPAAL is composed of nodes of the form $((l_1, v_1), \ldots, (l_n, v_n), Z, v)$ where l_i is the location (resp. v_i is the data valuation) for the ith automaton, Z is a zone over clocks of the n involved automata, and v is the valuation of global or shared data variables. An example of such node is $((Listen_1, v_0^1), (Init, v_0^2), node_1.clk \leq 4, v_0)$ with notation of Fig. 3, v_0 associates Trickle constants to their values, it sets queues to empty at start. The exploration of the graph uses inclusion on zones which checks whether a zone of a successor node in the graph is already covered by some zones of previously explored nodes. In case of inclusion, data valuations must coincide in order to prune the search. This helps master the search when infinite cycles exist. Intuitively, a typical cycle is when all nodes reach I_{max}, share the same version and the content of the queues coincides, then same behaviours will start over again. To enable detect this situation: (i) we choose small values for I_{max} and (ii) we stop increment the counter c once it reaches k (see transition $Check_1 \rightarrow Listen_1$ in Fig. 4). Note that *saturation* is an extra clock of the node that will be discussed later; obviously, this has no effect on Trickle behaviour since the decision to suppress transmission depends only on reaching exactly k. In fact, after exchanging k or many more redundant versions is similar concerning subsequent behaviours. Otherwise, counter c will be assigned differently depending on the number of received versions. In which case, matching data valuations fails despite zone inclusion, and the cycle never exit. UPPAAL provides classical search strategies Depth-First Search (DFS) and Breadth-First Search (BFS), as well as Random Depth-First Search (RDFS). As we consider reachability, so one solution is wanted, DFS or RDFS are typically the most efficient option according to the tool documentation. When applying a DFS (or RDFS), inclusion on zones is of practical use as is it avoids getting lost in an infinite cycle.

Reachability Properties in UPPAAL. The tool supports a subset of Computation Tree Logic (CTL) [10]. As we are interested in reachability, we propose to use CTL formulae of the form $E \lozenge \phi$ where $\phi = f \wedge g$ is a formula on data variables and clocks. The satisfaction of such formula is defined on the tree with root an S_0 extracted from the labelled transition system of the network (see Sect. 2). The operator E quantifies over paths (or runs) of such a tree: it checks if there exists a path (with root S_0) in the tree satisfying the sub formula $\lozenge \phi$, the latter on the other hand is satisfied by that path if a state S satisfying ϕ occurs in the path. A simple property is $E \lozenge (node_2.c \geq k \wedge node_2.clk = node_2.I)$. The property is satisfied by the run discussed in Fig. 3, in which the node $node_2$ suppresses its transmission. Let us discuss the following two properties expressed for the four-nodes topology of Fig. 2.

Updated: $E \lozenge ((node_1.myv = NEW) \wedge (node_2.myv = NEW) \wedge$
$$(node_3.myv = NEW) \wedge (node_4.myv = NEW))$$
Outdated: $E \lozenge ((node_4.isStarted) \wedge (node_4.myv = OLD) \wedge$
$$(node_2.myv = NEW) \wedge (node_2.c \geq k) \wedge (node_3.myv = NEW) \wedge (node_3.c \geq k)) \wedge$$
$$((node_2.saturation \geq D) \wedge (node_3.saturation \geq D))$$

The first property states that it is possible that all the nodes are updated. The second property states that there exists a node which is still outdated (holds an old version) while its neighbours are all updated, yet they have suppressed their transmissions. We use an extra clock *saturation* per node which is reset when the counter c reaches k (see Fig. 4). The clock measures the delay elapsed since then, and the formula requires that such delay is bounded by a parameter $D > 0$. This situation is not desirable, especially after having observed numerous exchanges of messages in the networks.

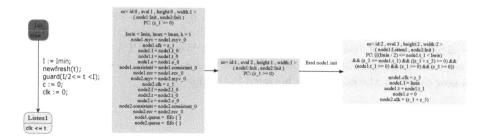

Fig. 5. Symbolic execution of a DIVERSITY transition.

DIVERSITY Models and Symbolic Execution. DIVERSITY [3] tools provides symbolic execution for state-based models (e.g., [4]) involving data expressions, data and clock guards. Input parameters or fresh symbols (they are used only once) can substitute uninitialized variables, reception variables used in communication with the external environment or any variable using a dedicated explicit newfresh statement. The latter is of the form newfresh(x); it associates the variable x with a new fresh symbol. We have developed a DIVERSITY model of the XTA network for Trickle, as the UPPAAL model it has a similar structure in terms of states and transitions. DIVERSITY provides communication over unbounded fifo queues. We declare a single queue per node as each node owns only one port for internal communications. Those are initially empty, and their size is automatically adjusted by the tool as communication actions are evaluated. Figure 5 depicts a DIVERSITY transition ($Init \rightarrow Listen_1$). It suggests a pattern in DIVERSITY which allows to assign the variable t with a random value within current interval $[I/2, I[$: newfresh(t) associates with t with a new fresh symbol, the latter is constrained by subsequent *guard statement* $I/2 \leq t < I$. It is possible in DIVERSITY to declare I_{min}, I_{max}, I and t to be typed as a positive rational numbers ($\mathbb{Q}_+$) so as to be compatible with clock clk. DIVERSITY computes the so-called symbolic tree in which nodes are called *execution contexts* ec: they store pieces of information about the execution including the current location, about the transition which allows reaching the context, and importantly about Path Conditions and Substitutions of data variables, clocks, queue places, ... by arithmetical expressions over input parameters. Figure 5 depicts the symbolic execution step of the previous transition (being of $node_1$) from ec_1. The context ec_2 is reached, the transmission variable t is substitutes by a new symbol $node_1.t_1$ (substituted by t_0 in initial context ec_0), t_1 is constrained by the PC sub-formula (($I_{min}/2$) $\leq node_1.t_1 < I_{min}$). Note that sub-formula

($z_3 \leq node1.t_1$) shows that time elapsing in ec_2 (denoted by duration symbol z_3) is bounded by the value denoted by $node1.t_1$. This condition corresponds to the evaluation of clock invariant $clk \leq t$ in location $Init$ for $node_1$ ($node_1.clk$ is substituted by z_3 in ec_2). Symbolic execution techniques characterize all intended runs. DIVERSITY provides different classical search strategies which can be used to unfold the symbolic tree from the initial context ec_0 up to criteria on tree size (depth, width or number of nodes). Naturally, this results in a huge tree. DIVERSITY provides heuristic search [3] guided by a user-specified sequence of transitions, possibly non-consecutive as it is difficult in general to guess strict sequencing when it comes to automata network. We use UPPAAL to find such a sequence corresponding to some runs satisfying a user-specified property. Let us now overview the connection between both tools.

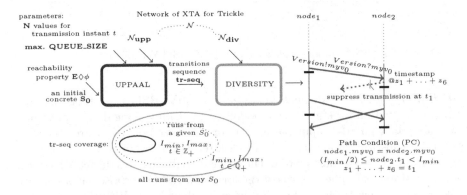

Fig. 6. Workflow UPPAAL-DIVERSITY. (Color figure online)

Tools Workflow and Experiments. The workflow is given in Fig. 6. UPPAAL takes as input a user-specified property $E\Diamond\phi$. The aim is to check the property from an initial state S_0. Parameters on the number N of transmission instants t to be selected within the Trickle interval have to be given together with a bound QUEUE_SIZE on communication queues. The property is assessed on the UPPAAL model $\mathcal{N}_{upp}$. In case of the property is verified, i.e., there exists at least a run from S_0 which satisfies ϕ (such runs are schematically depicted by a blue ellipse), then the sequence of covering transitions tr-seq is derived from the UPPAAL solution. The idea now is to compute the equivalence class composed by all runs from any sates S_0 which are covered by the sequence tr-seq. For this, a symbolic exploration guided by the sequence is conducted on the DIVERSITY model $\mathcal{N}_{div}$, a symbolic path together with its Path Condition (PC) is obtained then. The path is naturally feasible (satisfiability of its PC is assessed with SMT solvers). It identifies all runs covered by tr-seq with dense domain for I_{min}, I_{max} and t as being positive rationals (those are schematically depicted by a green ellipse). Since the path often represents pairwise communication actions from different automata, it can be depicted in a natural manner as a Sequence Diagram (SD). Figure 7 depicts an SD which highlights an outdated node situation, that of $node_4$. It has been computed by DIVERSITY for the four-nodes grid topology given in Fig. 2. The situation is atypical: neighbors of $node_4$, that is $node_2$ and $node_3$ are first updated by gateway $node_1$ with a new version (green messages), they hence reset their interval to I_{min}; right away, $node_4$ gets them to reset their interval again by transmitting its old version (blue messages), their transmissions are postponed; this somehow gives $node_1$ time to retransmit the new version and saturate them (orange messages); therefore they suppress their transmissions for $node_4$. This unfortunate circumstance for $node_4$ can be prevented by increasing the redundancy constant so that its neighbors, $node_2$ and $node_3$, can still transmit, yet this comes at a cost, the number of messages increases for the entire nodes lifetime. Or $node_4$ can still be updated later because it together with $node_1$ will get their intervals doubled, and their transmission instants are at least dephased of I_{min} of those of $node_2$ and $node_3$ which leaves them time to update $node_4$. This is in favour of using Trickle, even if a node is in such outdated situation, it will not remain for a long time, thanks to the dynamic interval adjustment which avoids flood the network with messages. We have experimented with more nodes in the grid (up to 9), Table 1 reports on those. *Updated* and *Outdated* properties were successfully checked, which is satisfactory given the non-trivial kind of interactions in case of outdated nodes.

Table 1. The nodes graph is bidirectional in the form of a grid topology (See Fig. 2), 7(2) (resp. 7(3)) denotes that $node_7$ is two blocks (resp. three blocks) from the gateway $node_1$. Results measured on an Intel Core i7-7920HQ processor with RAM 32 GB, the redundancy constant k was set to 1 the minimum transmission case in Trickle. DIVERSITY time includes PC check with CVC4. UPPAAL concluded in few more trials inline with the exponential growth in running time.

Nodes	Updated			Outdated		
	UPPAAL	DIVERSITY	Messages	UPPAAL	DIVERSITY	Messages
3	1 ms	1 s 542 ms	7	12 ms	4 s 156 ms	8
4	3 ms	2 s 731 ms	16	984 ms	9 s 796 ms	12
5	4 ms	9 s 395 ms	12	168 ms	11 s 828 ms	12
6	7 ms	32 s 750 ms	21	7 s 621 ms	1 m 28 s 953 ms	23
7(2)	6 ms	29 s 453 ms	29	5 s 772 ms	2 m 5 s 375 ms	26
7(3)	5 ms	49 s 375 ms	29	3 s 227 ms	1 m 42 s 718 ms	24
8	8 ms	59 s 640 ms	41	8 m 9 s 503 ms	9 m 36 s 375 ms	42
9	9 ms	2 m 58 s 408 ms	64	9 m 19 s 22 ms	15 m 36 s 11 ms	62

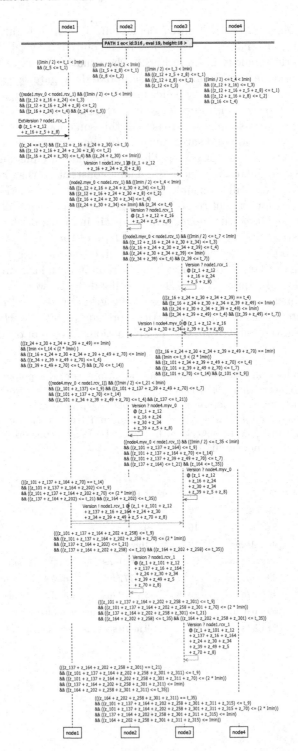

Fig. 7. Outdated node situation - Sequence Diagram generated by DIVERSITY. (Color figure online)

5 Conclusion

We have developed first models for desynchronized Trickle network. Those models use data to express adjustable transmission intervals and abstract transmitted information. To assess reachability properties, we combine model checking and symbolic execution. If the property is verified on the model in which data is concrete, we derive from the returned solution a sequence of transitions that guides the symbolic execution to compute the corresponding symbolic path. The latter is a compact representation of the equivalence class of behaviours for the transitions coverage and can be depicted in the user-friendly format of sequence diagrams to enable their understanding. For future work, we plan to extract from the model-checking solution more information about structural coverage of the mini-language of updates on transitions to refine the equivalence classes by symbolic execution. We also plan to experiment with other gossip protocols. We believe that our approach can be of practical use to highlight for those non-trivial nodes interactions and give hints on their benefit for transmissions control.

Acknowledgment. This work was financially supported by European commission through ECSEL-JU 2018 program under grant agreement No. 826276.

References

1. RPL: IPv6 routing protocol for low-power and lossy networks, request for comments: 6550. Technical report, Cooper Power Systems and Cisco Systems and Stanford University, March 2012 (2012)
2. Alur, R., Dill, D.: A theory of timed automata. J. Theoret. Comput. Sci. **126**, 183–235 (1994)
3. Arnaud, M., Bannour, B., Lapitre, A.: An illustrative use case of the DIVERSITY platform based on UML interaction scenarios. Electr. Notes Theoret. Comput. Sci. **320**, 21–34 (2016)
4. Bannour, B., Escobedo, J.P., Gaston, C., Le Gall, P.: Off-line test case generation for timed symbolic model-based conformance testing. In: Nielsen, B., Weise, C. (eds.) ICTSS 2012. LNCS, vol. 7641, pp. 119–135. Springer, Heidelberg (2012). https://doi.org/10.1007/978-3-642-34691-0_10
5. Bannour, B., Lapitre, A.: Heuristic-aided symbolic simulation for trickle-based wireless sensors networks configuration. In: International Workshop on RAPIDO@HiPEAC. ACM (2020)
6. Barrett, C., et al.: CVC4. In: Gopalakrishnan, G., Qadeer, S. (eds.) CAV 2011. LNCS, vol. 6806, pp. 171–177. Springer, Heidelberg (2011). https://doi.org/10.1007/978-3-642-22110-1_14
7. Becker, M., Kuladinithi, K., Görg, C.: Modelling and simulating the Trickle algorithm. In: Pentikousis, K., Aguiar, R., Sargento, S., Agüero, R. (eds.) MONAMI 2011. LNICST, vol. 97, pp. 135–144. Springer, Heidelberg (2012). https://doi.org/10.1007/978-3-642-30422-4_10
8. Breza, M.J., McCann, J.A.: Lessons in implementing bio-inspired algorithms on wireless sensor networks. In: International Conference on NASA/ESA. IEEE (2008)

9. Chen, Z., Zhang, D., Zhu, R., Ma, Y., Yin, P., Xie, F.: A review of automated formal verification of ad hoc routing protocols for wireless sensor networks. CoRR, abs/1305.7410 (2013)

10. Clarke, E.M., Emerson, E.A.: Design and synthesis of synchronization skeletons using branching time temporal logic. In: Grumberg, O., Veith, H. (eds.) 25 Years of Model Checking. LNCS, vol. 5000, pp. 196–215. Springer, Heidelberg (2008). https://doi.org/10.1007/978-3-540-69850-0_12

11. Clarke, E.M., Grumberg, O., Peled, D.A.: Model Checking. MIT Press, Cambridge (2001)

12. Coladon, T., Vucinic, M., Tourancheau, B.: Multiple redundancy constants with trickle. In: PIMRC. IEEE (2015)

13. de Moura, L., Bjørner, N.: Z3: an efficient SMT solver. In: Ramakrishnan, C.R., Rehof, J. (eds.) TACAS 2008. LNCS, vol. 4963, pp. 337–340. Springer, Heidelberg (2008). https://doi.org/10.1007/978-3-540-78800-3_24

14. Dill, D.L.: Timing assumptions and verification of finite-state concurrent systems. In: Sifakis, J. (ed.) CAV 1989. LNCS, vol. 407, pp. 197–212. Springer, Heidelberg (1990). https://doi.org/10.1007/3-540-52148-8_17

15. Dong, J.S., Sun, J., Sun, J., Taguchi, K., Zhang, X.: Specifying and verifying sensor networks: an experiment of formal methods. In: Liu, S., Maibaum, T., Araki, K. (eds.) ICFEM 2008. LNCS, vol. 5256, pp. 318–337. Springer, Heidelberg (2008). https://doi.org/10.1007/978-3-540-88194-0_20

16. Dunkels, A., Gronvall, B., Voigt, T.: Contiki - a lightweight and flexible operating system for tiny networked sensors. In: IEEE ICLCN (2004)

17. Hui, J., Kelsey, R.: Multicast protocol for low-power and lossy networks, request for comments: 7731. Technical report, Silicon Labs (2016)

18. King, J.C.: Symbolic execution and program testing. Commun. ACM **19**, 385–394 (1976)

19. Kermajani, H.R., Gomez, C., Arshad, M.H.: Modeling the message count of the Trickle algorithm in a steady-state, static wireless sensor network. IEEE Commun. Lett. **16**, 1960–1963 (2012)

20. Kwiatkowska, M.Z., Norman, G., Parker, D.: Analysis of a gossip protocol in PRISM. SIGMETRICS Perform. Eval. Rev. **36**, 17–22 (2008)

21. Kwiatkowska, M., Norman, G., Parker, D.: PRISM 4.0: verification of probabilistic real-time systems. In: Gopalakrishnan, G., Qadeer, S. (eds.) CAV 2011. LNCS, vol. 6806, pp. 585–591. Springer, Heidelberg (2011). https://doi.org/10.1007/978-3-642-22110-1_47

22. Lee, B., Song, H.K., Suh, Y., Oh, K.H., Youn, H.Y.: Energy-efficient gossiping protocol of WSN with realtime streaming data. In: International Conference on DASC (2014)

23. Levis, P., Clausen, T., Hui, J., Gnawali, O., Ko, J.: The Trickle algorithm, request for comments: 6206. Technical report, March 2011 (2011)

24. Levis, P., et al.: TinyOS: an operating system for sensor networks. In: Weber, W., Rabaey, J.M., Aarts, E. (eds.) Ambient Intelligence. Springer, Heidelberg (2005)

25. Levis, P., Patel, N., Culler, D., Shenker, S.: Trickle: a self-regulating algorithm for code propagation and maintenance in wireless sensor networks. In: International Symposium on NSDI. USENIX Association (2004)

26. Liu, Y., Sun, J., Dong, J.S.: PAT 3: an extensible architecture for building multi-domain model checkers. In: Dohi, T., Cukic, B. (eds.) International Conference on ISSRE. IEEE (2011)

27. Meyfroyt, T., Borst, S.C., Boxma, O.J., Denteneer, D.: On the scalability and message count of Trickle-based broadcasting schemes. Queueing Syst. **81**, 203–230 (2015)
28. Meyfroyt, T.M.M.: An analytic evaluation of the Trickle algorithm: towards efficient, fair, fast and reliable data dissemination. In: WoWMoM. IEEE (2015)
29. Nan, X., Fei, M., Yang, T.: Randomized and efficient time synchronization in dynamic wireless sensor networks: a gossip-consensus-based approach. Complexity **2018**, 1–16 (2018)
30. Nguyen, N.M.T., Bannour, B., Lapitre, A., Le Gall, P.: Behavioral models and scenario selection for testing IoT Trickle-based lossy multicast networks. In: International Workshop on VVIoT@ICST. IEEE (2019)
31. Vucinic, M., Król, M., Jonglez, B., Coladon, T., Tourancheau, B.: Trickle-D: high fairness and low transmission load with dynamic redundancy. IEEE IoT J. **4**, 1477–1488 (2017)
32. Webster, M., Breza, M., Dixon, C., Fisher, M., McCann, J.A.: Formal verification of synchronisation, gossip and environmental effects for wireless sensor networks. In: ECEASST (2018)
33. Woehrle, M., Bakhshi, R., Mousavi, M.R.: Mechanized extraction of topology anti-patterns in wireless networks. In: Derrick, J., Gnesi, S., Latella, D., Treharne, H. (eds.) IFM 2012. LNCS, vol. 7321, pp. 158–173. Springer, Heidelberg (2012). https://doi.org/10.1007/978-3-642-30729-4_12
34. Zheng, M., Sun, J., Liu, Y., Dong, J.S., Gu, Yu.: Towards a model checker for NesC and wireless sensor networks. In: Qin, S., Qiu, Z. (eds.) ICFEM 2011. LNCS, vol. 6991, pp. 372–387. Springer, Heidelberg (2011). https://doi.org/10.1007/978-3-642-24559-6_26

Broadcasting Information in Multi-hop Networks Prone to Mobile Byzantine Faults

Silvia Bonomi[1], Giovanni Farina[1,2(✉)], and Sébastien Tixeuil[2]

[1] Sapienza Università di Roma, Rome, Italy
bonomi@diag.uniroma1.it
[2] Sorbonne Université, CNRS, LIP6, 75005 Paris, France
{giovanni.farina,sebastien.tixeuil}@lip6.fr

Abstract. Every non-trivial distributed application needs to exchange information in order accomplish its task, and reliable communication primitives are fundamental in failures prone distributed systems to guarantee correct message exchanges between parties.

Their implementation becomes particularly challenging when considering distributed systems where processes are arranged in a multi-hop network and each of them may temporary and continuously be compromised by an attacker during the execution. Although some fundamental problems (such as the register implementation and the agreement) were investigated considering Mobile Byzantine Faults (MBF), most of the contributions consider a fully connected communication network.

In this paper we analyze the specific difficulty of ensuring reliable communication between parties in a distributed system affected by Mobile Byzantine Faults (compared to the case where the Byzantine failures are static), showing that such a problem is essentially impossible to solve in asynchronous systems with MBF, and we propose a synchronous protocol providing reliable communication both in complete networks and specific multi-hop topologies.

Keywords: Reliable communication · Mobile Byzantine Faults · Multi-hop networks

1 Introduction

Distributed systems are often prone to failures, given the multitude of interconnected components they are composed of, and protocols that are deployed on

This work was performed within Project ESTATE (Ref. ANR-16-CE25-0009-03), supported by French state funds managed by the ANR (Agence Nationale de la Recherche) and it has been partially supported by the INOCS Sapienza Ateneo 2017 Project (protocol number RM11715C816CE4CB). Giovanni Farina wishes to thank *Université Franco-Italienne/Università Italo-Francese* (UFI/UIF) for supporting his mobility through the Vinci grant 2018.

C. Georgiou and R. Majumdar (Eds.): NETYS 2020, LNCS 12129, pp. 112–128, 2021.
https://doi.org/10.1007/978-3-030-67087-0_8

them are usually designed to guarantee correct execution despite fault occurrences. Besides, distributed systems are more and more frequently subject also to external attackers, who aim to penetrate and compromise them.

Processes in a distributed system need to communicate in order to achieve non-trivial goals. Indeed, several reliable communication primitives have been defined to guarantee integrity, delivery and authorship of messages exchanged even in case of arbitrary failures. The reliable communication solutions proposed so far mostly put constraints on the spatial distribution of failures or on their duration. Such assumptions capture most of the internal misbehavior that may occurs in a system: data corruptions, link failures, machine faults, etc. On the other side, external malicious attackers commonly start compromising some machines and then they use them to move over the system till reaching their targets, and the research handling such kind of attacks mostly focus on their prevention, detection and reaction.

In this paper, we analyze the specific difficulties of ensuring reliable communication in distributed system affected by Mobile Byzantine Faults (compared to the case where the Byzantine failures are static), showing that reliable communication in asynchronous systems is essentially impossible, and then we propose a synchronous protocol solving reliable communication both in complete networks and specific multi-hop topologies.

2   Related Works

The reliable communication problem has been extensively investigated considering *static* Byzantine process failures. Dolev [10] provided the seminal contribution addressing this problem in general networks with a globally bounded number of faulty processes. Subsequently, several failure distributions have been considered, such as neighborhood-bounded [12,19,21,25], probabilistic [16,20], and the general adversary model [19]. Weaker problem specifications have been proposed to allow solving the reliable communication problem in loosely connected network [13,15], and dynamic networks have also been considered [2,17].

In complete communication networks, non-static Byzantine faulty processes were considered by Reischuk [22] who proposed an algorithm solving the Byzantine agreement in the case of f malicious agents that remain stationary on f processes only for a given period of time. Later, Ostrovsky and Yung [18] introduced the notion of an adversary that can inject and distribute faults in the system at a constant rate and they proposed solutions (mixing randomization and self-stabilization) for tolerating the attacks of mobile viruses. Then, Garay [11] considered processes proceedings in synchronous rounds composed by three phases (send, receive, and compute), and Byzantine mobile agents able to move between one process to another during the lifetime of the system. Several subsequent works later specialized his model, making alternative hypothesis on the unawareness of processes of being faulty [24], assuming correct processes sending non-equivocal messages [1], channels delays [23], decoupling the system evolution from the agents movements [5]. All aforementioned works for the mobile attacker model addressed either the Byzantine agreement, the approximate Byzantine agreement [7], or the register abstraction [4] problems in complete networks. Most related to our work is the solution by Sasaki et al. [24], that is detailed in Sect. 6.

3   System Model

Process Definition and Communication Model. We consider a distributed system composed by a set of n processes $\Pi = \{p_1, p_2, \ldots p_n\}$, each associated with an unique identifier. Processes communicate by exchanging messages via reliable and authenticated point-to-point links i.e., messages can neither be lost or altered by the links and the identity of the sender of any message cannot be forged. Processes and their links can be abstracted by an undirected graph $G = (\Pi, E)$ where the set of nodes is represented by the processes of the system and the set of edges E contains an element $e_{i,j}$ if and only if there exists a link between processes p_i and p_j. Two processes p_i and p_j can exchange messages only if there is a link between them.

Time Assumptions and Computational Model. Unless differently stated, we consider a *synchronous* system [9]. Specifically, we assume one where the computation evolves in sequential synchronous rounds $r_0, r_1, \ldots r_i \ldots$ (with $i \in \mathbb{N}$). Every round is divided in three phases: (i) *send* where processes send messages through their links for the current round, (ii) *receive* where processes receive all messages sent at the beginning of the current round, and (iii) *computation* where processes execute a deterministic distributed protocol $\mathcal{P}$ and generate the messages to be sent during the subsequent round. We assume a tamper-proof read-only memory on every process where the code of $\mathcal{P}$ is stored.

Failure Model. We assume that the system is affected by *Mobile Byzantine Faults* (MBF) [1,8,11,24]. Informally, in the mobile Byzantine failure model, faults are represented by f computationally unbounded agents that move between processes. When an agent is on a process p_i, it forces p_i to behave as a *Byzantine faulty* process (i.e., it may corrupt its local variables, forces it to execute an arbitrary protocol, to send arbitrary messages, to omit sending messages, etc.). We assume that, at every round r_i, every mobile Byzantine agent is placed on at most one process p_j and that it can move from p_j to another process p_k only if there is a link between the two. The movement of the Byzantine agents is characterized by the *roaming pace* parameter ρ, that is the minimum amount of time between two displacements of an agent. We assume that the Byzantine agents can only move in between the computation and the send phase [11,24], thus $\rho \geq 1$ round.

We alternatively consider either an *aware* [24] or *unaware* [11] mobile Byzantine failure model: in the former case a process knows about a mobile agent that is moving away from it, in the latter it does not. At every round r_i, a process p_j is either *correct* or *Byzantine faulty*. Precisely, p_j is faulty if a mobile

Byzantine agent is on it at r_i, or it is correct otherwise and it executes the distributed protocol $\mathcal{P}$. Notice that every process backs to execute protocol $\mathcal{P}$ right after a Byzantine agent moved away and that the failure state of a process cannot change during a message transmission (send - receive phases). In the aware mobile Byzantine failure model, we refer with *cured* process to a correct one at round r_i that was Byzantine faulty at round r_{i-1}. We assume that every cured process wipes all of its local variables at the beginning of the round.

Link Specifications. The point-to-point reliable and authenticated links guarantee the following properties [9]: *Reliable delivery* - if a correct process sends a message m to a correct process p_j, then p_j eventually receives m; *No duplication* - no message is delivered by a link to a process more than once; *Authenticity* - if some correct process p_j receives a message m with sender p_s, then m was previously sent to p_j by p_s.

3.1   Graph Metrics

We briefly recall some graph metrics that are employed to characterize reliable communication correctness conditions.

Sasaki et al. [24] defined $G(\alpha, \beta)$ as the class of graphs $G = (V, E)$ such that, for any pair i, j of vertices in V, there are α disjoint paths connecting i and j, whose length (in terms of the number of edges) is at most β.

A *k-clique community* is a graph defined as the union of all k-cliques (i.e., complete subgraphs of size k) that can be reached from each other through a series of adjacent k-cliques (where adjacency means sharing k-1 vertices).

Pelc and Peleg [21] defined the parameter $X(G)$ of a connected graph $G = (V, E)$: for every pair of nodes $i, j \in V$, $X(i, j)$ denotes the number of nodes $x \in \Gamma(i)^1$ that are closer to j than i; the parameter $X(G)$ is defined as the minimum $X(i, j)$ between any pair of not incident nodes, namely $X(G) := \min\{X(i, j) \mid i, j \in V, (i, j) \notin E\}$. The parameter $X(G)$ allows to arrange nodes of a graph G in disjoint level $L_0, L_1, \ldots L_j$ $(j \geq 1)$ with respect their distance to any chosen vertex $s \in V$ such that $L_0 = \{s\}$, $L_1 = \Gamma(s)$ and any node in a level L_i is at distance i from s and it has at least $X(G)$ neighbors in L_{i-1} (i.e. a *level ordering* [12]). A graphical example is provided in Fig. 1a.

Litsas et al. [12] defined the parameter $\Psi(G)$ of a graph G. Such a parameter allows to arrange nodes of graphs in disjoint level $L_0, L_1, \ldots L_j$ $(j \geq 1)$ with respect to any chosen vertex $s \in V$ such that $L_0 = \{s\}$, $L_1 = \Gamma(s)$ and any node in a level L_i has at least $\Psi(G)$ neighbors in levels $[L_1, L_{i-1}]$ (i.e. a *minimum level ordering* [12]). A graphical example is provided in Fig. 1b.

We refer with $\langle k, l \rangle$-*multipartite cycle* to a connected graph G composed by l sets of k not adjacent nodes, such that each set is part of exactly two complete bipartite subgraphs of $2k$ nodes. Figure 1c depicts an example of a $\langle 2, 4 \rangle$-multipartite cycle.

---

[1] $\Gamma(s)$ is the set of nodes in the neighborhood of node s in a graph.

All the graph parameters and topologies we recalled guarantee specific graph topological properties that will be leveraged addressing the reliable communication problem.

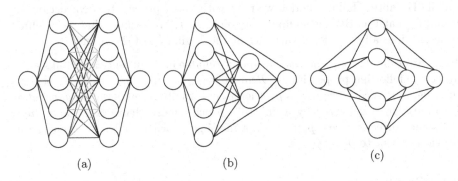

(a)   (b)   (c)

Fig. 1. (a) Level ordering with $X(G) = 5$. (b) Minimum Level ordering with $\Psi(G) = 5$. (c) $\langle 2, 4 \rangle$-multipartite cycle.

4 Mobile Byzantine Reliable Communication Problem Specification

Not all processes in a multi-hop network can directly exchange messages: some of them have to rely on intermediate nodes relaying their messages in order to communicate. Meanwhile, Byzantine faulty processes may diffuse *spurious messages*, i.e. messages that have not been sent by their advertised source. A reliable communication primitive prevent all correct processes from delivering spurious messages while allowing them to communicate.

We aim to define a mobile Byzantine fault tolerant *reliable communication* primitive in a multi-hop network of point-to-point reliable authenticated links, namely to enable message exchanges between every pair of processes extending the guarantees provided by the point-to-point links in a distributed system affected by Mobile Byzantine Faults.

The standard reliable communication (RC) specification [3,10,17,19,21] between a *source* process p_s and a *target* process p_t requires the following properties to be satisfied: *safety* - if a correct process p_t delivers a message m from p_s, then m has been sent by p_s; *liveness*: if a correct process p_s sends a message m to a correct process p_t, then m is eventually delivered by p_t.

In the system model we are considering, the failure state of processes change over time and no process is permanently correct. Furthermore, processes can be compromised while they are communicating, namely between the computation and send phase. It follows that every process which aims to communicate with a peer must remain correct for at least two consecutive rounds in order to diffuse any message, and thus, we define as *correct source* a process p_s that is correct for two consecutive rounds r_i and r_{i+1}, and computes a message m at r_i.

Another aspect to take into account is that a message may require several rounds to reach a target process, due to the network topology and to the protocol employed to diffuse it. As a matter of fact, the state of a process may change over time and a target process must not be permanently faulty in order to deliver a message sent by a source. Therefore, we say that a process p_j is *not permanently faulty* if for every round r_i there always exists a round $r' \geq r_i$ where p_j is correct.

Given all considerations stated above, we define a specification for the reliable communication problem with Mobile Byzantine Faults.

Reliable Communication with MBF Specification. Given a *correct source* process p_s and *target* process p_t, a reliable communication primitive guarantees that:

- *safety* - if p_t is correct at r_i and it delivers a message m from p_s, then m has been sent by p_s;
- *liveness*: if a correct source p_s sends a message m to a not permanently faulty process p_t, then p_t eventually delivers m.

5   Reliable Communication in Asynchronous Systems

In this section, we show that it is impossible to design a protocol $\mathcal{P}$ that is able to solve the reliable communication problem between a correct source p_s and a target p_t when the distributed system is asynchronous and there is only one mobile Byzantine agent. This motivates the subsequent assumptions for analyzing synchronous systems (see Sect. 6).

When assuming a fully asynchronous system, we consider that correct processes still execute a deterministic distributed protocol $\mathcal{P}$, but there is no known upper bound on the time demanded for local computation, neither on the time required to deliver point-to-point messages.

Theorem 1. *There exists no distributed protocol $\mathcal{P}$ that is able to solve the reliable communication problem specification with Mobile Byzantine Faults in an asynchronous system even if* (i) *the source process p_s is permanently correct,* (ii) *there exists only one mobile Byzantine agent, and* (iii) *processes are aware of their failure state.*

Proof. The reliable communication specification requires both safety and liveness property to be satisfied. We show that no protocol $\mathcal{P}$ can ensures the liveness property, even assuming an always correct source, only one mobile Byzantine agent and the aware failure model.

The reliable delivery property enforced by reliable and authenticated links is guaranteed only between correct processes. Given that there is no constraint on the link delay, even assuming a permanently correct source that continuously sends a message m, such a message may never be delivered by the link, because a target process p_t may be compromised during each transmission of m.   □

On the other hand, we highlight on the solvability of safe communication (i.e. enforcing only the safety property) in case of an asynchronous system.

The immediate consequence is that in the aware failure model, it is possible to design a "best-effort" protocol that ensures safety while trying to maximize the number of delivered messages.

Theorem 2. *Safe communication can be achieved with a non-degenerated protocol in an asynchronous distributed system in the aware mobile Byzantine failure model.*

Proof. We show a "best-effort" solution for the safe communication problem. Let us assume that every process p_j has access to a local clock T_j. It is reasonable to assume that a Byzantine agent which is forcing a process p_k to send a message m must remain on p_k till the end of its transmission to guarantee the link message delivery. Let us consider the following protocol:

- the source process p_s continuously sends $\langle s, t, m \rangle$;
- every process p_j stores every message $\langle s, t, m \rangle$ received from a process p_k jointly with timestamp $t^k_{\langle s,t,m \rangle}$ containing the value of T_j at the reception of $\langle s, t, m \rangle$;
- every process p_j stores and continuously relays any message $\langle s, t, m \rangle$ received from p_s;
- every process p_j that stores a set of $2f + 1$ tuples $M := [\langle \langle s, t, m \rangle, t^1_{\langle s,t,m \rangle} \rangle, \langle \langle s, t, m \rangle, t^2_{\langle s,t,m \rangle} \rangle, \ldots, \langle \langle s, t, m \rangle, t^{2f+1}_{\langle s,t,m \rangle} \rangle]$ received from distinct neighbors such that $\forall_{i<j}, t^i_{\langle s,t,m \rangle} < t^j_{\langle s,t,m \rangle}$ and $t^{2f+1}_{\langle s,t,m \rangle} - t^1_{\langle s,t,m \rangle} < \rho$ continuously relays $\langle s, t, m \rangle$;
- if process p_t relays $\langle s, t, m \rangle$ then it delivers m.

We show that the protocol defined above guarantees safety of reliable communication in an asynchronous system. Let us consider a single agent initially placed on a process $p_1 \neq p_s$, that starts the transmission of a spurious message $\tilde{m}$ to a process p_q at time t^{start}_1 and concludes at time t^{end}_1 when $\tilde{m}$ is received by p_q. Process p_q then stores $\tilde{m}$ and a timestamp $t^1_{\tilde{m}}$ obtained by its local clock at the reception of $\tilde{m}$. Subsequently, the Byzantine agent may move on a different process p_2 and start sending another copy of $\tilde{m}$ to p_q at time t^{start}_2, that it concludes at time t^{end}_2 when the message is received by p_q. Again, process p_q stores $\tilde{m}$ and a timestamp $t^2_{\tilde{m}}$. And once more, the agent can move another time on a process p_3 and iterate again the transmission of $\tilde{m}$. According with the absence of link latency guarantees, it could happen that $t^{end}_i - t^{start}_i \to 0$. On the other hand, $t^{j+2}_{\tilde{m}} - t^j_{\tilde{m}} > \rho$, because a mobile agent must move twice in order to send a spurious message for three distinct processes. It follows that, assuming f mobile Byzantine agents, if a process q receives more than $2f$ copies of a message m in a time windows shorter than ρ, then it can safely accept m. For ease of explanation, the execution stated above is depicted in Fig. 2. $\square$

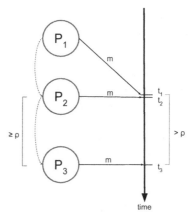

Fig. 2. Graphical execution example of Theorem 2.

6   Reliable Communication in Synchronous Systems

In this section, we briefly present the seminal reliable communication protocol defined by Sasaki et al. [24], and we define a new parameterized algorithm, *RCMB*.

Sasaki et al. [24] proposed a reliable communication protocol aimed to enable mobile Byzantine agreement on multi-hop networks. Their solution is based on the fact that mobile Byzantine agents may compromise at most f processes at every round: leveraging the disjoint paths available between all pairs of processes, they defined a reliable communication protocol that enables mobile Byzantine agreement in the unaware failure model in graphs $G(\alpha, \beta)$ where the inequality $\alpha > 2\beta f$ is satisfied. Specifically, messages between every pair of processes are routed over α disjoint paths and Byzantine agents may at most compromise βf of them.

RCMB Algorithm. We define a new protocol addressing the reliable communication problem, *RCMB*. With respect to the one proposed by Sasaki et al., it aims to keep the number of processes that concurrently send spurious messages bounded over time.

Algorithm *Reliable Communication Mobile Byzantines - RCMB:*

- the source process p_s computes message m addressed to a target process p_t at round r_i, and saves $\langle s, t, m \rangle$ in a set variable *delivered*.
- any message $\langle s, t, m \rangle$ stored in *delivered* is removed after τ rounds.
- every process p_j queues every message stored in *delivered* at round r_i to be sent in round r_{i+1} to itself and to all of its neighbors;
- if a correct process p_j receives a message $\langle s, t, m \rangle$ from p_s at round r_i, then p_j saves $\langle s, t, m \rangle$ in a set variable *delivered*, and delivers m from p_s if $j = t$;

– if a correct process p_j receives more than σ copies of a message $\langle s, t, m \rangle$ from distinct neighbors at round r_i, then p_j saves $\langle s, t, m \rangle$ in a set variable *delivered*, and delivers m from p_s if $j = t$;

The parameter σ is a safety threshold, corresponding to the number of copies of the same message that must concurrently be received to deliver it. The parameter τ allows processes that were faulty in the unaware failure model to remove spurious messages that may have been injected by malicious agents. It can be ignored in the aware failure model, because cured processes directly wipe their local variables. Notice that, in case of $\tau = 1$, every message stored in *delivered* at round r_i is queued to be sent at round r_{i+1} and then dropped.

6.1   Reliable Communication Correctness Conditions

We provide in this section several correctness conditions that enable to solve the reliable communication problem with one of the protocols presented in the previous subsection. We investigate the solvability of reliable communication in two scenarios: a correct source and a permanently correct source (that is, a source that is correct in every round r_i). The latter case is motivated by the fact that such additional assumption enables to solve the reliable communication problem in further topologies.

Unaware Failure Model

Theorem 3. *Reliable communication cannot be achieved in the unaware mobile Byzantine failure model with $n \leq 4f$.*

Proof. The result can be deduced from the lower bound implementing the safe register abstraction in the unaware mobile Byzantine failure model [4]. Let us consider a set of $4f$ processes connected through a complete communication network. Let us assume a correct source p_s that computes a message m at round r_0, that p_s sends it to all other processes at round r_1 and that p_t and other $f - 1$ processes are faulty at r_1. Thus, p_t is faulty while the reliable communication protocol is diffusing m according to a distributed protocol $\mathcal{P}$. Subsequently, the mobile Byzantine agents move on process p_s and on $f - 1$ other processes between rounds r_1 and r_2. It follows that at round r_2 there are $2f$ processes that share a state that contains m and $2f$ processes (f Byzantine faulty at r_2 and f that were faulty in r_1) that may share a state injected by the adversary, thus it is not possible to distinguish which set of processes is storing the message sent by the correct source. □

Theorem 4. *The RCMB protocol with $\sigma = (\tau + 1)f$ guarantees safety of reliable communication in the unaware mobile Byzantine failure model.*

Proof. Let us consider a set of n process connected through a complete network. Let us assume, for the ease of contradiction, that a target process p_t delivers a message m at round r_i from p_s but m has not been sent by its source (i.e. m is a spurious message).

The delivery of a message m in the $RCMB$ protocol is independent from the process local variables and it is only determined by the messages that are currently received in a round. On the other hand, the messages that are diffused in a round depends on the content of the *delivered* variable.

The message m has not been received by a process through a link with the source process p_s according to our hypothesis. It follows that there have been more than $\sigma = (\tau + 1)f$ processes that sent $\langle s, t, m \rangle$ to p_t at round r_i. Mobile Byzantine agents can force f processes to send $\langle s, t, m \rangle$ at round r_i and they can inject $\langle s, t, m \rangle$ in the *delivered* sent of the processes that were faulty at $r_{i-k}, k \in [1, \tau]$ if $\tau \geq 1$. Thus, at most τf correct processes may potentially relay $\langle s, t, m \rangle$ in a round because they were previously faulty, since after τ rounds $\langle s, t, m \rangle$ is dropped from the *delivered* set. Every other correct processes process $p_j \neq p_t$ sends $\langle s, t, m \rangle$ at r_i only if either p_j received such a message through a link with process p_s, or from more than $(\tau + 1)f$ neighbors. It follows that at most $(\tau + 1)f$ processes in the system may concurrently send $\langle s, t, m \rangle$. Thus message m has been sent by its source. This leads to a contradiction and the claim follows.   □

Theorem 5. *The RCMB protocol with $\tau = 1$ and $\sigma = (\tau + 1)f$ provides reliable communication in complete networks of size $n > 4f$ in the unaware mobile Byzantine failure model.*

Proof. We verified the safety property of the $RCMB$ protocol with $\sigma = (\tau + 1)f$ in the unaware mobile Byzantine failure model in Theorem 4. We need to prove the liveness property of reliable communication in a complete networks of size $n > 4f$ considering $\tau = 1$.

Let us assume a correct source p_s that computes a message m at r_0 and sends it at r_1 to itself and to all of its neighbors according to the $RCMB$ algorithm. It follows that more than $3f$ processes queue m to be sent at r_2, because m has been received through a link from its source. At any round r_i there are at most f processes that get faulty and at most f ones that were faulty in r_{i-1}. Thus, all correct processes receive at least $2f + 1$ copies of m from distinct nodes at any round $r_j \geq r_2$ and they relay it at the subsequent round. It follows that message m is relayed by at least $2f + 1 > \sigma$ processes on any round $r_j \geq r_2$, and that process p_t delivers it in a round $r_j \geq r_2$ it is correct.   □

Theorem 6. *The RCMB protocol with $\tau = 1$ and $\sigma = (\tau + 1)f$ provides reliable communication in the unaware mobile Byzantine failure model in a k-clique community network topology with $k > 4f + 1$.*

Proof. We verified the safety property of the $RCMB$ protocol with $\sigma = (\tau + 1)f$ in the unaware mobile Byzantine failure model in Theorem 4. We need to prove the liveness property of reliable communication in a k-clique community network topology with $k > 4f + 1$ considering $\tau = 1$.

Let us assume a correct source p_s that computes a message m at round r_0 and sends it at round r_1. Given a k-clique community network, two processes p_s and p_t are either both part of a k-clique or they are included in two distinct k-cliques that are connected through a sequence of adjacent ones.

Let us assume that p_s and p_t are both part of a k-clique $\mathcal{K}_0$. We showed in Theorem 5 that all correct processes in a complete network of at least $4f + 1$ nodes continuously relay a message m sent by a correct sender. It follows that t delivers m in a round $r_i \geq r_1$ it is correct.

Let us assume that p_t is part of a k-clique $\mathcal{K}_1$ adjacent to $\mathcal{K}_0$. All correct processes but $2f$ in $\mathcal{K}_0$ sends m at every round $r_j \geq r_{i+2}$ to all of their neighbors. It follows that p_t receives at least $2f+1 > \sigma$ copies of m on every round $r_j \geq r_{i+2}$ because it is connected to at least $4f + 1$ nodes in $\mathcal{K}_0$. Thus, it delivers m in a round $r_j \geq r_{i+2}$ it is correct.

Such an argumentation extends to any process in a k-clique reachable through a sequence of adjacent k-cliques.   □

Theorem 7. *The RCMB protocol with $\tau = 2$ and $\sigma = (\tau + 1)f$ provides reliable communication in the unaware mobile Byzantine failure model in a network topology G where $n > 6f$ and $X(G) > 6f$.*

Proof. The condition $X(G) > 6f$ allows to arrange nodes of a graph G in a level ordering of two or more levels $[L_0, \cdots L_k]$. Let us consider a correct source p_s that computes a message m at r_0 and sends it at round r_1.

Let us assume that the level ordering with respect to p_s is composed by 2 levels. It follows that all processes have a link with the source and that all the correct ones receive m at round r_1 directly from the source, thus they save it into their *delivered* set and relay it at r_2. Subsequently, the mobile Byzantine agents can move between r_1 and r_2. At round r_2 all correct processes are connected to at least $4f + 1 > \sigma$ processes that relays m. It follows they relay m at round r_3 and at all the subsequent rounds.

Let us assume that the level ordering with respect to p_s is composed by 3 or more levels. At round r_1 all correct processes in L_1 receive m directly from the source, thus they save it into their *delivered* set and they relay it at r_2. Subsequently, the mobile Byzantine agents can move between r_1 and r_2, and at round r_2 all correct processes in L_1 relay m to all nodes in L_2. Every process in L_2 has at least $6f + 1$ neighbors in L_1 and at least $4f + 1 > \sigma$ of them relay m. It follows they all save and relay m at round r_3. Between rounds r_2 and r_3 the mobile Byzantine agents move and compromise further f processes. It follows that at round r_3 every process in levels L_1, L_2 and L_3 receives m from at least $3f + 1 > \sigma$ processes, because each of them has at least $6f + 1$ neighbors inside the first three levels and at most $3f$ processes may have been compromised from the beginning of the transmission. It follows that all correct processes in the first three levels relay m at every round $r_i \geq r_4$. This reasoning extends considering more levels.   □

Theorem 8. *The RC Sasaki et al. protocol with $\sigma = \beta f$ provides reliable communication in the unaware mobile Byzantine failure model in networks where the inequality $\alpha > 2\beta f$ is satisfied [24].*

Proof. Every reliable communication instance between a source process p_s and a destination process p_t lasts exactly β rounds in the RC Sasaki et al. protocol. The inequality $\alpha > 2\beta f$ guarantees that between every pair of processes there exist at least $2\alpha + 1$ disjoint paths of length at most β. Any process can relay messages between peers p_s and p_t at only one defined round every β ones. It follows that the mobile Byzantine agents can compromise at most βf processes (and thus disjoint paths) in β rounds, and thus no correct process receive more than σ copies of a spurious message in a round. The assumption $\alpha > 2\beta f$ guarantees instead that there always exist $\beta f + 1$ disjoint paths that are not compromised by Byzantine agents in every communication instance. $\qquad\square$

Theorem 9. *The RCMB protocol with $\tau = 1$ and $\sigma = (\tau + 1)f$ provides reliable communication from a permanently correct source in the unaware mobile Byzantine failure model in networks where $\Psi(G) > 4f$.*

Proof. We verified the safety property of the RCMB algorithm with $\sigma = (\tau+1)f$ in the unaware mobile Byzantine failure model in Theorem 4. We need to prove the liveness property of reliable communication in networks where $\Psi(G) > 4f$ in case of a permanently correct source and $\tau = 1$.

The condition $\Psi(G) > 4f$ allows to arrange the nodes of a network G in a $(4f + 1)$-minimum level ordering with respect to every vertex of G.

Let us assume that process p_s sends a message m employing RCMB to process p_t at round r_i. Process p_t can either be in L_1 or in $L_{i>1}$. In the former case it receives m through a link from s starting from round $r_j \geq r_{i+1}$ it is correct, and thus it eventually delivers the message m. In the latter case, all correct processes in L_1 receive m at every round $r_j \geq r_{i+1}$. Thus, they queue m to be sent at every round $r_j \geq r_{i+2}$. At every round, there are at most f processes that can be faulty among all levels. It follows that at least $2f + 1$ processes in L_1 relay m to processes in L_2 at every round r_j, because f nodes may have been faulty at r_{j-1} and f ones are faulty at r_j. Therefore, all correct processes in L_2 relays m to all of their neighbors at every round $r_j \geq r_{i+3}$, and if process t is in L_2 then it delivers m at $r_j \geq r_{i+3}$ when it is correct. The reasoning extends to any other level given the assumption of $\Psi(G) > 4f$, and the claim follows. $\qquad\square$

Aware Failure Model

Theorem 10. *Reliable communication cannot be achieved in the aware mobile Byzantine failure model with $n \leq 3f$.*

Proof. The result can be deduced from the lower bound implementing the safe register abstraction in the aware mobile Byzantine failure model [4]. Let us consider a set of $3f$ processes connected through a complete communication network. Let us assume a correct source p_s that computes a message m at round

r_0, that p_s sends it to all other processes at round r_1 and that p_t and other $f - 1$ processes are faulty at r_1. Thus, p_t is faulty while the reliable communication protocol is diffusing m according to a distributed protocol $\mathcal{P}$. Subsequently, the mobile Byzantine agents moves on process p_s and on $f - 1$ other processes between rounds r_1 and r_2. It follows that at round r_2 there are f processes that share a state that contains m, f cured processes (i.e. with wiped local variables) and f faulty processes. Thus, it is not possible to distinguish which set of processes (the f faulty or the f not cured ones) is storing the message sent by the correct source. □

Theorem 11. *The RCMB protocol with $\sigma = f$ guarantees safety of reliable communication in the aware mobile Byzantine failure model.*

Proof. Let us consider a set of n process connected through a complete network. Let us assume, for the ease of contradiction, that a target process p_t has delivered a message m at round r_i from p_s but m has not been sent by its source (i.e. m is a spurious message).

The delivery of a message m in $RCMB$ is independent from the process local variables and it is only determined by the messages that are received in a round. The message m has been received by no process through a link with the source process p_s according to our hypothesis. It follows there have been more than $\sigma = f$ processes that sent $\langle s, t, m \rangle$ to p_t at round r_i. The mobile Byzantine agents can force f processes to send $\langle s, t, m \rangle$ at round r_i. The correct processes at r_i that were faulty at r_{i-1} turn to the cured state, thus they wipe their local variables (and thus their *delivered* set) and remove any message previously queued for the submission. Any correct process $p_j \neq p_t$ sends $\langle s, t, m \rangle$ at r_i only if either p_j has received such a message through a link with process p_s, or from more than f neighbors in a round. It follows that at most f processes in the system may concurrently send $\langle s, t, m \rangle$. Thus message m has been sent by its source. This leads to a contradiction and the claim follows. □

Theorem 12. *The RC Sasaki et al. protocol with $\sigma = (\beta - 1)f$ provides reliable communication in the aware mobile Byzantine failure model in networks where the inequality $\alpha > (2\beta - 1)f$ is satisfied.*

Proof. The cured processes remain silent, namely they drop every message previously queued for the submission. In the first round of a reliable communication instance, only the source is allowed to transmit. It follows that no process can diffuse spurious messages in such a round. Therefore, spurious messages can only traverse $(\beta - 1)f$ disjoint paths in a communication instance. On the other hand, Byzantine agents can still compromise f processes per round, preventing peers from receiving and relaying messages, and thus up to βf ones may be compromised in every communication instance. The inequality follow considering that $(\beta - 1)f + 1$ copies of a message received in a single round are sufficient to ensure safety and that at most βf process can be compromised during a communication instance. □

Theorem 13. *The RCMB protocol with $\sigma = f$ provides reliable communication in complete networks of size $n > 3f$ in the aware mobile Byzantine failure model.*

Proof. We verified the safety property of the RCMB algorithm with $\sigma = f$ in the aware mobile Byzantine failure model in Theorem 11. We need to prove the liveness property of reliable communication in a complete networks of size $n > 3f$.

Let us assume a correct source p_s that computes a message m at r_0 and sends it at r_1 to itself and to all of its neighbors according to the RCMB algorithm. It follows that p_s and at least $2f$ processes queue m to be sent at r_2, because m has been received through a link from its source. At any round r_i there are at most f processes that are faulty and at most f ones that were faulty in r_{i-1}. Thus, all correct processes receive at least $f + 1 > \sigma$ copies of m from distinct nodes at any round $r_j \geq r_2$ and they relay it in the subsequent round. It follows that message m is relayed by at least $f + 1$ processes at any round $r_j \geq r_2$, and that process p_t delivers it in a round $r_j \geq r_2$ it is correct. □

Theorem 14. *The RCMB protocol with $\sigma = f$ provides reliable communication in the aware mobile Byzantine failure model in (i) a k-clique community network topology with $k > 3f + 1$ and (ii) in topologies where $X(G) > 5f$.*

Proof. We verified the safety property of the RCMB algorithm with $\sigma = f$ in the unaware mobile Byzantine failure model in Theorem 11.

The liveness property in case of k-clique community networks with $k > 3f + 1$ or networks where $X(G) > 5f$ follows from the same argumentation provided respectively in Theorems 6 and 7 considering that σ is reduced to f. □

Theorem 15. *The RCMB protocol with $\sigma = f$ provides reliable communication from a permanent correct source in the aware mobile Byzantine failure model in networks where $\Psi(G) > 3f$.*

Proof. We verified the safety property of the RCMB algorithm with $\sigma = f$ in Theorem 11.

The liveness property in networks where $\Psi(G) > 3f$ follows from the same argumentation provided in Theorem 9 considering that σ is reduced to f. □

6.2   Graph Parameters Comparison

In this section we provide some examples of topology where the condition $\alpha > 2\beta f$ by Sasaki et al. [24] is not satisfied, but the reliable communication problem remains solvable.

Theorems 6 and 14 identify k-clique communities as a topology where the reliable communication problem is solvable. There exist topologies where $\alpha \leq 2\beta f$ but $k > 4f + 1$, and an example is depicted in Fig. 3a: a 6-clique community graph. According with Theorem 6, it is possible to provide reliable communication tolerating one mobile Byzantine agents ($f = 1$) in such a topology (indeed, $k > 4f + 1 = 5$) considering the unaware failure model with algorithm RCMB.

On the other hand, in such a graph $\beta = 3$ and $\alpha = 5$, thus the inequality $\alpha > 2\beta f$ is not satisfied for $f \geq 1$, so the algorithm by Sasaki et al. [24] does not guarantee reliable communication in such a network.

Theorems 9 and 15 identify graphs where the parameter $\Psi(G)$ is greater than certain values as topologies where the reliable communication problem is solvable from a permanent correct source. There exist topologies where $\alpha \leq 2\beta f$ but $\Psi(G) > 4f$, and an example is depicted in Fig. 3b. According with Theorem 8, one mobile Byzantine agent ($f = 1$) cannot be tolerated by the algorithm by Sasaki et al. [24], indeed $\alpha = 5$ and $\beta = 3$. Instead, $\Psi(G) > 4f$ in such an example, allowing to achieve reliable communication against one mobile Byzantine agent with algorithm RCMB.

The conditions defined in Theorems 7 and 14 identify new topologies where it is possible to solve the reliable communication problem. Specifically, there exist topologies where $\alpha \leq 2\beta f$ but $X(G) > 6f$. An example is depicted in Fig. 3c: a $\langle 7, 14 \rangle$-multipartite cycle. In such a network, $X(G) = 7$, $\alpha = 14$ and $\beta = 7$. According with Theorem 7 it is possible to achieve reliable communication against one mobile Byzantine agents (indeed, $X(G) > 6f$) with Algorithm RCMB. On the other hand the inequality $\alpha > 2\beta f$ is not satisfied in such a topology, so the algorithm by Sasaki et al. [24] cannot guarantee reliable communication in such a setting.

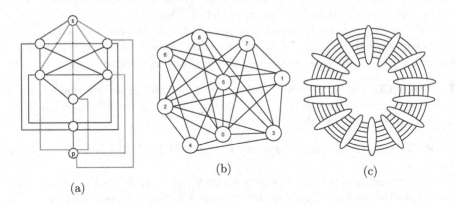

(a)   (b)   (c)

Fig. 3. (a) 6-clique community example. (b) $\Psi(G) = 5$, $\alpha > 2\beta f$ not satisfied with $f > 1$. (c) $\langle 7, 14 \rangle$-multipartite cycle.

7   Conclusion

We analyzed the reliable communication problem in distributed systems affected by Mobile Byzantine Faults. We highlighted the specific difficulties that arise when considering mobile malicious agents able to move in the system and to continuously compromise nodes. We shown that the reliable communication problem arises even in complete communication networks, and that it is not possible to address it in an asynchronous system. Then, starting from the only solution available in the literature (the one proposed by Sasaki et al. [24]), we provided additional insights about the specific properties that such protocols are able to guarantee. In more details, we defined a new reliable communication protocol, *RCMB*, and we identified new multi-hop topologies where reliable communication primitives remain feasible.

Our work paves the way toward deeper analyzes about reliable communication and others related distributed system problems with mobile Byzantine faults in multi-hop networks. A particularly interesting question is the feasibility of tolerating both mobile Byzantine failures and self-stabilization (as in the register construction of Bonomi et al. [6]) for the purpose of reliable communication. To our knowledge, this problem was only shown solvable by Maurer et al. [14] for the static Byzantine case.

References

1. Bonnet, F., Défago, X., Nguyen, T.D., Potop-Butucaru, M.: Tight bound on mobile Byzantine agreement. Theoret. Comput. Sci. **609**, 361–373 (2016). https://doi.org/10.1016/j.tcs.2015.10.019
2. Bonomi, S., Farina, G., Tixeuil, S.: Reliable broadcast in dynamic networks with locally bounded Byzantine failures. In: Izumi, T., Kuznetsov, P. (eds.) SSS 2018. LNCS, vol. 11201, pp. 170–185. Springer, Cham (2018). https://doi.org/10.1007/978-3-030-03232-6_12
3. Bonomi, S., Farina, G., Tixeuil, S.: Multi-hop Byzantine reliable broadcast with honest dealer made practical. J. Braz. Comput. Soc. **25**(1), 9:1–9:23 (2019). https://doi.org/10.1186/s13173-019-0090-x
4. Bonomi, S., Pozzo, A.D., Potop-Butucaru, M.: Optimal self-stabilizing synchronous mobile Byzantine-tolerant atomic register. Theoret. Comput. Sci. **709**, 64–79 (2018). https://doi.org/10.1016/j.tcs.2017.08.020
5. Bonomi, S., Pozzo, A.D., Potop-Butucaru, M., Tixeuil, S.: Optimal storage under unsynchronized mobile Byzantine faults. In: 36th IEEE Symposium on Reliable Distributed Systems, SRDS 2017, Hong Kong, 26–29 September 2017, pp. 154–163. IEEE Computer Society (2017). https://doi.org/10.1109/SRDS.2017.20
6. Bonomi, S., Del Pozzo, A., Potop-Butucaru, M., Tixeuil, S.: Brief announcement: optimal self-stabilizing mobile Byzantine-tolerant regular register with bounded timestamps. In: Izumi, T., Kuznetsov, P. (eds.) SSS 2018. LNCS, vol. 11201, pp. 398–403. Springer, Cham (2018). https://doi.org/10.1007/978-3-030-03232-6_28
7. Bonomi, S., Pozzo, A.D., Potop-Butucaru, M., Tixeuil, S.: Approximate agreement under mobile Byzantine faults. Theoret. Comput. Sci. **758**, 17–29 (2019). https://doi.org/10.1016/j.tcs.2018.08.001
8. Buhrman, H., Garay, J.A., Hoepman, J.: Optimal resiliency against mobile faults. In: Digest of Papers: FTCS-25, The Twenty-Fifth International Symposium on Fault-Tolerant Computing, Pasadena, California, USA, 27–30 June 1995, pp. 83–88. IEEE Computer Society (1995). https://doi.org/10.1109/FTCS.1995.466995
9. Cachin, C., Guerraoui, R., Rodrigues, L.E.T.: Introduction to Reliable and Secure Distributed Programming, 2nd edn. Springer, Heidelberg (2011). https://doi.org/10.1007/978-3-642-15260-3
10. Dolev, D.: Unanimity in an unknown and unreliable environment. In: 22nd Annual Symposium on Foundations of Computer Science, Nashville, Tennessee, USA, 28–30 October 1981, pp. 159–168 (1981). https://doi.org/10.1109/SFCS.1981.53

11. Garay, J.A.: Reaching (and maintaining) agreement in the presence of mobile faults (extended abstract). In: Tel, G., Vitányi, P. (eds.) WDAG 1994. LNCS, vol. 857, pp. 253–264. Springer, Heidelberg (1994). https://doi.org/10.1007/BFb0020438

12. Litsas, C., Pagourtzis, A., Sakavalas, D.: A graph parameter that matches the resilience of the certified propagation algorithm. In: Cichoń, J., Gębala, M., Klonowski, M. (eds.) ADHOC-NOW 2013. LNCS, vol. 7960, pp. 269–280. Springer, Heidelberg (2013). https://doi.org/10.1007/978-3-642-39247-4_23

13. Maurer, A., Tixeuil, S.: Byzantine broadcast with fixed disjoint paths. J. Parallel Distrib. Comput. **74**(11), 3153–3160 (2014). https://doi.org/10.1016/j.jpdc.2014.07.010

14. Maurer, A., Tixeuil, S.: Self-stabilizing Byzantine broadcast. In: 33rd IEEE International Symposium on Reliable Distributed Systems, SRDS 2014, Nara, Japan, 6–9 October 2014, pp. 152–160. IEEE Computer Society (2014). https://doi.org/10.1109/SRDS.2014.10

15. Maurer, A., Tixeuil, S.: Containing Byzantine failures with control zones. IEEE Trans. Parallel Distrib. Syst. **26**(2), 362–370 (2015). https://doi.org/10.1109/TPDS.2014.2308190

16. Maurer, A., Tixeuil, S.: Tolerating random Byzantine failures in an unbounded network. Parallel Process. Lett. **26**(1), 1650003:1–1650003:12 (2016). https://doi.org/10.1142/S0129626416500031

17. Maurer, A., Tixeuil, S., Défago, X.: Communicating reliably in multihop dynamic networks despite Byzantine failures. In: 34th IEEE Symposium on Reliable Distributed Systems, SRDS 2015, Montreal, QC, Canada, 28 September–1 October 2015, pp. 238–245. IEEE Computer Society (2015). https://doi.org/10.1109/SRDS.2015.10

18. Ostrovsky, R., Yung, M.: How to withstand mobile virus attacks (extended abstract). In: Logrippo, L. (ed.) Proceedings of the Tenth Annual ACM Symposium on Principles of Distributed Computing, Montreal, Quebec, Canada, 19–21 August 1991, pp. 51–59. ACM (1991). https://doi.org/10.1145/112600.112605

19. Pagourtzis, A., Panagiotakos, G., Sakavalas, D.: Reliable broadcast with respect to topology knowledge. Distrib. Comput. **30**(2), 87–102 (2017). https://doi.org/10.1007/s00446-016-0279-6

20. Pelc, A.: Reliable communication in networks with Byzantine link failures. Networks **22**(5), 441–459 (1992). https://doi.org/10.1002/net.3230220503

21. Pelc, A., Peleg, D.: Broadcasting with locally bounded Byzantine faults. Inf. Process. Lett. **93**(3), 109–115 (2005). https://doi.org/10.1016/j.ipl.2004.10.007

22. Reischuk, R.: A new solution for the Byzantine generals problem. Inf. Control **64**(1–3), 23–42 (1985). https://doi.org/10.1016/S0019-9958(85)80042-5

23. Sakavalas, D., Tseng, L.: Delivery delay and mobile faults. In: 17th IEEE International Symposium on Network Computing and Applications, NCA 2018, Cambridge, MA, USA, 1–3 November 2018, pp. 1–8. IEEE (2018). https://doi.org/10.1109/NCA.2018.8548345

24. Sasaki, T., Yamauchi, Y., Kijima, S., Yamashita, M.: Mobile Byzantine agreement on arbitrary network. In: Baldoni, R., Nisse, N., van Steen, M. (eds.) OPODIS 2013. LNCS, vol. 8304, pp. 236–250. Springer, Cham (2013). https://doi.org/10.1007/978-3-319-03850-6_17

25. Tseng, L., Vaidya, N.H., Bhandari, V.: Broadcast using certified propagation algorithm in presence of Byzantine faults. Inf. Process. Lett. **115**(4), 512–514 (2015). https://doi.org/10.1016/j.ipl.2014.11.010

Infinite Grid Exploration by Disoriented Robots

Quentin Bramas[1], Stéphane Devismes[2(✉)], and Pascal Lafourcade[3]

[1] University of Strasbourg, ICUBE, CNRS, Strasbourg, France
[2] Université Grenoble Alpes, VERIMAG, Saint-Martin-d'Héres, France
`stephane.devismes@univ-grenoble-alpes.fr`
[3] University Clermont Auvergne, CNRS UMR 6158, LIMOS, Clermont-Ferrand, France

Abstract. We study the *infinite grid exploration* (IGE) problem by a swarm of autonomous mobile robots. Those robots are opaque, have limited visibility capabilities, and run using synchronous Look-Compute-Move cycles. They all agree on a common chirality, but have no global compass. Finally, they may use lights of different colors that can be seen by robots in their surroundings, but except from that, robots have neither persistent memories, nor communication mean. We show that using only three fixed colors, six robots, with a visibility range restricted to one, are necessary and sufficient to solve the non-exclusive IGE problem. We show that using modifiable colors with only five states, five such robots, with a visibility range restricted to one, are necessary and sufficient to solve the (exclusive) IGE problem. Assuming a visibility range of two, we also provide an algorithm that solves the IGE problem using only seven identical robots without any light.

1   Introduction

We deal with a swarm of mobile robots having low computation and communication capabilities. The robots we consider are opaque (*i.e.*, a robot is able to see another robot if and only if no other robot lies in the line segment joining them) and run in synchronous Look-Compute-Move cycles, where they can sense their surroundings within a limited visibility range. All robots agree on a common chirality (*i.e.*, when a robot is located on an axis of symmetry in its surroundings, it is able to distinguish its two sides one from another), but have no global compass (they agree neither on a North-South, nor a East-West direction). However, they may use lights of different colors [17]. These lights can be seen by robots in their surroundings. However, except from those lights, robots have neither persistent memories nor communication capabilities.

We are interested in coordinating such weak robots, endowed with both typically small visibility range (*i.e.*, one or two) and few light colors (only a constant number of them), to solve an infinite task in an infinite discrete environment. As an attempt to tackle this general problem, we consider the exploration of an infinite grid, where nodes represent locations that can be sensed by robots and edges represent the possibility for a robot to move from one location to another. The exploration task requires each node

This study has been partially supported by the ANR projects DESCARTES (ANR-16-CE40-0023) and ESTATE (ANR-16-CE25-0009). Moreover, a preliminary version of this paper has been presented as a *brief announcement* at SIROCCO'2019 [5].

© Springer Nature Switzerland AG 2021
C. Georgiou and R. Majumdar (Eds.): NETYS 2020, LNCS 12129, pp. 129–145, 2021.
https://doi.org/10.1007/978-3-030-67087-0_9

to be visited within finite time by at least one robot. In the following, we refer to it as the *Infinite Grid Exploration* (IGE) problem.

Contribution. We give both negative and positive results. We first show that if robots have a common chirality but a bounded visibility range, the IGE problem is unsolvable with:

- two robots, even if those robots agree on common North (the proof of this result is essentially an adaptation to our context of the impossibility proof given in [13]);
- three or four robots equipped with self-inconsistent compasses (*i.e.*, the compasses may change throughout the execution).
- five robots equipped with self-inconsistent compasses if the visibility range is restricted to one, and the lights have fixed (*i.e.*, non-modifiable) colors.

We then propose three algorithms, respectively called $\mathcal{A}_1^{Fixed}$, $\mathcal{A}_1^{Modifiable}$, and $\mathcal{A}_2^{nolight}$, for solving the IGE problem using opaque robots equipped with self-inconsistent compass, yet agreeing on a common chirality. In particular, $\mathcal{A}_1^{Modifiable}$ and $\mathcal{A}_2^{nolight}$ additionally satisfy *exclusiveness* [2], which requires any two robots to never simultaneously occupy the same position nor traverse the same edge. In more detail, Algorithm $\mathcal{A}_1^{Fixed}$ solves the non-exclusive IGE problem using six robots with visibility range restricted to one, and only three fixed (*i.e.*, non-modifiable) colors. In this setting, the algorithm is optimal in terms of number of robots. In Algorithm $\mathcal{A}_1^{Modifiable}$, five robots use modifiable colors with only five states, still with visibility range one. In this setting, the algorithm is optimal in terms of number of robots; moreover it ensures exclusiveness. Algorithm $\mathcal{A}_2^{nolight}$ requires seven identical robots without light (*i.e.*, seven anonymous oblivious[1] robots) and ensures exclusiveness, yet assuming visibility range two. In order to help the reader, animations are available online [6], for each of the three algorithms.

Related Work. The model of robots with lights (also called luminous robots) has been proposed by Peleg in [17]. In [8], the authors use robots with lights and compare the computational power of such robots with respect to the three main execution models: fully-synchronous, semi-synchronous, and asynchronous. Solutions for dedicated problems such as *weak gathering* or *mutual visibility* have been respectively investigated in [15] and [16].

Mobile robot computing in infinite environments has been first studied in the continuous two-dimensional Euclidean space. In this context, studied problems are mostly *terminating* tasks, such as *pattern formation* [11] and *gathering* [14], *i.e.*, problems where robots aim at eventually stopping in a particular configuration specified by their relative positions. A notable exception is the *flocking* problem [18], *i.e.*, the infinite task consisting of forming a desired pattern with the robots and make them moving together while maintaining that formation.

When considering a discrete environment, space is defined as a graph, where the nodes represent the possible locations that a robot can take and the edges the possibility for a robot to move from one location to another. In this setting, researchers have first considered finite graphs and two variants of the exploration problem, respectively called the *terminating* and *perpetual* exploration. The terminating exploration requires

---

[1] *Oblivious* means that robots cannot remember the past.

every possible location to be eventually visited by at least one robot, with the additional constraint that all robots stop moving after task completion. In contrast, the perpetual exploration requires each location to be visited infinitely often by all or a part of robots. In [9], authors solve terminating exploration of any finite grid using few asynchronous anonymous oblivious robots, yet assuming unbounded visibility range. The exclusive perpetual exploration of a finite grid is considered in the same model in [3].

Various terminating problems have been investigated in infinite grids such as *arbitrary pattern formation* [4], *mutual visibility* [1], and *gathering* [10, 12]. The possibly closest related work to our paper is that of Emek *et al.* [13]. They consider the *treasure search problem in an unbounded-size grid* which is closely related to the IGE problem; see [7]. They consider robots that operate in two models: the semi-synchronous and synchronous ones. However, they do not impose the exclusivity at all since their robots can only sense the states of the robots located at the same node (in that sense, the visibility range is zero). The main difference with our settings is that they assume all robots agree on a *global compass*, *i.e.*, they all agree on the same directions North-South and East-West; while we only assume here a *common chirality*. This difference makes the problem somehow easier to solve, indeed they propose two algorithms that respectively need three synchronous and four semi-synchronous robots, while in our settings we show that at least five robots are necessary to solve the IGE problem (even in its non-exclusive variant). Notice that they also exclude solutions for two robots.

In a followup paper [7], Brandt *et al.* extend the impossibility result of Emek *et al.* Indeed, they show the impossibility of *exploring an infinite grid* with three semi-synchronous deterministic robots that agree on a common coordinate system. Although proven using similar techniques, this result is not correlated to ours. Indeed, the lower bound of Brandt *et al.* holds for robots that are weaker in terms of synchrony assumption (semi-synchrony *vs.* fully synchrony in our case), but stronger in terms of coordination capabilities (common coordinate system *vs.* self-inconsistent compass with a common chirality in our case). In other words, our impossibility results do not (even indirectly) follow from those of Brandt *et al.* since in our model difficulties arise from the lack of coordination capabilities and not the level asynchrony. As a matter of facts, based on the results of Emek *et al.* [13], four (asynchronous) robots are actually necessary and sufficient in their settings, while we show that it is five in our context.

Roadmap. In the next section, we define our computational model. In Sect. 3, we present several lower bounds on the number of robots to solve the IGE problem. In Sect. 4 and Sect. 5, we propose algorithms solving the IGE problem under visibility range one and two, respectively. We conclude with some perspectives in Sect. 6.

Due to the lack of space, some technical results are omitted.

2   Model

We consider a set of $n > 0$ robots located on an *infinite grid* graph with vertex set in $\mathbb{Z} \times \mathbb{Z}$, *i.e.*, there is an edge between two nodes (i, j) and (k, l) if and only if the *Manhattan distance* between those two nodes, *i.e.*, $|i - k| + |j - l|$, is one. Notice that coordinates are used for the analysis only, *i.e.*, robots cannot access them.

We assume time is discrete and at each *round*, the robots synchronously perform a *Look-Compute-Move* cycle. In the *Look* phase, a robot gets a snapshot of the subgraph induced by the nodes within distance $\Phi \in \mathbb{N}^*$ from its position. Φ is called the *visibility range* of the robots. The snapshot is not oriented in any way as the robots do not agree on a common North. However, it is implicitly ego-centered since the robot that performs a Look phase is located at the center of the subgraph in the obtained snapshot. Then, each robot *computes* a destination (either Up, Left, Down, Right or Idle) based only on the snapshot it received. Finally, it *moves* towards its computed destination. We also assume that robots are *opaque* and can obstruct the visibility so that if three robots are aligned, the two extremities cannot see each other.

Robots may have *lights* with different colors that can be seen by robots within distance Φ from them. Let Cl be the set of possible colors. Even when an algorithm does not achieve exclusiveness, we forbid any two robots to occupy the same node simultaneously. A node is *occupied* when a robot is located at this node, otherwise it is *empty*. The *state* of a node is either the light color of the robot located at this node, if it is occupied, or $\perp$ otherwise. In the Look phase, the snapshot includes the state of the nodes (at distance Φ). During the compute phase, and if colors are *modifiable*, a robot may decide to change its color. Otherwise, colors are said to be *fixed*.

Configurations. A *configuration* C is a set of pairs (p, c) where $p \in \mathbb{Z} \times \mathbb{Z}$ is an occupied node and $c \in Cl$ is the light color of the robot located at p. A node p is empty if and only if $\forall c, (p, c) \notin C$. We sometimes just write the set of occupied nodes when the colors are clear from the context. Also, for better readability, we sometimes partition the configuration into several subsets $C_1, \ldots, C_k$ and write $C = \{C_1, \ldots, C_k\}$ instead of writing $(C = C_1 \cup \ldots \cup C_k) \wedge (\forall i \neq j, C_i \cap C_j = \emptyset)$.

Views. We denote by G_r the *globally oriented view* centered at the robot r, *i.e.*, the subset of the configuration containing the states of the nodes at distance at most Φ from r, translated so that the coordinates of r is $(0, 0)$. We use this globally oriented view in our analysis to describe the movements of the robots: when we say "the robot moves Up", it is according to the globally oriented view. However, since robots do not agree on a common North, they have no access to the globally oriented view. Instead, when a robot looks at its surroundings, it obtains a snapshot. To model this, we assume that, the *local view* acquired by a robot r in the Look phase is the result of an arbitrary *indistinguishable transformation* on G_r. The set $\mathcal{IT}$ of indistinguishable transformations is closed by composition and depends on the assumptions we make on the robots. The rotations of angle $\pi/2$, and consequently of angle π and $3\pi/2$, centered at r are in $\mathcal{IT}$ if and only if the robots do not agree on a common North direction. A mirroring is in $\mathcal{IT}$ if and only if the robots do not agree on a common *chirality* (they cannot distinguish between clockwise and counterclockwise). Moreover, in the obstructed visibility model, the function that removes the state of a node u if there is another robot between u and r is in $\mathcal{IT}$ and is systematically applied. For a robot r, if the same transformation $f_r \in \mathcal{IT}$ is used for every look phase of r, we say that r is *self-consistent*. Otherwise, the adversary can choose a different transformation for each look phase, and r is said to be *self-inconsistent*.

In the remaining of the paper, all our algorithms assume that all robots agree on a common chirality, *i.e.*, they can distinguish two mirrored views, but we make no assumption on the self-consistency of the coordinate system. On the other hand, we give impossibility results for stronger models when possible.

When a robot r computes a destination d, it is relative to its local view $f(G_r)$, which is its globally oriented view G_r transformed by some $f \in \mathcal{IT}$. It is important to see that the actual movement of the robot in its globally oriented view G_r, and so in the configuration, is $f^{-1}(d)$. Indeed, if $d = Up$ but the robot sees the grid upside-down (f is the π-rotation), then the robot moves $Down = f^{-1}(Up)$. In a configuration C, $V_C(i,j)$ denotes the globally oriented view of a robot located at (i,j).

Algorithm. An algorithm $\mathcal{A}$ is a tuple (Cl, I, T) where Cl is the set of possible colors, I is the initial configuration, and T is the transition function $Views \rightarrow \{Idle, Up, Left, Down, Right\} \times Cl$, where $Views$ is the set of globally oriented views.

Recall that we assume in our algorithms that the robots are not self-consistent. In this context, we say that an algorithm (Cl, I, T) is *well-defined* if the global destination computed by a robot does not depend on the transformation f chosen by the adversary, *i.e.*, for every globally oriented view V, and every transformation $f \in \mathcal{IT}$, we have $T(V) = f^{-1}(T(f(V)))$. This is usually a property obtained by construction of the algorithm, as we describe the destination d for a given globally oriented view V and then assume that the destination computed from local view $f(V)$ is $f(d)$, for any $f \in \mathcal{IT}$. We can extend the transition function T to the entire configuration. When the robots are in configuration C, the configuration obtained after one round of execution is denoted $T(C)$ and contains the pair $((i,j),c)$ if and only if $\exists c' \in Cl$ for which one of the following conditions holds

- $((i,j),c') \in C$ and $T(V_C(i,j)) = (Idle, c)$,
- $((i-1,j),c') \in C$ and $T(V_C(i-1,j)) = (Right, c)$,
- $((i+1,j),c') \in C$ and $T(V_C(i+1,j)) = (Left, c)$,
- $((i,j-1),c') \in C$ and $T(V_C(i,j-1)) = (Up, c)$,
- $((i,j+1),c') \in C$ and $T(V_C(i,j+1)) = (Down, c)$.

The execution of algorithm $\mathcal{A}$ is the sequence $(C_i)_{i \in \mathbb{N}}$ of configurations such that $C_0 = I$ and $\forall i \geq 0$, $C_{i+1} = T(C_i)$. We sometimes write $\mathcal{A}(C)$ instead of $T(C)$.

Infinite Grid Exploration. An algorithm $\mathcal{A}$ solves the *infinite grid exploration* (IGE) problem if in the execution $(C_i)_{i \in \mathbb{N}}$ of $\mathcal{A}$ and for every node $(i,j) \in \mathbb{Z} \times \mathbb{Z}$ of the grid, there exists $t \in \mathbb{N}$ such that (i,j) is occupied in C_t.

Notations. $t_{(i,j)}(C)$ denotes the translation of the configuration C of vector (i,j).

3   Impossibility Results

The lemma below states the intuitive, yet non trivial, idea that, to explore an infinite grid, the maximum distance between the two farthest robots should tend to infinity. This claim is the cornerstone of our impossibility results.

Lemma 1. *Let $(C_i)_{i \in \mathbb{N}}$ be an execution of an algorithm $\mathcal{A}$. Let d_i be the distance between the two farthest robots in C_i. If $\mathcal{A}$ solves the IGE problem, then $\lim\limits_{i \to +\infty} d_i = +\infty$.*

Proof. We proceed by the contradiction. So we suppose there exists a bound $B > 0$ such that there are infinitely many configurations in the execution where the distance between every pair of robots is less than B. In other words, there is a subsequence of $(C_i)_{i \in \mathbb{N}}$ where the distance between every pair of robots is less than B. Let $(b_i)_{i \in \mathbb{N}}$ be the sequence of indices of this subsequence, *i.e.*, $(b_i)_{i \in \mathbb{N}}$ is a strictly increasing sequence of integers such that $d_{b_i} < B$.

When all robots are at distance less than B, then the occupied positions are included in a square sub-grid of size $B \times B$. Since the number of possible configurations included in a sub-grid of size $B \times B$ is finite, there must be two indices k and l such that $C_{b_l} = t(C_{b_k})$ and $k < l$ for a given translation t. The movements done by the robots in configurations C_{b_k} and C_{b_l} are the same because each robot has the same globally oriented view in both configurations, only their positions change. Thus $C_{b_l+1} = t(C_{b_k+1})$ and so on so forth, so that $\forall i$, $C_{b_l+i} = t(C_{b_k+i})$. We obtain that the configurations are periodic (with period $P = b_l - b_k$) and a node u is visited if and only if it is visited before round b_l or if there exists a node v visited between round b_k and b_l such that $u = t^q(v)$ with $q > 0$. So, we claim that there exists a node that is never visited.

To prove this claim, we now exhibit such a node. Let I be the set of integers i such that $(t^{-1})^i(0,0)$ is visited before round b_l applied i times. I is finite because the number of nodes visited before b_l is finite. Let m be the maximum integer in I (or 0 if I is empty). Let $u = (t^{-1})^{m+1}(0,0)$. Then, clearly u is not visited before round b_l, otherwise we have a contradiction with the maximality of m. Moreover, u cannot be visited after round b_l, otherwise u would be equals to $t^q(v)$ for a given integer q and a given node v, visited between round b_k and b_l, *i.e.*, $v = (t^{-1})^q(u) = (t^{-1})^{q+m+1}(0,0)$, which also contradicts the maximality of m. Thus u is never visited.

Theorem 1. *No algorithm can solve the IGE problem using two robots, even if robots agree on common North and chirality.*

Proof. By Lemma 1, there is a configuration from which the two robots will no more see each other (their distance will remain greater than an arbitrary bound $B \geq \Phi$). For each robot, its next move will only depend on its color. Since the number of color is finite, the movements of each robot are then periodic. So, from that point, each robot r moves by periodically performing the same translation t_r, and thus some nodes are never visited. $\qquad\square$

Lemma 2. *Assume the robots are equipped with self-inconsistent compasses, yet agree on a common chirality. Whenever a robot does not see any other one, it either stays idle or the adversary can make it alternatively move between two chosen adjacent nodes.*

Proof. If such a robot does not stay idle, it moves toward a direction $d \in \{Up, Down, Left, Right\}$ but since its orientation is not self-consistent, the adversary can choose, for each activation, a transformation $f \in \mathcal{IT}$ such that the destination $f^{-1}(d)$ in the globally oriented view alternate between two chosen directions (*e.g.*, Up and $Down$). $\qquad\square$

Theorem 2. *It is impossible to solve the IGE problem using three robots equipped with self-inconsistent compasses that agree on a common chirality.*

Proof. By Lemma 1, there is a configuration where two robots are always at distance at least B (say $B > 2 \cdot \Phi + 2$), so that it is impossible for any robot to see the all others in the same snapshot. Now, since there are three robots, at least one robot r does not see any other robot. By Lemma 2, if r stays alone, then it remains idle or the adversary can make it alternatively move between two nodes infinitely often. Moreover, the two other robots cannot explore the grid alone, by Theorem 1. Now, they cannot both move towards r because in such a case the distance between the farthest robots would become less than B, a contradiction. Finally, if one of the two other robots moves towards r, at some point all robots are out of the visibility range of each other. In that case, the adversary can make the exploration fail, by Lemma 2.   □

Due to the lack of space, the proofs of the next two theorems are only sketched.

Theorem 3. *It is impossible to solve the IGE problem using four robots equipped with self-inconsistent compasses that agree on a common chirality.*

Proof Outline. Assume, by contradiction, that an algorithm $\mathcal{A}$ solves the IGE problem using four robots equipped with self-inconsistent compasses that agree on a common chirality. Then, using Lemma 1, we consider a round where the two farthest robots, called here *extremities*, are always at distance $B \gg \Phi$. Since we know three robots are not enough, no robot stays alone forever. Therefore, infinitely often, there is a moving group of two robots traveling from one extremity to the other. Moreover, whenever traveling an arbitrary long distance, a group of robots necessarily uses periodic movements. We can then show that these periodic movements induce that after some time, the moving group travels infinitely often between two extremities by periodically performing the same translation. This latter claim implies that, after some time, the movements of the robots depend only on configurations of bounded size, which in turn implies that the movements of the two extremities are periodic. Since extremities eventually perform periodic movements, they each one move inside a strip of bounded width that grows in only one direction. Hence, whether they move along collinear vectors or not, the algorithm misses nodes forever in the exploration process.   □

Theorem 4. *It is impossible to solve the IGE problem using five robots with self-inconsistent compasses, a common chirality, fixed colors, and visibility range one.*

Proof Outline. First, one can generalize the notion of extremities, not only to be the two farthest robots, but to be a set of k gathering of robots, whose pairwise distances tend to infinity. Similarly to the previous theorem, one can prove that each extremity eventually follows a single vector, even if two robots remains close to an extremity. This is because the movements of the robots near an extremity are independent from the distances to the other extremities, and hence are periodic.

Since there are at least two robots in the moving group, there are at most three extremities. If there are only two extremities, the same conclusions as the previous theorem applies, hence one can assume there are three extremities, delimiting a triangle. Moreover, since colors are fixed, the moving group can only travel between two extremities in a straight line (vertically or horizontally). Hence the extremities form a right triangle (or a line but in this case again the previous result applies) and the moving group cannot travel along the hypotenuse, so that the algorithm misses nodes forever in the exploration process.   □

4 Infinite Grid Exploration with $\Phi = 1$

In this section, we present two algorithms assuming visibility range one. The former, Algorithm $\mathcal{A}_1^{Fixed}$, uses six robots with three fixed colors. The latter, Algorithm $\mathcal{A}_1^{Modifiable}$, uses five robots with five modifiable colors and additionally achieves exclusiveness. Recall that animations of these two algorithms are available in our complementary material [6]. The fact that the rules of these algorithms are well-defined has been checked by the script that generated those animations. This has been done by making sure that (1) the view of any rule cannot be transformed into the view of another rule using a combination of $\frac{\pi}{2}$-rotations, and (2) for each rule, the global destination does not depend on the applied local indistinguishable transformation.

4.1 An Algorithm Using Six Robots and Three Fixed Colors

Algorithm Overview. First, our robots are divided into two categories: the *beacon robots*—four robots with color B—and the *moving group*—two robots with respective color L and F. The beacons are used to delimit the area which is already explored. The moving group aims at reaching the beacons one by one. Each time a beacon is reached by the moving group, it moves once in the diagonal (two hops) to take the newly explored nodes into account. The moving group then continues toward the next beacon, and so on. Each time the moving group comes back to the first beacon, a so-called *phase* terminates: the border of the area initially delimited by the four beacons is now fully visited, and the area newly delimited by the beacons is bigger; see Fig. 2 to visualize the increasing area that is explored by the moving group (r_L is a particular robot of the moving group, whose role will be explained later).

The moving group successfully performs a phase independently of the distance between the beacons, so that infinitely many growing phases are achieved in sequence. The IGE is then solved as any node of the grid is eventually included in the area delimited by the beacons. Note that we use the same technique for the two other algorithms, yet using areas of different shapes.

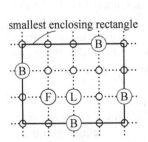

Fig. 1. Initial configuration of Algorithm $\mathcal{A}_1^{Fixed}$.

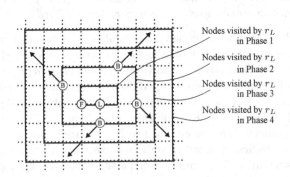

Fig. 2. Visited area after four phases for $\mathcal{A}_1^{fixed}$.

Definition of Algorithm $\mathcal{A}_1^{Fixed}$. We use the set of colors $Cl = \{L, F, B\}$ to partially distinguish robots. The moving group is composed of two robots: one with light color L called the *leader*, and the other with light color F called the *follower*. The four remaining robots, *i.e.*, the beacons, have light color B. The initial configuration I of $\mathcal{A}_1^{Fixed}$ is defined as follows: $I = \{((-1,0), F), ((0,0), L), ((0,-1), B), ((2,0), B), ((1,2), B), ((-2,1), B)\}$; see Fig. 1.

Recall that $\mathcal{A}_1^{Fixed}$ executes in phases. At the beginning of each phase, we consider the smallest enclosing rectangle, denoted by SER, that encloses the four beacon robots, *e.g.*, in Fig. 1, the SER of the initial configuration I is drawn with solid lines. During a phase, the follower robot r_F explores the borders of the SER, while the leader robot r_L visits the borders of the largest rectangle strictly inside the SER. First, the moving group $\{r_L, r_F\}$ moves straight until the leader robot becomes a neighbor of a beacon robot.

Then, the positions of three robots are *adjusted* so that (1) the moving group $\{r_L, r_F\}$ makes a turn, and (2) the beacon robot moves diagonally (two hops) in order to expand the SER. (Notice the execution starts by an adjustment.) Overall, at the end of Phase i (and so at the beginning of Phase $i + 1$), both the length and width of SER increases by two.

The rules of $\mathcal{A}_1^{Fixed}$ are defined in Figs. 4, 5, and 6. Some rules aim at moving the group of robots $\{r_L, r_F\}$ straight and the others are used to manage an *adjustment*. In the following, we detail how $\{r_L, r_F\}$ moves straight toward a beacon robot, does a left turn, and how the reached beacon robot moves diagonally. Recall that the rules below also describe the algorithm behavior on equivalent, rotated, local views.

Using Rules of Fig. 6, if we apply $\mathcal{A}_1^{Fixed}$ to $\{((i,j), L), ((i+1,j), F)\}$, we obtain $\{((i, j+1), L), ((i+1, j+1), F)\}$, *i.e.*, the two robots go through the translation $t_{(0,1)}$. So, the group $\{r_L, r_F\}$ moves on a straight line when isolated. If we rotate the two robots with angle $\pi/2$, π, or $3\pi/2$, then the moving group will move to the left, down, or right, respectively. In fact, the direction of the translation actually depends on the relative positions of r_L and r_F.

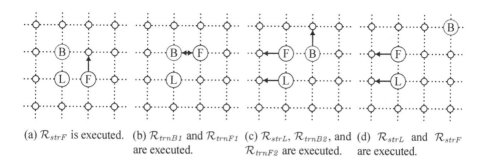

(a) $\mathcal{R}_{strF}$ is executed. (b) $\mathcal{R}_{trnB1}$ and $\mathcal{R}_{trnF1}$ (c) $\mathcal{R}_{strL}$, $\mathcal{R}_{trnB2}$, and (d) $\mathcal{R}_{strL}$ and $\mathcal{R}_{strF}$
                                      are executed. $\mathcal{R}_{trnF2}$ are executed.   are executed.

Fig. 3. Robots performing a turn.

Before giving the rules for the adjustments and in order to clearly explain how our algorithm works, we show in Fig. 3 the global configurations that occur when the

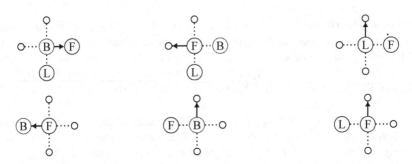

Fig. 4. $\mathcal{R}_{trnB1}$ and $\mathcal{R}_{trnF1}$.   **Fig. 5.** $\mathcal{R}_{trnB2}$ and $\mathcal{R}_{trnF2}$.   **Fig. 6.** $\mathcal{R}_{strL}$ and $\mathcal{R}_{strF}$.

moving group reaches the upper right beacon robot. In the first round, the follower (only) moves straight, as previously, to become neighbor of the beacon. In the second round, the beacon and the follower swap their positions, while the leader stays idle. In the third round, the beacon moves up to finalize its diagonal motion, while the moving group $\{r_L, r_F\}$ starts to move again in a straight line toward the left.

In more details, for the first round, there is no rule when r_L sees a beacon robot, thus, when it happens r_L stays idle and r_F continues to move one more time. For the second round, according to the rules of Fig. 4, when r_F only sees the beacon robot, it moves towards it, and when the beacon sees both r_F and r_L, it moves toward r_F, so that they swap their positions, while r_L stays idle. Finally, the beacon robot makes a last move up, and the moving group moves away from the beacon, according to the two rules of Fig. 5 and the rule of Fig. 6 that makes the leader move straight. With those rules, and with $M = \{((i,j), L), ((i+1,j), F)\}$, $X = \{((i, j+1), B)\}$, we can see that by applying $\mathcal{A}_1^{Fixed}$ three times starting from $\{M, X\}$ we obtain $\{((i-1,j), L), ((i-1, j+1), F), ((i+1, j+2), B)\}$, i.e., $\{\rho(M), \boldsymbol{t}_{(1,1)}(X)\}$, where ρ is the rotation centered at $(i-0.5, j-0.5)$ of angle $\pi/2$.

Theorem 5. *Algorithm $\mathcal{A}_1^{Fixed}$ solves the IGE problem using six robots and fixed colors having common chirality and a visibility range of one.*

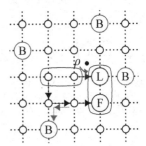

Fig. 7. Configuration after three rounds from C^0.

Proof. We denote by $I = C^0 = \{M^0, C_0^0, C_1^0, C_2^0, C_3^0\}$ the initial configuration given in Fig. 1, where $M^0 = \{((-1,0), F), ((0,0), L)\}$, $C_0^0 = \{((0,-1), B)\}$, $C_1^0 = \{((2,0), B)\}$, $C_2^0 = \{((1,2), B)\}$, and $C_3^0 = \{((-2,1), B)\}$. We define the configuration $C^i = \{M^i, C_0^i, C_1^i, C_2^i, C_3^i\}$ in Phase i, where $M^i = \boldsymbol{t}_{(-i,-i)}(M^0)$, $C_0^i = \boldsymbol{t}_{(-i,-i)}(C_0^0)$, $C_1^i = \boldsymbol{t}_{(i,-i)}(C_1^0)$, $C_2^i = \boldsymbol{t}_{(i,i)}(C_2^0)$, and $C_3^i = \boldsymbol{t}_{(-i,i)}(C_3^0)$. We now prove that starting with a configuration C^i, the configuration C^{i+1} is eventually reached. Since the initial configuration of our algorithm is C^0, this implies that every configuration C^i, for every $i \geq 0$, is gradually reached. By doing so, the leader robot visits all edges of growing rectangles. Consider the first configuration C^i of Phase i. In C^i, the distance between r_L and the beacon robot on its right is $2i + 2$. Indeed, starting from C^i, the robot r_L starts from $(-i, -i)$ and that beacon robot starts from $(i + 2, -i)$.

By executing the algorithm, we remark (see Fig. 7) that after three rounds (1) the configuration is $\{\rho(M^i),\ C_0^{i+1},\ C_1^i,\ C_2^i,\ C_3^i\}$ (where ρ is the rotation with center $(0.5, 0.5)$ of angle $\pi/2$) and (2) r_L is at distance $2i + 1$ from the bottom down beacon. From that point, the moving group $\{r_L, r_F\}$ starts moving one node to the right at each round (due to the first two rules) until robot r_L sees a beacon robot r in C_1^i; this event occurs at round $3 + 2i$, i.e., three plus the number of empty nodes between r_L and r. After three more rounds, the moving group performs a left turn again and bottom right beacon robot is translated by a vector $(1, -1)$.

Thus, at round $3 + 2i + 3$, the configuration is $\{t_{(2i,0)}(\rho^2(M^i)),\ C_0^{i+1},\ C_1^{i+1}, C_2^i, C_3^i\}$. After $2i + 3$ more rounds, the moving group reaches the top right beacon robot, and performs another left turn. So, at round $3 + 2(2i + 3)$ the configuration is $\{t_{(2i,2i)}(\rho^3(M^i)),\ C_0^{i+1}, C_1^{i+1}, C_2^{i+1}, C_3^i\}$. Similarly, at round $3 + 3(2i + 3) + 1$ the configuration is $\{t_{(-1,2i)}(\rho^4(M^i)),\ C_0^{i+1}, C_1^{i+1}, C_2^{i+1}, C_3^{i+1}\}$. We can observe that the moving group $\{r_L, r_F\}$ required one extra round (as compared to other beacon robots) to reach the beacon robot in C_3^i.

Then, after $2i + 1$ more rounds, the group of robots $\{r_L, r_F\}$ moves $2i + 1$ nodes down to reach the bottom left beacon robot again, so that, at round $(3 + 3(2i + 3) + 1) + 2i + 1$, the configuration is $\{t_{(-1,-1)}(\rho^4(M^i)),\ C_0^{i+1}, C_1^{i+1}, C_2^{i+1}, C_3^i\} = C^{i+1}$.

Recursively, if the robots start from configuration C^0, they reach configuration C^i in finite time, for any $i \geq 0$. Also, the nodes V_i visited by r_L between Phase i and $i + 1$ contains the edges of the rectangle $\{t_{(-i,-i)}(-1, 0), t_{(i,-i)}(1, 0),$ $t_{(i,i)}(1, 1), t_{(-i,i)}(-1, 1)\}$; see Fig. 2. Since $\bigcup_{i \geq 0} V_i = \mathbb{Z} \times \mathbb{Z}$, our algorithm solves the infinite grid exploration problem.   □

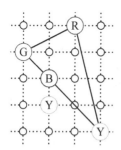

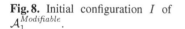

Fig. 8. Initial configuration I of $\mathcal{A}_1^{Modifiable}$.

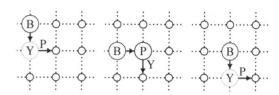

Fig. 9. Sequence of moves for a diagonal motion.

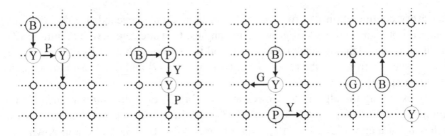

Fig. 10. Sequence of moves for a turn at the bottom beacon robot. A letter is written near each arrow to define the new color of the moving robot in case of change.

4.2 An Algorithm Using Five Robots and Five Modifiable Colors

Algorithm $\mathcal{A}_1^{Modifiable}$ we present now solves the exclusive IGE problem using a minimum number of robots. As compared to the previous algorithm, to use one less robot, the moving group of two robots moves along a triangle, delimited by three beacon robots, instead of a rectangle. Except the shape of the growing polygonal, the principles are similar to the previous algorithm. Notice that we require modifiable colors to allow the moving group to follow a diagonal and to make adjustments without violating exclusiveness.

The set of colors is $Cl = \{R, Y, G, B, P\}$. Notice that, to reduce the number of used colors, the meaning of each color changes according to the stage of the exploration, *i.e.*, along the exploration they are used for different purposes. The initial configuration I is given in Fig. 8. The three beacon robots at the corners of the growing triangle respectively hold light colors Y, G, and R. The principle of the algorithm is as follows: starting from the initial configuration I and using the diagonal movements described in Fig. 9, the moving group, composed of the two robots initially with lights colored B and Y, goes to the bottom beacon robot Y. During a diagonal move, the color of the light of the robot in the moving group initially colored Y alternates at each move between Y and P, while the light of the robot initially colored B has a fixed color. Robots in the group alternatively move horizontally and vertically (when one moves horizontally, the other moves vertically) according to the colors of the group, either $\{B, Y\}$ or $\{B, P\}$. After the turn at the bottom beacon robot, described in Fig. 10, the lights of the moving group are now colored G and B and the group moves with fixed colors similarly to the previous algorithm, until reaching the third beacon robot. Precisely, they move up towards the top right beacon robot, turns left, and then moves

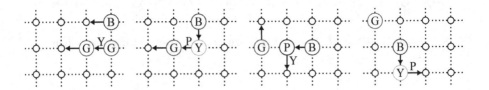

Fig. 11. Sequence of moves of a left turn at the top left beacon robot.

straight to the left towards the third beacon robot, following rules that are identical to the previous algorithm, except that at some point two robots swap their color (and so their role) instead of swapping positions so that the algorithm remains exclusive; precisely a member of the moving group becomes a beacon and conversely. Upon reaching the third beacon robot, the robots perform a turn following the sequence described in Fig. 11. After the turn at the top left beacon robot, the lights of the moving group have again colors B and Y and again moves in diagonal. All rules are given in Fig. 12.

Due to the lack of space, the proof of the next theorem (which follows the same sketch as the one of Theorem 5) has been omitted.

Theorem 6. *Algorithm $\mathcal{A}_1^{Modifiable}$ solves the exclusive IGE problem using five robots, five modifiable colors, and a visibility range of one.*

Rules for the diagonal move (the fourth rule is also used during the first and the last turns):

For the first turn:

The rules below allow two robots to move in straight line toward a beacon, turn left, and then move in straight line towards the next beacon. Actually, they are identical to the previous algorithm, except that the two robots swap their colors instead of swapping their positions.

Rules for the last turn:

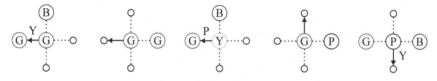

Fig. 12. Rules for Algorithm $\mathcal{A}_1^{Modifiable}$.

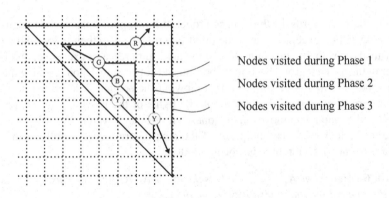

Nodes visited during Phase 1

Nodes visited during Phase 2

Nodes visited during Phase 3

Fig. 13. Visited triangles after three phases for $\mathcal{A}_1^{Modifiable}$.

5   Infinite Grid Exploration with $\Phi = 2$ and No Light

In this section, we describe Algorithm $\mathcal{A}_2^{nolight}$ which solves the exclusive IGE problem assuming visibility range two, yet using no light (or equivalently, using lights with the same fixed color for all robots), *i.e.*, using anonymous oblivious robots. Recall that an animation of this algorithm is available in our complementary material [6]. As previously, the fact that the rules of this algorithm are well-defined and unambiguous has been checked by the script that generated those animations.

First, one can observe that since the visibility range is two, the obstructed visibility can impact the local view of a robot because a robot at distance one can hide a robot behind it at distance two. So, the rules of $\mathcal{A}_2^{nolight}$ should not depend on the states of the nodes that are hidden by a robot. To make it clear, those nodes will be crossed out in the illustrations of our rules, in Figs. 15, 16, and 17.

The principle of our algorithm is similar to the first two ones. We still proceed by phases. In Phase i ($i \geq 1$), a moving group, this time of three robots, traverses the edges of a square of length $2i$ (see Fig. 14). The three *moving* robots are always placed in such a way that exactly one of them, the *leader*, has one robot of the group on its horizontal axis and the other on its vertical axis. Again, the two non-leader robots of the group are called the *followers*. Notice however that the leadership changes during a phase. Finally, as previously, the non-members of the moving group are called the *beacon* robots.

The overall idea is that the moving group moves straight according to the relative positions of its members until a follower detects a beacon at distance two. Then, an adjustment is performed in two rounds to push away the beacon and to make the moving group turn left.

The initial configuration is presented in Fig. 14 and the rules are given in Figs. 15, 16, and 17. During Phase i ($i \geq 1$), the visited square is actually the one of length $2i$ whose center is the initial position of the bottom follower; see Fig. 14. For the movements along a straight line, the moving group forms a right angle. Each of the three moving robots sees the others, can determine its position in the group, and so knows the current direction to follow. Then, when the moving group is close enough from a beacon robot (see the first configuration in Fig. 18), an adjustment is done in

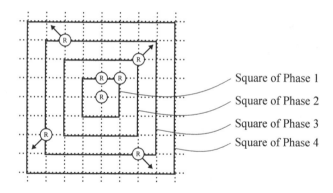

Fig. 14. Initial configuration I of $\mathcal{A}_2^{nolight}$ and visited squares after four phases.

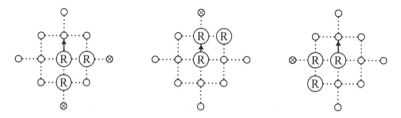

Fig. 15. Moving on a straight line for $\mathcal{A}_2^{nolight}$.

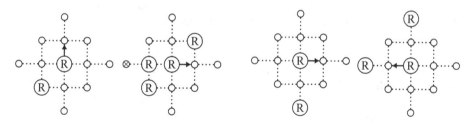

Fig. 16. First round.   **Fig. 17.** Second round.

two rounds. In the first round, a beacon robot sees a follower in diagonal and moves up. Simultaneously, that follower moves towards the node on the right of that beacon robot. The two other members of the moving group move straight, as previously. In the second round, the beacon robot moves away, on the left of the aforementioned follower it sees at distance two (*i.e.*, on the right from a global point of view described in Fig. 18). Simultaneously, that follower, which sees the beacon robot at distance two, catches up with the other robots of the moving group that are on its left and stay idle. Then, the moving group moves again along a straight line, and so on.

Due to the lack of space, the proof of the next theorem has been omitted. Again it follows the same sketch of the proof of Theorem 5.

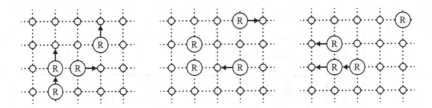

Fig. 18. Sequence moves for a left turn.

Theorem 7. *Algorithm $\mathcal{A}_2^{nolight}$ solves the exclusive IGE problem using seven robots without lights and a visibility range of two.*

6   Conclusion and Perspectives

We have considered the problem of exploring an infinite discrete environment, namely an infinite grid-shaped graph, using a small number of mobile synchronous robots with low computation and communication capabilities. In particular, our robots are opaque and only agree on a common chirality. We have shown that using few fixed colors (actually three), six robots, with a visibility range restricted to one, are necessary and sufficient to solve the non-exclusive IGE problem. We have also shown that using modifiable colors with few states (actually five), five such robots, with a visibility range restricted to one, are necessary and sufficient to solve the (exclusive) Infinite Grid Exploration (IGE) problem. We also provide an algorithm that the exclusive IGE problem using seven oblivious anonymous robots, yet assuming visibility range two.

A direct perspective of this work is to study the optimality, in terms of number of robots, when we consider the case of anonymous oblivious robots (*i.e.*, robots without any light). Another line of research would be to study the impact of removing the chirality assumption. As a long-term perspective, we envision to study the IGE problem in fully asynchronous settings.

References

1. Gilbert, S., Hughes, D., Krishnamachari, B. (eds.): ALGOSENSORS 2018. LNCS, vol. 11410. Springer, Cham (2019). https://doi.org/10.1007/978-3-030-14094-6
2. Baldoni, R., Bonnet, F., Milani, A., Raynal, M.: Anonymous graph exploration without collision by mobile robots. Inf. Process. Lett. **109**(2), 98–103 (2008)
3. Bonnet, F., Milani, A., Potop-Butucaru, M., Tixeuil, S.: Asynchronous exclusive perpetual grid exploration without sense of direction. In: OPODIS, Toulouse, France, pp. 251–265 (2011)
4. Bose, K., Adhikary, R., Kundu, M.K., Sau, B.: Arbitrary pattern formation on infinite grid by asynchronous oblivious robots. In: WALCOM, pp. 354–366 (2019)
5. Bramas, Q., Devismes, S., Lafourcade, P.: Infinite grid exploration by disoriented robots. In: SIROCCO, pp. 340–344 (2019)
6. Bramas, Q., Devismes, S., Lafourcade, P.: Infinite Grid Exploration by Disoriented Robots: Animations (September 2019). https://doi.org/10.5281/zenodo.2625730

7. Brandt, S., Uitto, J., Wattenhofer, R.: A tight bound for semi-synchronous collaborative grid exploration. In: DISC (2018)
8. Das, S., Flocchini, P., Prencipe, G., Santoro, N., Yamashita, M.: Autonomous mobile robots with lights. Theor. Comput. Sci. **609**(P1), 171–184 (2016)
9. Devismes, S., Lamani, A., Petit, F., Raymond, P., Tixeuil, S.: Optimal grid exploration by asynchronous oblivious robots. In: Richa, A.W., Scheideler, C. (eds.) SSS 2012. LNCS, vol. 7596, pp. 64–76. Springer, Heidelberg (2012). https://doi.org/10.1007/978-3-642-33536-5_7
10. Di Stefano, G., Navarra, A.: Gathering of oblivious robots on infinite grids with minimum traveled distance. Inf. Comput. **254**, 377–391 (2016)
11. Dieudonné, Y., Petit, F.: Circle formation of weak robots and Lyndon words. Inf. Process. Lett. **101**(4), 156–162 (2007)
12. Dutta, D., Dey, T., Chaudhuri, S.G.: Gathering multiple robots in a ring and an infinite grid. In: Krishnan, P., Radha Krishna, P., Parida, L. (eds.) ICDCIT 2017. LNCS, vol. 10109, pp. 15–26. Springer, Cham (2017). https://doi.org/10.1007/978-3-319-50472-8_2
13. Emek, Y., Langner, T., Stolz, D., Uitto, J., Wattenhofer, R.: How many ants does it take to find the food? Theor. Comput. Sci. **608**(P3), 255–267 (2015)
14. Flocchini, P., Prencipe, G., Santoro, N., Widmayer, P.: Gathering of asynchronous robots with limited visibility. Theor. Comput. Sci. **337**(1), 147–168 (2005)
15. Luna, G.A.D., Flocchini, P., Chaudhuri, S.G., Poloni, F., Santoro, N., Viglietta, G.: Mutual visibility by luminous robots without collisions. Inf. Comput. **254**, 392–418 (2017)
16. Ooshita, F., Datta, A.K.: Brief announcement: feasibility of weak gathering in connected-over-time dynamic rings. In: Izumi, T., Kuznetsov, P. (eds.) SSS 2018. LNCS, vol. 11201, pp. 393–397. Springer, Cham (2018). https://doi.org/10.1007/978-3-030-03232-6_27
17. Peleg, D.: Distributed coordination algorithms for mobile robot swarms: new directions and challenges. In: Pal, A., Kshemkalyani, A.D., Kumar, R., Gupta, A. (eds.) IWDC 2005. LNCS, vol. 3741, pp. 1–12. Springer, Heidelberg (2005). https://doi.org/10.1007/11603771_1
18. Yang, Y., Souissi, S., Défago, X., Takizawa, M.: Fault-tolerant flocking for a group of autonomous mobile robots. J. Syst. Softw. **84**(1), 29–36 (2011)

Wireless Broadcast with Short Labels

Gewu Bu$^{(\boxtimes)}$, Maria Potop-Butucaru, and Mikaël Rabie

Sorbonne University, LIP6 CNRS UMR 7606, Paris, France
{gewu.bu,maria.potop-butucaru,mikael.rabie}@lip6.fr

Abstract. In this paper, we study the broadcast problem in wireless networks when the broadcast is helped by a labelling scheme. We focus on two variants of broadcast: broadcast without acknowledgment (i.e. the initiator of the broadcast is not notified at the end of broadcast) and broadcast with acknowledgment. Our contribution is threefold. *First*, we improve in terms of memory complexity a recent [12] labelling-based broadcast scheme with acknowledgment designed for arbitrary networks. *Second*, we propose label optimal broadcast algorithms in *level separable networks* (a class of networks issued from recent studies in Wireless Body Area Networks). In this class of networks we propose an acknowledgment-free broadcast strategy using 1-bit labels and broadcast with acknowledgment using 2-bits labels. In the class of level-separable networks, our algorithms finish within $2D$ rounds, where D is the eccentricity of the broadcast initiator. Interestingly, the time complexity of broadcast in the case of level-separable networks does not depend on the size of the network but rather on the initiator eccentricity which makes this class of graphs interesting for further investigation. *Finally*, we study the hardness of determining that a graph is level separable. Our study shows that even though checking that a separation is a level separation can be done in polynomial time, determining that a graph has the level separable property is NP-complete. This result opens interesting independent research directions.

Keywords: Labelling scheme · Broadcast · Wireless networks

1 Introduction

Broadcast is the most studied communication primitive in networks and distributed systems. Broadcast ensures that once a *source node* (a.k.a. the broadcast initiator) sends a message, all other nodes in the network should receive this message in a finite time. Limited by the transmission range, messages might not be sent directly from one node to some other node in the network. Therefore relay nodes need to assist the source node during the message propagation by re-propagating it. Deterministic centralized broadcast, where nodes have complete network knowledge, has been studied by Kowalski *et al.* in [23]. The authors propose an optimal solution that completes within $O(D \log^2 n)$ rounds, where n is the number of nodes in the network and D is the largest distance from the source to any node of the network. For deterministic distributed broadcast, assuming that nodes only know their IDs (i.e. they do not know the IDs of their

© Springer Nature Switzerland AG 2021
C. Georgiou and R. Majumdar (Eds.): NETYS 2020, LNCS 12129, pp. 146–169, 2021.
https://doi.org/10.1007/978-3-030-67087-0_10

neighbours nor the network topology), in [9] is proposed the fastest broadcast within $O(n \log D \log \log D)$ rounds, where D is the diameter of the network. The lower bound in this case, proposed in [10], is $\Omega(n \log D)$.

In wireless networks, when a message is sent from a node it goes into the wireless channel in the form of a wireless signal which may be received by all the nodes within the transmission range of the sender node. However, when a node is located in the range of more than one node that sends messages simultaneously, the multiple wireless signals may generate *collisions* at the receiver. The receiver cannot decode any useful information from the superimposed interference signals. At the MAC layer, several solutions have been proposed in the last two decades in order to reduce collisions. All of them offer probabilistic guarantees. Our study follows the recent work that addresses this problem at the application layer. More specifically, we are interested in deterministic solutions for broadcasting messages based on the use of extra information or advise (also referred to as *labelling*) precomputed before the broadcast invocation.

Labelling schemes have been designed to compute network size, the father-son relationship and the geographic distance between arbitrary nodes in the network (e.g. [1,15,17]). Labelling schemes have been also used in [14,16] in order to improve the efficiency of Minimum Spanning Tree or Leader Election algorithms. Furthermore, [11,13] exploit labelling in order to improve the existing solutions for network exploration by a robot/agent moving in the network.

Very few works (e.g. [12,20]) exploit labelling schemes to design efficient *broadcast* primitives. When using labelling schemes, nodes record less information than in the case of centralized broadcast, where nodes need to know complete network information. Compared with the existing solutions for deterministic distributed broadcast the time complexity is improved. In [20] the authors prove that for an arbitrary network, to achieve broadcast within a constant number of rounds, a $O(n)$ bits of advice is sufficient but not $o(n)$. Very recently, a labelling scheme with 2-bits advice (3 bits for broadcast with acknowledgment) is proposed in [12]. The authors prove that their algorithms need $2n - 3$ rounds for the broadcast without acknowledgment and $3n - 4$ rounds for broadcast with acknowledgment in an arbitrary network.

Contribution: Our work is in the line of research described in [12]. We first study in terms of memory complexity the broadcast scheme proposed in [12], where 3-bits labelling based broadcast algorithm with acknowledgment is proposed for an arbitrary network. However, the utilization of the 3-bits labelling is not optimal. We propose therefore an improvement to optimal the memory complexity for the proposition in [12]. Due to the pages limitation, please see our technical rapport [8] for detailed description and preuve. Then, we study labelling-based broadcast in a new family of networks, called level-separable networks issued from Wireless Body Area Networks (e.g. [2–4,6,7]). In this class of networks we propose an acknowledgment-free broadcast strategy using 1-bit labels and a broadcast scheme with acknowledgment using 2-bits labels. Our algorithms terminate within $2D$ rounds for both types of broadcast primitives, where D is the eccentricity of the broadcast source. Interestingly, the time complexity of broadcast in the case of level separable networks does not directly depend on the network size which makes the study of level separable networks of independent interest. We further investigate the hardness of determining if a graph is level separable. Our study shows that even though checking that a separation is a level separation can be done in polynomial time, determining that a graph has the level separable property is NP-complete. This result opens interesting independent research directions that will be discussed in the conclusion of this document.

2   Model and Problem Definition

We model the network as a *graph* $G = (V, E)$ where V, the set of *vertices*, represents the set of nodes in the network and E, the set of *edges*, is a set of unordered pairs $e = (u, v)$, $u, v \in V$, that represents the communications links between nodes u and v. In the following $d(u)$ denotes the set of neighbours of node u. We assume that the network is connected, i.e., there is a path between any two nodes in the network.

We assume that nodes execute the same algorithm and are *time synchronized*. The system execution is decomposed in *rounds*. When a node u sends a message at round x, all nodes in $d(u)$ receive the message at the end of round x. Collisions occur at node u in round x if a set of nodes, $M \subseteq d(u)$ and $|M| > 1$, send a message in round x. In that case, it is considered that u has not received any message.

In the following we are interested in solving the *Broadcast problem*: when a source node s sends a data message μ, this μ should be received by all the nodes in the network in a finite bounded time. We are also interested in solving *Broadcast with acknowledgment problem*: once all nodes received μ, an acknowledgment message, called ACK, will be generated and sent backward to the source node s in a finite bounded time.

3   Level-Separable Networks

In this section, we define a family of networks, *Level-Separable Network*, issued from WBAN (Wireless Body Area Networks) area (e.g. [2–4, 6, 7, 21, 24, 26]), due to the pages limitation, please see our technical rapport [8] for detailed description and specification of WBAN. We therefore investigate the broadcast problem in these networks.

3.1   Formal Definition of Level-Separable Networks

We say that an arbitrary network is a Level-Separable Network if the underlay communication graph $G = (V, E)$ of the network verifies the *Level-Separable* property defined below. To define the *Level-Separable* property, we introduce some preliminary notations.

Let $G(V, E)$ be a network and let $s \in V$, a predefined vertex, be the source node of the broadcast. Each vertex $u \in V$ has a geometric distance with respect to s denoted $d(s, u)$. The eccentricity of vertex s, $\varepsilon_G(s)$, is the farthest distance from s to any other vertex. In the rest of the paper, we denote $\varepsilon_G(s)$ by D.

Definition 1 (Level). *Let $G(V, E)$ be a network and s the source node. For any vertex u in $G(V, E)$, the level of u is $l(u) = d(s, u)$ is its geometric distance to s. Let $S_i = \{u \mid u \in V, \ l(u) = i\}$ denote the set containing all the vertices at level i.*

Definition 2 (Parents and Sons). *Let $G(V, E)$ be a network. A vertex u is parent of vertex v (a vertex v is son of vertex u) in graph G with the root source node s: if $l(v) - l(u) = 1 \ \wedge \ \{u, v\} \in E$. Let $S(u)$ $(P(u))$ be the set of sons (parents) of u (v). If $v \in S(u)$ $(u \in P(v))$, we say that u (v) has v (u) as son (parent).*

Level-Separable property below defines how to filter nodes in the same level i into two disjoint subsets.

Definition 3 (Level-Separable Subsets). *Given $G(V, E)$ a network and the set S_i (the set of all vertices in the same level i of G), the level-separable subsets of S_i are $S_{i,1}$ and $S_{i,2}$, such that $S_{i,1} \cap S_{i,2} = \varnothing$, $S_{i,1} \cup S_{i,2} = S_i$*

There may be many possible pairs of $S_{i,1}$ and $S_{i,2}$ for a level i. Let T_i be the set of all possible pairs of *Level-Separable Subsets*:

$$T_i = \{(S_{i,1}^{(1)}, S_{i,2}^{(1)}), (S_{i,1}^{(2)}, S_{i,2}^{(2)}), \ldots, (S_{i,1}^{(2^x)}, S_{i,2}^{(2^x)})\}$$

where (m) on right-top of each pair represent the index of pairs (the mth pairs) in T_i, and $x = |S_i|$.

Definition 4 (Level-Separable Property). *Given an arbitrary graph $G(V, E)$, for all level $i \in [1, D-1]$, where D is the eccentricity of the source node, G verifies the Level-Separable property, if there are pairs for every T_i, $(S_{i,1}^{(k)}, S_{i,2}^{(k)})$, such that: $\forall u \in S_{i+1}, |P(u) \cap S_{i,1}^{(k)}| = 1 \vee |P(u) \cap S_{i,2}^{(k)}| = 1$ i.e., for every vertex u at level $i+1$, u has only one parent in $S_{i,1}$ or $S_{i,2}$.*

Note that when $S_{i,1}$ is fixed, $S_{i,2}$ is $S_i \setminus S_{i,1}$.

Definition 5 (Level-Separable Network). *A network $G(V, E)$ is a Level-Separable Network if its underlay graph verifies the Level-Separable property.*

Note that *Level-Separable Graph* has a similar flavour with *Bipartite Graph* [18]. A graph $G = (V, E)$ is said to be Bipartite if and only if there exists a partition $V = A \cup B$ and $A \cap B = \varnothing$. So that all edges share a vertex from both sets A and B, and there is no edge containing two vertices in the same set. A bipartite graph separates nodes into two independent sets. In a level-separable network, we aim at separating nodes of the same level. Moreover, we are interested in the relation between the two separated sets at level i and nodes in level $i+1$, i.e.,

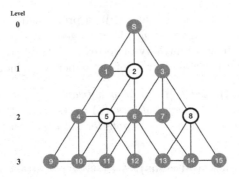

Fig. 1. Example of a Level-2 separable network, which is not a tree network

the node's father-son relationship. However, note that being bipartite does not necessarily means that the graph is level-separable.

Note that a level-separable network is not necessary for being a tree network. However, a tree is a level-separable network. A simple example of a level-separable network is a tree network, where the source node s can be seen as the root of the tree who begins the broadcast. In a tree topology, all non-source nodes have only one parent, i.e. $\forall u \in V - s$, $|P(u)| = 1$. Hence, we can choose $S_{i,1} = S_i$ and $S_{i,2} = \emptyset$. The Level-Separable property is therefore verified. Figure 1 shows an example of a level-separable network that is not a tree.

Note that studies conducted in wireless body area networks (e.g. [2–4,6,7]) fit our definition of level-separable network.

4   Broadcast in Level-Separable Network

In this section, we propose a 1-bit constant-length labelling broadcast Algorithm β^{LS} detailed in Algorithm 1. The algorithm needs $2D$ rounds to terminate, where D is the eccentricity of the broadcast source node.

4.1   Broadcast with 1-bit Labelling

Given a level-separable network whose root is the source of the broadcast, we propose Algorithm β^{LS} to achieve the wireless broadcast, when a 1-bit labelling scheme λ^{LS} is used. Each node in the network has a 1-bit label, X_1. X_1 is set to 1 or 0 following the labelling scheme λ^{LS} described below. The idea of the broadcast algorithm is to separate nodes at each level into two independent sets. Nodes in the first set transmit at round x and nodes in the second set transmit at round $x + 1$ (the next round), so they will not generate valid collisions[1].

---

[1] Note that collisions that occur at a node who has already received the message successfully are not considered as valid collisions.

The broadcast Algorithm β^{LS} using the labelling scheme λ^{LS} is as follows: the source node sends the message, μ, at round 0. Nodes at level 1 receive μ at the end of round 0. When nodes with $X_1 = 1$ receive message μ at round $2i - 3$ ($i > 1$) or $2i - 2$ ($i > 0$), where i is the level, they send μ at round $2i - 1$. When nodes with $X_1 = 0$ receive μ at round $2i - 3$ ($i > 1$) or $2i - 2$ ($i > 0$), they send μ at rounds $2i$. That is, nodes at level $i > 0$ will receive μ from their parents (nodes at level $i - 1$) at round $2i - 3$ ($i > 1$) or $2i - 2$ ($i > 0$), and they will send μ at round $2i$ or $2i - 1$ according to X_1. In other words, at each level i, nodes take two rounds to propagate μ to all nodes at level $i + 1$.

4.2   1-bit Labelling Scheme λ^{LS}

To achieve collision-free transmission, 1-bit Labelling Scheme λ^{LS} X_1 of all nodes in $S_{i,1}$ for level $i > 0$ is 1, and X_1 of all nodes in $S_{i,2}$ for level $i > 0$ is 0 where $S_{i,1}$ and $S_{i,2}$ are the sets identified in Definition 4.

4.3   Correctness of Algorithm β^{LS}

In the following, we prove that Algorithm β^{LS} is correct.

Theorem 1. *Algorithm β^{LS} with 1-bit constant Labelling Scheme λ^{LS} implements broadcast in a level-separable network within $2D$ rounds.*

The proof of this theorem is a direct consequence of Lemmas 1, 2 and 3 below.

Note 1. *Note that the 1-bit labelling scheme is optimal for broadcast in a level-separable network. That is, with 0-bit labelling (i.e. without using any labelling) it is possible that some nodes in the network do not receive the broadcasted message due to the collisions since nodes are synchronized and transmit at the same time.*

Lemma 1. *Let $G = (V, E)$ be a level-separable network such that each node has a label according to the labelling scheme λ^{LS}. If nodes with $X_1 = 1$ at the same level $i \in [1, D - 1]$ are the only one to send a message concurrently at round j and on the next round $j + 1$ nodes with $X_1 = 0$ at the same level i are the only one to send a message concurrently, all nodes at level $i + 1$ have received the message without collision either at round j or round $j + 1$.*

Proof. Let $u \in S_{i+1}$. By construction, u has exactly one parent in $S_{i,1}$ or $S_{i,2}$. In the first case, u has received the message without collision at round j, and it has received it at round $j + 1$ in the second case.

Lemma 2. *Given a level-separable network whose root is the source node by applying β^{LS} and λ^{LS}, all nodes in level $i > 0$ finish receiving the message μ at round $2i - 2$.*

Algorithm 1. $\beta^{LS}(\mu)$ executed at each node v

%Each node has a variable *sourcemsg*. The source node has this variable initially set to μ, all other nodes have it initially set to *null*. A variable k initially set to 0 to ensure each node sends μ only once.

for each round r from 0 **do**
　　if v is the source node and $r = 0$ **then**
　　　　transmit *sourcemsg*
　　if v is not source node and receives μ **then**
　　　　if $k = 0$ **then**
　　　　　　sourcemsg $\leftarrow \mu$
　　　　　　if r is odd number **then**
　　　　　　　　if $X_1 = 0$ **then**
　　　　　　　　　　transmit *sourcemsg* at round $r + 3$
　　　　　　　　else if $X_1 = 1$ **then**
　　　　　　　　　　transmit *sourcemsg* at round $r + 2$
　　　　　　else if r is even number **then**
　　　　　　　　if $X_1 = 0$ **then**
　　　　　　　　　　transmit *sourcemsg* at round $r + 2$
　　　　　　　　else if $X_1 = 1$ **then**
　　　　　　　　　　transmit *sourcemsg* at round $r + 1$
　　　　　　set $k = 1$

Proof. We begin from the base case where $i = 1$, nodes at level $i = 1$ means nodes that are only one hop away from the source node. At round 0, which is round $2 \times i - 2 = 2 \times 1 - 2 = 0$, the source sends the message. All nodes at level 1 will receive the message at the end of round 0. For $i = 2$, as all nodes at level 1 can receive the message at round 0, they will begin to send at round 1 and round 2 for nodes in $S_{i,1}$ and $S_{i,2}$, respectively. According to Lemma 1, all nodes received the message without collision at round 2, which is round $2 \times i - 2 = 2 \times 2 - 2 = 2$ and they begin to send the message at round 3 and 4. For the general case, we assume that all nodes at level i, $i > 2$, finish receiving the message at round $2i - 2$. So that nodes begin to send the received message at round $2(i+1) - 3$ and $2(i+1) - 2$, and nodes at level $i + 1$ receive the message at $2(i+1) - 3$ and $2(i+1) - 2$, that is nodes at level $i + 1$ finish receiving the message at round $2(i+1) - 2$.

Lemma 3. *Given a level-separable network whose root is the source node by applying β^{LS} and λ^{LS}, the broadcast finishes in $2D$ rounds.*

Proof. From Lemma 2, nodes having the longest distance to the source will receive the message at round $2D - 2$, where D is the source eccentricity. After receiving the message, these nodes will send it according to the broadcast algorithm, even though they are already the ending nodes in the network which takes two more rounds. Therefore the broadcast finishes at round $2D$.

Consider the execution of the Algorithm β^{LS} in a level-separable network with labelling scheme λ^{LS}, where nodes in level i have been separated into two sets $S_{i,1}$ and $S_{i,2}$ verifying the level-separable property at level i, $\forall i > 0$. Nodes in $S_{i,1}$ have $X_1 = 1$, and nodes in $S_{i,2}$ have $X_1 = 0$. The main idea of β^{LS} is that, nodes in each level i separated into two different sets transmit their received messages μ in different execution rounds to reduce the impact of the collision at nodes in level $i + 1$.

According to Algorithm β^{LS}, the message μ will be propagated from level to level. Each propagation from a level to the next one takes two execution rounds. In the first round all nodes in $S_{i,1}$ send the received message μ. At the end of this round all the nodes that are the sons of nodes in $S_{i,1}$ receive μ, without collision, see Lemma 1. Therefore sons of nodes in $S_{i,1}$ contain all the nodes at level $i+1$ who have multi-parents, that means it remains only nodes at level $i+1$ having only one parent and did not receive μ yet. In the second round, all nodes in $S_{i,2}$ send μ, and the remaining part of the nodes at level $i+1$ can therefore receive μ from their unique parent. So that after these two rounds of transmission from level i, all the nodes at $i+1$ will successfully receive the message μ. It takes therefore $2D$ rounds to finish the broadcast. Note that nodes will only send once according to β^{LS}. Therefore the algorithm terminates.

5   Broadcast with ACK in Level-Separable Network

In this section, we propose a broadcast algorithm with ACK, β^{LS}_{ACK}, and a Labelling Scheme, λ^{LS}_{ACK}, for level-separable networks. Our algorithm β^{LS}_{ACK} (Algorithm 2) uses only 2-bits labelling and the broadcast finishes within $2D$ rounds. In our solution, ACK goes back to the source node in at most $2D$ rounds, where D is the eccentricity of s (the broadcast source node). That means the ACK can be received by the source node at the same round of the broadcast termination.

5.1   2-bits Labelling Broadcast with ACK

According to Theorem 1 the broadcast finishes in a level-separable network within $2D$ rounds where D is the eccentricity of the source node. If the source node has the knowledge of D, then it automatically can decide if the broadcast is finished. However, when an ACK is necessary to inform the source node to trigger some additional functions then the source waits for the reception of this message. In order to avoid that ACK takes additional time after the end of the broadcast, we propose to send in advance the ACK message at the halfway of the transmission during the broadcast execution. Since in a level-separable network, informing nodes from level to level takes exactly 2 rounds, then ACK also takes 2 rounds to go back one level above. Therefore, when the last node receives μ, the source node receives ACK at the same round. Interestingly, compared with non-ACK broadcasting, our solution uses one extra bit for labelling and no additional rounds to forwarding ACK back to the source.

Figure 2 gives the intuition of how to send in advance the ACK: the half-way ACK mechanism. In Fig. 2, the network is represented in abstract levels to simplify the presentation. Packets flow shown in the figure represent the propagation of messages μ and ACK.

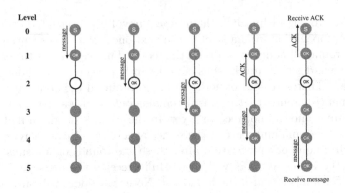

Fig. 2. Anticipating the ACK in a level-separable network

5.2 2-bits Labelling Scheme λ_{ACK}^{LS}

We use λ^{LS} to set X_1 in λ_{ACK}^{LS} in order to verify Lemma 1. Let X_2 be the second bit of the λ_{ACK}^{LS} labelling scheme. $X_2 = 1$ for a set of nodes if they are on the way back path from a node at level $\lfloor D/2 \rfloor - 1$ to the source node, where D is the eccentricity of s and s is the broadcast source. For the other nodes, $X_2 = 0$. In Sect. 5.3, we explain why we choose nodes at level $\lfloor D/2 \rfloor - 1$ to begin sending the ACK.

Note 2. *Note that the 2-bits labelling scheme is optimal to achieve broadcast with acknowledgment in a level-separable network. From Note 1 1-bit is necessary for broadcast without acknowledgment. When an acknowledgment has to be sent back to the source node, at least one additional bit is necessary to indicate the node to generate the acknowledgment message and send it back to the source node. Without this additional bit no node can decide (unless it uses extra local memory) if it is the last receiving node, and who should send ACK back.*

5.3 Correctness of Algorithm β_{ACK}^{LS}

Theorem 2 below proves the correctness of Algorithm β_{ACK}^{LS}.

Theorem 2. *Algorithm β_{ACK}^{LS} with 2-bits labelling scheme λ_{ACK}^{LS} implements broadcast in a level-separable network. The broadcast terminates in $2D$ rounds. The ACK message is transmitted back to the source at round $2(D-1)$, if D is odd or $2D$, if D is even.*

The proof of the theorem is the direct consequence of Lemmas 4, 5 and 6 below.

Lemma 4. *Given a level-separable network whose root is the source node by applying β_{ACK}^{LS} and λ_{ACK}^{LS}, nodes in level $i > 0$ receive message μ at round $2i - 2$. The broadcast finishes at round $2D$.*

Proof. β_{ACK}^{LS} follows the same idea as β^{LS}. The additional ACK transmission will not have any impact according to Lemma 2 and 3. Hence the proof follows.

Lemma 5. *Given a level-separable network whose root is the source node by applying β_{ACK}^{LS} and λ_{ACK}^{LS}, ACK goes back to the source node at round $2(D-1)$, if D is odd; or $2D$, if D is even.*

Proof. When D is odd, ACK and μ will begin to be sent to source and to the ending nodes from levels l_{ACK} and l_{MSG}, respectively. The distances from levels l_{ACK} back to the source are the same as that from l_{MSG} to the ending nodes. ACK arrives at the source at the same round as μ arrives at the ending nodes. According to Lemma 4, this is round $2(D-1)$. When D is even ACK needs to go one level farther compared with μ. Therefore, it takes two extra rounds when D is even. Therefore, when D is even the ACK message goes back to the source node in $2D$ rounds.

Lemma 6. *Given a Level-Separable Network whose root is the source node by applying β_{ACK}^{LS} and λ_{ACK}^{LS} , the algorithm finishes within $2D$ rounds.*

Proof. The idea of the correctness proof is as follows. Consider a level-separable network with the labelling scheme λ_{ACK}^{LS}, where all nodes in level i have been separated into two sets $S_{i,1}$ and $S_{i,2}$. Nodes in $S_{i,1}$ have $X_1 = 1$, and nodes in $S_{i,2}$ have $X_1 = 0$. A way back path is marked with $X_2 = 1$ between source s and an arbitrary node at level $\lfloor D/2 \rfloor - 1$, where D is the eccentricity of s, i.e., we only mark the way back path from the half-way level $\lfloor D/2 \rfloor - 1$ of the network in this case.

The idea is that when the message μ propagates to the half-way level of the network, a node at that level will begin ACK transmission processing, so that when the μ reaches to the ending node(s) at level D, ACK reaches the source s at (almost) the same round. As nodes cannot decide if they are the ones at the half-way of the network who should generate and send ACK, we use a *Waiting Period* and an extra $pACK$ message.

According to the β_{ACK}^{LS}, when a node with $X_2 = 1$, receives μ and finishes the μ retransmission, it cannot decide its position in the way back path. Therefore, it sends a $pACK$ and begins to wait for $pACK$ message sent to him in the following rounds. When a node with $X_2 = 1$ receives a $pACK$ within the *WaitingPeriod*, that means it is not the ending node, because there is another node with $X_2 = 1$ that received μ and sent $pACK$ to him. When a node with $X_2 = 1$ does not receive any $pACK$ within its *WaitingPeriod*, this means no node in the next level has $X_2 = 1$, i.e., it is the half-way ending node, so it generates and sends the ACK. All the nodes with $X_2 = 1$ will forward ACK from the ending node to the source s according to the marked way back path. In the β_{ACK}^{LS}, the *WaitingPeriod* is delayed two rounds after a node sends $pACK$ to avoid the collision between $pACK/ACK$ and μ.

A node with $X_2 = 1$ that receives μ at round x, transmits μ at round $x + 2$, then it sends $pACK$ to its parents at round $x+4$, then it waits a *Waiting Period* until round $x + 6$. If it doesn't receive another $pACK$, then it sends ACK at round $x + 8$. That means, for the half-way ending node, it needs to wait for 6 rounds to begin sending ACK. What we want for this half-way mechanism is that the source node can receive ACK as fast as possible, after the broadcast

---

Algorithm 2. $\beta_{ACK}^{LS}(\mu)$ executed at each node v

%Each node has a variable *sourcemsg*. The source node has this variable initially set to μ, all
other nodes have it initially set to *null*. A variable k and k_{ack} initially set to 0 to ensure each
node send μ only once.
for each round r from 0 **do**
   if v is source node and $r = 0$ **then**
      transmit *sourcemsg*
   if v is not source node and received μ **then**
      sourcemsg $\leftarrow \mu$
      if $k = 0$ **then**
         if r is odd number **then**
            if $X_1 = 0$ **then**
               transmit *sourcemsg* at round $r + 3$
               if $X_2 = 1$ **then**
                  transmit "pACK" at round $r + 4$
                  if v does not received "pACK" at $r + 6$ **then**
                     transmit "ACK" at round $r + 6$, set $k_{ack} = 1$
            else if $X_1 = 1$ **then**
               transmit *sourcemsg* at round $r + 2$
               if $X_2 = 1$ **then**
                  transmit "pACK" at round $r + 4$
                  if v has not received "pACK" at $r + 6$ **then**
                     transmit "ACK" at round $r + 6$, set $k_{ack} = 1$
         else if r is even number **then**
            if $X_1 = 0$ **then**
               transmit *sourcemsg* at round $r + 2$
               if $X_2 = 1$ **then**
                  transmit "pACK" at round $r + 3$
                  if v has not received "pACK" at $r + 5$ **then**
                     transmit "ACK" at round $r + 5$, set $k_{ack} = 1$
            else if $X_1 = 1$ **then**
               transmit *sourcemsg* at round $r + 1$
               if $X_2 = 1$ **then**
                  transmit "pACK" at round $r + 3$
                  if v has not received "pACK" at $r + 5$ **then**
                     transmit "ACK" at round $r + 5$, set $k_{ack} = 1$
      set $k = 1$
   if v is not source node and received ACK **then**
      if $X_2 = 1$ and $k_{ack} = 0$ **then**
         transmit ACK at round $r + 2$
         set $k_{ack} = 1$

---

finishes. When D (the eccentricity of the broadcast source s) is odd, then if
we chose the node at level $\lfloor D/2 \rfloor - 1$ as the half-way ending node, then the
ACK can be received by the source node at the same round as the end of the
broadcast. Because after waiting for 6 rounds at level $\lfloor D/2 \rfloor - 1$, μ has already
been transmitted to level $\lfloor D/2 \rfloor - 1 + 3 = \lfloor D/2 \rfloor + 2$. The distance from node
sending ACK to source node is $d(s, \lfloor D/2 \rfloor - 1) = \lfloor D/2 \rfloor - 1$; the distance from
node sending μ to nodes at level D is also $d(\lfloor D/2 \rfloor + 2, D) = \lfloor D/2 \rfloor - 1$. When
D is even, if we chose the node at level $\lfloor D/2 \rfloor - 1$ as the half-way ending node,
then the ACK can be received by the source node only two rounds after the
round of the ending of the broadcast.

Therefore it takes $2D$ rounds to finish the broadcast and ACK can be transmitted back to the source node at round $2(D-1)$ or round $2D$. Note that nodes
will only send (both for μ and ACK) once according to β_{ACK}^{LS}. Therefore the
algorithm terminates.

6   Hardness of Level Separation

It should be noted that checking that a separation is a Level-Separation is polynomial: it is sufficient to check that for each node u, $|P(u) \cap S_{l(u),1}| = 1 \vee |P(u) \cap S_{l(u),2}| = 1$. In this section we will prove that determining if a graph has the level-separable property is NP-Hard. To do so, we will reduce 1-IN-3-SAT [22] to the level separable problem. 1-IN-3-SAT is a NP-Complete variant of the usual NP-complete problem 3-SAT, where exactly a single literal in each clause must be true. As input, we have a list of variables $X = \{x_1, \ldots, x_k\}$ and a formula ϕ which is a conjunction of clauses $c_1, \ldots, c_l$ that are each composed of exactly 3 literals of the form x_i or $\overline{x_i}$. The goal is to find an assignation for the variables $A : X \rightarrow \{\top, \bot\}$ such that, for every clause c_i, exactly one variable is satisfied (i.e. has the assignation $\top$ if it appears positively, $\bot$ if it appears negatively).

Theorem 3. *Determining if a graph with a source has the Level-Separable property is NP-complete.*

Proof. Let (X, ϕ) be an instance of 1-IN-3-SAT. We will build $G = (V, E)$ such that $V = \{s\} \cup S_1 \cup S_2$, S_1 being the neighborhood of s, and S_2 all the other nodes, that will actually be at distance 2 from s. We have:

- $S_1 = \{u_{n_a}, u_{n_b}, u_y\} \cup \{u_{y_i}, u_{n_i}\}_{i \leq k}$.
- $S_2 = \{v_a, v_b\} \cup \{v_{x_i}\}_{i \leq k} \cup \{v_{c_j}\}_{j \leq l}$.
- $\{s\} \times S_1 \subset E$, $\{(u_{n_a}, v_a), (u_{n_b}, v_b), (u_y, v_a), (u_y, v_b)\} \subset E$.
- $\forall i \leq k$, we have $\{(u_{y_i}, v_{x_i}), (u_{n_i}, v_{x_i})\} \subset E$. If $x_i \in c_j$, then we have $(u_{y_i}, v_{c_j}) \in E$. If $\overline{x_i} \in c_j$, then we have $(u_{n_i}, v_{c_j}) \in E$.
- $\forall j \leq l$, we have $\{(u_{n_a}, v_{c_j}), (u_{n_b}, v_{c_j})\} \subset E$.

An abstract graph can be seen in Fig. 3 corresponding to the description above.

Let's suppose that we have a solution $S_{1,1}, S_{1,2}$ to the problem (any partition of S_2 works, as there are the farthest nodes from s). We will call $Y \in \{1, 2\}$ the index of the node u_y, and $N = 3 - Y$ the index that is different from Y. Here below a list of observations:

1. If a node in S_2 has exactly two parents, then the index of its parents must be different.
2. u_{n_a} (resp. u_{n_b}) must have index N, as v_a (resp. v_b) is only connected to it and to u_y.
3. $\forall i \leq k$, u_{y_i} and u_{n_i} have different indexes, as they are the only parents of v_{x_i}.
4. $\forall j \leq l$, v_{c_j} has exactly one parent of index Y, as it has at least two parents of index N: u_{n_a} and u_{n_b}.

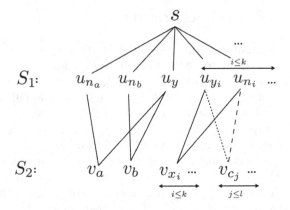

Fig. 3. Solid lines represent the edges that always exist. Dense dotted lines represent the edges that exist if $x_i \in c_j$. Loose dotted lines represent the edges that exist if $\overline{x_i} \in c_j$

A solution for the corresponding 1-IN-3-SAT instance is to choose, for each variable x_i such that u_{y_i} has index Y, valuation $\top$, and $\bot$ for the others. Let c_j be a clause. The node v_{c_j} has exactly one parent of index Y among the ones corresponding to variables. If it is a node of the form u_{y_i}, then x_i appears positively in c_j (otherwise, it is of the form u_{n_i} and x_i appears negatively in c_j). Let be another node corresponding to a variable connected to v_{c_j}. Its index must be N, and it appears positively in c_j iff the node is some u_{y_i} iff we chose $\bot$ for x_i. Hence, c_j has exactly one variable satisfied.

Reversely, let's suppose that we have an assignation A to the 1-IN-3-SAT instance. We choose $S_{1,1} = \{u_y\} \cup \{u_{y_i} : A(x_i) = \top\} \cup \{u_{n_i} : A(x_i) = \bot\}$ and $S_{1,2} = S_1 \setminus S_{1,1}$. Let's prove that each node in S_2 has exactly one parent in $S_{1,1}$. For v_a and v_b, it is u_y. For a node v_{c_j}, we know that exactly one variable of c_j is satisfied. Its corresponding node is in $S_{1,1}$ by construction, and the corresponding node of the two other variables are in $S_{1,2}$ by construction. As v_{n_a} and v_{n_b} are also in $S_{1,2}$, this concludes the proof.

7 Conclusion

We proposed solutions for implementing broadcast in wireless networks when the broadcast is helped by a labelling scheme. We studied broadcast without acknowledgment (i.e. the initiator of the broadcast is not notified at the end of the broadcast) and broadcast with acknowledgment. We first improved in terms of memory complexity the scheme proposed in [12] for arbitrary networks. Then we propose an optimal acknowledgment-free broadcast strategy using only 1-bit labelling and a broadcast with acknowledgment using a 2-bits labelling in level 2-separable networks. The complexity of both algorithms is $2D$ where D is the eccentricity of the broadcast initiator. Level 2-separable networks have a practical interest in the large literature of WBAN.

In Sect. 6, we proved that the verification of the level-separable property can be done in polynomial time while determining if a graph has the level separable property is NP-hard. This result may be considered as a serious break in exploiting the level separable property in labelling-based algorithms. However, in the case of small scale networks such as WBAN, polynomial algorithms may be of practical interest. For the case of large scale networks, since the verification of the level-separable property is NP-hard, we recommend to exploit $MIMO$ antenna technology [19,25] (wireless devices having the capability to focus the wireless transmission on several dedicated directions). Thanks to this technology the connections from a node to several of its neighbours can be disabled. This simple mechanism can help in constructing networks with built-in level separable property according to the description in Sect. 3. In this case, our algorithms are the best to date for labelling-based broadcast.

Independent of the practical interest of our work, an interesting theoretical research direction is opened by our study: the generalization of our results to level k-separable networks. In this framework, it would be interesting to find optimal separations for a graph and the tradeoff between the time and the bit complexity of broadcast in level k-separable networks.

Appendix A: Broadcast with ACK for Arbitrary Networks

In [12] the authors propose a broadcast with acknowledgment algorithm β_{ACK} for general networks using a 3-bits labelling scheme λ_{ACK}. The idea of the broadcast algorithm β_{ACK} is an extension of algorithm β also described in [12] which implements the broadcast of a message μ within bounded time. At each round, only nodes that received μ in specified previous rounds can send it to avoid the potential collisions. Initially, the source node s sends μ to all its neighbours. A *Frontier Set*, *Frnt*, is defined where *Frnt* contains all nodes that have not received μ and that have direct connections with nodes received μ at the end of that round. Then a *Minimal Dominating Set*, *miniD* is defined over the nodes that already have received μ such that nodes in *Frnt* are dominated by nodes in *miniD*. Nodes in *miniD* then send μ, so that some of nodes in *Frnt* can receive μ. *Frnt* and *miniD* are therefore updated since some nodes will leave *Frnt* and may join *miniD* in the next round. Nodes in new *miniD* will continue send μ until $Frnt = \varnothing$. The broadcast then finishes. Note that during the execution, a node in *miniD* at round i may stay in the *miniD* till round j, where $i < j$. In this case, additional notification message *Stay* is needed to be sent to nodes who need to stay in *miniD*.

Algorithm β_{ACK} extends β by adding an additional ACK message, that is, when the last nodes receive μ, one of them will generate an ACK message that will be forwarded back to s. During the execution, nodes will store the round number at which they received and sent μ with two variables *informedRound* and *transmitRounds*. So that nodes know which path the ACK should follow back to s. β_{ACK} is based on a 3 bits labelling scheme λ_{ACK}. The first bit, X_1, indicates if a node u will be in *miniD* at least once during the broadcast. If yes,

---

Algorithm 3. $\beta_{oACK}(\mu)$ executed at each node v

%Each node has a variable *sourcemsg*. The source node has this variable initially set to μ, all other nodes have it initially set to *null*.

for each round r from 0 **do**
    if v is source node and $r = 0$ **then**
        transmit *sourcemsg*
    if v is not source node **then**
        if message m is received AND m $\neq$ "stay" **then**
            sourcemsg $\leftarrow m$
    else if The node received μ before round r **then**
        if v received *sourcemsg* for first time in round $r - 2$ **then**
            if $X_1 = 1$ **then**
                transmit *sourcemsg*
        else if v received *sourcemsg* for first time in round $r - 1$ **then**
            if $X_1 = 0$ and $X_2 = 0$ and $X_3 = 1$ **then**
                transmit "ACK"
            else if $X_2 = 1$ **then**
                transmit "stay"
        else if v received "stay" in round $r - 1$ **then**
            if v transmitted *sourcemsg* in round $r - 2$ **then**
                transmit *sourcemsg*
        else if v received "ACK" in round $r - 1$ **then**
            if $X_3 = 1$ **then**
                transmit "ACK"

---

then X_1 of u equals 1; if not, it equals 0. If X_1 of u equals 1, when u receives message μ, u can re-send it once. The second bit X_2 of u equal to 1 means that u needs to send a *Stay* when it receives μ to notify the sender of μ to stay in *miniD* for the next round. Only one of the informed nodes will have the third bit X_3 equal to 1. This node will generate the ACK to be sent back to s. At the end of the broadcasting, which finishes in $2n - 3$ rounds, the last informed node generates and sends back to the source node the ACK within additional $n - 2$ rounds, where n is the number of nodes in the network.

Our optimization with respect to the λ_{ACK} proposed in [12] comes from the following simple observation: in a 3-bits labelling, there are 8 possible states: 000, 001, 010, 011, 100, 101, 110 and 111. The algorithm in [12] uses only 5 of them: 000, 001, 010, 100 and 110. In this section, we propose a labelling scheme, λ_{oACK} and a broadcast scheme with ACK algorithm that use all the 8 states of the 3-bits labelling in order to improve the memory complexity of the solution proposed in [12]. The idea of our optimization is as follows: instead of only using the last bit X_3 (the third bit) as a marker to point who is (one of) the last informed node(s) during the broadcast, we use also this third bit to show a path back to the source node s from the last informed node. Differently, from the solution proposed in [12], nodes do not need to keep additional variables in order to send back the ACK during the execution. Our proposition can therefore, save node's memory and computational power.

In the following, we present our λ_{oACK} labelling scheme and β_{oACK} algorithm.

3-bits Labelling Scheme λ_{oACK}

The first two bits of the labelling scheme X_1 and X_2 have the same functionality as in the λ_{ACK} scheme of [12]. The intuitive idea is as follows: 1) $X_1 = 1$ for nodes who should propagate μ when they receive it; 2) $X_2 = 1$ for nodes that need to send $Stay$ back to their sender neighbour to notice that they need to stay in $miniD$ and send μ one more time in the next round; 3) $X_3 = 1$ for one of the last receiving nodes to generate ACK and send it back to the source node s. In our scheme λ_{oACK} we also set X_3 (the third bit) to 1 for all nodes on the path back from the last informed node (who holds 001) to s. Note that, nodes on that path could have four kinds of different labels: 101, 011, 111 and 001, where 001 is the label of the last informed node. Label states 101, 011 and 111 are not used in the original β_{ACK}, therefore nodes can easily recognize if they are on the path to transmit ACK back to s. Note that we do not change the main architecture of the algorithm β_{ACK} with labelling scheme λ proposed in [12], therefore the correctness proof of our algorithm is very similar to the one in [12]. See Sect. 7 for a detailed proof that follows the lines of the proof in [12].

Broadcast Algorithm β_{oACK}

Our broadcast algorithm β_{oACK} that uses λ_{oACK} described above is described as Algorithm 3. Nodes with $X_1 = 1$ receiving a message at round $i - 1$ send it at round i. Then nodes who send at round i wait for the $stay$ message, at round $i + 1$, from nodes with $X_2 = 1$. If nodes who send at round i receive a $stay$ at round $x + 1$, they continue to send one more time μ at round $i + 2$, otherwise, they stay silent. When nodes with label 001 receive the message, they generate an ACK and send it. Since λ_{oACK} already marked the path back to the source node, in Algorithm β_{oACK}, the ACK message will only be re-propagated by nodes with $X_3 = 1$. i.e., nodes with label 101, 111 and 011.

Note that our proposed Algorithm β_{oACK} does not need additional variables to reconstruct the path back to s during the broadcast execution. In Algorithm β_{ACK} [12], two additional variables $informedRound$ (type int) and $transmitRounds$ (type $table$ of int) are needed to rebuild the back-way path. $informedRound$ is used to record the round number in which a node received μ; $transmitRounds$ is a table used to record all the round numbers in which one node transmits μ. However, by using β_{oACK}, the ACK transmission processing can be completed only by checking the third bit, X_3. Our Algorithm β_{oACK} does not need any extra local storage for detecting the path for ACK.

Correctness of β_{oACK}

Our proposition of β_{oACK} with λ_{oACK} is based on the algorithm β with labelling scheme λ proposed in [12]. The algorithm β_{oACK} can be seen as the combination of two phases: $Broadcast$ $Phase$ and ACK $Phase$. The aim of the broadcast phase of β_{oACK} is to finish first the broadcast: every node in the network should be informed of the message μ sent by the source node. In the second phase, one of the last informed nodes will generate ACK and send it back to the source node through a specific path marked according to the labelling scheme λ_{oACK}.

These two phases are well separated, because ACK will only be generated and sent to the network after one of the last informed nodes received μ sent by the source node. Therefore, there will be no collisions between μ and ACK during the execution of λ_{oACK}.

During the first broadcast phase, we use exactly the same idea of the algorithm β with labelling scheme λ in [12]. The correctness of this phase is given as Theorem 4 in [12], as follows:

Theorem 4 *[12].* *Consider any n-node unlabelled graph G with a designated source node s with μ. By applying the 2-bits labelling scheme λ and then executing algorithm beta, all nodes in $G \setminus \{s\}$ are informed within $2n - 3$ rounds.*

As described in Sect. 7, the idea is that every two rounds, if there are still nodes that have not received μ yet, a non-null subset of these nodes will form the new $Frnt$. When the new $miniD$ set of nodes send μ, some nodes belonging to $Frnt$ will receive it. Then the number of the non-informed nodes will decrease until 0. In the worst case, when the topology of the network is a line, μ has to go through all of them one by one to reach every node. The algorithm therefore finishes within $2n$ rounds.

We then prove that the ACK phase of β_{oACK}, finishes within n rounds.

Lemma 7. *After the broadcast phase finishes during the execution of β_{oACK}, ACK will be sent back to the source node within n rounds.*

Proof. By using λ_{oACK} described in Sect. 7, only one of the last informed nodes u will have its three bits equal to 001. Then u will send ACK, and only nodes with $X_3 = 1$ can forward ACK back only when they received it. The back-forward path to the source node is chosen by λ_{oACK}. In the worst case, when the topology of the network is a line, then the ACK has to go through all the nodes to reach the source node. Therefore, during the execution of β_{oACK}, ACK will need at most n rounds to reach the source node.

The Theorem 4 and Lemma 7 therefore complete the correctness proof of β_{oACK}.

Appendix B: Wireless Network Specification

The motivation of the study of level-separable networks comes from the recent studies of WBAN. WBAN is similar to WSN (Wireless Sensor Networks) in terms of devices functionalities and architecture. However, WBAN still has important differences with WSN. The deployment environment and application scenario make them totally different: WSN is usually deployed in wide range areas; WBAN on the other hand, is deployed on (or inside) the human body, to detect various physiological parameters of the human body. WBAN devices are in close contact with the body, therefore the transmission power cannot has a setting as high as in the case of WSN. Using a relatively small transmission power in WBAN might be greatly affected by the absorption, interference and refraction of the human body.

Furthermore, WBAN has to face the challenge of the human body mobility, which makes the connection between nodes appear and disappear from time to time. The challenge in WBAN is how to improve the communication reliability of the network by taking into consideration the human mobility and the changes in the communication channels.

To our best knowledge, Naganawa *et al.* [27] proposed the first simulation-based *Data Sets* of the human mobility and the channel quality change. These data sets provide measurement results of channel attenuation between different WBAN devices deployed on different positions of the human body during different human movement actions. The data sets have been validated by comparing to massive real-human based measurement results.

The network architecture of proposed environment is composed of seven WBAN devices distributed on the body as follows: Navel, Chest, Head, Upper Arm, Ankle, Thigh and Wrist. The authors measure the connectivity between every two nodes in seven different postures: 1) Walking, 2) Running, 3) Walking weakly, 4) Sitting down, 5) Lying down, 6) Sleeping and 7) Putting on a jacket, respectively (see Fig. 4).

In each posture, a continuous human action has been decomposed into a set of frames. Each single human body picture with a corresponding frame number, x, is a screenshot of this continuous human action at the xth frame. For example, in posture 1) Walking (see Fig. 4), the continuous action takes 30 frame, and it uses four screenshots at 1st frame, 10th frame, 20th frame and the 30th frame, respectively to represent this action. The red diamonds in the figures represent sensors on the human body while the body is moving.

Tables 1, 2, 3, 4, 5, 6, and to 7 show the measurement results of channel attenuation between two nodes pair in seven different human mobility postures. Values above the main diagonal represent the mean values of the random channel attenuation between any two WBAN nodes of the body. Based on data sets from [27], authors of [2] propose a channel-mobility model: for every wireless signal sent from a WBAN node, a random attenuation is added to the outgoing communication channel. If the signal strength after the attenuation is smaller than the sensitivity of the receiver, it will be dropped. The random attenuation is calculated by different normal distributions specified by means and standard deviations for each couple of nodes (e.g., the random channel attenuation between nodes on head and on upper arm in posture 1) Walking has the mean 45.4 dB and the standard deviations 5.1 dB).

Table 1. Means and Standards Deviations of Path Loss for all the links in Posture 1) Walking [27]

T_X or R_X	navel	chest	head	upper arm	ankle	thigh	wrist	
navel		30.6	45.1	44.4	57.4	45.8	41.0	
chest	0.5		38.5	40.6	58.2	51.6	45.1	
head	0.8	0.5		45.4	64.0	61.3	49.7	
upper arm	5.8	5.2	5.1		54.2	45.5	34.0	Mean[dB]
ankle	4.3	3.4	5.0	3.1		40.6	48.9	
thigh	2.0	2.5	6.8	4.8	1.0		35.0	
wrist	5.0	3.6	3.8	2.5	3.8	3.3		

Standard deviation [dB]

Table 2. Means and Standards Deviations of Path Loss for all the links in Posture 2) Running [27]

T_X or R_X	navel	chest	head	upper arm	ankle	thigh	wrist	
navel		31.4	47.4	54.5	57.9	44.8	45.9	
chest	1.4		41.0	39.2	61.0	49.9	41.2	
head	3.5	2.9		41.3	65.6	59.3	45.5	
upper arm	9.9	8.4	8.4		58.0	52.4	33.8	Mean[dB]
ankle	6.9	6.9	5.7	8.2		39.0	56.9	
thigh	2.0	2.5	6.8	4.8	1.0		49.6	
wrist	6.1	8.2	3.5	4.6	7.5	11.6		

Standard deviation [dB]

Table 3. Means and Standards Deviations of Path Loss for all the links in Posture 3) Walking weakly [27]

T_X or R_X	navel	chest	head	upper arm	ankle	thigh	wrist	
navel		26.1	42.4	44.3	55.4	44.9	34.0	
chest	0.4		38.1	37.3	58.8	47.1	41.7	
head	1.3	0.7		44.5	52.4	60.0	42.8	
upper arm	5.5	5.5	6.8		53.7	45.1	34.5	Mean[dB]
ankle	4.2	4.6	3.3	6.1		42.4	49.2	
thigh	2.2	5.3	5.4	4.8	2.2		37.9	
wrist	2.8	2.5	1.5	3.1	4.8	4.4		

Standard deviation [dB]

Fig. 4. 7 Different Human Postures [27]

Table 4. Means and Standards Deviations of Path Loss for all the links in Posture 4) Sitting down [27]

T_X or R_X	navel	chest	head	upper arm	ankle	thigh	wrist	
navel		27.9	41.1	41.5	59.6	48.3	38.6	
chest	1.0		37.0	36.0	60.0	51.0	43.2	
head	1.6	0.8		42.1	63.7	59.1	46.9	
upper arm	5.3	4.8	6.3		63.7	49.0	37.7	Mean[dB]
ankle	8.4	8.0	8.7	8.1		40.9	60.2	
thigh	6.3	5.3	7.8	5.5	6.3		35.1	
wrist	4.6	5.3	5.5	5.7	9.6	6.9		
			Standard deviation [dB]					

Table 5. Means and Standards Deviations of Path Loss for all the links in Posture 5) Lying down [27]

T_X or R_X	navel	chest	head	upper arm	ankle	thigh	wrist	
navel		30.5	45.1	54.1	65.0	55.8	49.7	
chest	2.2		38.2	43.4	63.6	54.3	46.5	
head	3.3	1.3		40.0	61.8	58.6	45.5	
upper arm	5.9	4.2	4.2		58.3	50.1	38.8	Mean[dB]
ankle	6.9	5.8	7.0	5.1		41.2	44.7	
thigh	12.4	10.1	10.1	10.1	7.2		41.6	
wrist	6.3	4.9	3.8	1.9	9.6	8.8		
			Standard deviation [dB]					

Table 6. Means and Standards Deviations of Path Loss for all the links in Posture 6) Sleeping [27]

T_X or R_X	navel	chest	head	upper arm	ankle	thigh	wrist	
navel		31.7	64.3	66.5	72.5	56.3	58.6	
chest	4.3		50.9	51.9	72.4	51.3	44.1	
head	10.4	10.6		39.0	69.4	59.9	42.5	
upper arm	4.6	2.7	11.3		51.5	42.7	30.9	Mean[dB]
ankle	5.7	7.5	9.3	0.8		35.7	56.8	
thigh	5.0	2.1	10.8	2.6	0.9		48.9	
wrist	7.8	4.1	7.2	3.6	2.8	2.5		
			Standard deviation [dB]					

Studies [4,6] conducted in WBAN show that various postural mobilities can be modeled as graphs (one for each human posture), see Fig. 5. Moreover, the authors in [5] proved that the performances of any protocol for wireless body area networks strongly depend on the topology of the graph and it should be noted that none of the graphs corresponds to the classical classes (e.g. planar or minor-free).

In the case presented above (the only available to date benchmark for practical WBAN), each graph is a level-separable network defined below.

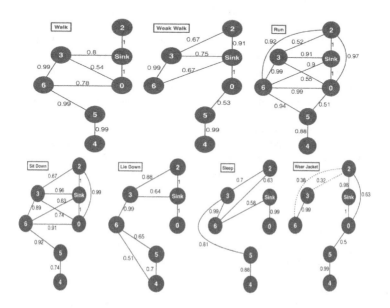

Fig. 5. Graphs that model human postures in WBAN. Numbers on the edges represent the edge reliability [4]

Table 7. Means and Standards Deviations of Path Loss for all the links in Posture 6) Wearing a jack [27]

T_X or R_X	navel	chest	head	upper arm	ankle	thigh	wrist	
navel		27.4	43.3	56.8	62.8	45.0	52.0	
chest	3.4		37.4	51.4	60.4	47.7	50.9	
head	4.9	3.6		49.2	64.0	51.7	46.8	
upper arm	6.7	5.1	9.2		52.3	52.9	31.1	Mean[dB]
ankle	7.1	9.9	8.8	4.1		39.5	55.1	
thigh	2.5	6.3	7.0	5.1	1.7		52.3	
wrist	7.4	5.9	5.9	4.8	10.8	7.7		
			Standard deviation [dB]					

References

1. Abiteboul, S., Kaplan, H., Milo, T.: Compact labeling schemes for ancestor queries. In: Proceedings of the 12th Annual ACM-SIAM Symposium on Discrete Algorithms, pp. 547–556. Society for Industrial and Applied Mathematics (2001)
2. Badreddine, W., Chaudet, C., Petruzzi, F., Potop-Butucaru, M.: Broadcast strategies in wireless body area networks. In: Proceedings of the 18th ACM International Conference on Modeling, Analysis and Simulation of Wireless and Mobile Systems, pp. 83–90. ACM (2015)
3. Badreddine, W., Khernane, N., Potop-Butucaru, M., Chaudet, C.: Convergecast in wireless body area networks. Ad Hoc Netw. **66**, 40–51 (2017)
4. Badreddine, W., Potop-Butucaru, M.: Peak transmission rate resilient crosslayer broadcast for body area networks. arXiv preprint arXiv:1702.05031 (2017)
5. Bruno, B., Gewu, B., Maria, P.-B.: Markovian model for broadcast in wireless body area networks. In: Proceedings of the 17th ACM International Symposium on Mobility Management and Wireless. ACM (2019)
6. Bu, G., Potop-Butucaru, M.: Total order reliable convergecast in WBAN. In: Proceedings of the 18th International Conference on Distributed Computing and Networking, p. 26. ACM (2017)
7. Gewu, B., Potop-Butucaru, M.: BAN-GZKP: optimal zero knowledge proof based scheme for wireless body area networks. Ad Hoc Netw. **77**, 28–41 (2018)
8. Bu, G., Potop-Butucaru, M.: Wireless Broadcast with short labelling. arXiv arXiv:1901.08919v2 (February 2019)
9. Cicalese, F., Manne, F., Xin, Q.: Faster deterministic communication in radio networks. Algorithmica **54**(2), 226–242 (2009)
10. Clementi, A.E.F., Monti, A., Silvestri, R.: Selective families, superimposed codes, and broadcasting on unknown radio networks. In: Proceedings of the 12th Annual ACM-SIAM Symposium on Discrete Algorithms, pp. 709–718. Society for Industrial and Applied Mathematics (2001)
11. Cohen, R., Fraigniaud, P., Ilcinkas, D., Korman, A., Peleg, D.: Label-guided graph exploration by a finite automaton. ACM Trans. Algorithms (TALG) **4**(4), 42 (2008)
12. Ellen, F., Gorain, B., Miller, A., Pelc, A.: Constant-length labeling schemes for deterministic radio broadcast. In: The 31st ACM on Symposium on Parallelism in Algorithms and Architectures, pp. 171–178. ACM (2019)
13. Fraigniaud, P., Ilcinkas, D., Pelc, A.: Tree exploration with advice. Inf. Comput. **206**(11), 1276–1287 (2008)
14. Fraigniaud, P., Korman, A., Lebhar, E.: Local MST computation with short advice. Theor. Comput. Syst **47**(4), 920–933 (2010). https://doi.org/10.1007/s00224-010-9280-9
15. Gavoille, C., Peleg, D., Pérennes, S., Raz, R.: Distance labeling in graphs. J. Algorithms **53**(1), 85–112 (2004)
16. Glacet, C., Miller, A., Pelc, A.: Time vs. information tradeoffs for leader election in anonymous trees. ACM Trans. Algorithms (TALG) **13**(3), 31 (2017)
17. Gorain, B., Pelc, A.: Finding the size of a radio network with short labels. In: Proceedings of the 19th International Conference on Distributed Computing and Networking, p. 10. ACM (2018)
18. Gross, J.L., Yellen, J.: Graph Theory and its Applications. CRC Press, Boca Raton (2005)
19. Haimovich, A.M., Blum, R.S., Cimini, L.J.: MIMO radar with widely separated antennas. IEEE Sig. Process. Mag. **25**(1), 116–129 (2007)

20. Ilcinkas, D., Kowalski, D.R., Pelc, A.: Fast radio broadcasting with advice. Theor. Comput. Sci **411**(14–15), 1544–1557 (2010)
21. Javaid, N., Khan, N.A., Shakir, M., Khan, M.A., Bouk, S.H., Khan, Z.A.: Ubiquitous healthcare in wireless body area networks - A survey. CoRR, abs/1303.2062 (March 2013)
22. Johnson, D.S., Garey, M.R.: Computers and Intractability: A Guide to the Theory of NP-Completeness, vol. 1. WH Freeman, San Francisco (1979)
23. Kowalski, D.R., Pelc, A.: Optimal deterministic broadcasting in known topology radio networks. Distrib. Comput. **19**(3), 185–195 (2007)
24. Latré, B., Braem, B., Moerman, I., Blondia, C., Demeester, P.: A survey on wireless body area networks. Wirel. Netw. **17**(1), 1–18 (2011)
25. Li, J., Stoica, P.: MIMO radar with colocated antennas. IEEE Sig. Process. Mag. **24**(5), 106–114 (2007)
26. Movassaghi, S., Abolhasan, M., Lipman, J., Smith, D., Jamalipour, A.: Wireless body area networks: a survey. IEEE Commun. Surv. Tut. **16**(3), 1658–1686 (2014)
27. Naganawa, J., Wangchuk, K., Kim, M., Aoyagi, T., Takada, J.: Simulation-based scenario-specific channel modeling for WBAN cooperative transmission schemes. IEEE J. Biomed. Health Inform. **19**, 559–570 (2015)

The Imitation Game: Algorithm Selection by Exploiting Black-Box Recommenders

Georgios Damaskinos[1]([✉]), Rachid Guerraoui[1], Erwan Le Merrer[2], and Christoph Neumann[3]

[1] Ecole Polytechnique Fédérale de Lausanne, Lausanne, Switzerland
georgios.damaskinos@gmail.com,
{georgios.damaskinos,rachid.guerraoui}@epfl.ch
[2] Université de Rennes, Inria, CNRS, IRISA, Rennes, France
erwan.le-merrer@inria.fr
[3] InterDigital, Rennes, France
christoph.neumann@interdigital.com

Abstract. Cross-validation is commonly used to select the recommendation algorithms that will generalize best on yet unknown data. Yet, in many situations the available dataset used for cross-validation is scarce and the selected algorithm might not be the best suited for the unknown data. In contrast, established companies have a large amount of data available to select and tune their recommender algorithms, which therefore should generalize better. These companies often make their recommender systems available as black-boxes, i.e., users query the recommender through an API or a browser. This paper proposes RECRANK, a technique that exploits a black-box recommender system, in addition to classic cross-validation. RECRANK employs graph similarity measures to compute a *distance* between the output recommendations of the black-box and of the considered algorithms. We empirically show that RECRANK provides a substantial improvement (33%) for the selection of algorithms for the MovieLens dataset, in comparison with standalone cross-validation.

Keywords: Recommender algorithm selection · Black-box exploitation · Cross-validation · Graph similarity · Spearman ranking

1 Introduction

The availability of open source recommendation algorithms and engines is appealing for startups or institutions that bootstrap their online services. A plethora of approaches, from collaborative filtering techniques to neural network based approaches are now at disposal [9], along with the deluge of research results that are thoroughly described (but not open-sourced). The users of online services generate a huge volume of data thus triggering the advantage shift from solely leveraging a good item recommendation algorithm, to having access to

G. Damaskinos—Work done during an internship at Technicolor - Rennes.

both a good algorithm and a considerable amount of data for training or parameterizing it. In that context, it is clear that the big industrial players, have a steady and decisive advantage over potential newcomers on the market since they have both significant engineering work-forces and a large audience to get data from. Those established companies propose recommendation services, that interact with users through queries from browser-interactions or standard APIs. The recommendation algorithm acts as a black-box from the perspective of the user, and for potential observers such as those newcomers.

We present RECRANK, a method to sort a list of available recommendation algorithms based on their ability to generalize on unknown data. In stark contrast with cross-validation, this method exploits the recommendations of an established black-box recommender, and captures how well each of the available recommendation algorithms *imitates* the black-box recommender. We evaluate RECRANK and depict its superiority against classic cross-validation and an alternative ranking method. Our code is available [3].

Problem Setting. Let $\mathcal{D}$ be the corpus of data that the recommender interacts with. This data includes tuples of the form $\langle u, i, l \rangle$ where a user u gives feedback l (implicit or explicit) for a certain item i. We split $\mathcal{D}$ into three parts: $\mathcal{D} = \{\mathcal{D}_a \cup \mathcal{D}_b \cup \mathcal{D}_u\}$.

On the one hand, an entity (e.g., a startup) targets to bootstrap a recommender. This entity has access to an *available dataset* $\mathcal{D}_a$, typically limited in size. This entity has also access to a set of open-sourced or in-house *candidate* recommendation algorithms, and needs to select the ones that will generalize best (i.e., provide good recommendations) on an *unknown dataset* $\mathcal{D}_u$.

On the other hand, a well-established recommendation service (e.g., IMDB, Spotify) enables *queries* to its recommender, typically through an API. We assume that the well-established recommender was trained using a private (i.e., available only to itself) dataset $\mathcal{D}_b$ (typically significantly larger than $\mathcal{D}_a$) and a private algorithm. This algorithm is a black-box to a user, and we denote it as $f(\mathcal{D}_b)$. The inputs to the black-box recommender are queries of the form $\langle u, i, l \rangle$ and the output is a ranked list of the top-N recommendations for user u, typically based on knowledge of the black-box recommender regarding u and i. For example, users make queries such as $\langle user, song, click \rangle$ (Spotify), $\langle user, video, like \rangle$ (YouTube) or $\langle user, movie, rating \rangle$ (IMDB) and get a ranked list of recommendations such as "Made for Alice" (Spotify), "Up next" (YouTube) or "Recommended For You" (IMDB), respectively.

Let $\mathcal{A}$ be the set of considered recommendation algorithms, along with their hyper-parameters. We define $P_A(\mathcal{D}) \in \mathbb{R}$ as the performance measure of an algorithm $A \in \mathcal{A}$ given a dataset $\mathcal{D}$ (e.g., the precision of A after splitting $\mathcal{D}$ into a training and validation set). Let $\mathcal{K}$ be *any* side knowledge. We consider $r(\mathcal{A}, \mathcal{D}, \mathcal{K})$ to be a ranking function producing a sorted array $[A_0, A_1, \ldots, A_{n-1}]$, such that $P_{A_0}(\mathcal{D}) \geq P_{A_1}(\mathcal{D}) \geq \cdots \geq P_{A_{n-1}}(\mathcal{D})$. Each algorithm in $\mathcal{A}$ is solely trained and cross-validated using $\mathcal{D}_a$. We define the optimal ranking as $r^* :=$

$r(\mathcal{A}, \mathcal{D}_a \cup \mathcal{D}_u, \emptyset)$, i.e., the perfect ranking for the available trained algorithms after taking into account the yet unknown data $\mathcal{D}_u$.

Black-Box Exploitation. We define the problem of exploiting a black-box recommender for algorithm selection as finding the ranking:

$$r := \arg \max_{r\prime} \rho(r^*, r\prime(\mathcal{A}, \mathcal{D}_a, f(\mathcal{D}_b))) \tag{1}$$

with ρ being the Spearman ranking correlation score (Sect. 3). The goal is to obtain side knowledge from the black-box in order to produce a ranking that gets closer to the optimal ranking. Our working hypothesis is that:

$$\rho(r^*, r(\mathcal{A}, \mathcal{D}_a, f(\mathcal{D}_b))) > \rho(r^*, r(\mathcal{A}, \mathcal{D}_a, \emptyset))) \tag{2}$$

i.e., there exists a gain (in comparison with cross-validation) from the information $f(\mathcal{D}_b)$ leaked from the black-box.

Noteworthy, the option of building a proxy recommender that always employs the black-box is not practical. Sending all the data to the black-box implies potential privacy violations as the user feedback (e.g., movie ratings) is forwarded to a third-party. From the system performance perspective, there are significant additional bandwidth costs and the service throughput is bounded by the query APIs limits (e.g., IMDB via RapidAPI has a limit of 1000 requests per day [17]). Therefore, the goal is to bootstrap the service and then only utilize the selected algorithm locally.

2   RECRANK

We introduce, RECRANK, a ranking function that exploits the outputs of a black-box (series of top-N recommendations) to compute a *distance* between each algorithm in $\mathcal{A}$ and a black-box recommender, under the assumption that the black-box generalizes better due to its larger dataset (we validate this assumption in Sect. 3). The final ranking of RECRANK follows the ascending order of this distance: the better an algorithm imitates the black-box, the higher its ranking.

RECRANK consists of two components as shown in Fig. 1. REC2GRAPH transforms the output of a recommender into a graph data structure. The graph obtained from the outputs of the black-box is compared to the graph obtained from the outputs of each algorithm in $\mathcal{A}$, in order to compute a distance D with GRAPHDIST. The graph representation captures latent information about the recommender outputs (e.g., popularity of certain items among different subsets of users). This information is important for the performance of RECRANK, as we empirically show in Sect. 3 by using a baseline that directly compares the outputs of the two algorithms. RECRANK is shown in Algorithm 1, where $get\_rec(X, \mathcal{D}_q)$ returns the top-N recommendations of algorithm X given inputs in *query dataset* $\mathcal{D}_q$.

REC2GRAPH. This method transforms the output of the queried recommender into a graph. Building a graph from recommendations was recently shown to be

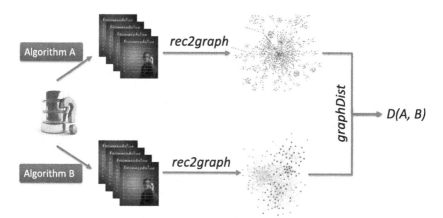

Fig. 1. Core components of RecRank. Algorithm A is each algorithm in set $\mathcal{A}$ using the available dataset $\mathcal{D}_a$, while B is the black-box recommender. RecRank builds a graph for each algorithm using Rec2Graph and computes a distance between graphs using GraphDist.

Algorithm 1: RecRank

Input: Candidate algorithm set $\mathcal{A}$, black-box B, query set $\mathcal{D}_q$
1   $G_b = $ Rec2Graph $(get\_rec(B, \mathcal{D}_q))$
2   **for** A **in** $\mathcal{A}$ **do**
3      $G_a = $ Rec2Graph $(get\_rec(A, \mathcal{D}_q))$
4      $D(A, B) = $ GraphDist (G_a, G_b)
5      $distances.append(D(A, B))$
6   **end**
7   **return** $sort(distances)$

---

interesting for several applications [7,13]. For each query $\langle u, i, l \rangle$ in the query dataset, we denote as $\mathcal{D}_q$, the recommender outputs a list of the top-N recommendations. Rec2Graph constructs the graph according to the following rules.

- *Vertex i*: There exists a recommendation for item i and/or there exists a query for item i in $\mathcal{D}_q$ (e.g., a movie rating).
- *Edge e_{ij}*: Item j is at least in one of the top-N recommendation lists given as an output to a query for item i.
- *Weight* $w_{ij} = \dfrac{\sum_{e_{ij}} ranking\_score}{\sum_{e \in E} \sum_e ranking\_score}$

where $\sum_{e_{ij}} ranking\_score$ is the summation of the recommender output over all recommendations for item j triggered by a query for item i.[1]

---

[1] If the recommender only outputs a top-N list, the output for each item is the rank (e.g., value $\in [1, 5]$ for top-5 outputs).

The edge weight captures the fact that there are typically multiple recommendations between the same items. For example, a user might receive the same item in multiple top-N recommendations before she either clicks it or the recommender lowers its ranking and removes it from the top-N list. The denominator normalizes each weight in order for the graphs of different algorithms to be comparable, given that the scores of each recommender have different scales.

GRAPHDIST. In order to compare the two graphs, GRAPHDIST extracts a set of features for each graph (denoted as $\mathbf{X}_A$ and $\mathbf{X}_B$) and computes the distance between the two algorithms:

$$D(A, B) := \|\mathbf{X}_A - \mathbf{X}_B\| \tag{3}$$

GRAPHDIST extracts features that capture the state of the algorithm recommendations. For the features that involve distributions, we employ statistical values depending on whether we assume a Gaussian prior or not. We list a subset of these features below, and note that $\mathbf{X} \in \mathbb{R}^{31}$; the full set of the 31 features that GRAPHDIST employs is available in our code [3]. We normalize the feature vectors by using z-score normalization.

- *Number vertices and number of edges.* These illustrate the number of distinct recommendations.
- *Vertex in-degree.* This shows how polarized the recommendations are, i.e., how many popular items are recommended and how much is their popularity.
- *PageRank.* This indicates the PageRank centrality in the graph of the recommended items.
- *Eigenvector and betweeness centrality.* These centrality measures show how many items are the most central, i.e., most popular among the recommendations.
- *Closeness centrality.* This also captures the topological proximity of a given item to the others in the graph.
- *Assortativity.* This shows the connectivity between nodes of similar degree, i.e., how much popular items are connected to other popular items.
- *Shortest distances.* For each vertex, we compute the mean value of its shortest distances with each other vertex. We then average these mean values across all vertexes. This feature captures how close each item node is to the others.

The construction of GRAPHDIST boosts the *interpretability* of RECRANK. Given the output of RECRANK, one can determine the contributing factor of each feature to this output. For example, if the *Vertex in-degree* feature has a very similar value for the candidate algorithm and the black box (i.e., contribution to the distance is minimal) comparing to the other features, then one can conclude that recommending popular items is an important factor for the final rank (output of RECRANK) of this candidate algorithm.

3   Evaluation

We study the performance of RecRank on the *MovieLens* dataset[2] that consists of 100,000 ratings from 943 users on 1682 movies.

Table 1. Candidate recommendation algorithms. Information regarding the hyperparameters is available in our open-source repository [3].

Library	Model-based	Memory-based	Baselines
Librec	AOBPR, BIASEDMFlib, BPMFlib, EALSlib, LDAlib, LLORMAlib, NMFlib, SVDPPlib, PMF2lib PMFlib, RBMlib	KNNlib	MPOPlib, RANDlib
Surpriselib	NMF, PMF, SVD, SVDpp	KNNWithMeans	

Recommendation Algorithms. We collect recommendation algorithms from open-source libraries: 14 algorithms from Librec[3] and 5 algorithms from SurpriseLib,[4] as summarized in Table 1. We consider that a different implementation of the same algorithm constitutes a new candidate recommendation algorithm (e.g., KNNlib and KNNWithMeans): the output recommendations depend on various factors that differ among the two libraries (e.g., the formula for calculating the rating prediction). Additionally, we include two versions of the PMF algorithm (denoted as PMFlib and PMF2lib) with a different hyper-parameter tuning setup. Therefore, we illustrate that a different tuning (that can be the result of a difference in the resources for the A/B testing phase) leads to a different recommendation behavior (Table 2), thus to a different candidate recommendation algorithm.

Evaluation Metrics. We now describe the metrics used for reflecting the performance of the candidate recommender and for demonstrating the efficacy of RecRank.

Precision. We adopt this metric to test the accuracy of the recommendations. Given that $\mathcal{H}_u$ is the set of recommended items that were clicked by a user u (hits), and $\mathcal{R}_u$ is the set of items recommended to u, we denote the precision for u by $Precision_u$ and define it as follows.

$$Precision_u = \frac{|\mathcal{H}_u|}{|\mathcal{R}_u|} \tag{4}$$

---

[2] http://grouplens.org/datasets/movielens/.
[3] https://www.librec.net/.
[4] https://www.surpriselib.com/.

The overall precision over the whole test set is the average over the precision values for all users in the test set. Note that a recommended item is considered as a *hit*, if the user rates that item anytime later than the time of the recommendation with a rating score larger than 50% of the maximum score [4]. *Recall.* We use this metric to capture the sensitivity of a recommender to the frequency of updates. Given that $\mathcal{C}_u$ is the set of items clicked by a user u, we denote the recall for u by $Recall_u$ and define it as follows.

$$Recall_u = \frac{|\mathcal{H}_u|}{|\mathcal{C}_u|} \tag{5}$$

The overall recall is the average over the recall values for all the users in the test set.

F1-score. We employ this standard metric to measure the recommendation accuracy in order to combine the precision and recall into a single score.

$$F1_u = 2 * \frac{Precision_u * Recall_u}{Precision_u + Recall_u}$$

Spearman Correlation. We use this metric to evaluate the ranking quality of RecRank. Moreover, we compute the Spearman rank-order correlation coefficient between the output ranking and the optimal ranking r^*, i.e., the ranking after evaluating the candidates on the dataset $\mathcal{D}_u$. A value of 0 indicates no correlation and a value of 1 an exact monotonic relationship; thus the higher the value of this metric, the better the performance. This metric is computed as follows [5]:

$$\rho = 1 - \frac{6 \sum d_i^2}{n(n^2 - 1)}, \ 1 \leq i \leq C \tag{6}$$

where $d_i = rank(A_i) - optimal\_rank(A_i)$, is the difference between the two ranks for each candidate algorithm and n is the number of candidates.

The impact of an ordering mismatch does not depend on the rank of the mismatch. For example, the Spearman correlation between $\{1, 2, 3, 4\}$ and $\{1, 2, 4, 3\}$ is the same as $\{1, 2, 3, 4\}$ and $\{2, 1, 4, 3\}$. This ensures an equal weight for all the ranked candidates based on the fact that the entity that employs RecRank can have access to any subset of these candidates.

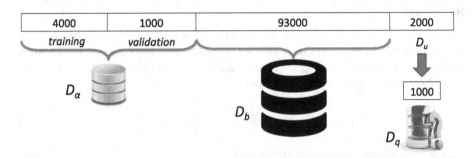

Fig. 2. Chronological data split for MovieLens. The first part is used for $\mathcal{D}_a$, the largest part for the black-box $\mathcal{D}_b$, and the last part is the yet unknown data $\mathcal{D}_u$.

Evaluation Scheme. We replay the dataset, ordered by the timestamp, to capture the original temporal behavior. We split the dataset into $\mathcal{D}_a, \mathcal{D}_b, \mathcal{D}_u, \mathcal{D}_q$, according to Fig. 2, and derive $\mathcal{D}_q$ by randomly sampling 1000 ratings from $\mathcal{D}_u$. We then train all the available recommendation algorithms on $\mathcal{D}_b$ and evaluate them on $\mathcal{D}_u$. Given our assumption regarding a black-box recommender with (a) significantly more data available for training and (b) superior algorithm (Sect. 1), we (a) make $\mathcal{D}_b$ significantly larger than $\mathcal{D}_a$ and (b) select the recommendation algorithm with the highest F1-score as the black-box. The remaining recommendation algorithms constitute our *candidate recommendation algorithms*. Finally, we re-train each candidate recommendation algorithm on the training set (first split of $\mathcal{D}_a$) and tune on the validation set (second split of $\mathcal{D}_a$, i.e., most recent 1000 ratings, based on the benchmark for evaluating stream-based recommenders [10]). Further information regarding our training setup (e.g., choice of hyperparameters) is available in our open-source repository [3].

Baselines. We compare RECRANK with the traditional ranking approach (i.e., cross-validation) along with a baseline algorithm, namely SETDISTRANK. SETDISTRANK computes the distance between algorithms directly from their outputs (i.e., without the REC2GRAPH and GRAPHDIST methods). The comparison with SETDISTRANK illustrates the importance of these two methods for the performance of RECRANK. SETDISTRANK computes the distance as follows:

$$D(A, B) = \frac{|\bigcap_{u \in \mathcal{U}} Recommended_u| + |\bigcap_{i \in \mathcal{I}} Recommended_i|}{2} \quad (7)$$

where $\mathcal{U}$ is the set of users and $\mathcal{I}$ is the set of items. $Recommended_u$ is the per-user recommendation set, i.e., the set of all the items recommended after a query from user u. $\bigcap_{u \in \mathcal{U}} Recommended_u$ denotes the intersection among all the per-user recommendation sets of the algorithms A, B. $Recommended_i$ is defined respectively.

Experimental Results. We train the candidate recommendation algorithms (Table 1) by using the data scheme in Fig. 2 and present the results in Table 2. First, we observe that the ranking derived from cross-validation on $\mathcal{D}_u$ (2nd column) is different than the optimal ranking (3rd column). Therefore, there is room for RECRANK to get a better ranking. We train all the algorithms with the black-box dataset $\mathcal{D}_b$ in order to select the black-box recommender. According to the results shown in the 4th column, this algorithm is LLORMAlib. The 5th column contains the results when training each algorithm on the training set and evaluating on the query set $\mathcal{D}_q$, which constitutes the comparison case for all presented competitors.

We compare the performance of the ranking algorithms by comparing the Spearman correlation with respect to the third column of Table 2. Table 3 depicts the results. The poor performance of the cross-validation on the query set $\mathcal{D}_q$ can be attributed to the chronological sorting of the ratings; the cross-validation becomes accurate if the validation and training set are closer in time and

Table 2. F1 @ top-20 recommendations (and rank) of candidate algorithms (black-box algorithm is in bold).

	Standard cross-validation	Optimal ranking	Black-box ranking	Cross-validation on query set
Training set Evaluation set	$\mathcal{D}_a^{training}$ $\mathcal{D}_a^{validation}$	$\mathcal{D}_a^{training}$ $\mathcal{D}_u$	$\mathcal{D}_b$ $\mathcal{D}_u$	$\mathcal{D}_a^{training}$ $\mathcal{D}_q$
AOBPRlib	0.213 (4)	0.087 (5)	0.156 (5)	0.046 (4)
BIASEDMFlib	0.136 (9)	0.054 (11)	0.057 (11)	0.028 (13)
BPMFlib	0.618 (1)	0.419 (2)	0.408 (2)	0.374 (2)
EALSlib	0.1973 (7)	0.084 (7)	0.138 (6)	0.046 (4)
KNNlib	0.206 (6)	0.085 (6)	0.126 (7)	0.046 (4)
KNNWithMeans	0.039 (19)	0.024 (18)	0.027 (15)	0.016 (18)
LDAlib	0.210 (5)	0.095 (4)	0.164 (4)	0.046 (4)
LLORMAlib	0.611 (2)	0.420 (1)	**0.412** (1)	0.377 (1)
MPOPlib	0.188 (8)	0.074 (9)	0.115 (8)	0.042 (8)
NMF	0.115 (13)	0.048 (15)	0.023 (16)	0.032 (11)
NMFlib	0.045 (18)	0.016 (19)	0.002 (19)	0.012 (19)
PMF	0.083 (16)	0.043 (16)	0.016 (18)	0.022 (17)
PMF2lib	0.133 (10)	0.076 (8)	0.058 (10)	0.037 (9)
PMFlib	0.106 (15)	0.050 (13)	0.030 (14)	0.027 (14)
RANDlib	0.083 (16)	0.039 (17)	0.023 (16)	0.024 (16)
RBMlib	0.565 (3)	0.398 (3)	0.403 (3)	0.358 (3)
SVD	0.123 (11)	0.049 (14)	0.059 (9)	0.033 (10)
SVDpp	0.120 (12)	0.052 (12)	0.051 (12)	0.031 (12)
SVDpplib	0.109 (14)	0.055 (10)	0.031 (13)	0.027 (14)

Table 3. Candidate algorithms ranking evaluation. The correlation factors are computed based on the output ranking of each method and the optimal ranking (third column of Table 2).

Ranking method	Spearman correlation
Standard cross-validation	0.53
Cross-validation on query set	−0.44
SETDISTRANK	0.68
RECRANK	**0.79**

thus have significant overlap in the user sets. We then observe the substantial improvement (33%) that RECRANK provides in comparison with the standard

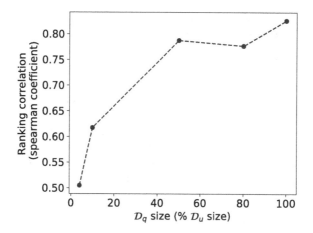

Fig. 3. Effect of the amount of queries on the performance of RECRANK.

cross-validation. The fact that SETDISTRANK also outperforms the cross-validation approach confirms that the information provided by the black-box recommender is valuable even without REC2GRAPH and GRAPHDIST.

Figure 3 depicts the effect that the size of the query set has to the performance of RECRANK. As the portion of $\mathcal{D}_q$ used to query recommenders increases, RECRANK exploits more information to compute better distance values, resulting in a better final ranking. The results of Table 3 have been obtained with a query set $\mathcal{D}_q$ by sampling 50% of $\mathcal{D}_u$ (1000 out of 2000 ratings shown in Fig. 2).

4   Related Work

RECRANK proceeds by comparing the outputs of recommenders similar to benchmarking frameworks [12,18]. These frameworks enable the ranking of a set of recommendation algorithms according to some metric (e.g., F1-score) - similar to what RECRANK does based on $\mathcal{D}_a$ and the output of a black-box service. These frameworks do not allow to compare against the output recommendations of a black-box service that has been trained and tuned on an unknown set of data.

Evaluation of recommenders is very challenging when using offline datasets such as MovieLens. We plan to evaluate RECRANK with additional metrics such as propensity-weighting techniques [1], as well as employ alternative online methodologies and user studies [2]. We also plan to include additional baselines to the standard (i.e., leave-one-out) cross-validation, e.g., based on k-fold validation [11]. Nevertheless, the functionality of RECRANK is independent of the evaluation methodology.

Black-box analysis of recommendation algorithms has been also studied for the goal of algorithmic transparency. Xray [14] infers which user data (e.g. e-mails, searches) a recommender is using. Le Merrer et al. [13] propose a framework for detecting bias in recommended items. Hou et al. [7] proposed to operate random walks on the graph extracted from the recommendations to a user by the Amazon book platform. While these related works try to understand how the remote recommender system works, they do not try build their own recommendation system (i.e. they do not try to benefit from the gained insights to tune a recommender).

Imitation learning [8] and knowledge distillation [6,16] apply the broad idea of learning a policy, a reward function or prediction function by observing an expert system. In that sense, RECRANK is the first attempt to improve the selection of a recommender algorithm by imitating an expert recommender system, typically in production.

RECRANK targets to boost the recommendation quality given a limited amount of data, a problem also known as cold-start. Techniques that boost the quality of a specific recommender, e.g., transfer learning [15], or meta-learning [19] can be used for creating better candidate recommendation algorithms as input to RECRANK.

5   Discussion and Limitations

It is important to notice that, while RECRANK is the first tool to exploit black-box recommender systems for algorithm selection, we do not claim it to be a silver bullet. We discuss the limitations of our work in the following.

Black-Box Recommender Bias. The recommendations of the black-box during the operation of RECRANK may be biased, i.e., not solely targeting the relevance to the users. For example, a commercial music recommender may promote songs from certain premium producers with the goal of direct financial gain. As a second example, the black-box may be a relatively new service that undergoes an A/B testing phase or some "exploration" phase (e.g., with random recommendations). In such cases, we expect RECRANK to output a biased ranking. Given that it is impossible for the user of RECRANK to determine whether the black-box is biased at a given time, we propose multiple deployments of RECRANK across different times. The similarities between the outputs of these deployments could help indicate the deployments that are biased; if the bias is not transient, multiple deployments will not be effective.

Advancing the State-of-the-Art. The goal of RECRANK is not to directly create new recommendation algorithms but to select the most promising ones among a list of candidates. Nevertheless, this selection could be instrumental in developing a new state-of-the-art recommender that is an ensemble of multiple recommendation algorithms. For example, the cold-start component could be intentionally designed to mimic the cold-start behaviour of a well-established service; in that case RECRANK would be of great interest.

Local VS Black-Box Data. A question that may arise in our problem setup is whether there are any constraints for the relation between the training data of the candidate algorithms (local) and the training data of the black-box. In our evaluation (Sect. 3), this relation is that the data has no overlap but comes from the same dataset, i.e., the user rating behaviour follows the preference and behavioural drifts of the MovieLens dataset [4]. We plan to evaluate the performance of RECRANK under alternative relation scenarios (e.g., the data comes from different datasets) as part of our future work.

We expect the performance of RECRANK to degrade as the difference between the characteristics (e.g., how frequent are popular items rated and with what scores) of the local and black-box training data grows. Nevertheless, we highlight that the operation of RECRANK does not have any constraints regarding the training data as the query data is the same both for the candidate algorithms and the black-box. The smaller the relevance between the query data and the training data, the less the performance degradation of RECRANK due to differences in the training data. For example, if the query data only contains new users and new items, then RECRANK is essentially imitating the cold-start behaviour of the black-box and we thus do not expect differences in the training data to significantly degrade RECRANK performance.

The only requirement is for the input and output format of the query dataset to be compliant with the black-box. This requirement is easily satisfied given our generic form of input (tuples of the form $\langle u, i, l \rangle$) and output (ranking list of top-N recommendations) as mentioned in Sect. 1.

6 Concluding Remarks

We present RECRANK, an algorithm that facilitates recommender algorithm selection, traditionally made solely via cross-validation. Our initial results show a promising potential for this tool. Nevertheless, these results do not constitute an in-depth experimental validation and there is work towards measuring the true potential of RECRANK. We also plan to compare REC2GRAPH with alternative methods for transforming the recommender outputs into graphs [7,13]. Finally, we propose RECRANK as one instance of an algorithm that exploits a black-box recommender; we believe this proposal will motivate related works for finding other good performing alternatives with a similar goal.

References

1. Agarwal, A., Wang, X., Li, C., Bendersky, M., Najork, M.: Offline comparison of ranking functions using randomized data. In: REVEAL (2018)
2. Beel, J., Langer, S.: A comparison of offline evaluations, online evaluations, and user studies in the context of research-paper recommender systems. In: Kapidakis, S., Mazurek, C., Werla, M. (eds.) TPDL 2015. LNCS, vol. 9316, pp. 153–168. Springer, Cham (2015). https://doi.org/10.1007/978-3-319-24592-8_12
3. Damaskinos, G.: RecRank source-code. https://github.com/gdamaskinos/RecRank

4. Damaskinos, G., Guerraoui, R., Patra, R.: Capturing the moment: lightweight similarity computations. In: ICDE, pp. 747–758. IEEE (2017). https://doi.org/10.1109/ICDE.2017.126
5. Dodge, Y.: The Concise Encyclopedia of Statistics. Springer Science & Business Media, New York (2008). https://doi.org/10.1007/978-0-387-32833-1
6. Hinton, G., Vinyals, O., Dean, J.: Distilling the knowledge in a neural network. arXiv preprint arXiv:1503.02531 (2015)
7. Hou, L., Liu, K., Liu, J.: Navigated random walks on Amazon book recommendation network. In: Cherifi, C., Cherifi, H., Karsai, M., Musolesi, M. (eds.) COMPLEX NETWORKS 2017 2017. SCI, vol. 689, pp. 935–945. Springer, Cham (2018). https://doi.org/10.1007/978-3-319-72150-7_75
8. Hussein, A., Gaber, M.M., Elyan, E., Jayne, C.: Imitation learning: a survey of learning methods. CSUR **50**(2), 21 (2017)
9. Jenson, G.: Recommenders list (2019). https://github.com/grahamjenson/list_of_recommender_systems
10. Kille, B., et al.: Overview of CLEF newsreel 2015: news recommendation evaluation lab. In: International Conference of the CLEF Initiative (2015)
11. Košir, A., Odić, A., Tkalčič, M.: How to improve the statistical power of the 10-fold cross validation scheme in recommender systems. In: RepSys, pp. 3–6. ACM (2013)
12. Kowald, D., Kopeinik, S., Lex, E.: The TagRec framework as a toolkit for the development of tag-based recommender systems. In: UMAP, pp. 23–28. ACM, New York (2017). https://doi.org/10.1145/3099023.3099069
13. Le Merrer, E., Trédan, G.: The topological face of recommendation. In: Cherifi, C., Cherifi, H., Karsai, M., Musolesi, M. (eds.) COMPLEX NETWORKS 2017 2017. SCI, vol. 689, pp. 897–908. Springer, Cham (2018). https://doi.org/10.1007/978-3-319-72150-7_72
14. Lécuyer, M., et al.: XRay: enhancing the web's transparency with differential correlation. In: USENIX Security Symposium, pp. 49–64 (2014)
15. Pan, W., Xiang, E.W., Liu, N.N., Yang, Q.: Transfer learning in collaborative filtering for sparsity reduction. In: AAAI (2010)
16. Polino, A., Pascanu, R., Alistarh, D.: Model compression via distillation and quantization. In: ICLR (2018)
17. IMDB via RapidAPI query limit. https://rapidapi.com/blog/how-to-use-imdb-api/
18. Said, A., Bellogín, A.: Rival: a toolkit to foster reproducibility in recommender system evaluation. In: RecSys, pp. 371–372. ACM (2014)
19. Vartak, M., Thiagarajan, A., Miranda, C., Bratman, J., Larochelle, H.: A meta-learning perspective on cold-start recommendations for items. In: NIPS, pp. 6904–6914 (2017)

Byzantine k-Set Agreement

Carole Delporte-Gallet[1]([⊠]), Hugues Fauconnier[1], and Mouna Safir[2]

[1] IRIF, Université de Paris, Paris, France
{cd,hf}@irif.fr
[2] Université Polytechnique Mohammed 6, Ben Guerir, Maroc
mouna.safir@um6p.ma

Abstract. In the k-set agreement, each process must decide on a value in such a way that no more than k different values are decided by the processes. The case where $k = 1$ corresponds to the consensus problem. For both theoretical (possibility and impossibility results) and practical (state machine replication) reasons, this problem remains crucial in distributed computing.

In this paper, we study k-set agreement in the synchronous case with Byzantine failures. By extending and fixing the results in [3], we present an (almost) complete cartography of possibility and impossibility results on the Byzantine k-set agreement in synchronous systems depending on the number of processes n, and the number of Byzantine processes t and k.

Keywords: Byzantine failures · Synchronous systems · Set-agreement algorithm

1 Introduction

The k-set agreement problem [4] has been extensively studied in distributed computing [13]. Beyond the practical interest of this problem, particularly regarding fault-tolerant distributed computing, one of the main reasons behind the focus on k-set agreement problem is the fact that it can be used to define and compare computational power properties of systems.

In k-set agreement, each process must decide on value such that no more than k different values are decided by processes. In addition, the processes must guarantee a validity condition according to the failure models of the processes. Therefore, with crash process failures, the validity condition ensures that the decided values are initial values proposed by processes. In the case where $k = 1$, the k-set agreement is the very classical consensus problem which is fundamental for fault tolerant distributed algorithms. An important result in distributed computing is the impossibility of consensus in asynchronous systems when at most one process can crash [6]. Regarding k-set agreement in asynchronous models one of the most famous (and difficult) results is the extension of this impossibility result to the k-set agreement [2,9,14]: the k-set agreement can be resolved if

© Springer Nature Switzerland AG 2021
C. Georgiou and R. Majumdar (Eds.): NETYS 2020, LNCS 12129, pp. 183–191, 2021.
https://doi.org/10.1007/978-3-030-67087-0_12

and only if, at most, $k - 1$ processes may crash. In particular, in the wait-free case (in which at most $n - 1$ processes may crash) we obtain the impossibility of the set-consensus (another name for the $n - 1$ set agreement) whose proof uses techniques of combinatorial topology [8,10]. An important interest of the k-set agreement is its universality in the sense where the k-set agreement allows state machine (with some liveness condition) replication [7].

The results are of course different when we consider synchronous systems when processes may crash. In this case, we have no impossibility results as in the asynchronous case: in synchronous systems with crash process failures, consensus and the k-set agreement become solvable. Therefore, in synchronous models, the main results concern the lower bound of the number of synchronous rounds to achieve k-set agreement. In [5] it is proved that $\lfloor \frac{n}{k} \rfloor + 1$ rounds are needed to solve k-set agreement in synchronous systems.

The results we mentioned concern process crash failures. However, in this paper, we discuss the k-set agreement with Byzantine process failures (recalling that a Byzantine process can do anything and acts as an adversary without the limit of computational power). With Byzantine failures, the validity condition is obtained only in the case where all correct processes propose the same value, this value is the only possible decision value for the correct processes. The case $k = 1$, that is to say the consensus problem with Byzantine process failures and synchronous systems has been widely studied. In terms of possibility and the impossibility, the main results found are that for n processes among them at most t can be Byzantine, there is a solution for consensus if and only if $n > 3t$ and $t + 1$ rounds are necessary for the consensus [1,11,12].

Following Bouzid et al. [3], we study in this paper the possibility and the impossibility of k-set agreement with Byzantine process failures. [3] affirms that there is no k-set agreement with Byzantine failure, if $n < 2t + \frac{t}{k}$.

A first of our results shows that this assertion is valid only when $n - t \geq k + 1$. Then we generalize the possibility and impossibility conditions for Byzantine k-set and provide an almost exhaustive cartography according to the values of the three parameters n, k and t.

These results are summarized in Fig. 1 for $n = 18$ and $n = 19$. The number of failures t is on the abscissa and k on the ordinate. For a (t, k) point on the left part up to blue line, the k-set agreement is solvable with t byzantine processes. For a (t, k) point in a aera colored in blue, k-set agreement is impossible with t byzantine processes. One aera comes from the result of [3] and the other (at the right surrounded by points in green), from our results. For a (t, k) point with a red cross, we don't know if the k-set agreement with t byzantine processes is solvable or not.

An interesting point that can be drawn is the fact that the possibility results presented here (with the exception of the consensus case) are using a very simple algorithm in only one round. This very simple algorithm is clearly optimal concerning the number of rounds (only one) and very close to being optimal concerning the k of the k-set agreement which it allows to obtain.

2 Model and Definitions

2.1 Computation Models

A distributed system is made up of n sequential processes $\Pi = \{p_1, p_2, ..., p_n\}$ that communicate by message passing.

Processes may experience Byzantine failures [11], a Byzantine process may crash, fail to communicate but also may deviate from its code. In this case, they may send bogus values to some processes. Moreover, the Byzantine processes may collude to perturb the computation. Henceforth, a Byzantine process may act as an adversary without any computational limit.

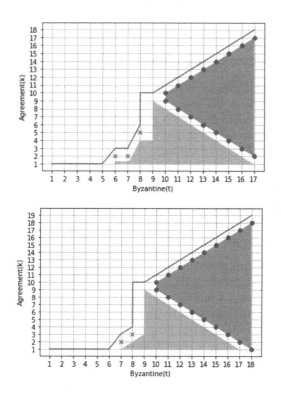

Fig. 1. Case study : n = 18 (Above), n = 19 (Below)

Processes communicate by message passing. Any process may send a message to any other process. We assume that the communication is reliable with no loss, corruption, duplication or creation of messages. In addition, when the process p receives a message from another process q, it knows that q is the sender of the message and that there is no impersonation (but the messages are not authenticated). To simplify the presentation, we assume that when a process sends a message to all processes, it "receives" its own message.

A process that takes an infinite number of steps without deviating from its code, as defined by its algorithm, is said to be correct. A process that deviates from its code or stops taking steps is said to be faulty or Byzantine. t denotes the maximum number of processes which may be Byzantine. We assume that there is at least one correct process i.e $t < n$.

In the synchronous model, the processes execute a sequence of rounds in a lock-step manner. In every round, a process first sends a message to all processes then receives messages from processes, and executes a local computation. The message to be sent and the local computation is defined by the algorithm. The process receives all the messages sent by correct processes, including itself, in the very same round and some messages sent by Byzantine processes. As we assume at most t Byzantine failures, in each round a correct process receives at least $n - t$ messages.

2.2   The k-Set Agreement Problem

The k-set agreement problem, introduced by Chaudhuri [4], is a generalization of the consensus problem [6].

Let V be a finite set of at least n values. Each process has an initial value v in some set V and proposes its initial value to the k-set agreement. Each process has to irrevocably decide on a value.

The k-set agreement is formally defined by the following properties :

- Agreement: At most k values are decided by the correct processes.
- Validity : If all the correct processes propose the same value, no correct process can decide on another value.
- Termination: Eventually, a correct process decides.

The classic consensus problem is the k-set agreement problem for $k = 1$.

We say that an algorithm solving a problem $\mathcal{P}$ is t-resilient if it solves the problem $\mathcal{P}$ when at most t processes are faulty.

If the failures are only process crash failures, it is possible to solve t-resilient k-set agreement, for any t and k, in a synchronous system for $\lfloor \frac{n}{k} \rfloor + 1$ rounds (moreover $\lfloor \frac{n}{k} \rfloor + 1$ rounds is a lower bound for t-resilient k-set agreement) [5].

In asynchronous system with process crash failures, t-resilient k-set agreement can be solved if and only if $t + 1 \le k$ [2,9,14].

3   Algorithms

In this section, we present Algorithm 1 a very simple al t-resilient algorithm that solves the k-set agreement problem.

Each process executes only one round. It sends its input value and collects all the values that it receives from the other processes in the round.

Each process receives at least $n - t$ values and among them all the values sent by correct processes. If its value is the same as the received values from at least $n - t - 1$ processes, it is possible that the initial value of all correct processes is

---

Algorithm 1: t-resilient k-set agreement algorithm: code for process p_i

---

Input: v_i initial value of p_i;
Local Variable: multiset $\mathbf{S} = \emptyset$
Output: decision value

1   send v_i to all processes
2   receive values from all other processes (including the value from p_i)
3   Let $\mathbf{S}$ be the multiset of received values
4   **if**   *the multiplicity of v_i in S is at least $n - t$* **then**
5 | decide v_i
6   **else**
7 | decide 0
8   **end**

---

this value and then by the Validity property of the k-set agreement, the decision value has to be this value. Hence when a process receives from $n - t - 1$ processes a value equal to its own value it decides its own value.

When this previous condition is not fulfilled, by the Validity property, a process can decide on any value. To avoid that many values are decided, we choose a default value in V for this case: This default value is denoted 0.

When $n \leq 2t$, it may be possible that a correct process receives $n - t - 1$ times its value v (and hence decide v) and all these values come from Byzantine processes. Hence with at least $n - t - 1$ Byzantine processes in the run, each Byzantine process may send the initial value v_p of each correct process p to p. In this way all the correct processes decide their own value. When $n \leq 2t$, we have at most $t + 1$ correct processes, and no more than $t + 1$ values are decided by correct processes, satisfying the Agreement property. If we have less Byzantine processes in the run, to get $n - t - 1$ times its value v a correct process has to receive v from some correct processes. Hence every correct process decides either 0 or value that is initial value of some correct processes. In this way, no more than $t + 1$ values are decided by correct processes.

When $n \geq 2t + 1$, if a correct process p with value v receives v from $n - t - 1$ different processes among them there are at least $n - 2t - 1$ correct processes. These processes decide v or 0.

When $n > 3t$, in our algorithm, at most 2 values are decided by correct processes. Which is not optimal, see [11] for example, they give a t resilient consensus algorithm when $n > 3t$.

Which lead us to have the following Theorem:

Theorem 1. *The Algorithm 1 solves t-resilient k-set agreement problem (1) if $n \geq 2t + 1$, for $\lfloor \frac{n - t}{n - 2t} \rfloor + 1 \leq k$, and (2) if $n \leq 2t$, for $t + 1 \leq k$.*

Proof. Let e be any execution of the algorithm. In e, there is at most t Byzantine failures. Let $0 \leq f \leq t$ the actual number of Byzantine failures in e.

We prove first that if $n \geq 2t + 1$, the correct processes in e decide at most $\lfloor \frac{n-t}{n-2t} \rfloor + 1$ values in Algorithm 1.

If a correct process p decides a value v different from 0, then there is at least $n - t - f$ processes, including p, that have this value as input.

We have $n \geq 2t + 1$ that implies $n - t \geq t + 1$. As we have $n - t \geq t + 1$, then $n - t - f \geq 1$, which leads to two cases:

(1) If $n - t - f = 1$ then $t = f$, there are $n - t$ correct processes, even if each of them decided a different value, there are at most $n - t = \lfloor \frac{n-t}{n-2t} \rfloor$ decided values by correct processes in e.

(2) if $n - t - f \geq 2$, the pcorrect rocesses with input values v may decide v or 0 if it doesn't receive the value v from Byzantine processes. Then at most $\lfloor \frac{n-f}{n-t-f} \rfloor + 1$ are decided by correct processes in e. The function $\lfloor \frac{n-f}{n-t-f} \rfloor + 1$ of f is growing, as $f \leq t$, its maximum is for $f = t$, consequently at most $\lfloor \frac{n-t}{n-2t} \rfloor + 1$ values are decided by correct processes in e.

In both cases, at most $\lfloor \frac{n-t}{n-2t} \rfloor + 1$ values are decided by correct processes in e.

We now demonstrate that if $n \leq 2t$, the correct processes in e decide at most $t + 1$ values in Algorithm 1.

$n \leq 2t$ implies $n - t \leq t$, the number of processes that a process considers at Line 4 is less that the number of tolerate failures, so it is possible that the considered values by a correct processes comes from Byzantine processes.

If $f \geq n - t - 1$, there are $n - f$ correct processes in e, as $n - f \leq t + 1$, there are at most $t + 1$ values decided by correct processes in e.

If $f < n - t - 1$, then $n - t \geq f + 2$. A correct process (Line 4) considers $n - t$ values, at least 2 of them come from correct processes then there are at most $\lfloor \frac{(n-f)}{2} \rfloor + 1$ decided values by correct processes. As $f \geq 0$, $\lfloor \frac{(n-f)}{2} \rfloor + 1 \leq \frac{n}{2} + 1 \leq t + 1$, proving that at most $t + 1$ values are decided in e by correct processes.

4   Impossibility

In this section, we focus on the case where k-set agreement problem is impossible to solve t-resilient. Our starting point is the paper of Bouzid and al. [3], which demonstrates that:

Theorem 2. *(from [3]) There is no t-resilient algorithm that solves k-set agreement when $n \leq 2t + \frac{t}{k}$*

Their theorem implies that there is no t-resilient algorithm that solves any k-set agreement ($k < n$) when $n \leq 2t$. But we have seen in Sect. 3 that in this case we can solve t-resilient $(t + 1)$-set agreement.

To prove their theorem, they have split the system of n processes into $(k+1)$ subsets $S_1, ..., S_{k+1}$ of size $\lceil \frac{n-t}{k+1} \rceil$ or $\lfloor \frac{n-t}{k+1} \rfloor$ such that $card(\bigcup\limits_{j=1}^{j=k+1} S_j) = n-t$. They show that if $n \leq 2t + \frac{t}{k}$ then each set S_i is a subset of the correct processes and processes of S_i decide a value v_i (with $v_i \neq v_j$). However, they have missed the idea that this is only true if every set contains at least one process i.e $\frac{n-t}{k+1} \geq 1$.

In fact, they proved:

Theorem 3. *(revised from [3]) If $n-t \geq k+1$, there is no t-resilient algorithm that solves k-set agreement when $n \leq 2t + \frac{t}{k}$*

In this section, we complete their results when $n - t < k + 1$. In Fig. 1, the results from [3] are in light blue and our impossibility result are in dark blue.

Theorem 4 and Theorem 1 show that our bound is tight when $n \leq 2t + 1$.

Theorem 4. *If $n - t < k + 1$ and $n \leq 2t + 1$, there is no t-resilient algorithm that solves k-set agreement when $k \leq t$.*

Proof. If $n - t < k + 1$ and $n \leq 2t + 1$, if there is a t-resilient k-set agreement algorithm, we prove that there is an execution of this algorithm where there are at least $t + 1$ different values that are decided by correct processes, proving that $k \geq t+1$. Consequently there is no t-resilient k-set agreement algorithm if $k \leq t$.

We proceed as in the proof of [3]. Let $\mathcal{A}$ be a t-resilient k-set agreement algorithm. Let $v_1, ..., v_{t+1}$ be $t + 1$ different values of V

In our system there is always at least one correct process, then there exists $t + 1$ non empty subsets of processes: $S_1 = \{p_1\}$ $S_2 = \{p_2\}$, ..., $S_{t+1} = \{p_{t+1}\}$ of Π.

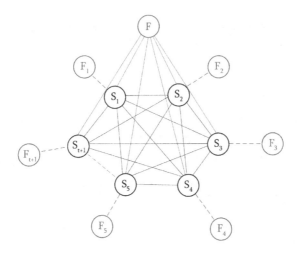

Fig. 2. The behavior of the t Byzantine processes

Let $\bar{S}_i$ be $(\bigcup_{j=1}^{j=t+1} S_j) \setminus S_i$. By construction $\bar{S}_i$ contains t processes. As $n \leq 2t + 1$ then $\bar{S}_i$ contains at least $n - t - 1$ processes. Let F be $\Pi \setminus \bigcup_{i=1}^{i=t+1} S_i$. By construction F contains $n - t - 1$ processes. As $n \leq 2t + 1$, F contains at most t processes.

For each i from 1 to $t + 1$, the process of S_i executes the algorithm $\mathcal{A}$ with input value v_i.

If F is an empty set, we have $n = t + 1$. Then for p_i, all processes in $\bar{S}_i$ may be Byzantine, to achieve Validity, p_i has to decide its own values. Hence $t+1$ different values are decided by correct processes. Assuming that F is not an empty set. We specify the behavior of the Byzantine processes in F, as seen in Fig. 2. The Byzantine processes in F simulate $(t + 1)$ sets of processes $F_1, \ldots, F_{t+1}$, such that processes of each set F_i execute correctly $\mathcal{A}$ with the input value v_i. Moreover, the processes of F_i ignore the messages sent by $\bar{S}_i$ and receive those from $F_i \cup S_i$. Thus, the processes F_i appear as being correct to S_i and $\bar{S}_i$ appear to be Byzantine. Besides, the processes of F_i ignore the messages sent by $\bar{S}_i$ and receive those from $F_i \cup S_i$.

As $\bar{S}_i$ contains t processes and at least $n - t - 1$ processes and F contains $n - t - 1$ and at most t processes, the process in S_i cannot distinguish the case where the processes of F are Byzantine and the processes of $S_i \cup \bar{S}_i$ are correct, and the case where processes of $\bar{S}_i$ are Byzantine and the processes of $F \cup S_i$ are correct. Consequently, by assumption, $\mathcal{A}$ is a t-resilient k-set agreement algorithm, it follows from the Termination and the Validity properties that, for each i from 1 to $t + 1$, the correct processes in S_i decide v_i.

Consequently, $t + 1$ different values are decided by correct processes.

5   Conclusion

We have proved that it is possible to solve t-resilient k-set agreement problem by a simple algorithm in one round in the following cases:

1. if $n \geq 2t + 1$, for $\lfloor \dfrac{n - t}{n - 2t} \rfloor + 1 \leq k$, and
2. if $n \leq 2t$, for $t + 1 \leq k$.

We have also proved that if $n - t < k + 1$ and $n \leq 2t + 1$, there is no t-resilient algorithm that solves k-set agreement when $k \leq t$.

Combined with the results of [3] and the consensus algorithm in Byzantine setting with $3t < n$ in, for example, [11], we conclude that we know for every values of k and t if it is possible or not to solve k-set agreement t resilient except for $n/3 \geq t \geq n/2$ and $k = \lfloor \dfrac{n - t}{n - 2t} \rfloor$

Acknowledgments. This work was partially supported by the French ANR project DESCARTES 16-CE40-0023-03 devoted to layered and modular structures in distributed computing and FREDDA ANR-17-CE40-0013 devoted to Formal methods for the design of distributed algorithms.

References

1. Aguilera, M.K., Toueg, S.: A simple bivalency proof that t-resilient consensus requires t+ 1 rounds. Inform. Process. Lett. **71**(3–4), 155–158 (1999)
2. Borowsky, E., Gafni, E.: Generalized FLP impossibility result for t-resilient asynchronous computations. In: Proceedings of the Twenty-Fifth Annual ACM Symposium on Theory of Computing, May 16–18, 1993, San Diego, CA, USA pp. 91–100. ACM (1993)
3. Bouzid, Z., Imbs, D., Raynal, M.: A necessary condition for byzantine k-set agreement. Inform. Process. Lett. **116**(12), 757–759 (2016)
4. Chaudhuri, S.: More choices allow more faults: Set consensus problems in totally asynchronous systems. Inform. Comput. **105**(1), 132–158 (1993)
5. Chaudhuri, S., Herlihy, M., Lynch, N.A., Tuttle, M.R.: Tight bounds for k-set agreement. J. ACM **47**(5), 912–943 (2000)
6. Fischer, M.J., Lynch, N.A., Paterson, M.: Impossibility of distributed consensus with one faulty process. J. ACM **32**(2), 374–382 (1985)
7. Gafni, E., Guerraoui, R.: Generalized universality. In: Katoen, J.-P., König, B. (eds.) CONCUR 2011. LNCS, vol. 6901, pp. 17–27. Springer, Heidelberg (2011). https://doi.org/10.1007/978-3-642-23217-6_2
8. Herlihy, M., Kozlov, D.N., Rajsbaum, S.: Distributed Computing Through Combinatorial Topology. Morgan Kaufmann, Burlington (2013)
9. Herlihy, M., Shavit, N.: The asynchronous computability theorem for t-resilient tasks. In: Proceedings of the Twenty-Fifth Annual ACM Symposium on Theory of Computing, May 16–18, 1993, San Diego, CA, USA. pp. 111–120. ACM (1993)
10. Herlihy, M., Shavit, N.: The topological structure of asynchronous computability. J. ACM **46**(6), 858–923 (1999)
11. Lamport, L., Shostak, R., Pease, M.: The byzantine generals problem. ACM Trans. Program. Lang. Syst. (TOPLAS) **4**(3), 382–401 (1982)
12. Pease, M.C., Shostak, R.E., Lamport, L.: Reaching agreement in the presence of faults. J. ACM **27**(2), 228–234 (1980)
13. Raynal, M.: Fault-tolerant agreement in synchronous message-passing systems. Synth. Lect. Distrib. Comput. Theory **1**(1), 1–189 (2010)
14. Saks, M., Zaharoglou, F.: Wait-free k-set agreement is impossible: the topology of public knowledge. SIAM J. Comput. **29**(5), 1449–1483 (2000)

Fissile Locks

Dave Dice[(✉)] and Alex Kogan

Oracle Labs, Austin, USA
{dave.dice,alex.kogan}@oracle.com

Abstract. Classic test-and-test (TS) mutual exclusion locks are simple, and enjoy high performance and low latency of ownership transfer under light or no contention. They do not, however, scale gracefully under high contention and do not provide any admission order guarantees. Such concerns led to the development of scalable queue-based locks, such as a recent *Compact NUMA-aware* (CNA) lock, a variant of another popular queue-based *MCS* lock. CNA scales well under load and provides certain admission guarantees, but has more complicated lock handover operations than TS and incurs higher latencies at low contention.

We propose **Fissile** locks, which capture the most desirable properties of both TS and CNA. A Fissile lock consists of two underlying locks: a TS lock, which serves as a fast path, and a CNA lock, which serves as a slow path. The key feature of Fissile locks is the ability of threads on the fast path to bypass threads enqueued on the slow path, and acquire the lock with less overhead than CNA. Bypass is bounded (by a tunable parameter) to avoid starvation and ensure long-term fairness. The result is a highly scalable NUMA-aware lock with progress guarantees that performs like TS at low contention and like CNA at high contention.

Keywords: Locks · Mutexes · Mutual exclusion · Synchronization · Concurrency control

1 Introduction

TS: Test-and-test locks (TS) [3] are compact – consisting of a single *lock word* – simple, and provide excellent latency under light or no contention. They fail to scale, however, as contention increases.

Acquiring threads simply busy-wait, or *spin* attempting to change the lock word state from *unlocked* to *locked* with an atomic read-modify-write instruction, such as compare-and-swap (CAS) or exchange (SWAP). If the atomic operation was successful, then the thread has acquired the lock and may enter the critical section. Releasing the lock requires only a simple store to set the state to unlocked. So-called "polite" test-and-test-and-set locks (TTS), a variation on TS, first fetch the lock value and only attempt the atomic instruction if the lock was observed to be not held. That is, acquiring threads busy-wait until the lock is clear, at which point they execute an atomic instruction to try to

An extended version of this paper is available at https://arxiv.org/abs/2003.05025.

© Springer Nature Switzerland AG 2021
C. Georgiou and R. Majumdar (Eds.): NETYS 2020, LNCS 12129, pp. 192–208, 2021.
https://doi.org/10.1007/978-3-030-67087-0_13

gain ownership. TTS acts to avoid unnecessary write invalidation arising from failed atomic operations. Simple "impolite" TS locks do not bother to first load the value, so each *probe* of the lock causes writing via the atomic instruction. TS and TTS locks are usually augmented with back-off – delays between probes – to moderate contention.

MCS: The *MCS lock* [30], is the usual alternative to simple test-and-set-based locks, performing better under high contention, but also having a more complex path and often lagging behind simple locks under no or light contention. In MCS, arriving threads use an atomic operation to append an element to the tail of a linked list of waiting threads, and then busy wait on a field within that element, avoiding global spinning as found in TS. The list forms a queue of waiting threads. The lock's tail variable is explicit and the head – the current owner – is implicit. When the owner releases the lock it reclaims the element it originally enqueued and sets the flag in the next element, passing ownership. To convey ownership, the MCS unlock operator must identify the successor, if any, and then store to the location where the successor busy waits. The list forms a multiple-producer-single-consumer (MPSC) queue where any thread can enqueue but only the current owner can dequeue itself and pass ownership. The handover path is longer than that of TS locks and accesses more distinct shared locations.

MCS uses so-called local waiting where at most one thread is waiting on a given location at any one time. As such, an unlock operation will normally need to invalidate just one cache line – the line underlying the flag where the successor busy waits – in one remote cache. Under contention, the unlock operator must fetch the address of the successor element from its own element, and then store into the flag in the successor's element, accessing two distinct cache lines, and incurring a dependent memory access to reach the successor. Absent contention, the unlock operator uses an atomic compare-and-swap (CAS) operator to try to detach the owner's element and set the tail variable to `null`.

MCS locks provide strict FIFO order. They are also compact, with the lock body requiring just a pointer to the tail of the chain of queue elements.

One MCS queue element instance is required for each lock a thread currently holds, and an additional queue element is required while a thread is waiting on a lock. Queue elements can not be shared concurrently and can appear on at most one queue – be associated with at most one lock – at a given time. The standard POSIX `pthread_mutex_lock` and `pthread_mutex_unlock` operators do not require scoped or lexically balanced locking. As such, queue element can not be allocated on stack. Instead, MCS implementations that expose a standard POSIX interface will typically allocate elements from thread-local free lists, populated on demand[1].

The standard POSIX interface does not provide any means to pass information from a lock operation to the corresponding unlock operator. As such, the address of the MCS queue element inserted by the owner thread is usually recorded in the lock instance so it can be conveyed to the subsequent unlock

---

[1] We note that the MCS "K42" variant [28,33] allows queue elements to be allocated on stack – they are required only while a thread waits – but at the cost of a longer path with more accesses to shared locations.

operation to identify the successor, if any. That field is protected by the lock itself and accessed within the critical section. Accesses to the field that records the owner's queue element address may themselves generate additional coherence traffic, although some implementations may avoid such accesses to shared fields by storing the queue element address in a thread-local associative structure that maps lock addresses to the owner's queue element address.

CNA: Compact NUMA-Aware locks (CNA) [15] are based on MCS, but add NUMA-awareness. At arrival time, threads annotate their queue element with their NUMA node number. At unlock-time, the owner scans forward into the primary MCS chain and culls remote elements, transferring them to a secondary chain of remote threads. That secondary chain is propagated from the unlock operator to the successor via the queue elements, so the lock structure remains compact. Reducing the NUMA diversity of the primary chain acts to reduce *lock migration* [17] and improve performance. To avoid indefinite starvation of threads on the secondary chain, the unlock operator periodically flushes the secondary chain back into the primary chain to shift the currently preferred NUMA node. At unlock-time, if the primary chain is found empty, the secondary is flushed back into the primary to reprovision the primary chain. CNA unlock prefers to dispatch to threads on the primary, but will revert to the secondary list if the primary is empty. The secondary chain is manipulated under the lock itself, in the unlock operation. While CNA is NUMA-aware, compared to MCS, a number of additional CNA-specific administrative steps – culling, reprovisioning, periodic flushing – execute while the lock is held and are subsumed into the critical section, potentially increasing the effective hold time of the lock. We observe that all NUMA-aware locks trade-off short-term fairness for improved overall throughput.

2   The Fissile Algorithm

Fissile augments CNA with a TS fast-path using the *LOITER* lock construction (Locking : Outer-Inner Tranformation) [12] where the *outer lock* is a TS lock and the *inner lock* is a CNA lock. Acquiring ownership of the outer TS lock confers ownership of the compound Fissile lock. Arriving threads first try the fast-path TS lock and, if successful, immediately enter the critical section. Otherwise control diverts into the slow path where the thread acquires the inner CNA lock. We refer to the owner of the inner CNA lock as the *alpha* thread. Once the CNA lock has been acquired, the alpha thread then busy-waits on the TS outer lock. At most one thread at any one time busy-waits on the outer TS lock, avoiding the scalability impact of global spinning, where multiple threads simultaneously busy-wait on a given location. As there is at most one thread busy-waiting on the outer lock, we use TS instead of TTS. Once the outer lock has been acquired, we release the inner lock and enter the critical section. To release a Fissile lock, we simply release the outer TS lock, regardless of whether the corresponding acquisition took the fast path or slow path.

A thread holds the inner CNA lock only within the Fissile lock acquisition operator. Specifically, Fissile releases the inner CNA lock within the Fissile acquire operation, but while still holding the outer TS lock, potentially extending the hold-time of the outer lock. This choice, however, allows us to allocate the MCS queue element on-stack, which is a distinct advantage, avoiding MCS queue element allocation and deallocation. (Classic MCS requires one allocated queue element for each lock concurrently held by a thread whereas our approach avoids that expense). Furthermore the queue element of the alpha thread does not need to be communicated from the Fissile acquire operation to the unlock operation, as is the case for normal MCS and CNA. We employ a specialized CNA implementation, described below, which shifts much of the administrative overhead specific to CNA and normally found in the unlock operator to run before we acquire the outer TS lock, so the overhead of releasing the CNA inner lock while holding the outer TS lock is minimized.

In Listing-1.1 we provide a sketch of the Fissile algorithm. The `Outer` field is a TS lock word which can take on 3 values: 0 indicates *unlocked*; 1 indicates *locked* and 2 encodes a special locked state used when the alpha thread is impatient and the previous owner is transferring ownership of the outer TS lock directly to the alpha thread. `Inner` is the CNA inner lock, and `Impatient` reflects the state of the alpha thread.

Absent remediation, simple TS allows indefinite bypass and starvation of waiting threads. To avoid this issue, the alpha threads busy-waits on the TS lock for a short *grace period* but will then become "impatient" and cue direct handover of ownership the next time the TS lock is released, bounding bypass.

When the alpha thread becomes impatient, having failed to acquire the outer lock within the grace period, it sets the `Impatient` field from the normal state of 0 to 2. The unlock operator fetches from `Impatient` and stores that value into the TS lock word. In typical circumstances when unlock runs after the alpha has become impatient, it will observe and fetch 2 from `Impatient` and store that value into the TS lock word. The alpha will then notice that the value 2 has propagate from `Impatient` into the lock word, and takes direct handoff of ownership from that previous owner, restoring the lock word from 2 back to 1. If the unlock operation happens to run concurrently with the alpha thread becoming impatient, the unlock may race and fetch 0 from `Impatient` instead of 2. In this case either the alpha manages to seize the TS lock and acquire it when it becomes 0, or some other thread managed to pounce on the TS lock, in which case the alpha thread must wait one more lock cycle to take ownership. At worst, impatient handover is delayed by one acquire-release cycle. Once the value of 2 is visible to threads in unlock, immediate handover to the alpha is assured. Threads arriving in the fast-path that observe 2 will divert immediately into the CNA slow-path.

The grace period serves as tunable parameter reflecting the trade-off and tension between throughput and short-term fairness. A shorter grace periods yields less bypass and fairer admission, while longer periods may allow better throughput but worse short-term fairness.

Fissile provides hybrid succession, employing *competitive succession* [12] when there is no contention, but switching to more conservative *direct succession* when the alpha thread becomes impatient. Under competitive succession, the owner releases the lock, allowing other waiting or arriving threads to acquire the lock. Unfettered competitive succession admits undesirable long-term unfairness and starvation but typically performs well under light load. In addition, competitive succession tends to provide more graceful throughput under preemption. In direct succession, as used by MCS, for instance, the lock holder directly transfers ownership to a waiting successor without any intermediate or intervening transition to an unlocked state. All strict FIFO locks employ direct succession. Direct succession suffers under preemption, however, as ownership may be conveyed to a preempted thread, and we have to wait for operating system time-slicing to dispatch the owner onto a processor.

By restricting the number of threads competing for the outer TS lock, we improve the odds that an arriving thread will find the lock clear and manage to acquire via the TS outer fast path. Under fixed load, ithe system will tend to reach a balanced steady state where many circulating threads tend to acquire the TS lock without waiting.

As shown in [13], as more threads busy-wait on a given location, as is the case in TS, stores to that location take longer to propagate. (Concurrent reads to a given location scale, but concurrent writes or atomics do not [32]). Fissile addresses that concern by ensuring that only the alpha thread busy-waits on the outer TS lock at any given time, accelerating handover.

The TS fast path provides the following benefits. First, latency is reduced, relative to MCS and CNA, for the uncontended case. Acquisition requires an atomic instruction and just a simple store to release. Second, the slow-path CNA MCS nodes can be allocated on-stack, simplifying the CNA implementation and avoiding the need to communicate or convey the owner's MCS node from the lock operation to the corresponding unlock. Third, TS with bounded bypass performs well under preemption, relative to MCS. Finally, and less obviously, the TS fast path provides benefit in the contended case. Fissile provides significant improvement over CNA when the critical section is small, and CNA has a hard time "keeping up" with the flow of arriving threads. That is, for very short critical sections, CNA itself – CNA overheads – becomes the bottleneck for throughput [18]. Under intense contention the TS lock allows more throughput, serving as an alternative bypass channel, giving contention "pressure" a way to get around CNA when CNA becomes the bottleneck. When the critical sections are longer, fissile performs like CNA. Allowing some threads to pass through the CNA slow path and some fraction over the TS fast path would appear to dilute CNA's NUMA benefits, but in practice, we find that CNA still quickly acts to filter out remote threads from a set of threads circulating over a contended lock.

The result is a highly scalable NUMA-aware lock that performs like TS at low contention and as well or better than CNA at high contention. Fissile provides short-term *concurrency restriction* [12] which may improve overall throughput over a contended lock. Fissile locks are compact and also tolerate preemption, by virtue of the TS outer lock, more gracefully than does CNA or MCS.

2.1 Specialized CNA

Classic CNA performs reorganization of the MCS chain – to be more NUMA-friendly and reduce NUMA lock transitions – while holding the CNA lock itself, extending the effective critical section length and delaying handover to a successor. Handover time impacts the scalability as the lock is held throughout handover, increasing the effective length of the critical section. At extreme contention, the critical section length determines throughput [2,18]. Fissile uses a specialized variant of CNA which reorganizes the chain of waiting threads early, immediately after acquiring the CNA lock. As such, reorganization runs outside and before the TS critical section, off the critical path, and potentially allows pipelining and overlap with the critical section execution. (Arguably, earlier reorganization may suffer as there are fewer threads enqueued from which to schedule, but we have not observed any performance penalty related to this concern).

The variant of CNA used by Fissile differs from the original [15] as follows. Classic CNA, at unlock-time, culls the entire remote suffix of the primary chain into the remote list. Our variant looks ahead only one thread into the primary MCS chain, and provides constant-time culling costs, yielding less potentially futile scanning of the chain, and more predictable overheads. In addition, our look-ahead-one policy generates less coherence traffic accessing the MCS chain elements, as the element examine for potential culling would also be accessed in the near future when we subsequently release the CNA lock.

Finally, our version of CNA performs CNA administrative duties – flushing and culling – immediately after the owner acquires the CNA lock, whereas classic CNA defers those operations until unlock-time. Specifically, we reorganize outside and before the outer TS critical section, allowing more overlap between CNA administrative duties and the execution of the critical section, and accelerating CNA lock handover.

All the changes above are optional optimizations and are not required to use CNA within Fissile, but they serve to enhance performance.

3 Related Work

While mutual exclusion remains an active research topic [2,4–6,11,14,18–20,22–24] we focus on locks closely related to our design.

NUMA-aware locks attempt to restrict ownership of a lock to threads on a given NUMA node over the short term, reducing so-called *lock migration*, which can result in expensive inter-node coherence traffic. The first NUMA-aware lock was HBO (Hierarchical Back Off) [31], a test-and-set lock where busy-waiting threads running on the same NUMA node as the current owner would use shorter back-off durations, favoring the odds of handover to such proximal threads relative to most distant threads. While simple, HBO suffers from the same issues as other TS locks.

```
1    class Fissile :
2    |  ## Outer : TTS Lock
3    |  atomic<int> Outer      = 0 ;
4    |
5    |  ## anti-starvation
6    |  atomic<int> Impatient = 0 ;
7    |
8    |  ## Inner : CNA-MCS lock
9    |  ## Represented by tail pointer
10   |  CNAMCSLock Inner {} ;
11
12   def Lock (Fissile * L) :
13   |  ## try fast-path outer : trylock
14   |  ## Thread that acquired the outer lock owns the
15   |  ## compound fissile lock
16   |  if AtomicCAS (&L->Outer, 0, 1) == 0 :
17   |  |  return
18   |
19   |  ## Contention : Revert to slow path ...
20   |  ## Acquire the inner CNA-MCS lock
21   |  ## MCS queue element allocated on-stack
22   |  auto QueueElement I {} ;
23   |
24   |  CNAAcquire (&L->Inner, &I) ;
25   |  ## This thread holds the inner CNA lock
26   |  ## and assumes the role of the "alpha" thread.
27   |
28   |  ## Execute CNA administrative operation to cull
29   |  ## remotes from primary into remote or to flush
30   |  ## elements from remote into primary
31   |  CNACullOrFlush (&L->Inner, &I) ;
32   |
33   |  ## Acquire the outer lock
34   |  ## Patient waiting phase - grace period
35   |  ## allow bypass over outer TTS lock
36   |  for :
37   |  |  if AtomicSwap (&L->Outer, 1) == 0 :
38   |  |  |  goto Exeunt
39   |  |  if PatienceExhausted() : break
40   |  |  Pause() ;
41   |
42   |  ## Enter impatient waiting phase
43   |  ## suppress bypass to avoid starvation
44   |  assert L->Impatient == 0 ;
45   |  L->Impatient = 2 ;
46   |  for
47   |  |  ## Wait for swap to overwrite either 0 or 2
48   |  |  if AtomicSwap (&L->Inner, 1) != 1 :
49   |  |  |  break ;
50   |  |  Pause() ;
51   |  L->Impatient = 0 ;
52   |
53   |  Exeunt:
54   |  ## We hold the outer lock
55   |  ## Release the inner lock
56   |  assert L->Outer == 1 ;
57   |  CNARelease (&L->Inner, &I) ;
58
59   def Unlock (Fissile * L) :
60   |  ## Release the outer lock
61   |  assert L->Outer != 0 ;
62   |  L->Outer = L->Impatient ;
```

Listing 1.1: Simplified Pseudocode Implementation of Fissile

Luchangco et al. [27] introducing HCLH, a NUMA-aware hierarchical version of the CLH queue-lock [10,29]. The HCLH algorithm collects requests on each node into a local CLH-style queue, and then has the thread at the head of the queue integrate each node's queue into a single global queue. This avoids the overhead of spinning on a shared location and eliminates fairness and starvation issues. HCLH intentionally inserts non work-conserving combining delays to increase the size of groups of threads to be merged into the global queue. It was subsequently discovered that HCLH required threads to be bound to one processor for the thread's lifetime. Failure to bind could result in exclusion and progress failures, and as such we will not consider HCLH further.

NUMA-aware Cohort locks [16,17] spawned various derivatives [7,8]. While cohort locks scale well, they have a large variable-sized footprint. The size of a cohort lock instance is a function of the number of NUMA nodes, and is thus not generally known until run-time, complicating static allocation of cohort locks. Being hierarchical in nature, they suffer increased latency under low or no contention as acquisition requires acquiring both node-level locks and top-level lock. CNA avoids all these concerns and is superior to cohort locks. A changeset to convert the Linux kernel *qspinlock* low-level spin lock [9,26] implementation from an MCS-based design to CNA is under submission at the time of writing[2]. Similarly, Fissile locks are readily portable into the kernel environment.

Kashyap's et al. [23] *Shuffling Lock* also performs NUMA-aware reorganization of MCS chains of waiters off the critical path, by waiting threads. They also use a LOITER-based design, but do not allow bypass. In the evaluation section, below, we compare Fissile against their user-mode implementation.

LOITER-base designs [12] first appeared, to our knowledge, in the HotSpot Java Virtual Machine implementation[3] in 2007. The "Go" language runtime mutex [1] uses a LOITER-based scheme where the inner lock is implemented via a semaphore and time-bounded bypass is allowed. The linux kernel *QSpinlock* [26] construct also has a dual path TS and MCS lock, but does not allow bypass. The QSpinlock TS fast-path avoids MCS latency overheads in the uncontended case.

Various authors [4,21] have suggested switching adaptively between MCS and lower latency locks depending on the contention level. While workable, this adds considerable algorithmic complexity, particularly for the changeover phase, and requires tuning. Lim et al. [25] suggested a more general framework for switching locks at runtime.

4   Empirical Evaluation

Unless otherwise noted, all data was collected on an Oracle X5-2 system. The system has 2 sockets, each populated with an Intel Xeon E5–2699 v3 CPU running at 2.30 GHz. Each socket has 18 cores, and each core is 2-way hyperthreaded, yielding 72 logical CPUs in total. The system was running Ubuntu 18.04 with

---

[2] https://lwn.net/Articles/805655/.

[3] https://github.com/openjdk-mirror/jdk7u-hotspot/blob/master/src/share/vm/runtime/mutex.cpp#L168.

a stock Linux version 4.15 kernel, and all software was compiled using the provided GCC version 7.3 toolchain at optimization level "-O3". 64-bit C or C++ code was used for all experiments. Factory-provided system defaults were used in all cases, and Turbo mode [35] was left enabled. In all cases default free-range unbound threads were used.

We implemented all user-mode locks within LD_PRELOAD interposition libraries that expose the standard POSIX pthread_mutex_t programming interface using the framework from [17]. This allows us to change lock implementations by varying the LD_PRELOAD environment variable and without modifying the application code that uses locks. The C++ std::mutex construct maps directly to pthread_mutex primitives, so interposition works for both C and C++ code. All busy-wait loops used the Intel PAUSE instruction. We note that user-mode locks are not typically implemented as pure spin locks, instead often using a spin-then-park waiting policy which voluntarily surrenders the CPUs of waiting threads after a brief optimistic spinning period designed to reduce the context switching rate. In our case, we find that user-mode is convenient venue for experiments, and note in passing that threads in the CNA slow-path are easily made to park.

4.1 MutexBench

The MutexBench benchmark spawns T concurrent threads. Each thread loops as follows: acquire a central lock L; execute a critical section; release L; execute a non-critical section. At the end of a 10 s measurement interval the benchmark reports the total number of aggregate iterations completed by all the threads. We report the median of 7 independent runs in Fig. 1. The critical section advances a C++ std::mt19937 pseudo-random generator (PRNG) 2 steps. The non-critical section is empty. For clarity and to convey the maximum amount of information to allow a comparision the algorithms, the X-axis is offset to the minimum score and the Y-axis is logarithmic.

Immediately before acquiring the lock, each thread fetches the value of a shared *lock clock* value. The critical section advances that value. Subtracting the clock value fetched in the critical section from the value fetched before acquiring the lock gives a useful approximation of the thread's waiting time, given in units of lock acquisitions. Within the critical section, we record that waiting time value into a global log. After the measurement interval the benchmark harness postprocesses the log to produce statistics describing the distribution of the waiting time values, which reflect short-term fairness of the lock algorithm. The critical section also tallies lock migrations. These activities increase the effective length of the critical section.

We ran the benchmark under the following lock algorithms: **TTS** is a simple test-and-test-and-set lock using classic truncated randomized binary exponential back-off [3,30] with the back-off duration capped to 100000 iterations of a PAUSE loop; **MCS** is classic MCS; **CNA** is described in [15] with the probability of flushing the secondary chain into the primary configured as $P = 1/256^4$; **Shuffle**

---

^{4} We picked $P = 1/256$ to match the default value used by the Shuffle Lock, allowing a fair comparison between that lock and CNA.

is Kashyap's *Shuffle Lock* [23] *aqswonode* variant[5]; **Fissile** is the Fissile algorithm described above with the grace period configured as 50 steps of the TS loop executed by the alpha thread and the CNA flush probability configured for $P = 1/256$.

In Fig. 1 we make the following observations regarding operation at maximal contention with an empty critical section:

- At 1 thread the benchmark measures the latency of uncontended acquire and release operations. MCS and CNA lag behind TTS, Shuffle and Fissile as they lack a fast-path.
- At or above 2 threads, most algorithms fall behind TTS as TTS starves all but one thread for long periods, effectively yielding performance near that found at just one thread.
- Broadly, Fissile outperforms CNA and CNA outperforms Shuffle.
- Above 72 threads we encounter preemption via time slicing. TTS and Fissile are tolerant of preemption where the other forms with direct handover encounter a precipitous drop in performance.

In Table 1 we provide additional details for execution at 10 threads. **Throughput** is given in units of millions of acquires per second aggregate throughput for all threads; **Spread** reflects long-term fairness between threads, computed as the maximum number of iterations completed by any thread within the measurement interval divided by the minimum; **Migration** is the reciprocal of the NUMA lock migration rate. (A Migration value of N indicates that the lock migrated between NUMA nodes 1 out of every N lock acquisitions, on average). The remaining columns describe the distribution of the observed waiting times, which we use to measure short-term fairness. **RSTDDEV** is the relative standard deviation [36]; **Theil-T** is the normalized Theil-T index [34,38] – used in the field of econometrics as a metric of income disparity and unfairness – where a value of 0 is ideally fair and 1 is maximally unfair.

We observe that TTS is deeply unfair over the long term and short term. TTS also exhibits a surprisingly low lock migration rate – on average 1 migration per 323 acquisitions – presumably arising from platform-specific cache line arbitration phenomena. Somewhat perversely, this makes TTS implicitly NUMA-friendly, reducing migration rates. TTS is vulnerable to the *Matthew Effect* [37][6] – once a thread has entered deeper back-off, it is less likely to acquire the lock in unit time, amplifying subsequent unfairness. The remaining locks show reasonable long-term and short-term fairness.

In Fig. 2 we configure the benchmark so the non-critical section generates a uniformly distributed random value in $[0 - 200)$ and steps the thread-local random number generator that many steps, admitting potential positive scalability. In this moderate contention case we can see that Fissile and TTS locks tend to provide the best performance although TTS is again unfair. Shuffle, CNA,

---

[5] Taken verbatim from https://github.com/sslab-gatech/shfllock/blob/master/ulocks/src/litl/src/aqswonode.c and integrated into our LD_PRELOAD framework.

[6] Sometimes called the *capture effect*.

and Fissile show a positive inflection around 12 threads, as there are sufficient waiting threads to allow NUMA-friendly intra-node handover. Again, we see an abrupt drop in throughput above 72 threads when preemption is active, but note that Fissile and TTS more gracefully tolerate preemption.

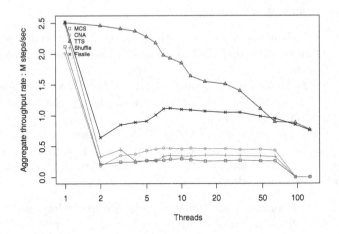

Fig. 1. MutexBench: Maximum Contention

Table 1. Detailed execution analysis

	Throughput	Spread	Migration	RSTDDEV	Theil-T
MCS	.297	1.00	1.83	0.01	0.00
CNA	.458	1.06	254	13.5	0.17
TTS	1.85	7.89	323	102	0.44
Shuffle	.344	1.86	234	11.3	0.15
Fissile	1.11	1.26	374	11.8	0.17

4.2   Std::atomic

In Fig. 3 we use a benchmark harness similar to that of MutexBench but with the following differences. The non-critical section uses a thread-local std::mt19937 pseudo-random number generator (PRNG) to compute a value distributed uniformly in $[0, 200)$ and then advances the PRNG that many steps. Each iteration executes A.load() where A is shared an instance of std::atomic<T> and T is a simple *struct* containing 5 32-bit integer fields. The C++ compiler and runtime implement std::atomic for such objects by hashing the address of the instance

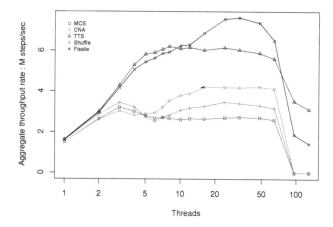

Fig. 2. MutexBench: Moderate Contention

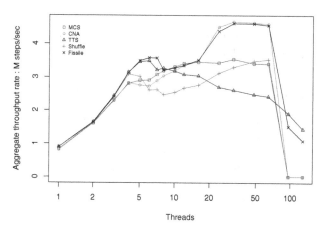

Fig. 3. C++ std::atomic

into an array of mutexes, and acquiring those as needed to implement the desired atomic action. Interestingly, the NUMA-aware locks, CNA, Shuffle and Fissile, exhibit fading performance between 5 and 10 threads, but performance recovers at higher thread counts when there are sufficient waiting threads to profitably reorder for a NUMA-friendly admission schedule. Below 10 threads, contention is sufficiently low that Fissile exceeds CNA by virtue of its fast-path. Fissile and TTS provide similar performance in this region. Above 10 threads, the critical section is sufficiently long in duration that CNA and Fissile yield approximately the same performance.

In Fig. 4 we repeat the experiment in Fig. 3 on an Oracle X5-4, which has 4 NUMA nodes, 18 cores per socket and 2 hyperthreads per core, for 144 logical CPUs, demonstrating that our approach generalizes to larger NUMA systems. The onset of benefit provided by NUMA-aware locks is somewhat delayed as

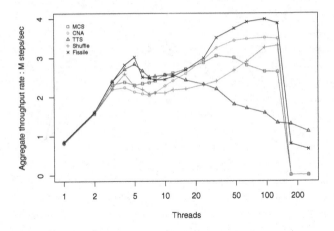

Fig. 4. C++ std::atomic on 4-node System

we have 4 nodes instead of 2 and, at a given thread count, threads are more dispersed and the socket is less populated.

4.3   FIFO Support

Fissile allows bypass both over the outer lock and within the CNA inner lock. We can, however, easily modify Fissile to provide expedited FIFO-like admission service as follows. First, FIFO locking requests that pass into the slow path mark their CNA MCS queue element with a "FIFO" flag. CNA culling refrains from shifting such elements into the CNA secondary list. Critically, if element S is marked as FIFO, then no requests that arrive after S on the inner CNA lock will acquire that lock before S. We also suppress bypass over the outer lock while FIFO requests are waiting. To that end, instead of setting and clearing the Impatient field we modify Fissile slightly to atomically fetch-and-add Impatient by 2 or -2, respectively. (We also make a corresponding change to the comparison in the grace period loop from == 0 to != 1). When a FIFO request diverts into the slow path, it increments Impatient by 2 before acquiring the CNA inner lock, and decrements by 2 after acquiring the outer lock. The request will be serviced in FIFO order, without being bypassed by more recently arrived threads, once it increments Impatient – and that value has become visible to threads in the unlock path – and has executed the SWAP instruction that appends the request to the CNA MCS chain.

To avoid fairness anomalies and make fairness analysis more tractable, we explicitly do no change the preferred NUMA when servicing a FIFO request.

To demonstrate the efficacy of FIFO-enabled Fissile, we extended the MutexBench benchmark harness to allow a mixture of normal and FIFO-designated threads, both competing for a common lock. We used 25 normal threads, and 2 FIFO threads. Normal threads advance the global PRNG 2 times in the critical section, as described above, and in the non-critical section compute a uniformly distributed random number in $[0-100)$ and advance a thread-local PRNG instance that many steps. FIFO threads execute the same critical section, but use a non-critical section duration randomly selected from the range $[0-2000)$, reflecting intermittent low duty-cycle FIFO operations. The FIFO attribute is per-thread (but could also be specified for individual locking operations) and is ignored by all lock implementations except FIFO-enabled Fissile. All FIFO data was taken on the X5-2.

Table 2 shows the results, comparing Fissile, FIFO-enabled Fissile, and MCS. We report throughput over a 10 s measurement interval broken out for the normal threads and the FIFO threads. We also report statistics describing the observed wait times, computed in logical *lock clock* units, for the FIFO threads in isolation. As we can see `Fissile+FIFO` provides wait times very close to that afforded by MCS, and with greater throughput for both normal and FIFO threads.

Table 2. FIFO performance

	Throughput		Wait times for FIFO			
	FIFO	Normal	RSTDDEV	Worst	Avg	Median
MCS	1.3M	23.0M	0.03	29	24.4	25
Fissile	1.5M	43.9M	52.3	531294	40.7	15
Fissile+FIFO	2.7M	38.8M	0.33	41	11.9	12

5 Conclusion

Fissile locks are compact, NUMA-aware, preemption tolerant, and scalable, but also provide excellent latency at low or no contention. The algorithm is straightforward and easily integrated into existing locking infrastructures. They are particularly helpful under contention with high arrival rates and short critical sections. Contended locking uses the CNA lock while uncontended operations use the TS lock. Fissile locks deflect contention away from TS lock into the CNA lock.

Bypass over the outer lock via the fast path is the key to Fissile. While the slow path provides a higher quality NUMA-friendly admission schedule, it also suffers higher latency arising from the more complex lock mechanism. The fast path allows for low latency in the uncontended case, but also improves scalability under contention by augmenting the slow path with an alternative if the slow path lock overheads prove a bottleneck.

References

1. Go runtime : mutex implementation (2020). https://github.com/golang/go/blob/master/src/sync/mutex.go

2. Aksenov, V., Alistarh, D., Kuznetsov, P.: Brief announcement: performance prediction for coarse-grained locking. In: Proceedings of the 2018 ACM Symposium on Principles of Distributed Computing. PODC 2018 (2018). http://doi.acm.org/10.1145/3212734.3212785

3. Anderson, T.E.: The performance of spin lock alternatives for shared-money multiprocessors. IEEE Transactions on Parallel and Distributed Systems (1990)

4. Antić, J., Chatzopoulos, G., Guerraoui, R., Trigonakis, V.: Locking made easy. In: Proceedings of the 17th International Middleware Conference. Middleware 2016 (2016). http://doi.acm.org/10.1145/2988336.2988357

5. Boyd-Wickizer, S., Kaashoek, M.F., Morris, R., Zeldovich, N.: Non-scalable locks are dangerous. Ottawa Linux Symposium (OLS) (2012). https://www.kernel.org/doc/ols/2012/ols2012-zeldovich.pdf

6. Bueso, D.: Scalability techniques for practical synchronization primitives. Commun. ACM (2014). http://doi.acm.org/10.1145/2687882

7. Chabbi, M., Fagan, M., Mellor-Crummey, J.: High performance locks for multi-level numa systems. Association for Computing Machinery (2015). https://doi.org/10.1145/2688500.2688503

8. Chabbi, M., Mellor-Crummey, J.: Contention-conscious, locality-preserving locks. Association for Computing Machinery (2016). https://doi.org/10.1145/2851141.2851166

9. Corbet, J.: MCS locks and qspinlocks, 11 March 2014. https://lwn.net/Articles/590243. Accessed 12 Sept 2018

10. Craig, T.: Building fifo and priority-queueing spin locks from atomic swap (1993)

11. David, T., Guerraoui, R., Trigonakis, V.: Everything you always wanted to know about synchronization but were afraid to ask. In: Proceedings of the Twenty-Fourth ACM Symposium on Operating Systems Principles. SOSP 2013 (2013). http://doi.acm.org/10.1145/2517349.2522714

12. Dice, D.: Malthusian locks. CoRR abs/1511.06035 (2015). http://arxiv.org/abs/1511.06035

13. Dice, D., Kogan, A.: TWA - ticket locks augmented with a waiting array. CoRR abs/1810.01573 (2018). http://arxiv.org/abs/1810.01573

14. Dice, D., Kogan, A.: Avoiding scalability collapse by restricting concurrency. In: Yahyapour, R. (ed.) Euro-Par 2019. LNCS, vol. 11725, pp. 363–376. Springer, Cham (2019). https://doi.org/10.1007/978-3-030-29400-7_26

15. Dice, D., Kogan, A.: Compact numa-aware locks. Association for Computing Machinery (2019). https://doi.org/10.1145/3302424.3303984

16. Dice, D., Marathe, V.J., Shavit, N.: Lock cohorting: A general technique for designing numa locks. Association for Computing Machinery (2012). https://doi.org/10.1145/2145816.2145848

17. Dice, D., Marathe, V.J., Shavit, N.: Lock cohorting: A general technique for designing numa locks. ACM Trans. Parallel Comput. (2015). http://doi.acm.org/10.1145/2686884

18. Eyerman, S., Eeckhout, L.: Modeling critical sections in amdahl's law and its implications for multicore design. In: Proceedings of the 37th Annual International Symposium on Computer Architecture. ISCA 2010 (2010). http://doi.acm.org/10.1145/1815961.1816011

19. Guerraoui, R., Guiroux, H., Lachaize, R., Quéma, V., Trigonakis, V.: Lock-unlock: Is that all? a pragmatic analysis of locking in software systems (2019). https://doi.org/10.1145/3301501

20. Guiroux, H., Lachaize, R., Quéma, V.: Multicore locks: the case is not closed yet. In: 2016 USENIX Annual Technical Conference (USENIX ATC 16). USENIX Association (2016). https://www.usenix.org/conference/atc16/technical-sessions/presentation/guiroux
21. Ha, P.H., Papatriantafilou, M., Tsigas, P.: Reactive spin-locks: a self-tuning approach. In: 8th International Symposium on Parallel Architectures, Algorithms and Networks (ISPAN 2005) (2005)
22. Jayanti, P., Jayanti, S., Jayanti, S.: Towards an ideal queue lock. In: Proceedings of the 21st International Conference on Distributed Computing and Networking. ICDCN 2020, Association for Computing Machinery (2020). https://doi.org/10.1145/3369740.3369784
23. Kashyap, S., Calciu, I., Cheng, X., Min, C., Kim, T.: Scalable and practical locking with shuffling. In: Proceedings of the 27th ACM Symposium on Operating Systems Principles. SOSP 2019, Association for Computing Machinery (2019). https://doi.org/10.1145/3341301.3359629
24. Kashyap, S., Min, C., Kim, T.: Scalable numa-aware blocking synchronization primitives. In: 2017 USENIX Annual Technical Conference (USENIX ATC 2017). USENIX Association (2017). https://www.usenix.org/conference/atc17/technical-sessions/presentation/kashyap
25. Lim, B.H., Agarwal, A.: Reactive synchronization algorithms for multiprocessors. In: Proceedings of the Sixth International Conference on Architectural Support for Programming Languages and Operating Systems. ASPLOS VI (1994). http://doi.acm.org/10.1145/195473.195490
26. Long, W.: qspinlock: Introducing a 4-byte queue spinlock implementation. https://lwn.net/Articles/561775, July 31, 2013 (2013). Accessed 19 Sept. 2018
27. Luchangco, V., Nussbaum, D., Shavit, N.: Hierarchical clh queue lock. In: Euro-Par 2006 Parallel Processing. Springer, Heidelberg (2006). https://doi.org/10.1007/11823285_84
28. Auslander, M., Edelsohn, D., Wisniewski, O.K.B.R.: Enhancement to the mcs lock for increased functionality and improved programmability - u.s. patent application number 20030200457 (2003). https://patents.google.com/patent/US20030200457
29. Magnusson, P., Landin, A., Hagersten, E.: Queue locks on cache coherent multiprocessors. In: Proceedings of 8th International Parallel Processing Symposium (1994)
30. Mellor-Crummey, J.M., Scott, M.L.: Algorithms for scalable synchronization on shared-memory multiprocessors. ACM Trans. Comput. Syst. (1991). http://doi.acm.org/10.1145/103727.103729
31. Radović, Z., Hagersten, E.: Hierarchical Backoff Locks for Nonuniform Communication Architectures. In: International Symposium on High Performance Computer Architecture - HPCA. IEEE Computer Society (2003). http://dl.acm.org/citation.cfm?id=822080.822810
32. Schweizer, H., Besta, M., Hoefler, T.: Evaluating the cost of atomic operations on modern architectures. In: 2015 International Conference on Parallel Architecture and Compilation (PACT) (2015)
33. Scott, M.L.: Shared-Memory Synchronization. Morgan & Claypool Publishers (2013)
34. Theil, H.: Economics and Information Theory. North-Holland (1967)
35. Verner, U., Mendelson, A., Schuster, A.: Extending amdahl's law for multicores with turbo boost. IEEE Computer Architecture Letters (2017). https://doi.org/10.1109/LCA.2015.2512982

36. Wikipedia Contributors: Coefficient of variation (2020). https://en.wikipedia.org/wiki/Coefficient_of_variation
37. Wikipedia Contributors: Matthew effect (2020). https://en.wikipedia.org/wiki/Matthew_effect
38. Wikipedia Contributors: Theil index (2020). https://en.wikipedia.org/wiki/Theil_index

Verifying Safety of Parameterized Heard-Of Algorithms

Zeinab Ganjei, Ahmed Rezine[✉], Petru Eles, and Zebo Peng

Linköping University, Linköping, Sweden
{zeinab.ganjei,ahmed.rezine,petru.eles,zebo.peng}@liu.se

Abstract. We consider the problem of automatically checking safety properties of fault-tolerant distributed algorithms. We express the considered class of distributed algorithms in terms of the Heard-Of Model where arbitrary many processes proceed in infinite rounds in the presence of failures such as message losses or message corruptions. We propose, for the considered class, a sound but (in general) incomplete procedure that is guaranteed to terminate even in the presence of unbounded numbers of processes. In addition, we report on preliminary experiments for which either correctness is proved by our approach or a concrete trace violating the considered safety property is automatically found.

1 Introduction

Fault-tolerant distributed algorithms are difficult to prove correct. Such algorithms are meant to operate in the presence of faults ranging from process crashes to message losses or corruption. We consider the parameterized case where arbitrarily many identical processes participate in running the distributed algorithm. We adopt the popular Heard-Of model [3,4]. This model uniformly describes distributed algorithms in the presence of transmission-based failures whether static or dynamic, permanent or transient. Algorithms proceed in rounds where, at each round, each process sends a message to other processes, hears from some of them, and updates its state. Hence, at each round, a process "hears" from a set of other processes. Fault descriptions are captured by stating constraints on the possible sets of processes and messages each process hears from (e.g. each process hears from at least half the processes or at most a third of the sent messages have been corrupted).

We consider the problem of automatically establishing the correctness of safety properties for parameterized distributed algorithms expressed in the Heard-Of model. The safety properties we consider concern checking state reachability, i.e., reachability of configurations where a given number of processes are in some forbidden combination of states. Observe that we do not check whether the algorithms make progress. This would require us to account for communication predicates that ensure the processes eventually hear from enough other processes. We need however to constrain, depending on the environment we want to capture, that messages may be lost (benign crashes or transmission failures)

© Springer Nature Switzerland AG 2021
C. Georgiou and R. Majumdar (Eds.): NETYS 2020, LNCS 12129, pp. 209–226, 2021.
https://doi.org/10.1007/978-3-030-67087-0_14

or altered (corruption failure). For consensus protocols, this is enough to capture all executions that violate agreement (two processes decide on different values), validity (a value is decided although no process proposed it) or irrevocability (a decided value is revoked). The verification problem is made difficult by the parameterization in the number of processes and by the allowed faults. Parameterization requires us to verify infinite families of algorithms, one for each number of participating processes. The transmission model allows each process to receive a subset of the sent messages (benign failures) in addition to a number of altered messages (corrupted communication), making this information local to the processes.

Related work. Abstractions for threshold-based fault-tolerant distributed systems were introduced in [11,12]. The work is extended to synchronous round-based semantics in [17]. These works can handle interesting fault-tolerant algorithms in presence of different faults such as Byzantine faults, but have the limitation of requiring the user to encode the distributed system in terms of threshold automata and propose interval-based over-approximations or bounded-model checking based under-approximations for the parameterized verification problem. The models we consider directly target al.gorithms expressed in the Heard-Of model with a sound over-approximation and can account for message losses (omission fault) and message alteration (corruption fault). The work in [14] has the merit of proposing cutoffs for a syntactically restricted class of consensus algorithms. The class is also expressed in the Heard-Of model. While we do not provide such cutoffs, our work can afford to check correctness for richer fragments that can more faithfully capture constructs such as "the number of received messages with value v_0 is at least two thirds the number of processes" as opposed to "the number of received messages is at least two thirds the number of processes, and all of them have value v_0". The approach in [14] can verify Heard-Of algorithms such as Paxos that we cannot verify in our current approach. Because in our current setting, we have only many-to-many transmissions, while we need to account for one-to-many and many-to-one transmissions to be able to capture those algorithms. However, they only consider benign faults for the algorithms, but our approach can handle both benign and corruption faults. To the best of our knowledge, we are the first ones to verify Heard-of algorithms in presence of corruption faults.

Ongoing works [1,13] study automatizing deciding satisfiability of constraints involving arbitrarily many processes and cardinality constraints over sets of received messages with specific properties. Such constraints naturally arise when verifying fault-tolerant distributed algorithms. For instance, [7,15] consider a rich class of algorithms but require the user to supply such constraints in order to automatically establish correctness. The work in [15] abstracts the quorum of threads in the Paxos algorithm by introducing a new sort for quorum and adding an axiom to capture the fact that the intersection of two quorums is non-empty. While this abstraction is enough for verifying Paxos, it is too coarse for the algorithms we consider, since the *size* of the intersection of quorums are essential for proving the correctness of them. Other approaches [6,8–10] can tackle wider classes of systems but adopt an interactive approach to verification, while our approach is fully automatic.

Contributions. We propose a sound and automatic approach to check safety properties. More specifically:

1. We identify a subclass of fault-tolerant distributed algorithms in terms of the Heard-Of model and describe the considered safety properties.
2. We introduce a symbolic representation where we capture cardinality constraints on multisets (formed by values of variables or heard-of sets) using integer counters, hence avoiding the challenge of implementing quantifier elimination for theories with cardinality constraints.
3. We show how to use the symbolic representation in a sound but (in general) incomplete procedure for checking state reachability in the presence of lossy or corrupt communication.
4. We show termination of the procedure even in the presence of arbitrarily many processes.
5. We report on preliminary experiments with correct and buggy examples.

Outline. We describe the challenges of the verification problem using a motivating example in Sect. 2. We then introduce the class of distributed algorithms and the properties we aim to verify in Sect. 3. We formalize the symbolic representations in Sect. 4 and use them in Sect. 5 in a sound (but in general incomplete) verification algorithm for which we show termination. We describe preliminary experiments in Sect. 6 and conclude in Sect. 7.

```
init:  x, res = -1
r  mod 1 = 0:
    send x;
    1.  |HO| > 2n/3 ∧ |HO¹| ≤ |HO⁰| ≤ 2n/3  →  x:=0
    2.  |HO| > 2n/3 ∧ |HO⁰| < |HO¹| ≤ 2n/3  →  x:=1
    3.  |HO⁰| > 2n/3  →  x,res:=0,0
    4.  |HO¹| > 2n/3  →  x,res:=1,1
    5.  |HO| ≤ 2n/3  →  skip
```

Fig. 1. The One-Third-Rule consensus algorithm. An arbitrary number of processes synchronize in rounds and try to choose the same value for **res**. HO is the multiset of values received from other processes and $|HO^d|$ is the number of those messages equal to d.

2   Motivating Example

The One-Third-Rule algorithm listed in Fig. 1 is a simple consensus protocol that can tolerate benign transmission failures such as process crashes and message losses. Each process p has two local variables x_p and res_p ranging over finite domains. The values of each variable x_p range over the set $\{0, 1\}$. They are used to capture the candidate of process p in the consensus algorithm. The values of each variable res_p range over $\{-1, 0, 1\}$ and are used to capture the decisions of the process. The initial value –1 captures that the process did not decide yet. The example is formalized in the Heard-Of model where n processes operate in infinite rounds in lock-step. The goal of the protocol is for the processes to agree on one of the initial values as a common output.

In each round, a process first sends its local candidate value x_p to all other processes and receives values sent by other processes. Then, it executes one of the guarded commands that follow the send operation and whose guard is satisfied. In the original HO model [4] it is assumed that process ids of those processes a process p hears from is stored in the set HO_p. We make a small modification and assume that the values received from those processes by process p are stored in a local multiset HO_p called the heard-of multiset of p. At each round, there are as many HO_p multisets as there are processes. These are used to uniformly capture different failures (e.g., delays, losses, crashes, corruption). For instance, if $\bar{x}$ is the multiset obtained by collecting the values of all variables x_p just sent by all processes, and in case of benign transmission failures (e.g. process crashes or message losses), each HO_p will be smaller than $\bar{x}$ for each value, written $HO_p \preceq \bar{x}$. For a multiset $\bar{m}$, we write $|\bar{m}|$ to mean the cardinality of $\bar{m}$. For instance, $|\bar{x}|$ is the number n of processes running the algorithm while $|HO_p|$ captures the total number of messages received by process p (i.e. the total number of processes that p heard from). Moreover, for any value d in the domain of the sent variables, we write $|HO_p^d|$ to mean the number of those messages that are equal to d.

In Fig. 1, a process p that receives more messages than two-thirds of the total number of processes (i.e. $|HO_p| > 2n/3$) will update the value of its local candidate x_p with the smallest most often received value (lines 1 to 4). Besides, if among the received messages, more than two-thirds of the number of processes have the same value (here $|HO_p^0| > 2n/3$ or $|HO_p^1| > 2n/3$), then both variables x_p and res_p are updated to the said value (lines 3 and 4). The process is then said to have decided on the value of res_p. Observe that if a process does not receive its candidate value x_p from more than $2n/3$ processes, then it will not decide on it (lines 1 and 2). Furthermore, if a process has only heard from less than $2n/3$ processes then it will not update its local variables (line 5).

Typical safety properties for such consensus protocols include:

- Agreement: whenever two processes have reached a decision, the values they have decided on must be equal.
- Validity: if all processes propose the same initial value, then the processes who have reached a decision must have decided on that initial value.
- Irrevocability: if a process has decided on a value, it does not revoke its decision later.

Detecting violations of the above properties boils down to checking reachability of sets of configurations for unbounded numbers of processes. However, the correctness of the One-Third-Rule algorithm is independent of the number of processes. In fact, its correctness lies in the fact that: (1) in each round, $\mathrm{HO}_p \preceq \bar{x}$ for each process p, (2) only those processes can update their x who have heard from more than two thirds of the total number of processes and (3) only those can decide who have heard the same value from more than two thirds of the processes.

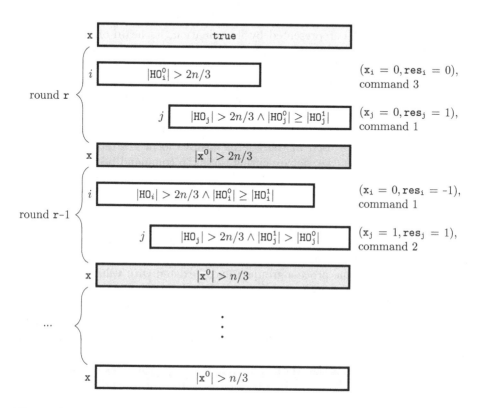

Fig. 2. A run of the One-Third-Rule algorithm by two process groups i and j in backward from configurations with processes having decided on different values of res. The widths of the bars model the size of the corresponding multisets. Different colors correspond to different rounds.

In order to capture unbounded numbers of processes, we use constraints that group the processes based on the valuations of their local variables. Observe there are finitely many such valuations. We then describe bad configurations using such constraints. For instance, in order to check the agreement property for the One-Third-Rule algorithm, we need to check reachability of all constraints capturing all configurations where at least two groups of processes, namely i and j have $\mathrm{res}_i = 0$ and $\mathrm{res}_j = 1$. Assume this constraint had been reached after r rounds. It is not difficult to see that process groups i and j could not have executed the guarded commands 3 and 4 during the same round r and assign 0 and 1 to res_i

and res_j respectively. This is because they would have had to satisfy both of the guards $|\text{HO}_i^0| > 2n/3$ and $|\text{HO}_j^1| > 2n/3$. Combined with $\text{HO}_p \preceq \overline{\text{x}}$ for each process p (since message loss is the only fault), we get $|\overline{\text{x}}^0| > 2n/3$ and $|\overline{\text{x}}^1| > 2n/3$. This would give $|\overline{\text{x}}| > 4n/3$, which contradicts the assumption that the number of processes in the system is n. Thus, we should look for runs in which res_i and res_j are set to 0 and 1 in separate rounds.

A possible run in backwards is shown in Fig. 2 in which each group of processes in each round is represented by its valuation, its heard-of multiset and the weakest predicate on its local variables that needs to be satisfied to make the run possible. In this description, we do not account for corruption or duplication of messages and therefore assume heard-of multisets are smaller (because of message loss) than the multiset of sent values $\overline{\text{x}}$. Accounting for corruption or duplication of messages is a matter of assuming other relations between $\overline{\text{x}}$ and the heard-of multisets. A key to the correctness of the algorithm is the fact that the fraction $2n/3$ used in the guards ensures local heard-of multisets of participating processes (i.e. not executing the skip command because they did not receive enough messages) have large intersections (in fact larger than $n/3$ for any pair of such multisets).

We start the run without any assumption on $\overline{\text{x}}$, therefore it satisfies true. If all processes in group i and all those in group j had executed the commands 1 and 3 respectively during round r (note that each group could have also executed more commands, and we might need to split groups), one of the possible predecessors would be that the same process groups i and j existed with valuations $\text{res}_i = -1$ and $\text{res}_j = 0$. Moreover, the predicate $|\overline{\text{x}}^0| > 2n/3$ needs to hold at the beginning of round r. This is implied by the guards of the commands 1 and 3, $|\text{HO}_i| > 2n/3 \ \wedge \ |\text{HO}_i^1| \leq |\text{HO}_i^0| \leq 2n/3$ and $|\text{HO}_j^0| > 2n/3$, as well as the invariant $\text{HO}_p \preceq \overline{\text{x}}$ for each process p. We could unroll the loop once more, assuming that in round $r - 1$ the two process groups had executed commands 1 and 2 respectively and assigned different values to their variables x_i and x_j (this does not contradict $|\overline{\text{x}}^0| > 2n/3$). The guards of the corresponding commands together with the invariant $\text{HO}_p \preceq \overline{\text{x}}$ for each process p entail that the predicate $|\overline{\text{x}}^0| > n/3$ held at the beginning of the round $r - 1$. Further unrollings of the loop in backward for any number of times will maintain $|\overline{\text{x}}^0| > n/3$. As a result, firing command 4 in some previous iteration would have been impossible as it requires $|\text{HO}^1| > 2n/3$. This command is however needed to reach to the initial state. A systematic exploration of similar constraints allows us to conclude the impossibility of deciding on different values.

The work in [3] introduced algorithms in Heard-Of model where received messages might be corrupted. One such algorithm is demonstrated in Fig. 3. We can handle such algorithms and the analysis is similar to the case where we have omission faults. The only difference is that the invariant in presence of corruption faults is that no more than α messages received per round, per process and per data value will be corrupted. Therefore, the invariant is that $|\text{HO}_p^d| \leq |\overline{\text{x}}^d| + \alpha$.

Our work proposes a sound but (in general) incomplete algorithm for checking control state reachability for unbounded number of processes. The algorithm is

```
init :  x, res = -1
r  mod 1 = 0:
   send x;
   1.  |HO| > T  ∧  |HO¹| ≤ |HO⁰| ≤ E  →  x:=0
   2.  |HO| > T  ∧  |HO⁰| < |HO¹| ≤ E  →  x:=1
   3.  |HO⁰| > E  →  x,res:=0,0
   4.  |HO¹| > E  →  x,res:=1,1
   5.  |HO| ≤ T  →  skip
```

Fig. 3. The $\mathcal{A}_{E,T}$ consensus algorithm [3]. An arbitrary number of processes synchronize in rounds and try to choose the same value for **res**. The messages might get lost or corrupted. Per each round, process, and data value, there will be at most α corrupted messages. T is the threshold on the number of received messages and E is enough number of received messages with a certain value. According to [3], for correctness of the algorithm, it is sufficient that $T \geq 2(n + 2\alpha - E)$, $E \geq \frac{n}{2} + \alpha$ and $n > T \geq E$. We check correctness by adding these predicates as invariants.

guaranteed to terminate and starts from a symbolic representation of all bad configurations. It successively computes representations of over-approximations of predecessor configurations.

3 Heard-Of Programs

To simplify the presentation, we use a unique domain for all local variables and assume programs to proceed in infinite rounds where the state of each process is captured by the local variables. Introducing specific data domains for each variable or explicit local states in the transitions is straightforward. We use *valuations* (i.e., mapping from the set of local variables of a process to its domain) to capture the values of process variables. We define the syntax and semantics of a language to capture a class of heard-of programs. A heard-of program $\mathbf{prg} = (\mathbf{V}, \mathbf{D}, \mathbf{Init}, \mathbf{Tr})$ involves:

- A set **V** of variables local to each process.
- A finite set $\mathbf{D} \subset \mathbb{Z}$ of possible data values,
- An initial set of valuations **Init** sending local variables **V** to **D**,
- A set of transitions **Tr**.

The syntax of such programs is as follows.

$$
\begin{aligned}
\mathbf{prg} \quad &::= \mathbf{init} \ \mathbf{tr}_1 \dots \mathbf{tr}_{|\mathbf{Tr}|} \\
\mathbf{init} \quad &::= v \mid v := d \\
\mathbf{tr} \quad &::= \left(\mathbf{r} \ \mathbf{mod} \ |\mathbf{Tr}| = e : \mathbf{send} \ v; \ \mathbf{cmd}_1, \dots \mathbf{cmd}_K\right) \\
\mathbf{cmd} \quad &::= \left(\mathbf{guard}, \mathbf{val}^1 \to \mathbf{val}^2\right) \\
\mathbf{guard} \quad &::= \mathbf{guard} \lor \mathbf{guard} \mid \mathbf{guard} \land \mathbf{guard} \mid \mathbf{true} \mid \mathbf{false} \mid \mathbf{atom} \\
\mathbf{atom} \quad &::= |\mathbf{HO}^{d_i}| \ \mathbf{cmp} \ |\mathbf{HO}^{d_j}| \mid |\mathbf{HO}^d| \ \mathbf{cmp} \ \mathbf{c.n} \mid |\mathbf{HO}| \ \mathbf{cmp} \ \mathbf{c.n} \\
\mathbf{cmp} \quad &::= > \mid < \mid \geq \mid \leq
\end{aligned}
$$

Each process starts by setting the initial values to its local variables. Then, all processes execute the transitions in a lock-step manner. Each program consists of a macro-round which is a sequence of $|\text{Tr}|$ consecutive rounds (r mod $|\text{Tr}|$) = 0, ..., (r mod $|\text{Tr}|$) = $|\text{Tr}| - 1$. The program starts in round $\text{r} = 0$ and at each round r, all the processes will execute the transition designated with (r mod $|\text{Tr}|$). r is incremented after each transition.

In each transition (r mod $|\text{Tr}| = e : \text{send } v; \text{cmd}_1, \ldots \text{cmd}_K$), first, all processes send the value of their local variable v. After send, there is an implicit receive step in which the processes receive the values sent by others. Between the send and receive of the messages, an adversarial environment can choose to drop or alter messages. The received values are stored in a HO (heard-of) multiset that is local to each process. The impact of the environment is captured by the heard-of multiset.

After send and receive, each process p with heard-of multiset HO_p executes a guarded command $\text{cmd}_k = (\text{guard}_k : \text{val}_k^1 \rightarrow \text{val}_k^2)$ where $\text{HO}_p \models \text{guard}_k$. A guard mainly focuses on capturing cardinality of some HO multiset(s). This cardinality is in many cases compared to a fraction of the total number of processes, i.e. c.n. In order to simplify the presentation, we consider each cmd to be a change in the local valuation of a process . A skip command can easily be transformed to this format by choosing identical values for the command. Introducing explicit local states is simple but would not improve readability.

Configurations. Configurations of a heard-of program describe the round number, as well as the local state of the processes, i.e. their valuations and heard-of multisets. More formally, a configuration of $\text{prg} = (\text{V}, \text{D}, \text{Init}, \text{Tr})$ is a tuple $(\text{r}, [\text{p}_1, \ldots, \text{p}_a])$ where:

- r is the round number.
- for all i in $0 \leq i \leq a$, $\text{p}_i = (\text{val}_i, \text{HO}_i)$ is a process where:
  - val_i is a mapping $\text{V} \rightarrow \text{D}$. In other words, the valuation val_i maps each local variable of the process to a value in the domain.
  - $\text{HO}_i : \text{D} \rightarrow \mathbb{N}$ is a multiset of integer values.

Values of a configuration. For a configuration $c = (\text{r}, [\text{p}_1, \ldots, \text{p}_a])$ and for any variable $v \in \text{V}$ we define $\text{valuesOf}(c, v)$ to be a multiset containing all the local values of v in all the processes. More formally, for all $d \in \text{D}$, $\text{valuesOf}(c, v)(d) = |\{\text{p}_i | \text{p}_i = (\text{val}_i, \text{HO}_i) \text{ with } \text{val}_i(v) = d\}|$.

Example 1. For the program in Fig. 1, consider the following processes at round $\text{r} = 0$.

- $\text{p}_1 = ((\text{x}_1 = 1, \text{r}_1 = \text{-1}), \varnothing)$
- $\text{p}_2 = ((\text{x}_2 = 1, \text{r}_2 = \text{-1}), \varnothing)$
- $\text{p}_3 = ((\text{x}_3 = 0, \text{r}_3 = \text{-1}), \varnothing)$
- $\text{p}_4 = ((\text{x}_4 = 1, \text{r}_4 = \text{-1}), \varnothing)$

The configuration $c = (0, [\text{p}_1, \text{p}_2, \text{p}_3, \text{p}_4])$ captures initial configuration. The heard-of multisets of the processes are empty initially. The values of variable x are captured by the multiset $\text{valuesOf}(c, \text{x}) = [0, 1, 1, 1]$.

Semantics. Given a program $\mathtt{prg} = (\mathtt{V}, \mathtt{D}, \mathtt{Init}, \mathtt{Tr})$, the processes start executing $\mathtt{Tr}$ from an initial configuration $\mathtt{c}_{init} = \left(\mathtt{r}^{init}, \left[\mathtt{p}_1^{init}, \ldots, \mathtt{p}_a^{init}\right]\right)$ where $\mathtt{r}^{init} = 0$, and for all $1 \le i \le a$, $\mathtt{p}_i^{init} = (\mathtt{val}_i, \emptyset)$, and $\mathtt{val}_i \in \mathtt{Init}$. Suppose configurations $\mathtt{c}$ and $\mathtt{c}'$ can be written (up to a renaming of the processes) as $\mathtt{c} = (\mathtt{r}, [(\mathtt{val}_1, \mathtt{HO}_1), \ldots (\mathtt{val}_a, \mathtt{HO}_a)])$, $\mathtt{c}' = (\mathtt{r}', [(\mathtt{val}'_1, \mathtt{HO}'_1), \ldots (\mathtt{val}'_a, \mathtt{HO}'_a)])$, and $\mathtt{tr} = (\mathtt{r} \bmod |\mathtt{Tr}| = \mathtt{e} : \mathtt{send}\ \mathtt{v};\ \mathtt{cmd}_1, \ldots \mathtt{cmd}_K)$ with $\mathtt{cmd}_k = \left(\mathtt{guard}_k, \mathtt{val}_k^1 \to \mathtt{val}_k^2\right)$ for each $k : 1 \le k \le K$. We write $\mathtt{c} \xrightarrow{\mathtt{tr}} \mathtt{c}'$ to mean that $\mathtt{r}' = \mathtt{r} + 1$ and there is a total function $\mathtt{F} : \{1, \ldots a\} \to \{1, \ldots K\}$ where for each $i : 1 \le i \le a$, $\mathtt{val}_i = \mathtt{val}^1_{\mathtt{F}(i)}$, $\mathtt{val}'_i = \mathtt{val}^2_{\mathtt{F}(i)}$ and $\mathtt{HO}_i \models \mathtt{guard}_{\mathtt{F}(i)}$. Note that the numbers of processes in $\mathtt{c}$ and $\mathtt{c}'$ are finite, arbitrary large and equal.

Example 2. Consider Example 1 and $\mathtt{tr}$ being the transition $\mathtt{tr}$ in Fig. 1. Processes 1 to 4 can take guarded commands 2, 2, 5 and 4 respectively and result in the configuration $\mathtt{c}' = (1, [\mathtt{p}'_1, \mathtt{p}'_2, \mathtt{p}'_3, \mathtt{p}'_4])$ where:

- $\mathtt{p}'_1 = ((x_1 = 1, r_1 = \text{-}1), [1, 0, 1])$
- $\mathtt{p}'_2 = ((x_2 = 1, r_2 = \text{-}1), [1, 1, 0])$
- $\mathtt{p}'_3 = ((x_3 = 0, r_3 = \text{-}1), [0, 1])$
- $\mathtt{p}'_4 = ((x_4 = 1, r_4 = 1), [1, 1, 1])$

Here $\mathtt{F} = \{(1, 2), (2, 2), (3, 5), (4, 4)\}$ witnesses $\mathtt{c} \xrightarrow{\mathtt{tr}} \mathtt{c}'$.

4   Symbolic Representation

In this section, we formally define our symbolic representation and describe a corresponding entailment relation. We assume a program $\mathtt{prg} = (\mathtt{V}, \mathtt{D}, \mathtt{Init}, \mathtt{Tr})$.

Constraints. A constraint ϕ is a tuple $(\mathtt{e}, \mathtt{gl}, \{\mathtt{val}_1, \ldots, \mathtt{val}_b\})$ that denotes a possibly infinite set of configurations such that:

- An integer $\mathtt{e}$ in $\{0, \ldots |\mathtt{Tr}| \text{-} 1\}$ capturing the control location of the execution.
- A *global condition* $\mathtt{gl}$ in the form of a Presburger predicate with a free variable n (for the number of processes) and a set of $|\mathtt{V}| \times |\mathtt{D}|$ free variables $\#\mathtt{V} = \{\#\mathtt{v}^\mathtt{d} \mid \mathtt{v} \in \mathtt{V} \text{ and } \mathtt{d} \in \mathtt{D}\}$, where each $\#\mathtt{v}^\mathtt{d}$ accounts for the number of occurrences of value $\mathtt{d}$ among variables $\mathtt{v}$ of all processes.
- A *base* formed by a set of valuations $\{\mathtt{val}_1, \ldots \mathtt{val}_b\}$. The valuations are similar to those used by the configurations and represent groups of processes with the same valuations.

Each valuation in the base of a constraint corresponds to one or more processes with that valuation in a denoted configuration. Besides, a constraint does not explicitly represent conditions on heard-of multisets; instead, we maintain a global condition $\mathtt{gl}$ which is a predicate on the number of occurrences of values in program variables of all processes (i.e.global state). The intuition is that heard-of sets ultimately originate from the global state. Hence constraining their values (to satisfy some guarded commands) is a matter of constraining the global state and accounting for possible faults (see Sect. 5). For a predicate p that might depend on a set of integer variables $X = \{x_1, \ldots, x_q\}$, we write $p(X)$ to clarify that p might have a subset of X as free variables. To simplify the presentation, we typically omit to mention that a predicate might have n (for the number of processes) as a free variable. For instance, we write $\mathtt{gl}(^{\#}\mathtt{V})$ to clarify that $\mathtt{gl}$ might have as free variables a subset of $^{\#}\mathtt{V}$ in addition to the variable n.

Denotations. For a constraint $\phi = \left(\mathbf{e}, \mathtt{gl}^{\phi}, \left\{ \mathtt{val}_1^{\phi}, \ldots, \mathtt{val}_b^{\phi} \right\} \right)$ we write $\mathbf{c} \models \phi$ to mean ϕ denotes the configuration $\mathbf{c} = (\mathbf{r}, (\mathtt{val}_1^c, \mathtt{HO}_1^c), \ldots, (\mathtt{val}_a^c, \mathtt{HO}_a^c))$. Intuitively, ϕ should account for all local valuations in $\mathbf{c}$ (captured by a surjection from $\{1, \ldots a\}$ to $\{1, \ldots b\}$). Moreover, the predicate $\mathtt{gl}^{\phi}$ must be compatible with the multiset of all local valuations of the processes. More formally:

1. $\mathbf{r} \mod |\mathtt{Tr}| = \mathbf{e}$.
2. Replacing in the global condition $\mathtt{gl}$ each occurrence of $^{\#}\mathtt{v}^{\mathtt{d}}$ by the number of occurrences of $\mathtt{d}$ in $\mathbf{c}$ (i.e., $\mathtt{valuesOf}(\mathbf{c}, \mathtt{v})(\mathtt{d})$) and each occurrence of n by the number of processes in $\mathbf{c}$ (i.e., a) results in a valid formula.
3. There is a surjection $\mathtt{S} :: \{1, \ldots a\} \to \{1, \ldots b\}$ such that for all $1 \le i \le a$, $\mathtt{val}_i^c = \mathtt{val}_{\mathtt{S}(i)}^{\phi}$

Observe that a constraint $(\mathbf{e}, \mathtt{gl}, \{\mathtt{val}_1, \ldots, \mathtt{val}_b\})$ will have an empty denotation if its base requires the presence of valuations forbidden by the global condition, or if the global condition requires valuations forbidden by the base (since we require a surjection). It is safe to systematically discard such constraints in our analysis presented in Sect. 5.

Example 3. The configuration $\mathbf{c}'$ in Example 2 is in the denotation of the constraint
$$\phi' = (1, ^{\#}\mathtt{x}^1 > 2n/3, \{(\mathtt{x}_1 = 1, \mathbf{r}_1 = \text{-}1), (\mathtt{x}_1 = 0, \mathbf{r}_2 = \text{-}1), (\mathtt{x}_3 = 1, \mathbf{r}_3 = 1)\})$$
with $\mathtt{S}$ being $\{(1, 1), (2, 1), (3, 2), (4, 3)\}$.

Entailment. We write $\phi_1 \sqsubseteq \phi_2$ to mean $\phi_1 = \left(\mathbf{e}, \mathtt{gl}^1, \{\mathtt{val}_1^1, \ldots, \mathtt{val}_{b_1}^1\} \right)$ is entailed by $\phi_2 = \left(\mathbf{e}, \mathtt{gl}^2, \{\mathtt{val}_1^2, \ldots, \mathtt{val}_{b_2}^2\} \right)$. This will ensure that configurations denoted by ϕ_2 are also denoted by ϕ_1. Intuitively, ϕ_1 and ϕ_2 must have the same round number modulo $|\mathtt{Tr}|$, and

- There is a bijection $\mathtt{Y} :: \{1, \ldots b_2\} \to \{1, \ldots b_1\}$ with $\mathtt{val}_j^2 = \mathtt{val}_{\mathtt{Y}(j)}^1$ for all $1 \le j \le b_2$.
- $\mathtt{gl}^2 \Rightarrow \mathtt{gl}^1$.

5   A Symbolic Verification Procedure

We use the constraints defined in Sect. 4 as a symbolic representation to denote sets of configurations. We adopt a working-list procedure that checks reachability of a $\sqsubseteq$-minimal set Φ of target constraints by a program $\mathtt{prg} = (\mathtt{V}, \mathtt{D}, \mathtt{Init}, \mathtt{Tr})$.

For a bad set $B = \{\text{val}_1, \ldots \text{val}_x\}$ of valuations, the set of target constraints Φ_B contains each $(\text{e}, \text{true}, \text{val}_1, \ldots, \text{val}_x)$ where e is a value in $\{0, \ldots, |\text{Tr}|-1\}$. In addition, it contains each constraint obtained from such a constraint by adding some unique valuations that were not in its base (since we require surjections for the denotations in Sect. 4).

The procedure computes a fixpoint using the entailment relation $\sqsubseteq$ and a predecessor computation that results, for a constraint ϕ and a transition tr, in a finite set $\text{pre}_{\text{tr}}(\phi)$. In fact, $\text{pre}_{\text{tr}}(\phi)$ is the set of constraints that capture an over-approximation of all the configurations that might reach in one round a configuration denoted by ϕ. Figure 4 captures this computations and uses several sets of integer variables. The variables $^{\#}\text{V} = \{^{\#}\text{v}^{\text{d}} \mid \text{v} \in \text{V} \text{ and } \text{d} \in \text{D}\}$ (resp. $^{\#}\text{V}' = \{^{\#}\text{v}'^{\text{d}} \mid \text{v} \in \text{V} \text{ and } \text{d} \in \text{D}\}$) are used to constrain values of process variables in the successor constraint ϕ (resp. predecessor constraint ϕ'). The variables $^{\#}\text{HO}_k = \{^{\#}\text{ho}_k^{\text{d}} \mid \text{d} \in \text{D}\}$ are used to constrain values in the heard-of multisets of processes taking a guarded command cmd_k in tr. The remaining text in this Section describes the over-approximation.

$$\phi = (\text{e}, \text{gl}, \{\text{val}_1, \ldots, \text{val}_b\})$$
$$\text{tr} = (\text{r} \bmod |\text{Tr}| = \text{e} : \text{send v}; \text{cmd}_1, \ldots \text{cmd}_K)$$
$$1 \leq k \leq K \implies \text{cmd}_k = \left(\text{guard}_k, \text{val}_k^1 \to \text{val}_k^2\right)$$
$$\text{I} \subseteq \{1, \ldots K\} \times \{1, \ldots b\} \text{ st. } \text{I}_{|\{1, \ldots b\}} = \{1, \ldots b\}$$
$$\text{H} :: \{1, \ldots |\text{I}|\} \to \text{I} \text{ is an enumeration of I}$$
$$1 \leq i \leq |\text{I}| \land \text{H}(i) = (k, j) \implies \text{val}_i' = \text{val}_k^1 \land \text{val}_k^2 = \text{val}_j$$
$$\Gamma = \{\gamma_k \mid k : 1 \leq k \leq K\} \text{ with}$$
$$\gamma_k(^{\#}\text{V}') = \exists^{\#}\text{HO}_k.\xi(\text{guard}_k)(^{\#}\text{HO}_k) \land \text{HAX}_k(^{\#}\text{HO}_k, {}^{\#}\text{V}')$$
$$\text{gl}'(^{\#}\text{V}') = \left(\text{Inv} \land \bigwedge_{(k,\_)\in \text{I}} \gamma_k(^{\#}\text{V}') \land \text{PrAbs}_{[\Gamma]}\left(\exists^{\#}\text{V}. \text{DAX}(^{\#}\text{V}, {}^{\#}\text{V}') \land \text{gl}(^{\#}\text{V})\right)\right)$$
$$\text{Inv} = \left(\sum_{d \in D} {}^{\#}\text{v}'^{\text{d}} = n\right)$$
$$\phi' = \left((\text{e} - 1) \bmod |\text{Tr}|, \text{gl}'\left[^{\#}\text{v}'/^{\#}\text{v}\right], \text{setOf}(\text{val}_1', \ldots, \text{val}_{|\text{I}|}')\right)$$
$$\rule{6cm}{0.4pt}$$
$$\phi' \in \text{pre}_{\text{tr}}(\phi)$$

Fig. 4. Predecessors computation for constraint ϕ and transition tr.

Choice of guarded commands and resulting bases. Intuitively, the set I corresponds to combinations of processes in the successors (i.e., ϕ) and guarded commands in the transition (i.e., tr). Each pair $(k, j) \in \text{I}$ corresponds to a group of processes with the same valuation $\text{val}'_{H^{-1}((k,j))}$ in the predecessors (i.e., ϕ') that took the guarded command cmd_k in the transition tr resulting in a valuations val_j in ϕ. Observe there are finitely many such combinations, and hence finitely many such sets I. The definition of I ensures that the set $\{1, \ldots b\}$ of process groups of ϕ is covered. In addition, two pairs (k_1, j_1) and (k_2, j_2) may result in equal valuations $\text{val}'_{H^{-1}((k_1,j_1))}$ and $\text{val}'_{H^{-1}((k_2,j_2))}$. We keep only one representative in ϕ' by making a set $\mathtt{setOf}(\mathtt{val}'_1, \ldots, \mathtt{val}'_{|\mathrm{I}|})$ of the multiset $[\mathtt{val}'_1, \ldots, \mathtt{val}'_{|\mathrm{I}|}]$

Constraints imposed by the guards. Given a guarded command $\mathtt{cmd}_k$, we use the predicate $\xi(\mathtt{guard}_k)$ to encode the fact that the heard-of multisets of predecessor configurations denoted by ϕ' satisfy the guard $\mathtt{guard}_k$ of $\mathtt{cmd}_k$. For this, we use an integer variable $\#\mathtt{ho}_k^\mathtt{d}$ for each value $\mathtt{d}$ and index $k : 1 \le k \le K$ to count the occurrences of $\mathtt{d}$ in the heard-of multiset of the processes taking $\mathtt{cmd}_k$. We write $\#\mathtt{HO}_k = \{\#\mathtt{ho}_k^\mathtt{d} \mid \mathtt{d} \in \mathtt{D}\}$ to mean the set of all such variables for all values in $\mathtt{D}$. For instance, $\mathtt{guard}_3$ is $|\mathtt{HO}^0| > 2n/3$ in Fig. 1 and is encoded with the predicate $(\#\mathtt{ho}_3^0 > 2n/3)$. We also need to relate the constraints on the heard-of multisets to the constraints on the variables values in the predecessor constraint ϕ'. Assume ϕ' denotes a configuration $\mathtt{c}'$ resulting, via $\mathtt{tr}$, in a configuration $\mathtt{c}$ denoted by ϕ. Suppose $\mathtt{tr}$ sends values of variable $\mathtt{v}$. In the case of benign failures (e.g., message losses), any heard-of multiset $\mathtt{HO}_k$ of some process that took a guarded command $\mathtt{cmd}_k$ in $\mathtt{tr}$ needs to get its values from the multiset $\mathtt{valuesOf}(\mathtt{c}', \mathtt{v})$ of values of $\mathtt{v}$ in $\mathtt{c}'$. We therefore enforce $\mathtt{HO}_k \preceq \mathtt{valuesOf}(\mathtt{c}', \mathtt{v})$. This is captured by $\mathtt{HAX}_k(\#\mathtt{HO}_k, \#\mathtt{V}') = \bigwedge_{\mathtt{d} \in \mathtt{D}} 0 \le \#\mathtt{ho}_k^\mathtt{d} \le \#\mathtt{v}'^\mathtt{d}$. For each guarded command $\mathtt{cmd}_k$, the predicate $\gamma_k(\#\mathtt{V}') = \exists \#\mathtt{HO}_k . \left(\xi(\mathtt{guard}_k)(\#\mathtt{HO}_k) \wedge \mathtt{HAX}_k(\#\mathtt{HO}_k, \#\mathtt{V}') \right)$ captures the strongest constraints imposed, in the predecessor processes, by the guard of $\mathtt{cmd}_k$ on values of the variable that was sent (here $\mathtt{v}$). We explain later in this section how we handle corrupt communication. These predicates are only dependent on the chosen guarded commands and the sent variables. We collect them in a set $\Gamma = \{\gamma_k \mid k : 1 \le k \le K\}$. Observe the set Γ is finite.

Constraints imposed by the commands. Each time a process takes a chosen guarded command $\mathtt{cmd}_k = (\mathtt{guard}_k, \mathtt{val}_k^1 \to \mathtt{val}_k^2)$ with (k,j) in I for some j, it transforms its valuation from $\mathtt{val}_k^1$ to $\mathtt{val}_k^2$. This affects the relation between $\mathtt{gl}(\#\mathtt{V})$ and $\mathtt{gl}'(\#\mathtt{V}')$ as the number of occurrences of a variable with a given value depends on the proportions of processes that take each guarded command. We first illustrate how this relation can be captured exactly by introducing auxiliary variables to represent the number of processes that took each one of the chosen guarded commands. Then we describe how we can over-approximate this relation and avoid the introduction of the variables.

First, we introduce an integer variable δ_k, for each $k \in \{1, \ldots, K\}$, to capture the number of processes in some configuration $\mathtt{c}'$ denoted by ϕ' that executed the guarded command $\mathtt{cmd}_k = (\mathtt{guard}_k, \mathtt{val}_k^1 \to \mathtt{val}_k^2)$. If $\mathtt{d}_1 = \mathtt{val}_k^1(\mathtt{v})$ and $\mathtt{d}_2 = \mathtt{val}_k^2(\mathtt{v})$, then each process taking the guarded command $\mathtt{cmd}_k$ will decrease the number of occurrences of $\mathtt{d}_1$ and increase the number of occurrences of $\mathtt{d}_2$. More precisely, for each variable $\mathtt{v}$, the following relation holds:

$$\mathtt{DAX}_e(\#\mathtt{V}, \#\mathtt{V}') = \left(\begin{array}{c} \exists \{\delta_k \mid k \in \{1, \ldots, K\}\} . \wedge \bigwedge_{(k,\_) \in \mathrm{I}} \delta_k \ge 1 \\ \wedge \bigwedge_{\substack{\mathtt{v} \in \mathtt{V} \\ \mathtt{d} \in \mathtt{D}}} \#\mathtt{v}'^\mathtt{d} = \sum_{\substack{\mathtt{d} = \mathtt{val}_k^1(\mathtt{v}) \\ (k,\_) \in \mathrm{I}}} \delta_k \wedge \#\mathtt{v}^\mathtt{d} = \sum_{\substack{\mathtt{d} = \mathtt{val}_k^2(\mathtt{v}) \\ (k,\_) \in \mathrm{I}}} \delta_k \end{array} \right)$$

The relation $\mathtt{DAX}_e$ is expensive to compute. Instead, we over-approximate it with $\mathtt{DAX}$ (see below) where we identify two cases in which we can relate variables in $^\#\mathtt{V}$ and $^\#\mathtt{V}'$. For each variable $\mathtt{v} \in \mathtt{V}$, the first case (captured with the predicate $\mathtt{preserved}_\mathtt{I}(\mathtt{v})$) is true when each chosen guarded command $\left(\mathtt{guard}_k, \mathtt{val}_k^1 \to \mathtt{val}_k^2\right)$ with $(k, \_) \in \mathtt{I}$ preserves the variable $\mathtt{v}$ (i.e., $\mathtt{val}_k^1(\mathtt{v}) = \mathtt{val}_k^2(\mathtt{v})$). The second (captured with the predicate $\mathtt{uniqueChange}_\mathtt{I}(\mathtt{v}, \mathtt{d})$) corresponds to the situation when the only allowed changes for variable $\mathtt{v}$ are to some value $\mathtt{d}$ (i.e., for all k, k' with $(k, \_), (k', \_) \in \mathtt{I}$, if $\mathtt{val}_k^1(\mathtt{v}) \neq \mathtt{val}_k^2(\mathtt{v})$ and $\mathtt{val}_{k'}^1(\mathtt{v}) \neq \mathtt{val}_{k'}^2(\mathtt{v})$ then $\mathtt{val}_k^2(\mathtt{v}) = \mathtt{val}_{k'}^2(\mathtt{v}) = \mathtt{d}$). The over-approximation $\mathtt{DAX}$ of $\mathtt{DAX}_e$ is defined as:

$$\mathtt{DAX}(^\#\mathtt{V}, {}^\#\mathtt{V}') = \bigwedge_{\mathtt{v} \in \mathtt{V}} \left(\begin{array}{l} \mathtt{preserved}_\mathtt{I}(\mathtt{v}) \implies \bigwedge_{\mathtt{d} \in \mathtt{D}} {}^\#\mathtt{v}'^\mathtt{d} = {}^\#\mathtt{v}^\mathtt{d} \\ \wedge \bigwedge_{\mathtt{d} \in \mathtt{D}} \left(\mathtt{uniqueChange}_\mathtt{I}(\mathtt{v}, \mathtt{d}) \implies {}^\#\mathtt{v}'^\mathtt{d} \leq {}^\#\mathtt{v}^\mathtt{d} \right) \end{array} \right)$$

To achieve the computation of $\mathtt{gl}'(^\#\mathtt{V}')$, we account for the global condition of the successor constraint (using $\mathtt{gl}(^\#\mathtt{V})$) and deduce constraints on $\mathtt{V}'$ via the relation $\mathtt{DAX}(^\#\mathtt{V}, {}^\#\mathtt{V}')$. More precisely, we compute: $\pi(^\#\mathtt{V}') = \exists^\#\mathtt{V}. \mathtt{DAX}(^\#\mathtt{V}, {}^\#\mathtt{V}') \wedge \mathtt{gl}(^\#\mathtt{V})$. In general, arbitrarily many different such predicates may be generated in the fixpoint iteration. To help termination, we use the abstraction $\mathtt{PrAbs}_{[\Gamma]}(\pi)$ of π with respect to the predicates $\Gamma = \{\gamma_k \mid k : 1 \leq k \leq K\}$ obtained from all the guards.

Example 4. Consider the configurations c, c' and the constraint ϕ' in the Examples 1, 2 and 3. We have shown $c \xrightarrow{\mathtt{tr}} c'$ using $\mathtt{F}$ and $c' \models \phi'$ using $\mathtt{S}$. Consider now the constraint $\phi = (0, {}^\#\mathtt{x}^1 > 2n/3, \{(\mathtt{x}_1 = 1, \mathtt{r}_1 = -1), (\mathtt{x}_1 = 0, \mathtt{r}_2 = -1)\})$. We define $\mathtt{H} = \{(1, (2, 1)), (2, (5, 2)), (1, (4, 3))\}$ to show $\phi' \in \mathtt{pre}_\mathtt{tr}(\phi)$. Moreover, there is a surjection $\mathtt{S}' = \{(1, 1), (2, 1), (3, 2), (4, 1)\}$ that witnesses $c \models \phi$.

Corrupted communications. As in [3], corrupted communications or value faults are related to the classical Byzantine Faults in which a portion of the received messages are corrupted. Note that in the classical Byzantine setting, also the state of a process can be corrupted, which is not the case in this model. All processes follow the algorithm but may receive a number of corrupted messages (whether accidental or malicious). We weaken this assumption so that in each round, for each process and for each data value, no more than α (given as a fraction of n) messages received by a process may have been corrupted. This assumption is weaker than the one in [14]. We model this by enforcing the following invariants. $\mathtt{DAX}$ remains unchanged because of the assumption that states of processes are not corrupted. It is the relation between the heard-of multisets and process variables that change: $\mathtt{HAX}_k = \bigwedge_{\mathtt{d} \in \mathtt{D}} (0 \leq {}^\#\mathtt{ho}_k^\mathtt{d} \leq {}^\#\mathtt{v}'^\mathtt{d} + \alpha)$.
The rest of the computation of predecessors remains unchanged.

Theorem 1. *The proposed predecessor computation method introduced in Fig. 4 is a sound over-approximation for parameterized Heard-Of programs.*

Proof. Sketch. Assume configurations c, c' and constraint ϕ as described in Fig. 5. The total function F witnesses $c' \to c$ and surjection S witnesses $c \models \phi$. We show a constraint ϕ' that denotes c' is generated by the procedure. All generated e' capture r' if $c' \to c$ and $c \models \phi$. Observe each $\mathtt{val}_j^\phi$ is mapped to (via S) at least some $\mathtt{val}_i^c$. By choosing $I = \{(F(i), S(i)) \mid i : 1 \le i \le a\}$ we ensure the existence of a surjection S' that maps each $\mathtt{val}_i^{c'}$ to some $\mathtt{val}_{j'}^{\phi'}$. In addition, the values $\mathtt{valuesOf}(c', v)$, for each $v \in V$, resulted in heard-of multisets that satisfied the guarded commands $\{\mathtt{cmd}_{F(i)} \mid i : 1 \le i \le a\}$. Moreover, $\mathtt{valuesOf}(c', v)$ satisfies $\mathtt{gl}'$ because of the following. Indeed, $\mathtt{valuesOf}(c, v)$ satisfy $\mathtt{gl}$ and are related to $\mathtt{valuesOf}(c', v)$ with $\mathtt{DAX}_e$ and its over-approximations $\mathtt{DAX}$ and its predicate abstraction with respect to some predicates. Finally, $\mathtt{Inv}$ restricts $\mathtt{valuesOf}(c', v)$ to possible values (e.g., sum of all occurrences per variable should be n) or relevant values (e.g., enforcing invariants under which correctness is checked).

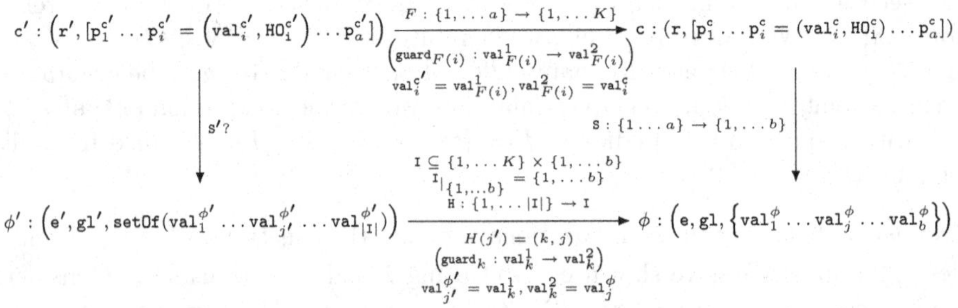

Fig. 5. Given $c' \to c$ and $c \models \phi$, soundness boils down to showing the existence of $\phi' \in \mathtt{pre}_{\mathtt{tr}}(\phi)$ for which $c' \models \phi'$.

Theorem 2. *The proposed procedure terminates.*

Termination is obtained by the fact that at most a finite number of constraints might be generated. To see this, observe that constraints consist of an integer capturing control location, a predicate (the global condition), and a set of local valuations of processes (the base). The number of control locations and that of the local valuations of processes is finite. In addition, the number of combinations of subsets of guarded commands is finite and the strengthening invariants do not change.

6   Experimental Results

We report on experiments with our open-source prototype SyncV which is publically available online at https://gitlab.liu.se/live/syncv for the verification of a class of HO algorithms. The experiments were conducted on a 2.9 GHz processor with 8 GB of memory. We conducted experiments on several variations of the One-Third-Rule and $\mathcal{A}_{E,T}$ algorithms. In fact, these variations correspond to checking the correctness properties of agreement, validity, and irrevocability for correct and buggy versions of the considered algorithms and for an unbounded number of processes. For each property, a correct version and a buggy version were tested. The buggy versions differ from the correct ones by the considered guards in the commands. For verification of the $\mathcal{A}_{E,T}$ algorithm, we strengthened our invariant Inv in Fig. 4 with the invariants represented in Fig. 3 that according [3] are essential for correctness of the algorithm.

For all the correct versions, our tool reported that the program is safe and for all the buggy ones, it presented a valid trace violating the considered property. Our implemented procedure does not eagerly concretize local valuations of processes. Instead, we concretize on demand. All benchmarks are available on the tool homepage.

Checking different correctness properties. We discussed in depth checking the agreement correctness property in Sects. 2 and 5. Checking the validity property is similar in the sense that it also uses a finite set of forbidden valuations to characterize the set of bad constraints. In order to check irrevocability, one needs to see if a process can make a decision and revoke it later. In order to make such checks, we take into account a *history* of the changes. We do that by augmenting each process group in a constraint by a list of possible decisions as its history. This list is empty by default. A bad constraint that violates irrevocability has at least one process group with a minimum of two different values in its history.

7   Conclusion and Future Work

We have studied a subclass of fault-tolerant distributed algorithms in terms of the Heard-Of model and proposed a symbolic representation using cardinality constraints on multisets to model sets of configurations generated during the analysis of such programs. We have also introduced a sound procedure for checking state reachability to check various correctness properties for consensus programs such as agreement, validity, and irrevocability in the presence of lossy or corrupt communications. We showed that the introduced procedure terminates even for an unbounded number of processes. To the best of our knowledge, this is the first fully-automatic approach to verify Heard-Of protocols in the presence of corrupt communication. We reported on preliminary experiments with correct and buggy variations of the protocols (Table 1).

Table 1. The result of checking safety properties for some HO protocols with SyncV. For each algorithm, a correct and a buggy version were tested by the tool. The buggy versions differ from the correct ones by the guards of their commands. For all the correct versions our tool reported that the program is safe and for all the buggy ones, it presented a valid trace violating the considered property.

Program	Property	Safe?	Result	Time(m)
simple	agreement	✓	safe	2
	validity	✓	safe	0
	irrevocability	✓	safe	1
$\frac{1}{3}$-rule	agreement	✓	safe	19
		✗	trace	0
	validity	✓	safe	2
		✗	trace	0
	irrevocability	✓	safe	7
		✗	trace	0
$\mathcal{A}_{E,T}$	agreement	✓	safe	54
		✗	trace	1
	validity	✓	safe	5
		✗	trace	0
	irrevocability	✓	safe	21
		✗	trace	0

Future Work. Future work can consider improving the scalability of the tool, and also extending the presented technique to more general models and more sophisticated faults such as Byzantine faults. Besides, the current technique assumes symmetric processes in the sense that all of them execute the same operation in each round. One can extend the model to non-symmetric processes as in the Heard-Of examples having coordinators, for instance in *CoordUniformVoting* and *LastVoting* algorithms in [4], or the *Phase King* and *Phase Queen* algorithms introduced in [2] in which a *King* or *Queen* is distinguished in each round, or the reliable broadcast algorithm in [16]. It will also be interesting to combine the approach with abstract interpretation for loops to be able to capture the distributed algorithms in which the number of iterations is crucial for the correctness of the algorithm, for example, the *FloodMin* algorithm in [5]. Moreover, identification of conditions for completeness of the approach, automatic refinement of the over-approximation and combination with richer theories are interesting directions for future work.

References

1. Alberti, F., Ghilardi, S., Pagani, E.: Cardinality constraints for arrays (decidability results and applications). Form. Methods Syst. Des. **51**(3), 545–574 (2017). https://doi.org/10.1007/s10703-017-0279-6
2. Berman, P., Garay, J.A., Perry, K.J.: Optimal early stopping in distributed consensus. In: Segall, A., Zaks, S. (eds.) WDAG 1992. LNCS, vol. 647, pp. 221–237. Springer, Heidelberg (1992). https://doi.org/10.1007/3-540-56188-9_15
3. Biely, M., Widder, J., Charron-Bost, B., Gaillard, A., Hutle, M., Schiper, A.: Tolerating corrupted communication. In: Proceedings of the Twenty-sixth Annual ACM Symposium on Principles of Distributed Computing - PODC 2007. ACM Press (2007). https://doi.org/10.1145/1281100.1281136
4. Charron-Bost, B., Schiper, A.: The heard-of model: computing in distributed systems with benign faults. Distrib. Comput. **22**(1), 49–71 (2009). https://doi.org/10.1007/s00446-009-0084-6
5. Chaudhuri, S., Erlihy, M., Lynch, N.A., Tuttle, M.R.: Tight bounds for k-set agreement. J. ACM (JACM) **47**(5), 912–943 (2000)
6. Debrat, H., Merz, S.: Verifying fault-tolerant distributed algorithms in the heard-of model. Archive of Formal Proofs (2012) https://www.isa-afp.org/entries/HeardOf.shtml
7. Drăgoi, C., Henzinger, T.A., Zufferey, D.: PSync: a partially synchronous language for fault-tolerant distributed algorithms. In: Proceedings of the 43rd Annual ACM SIGPLAN-SIGACT Symposium on Principles of Programming Languages - POPL 2016. ACM Press (2016). https://doi.org/10.1145/2837614.2837650
8. Gleissenthall, K.v., Bjørner, N., Rybalchenko, A.: Cardinalities and universal quantifiers for verifying parameterized systems. In: Proceedings of the 37th ACM SIGPLAN Conference on Programming Language Design and Implementation, pp. 599–613 (2016)
9. Hawblitzel, C., Howell, J., Kapritsos, M., Lorch, J.R., Parno, B., Roberts, M.L., Setty, S., Zill, B.: IronFleet. In: Proceedings of the 25th Symposium on Operating Systems Principles - SOSP 2015. ACM Press (2015). https://doi.org/10.1145/2815400.2815428
10. Jaskelioff, M., Merz, S.: Proving the correctness of disk paxos. Archive of Formal Proofs (2005). https://www.isa-afp.org/entries/DiskPaxos.shtml
11. John, A., Konnov, I., Schmid, U., Veith, H., Widder, J.: Parameterized model checking of fault-tolerant distributed algorithms by abstraction. In: 2013 Formal Methods in Computer-Aided Design. IEEE (2013). https://doi.org/10.1109/fmcad.2013.6679411
12. Konnov, I., Veith, H., Widder, J.: On the completeness of bounded model checking for threshold-based distributed algorithms: reachability. Inform.Comput. **252**, 95–109 (2017). https://doi.org/10.1016/j.ic.2016.03.006
13. Kuncak, V., Nguyen, H.H., Rinard, M.: An algorithm for deciding BAPA: Boolean algebra with presburger arithmetic. In: Nieuwenhuis, R. (ed.) CADE 2005. LNCS (LNAI), vol. 3632, pp. 260–277. Springer, Heidelberg (2005). https://doi.org/10.1007/11532231_20
14. Marić, O., Sprenger, C., Basin, D.: Cutoff bounds for consensus algorithms. In: Majumdar, R., Kunčak, V. (eds.) CAV 2017. LNCS, vol. 10427, pp. 217–237. Springer, Cham (2017). https://doi.org/10.1007/978-3-319-63390-9_12
15. Padon, O., Losa, G., Sagiv, M., Shoham, S.: Paxos made EPR: decidable reasoning about distributed protocols. In: Proceedings of the ACM on Programming Languages 1(OOPSLA), pp. 1–31 (2017). https://doi.org/10.1145/3140568

16. Srikanth, T., Toueg, S.: Simulating authenticated broadcasts to derive simple fault-tolerant algorithms. Distrib. Comput. **2**(2), 80–94 (1987)
17. Stoilkovska, I., Konnov, I., Widder, J., Zuleger, F.: Verifying safety of synchronous fault-tolerant algorithms by bounded model checking. In: Vojnar, T., Zhang, L. (eds.) TACAS 2019. LNCS, vol. 11428, pp. 357–374. Springer, Cham (2019). https://doi.org/10.1007/978-3-030-17465-1_20

Staleness and Local Progress in Transactional Memory

Hagit Attiya[1], Panagiota Fatourou[2], Sandeep Hans[3], and Eleni Kanellou[4(✉)]

[1] Technion, Haifa, Israel
hagit@cs.technion.ac.il
[2] ICS-FORTH and University of Crete, Heraklion, Greece
faturu@ics.forth.gr
[3] IBM Research India, New Delhi, India
shans001@in.ibm.com
[4] ICS-FORTH, Heraklion, Greece
kanellou@ics.forth.gr

Abstract. A key goal in the design of *Transactional Memory* (TM) systems is ensuring liveness. *Local progress* is a liveness condition which ensures that a process successfully completes every transaction it initiates, if it continually re-invokes it each time it aborts. In order to facilitate this, several state-of-the-art TM systems keep multiple versions of data items. However, this method can lead to high space-related overheads in the TM implementation. Therefore, it is desirable to strike a balance between the progress that a TM can provide and its practicality, while ensuring correctness. A consistency property that limits the number of previous versions a TM may rely on, is *k-staleness*. It is a condition derivative of snapshot isolation, in which a transaction is not allowed to access more than k previous versions of a data item. This facilitates implementations that can take advantage of multi-versioning, while at the same time, contributing to the restriction of the space overhead introduced by the TM.

In this paper, we prove that no TM can ensure both local progress and *k-staleness*, if it is unaware of the transaction's accesses and can only keep a bounded number of versions for each data item.

Keywords: Transactional memory · Progress · Consistency · Impossibility

1 Introduction

Transactional memory (TM) [13] is an important programming paradigm, which offers synchronization of processes by providing the abstraction of the *transaction* to the programmer. A transaction contains several read and/or write accesses to shared memory, determined by a piece of sequential code, which the transaction encapsulates, in order to ensure that its execution is safe when it is concurrent with other transactions. The *data items* accessed by a transaction form its *data*

© Springer Nature Switzerland AG 2021
C. Georgiou and R. Majumdar (Eds.): NETYS 2020, LNCS 12129, pp. 227–243, 2021.
https://doi.org/10.1007/978-3-030-67087-0_15

set. If the execution of the transaction does not violate consistency, then it can terminate successfully (*commit*) and its writes to data items take effect atomically. Otherwise, all the updates of the transaction are discarded and the transaction *aborts*, i.e. it appears as if it had never taken place.

The possibility of aborting a transaction is an important feature that helps ensure consistency. At the same time, however, it can hinder liveness given that if a process finds itself in a situation where its transactions repeatedly aborts (and possibly have to be restarted), it spends computation time and resources without advancing its computational task.

Thus, it is desirable for a TM implementation to provide liveness guarantees that avoid such scenarios. *Local progress* (LP) [5] is such a desirable property. A TM implementation that ensures LP guarantees that even a transaction that is aborted will have to be restarted and re-executed a finite number of times before it finally commits. However, it was shown in [5] that LP cannot be achieved if the TM implementation has to provide *strict serializability* [17], traditionally implemented by database systems. This means that a TM implementation that ensures the stronger consistency property of *opacity* [11] cannot guarantee LP.

Snapshot isolation (SI) [2] is a consistency property weaker than opacity and strict serializability. While strict serializability requires that a single serialization point $*_T$ be found for each committed transaction T, so that T appears as if it had been atomically executed at $*_T$, snapshot isolation allows two serialization points, i.e. $*_{T|r}$, a read serialization point, and $*_{T|w}$, a write serialization point, for each committed transaction T, so that T's reads on data items appear as if they had atomically occurred at point $*_{T|r}$, while its writes appear as if they had atomically occurred at $*_{T|w}$. We define a condition that is derivative of snapshot isolation, called *k-staleness* (*k*-SL), where a read operation of some transaction may read one of the k last values that the data item has had.

Multi-version TMs that keep an unbounded number of previous versions may end up in implementations with high space complexity. Even more so, in practice, data items have shared representation, which results in even higher space overheads in real-life implementations. *k*-SL restricts the number of previous versions that a transaction may access in order to be consistent, i.e., in order to make it possible to assign it serialization points. In practice, then, this can lead to implementations that are more parsimonious in the use of space.

We extend the impossibility result of [5] to *k*-staleness, by showing that even a TM implementation that provides only *k*-SL cannot guarantee LP. This result concerns TM implementations where there is the underlying assumption that transactions may be unaware of each others' data sets and where a transaction T may not execute a read or write to some data item on behalf of some other transaction T'. This means that in such TMs, one transaction does not have access to the code executed by another transaction. We remark that this assumption is kind of standard in TM computing (and is needed also for the result of [3]).

To prove our results we present a comprehensive set of formal definitions, some introducing new concepts and others formalizing existing ones that are

Table 1. Properties of popular TM implementations.

STM	Consistency	Progress	Version	Other
DSTM [12]	Opacity	Obstruction free	1	–
TL2 [7]	Opacity	Minimal progressiveness	1	Invisible reads
NoREC [6]	Opacity	Lock-Free	1	–
PermiSTM	Opacity	Wait-free (RO)	1	–
Pessimistic LE	Opacity	Wait-free (RO)	1	–
SI-STM [21]	Snapshot isolation	Obstruction free	k	No revalidation
SI-TM [15]	Snapshot isolation	Wait-free (RO)	k	–

often met only in an informal way and, thus, they are mostly understood intuitively. We consider this as one of the contributions of the paper and we believe that Sect. 2 is interesting on its own.

For instance, the notion of data item *versioning* plays an important role in some theoretical results about transactional memory [18,19] and in several TM implementations [1,10,14,16,20,21]. These works only give informal descriptions of the term or rely on the intuitive understanding by the reader. Occasionally, the term is even used in order to refer to past values of a data item or to intermediate values that are used for local bookkeeping by an implementation.

To provide a clear model for our results, we present a formal definition of the concept of versions in TM, which reflects the way versioning is used in some of the prior theoretical results. For example, the limitations of keeping multiple versions for TM implementations are examined in [19]. The authors use a design principle by which a new version of a t-object is produced by an update transaction that has the t-object in its write set and commits, similar to our concept of past committed transaction. Similarly, in [18], reads on t-objects are considered to access values installed by transactions that have committed. Our definition is also compatible with existing k-version implementations. Table 1 summarizes some well-known TM implementations, presenting their properties according to the parameters we consider. Some of our definitions follow those in [4,8].

The rest of the paper is organized as follows: Sect. 2 provides the model on which we base our results, while Sect. 3 outlines the impossibility result. Finally, Sect. 4 summarizes our result and discusses its implication and context.

2   Definitions

2.1   Basic TM Concepts

We assume a system of n asynchronous processes that communicate through a shared memory. The shared memory is modeled as a collection of *base objects*, provided by hardware, which can be accessed by executing *primitives*, such as read, write, or CAS, on them.

A *transactional memory* (*TM*) supports the execution of pieces of sequential code in a concurrent setting through the use of *transactions*. Transactions contain read and write accesses to pieces of data, referred to as *data items*. Data items may be accessed simultaneously by multiple processes in a concurrent setting. A data item has a *shared representation*, also called *t-object*, out of base objects. A transaction T may *commit* or *abort*. If it commits, its updates on t-objects take effect, whereas if it aborts, its updates are discarded.

A *TM implementation* provides, for each process, the implementation of a set of routines, also called *t-operations*, which are invoked in order to execute transactions. Common such routines are listed in Table 2. *BeginTx* is called in order to start the execution of a transaction and *CommitTx* is called in order to attempt to commit a transaction. T-objects are accessed by calling t-operations *Read* and *Write*. When a transaction initiates the execution of a t-operation, we say that it *invokes* it, and a *response* is returned to the transaction when the t-operation execution terminates. Invocations and responses are referred to as *actions*.

Table 2. Invocations and possible responses of t-operations by a transaction T.

t-operation	Invocation	Valid response	Description
BeginTx	T.BeginTx	T.ACK	Initiates transaction T
CommitTx	T.CommitTx	T.committed or T.aborted	Attempts to terminate T successfully
Read	T.Read(x)	value v in some domain V or T.aborted	Reads the value of t-object x
Write	T.Write(x, v)	T.ACK or T.aborted	Writes value v to t-object x

In the following, $Read(x, v)$ denotes an instance of a *Read* t-operation executed by some transaction. It accesses t-object x and receives response v. Furthermore, $Write(x, v)$ denotes an instance of a *Write* t-operation that writes v to t-object x. We say that a transaction *reads* a data item when it invokes an instance of *Read* on the t-object of the data item, and that it *writes* to a data item when it invokes an instance of *Write* on the t-object of the data item. (In such cases, we may abuse terminology and say that a transaction reads or writes a t-object, respectively.) The *read set* of a transaction T, denoted rset(T), is the set of data items that T reads, while its *write set*, denoted wset(T), is the set of data items that T writes to. The union of read set and write set is the *data set* of T.[1]

---

[1]   The definitions of read set, write set, and data set are formulated under the implicit assumption that transactions only execute their own code and do not perform reads

A *history* is a (possibly infinite) sequence of invocations and responses of t-operations. For a history H, $H|p$ denotes the subsequence of all those actions pertaining to process p. Similarly, $H|T$ denotes the subsequence of all those actions pertaining to transaction T. We remark that any of those subsequences may be empty. We denote by λ the empty sequence.

If $H|T$ is not empty, then T *is in* H. We denote by $\mathsf{txns}(H)$ the set of all transactions in H. Two histories H and H' are *equivalent*, denoted $H \equiv H'$, if $\mathsf{txns}(H) = \mathsf{txns}(H')$ and for every transaction $T \in \mathsf{txns}(H)$ and every process p, it holds that $H|T = H'|T$ and $H|p = H'|p$.

A history H is *well-formed* if for every transaction T in $\mathsf{txns}(H)$, $H|T$ is an alternating sequence of invocations of t-operations and their valid responses, starting with $T.BeginTx$, such that (i) no further invocation follows a T.committed or T.aborted response in $H|T$, and (ii) given another transaction $T' \in \mathsf{txns}(H)$ executed by the same process as T, either the last action of $H|T$ is T.committed or T.aborted and precedes the first action of $H|T'$ in H or the last action of $H|T'$ is T'.committed or T'.aborted and precedes the first action of $H|T$ in H. We only consider well-formed histories.

T is *committed* in H, if $H|T$ ends with T.committed. It is *aborted* in H, if $H|T$ ends with T.aborted. T is *completed* in H, if it is either committed or aborted in H; otherwise, it is *live*. If $H|T$ ends with an invocation of $T.CommitTx$, then T is *commit-pending* in H. A history H is *complete* if all transactions in $\mathsf{txns}(H)$ are completed. Let $H|$com be the projection of H on actions performed by the committed transactions in H. A *completion* of a finite history H is a (well-formed) complete history H' such that $H' = HH''$, where H'' is a sequence of actions where any action is either T.committed or T.aborted, for every transaction T that is commit-pending in H. The set of completions of H is denoted $\mathsf{comp}(H)$.

A history H imposes a partial order, called *real-time order*, on t-operations: For two t-operations o_i, o_j in H, we say that o_i *precedes* o_j in H, denoted $o_i \prec^o_H o_j$, if the response of o_i occurs before the invocation of o_j in H. A history H is *operation-wise sequential* if for every pair of t-operations o_i, o_j in H, either $o_i \prec^o_H o_j$ or $o_j \prec^o_H o_i$. A history H further imposes a partial (real-time) order on transactions in it. For two transactions $T_i, T_j \in \mathsf{txns}(H)$, we say that T_i *precedes* T_j in H, denoted $T_i \prec^T_H T_j$, if T_i is complete in H and the last action of $H|T_i$ appears in H before the first action of $H|T_j$. A history H is *sequential* if for every pair of transactions $T_i, T_j \in \mathsf{txns}(H)$, either $T_i \prec^T_H T_j$ or $T_j \prec^T_H T_i$.

A $Read(x, v)$ t-operation r executed by transaction T in a *sequential* history S is *legal* if either (i) T contains a $Write(x, v)$ t-operation w which precedes r; or in case (i) does not hold, if (ii) $\mathsf{txns}(S)$ contains a committed transaction T', which executes a $Write(x, v)$ t-operation w', and w' is the last such t-operation by a committed transaction that precedes T; or in case neither (i) nor (ii) hold, if (iii) v is the initial value of x. A transaction T in S is *legal* if all its $Read$ t-operations that do not receive T.aborted as a response, are legal in S. A complete sequential history S is *legal* if every committed transaction T in S is legal in S.

---

or writes by executing code that pertains to other transactions or by other forms of light-weight helping.

We define a *configuration* of the system as a vector that contains the state of each process and the state of each base object. This vector describes the system at some point in time. In an initial configuration all processes are in initial states and all base objects hold initial values. A *step* by some process p consists of the application of a primitive on a base object by p, or of the invocation or the response of a t-operation by a transaction executed by p; the step may also contain some local computation by p which cannot cause changes to the state of the base objects but it may change local variables used by p.

An *execution* is a (finite or infinite) sequence of steps. We use $\alpha\beta$ to denote the execution α immediately followed by the execution β. An execution α may also contain a $stop(p)$ event, for each process $p \in P$, which indicates that, after that point, process p is faulty (i.e. it does not take any further steps in α). Denote by $F(\alpha)$ the set of faulty processes in α, i.e. for each process $p \in F(\alpha)$, there is a $stop(p)$ event in α.

An execution α of a TM implementation is *feasible*, starting from a configuration C, if the sequence of steps performed by each process follows the algorithm for that process (starting from its state in C) and, for each base object, the responses to the primitives performed on the object are in accordance with its specification (and the value stored in the object at configuration C). Let $H(\alpha)$ be the subsequence of α consisting only of the invocations and responses of t-operations in α. We refer to $H(\alpha)$ as the history of α.

2.2   TM Consistency

Commonly used consistency conditions for transactional memory include *strict serializability* [17] and *opacity* [11]. Roughly speaking, some history H is strictly serializable if it is possible to assign a *linearization point* between the invocation and the response of each transaction in $H|$com and possibly of some of the commit-pending transaction in H such that the sequential history resulting from executing the transactions in the order defined by their linearization points, is legal. Opacity is a consistency condition stronger than strict serializability, which further restricts the responses of t-operations obtained by live transactions.

Assigning a single linearization point for each transaction T provides an atomicity guarantee for all the accesses (reads and writes) to data items by T. However, in order to avoid the performance overhead that is usually incurred to ensure these guarantees, weaker consistency conditions are often employed. A way of relaxing the strict requirements imposed by the aforementioned conditions, is that of assigning two linearization points per transaction, one to (a subset of its) *Read* t-operations and another to the rest of its t-operations. *Snapshot isolation* [2] is a weaker consistency condition which employs this strategy. Roughly speaking, the effect that the two linearization points per transaction T have, is that of making T appear to be split into two subtransactions, where one of the subtransactions contains the *global Read* t-operations that T performs on data items (i.e. those t-operations that read data items which are never written to by T), while the second subtransaction contains all *Write* t-operations and all remaining *Read* t-operations performed by T. This practice is reminiscent of taking a "snapshot" of the values of the data items in T's read set (that are not written by T) at some point in the beginning of the transaction and of reading the data item values from that snapshot whenever necessary, hence the name of the consistency condition. This use of two linearization points allows for more flexibility, because when it comes to finding an equivalent legal sequential history, the two subtransactions can be treated as separate entities that do not have to be serialized together. Instead, they can be interleaved with the linearization points of other transactions. This allows a wider collection of histories to be considered correct under snapshot isolation. In the following, we formalize the intuitive notion of treating one transaction as split into two subtransactions and use this formalism in order to provide a definition for snapshot isolation.

Given a history H, a $Read(x)$ t-operation r invoked by some transaction $T \in txns(H)$ is *global*, if T did not invoke a $Write(x, v)$ before invoking r. Let $T|r_g$ be the longest subsequence of $H|T$ consisting only of global read invocations and their corresponding responses. Let $T|o$ be the subsequence of $H|T$ consisting of all $Read$ and $Write$ t-operations in $H|T$ other than those in $T|r_g$. Recall that λ is the empty sequence. For each committed transaction T, let $\mathsf{readTx}_g(T)$ and $\mathsf{other}(T)$ be the following histories:

- if $T|r_g = \lambda$ then $\mathsf{readTx}_g(T) = \lambda$, otherwise $\mathsf{readTx}_g(T) = T.\mathsf{BeginTx}, T.\mathsf{ACK},$ $T|r_g, T.\mathsf{CommitTx}, T.\mathsf{committed}.$
- if $T|o = \lambda$ then $\mathsf{other}(T) = \lambda$, otherwise $\mathsf{other}(T) = T.\mathsf{BeginTx}, T.\mathsf{ACK},$ $T|o, T.\mathsf{CommitTx}, T.\mathsf{committed}.$

Definition 1. *A history H satisfies* **snapshot isolation**, *if there exists a history $H' \in comp(H)$, such that for every committed transaction T in H' it is possible to insert a read point $*_{T,r}$ and a write point $*_{T,w}$ such that*

(i) $*_{T,r}$ *precedes* $*_{T,w}$,
(ii) *both $*_{T,r}$ and $*_{T,w}$ are inserted after the first action of T in H' and before the last action of T in H', and*
(iii) *if $\sigma_{H'}$ is the sequence defined by these points, in order, and S is the history obtained by replacing each $*_{T,r}$ with $\mathsf{readTx}_g(T)$ and each $*_{T,w}$ with $\mathsf{other}(T)$ in $\sigma_{H'}$, then S is legal.*

Snapshot isolation is weaker than strict serializability, i.e. all histories that are strictly serializable satisfy snapshot isolation as well. Definition 1 provides a weaker form of snapshot isolation in comparison to standard previous definitions provided in the literature [2,9,21]. This is so because, in addition to ensuring the conditions of Definition 1, the definitions in [2,9,21] impose the extra constraint that from any two concurrent transactions writing to the same data item, only one can commit. Note also that Definition 1 does not impose any restriction on the value returned by a $Read$ t-operation on some data item by a transaction, if the transaction has written to the data item before invoking this $Read$ t-operation.

Figure 1 shows a history H which satisfies snapshot isolation but not strict serializability. H contains two transactions, T_1 and T_2, which each perform a

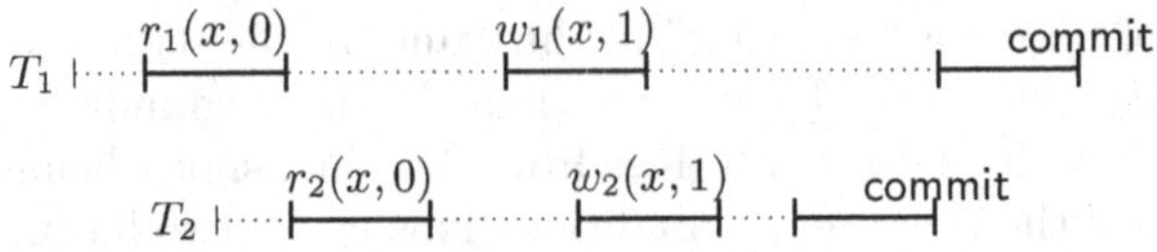

$$T_1 \vdash\!\!\!\cdots\overset{r_1(x,0)}{\longmapsto}\!\!\!\!\cdots\!\!\!\!\cdots\overset{w_1(x,1)}{\longmapsto}\!\!\!\!\cdots\!\!\!\!\cdots\overset{\text{commit}}{\longmapsto}$$

$$T_2 \vdash\!\!\!\cdots\overset{r_2(x,0)}{\longmapsto}\!\!\!\!\cdots\!\!\!\!\cdots\overset{w_2(x,1)}{\longmapsto}\!\!\!\cdots\overset{\text{commit}}{\longmapsto}$$

Fig. 1. An SI history which does not satisfy serializability.

Read and a *Write* t-operation on x. Both transactions read the value 0 for x and subsequently, write the value 1 to x. In order for this history to be strictly serializable, it should be possible to assign a single linearization point between the invocation and the response of T_1 and a single linearization point between the invocation and the response of T_2, so that an equivalent and legal sequential history can be constructed based on the order of these linearization points. Since the executions of T_1 and T_2 are overlapping, by assigning linearization points, we end up either with equivalent sequential history $S = T_1T_2$ or with equivalent sequential history $S' = T_2T_1$. Notice, however, that neither of those histories is legal, since for example, in S, the *Read* t-operation of T_2, r_2, returns the value 0 for x, although T_1, which writes the value 1 to x, has committed before T_2 in S. Conversely also for S'. Therefore, it isn't possible, by assigning a single linearization point to each transaction, to get an equivalent, legal sequential history, and therefore H is not strictly serializable.

On the contrary, it is possible to insert read points $*_{T_1,r}$, $*_{T_2,r}$ and write points $*_{T_1,w}$, $*_{T_2,w}$, for example in the order $*_{T_1,r}$, $*_{T_2,r}$, $*_{T_1,w}$, $*_{T_2,w}$, so that, by replacing $*_{T_1,r}$ with $\text{readTx}_g(T_1)$, $*_{T_2,r}$ with $\text{readTx}_g(T_2)$, $*_{T_1,w}$ with $\text{other}(T_1)$, and $*_{T_2,w}$ with $\text{other}(T_2)$, then, the equivalent sequential history that results, namely $S = \text{readTx}_g(T_1)\text{readTx}_g(T_2)\text{other}(T_1)\text{other}(T_2)$, is legal, given that in that case, both $\text{readTx}_g(T_1)$ and $\text{readTx}_g(T_2)$ contain a *Read*(x) t-operation which in either case, legally returns the value 0 for x, since both those transactions commit in S before the invocation of transactions $\text{other}(T_1)\text{other}(T_2)$, which are the ones containing *Write*$(x,1)$ t-operations, modifying the value of x.

2.3   Progress Conditions

A pair $\langle \alpha, F \rangle$ of an execution α produced by a TM implementation I and a set of processes $F \subset P$, is *fair*, if for each process $p \in P \setminus F$, the following holds:

- If α is finite, then p does not have a live transaction at the end of $H(\alpha)$ and p's last transaction in $H(\alpha)$ (if any) is not aborted,
- If α is infinite, then α contains either infinitely many steps by p or infinitely many configurations in which p does not have a live transaction.

For each TM implementation I, let $HF(I) = \{\langle H(\alpha), F(\alpha)\rangle | \forall \alpha$ produced by I s.t. $\langle \alpha, F(\alpha)\rangle$ is fair$\}$.

Local progress is a set $\mathcal{LP}$ of pairs s.t. for each pair $\langle H, F\rangle \in \mathcal{LP}$, H is a well-formed history and $F \subset P$ is a set of processes for which the following hold:

- If H is finite, then for each process $p \in P \setminus F$, p's last transaction in H (if any) is committed.
- If H is infinite, then for each process $p \in P \setminus F$, H contains either infinitely many *commit* events for p or there are infinitely many prefixes of H such that for each such prefix H' the last transaction (if any) executed by p in H' is committed (i.e. p does not have a live transaction at the end of H').

We say that a TM implementation I satisfies local progress (LP) if $HF(I) \subseteq \mathcal{LP}$. Intuitively, local progress guarantees that the transactions of any process not only terminate, but furthermore, that every non-faulty process eventually receives a commit response for each transaction it initiates, independently of the actions of the other processes in the system. This implies that, should a process decide to restart an aborted transaction, then this transaction will not indefinitely terminate by aborting.

3   Impossibility Result

In this section, we provide definitions regarding the staleness of values of data items in TM and use those to formally define k-staleness. Then, we use this definition in order to prove that it is not possible to come up with a TM system that can ensure local progress and k-staleness while tolerating failures, i.e. the existence of faulty processes.

3.1   Stale Values in TM

Consider an operation-wise sequential history H and a *Read* t-operation r on data item x by transaction T in H. Let T_{pw} be a committed transaction which writes x and its *CommitTx* t-operation c_{pw} is such that $c_{pw} \prec_H^o r$. Then, we say that T_{pw} is a *past committed write transaction* for r. We define the *last committed write transaction* for r as the past committed write transaction T_{lw} for r for which the following holds: if c_{lw} is the *CommitTx* t-operation of T_{lw}, then there is no other past committed transaction T' for r such that, if c' is the commit t-operation of T', then $c_{lw} \prec_H^o c'$.

Let Seq_r be the sequence of all past committed write transactions of r, defined by the order of their *CommitTx* t-operations. The last transaction in this sequence is T_{lw}. Let S_r^k be the set that contains those transactions that are determined by the k last transactions in Seq_r, if $|Seq_r| > k$, and the set that contains all transactions in Seq_r, otherwise. We refer to S_r^k as the set of the k *last committed transactions* for r. Each of the values written for x during the last *Write* performed for x by each of the transactions in S_r^k is referred to as a *previous value* of x. We denote by V_r^k the set of all these values. If $|S_r^k| < k$, let V_r^k contain also the initial value for x.

A *Read*(x) t-operation invoked by a transaction T in H is called *global* if T did not invoke a *Write* for x before invoking this *Read*. An operation-wise sequential history H is *k-value* if for every global *Read*(x, v) executed by a transaction T

in H, it holds that $v \in V_r^k$. A TM algorithm is *k-value* if every operation-wise sequential history that it produces is k-value. Notice that a TM implementation is *single-value* if in each operation-wise sequential history H that it produces, for every global $Read(x, v)$ t-operation r, v is the value written by the last write for x performed by the last committed write transaction for r; if such a transaction does not exist, then v is the initial value of x.

Definition 2. *An operation-wise sequential history H satisfies k-staleness, if it satisfies snapshot isolation and it is additionally k-value.*

A TM implementation satisfies k-staleness if every operation-wise sequential history it produces satisfies k-staleness. We remark that k-staleness is a weak property that does not provide any consistency guarantee for histories produced by the implementation that are not operation-wise sequential. This makes our impossibility result stronger.

3.2   Impossibility of k-staleness and Local Progress

In order to prove the following theorem, we construct a fair history based on the use of a transaction T_0 which reads two distinct data items x and y. We construct the history so that the $Read$ t-operations of T_0 are interleaved with $Write$ t-operations to x and y, and argue that T_0 can not commit.

$$C^0 \xdashrightarrow{\alpha^1\alpha^2\dots\alpha^{i-1}} C^{i-1} \xrightarrow[T_0.r_1]{\alpha_0^i} C_0^i \cdots \longrightarrow C_{j-1}^i \xrightarrow[T_j]{\alpha_j^i} C_j^i \cdots\cdots \longrightarrow C_k^i \xrightarrow[T_0.r_2]{\alpha_{k+1}^i} C^i$$

Fig. 2. Configurations in the proof of Theorem 1.

Theorem 1. *There is no TM implementation I that ensures both k-staleness and local progress and tolerates one process failure.*

Proof. The proof is by contradiction. Consider a TM implementation that ensures k-SL and LP, and assume that it tolerates one process failure. We will construct a troublesome history H in which a transaction T_0 never commits. H will be constructed to be an infinite fair history in which process p_0, which executes T_0, takes infinitely many steps. To construct H, we employ an instance of the following transaction (which, as we prove, repeatedly aborts forever in H):

– $T_0 = r_1(x)r_2(y)$, executed by p_0, where x and y are two distinct data items.

We also employ an infinite number of instances of the following k transactions, executed by a different process p_1:

– for every j, $1 \le j \le k$, $T_j = w_{j,1}(x, v_j^i), w_{j,2}(y, v_j^i)$, executed by p_1, where for every integer $i > 0$, v_j^i is a distinct value other than 0, used by the ith instance of T_j.

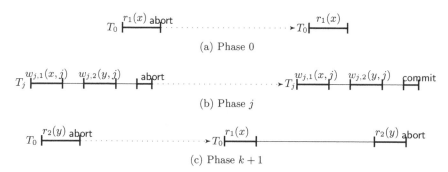

(a) Phase 0

(b) Phase j

(c) Phase $k+1$

Fig. 3. An illustration of the phases performed in the proof of Theorem 1

For simplicity, we have omitted the invocations of BeginTx and CommitTx when describing transactions $T_0, \ldots, T_k$ above.

Let the initial values of x and y be 0. An adversary constructs history H as described below:

Phase 0: Process p_0 starts executing solo from the initial configuration to perform transaction T_0 and invokes r_1 on x. As long as r_1 returns T_0.aborted, phase 0 is repeated until r_1 returns a value (we later prove that this indeed occurs). Then, Phase 1 starts.

Phases $j = 1$ to k: These phases are constructed inductively on j as follows. Fix j, $1 \le j \le k$, and assume that phases $1, \ldots, j-1$ have been constructed. Let C_{j-1} be the configuration at the end of phase $j-1$. Phase j starts from C_{j-1}. In phase j, process p_1 does the following: It starts executing transaction T_j. As long as the execution of T_j completes with T_j.aborted, p_1 restarts the execution of T_j from the resulting configuration. If T_j commits, Phase j ends. We later prove that T_j must indeed eventually commit, and we denote by C_j the resulting configuration.

Phase $k+1$: Process p_0 resumes executing solo from C_k to continue performing transaction T_0 and invokes r_2 on y. As long as r_2 returns T_0.aborted, the adversary repeats all phases from the resulting configuration, starting from phase 0. We later prove that r_2 must always return T_0.aborted. Therefore, the result is an infinite, fair history H. This history violates local progress since T_0 never commits.

Figure 3 illustrates the phases described above. Figure 4 illustrates the adversary's strategy for the case $k = 1$, namely, for a single-version TM.

The next claim shows that the adversary can indeed follow the strategy described above and that the resulting history has the required properties. We denote by C^0 the initial configuration.

Claim 1. *For each integer $i > 0$, the TM implementation I has a feasible execution α^i, starting from configuration C^{i-1}, such that $\alpha^i = \alpha_0^i \alpha_1^i \ldots \alpha_k^i \alpha_{k+1}^i$, where:*

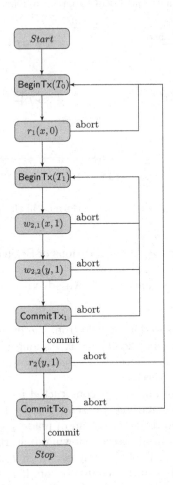

Fig. 4. Flowchart of the adversary's strategy for $k = 1$.

- α_0^i is a solo execution by p_0,
- α_j^i is a solo execution by p_1, for $1 \leq j \leq k$,
- α_{k+1}^i is a solo execution by p_0,

so that:

1. α_0^i is a finite execution in which p_0, starting from C^{i-1}, repeatedly executes T_0 until r_1 returns a value other than T_0.aborted; let C_0^i be the resulting configuration.
2. α_j^i, $\forall j$, $1 \leq j \leq k$, is a finite execution starting from C_{j-1}^i, in which T_j writes value v_j^i to x and y and commits; let C_j^i be the resulting configuration.
3. α_{k+1}^i is a finite execution by p_0 starting from configuration C_k^i such that T_0 is aborted in α_{k+1}^i; let C^i be the resulting configuration.

Proof. The proof is by induction on i. Fix any $i > 0$ and assume that we have constructed $\alpha^1, \ldots, \alpha^{i-1}$; let C^{i-1} be the configuration we reach when $\alpha^1, \ldots, \alpha^{i-1}$

is applied from C^0. We prove that the claim holds for i. Figure 2 shows the configurations.

We first show (1), i.e. that *there is a feasible execution α_0^i, starting from C^{i-1} with the required properties.*

Notice that no transaction is live at C_0. This and the induction hypothesis imply that no transaction is live at C^{i-1}. So, if process p_0 starts executing solo from configuration C^{i-1}, it (re-)initiates transaction T_0 and invokes r_1 on x. Assume, by the way of contradiction, that either, repeatedly forever, r_1 terminates in a T_0.aborted event and p_0 re-initiates T_0 and re-invokes r_1, or that one of these invocations of r_1 never terminates. Let γ_0^i be the infinite solo execution by p_0, starting from C^{i-1}, in which this occurs. Consider the execution $\delta_0^i = \alpha^1 \dots \alpha^{i-1} \gamma_0^i$. Then $\langle \delta_0^i, \emptyset \rangle$ is fair. This is so because δ_0^i is infinite and the induction hypothesis implies that the following hold: (1) there are infinitely many configurations in δ_0^i (namely, all configurations in γ_0^i) in which p_1 does not have a live or aborted last transaction, and (2) p_0 takes an infinite number of steps in δ_0^i. However, $\langle H(\delta_0^i), \emptyset \rangle \notin \mathcal{LP}$. We remark that p_0 never commits the transaction it executes in δ_0^i. To prove that $\langle H(\delta_0^i), \emptyset \rangle \notin \mathcal{LP}$, we consider the following two cases.

1. $H(\delta_0^i)$ is finite. Notice that this holds only if one of the invocations of r_1 never terminates. Then p_0, which is non-faulty, has a live transaction at the end of $H(\delta_0^i)$.
2. $H(\delta_0^i)$ is infinite. Notice that this holds if r_1 repeatedly forever returns T_0.aborted. Then, for p_0, it neither contains infinitely many commit events, nor are there infinitely many prefixes of $H(\delta_0^i)$, in which the last transaction executed by p_0 in the prefix, commits.

We now use similar arguments to prove point (2) of Claim 1, i.e. that *for each j, $1 \le j \le k$, there exists a finite execution α_j^i starting from C_{j-1}^i such that α_j^i is a solo execution by p_1 resulting in configuration C_j^i, in which T_j eventually commits, given that p_1 re-executes T_j each time it aborts.*

Let f, $1 \le f \le k$, be the first index for which the claim does not hold. Let γ_f^i be the infinite solo execution by p_1, starting from C_{f-1}^i, in which either some t-operation invoked by T_f never terminates, or repeatedly forever, some t-operation executed by T_f aborts, and T_f is re-initialized. Consider the execution $\delta_f^i = \alpha^1 \dots \alpha^{i-1} \alpha_0^i \, \mathtt{stop}_{p_0} \, \alpha_1^i \dots \alpha_{f-1}^i \gamma_f^i$. Then, $\langle \delta_f^i, \{p_0\} \rangle$ is fair. This is because δ_f^i is infinite and the following holds: (1) there are infinitely many configurations in δ_f^i (namely, all configurations in γ_f^i) in which p_1 does not have a live or aborted last transaction, and (2) p_1 takes an infinite number of steps in δ_f^i. However, $\langle H(\delta_f^i), \{p_0\} \rangle \notin \mathcal{LP}$. To prove this, we consider the following two cases.

1. $H(\delta_f^i)$ is finite. Then p_1, which is non-faulty, has a live transaction at the end of $H(\delta_f^i)$.
2. $H(\delta_f^i)$ is infinite. Then, for p_1, it neither contains infinitely many commit events, nor are there infinitely many prefixes of $H(\delta_f^i)$, in which the last transaction executed by p_1 in the prefix, commits.

This contradicts the fact that I ensures local progress. Therefore, it holds that for each j, $1 \leq j \leq k$, there exists a finite execution α_j^i starting from C_{j-1}^i such that α_j^i is a solo execution by p_1 resulting in configuration C_j^i, in which T_j eventually commits, given that p_1 re-executes T_j each time it aborts. Moreover $\alpha_0^i \dots \alpha_k^i$ is a feasible execution starting from C^{i-1}.

We finally show that point (3) of Claim 1 holds, i.e. that there is a feasible execution α_{k+1}^i by p_0 starting from configuration C_k^i such that T_0 is aborted in α_{k+1}^i. Starting from C_k, we let process p_0 execute solo to continue its execution with the invocation of r_2. Let α_{k+1}^i be the solo execution by p_0, starting from C_k^i, until r_2 completes; if this does not happen, let α_{k+1}^i be the infinite solo execution by p_0 starting from C_k^i. Let $\delta_{k+1}^i = \alpha^1 \dots \alpha^{i-1} \alpha_0^i \dots \alpha_k^i \alpha_{k+1}^i$.

We prove that if r_2 returns in δ_{k+1}^i, then it returns T_0.aborted. Assume, by the way of contradiction, that r_2 returns a value (and not T_0.aborted) in δ_{k+1}^i. By point (2) of Claim 1 (proved above), each of the transactions $T_1, \dots, T_k$ executed in δ_{k+1}^i eventually commits. This in turn means that each T_j, $1 \leq j \leq k$, writes value v_j^i to both t-objects x and y. Since I is a k-version TM implementation, it follows that r_2 returns one of the last k written values for y, i.e. a value v_j^i, $j \in \{1, 2, \dots, k\}$. However, neither of those values for t-object y is consistent with the value returned by r_1 in α_0^i which must be one of the k versions of x at configuration C^{i-1}. This contradicts the assumption that I satisfies snapshot isolation. Therefore, if r_2 returns, it returns T_0.aborted.

We finally prove that α_{k+1}^i *is finite.* Assume, by way of contradiction, that α_{k+1}^i is infinite. Then, $\langle \delta_{k+1}^i, \emptyset \rangle$ is fair. This is so because δ_{k+1}^i is infinite and the following holds: (1) there are infinitely many configurations in δ_{k+1}^i (namely, all configurations in α_{k+1}^i) in which p_1 does not have a live or aborted last transaction, and (2) p_0 takes an infinite number of steps in δ_{k+1}^i. However, $\langle H(\delta^i), \emptyset \rangle \notin \mathcal{LP}$. This is so because $H(\delta_{k+1}^i)$ is finite, and p_0, which is non-faulty, has a live transaction at the end of $H(\delta_{k+1}^i)$. This contradicts the fact that I ensures local progress. Therefore, it holds that α_{k+1}^i is a finite execution by p_0 starting from configuration C_k^i in which T_0 is aborted. Denote by C^i the resulting configuration. Notice that execution $\alpha^i = \alpha_0^i \dots \alpha_k^i \alpha_{k+1}^i$ is feasible from C^{i-1}. □

Notice that execution α_0^i corresponds to an execution of Phase 0. Since I satisfies snapshot isolation, the value returned by r_1 in α_0^i must be 0, i.e. the initial value for x. After Phase 0, the adversary moves to Phase 1. Notice that, for each j, $1 \leq j \leq k$, execution α_j^i corresponds to an execution of Phase j. In Phase j, T_j commits. After T_k commits, the adversary moves to Phase $k + 1$. Execution α_{k+1}^i corresponds to an execution of Phase $k + 1$. Claim 1 shows that each time the adversary executes phases $0, \dots, k + 1$, the resulting execution is finite.

The next claim shows that execution $\alpha = \alpha^0 \alpha^1 \alpha^2 \dots$ is a feasible fair execution of I which violates local progress.

Claim 2. *Let $\alpha = \alpha^0 \alpha^1 \alpha^2 \dots$. Then, the following hold:*

1. α is a feasible infinite execution starting from C^0;

2. the pair $\langle \alpha, \emptyset \rangle$ is fair

3. $\langle H(\alpha), \emptyset \rangle \notin \mathcal{LP}$.

Proof. Lemma 1 implies that, for each $i > 0$, α^i is a feasible execution starting from C^{i-1} in which T_0 is aborted. Therefore, α is a feasible infinite execution. Moreover, $\langle \alpha, \emptyset \rangle$ is fair. This is so because each process takes infinite steps in α. Since all t-operation invocations in α receive a response, $H(\alpha)$ is infinite as well. However, $\langle H(\alpha), \emptyset \rangle \notin \mathcal{LP}$. This is so since neither does $H(\alpha)$ contain infinite many commit responses for process p_0 (specifically, transaction T_0 that is repeatedly invoked by p_0 always completes by aborting in α), nor does $H(\alpha)$ contain infinitely many prefixes in which the last transaction executed by p_0 is committed. This contradicts the fact that I ensures local progress.   □

Theorem 1 is an immediate consequence of Claims 1 and 2.   □

4 Discussion

We have studied the progress that can be provided by a TM implementation that ensures k-staleness, a condition derivative of snapshot isolation, but where processes can crash, i.e., unexpectedly stop executing in between t-operations. Specifically, we have studied whether such a TM implementation can guarantee *local progress* for transactions. We provide a definition of local progress based on fair executions, which avoids the need to study other types of process malfunctions, such as the so-called *parasitic* processes. Parasitic processes have not suffered crash failures but still do not attempt to commit the transactions that they invoke, continuously invoking *Read* or *Write* t-operations instead [5].

Our impossibility result could possibly be extended to other, even weaker consistency conditions, for example, *adaptive consistency* [3], because most consistency conditions require that each transaction obtains a consistent view of its read set. In this case, and assuming that a system is k-version, an adversary can always come up with a troublesome strategy that executes more than k update transactions between two reads of some read-only transaction.

It is interesting to explore the use of stronger primitives, such as m-assignment, an operation that atomically writes values to m different base objects, and other objects, such as snapshots, for implementing stronger consistency conditions, such as serializability, in conjunction with local progress. Alternatively, the impossibility might be sidestepped for weaker consistency conditions also, by using other assumptions and primitives, which might be less complex.

Acknowledgment. This work has been supported by the European Commission under the 7th Framework Program through the TransForm (FP7-MC-ITN-238639) project. It has further been co-financed by the European Union and Greek national funds through the Operational Program Competitiveness, Entrepreneurship and Innovation, under the call RESEARCH – CREATE – INNOVATE (project code:T1EDK-02857)

References

1. Attiya, H., Hillel, E.: A single-version STM that is multi-versioned permissive. Theory Comput. Syst. **51**(4), 425–446 (2012)
2. Berenson, H., Bernstein, P., Gray, J., Melton, J., O'Neil, E., O'Neil, P.: A critique of ANSI SQL isolation levels. In: SIGMOD (1995)
3. Bushkov, V., Dziuma, D., Fatourou, P., Guerraoui, R.: The PCL theorem: transactions cannot be parallel, consistent and live. In: SPAA (2014)
4. Bushkov, V., Dziuma, D., Fatourou, P., Guerraoui, R.: The PCL theorem: transactions cannot be parallel, consistent, and live. J. ACM **66**(1), 2:1–2:66 (2019). https://doi.org/10.1145/3266141
5. Bushkov, V., Guerraoui, R., Kapalka, M.: On the liveness of transactional memory. In: PODC (2012)
6. Dalessandro, L., Spear, M.F., Scott, M.L.: Norec: streamlining STM by abolishing ownership records. In: PPoPP (2010)
7. Dice, D., Shalev, O., Shavit, N.: Transactional locking II. In: DISC (2006)
8. Dziuma, D., Fatourou, P., Kanellou, E.: Consistency for transactional memory computing. In: Guerraoui, R., Romano, P. (eds.) Transactional Memory. Foundations, Algorithms, Tools, and Applications. LNCS, vol. 8913, pp. 3–31. Springer, Cham (2015). https://doi.org/10.1007/978-3-319-14720-8_1
9. Fekete, A., Liarokapis, D., O'Neil, E., O'Neil, P., Shasha, D.: Making snapshot isolation serializable. ACM Trans. Database Syst. **30**(2), 492–528 (2005). https://doi.org/10.1145/1071610.1071615
10. Fernandes, S.M., Cachopo, J.a.: Lock-free and scalable multi-version software transactional memory. In: PPoPP (2011)
11. Guerraoui, R., Kapalka, M.: On the correctness of transactional memory. In: PPoPP (2008)
12. Herlihy, M., Luchangco, V., Moir, M., Scherer III, W.N.: Software transactional memory for dynamic-sized data structures. In: PODC (2003)
13. Herlihy, M., Moss, J.E.B.: Transactional memory: architectural support for lock-free data structures. SIGARCH Comput. Archit. News **21**(2), 289–300 (1993)
14. Kumar, P., Peri, S., Vidyasankar, K.: A timestamp based multi-version STM algorithm. In: Chatterjee, M., Cao, J., Kothapalli, K., Rajsbaum, S. (eds.) ICDCN 2014. LNCS, vol. 8314, pp. 212–226. Springer, Heidelberg (2014). https://doi.org/10.1007/978-3-642-45249-9_14
15. Litz, H., Cheriton, D.R., Firoozshahian, A., Azizi, O., Stevenson, J.P.: SI-TM: reducing transactional memory abort rates through snapshot isolation. In: ASPLOS (2014)
16. Lu, L., Scott, M.L.: Generic multiversion STM. In: Afek, Y. (ed.) DISC 2013. LNCS, vol. 8205, pp. 134–148. Springer, Heidelberg (2013). https://doi.org/10.1007/978-3-642-41527-2_10
17. Papadimitriou, C.H.: The serializability of concurrent database updates. J. ACM **26**(4), 631–653 (1979)
18. Perelman, D., Byshevsky, A., Litmanovich, O., Keidar, I.: SMV: selective multi-versioning STM. In: Peleg, D. (ed.) DISC 2011. LNCS, vol. 6950, pp. 125–140. Springer, Heidelberg (2011). https://doi.org/10.1007/978-3-642-24100-0_9

19. Perelman, D., Fan, R., Keidar, I.: On maintaining multiple versions in STM. In: PODC (2010)
20. Riegel, T., Felber, P., Fetzer, C.: A lazy snapshot algorithm with eager validation. In: DISC (2006)
21. Riegel, T., Fetzer, C., Felber, P.: Snapshot isolation for software transactional memory. In: TRANSACT (2006)

Generic Framework for Optimization of Local Dissemination in Wireless Networks

Dariusz R. Kowalski[1] , Miguel A. Mosteiro[2](✉) , and Krutika Wadhwa[2]

[1] School of Computer and Cyber Sciences, Augusta University, Augusta, GA, USA
dkowalski@augusta.edu
[2] Computer Science Department, Pace University, New York, NY, USA
{mmosteiro,kw62027n}@pace.edu

Abstract. We present a generic framework to compute transmission schedules for a comprehensive set of well-known local dissemination problems in Wireless Networks. In our framework, we formulate the communication restrictions to overcome while solving those problems as a mathematical optimization program, where the objective function is to minimize the transmissions schedule length. The program is solved by standard methods which may yield partial solutions. So, the method is iterated until the solution is complete. The schedules obtained achieve the desired dissemination under the general affectance model of interference. We prove the correctness of our model and we evaluate its efficiency through simulations.

1 Introduction

The algorithmic problem of disseminating information in ad-hoc wireless communication networks (for instance, embedded in the Internet of Things) has been well studied. Depending on the field of application, challenges such as communication-link interference or network-node limitations yield different models, but always the desired dissemination is an instance of the following general problem. Some nodes are the source of one or many data packets, and the goal is to deliver those packets to some destination nodes, possibly through multiple hops. The specific meaning of *some* defines the multiple versions of dissemination. Yet, to the best of our knowledge, the various versions of dissemination have been mostly studied independently until now.

Given that *local* dissemination is the atomic part of any network-wide communication task, in this work, we focus on different variants of the problem of passing information to nodes that are within reach of the sources of such information in *one* hop. Even in the local context, depending on whether it is enough to receive from (resp. send to) one or more neighboring nodes, application requirements yield different types of dissemination. Moreover, transmission

This work was partially supported by the National Science Center Poland (NCN) grant 2017/25/B/ST6/02553; the UK Royal Society International Exchanges 2017 Round 3 Grant #170293; and Pace University SRC Grant and Kenan Fund.

ⓒ Springer Nature Switzerland AG 2021
C. Georgiou and R. Majumdar (Eds.): NETYS 2020, LNCS 12129, pp. 244–260, 2021.
https://doi.org/10.1007/978-3-030-67087-0_16

to all neighboring nodes may be required to happen simultaneously, or may be enough to do it along multiple rounds of communication. Some of these local problems are known in the literature as *Local-broadcast* [10] (transmit to all neighbors in one slot), *Wake-up* [6,8] (receive from at least one neighbor), and *Link-scheduling* [12,13] (transmit through an input set of links). We define formally all the local dissemination problems studied in Sect. 2.

Motivated by current data-link layer technologies, we focus on settings with one task per node, which restricts Link-scheduling to one instance of each originator node in the input set of links[1].

We adopt the notation used in the Link-scheduling literature for our node-centered tasks. The set of nodes such that the local dissemination task needs to be solved for each of them is called the set of **requests**. Once the task is completed for a given node u, we say that u has been **realized**, or **pending** otherwise. Our framework is generic also with respect to the set of requests. That is, our methods can be applied to solve the dissemination problems on sets of requests that are proper subsets of the network nodes. We notice that this is not a simple reduction of the problem to a smaller subgraph. While solving for a subset, all the other nodes still participate (and produce interference). The definitions in Sect. 2 reflect this generalization.

We do not assume any underlying communication infrastructure. That is, **transmitters** (i.e. source nodes) attempt to deliver a **message** (i.e. the information to deliver) by radio broadcast but, if two or more nodes transmit at the same time, mutual interference may prevent the **receivers** from getting the message. To take into account this phenomenon, we study local dissemination under a general model of interference called **affectance**. As in [15,16] we parameterize affectance with a real value $0 \leqslant a(u,(v,w)) \leqslant 1$ that represents the affectance of each transmitter u on each link (v,w).

Affectance is a general model of interference in the sense that comprises other particular models studied before (cf. [16]). Moreover, previous models do not accurately represent the physical constraints in real-world deployments. For instance, in the Radio Network model [2] interference from non-neighboring nodes is neglected. Signal to Inteference-plus-Noise Ratio (SINR) [5,19] is a simplified model because other constraints, such as obstacles, are not taken into account. Yet, should the application require the use of Radio Network or SINR models, a simple instantiation of the affectance matrix allows the application of our generic framework, as we show below.

Customarily, we assume that time is slotted and we call the sequence of transmit/not-transmit states of the nodes a **transmissions schedule**.

Related Work. Before [15,16], the generalized affectance model was introduced and used only in the context of one-hop communication, more specifically, to

---

[1] If a Link-scheduling input contains multiple instances of the same originating node, representing different links/packets outgoing from that node, we can simply create virtual copies of the node. We keep the assumption of different link originators for the easy of presentation of the generic framework.

link scheduling by Kesselheim [12, 13]. He also showed how to use it for dynamic link scheduling in batches. This model was inspired by the affectance parameter introduced in the more restricted SINR setting [5]. They give a characteristic of a set of links, based on affectance, that influence the time of successful scheduling these links under the SINR model.

We note that interference measures for link scheduling cannot immediately be applied to local broadcast or wake up. Intuitively, the reason is that link scheduling is a link-oriented task whereas local broadcast and wake up are node-oriented. For instance, specific classes of power assignments (e.g. linear) are not well defined when a node has to transmit through many links simultaneously. So, later on, the interference characteristic was generalized in [15, 16], called the maximum average tree-layer affectance, to be applicable to multi-hop communication tasks such as broadcast, together with another characteristic, called the maximum path affectance.

The Wake Up, Local Broadcast, Link Scheduling, and other local dissemination problems have been thoroughly studied under various models [6, 8, 10, 12, 13]. In the SINR model, single-hop instances of broadcast in the ad-hoc setting were studied by Jurdzinski et al. [7, 9] and Daum et al. [3], who gave several deterministic and randomized algorithms working in time proportional to the diameter multiplied by a polylogarithmic factor of some model parameters. To the best of our knowledge, ours is the first formulation for these and other problems under the affectance model of interference.

Our Results and Approach. The main contribution of this work is the design of a *generic framework to compute transmission schedules for a comprehensive set of local dissemination problems.*

We start by formulating the communication restrictions to overcome in solving each of those problems in one mathematical optimization program, where the objective function is to minimize the transmissions schedule length. The formulation so obtained is an Integer Linear Program (ILP). The model obtained can be instantiated on each of the problems as needed by removing constraints. The local dissemination problems studied may require multiple rounds of communication for non-trivial network topologies. Note that our ILP entails an optimization over many rounds of communication, rather than a simple repeated application of one-round optimizations.

Even the seemingly simpler problem of deciding whether a given ILP with binary variables has a feasible solution, regardless of the objective function, is well known to be NP-complete (cf. 0–1 INTEGER PROGRAMMING [11]). Since the optimization version asks to minimize the value of the objective function, subject to all the constraints, it is also NP-complete. So, to apply our method in networks of significant size, LP-relaxation and Randomized rounding [4] are applied. That is, we relax the domain of the variables of the ILP to real numbers in the $[0, 1]$ interval, and we round the values in the solution at random.

Due to rounding, the schedule obtained may not solve the dissemination problem under consideration for all the requests. Thus, we repeat the above steps iteratively updating the set of requests until all are realized. That is, our generic framework tolerates multiple applications of the ILP (if needed) reducing the set of requests in each iteration, but with all the network nodes participating in the schedule and, hence, introducing interference.

Our approach provides a versatile engineering solution for a variety of fundamental communication problems in one tool. Specifically, given the network topology and the affectance of nodes on links, one can solve the mathematical formulation adequately tailored for the problem of interest using our framework, and use the transmission schedules obtained. The method requires knowledge of all affectance values. These values may be obtained geometrically for the Radio Network, SINR or similar models of interference, or may be measured in the field in advance for the most general model. Moreover, affectance may be even obtained by the network nodes as in Conflict Maps (CMAP) [20], where nodes probe the network to build a map of conflicting transmissions.

Evaluation. We apply our methods on two network topologies with obstacles. One of them is based on a real-world floor plan of an office building, the other is a simple square grid with obstacles spaced at regular intervals. Physical measurements of interference capture all the signal-attenuation factors that are present in the specific physical medium where the network is deployed. Distance, reflection, scattering, and diffraction all have an impact on signal attenuation in an environment with obstacles. Customarily, we simulated those effects computing attenuation as the inverse of the distance raised to the path-loss exponent. We considered boundary cases of high- and low interference. The distance was computed assuming that the signal sorts the obstacles by going around them.

In our experimental evaluations, we observed that the number of iterations that our method must be applied to obtain a transmissions schedule is constant with respect to the network size, even if the set of requests is all the nodes. Given that the cases studied are natural instances of real-world network deployments, these results show the effectiveness of our methods in practice.

To the best of our knowledge, this is the first comprehensive tool to compute local dissemination schedules for Wireless Networks under a general model of interference.

Roadmap. In Sect. 2 we specify the details of the affectance and network models. In Sect. 3 we specify our generic framework, including the ILP formulation in Sect. 3.1 and the proof of correctness in Sect. 3.2. In Sect. 4 we present our simulation results.

2   Model and Problems

We model the Wireless Network topology as a graph $G = (V, E)$, where V is a set of n nodes and E is the set of communication links among such nodes. That is, for each pair of nodes $u, v \in V$, the ordered pair $(u, v) \in E$ if an only if v is able to receive a radio transmission from u directly (if there is no interference). Without loss of generality, we assume that time is slotted so that the length of one slot is enough to achieve such communication, provided that interference from other communications is low enough as defined later.

Following [16], we model interference as **affectance** of nodes on links. That is, we define a matrix A of size $|V| \times |E|$, where $a(u, (v, w))$ quantifies the interference that a transmitting node $u \in V$ introduces to the communication through link $(v, w) \in E$. We normalize affectance to the range $[0, 1]$, that is, $0 \leqslant a(u, (v, w)) \leqslant 1$. The aim of the affectance matrix is to apply our framework to any interference scenario, given that the affectance values are part of the input. Hence, we do not fix any specific values even though, for instance, $a(u, (u, v))$ is naturally 0.

For convenience, we denote $a_{V'}((v, w))$ as the affectance of a set of nodes $V' \subseteq V$ on a link $(v, w) \in E$, and $a_{V'}(E')$ as the affectance of a set of nodes $V' \subseteq V$ on a set of links $E' \subseteq E$. In this model definition, we do not restrict affectance to a specific function, as long as its effect is additive, that is,

$$a_{V'}((v, w)) = \sum_{u \in V'} a(u, (v, w))$$

$$a_{V'}(E') = \sum_{(v, w) \in E'} a_{V'}((v, w)) \ .$$

Under the above affectance model, a **successful transmission** is defined as follows. For any pair of nodes $v, w \in V$ such that $(v, w) \in E$, a transmission from v is received at w in a time slot t if and only if: v transmits in time slot t, and $a_{\mathcal{T}(t)}((v, w)) < 1$, where $\mathcal{T}(t) \subseteq V$ is the set of nodes transmitting in time slot t. The event of a non-successful transmission, that is when the affectance is at least 1, is called a **collision**. We assume that a node listening to the channel cannot distinguish between a collision and background noise present in the channel in absence of transmissions.

The affectance model defined subsumes any other interference model as long as the impact of interference is additive. For instance, in the Radio Network model where a node receives a transmission at a given time t if and only if exactly one of the neighbors of w is transmitting at time t, for $u, v, w \in V$ and $u \neq v$ the affectance matrix is the following:

$$A(u, (v, w)) = \begin{cases} 0 \text{ if } (u, w) \notin E \ , \\ 1 \text{ otherwise} \ . \end{cases}$$

On the other hand, consider the SINR with uniform power assignment model in [5] where a node receives a transmission if and only if the following holds for a parametric threshold β':

$$\frac{P/d_{uv}^{\alpha}}{N + \sum_{w \neq u} P/d_{wv}^{\alpha}} > \beta' \ .$$

In the latter, P is the transmission power level, N is the background noise, d_{uv} is the Euclidean distance between nodes u and v, α denotes the path-loss exponent.

Then, the affectance matrix is

$$A(u,(v,w)) = \frac{P/d_{uw}^\alpha}{P/(\beta' d_{vw}^\alpha) - N} \ .$$

The proof of the latter is a simple application of the SINR model definition and it is left to the full version of this work for brevity.

2.1 Local Dissemination Problems

In this work, we study the following local dissemination problems. Recall that, with respect to the usual definition of these problems in the literature, ours parameterize the problem on subsets of network nodes, called a set of requests.

- **Wake Up**: Given a Wireless Network as defined and a set of requests $R \subseteq V$, the wake-up problem is solved at time slot t if, for every node $v \in R$, there exists some time slot $t' \leqslant t$ and some link $(u,v) \in E$ such that there was a successful transmission through (u,v) in t'. As a worst-case scenario definition, we assume that no nodes wake-up spontaneously.
- **Link Scheduling**: Given a Wireless Network as defined, a set of requests $R \subseteq V$, and a set of link-requests $\mathcal{R}$ such that link $(u,v) \in \mathcal{R}$ if and only if $u \in R$, the link-scheduling problem is solved at time slot t if, for every node $u \in R$ and every link $(u,v) \in \mathcal{R}$, there exists some time slot $t' \leqslant t$ such that there was a successful transmission through (u,v) in t'.
- **Local Broadcast**: Given a Wireless Network as defined and a set of requests $R \subseteq V$, the local-broadcast problem is solved at time slot t if, for every node $v \in R$, there exists some time slot $t' \leqslant t$ such that for every link $(v,w) \in E$ there was a successful transmission through (v,w) in t'. As a worst-case scenario definition, we assume that all links outgoing a node have to be scheduled in the same time slot.

We also consider extensions of the above known problems to the following generalizations.

- **Receive-One**: Given a Wireless Network as defined and a set of requests $R \subseteq V$, the problem is solved at time slot t if, for every node $v \in R$, there exists some time slot $t' \leqslant t$ and some link $(u,v) \in E$ such that there was a successful transmission through (u,v) in t'. (Equivalent to wake-up.)
- **Transmit-One**: Given a Wireless Network as defined and a set of requests $R \subseteq V$, the problem is solved at time slot t if, for every node $v \in R$, there exists some time slot $t' \leqslant t$ and some link $(v,u) \in E$ such that there was a successful transmission through (v,u) in t'.
- **Receive-All**: Given a Wireless Network as defined and a set of requests $R \subseteq V$, the problem is solved at time slot t if, for every node $v \in R$, and for every link $(u,v) \in E$, there exists some time slot $t' \leqslant t$ such that there was a successful transmission through (u,v) in t'.

– **Transmit-All**: Given a Wireless Network as defined and a set of requests $R \subseteq V$, the problem is solved at time slot t if, for every node $v \in R$, and for every link $(v, u) \in E$, there exists some time slot $t' \leq t$ such that there was a successful transmission through (v, u) in t'. (Equivalent to local broadcast if all links are scheduled in the same time slot.)

3 Generic Framework

In the following, a transmissions schedule is denoted as a matrix $X_V = (x_{ut})_{u \in V, t \in \mathbb{N}}$, where $x_{ut} \in \{0, 1\}$. We denote as $|X_V|$ the number of columns of X_V where $x_{ut} = 1$ for some $u \in V$, called the length of the schedule. Also, let $P \in \{$Receive-one, Receive-all, Transmit-one, Transmit-all, Local-broadcast, Link-scheduling$\}$ be one of the problems defined in Sect. 2.

The generic framework (described in Algorithm 1) includes the application of our ILP (cf. Sect. 3.1) to the particular problem to solve. The variables in the ILP are restricted to be either 0 or 1. The problem of deciding whether a given ILP with binary variables has a feasible solution, regardless of the objective function, is known as 0-1 INTEGER PROGRAMMING, and it is known to be NP-complete [11]. Hence, the optimization version, where the objective function is minimized subject to all the constraints, is also NP-complete. That is, unless P=NP, it would take an impractical amount of time to solve the ILP for networks of significant size.

---

input : network graph $G = (V, E)$, affectance matrix A, set of requests R,
problem P and, if $P =$ Link-scheduling, set of link-requests $\mathcal{R}$ such that
$\forall u \in R : \exists (u, v) \in E : (u, v) \in \mathcal{R}$ and
$\forall (u, v) \in \mathcal{R} : \forall w \in V : w \neq v \Rightarrow (u, w) \notin \mathcal{R}$
output: transmissions schedule X_V that solves P for R

1 **while** $R \neq \varnothing$ **do**
2   instantiate the ILP of Sect. 3.1 to compute X_V that solves P for R
3   relax the integrality constraints to reals in $[0, 1]$ (i.e. ILP → LP)
4   solve the LP to obtain a matrix $X'_V = (x'_{ut})_{u \in V, t \in \mathbb{N}}$, where $x'_{ut} \in [0, 1]$
5   set $x_{ut} \leftarrow 1$ with probability x'_{ut}, or $x_{ut} \leftarrow 0$ otherwise
6   verify the solution and remove all realized nodes from R
7 **end**

Algorithm 1: Generic Framework for Optimization of Local Dissemination in Wireless Networks.

To make it practical, our framework includes the application of standard approximation methods [4]. Specifically, LP-relaxation and rounding [18]. The solution of the LP can be obtained in polynomial time [14], but the solution values are reals in $[0, 1]$. To obtain integers in $\{0, 1\}$ as required by a transmissions schedule, we apply randomized rounding.

The integer assignments for the LP decision variables after rounding are a transmissions schedule, but due to rounding they may not preserve some of the constraints in the original ILP. In other words, the schedule may not solve the problem for all requests. An option would be to de-randomize the rounding step using the method of conditional probabilities, but given the number of constraints it would be computationally prohibitive. Thus, we include in our framework a final step when we verify the schedule obtained to identify the nodes that have been realized, and we iterate the method on the pending nodes. The total schedule length is the sum of the lengths of the sequence of schedules computed over this iterative process. Our simulations (cf. Sect. 4) show that in practice the number of iterations does not depend on the network size, and in fact it is very small.

In the following sections, we specify the details of our ILP formulation of local dissemination problems under affectance, and we prove its correctness.

3.1   Integer Linear Program Formulation

Definitions

- Indices:
  u, v, w: network nodes, $u, v, w \in V$.
  (v, w): directed network link, $(v, w) \in E$.
  t: time slot, $t \in [T]$.
- Input parameters:
  $a_u((v, w))$: affectance of node u on link (v, w), $0 \leqslant a_u((v, w)) \leqslant 1$.
  T: a large positive integer constant not less than the schedule length.
  $R \subseteq V$: set of requests.
  $\mathcal{R} \subseteq E$: set of link-requests, where $\forall u \in R : \exists (u, v) \in E : (u, v) \in \mathcal{R}$ and $\forall (u, v) \in \mathcal{R} : \forall w \in V : w \neq v \Rightarrow (u, w) \notin \mathcal{R}$.
- Decision variables:
  $x_{ut} = 1$ if node u transmits in time slot t, otherwise $x_{ut} = 0$.
- Auxiliary variables:
  $x_t = 1$ if some node transmits in time slot t, otherwise $x_t = 0$.
  $y_{vwt} = 1$ if total affectance on link (v, w) at time t is less than 1, otherwise $y_{vwt} = 0$.
  $z_{vwt} = 1$ if there is a successful transmission in link (v, w) at time t, otherwise $z_{vwt} = 0$.
  $z_{vt} = 1$ if there are successful transmissions in all links outgoing from v at time t, otherwise $z_{vt} = 0$.
  $\breve{z}_{vt} = 1$ if there is a successful transmission in some link outgoing from v at time t, otherwise $\breve{z}_{vt} = 0$.

Objective Function

The objective function is simply to minimize the length of the schedule. That is, to minimize the number of time slots when some node transmits.

Minimize

$$\sum_{t \in [T]} x_t$$

subject to the constraints that follow.

Transmission-Indicator Constraints

The following constraints restrict x_t to be an indicator of transmissions at time t. Given that x_t is restricted to be binary, Constraint 1 restricts $x_t = 0$ if $\sum_{u \in V} x_{ut} = 0$, and Constraint 2 restricts $x_t = 1$ if $\sum_{u \in V} x_{ut} > 0$:

$$\forall t \in [T] : x_t \leqslant \sum_{u \in V} x_{ut} \tag{1}$$

$$\forall t \in [T] : n x_t \geqslant \sum_{u \in V} x_{ut} . \tag{2}$$

Affectance-Indicator Constraints

The following constraints restrict y_{vwt} to be an indicator of "low" affectance on link (v, w) at time t. Given that y_{vwt} is restricted to be binary, Constraint 3 restricts $y_{vwt} = 1$ if $\sum_{u \in V} a_u((v, w)) x_{ut} < 1$, and Constraint 4 restricts $y_{vwt} = 0$ if $\sum_{u \in V} a_u((v, w)) x_{ut} \geqslant 1$:

$$\forall (v, w) \in E : \forall t \in [T] : \sum_{u \in V} a_u((v, w)) x_{ut} - 1 \geqslant -y_{vwt} \tag{3}$$

$$\forall (v, w) \in E : \forall t \in [T] : \sum_{u \in V} a_u((v, w)) x_{ut} - 1 < (n - 1)(1 - y_{vwt}) . \tag{4}$$

1-Link Successful-Transmission Constraints

The following constraints restrict z_{vwt} to be an indicator of successful transmission in link (v, w) at time t. Given that z_{vwt} is restricted to be binary, Constraint 5 restricts $x_{vt} = 1$ if $z_{vwt} = 1$, Constraint 6 restricts $y_{vwt} = 1$ if $z_{vwt} = 1$, and Constraint 7 restricts that it must be $y_{vwt} = 0$ or $x_{vt} = 0$ if $z_{vwt} = 0$:

$$\forall (v, w) \in E : \forall t \in [T] : z_{vwt} \leqslant x_{vt} \tag{5}$$

$$\forall (v, w) \in E : \forall t \in [T] : z_{vwt} \leqslant y_{vwt} \tag{6}$$

$$\forall (v, w) \in E : \forall t \in [T] : z_{vwt} \geqslant y_{vwt} + x_{vt} - 1 . \tag{7}$$

All-Outlinks Successful-Transmission Constraints

The following constraints restrict z_{vt} to be an indicator of successful transmission in *all* links outgoing from v at time t. Given that z_{vt} is restricted to be binary, Constraint 8 restricts $z_{vt} = 1$ if $\sum_{w \in out(v)} z_{vwt} = |out(v)|$, and Constraint 9 restricts $z_{vt} = 0$ if $\sum_{w \in out(v)} z_{vwt} < |out(v)|$:

$$\forall v \in V : \forall t \in [T] : (1 - z_{vt}) \leqslant |out(v)| - \sum_{w \in out(v)} z_{vwt} \qquad (8)$$

$$\forall v \in V : \forall t \in [T] : |out(v)|(1 - z_{vt}) \geqslant |out(v)| - \sum_{w \in out(v)} z_{vwt} . \qquad (9)$$

Some-Outlink Successful-Transmission Constraints

The following constraints restrict $\breve{z}_{vt}$ to be an indicator of successful transmission in *some* link outgoing from v at time t. Given that $\breve{z}_{vt}$ is restricted to be binary, Constraint 10 restricts $\breve{z}_{vt} = 1$ if $\sum_{w \in out(v)} z_{vwt} > 0$, and Constraint 11 restricts $\breve{z}_{vt} = 0$ if $\sum_{w \in out(v)} z_{vwt} = 0$:

$$\forall v \in V : \forall t \in [T] : |out(v)|\breve{z}_{vt} \geqslant \sum_{w \in out(v)} z_{vwt} \qquad (10)$$

$$\forall v \in V : \forall t \in [T] : \breve{z}_{vt} \leqslant \sum_{w \in out(v)} z_{vwt} . \qquad (11)$$

Integrality and Range Constraints

$$\forall v \in V : \forall t \in [T] : x_{vt} \in \{0, 1\} \qquad (12)$$
$$\forall t \in [T] : x_t \in \{0, 1\} \qquad (13)$$
$$\forall (v, w) \in E : \forall t \in [T] : y_{vwt} \in \{0, 1\} \qquad (14)$$
$$\forall (v, w) \in E : \forall t \in [T] : z_{vwt} \in \{0, 1\} \qquad (15)$$
$$\forall v \in V : \forall t \in [T] : z_{vt} \in \{0, 1\} \qquad (16)$$
$$\forall v \in V : \forall t \in [T] : \breve{z}_{vt} \in \{0, 1\} . \qquad (17)$$

Problem-Specific Constraints

- The model is completed with one of the constraints that follow, depending on the specific problem studied.
- <u>Receive-one</u>: there is at least one time slot when w receives, that is:

$$\forall w \in R : \sum_{t \in [T]} \sum_{v \in in(w)} z_{vwt} \geqslant 1. \qquad (18)$$

- Receive-all: there is at least one time slot when w receives from v:

$$\forall w \in R : \forall v \in in(w) : \sum_{t \in [T]} z_{vwt} \geqslant 1 . \tag{19}$$

- Transmit-one: there is at least one time slot when some neighbor of v receives from v:

$$\forall v \in R : \sum_{t \in [T]} \sum_{w \in out(v)} z_{vwt} \geqslant 1 . \tag{20}$$

- Transmit-all: there is at least one time slot when w receives from v:

$$\forall v \in R : \forall w \in out(v) : \sum_{t \in [T]} z_{vwt} \geqslant 1 . \tag{21}$$

- Local-broadcast: there is at least one time slot when all out-neighbors of v receive:

$$\forall v \in R : \sum_{t \in [T]} z_{vt} \geqslant 1 . \tag{22}$$

- Link-scheduling there is at least one time slot when w receives from v:

$$\forall v \in R : \forall (v, w) \in \mathcal{R} : \sum_{t \in [T]} z_{vwt} \geqslant 1 . \tag{23}$$

3.2   Correctness

Lemma 1. *The indicator variables in the Integer Program of Sect. 3.1 are well defined.*

Proof. We prove that each indicator variable is 1 if and only if the corresponding event occurred. For each new variable, we use that previous variables are well defined.

- x_{vt}, for $v \in V$ and $t \in [T]$: it is by definition $x_{vt} = 1$ if and only if node v transmits in time slot t.
- x_t, for $t \in [T]$: indicates that node v transmits at time t.

$$\exists u \in V : x_{ut} = 1 \Rightarrow \sum_{u \in V} x_{ut} \geqslant 1, \text{ using Constraint 2,}$$

$$\sum_{u \in V} x_{ut} \geqslant 1 \land n x_t \geqslant \sum_{u \in V} x_{ut} \Rightarrow n x_t \geqslant 1, \text{ using Constraint 13,}$$

$$n x_t \geqslant 1 \land x_t \in \{0, 1\} \Rightarrow x_t = 1 .$$

$$\forall u \in V : x_{ut} = 0 \Rightarrow \sum_{u \in V} x_{ut} = 0, \text{ using Constraint 1,}$$

$$\sum_{u \in V} x_{ut} = 0 \land x_t \leqslant \sum_{u \in V} x_{ut} \Rightarrow x_t \leqslant 0, \text{ using Constraint 13,}$$

$$x_t \leqslant 0 \land x_t \in \{0, 1\} \Rightarrow x_t = 0 .$$

- y_{vwt}, for $(v, w) \in E$ and $t \in [T]$: indicates low affectance on link (v, w) at time t. Using Constraints 3 and 14 we get:

$$\sum_{u \in V} a_u((v, w))x_{ut} < 1 \wedge \sum_{u \in V} a_u((v, w))x_{ut} - 1 \geqslant -y_{vwt} \Rightarrow 1 - y_{vwt} < 1,$$

$$1 - y_{vwt} < 1 \wedge y_{vwt} \in \{0, 1\} \Rightarrow y_{vwt} = 1 .$$

Using Constraints 4 and 14 we obtain:

$$\sum_{u \in V} a_u((v, w))x_{ut} \geqslant 1 \wedge$$

$$\sum_{u \in V} a_u((v, w))x_{ut} - 1 < (n-1)(1 - y_{vwt}) \Rightarrow (n-1)(1 - y_{vwt}) > 0$$

$$(n-1)(1 - y_{vwt}) > 0 \wedge y_{vwt} \in \{0, 1\} \Rightarrow y_{vwt} = 0.$$

- z_{vwt}, for $(v, w) \in E$ and $t \in [T]$: indicates a successful transmission in link (v, w) at time t. That is, it indicates whether the affectance on (v, w) is low and v transmits. Using Constraints 7 and 15, we get

$$x_{vt} = 1 \wedge y_{vwt} = 1 \wedge z_{vwt} \geqslant y_{vwt} + x_{vt} - 1 \Rightarrow z_{vwt} \geqslant 1$$

$$z_{vwt} \geqslant 1 \wedge z_{vwt} \in \{0, 1\} \Rightarrow z_{vwt} = 1 .$$

On the other hand, using Constraints 5 and 15, we have

$$x_{vt} = 0 \wedge z_{vwt} \leqslant x_{vt} \wedge z_{vwt} \in \{0, 1\} \Rightarrow z_{vwt} = 0 .$$

And using Constraints 6 and 15,

$$y_{vwt} = 0 \wedge z_{vwt} \leqslant y_{vwt} \wedge z_{vwt} \in \{0, 1\} \Rightarrow z_{vwt} = 0 .$$

- z_{vt}, for $v \in V$ and $t \in [T]$: indicates a successful transmission in all links outgoing from v at time t. Using Constraints 8 and 16, we obtain

$$\sum_{w \in out(v)} z_{vwt} = |out(v)| \wedge (1 - z_{vt}) \leqslant |out(v)| - \sum_{w \in out(v)} z_{vwt} \Rightarrow (1 - z_{vt}) = 0$$

$$(1 - z_{vt}) = 0 \wedge z_{vt} \in \{0, 1\} \Rightarrow z_{vt} = 1 .$$

Using Constraints 9 and 16, we get

$$\sum_{w \in out(v)} z_{vwt} < |out(v)| \wedge$$

$$|out(v)|(1 - z_{vt}) \geqslant |out(v)| - \sum_{w \in out(v)} z_{vwt} \Rightarrow |out(v)|(1 - z_{vt}) > 0$$

$$|out(v)|(1 - z_{vt}) > 0 \wedge z_{vt} \in \{0, 1\} \Rightarrow z_{vt} = 0.$$

- $\breve{z}_{vt}$, for $v \in V$ and $t \in [T]$: indicates a successful transmission in some link outgoing from v at time t. Using Constraints 10 and 17, we obtain

$$\sum_{w \in out(v)} z_{vwt} > 0 \wedge |out(v)|\breve{z}_{vt} \geqslant \sum_{w \in out(v)} z_{vwt} \Rightarrow |out(v)|\breve{z}_{vt} > 0$$

$$|out(v)|\breve{z}_{vt} > 0 \wedge \breve{z}_{vt} \in \{0, 1\} \Rightarrow \breve{z}_{vt} = 1 .$$

Using Constraints 11 and 17, we get

$$\sum_{w \in out(v)} z_{vwt} = 0 \wedge \breve{z}_{vt} \leqslant \sum_{w \in out(v)} z_{vwt} \Rightarrow \breve{z}_{vt} \leqslant 0$$

$$\breve{z}_{vt} \leqslant 0 \wedge \breve{z}_{vt} \in \{0,1\} \Rightarrow \breve{z}_{vt} = 0 \ .$$

□

Theorem 1. *The Integer Program of Sect. 3.1 is correct.*

Proof. To prove the correctness of our formulation it is enough to prove that, for each of the communication problems studied, if the corresponding constraint is true the problem is solved, and viceversa. We include such proof for the Receive-one problem. For the other problems the proof is similar.

Constraint 18 is true if, for each node $w \in R$, there is at least one time slot $t \in T$ and one node $v \in in(w)$ for which the indicator variable $z_{vwt} = 1$. By Lemma 1, if $z_{vwt} = 1$ there is at least one time slot when w receives, as required by the Receive-one problem.

On the other hand, the Receive-one problem is solved when, for each node $w' \in R$, there is at least one time slot t' when node w' receives successfully from at least one of its neighbors. Consider one of those neighbors $v' \in in(w')$. In that case, by Lemma 1 we know that $z_{v'w't'} = 1$. Hence, Constraint 18 is true.   □

4   Simulations

In this section we present applications of our generic framework to network deployments. We study two network topologies including obstacles: a grid and a layer network. We note that the cases studied are an illustration of our methods applied to networks that frequently appear in real world deployments, rather than examples of worst-case scenarios.

As a layer-network, i.e. a bipartite graph on a partition transmitters-receivers, we used as a model of obstacles the floorplan of the School of Computer Science and Information Systems at Pace University (see Fig. 1). We considered nodes installed in the intersections of each square of four ceiling panels. We focus on one layer of this network going across various offices. For simplicity, to evaluate performance as n grows, we replicated the same office multiple times in a layer.

The walls of these offices have a metallic structure. Hence, each office behaves as a Faraday cage blocking radio transmissions (specially millimeter wave). Consequently, most of the radio waves propagate through doors (which are not metallic). We fixed the radio transmission power to be large enough to reach five grid cells, so that transmissions from layer to layer are possible. Given the offices dimensions, transmitters within an office are connected to all receivers. On the other hand, the interference to other offices in the same layer is approximated by adding ten grid cells for each office of distance. The resulting topology can be seen in Fig. 2.

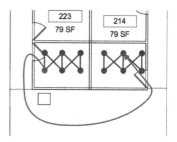

Fig. 2. Affectance example.

Fig. 1. A layer of the network grid.

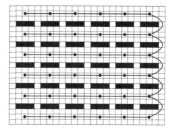

Fig. 3. Square grid.

In the second case studied, nodes are deployed in a square grid, but with a more intricate placement of obstacles among them, as shown in Fig. 3. In this case the range of communication is assumed to be 4 grid cells (measured in Manhattan distance for simplicity) so that connected nodes form paths, which we assume to be connected in one end by some other means.

Physical measurements of interference capture all the signal-attenuation factors present in the specific physical medium. In an environment with obstacles, those factors include distance, reflection, scattering, diffraction, etc. Customarily for synthetic inputs, we computed attenuation as the inverse of the distance between transmitter and receiver raised to the path-loss exponent α. To evaluate low- and high-interference scenarios, we considered boundary cases of $\alpha = 6$ and $\alpha = 2$ respectively [17].

The separation between transmitter and receiver was measured in Manhattan distance, assuming that the signal sorts the obstacles by going around them. Then, assuming a uniform transmission-power assignment, the affectance of each node u on each link (v, w) was computed as the ratio of the attenuation between u and w over the attenuation on (v, w).

For the network topologies described, and for various values of n, we applied our generic framework instantiated in each of the six local dissemination problems studied, using as a worst case scenario $R = V$. We measured the length of the schedules obtained and the number of iterations our framework needed to obtain the solution for all nodes. To solve the corresponding LP's we used IBM ILOG CPLEX Optimization Studio V12.8.0 in Java, on the Pace University

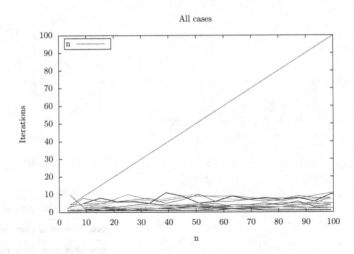

Fig. 4. Framework iterations for all cases studied.

Seidenberg School of CSIS Dell HPC cluster. (Head node with dual 12core Xeon processors, 192 GB memory, and 8 × 2.4TB HDs, and two GPU Compute nodes each with dual 12core Xeon processors, 384 GB memory, and 3 × NVIDIA Tesla V100 32 G Passive GPUs, with a Red Hat Enterprise Linux environment.)

The results of our evaluations are discussed in the following section.

5   Discusion of Results and Conclusions

In this work, we present a generic framework to compute transmission schedules to solve a comprehensive set of local dissemination problems frequently studied for Wireless Networks. Our framework provides an engineering solution with theoretical guarantees of correctness. Based on measurements of interference in the specific deployment area, one can obtain transmission schedules for any of the problems studied with one tool.

The practicality of our framework is shown by evaluating the number of iterations of LP-solver application until the solution is complete. It can be seen in Fig. 4 that the number of iterations remains constant when the network size grows, for all problems, topologies, and path-loss exponents studied, even though the set of requests used for the simulations was $R = V$. The length of the schedules obtained for the variety of problems studied, as the network size grows, under low- and high-interference, for two typical network topologies, and in a typical setting with obstacles are shown in Figs. 5 and 6.

To the best of our knowledge, this is the first comprehensive tool to compute local dissemination schedules for Wireless Networks under a general model of interference. A possible improvement, suggested by one of the reviewers and an interesting open direction, relates to the IP formulation - aimed to make it simpler and algorithmically more tractable.

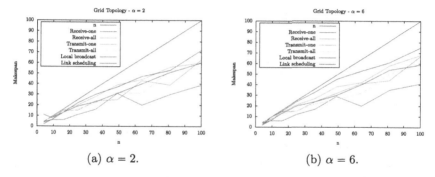

Fig. 5. Schedule length for grid topology.

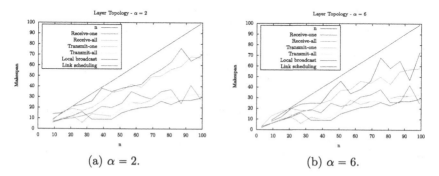

Fig. 6. Schedule length for layer topology.

References

1. Afek, Y. (ed.): DISC 2013. LNCS, vol. 8205. Springer, Heidelberg (2013). https://doi.org/10.1007/978-3-642-41527-2
2. Chlamtac, I., Kutten, S.: Tree-based broadcasting in multihop radio networks. IEEE Trans. Comput. **36**(10), 1209–1223 (1987)
3. Daum, S., Gilbert, S., Kuhn, F., Newport, C.C.: Broadcast in the ad hoc sinr model. In: Afek [1], pp. 358–372 (2013)
4. Genova, K., Guliashki, V.: Linear integer programming methods and approaches–a survey. J. Cybernetics Inf. Technol. **11**(1) 56 (2011)
5. Halldórsson, M.M., Wattenhofer, R.: Wireless communication is in apx. In: Proceedings of the 36th International Colloquium on Automata, Languages and Programming, Part I. pp. 525–536 (2009)
6. Kao, M.-Y. (ed.): Encyclopedia of Algorithms. Springer, New York (2016). https://doi.org/10.1007/978-1-4939-2864-4
7. Jurdzinski, T., Kowalski, D.R., Rozanski, M., Stachowiak, G.: Distributed randomized broadcasting in wireless networks under the sinr model. In: Afek [1], pp. 373–387 (2013)
8. Jurdzinski, T., Kowalski, D.R., Rozanski, M., Stachowiak, G.: Deterministic digital clustering of wireless ad hoc networks. In: Proceedings of the 2018 ACM Symposium on Principles of Distributed Computing, pp. 105–114 (2018)

9. Jurdzinski, T., Kowalski, D.R., Stachowiak, G.: Distributed deterministic broadcasting in uniform-power ad hoc wireless networks. In: Gasieniec, L., Wolter, F. (eds.) FCT 2013. LNCS, vol. 8070, pp. 195–209. Springer, Heidelberg (2013). https://doi.org/10.1007/978-3-642-40164-0_20

10. Jurdziński, T., Różański, M.: Deterministic oblivious local broadcast in the SINR model. In: Klasing, R., Zeitoun, M. (eds.) FCT 2017. LNCS, vol. 10472, pp. 312–325. Springer, Heidelberg (2017). https://doi.org/10.1007/978-3-662-55751-8_25

11. Karp, R.M.: Reducibility among combinatorial problems. In: Complexity of Computer Computations, pp. 85–103. Springer, Boston (1972). https://doi.org/10.1007/978-1-4684-2001-2_9

12. Kesselheim, T.: Dynamic packet scheduling in wireless networks. In: Proceedings of the 31st Annual ACM SIGACT-SIGOPS Symposium on Principles of Distributed Computing, pp. 281–290 (2012)

13. Kesselheim, T., Vöcking, B.: Distributed contention resolution in wireless networks. In: Lynch, N.A., Shvartsman, A.A. (eds.) DISC 2010. LNCS, vol. 6343, pp. 163–178. Springer, Heidelberg (2010). https://doi.org/10.1007/978-3-642-15763-9_16

14. Khachiyan, L.G.: A polynomial algorithm in linear programming. In: Doklady Akademii Nauk. vol. 244, pp. 1093–1096. Russian Academy of Sciences (1979)

15. Kowalski, D.R., Mosteiro, M.A., Rouse, T.: Dynamic multiple-message broadcast: bounding throughput in the affectance model. In: 10th ACM International Workshop on Foundations of Mobile Computing, FOMC 2014, Philadelphia, PA, USA, August 11, 2014, pp. 39–46 (2014)

16. Kowalski, D.R., Mosteiro, M.A., Zaki, K.: Dynamic multiple-message broadcast: Bounding throughput in the affectance model. CoRR abs/1512.00540 (2015), http://arxiv.org/abs/1512.00540

17. Kumar, A., Manjunath, D., Kuri, J.: Chapter 2 - wireless communication: Concepts, techniques, models. In: Kumar, A., Manjunath, D., Kuri, J. (eds.) Wireless Networking, pp. 15–51. The Morgan Kaufmann Series in Networking, Morgan Kaufmann, Burlington (2008). https://doi.org/10.1016/B978-012374254-4.50003-X, http://www.sciencedirect.com/science/article/pii/B978012374254450003X

18. Raghavan, P., Tompson, C.D.: Randomized rounding: a technique for provably good algorithms and algorithmic proofs. Combinatorica 7(4), 365–374 (1987)

19. Scheideler, C., Richa, A.W., Santi, P.: An o(log n) dominating set protocol for wireless ad-hoc networks under the physical interference model. In: Proceedings of the 9th ACM International Symposium on Mobile Ad Hoc Networking and Computing, pp. 91–100. ACM (2008)

20. Vutukuru, M., Jamieson, K., Balakrishnan, H.: Harnessing exposed terminals in wireless networks. In: Proceedings of the 5th USENIX Symposium on Networked Systems Design and Implementation, pp. 59–72 (2008)

Verifying Weakly Consistent Transactional Programs Using Symbolic Execution

Burcu Kulahcioglu Ozkan[✉]

Max Planck Institute for Software Systems (MPI-SWS), Kaiserslautern, Germany
burcu@mpi-sws.org

Abstract. We present a method for verifying whether all executions of a set of transactions satisfy a given invariant when run on weakly consistent systems. Existing approaches check that all executions under weak consistency are equivalent to some serial execution of the transactions, and separately that the serial executions satisfy the invariant. While sound, this can be overly strict. Programs running on systems with weak guarantees are usually designed to tolerate some anomalies w.r.t. the serial semantics and yet maintain some expected program invariants even on executions that are not serializable. In contrast, our technique does not restrict possible executions to be serializable, but directly checks whether given program properties hold w.r.t. all executions allowed under varying consistency models.

Our approach uses symbolic execution techniques and satisfiability checkers. We summarize the effects of transactions using symbolic execution and build a satisfiability formula that precisely captures all possible valuations of the data variables under a given consistency model. Then, we check whether the program invariants hold on the resulting symbolic set of behaviors. Our encoding is parameterized over the underlying consistency specification. Hence, the programmer can check the correctness of a program under several consistency models—eventual consistency, causal consistency, (parallel) snapshot isolation, serializability—and identify the level of consistency needed to satisfy the application-level invariants.

Keywords: Weak consistency · Transactions · Symbolic execution · Satisfiability

1 Introduction

Large-scale distributed systems rely on replicated databases that maintain data across a large number of nodes, potentially over a wide geographical span. Clients of the system can perform transactions at any node; the database is responsible to synchronize the data across the many nodes and maintain "consistency." Traditionally, consistency implied that the database was serializable [8]: the result

© Springer Nature Switzerland AG 2021
C. Georgiou and R. Majumdar (Eds.): NETYS 2020, LNCS 12129, pp. 261–278, 2021.
https://doi.org/10.1007/978-3-030-67087-0_17

of concurrently executing a set of transactions should be equivalent to executing the transactions serially in some order. Unfortunately, the synchronization cost of maintaining consistency is high; moreover, the CAP theorem [9] states that a distributed system cannot simultaneously guarantee consistency, availability, and partition tolerance. Thus, many modern systems sacrifice serializability in favor of weaker guarantees which allow executions that cannot be explained by any serial execution. A generic weaker guarantee is *eventual consistency* [13,31], which states that all replicas reach a consistent state if no more user updates arrive to the data centers.

Generally, eventual consistency guarantee is too weak by itself to satisfy the specifications of many applications: indeed, user updates never stop arriving in these systems. Hence, systems provide additional consistency guarantees which pose some restrictions on executions and specify which subset of anomalous (non-serializable) behaviors are allowed by a system, and which are not. Such weak consistency models include causal consistency [27], prefix consistency [14], parallel snapshot isolation [32], and snapshot isolation [6].

While weaker consistency models offer more availability and performance, they also make reasoning about programs more difficult. Under serializability, a programmer could argue about invariants one transaction at a time, disregarding concurrent interactions. Under weaker models, this is no longer possible.

Our goal in this work is to propose a method to verify safety properties of a program running under a weak consistency model. Existing work for analyzing safety properties of weakly consistent programs [4,5,10,11,28] take serializability as a reference model for correctness and decompose the safety verification problem into two steps: (1) show that the safety property holds under serializability, and separately, (2) show that a program is robust against a weak consistency model. Robustness against a weak consistency model [7] means that the program has exactly the same observable behaviors as with serializability guarantees. To show robustness, these methods build a dependency graph from the program executions and check for cycles in the graph which violate serializability.

While sound, this method is often too strict. Most programs designed for weak consistency are expected to tolerate some anomalies and yet satisfy application-level safety properties. Consider the two programs in Fig. 1. Neither program is robust against snapshot isolation, which allows concurrent transactions to commit if they write into a disjoint set of data variables. However, one of the programs exhibit buggy behavior with respect to the application-level invariant while the other one satisfies its application invariants under snapshot isolation.

The program in Fig. 1(a) considers a simple bank application. The example has two concurrent transactions operating on two bank accounts with an invariant that the total amount in both accounts is nonnegative. While the serial executions of the transactions satisfy the assertion, their execution under weaker consistency models do not. Under snapshot isolation (SI), both transactions can read from the initial snapshot and be unaware of each other's updates. Both

```
transaction T1()                        transaction T2()
  x = read accₓ in Accounts               x = read accₓ in Accounts
  y = read accᵧ in Accounts               y = read accᵧ in Accounts
  if (x + y) > 100                        if (x + y) > 100
    write accₓ (x-100) in Accounts          write accᵧ (y-100) in Accounts
              acc_x = acc_y = 60
              T1() || T2()
              assert(Accounts[accₓ] + Accounts[accᵧ]) > 0
```

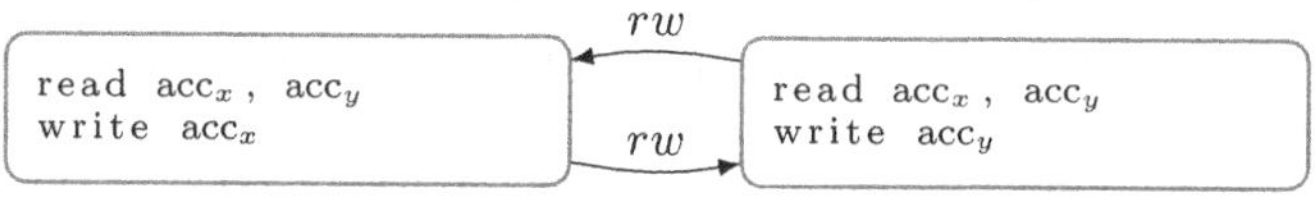

(a) Not robust against SI. Some executions under SI result in incorrect behavior.

```
transaction scheduleCourse(courseId)
    slots = read slot₁, ..., slotₙ in TimeTable
    index = findAvailable(slots, courseId)
    if index >= 0
        write slot_index courseId in TimeTable

  scheduleCourse(courseId₁) || scheduleCourse(courseId₂)
  assert(TimeTable[courseId₁] != TimeTable[courseId₂])
```

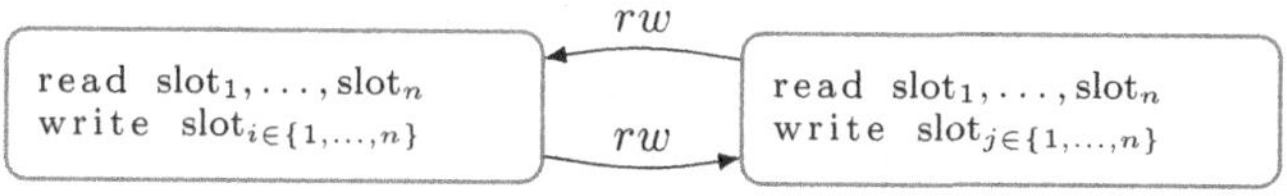

(b) Not robust against SI. However, its executions under SI are correct.

Fig. 1. Two programs both of which are not robust against SI. While the first example fails to provide its specifications, the second example satisfies them.

transactions can successfully commit under SI since they update disjoint sets of variables.

On the other hand, the non-serializable program in Fig. 1(b) is correct. This program considers a simple course scheduling application with an invariant that only a single course is assigned to a time slot. The example has two concurrent transactions to schedule the given courses into time slots which operate on a timetable database. The transactions concurrently read the timetable slots, check for a slot that is available and that satisfies the course requirements, and commit the assignment of course to the time slot by marking the allocated slot. Both transactions can successfully commit under snapshot isolation if they write to disjoint slots, e.g., if $i \neq j$ in Fig. 1(b). All executions under snapshot isolation satisfy the assertion.

In this paper, we describe a method to verify application-specific assertions in a transactional program running under a weak consistency model. Our method is parameterized over the underlying consistency model. Given a set of trans-actions on an underlying database, an assertion on the program state, and a consistency model, our method proceeds as follows. First, we use symbolic exe-cution to construct a summary for each transaction. The summary describes the relation between the before- and after-states for each transaction. Second, we symbolically encode an ordering of the transactions in the program, and compose the transaction summaries according to this ordering. The ordering specifies the data flow relationships between the transactions. Third, we use the axiomatic approach of [16] to encode constraints on valid executions under the weak consistency model. Altogether, this reduces the problem of assertion verification to a satisfiability checking question for the conjunction of all these constraints.

We show the applicability of our approach on a set of benchmarks written in the Boogie programming language [3] and used Symbooglix [26] for symbolic execution of transactions. Our approach allows the use of existing symbolic execution and satisfiability checking tools for the problem of verifying programs running on weakly consistent systems with complicated sets of behaviors.

2 Transactions on Weakly Consistent Systems

2.1 Abstract Executions

We formalize weakly consistent transactions in an axiomatic way, based on the framework presented by Cerone et al. [16]. We consider a database which keeps a set of *variables* $\mathtt{Vars} = \{x, y, \ldots\}$, replicated among a set of nodes in the distributed system. Clients interact with the database variables by running *transactions* $T \in \mathbb{T}$, which are programs issuing some read and write operations atomically on the database variables. For simplicity, we assume all the variables are integer valued and we define the operations on the variables as the set $\mathtt{Op} = \{\mathrm{rd}(x, n), \mathrm{wr}(x, n) \mid x \in \mathtt{Vars}, n \in \mathbb{Z}\}$. An *event* over $\mathtt{Op}$ is a labeled invocation $\mathrm{op}^\ell(x, n)$ of an operation. It consists of a unique identifier ℓ and an operation $\mathrm{op} \in \mathtt{Op}$ on a variable $x \in \mathtt{Vars}$ and a value $n \in \mathbb{Z}$. For example, the event $\mathrm{rd}^\ell(x, 0)$ represents an event with the (unique) label ℓ that reads the value 0 from variable x and $\mathrm{wr}^{\ell'}(x, 1)$ represents a write of value 1 to variable x. When the label is not important, we omit it and write $\mathrm{op}^{(\cdot)}(x, n)$.

Definition 1 (Transaction Trace and History). *A transaction trace is a pair* $(E, <_{po})$ *where E is a finite set of events over* $\mathtt{Op}$ *and program order $<_{po}$ is a total order over E. A history* $H = \langle \mathtt{Vars}, \{T_1, \ldots, T_n\} \rangle$ *consists of a set of variables* $\mathtt{Vars}$ *and a finite set of transaction traces with pairwise disjoint sets of identifiers. We assume all transactions are potentially concurrent to each other.*

Intuitively, a transaction trace records a successful sequence of operations on a database atomically executed by a client in a transaction and the order in which the operations were performed. A history records a concurrent set of transactions. On weakly consistent systems, the distributed nodes are not immediately synchronized after commiting a transaction. Therefore, the updates of a transaction on a replicated variable may not immediately be visible to all the nodes. Weakly consistent systems allow executing client transactions without the necessity of receiving all the updates committed on different replicas.

Systems providing weak consistency define a conflict resolution policy on the set of its operations to resolve conflicting updates made by concurrent transactions, such as last writer wins (LWW) for a register data type or add wins for a set data type [31]. For example, Cassandra [24] attaches a timestamp to each data update and applies LWW conflict resolution, i.e., it chooses the data with the most recent timestamp in case of concurrent updates to a data variable.

An abstract execution of a weakly consistent system is formally defined by the binary relations *visibility vis* and the *arbitration ar* between the transactions in a history. We write $T_1 \xrightarrow{vis} T_2$ if $(T_1, T2) \in vis$ and similarly $T_1 \xrightarrow{ar} T_2$ if $(T_1, T_2) \in ar$. The visibility relation is a strict pre-order (i.e., irreflexive and transitive), and models the delivery of updates between the replicas of a variable: $T_1 \xrightarrow{vis} T_2$ means that the updates of transaction T_1 are delivered to the node executing the transaction T_2 and therefore T_2 operates on variables that have been updated based on the operations in T_1. Two transactions are *concurrent* if neither of them sees the effects of the other, i.e., $T_1 \xrightarrow{vis} T_2$ and $T_2 \xrightarrow{vis} T_1$. The arbitration relation is a total order; $T_1 \xrightarrow{ar} T_2$ intuitively means that the version of variables written by T_2 supersede the versions written by T_1. The arbitration relation can be computed by Lamport timestamps [25].

Definition 2 (Abstract Execution). *An (abstract) execution of a history H is a tuple $A = \langle H, vis, ar \rangle$ of the history H with a visibility relation $vis \subseteq H \times H$ and an arbitration relation $ar \subseteq H \times H$ such that $vis \subseteq ar$.*

The constraint $vis \subseteq ar$ in an execution ensures that if T_2 is aware of T_1 (i.e., $T_1 \xrightarrow{vis} T_2$), then T_2's writes supersede T_1's writes (i.e., $T_1 \xrightarrow{ar} T_2$).

The weakest consistency specification is *eventual consistency* [13,31], which provides the basic guarantee that in a state where clients stop submitting transactions (which is called *quiescent state*) (i) all update transactions will eventually be visible to each node and (ii) the value of all the copies of the database variables will be the same. Eventual consistency is too weak by itself to satisfy the specifications of many applications. Hence, systems provide a spectrum of weak consistency models which provide additional guarantees on the system execution by requiring synchronization to some extent.

2.2 Axioms for Weak Consistency

In this section we recall a set of axioms summarized in [7,16] whose combination can be used to define weak consistency models.

We need some notation before we can formally describe the axioms. For a total order $< \subseteq A \times A$ on a set A and a non-empty set $B \subseteq A$, we define $\max(B, <)$ (respectively, $\min(B, <)$) as the unique event $b \in B$ such that, for all $a \in B$, we have $a < b$ or $a = b$ (respectively, $b < a$ or $b = a$). The operations max and min are undefined if B is empty. For an event $a \in A$, we write $\mathsf{bf}(a, <)$ for the set $\{b \in A \mid b < a\}$ of events preceding a and write $\mathsf{bf}(a, < \mid B)$ for $\mathsf{bf}(a, <) \cap B$. For a set of events E and $x \in \mathsf{Vars}$, we write E_x (resp. E_x^r, E_x^w) for the restriction of E to operations (resp. read, write operations) on variable x: $E_x = \{\mathsf{op}^\ell(\hat{x}, n) \in E \mid x = \hat{x}\}$, $E_x^r = \{\mathsf{rd}^\ell(\hat{x}, n) \in E \mid \hat{x} = x\}$, $E_x^w = \{\mathsf{wr}^\ell(\hat{x}, n) \in E \mid \hat{x} = x\}$.

The axiom INT is the *internal consistency axiom* which ensures that, within a transaction, the database provides sequential semantics: in a transaction $(E, <_{po})$, a read event e on a variable x returns the value of the last event on x preceding e. Formally,

$$\forall (E, <_{po}) \in H. \forall \mathrm{rd}^{\ell}(x, n)) \in E.$$

$$\mathrm{bf}(e, <_{po}| E_x) = \emptyset \lor \max(\mathrm{bf}(e, <_{po}| E_x)) \equiv \mathrm{op}^{(\cdot)}(x, n) \qquad (\mathrm{INT})$$

The axiom EXT is the *external consistency axiom* which ensures that, if in $(E, <_{po})$ a read e on x is not preceded by an operation on the same variable, then its value is determined in terms of writes by other transactions visible to it, if no transaction has written to x, by the initial value 0. For a transaction $T = (E, <_{po})$, we define the predicate $\langle T \text{ writes } (x, n)\rangle$ as $\max(E_x^w, <_{po}) \equiv \mathrm{wr}^{(\cdot)}(x, n)$ and the predicate $\langle T \text{ reads } (x, n)\rangle$ as $\min(E_x^r) \equiv \mathrm{rd}^{(\cdot)}(x, n)$. We also define $\langle T \text{ writes } x\rangle$ as $\exists n \in \mathbb{Z}.\langle T \text{ writes } (x, n)\rangle$. Formally, the EXT axiom states:

$$\forall (E, <_{po}) \in H. \forall x \in \mathbf{Vars}, \forall n \in \mathbb{Z}.\langle (E, <_{po}) \text{ reads } (x, n)\rangle \Rightarrow$$

$$(\mathrm{bf}(T, \xrightarrow{vis}| \mathrm{wr}(x)) = \emptyset \land n = 0) \lor \max(\mathrm{bf}(T, \xrightarrow{vis}| \mathrm{wr}(x)), \xrightarrow{ar}) \equiv \mathrm{op}^{(\cdot)}(x, n) \qquad (\mathrm{EXT})$$

where $\mathrm{wr}(x) = \{T \in H \mid \langle T \text{ writes } x\rangle\}$.

The NOCONFLICT axiom states that updates to the same variable by different transactions must be ordered by the visibility relation:

$$\forall T_1, T_2 \in H.(\exists x \in \mathbf{Vars}.T_1 \text{ writes } x \land T_2 \text{ writes } x) \Rightarrow$$

$$T_1 = T_2 \lor T_1 \xrightarrow{vis} T_2 \lor T_2 \xrightarrow{vis} T_1 \qquad (\mathrm{NOCONFLICT})$$

The axiom TRANSVIS states the transitivity of the *vis* relation:

$$\forall T_1, T_2, T_3 \in H.T_1 \xrightarrow{vis} T_2 \land T_2 \xrightarrow{vis} T_3 \implies T_1 \xrightarrow{vis} T_3 \qquad (\mathrm{TRANSVIS})$$

The PREFIX axiom states that if T_3 observes T_2, then it also observes any transaction before T_2 in the arbitration order and hence it is stricter than TRANSVIS:

$$\forall T_1, T_2, T_3 \in H : T_1 \xrightarrow{ar} T_2 \land T_2 \xrightarrow{vis} T_3 \implies T_1 \xrightarrow{vis} T_3 \qquad (\mathrm{PREFIX})$$

The axiom TOTALVIS states that *vis* is a total order, i.e., $vis = ar$, and hence it is stricter than PREFIX:

$$\forall T_1, T_2 \in H.T_1 = T_2 \lor T_1 \xrightarrow{vis} T_2 \lor T_2 \xrightarrow{vis} T_1 \qquad (\mathrm{TOTALVIS})$$

2.3 Weak Consistency Models

We now recall weak consistency models based on the axioms in Sect. 2.2 for which we provide symbolic encodings in Sect. 3. The definitions of the consistency models are summarized in Table 1.

Serializability (SER). [8] is a strong consistency model that guarantees the transactions to be executed serially and in the same order on every node. Formally, serializability allows executions which satisfy internal and external consistency for which the visibility relation is totally ordered.

Snapshot Isolation (SI). [6,19] weakens the serializability guarantee by allowing concurrent execution of two transactions that do not write to the same data variable. A transaction may not see all committed transactions in the system but it sees a prefix of the total order of transactions. However, it cannot commit if it updates an intersecting set of data variables with the set of updated variables of a concurrent transaction (formalized by NOCONFLICT axiom).

Table 1. Definitions of the consistency models

$$
\begin{aligned}
\text{SER} &= \text{INT} \wedge \text{EXT} \wedge \text{TOTALVIS} \\
\text{SI} &= \text{INT} \wedge \text{EXT} \wedge \text{PREFIX} \wedge \text{NOCONFLICT} \\
\text{PSI} &= \text{INT} \wedge \text{EXT} \wedge \text{TRANSVIS} \wedge \text{NOCONFLICT} \\
\text{PC} &= \text{INT} \wedge \text{EXT} \wedge \text{PREFIX} \\
\text{CC} &= \text{INT} \wedge \text{EXT} \wedge \text{TRANSVIS}
\end{aligned}
$$

Parallel Snapshot Isolation (PSI). [32] relaxes SI by weakening the PREFIX requirement which enforces a global ordering of transactions to causal delivery of transactions (TRANSVIS). Causal delivery ensures the ordered delivery of causally related updates. If a transaction T_i was visible to the execution of the transaction T_j, i.e., T_j operates on the effects produced by T_i, then T_j is causally related to T_j. In causally consistent systems, all the replicas see the transactions T_i and T_j in that order. This is formalized by the axiom TRANSVIS.

Prefix Consistency (PC). [14] is also a relaxation of SI which is not strictly stronger or weaker than PSI. PC is strict in the sense that it requires a transaction to see the updates of some prefix of all the updates w.r.t., ar relation, enforcing PREFIX. On the other hand, it is weak on its guarantees for committing transactions. It allows conflicting updates of concurrent transactions, not enforcing NOCONFLICT.

Causal Consistency (CC). [27] requires causally related transactions to be visible to other replicas in the causal order (TRANSVIS). Some variants of causal consistency are defined in the context of both memory and distributed systems (e.g., causal memory [1], causal convergence [12,13]). All these definitions are based on the requirement of causal delivery. Causal consistency guarantees are weaker than PSI as CC allows the transactions with conflicting set of updates to commit concurrently.

Verification Problem. In this work, we study the program verification problem parametrized over the consistency model. Given a history with a set of transactions on the database variables, a consistency model, and an assertion on the database variable, we ask whether there is an abstract execution of the system allowed by the consistency model which violates the program assertion.

Definition 3 (Verification Problem). *Given a history* $H = \langle \text{Vars}, \rangle$ $\{T_1, \ldots, T_n\}$, *a consistency model* $cm \in \{\text{SER}, \text{SI}, \text{PSI}, \text{PC}, \text{CC}\}$, *and a program assertion* ϕ_{PROG} *on the variables* Vars, *the verification problem asks whether there is an abstract execution* $A = \langle H, vis, ar \rangle$ *satisfying* cm *that violates* ϕ_{PROG} *after executing* $\{T_1, \ldots, T_n\}$.

In the next section, we present our method for answering the verification problem by using symbolic execution and encoding the possible set of program behaviors into a satisfiability formula.

3   Encoding Weakly Consistent Executions

Our method encodes the possible set of executions of a set of concurrent transactions under a given consistency model into a satisfiability formula Φ. Our encoding has three steps:

1. Symbolically executing each transaction to summarize its effects into symbolic valuation of variables (Sect. 3.1),
2. Connecting the symbolic valuations of the transactions together so that the composition captures only causally consistent sets of executions (Sect. 3.2)
3. Constraining the sets of executions w.r.t. a consistency model (Sect. 3.3)

3.1   Symbolic Execution of Transactions

In transactional programs, the effects of a transaction are made visible to other transactions *atomically*. The intermediate state of in-progress or rolling back transactions are not seen by any other transaction. This property allows for a modular encoding for each transaction independently of others.

Given a set of transactions $T_1, \ldots, T_n$, we execute each transaction on a symbolic state and obtain their symbolic summaries. The summary of the transaction is the relation between the initial symbolic snapshot and the final symbolic expressions for the variables. In order to track different sets of variables, for each transaction, we introduce two arrays of symbolic variables X and X'. These arrays keep the symbolic values for each variable before and after the execution of a transaction respectively. The contents of X'_i with $1 \le i \le n$ keeps the updates made by the transaction in the arbitration order i on state X_i in a symbolic way.

For each transaction $T_i \in \{T_1, \ldots, T_n\}$, the formula TRANSACTION-SUMMARY represents the relationship between its input valuation X and the

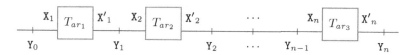

Fig. 2. The execution of transactions $T_{ar_1}, \ldots, T_{ar_n}$ in the arbitration order on the symbolic states $X_1, \ldots, X_n$ respectively.

output valuation X' along with a map $Wr : Vars \mapsto \mathbb{B}$. Wr maps a variable to a Boolean value such that $Wr.x$ is true if T_i modifies the data variable x. The valuation of the map Wr for a transaction is computed during its symbolic execution. This information is used later for detecting conflicts between concurrent transactions.

$$T_i(X, X', Wr) \qquad\qquad \text{(Transaction-Summary)}$$

In order to represent valid executions, we have to "tie together" different symbolic states. The symbolic states of transactions are tied together in their arbitration order. We model the arbitration as a symbolic permutation of transactions. We introduce variables $ar_1, \ldots, ar_n$ which has distinct values from $\{1, \ldots, n\}$. The variable ar_i represents the identifier of the transaction in the arbitration order i, that is $ar_i = j$ iff T_j is the ith transaction in the arbitration.

Figure 2 illustrates the execution of transactions on the symbolic states. Each transaction T_{ar_i} in the arbitration order i, reads a symbolic state X_i and updates it to X'_i. The first transaction is executed on X_0 which contains the initial variable valuation. The next transactions can operate on either the initial symbolic state or another state produced by an earlier transaction.

Our encoding nondeterministically picks a symbolic state X_i with $1 \le i \le n$ from the set of states produced by the earlier transactions X'_j with $i < j \le n$. We use an additional array of symbolic states Y_i to keep the effects of the first i transactions in the arbitration order. Initially, $Y_0 = X_0$. As we explain in the next subsection, the later values of Y are calculated by applying the transactions' effects in the arbitration order.

3.2   Encoding the Executions

In this subsection, we build a logical formula $\varPhi$ which brings together the symbolic execution summaries of $T_1, \ldots, T_n$. The resulting formula models the possible executions of transactions as illustrated in Fig. 2.

The set of symbolic valuations which satisfy $\varPhi$ models all possible variable valuations that can be obtained after the execution of the transactions. All possible executions of $T_1, \ldots, T_n$ satisfy the program properties iff the intersection of $\varPhi$ and the negation of the program properties is not satisfiable.

The encoding has three main components:

– The arbitration order of the transactions $T_1, \ldots, T_n$ (Arbitration)

– The input symbolic states transactions read from (INPUT-STATES)
– The symbolic states after the synchronization of updates (OUTPUT-STATES)

(ARBITRATION) encodes the arbitration order of the transaction summaries using the variables $ar_1, \ldots, ar_n$. The formula requires the variables $ar_1, \ldots, ar_n$ to have distinct values in $\{1, \ldots, n\}$. It also encodes that ar_i keeps the ith transaction T_j in the arbitration order.

$$\bigwedge_{1 \leq i \leq n} \bigvee_{1 \leq j \leq n} (ar_i = j) \wedge \bigwedge_{1 \leq i,j \leq n} (i \neq j \implies ar_i \neq ar_j)$$
$$\wedge \bigwedge_{1 \leq j \leq n} \bigvee_{1 \leq i \leq n} (ar_i = j \implies T_j(\mathbf{X}_i, \mathbf{X'}_i, \mathbf{Wr}_i))$$

(ARBITRATION)

(INPUT-STATES) encodes the possible sets of symbolic states $\mathbf{X}_i$ that a transaction in the arbitration order i can read from. A transaction in ith order can either read from the output snapshot of a transaction earlier than itself in the arbitration order or a symbolic state that has the effects of first $j < i$ transactions in the arbitration order. The formula $\phi_{\text{READ}}(cm)$ further restricts the set of symbolic values w.r.t. a consistency model $cm \in \{\text{CC}, \text{PSI}, \text{PC}, \text{SI}, \text{SER}\}$ as we explain in the next subsection.

$$\bigwedge_{0 < i \leq n} \bigvee_{0 \leq j < i} \left(\bigwedge_{x \in \mathsf{Vars}} (\mathbf{X}_i.x = \mathbf{X'}_j.x) \vee \bigwedge_{x \in \mathsf{Vars}} (\mathbf{X}_i.x = \mathbf{Y}_j.x) \right) \wedge \phi_{\text{READ}(cm)}$$

(INPUT-STATES)

(OUTPUT-STATES) encodes the valuation of the variables $\mathbf{Y}_{1 \leq i \leq n}$ which summarizes the effects of first i transactions in the arbitration order. For each variable $x \in \mathsf{Vars}$, if the ith transaction writes to x, $\mathbf{Y}_i.x$ is equal to the output value of ith transaction $\mathbf{X'}_i.x$. Otherwise, $\mathbf{Y}_i.x$ keeps the existing value of x, i.e., $\mathbf{Y}_{i-1}.x$.[1] The formula $\phi_{\text{WRITE}}(cm)$ further restricts the set of symbolic values w.r.t. a consistency model $cm \in \{\text{CC}, \text{PSI}, \text{PC}, \text{SI}, \text{SER}\}$.

$$\bigwedge_{0 < i \leq n} \bigwedge_{x \in \mathsf{Vars}} ((\mathbf{Wr}_i(x) \implies \mathbf{Y}_i = \mathbf{X'}_i.x) \wedge (\neg \mathbf{Wr}_i(x) \implies \mathbf{Y}_i.x = \mathbf{Y}_{i-1}.x)) \wedge \phi_{\text{WRITE}(cm)}$$

(OUTPUT-STATES)

(INITIAL) encodes the initial valuation of the variables. Initially, $\mathbf{Y}_0$ is equal to the initial variable valuation.

$$\bigwedge_{x \in \mathsf{Vars}} (\mathbf{Y}_0.x = \mathbf{X'}_0.x \wedge \mathbf{X}_0.x = \mathbf{X'}_0.x)$$

(INITIAL)

The formula Φ is the intersection of the formulas above, which encodes all possible executions of $T_1, \ldots, T_n$ satisfying INT, EXT and TRANSVIS:

$$\Phi = (\text{ARBITRATION}) \wedge (\text{INPUT-STATES}) \wedge (\text{OUTPUT-STATES}) \wedge (\text{INITIAL})$$

---

[1] Our encoding follows Last Writer Wins (LWW) policy.

We check whether some property ϕ_{PROG} on $x \in \textsf{Vars}$ holds for all possible executions of the program by using (PROGRAM-PROP). We obtain (PROGRAM-PROP) by replacing the accesses of $x \in \textsf{Vars}$ to the symbolic valuation $\textsf{Y}_n.x$, so that we evaluates ϕ on the symbolic valuation of the variables obtained after executing transactions $T_1, \ldots, T_n$.

$$\phi_{\text{PROG}}[\forall x \in \textsf{Vars}.\ \textsf{Y}_n.x/x] \qquad \text{(PROGRAM-PROP)}$$

Theorem 1. *The encoded set of variable valuations satisfies the property ϕ under causal consistency iff the formula $\Phi \wedge \neg(\text{PROGRAM-PROP})$ is not satisfiable with $\phi_{\text{READ}}(cm) = \mathsf{true}$ and $\phi_{\text{WRITE}}(cm) = \mathsf{true}$.*

The theorem follows from the fact that the encoded set of executions satisfies INT, EXT and TRANSVIS axioms. The axiom INT is trivially satisfied by the TRANSACTION-SUMMARY which is obtained by symbolically executing a transaction. EXT is satisfied by restricting the input symbolic valuation $\textsf{X}_i.x$ to the last visible value to the transaction in the arbitration order i. The axiom TRANSVIS is satisfied by the relation between the symbolic input/output states of transactions. For any three transactions T_{ar_i}, T_{ar_j} and T_{ar_k} such that $\textsf{X}_j = \textsf{X}'_i$ and $\textsf{X}_k = \textsf{X}'_j$, T_{ar_k} operating on the symbolic output state of T_{ar_j} sees the effect of T_{ar_j} as well as the effect of T_{ar_i} on whose output state T_{ar_j} operates. Therefore, for all $T_{ar_i} \xrightarrow{vis} T_{ar_j}$ and $T_{ar_i} \xrightarrow{vis} T_{ar_k}$, we have $T_{ar_i} \xrightarrow{vis} T_{ar_k}$.

Notice that all the program behaviors encoded by the formula—without any further restrictions on which symbolic values to read or which transactions to commit—are not allowed by all weak consistency models. In the next subsection, we restrict the executions for different consistency models.

3.3   Encoding the Consistency Model

We model the allowed set of executions $A = \langle H, vis, ar \rangle$ under the given consistency model $cm \in \{$ PSI, PC, SI, SER$\}$ by incorporating the restrictions of these consistency models into two additional constraints in the formula Φ:

$\phi_{\text{READ}}(cm)$ Constrains the visibility relation $vis \subseteq ar$, i.e., the effects of which transactions can be visible for a transaction by restricting the set of symbolic states a transaction can read from

$\phi_{\text{WRITE}}(cm)$ Constrains which transactions can commit concurrently based on the set of variables they write to

CC	$\phi_{\text{READ}}(\text{CC}) = \mathsf{true}$	$\phi_{\text{WRITE}}(\text{CC}) = \mathsf{true}$
PSI	$\phi_{\text{READ}}(\text{PSI}) = \mathsf{true}$	$\phi_{\text{WRITE}}(\text{PSI}) = \phi\text{-NOCONFLICT}$
PC	$\phi_{\text{READ}}(\text{PC}) = \phi\text{-PREFIX}$	$\phi_{\text{WRITE}}(\text{PC}) = \mathsf{true}$
SI	$\phi_{\text{READ}}(\text{SI}) = \phi\text{-PREFIX}$	$\phi_{\text{WRITE}}(\text{SI}) = \phi\text{-NOCONFLICT}$
SER	$\phi_{\text{READ}}(\text{SER}) = \phi\text{-TOTALVIS}$	$\phi_{\text{WRITE}}(\text{SER}) = \mathsf{true}$

Fig. 3. Encodings for ϕ_{READ} and ϕ_{WRITE} to constrain the set of executions.

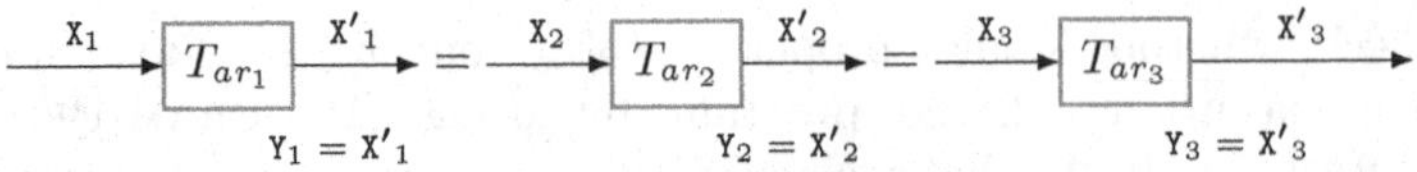

(a) The symbolic execution produces a serial execution of T_{ar_1}, T_{ar_2} and T_{ar_3}.

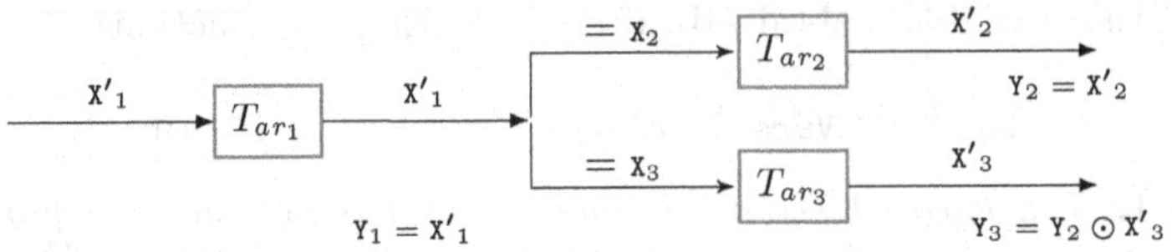

(b) The symbolic execution produces an execution under snapshot isolation. Both transactions T_{ar_2} and T_{ar_3} operate on the snapshot valuation X'_1 produced by T_{ar_1}.

Fig. 4. Two different executions of transactions $T_{ar_1}, T_{ar_2}, T_{ar_3}$. Initially, $Y_0 = X_0$.

In order to satisfy PREFIX, TOTALVIS and NOCONFLICT, we restrict the possible set of symbolic valuations which satisfy Φ. Figure 3 lists the formulas for constraining the executions to satisfy the axioms defined in Sect. 2.3.

(ϕ-PREFIX) requires the symbolic variable valuation X_i read by a transaction to be a prefix state, i.e., a valuation of variables obtained after the effect of a prefix of transactions in the arbitration order.

$$\bigwedge_{1 \leq i \leq n} \bigvee_{0 \leq j < i} \bigwedge_{x \in \text{Vars}} (X_i.x = Y_j.x) \qquad (\phi-\text{PREFIX})$$

(ϕ-TOTALVIS) requires the visibility relation to be a total order. It requires the input state X_i of the transaction in the ith arbitration order to be the output state of the transaction in the $(i-1)$th arbitration order, i.e., X'_{i-1}. In this case, X'_{i-1} is equal to Y_{i-1} since there are no concurrent transactions.

$$\bigwedge_{1 \leq i \leq n} \bigwedge_{x \in \text{Vars}} (X_i.x = Y_{i-1}.x) \qquad (\phi-\text{TOTALVIS})$$

(ϕ-NOCONFLICT) requires that if the transaction T_{ar_i} reads from the symbolic state of an earlier transaction T_{ar_k}, there are not any transactions T_{ar_j} in between T_{ar_k} and T_{ar_i} (where $T_{ar_j} \xrightarrow{vis} T_{ar_i}$ and $T_{ar_i} \xrightarrow{vis} T_{ar_j}$) which update the same variable with T_{ar_i}.

$$\bigwedge_{0 \leq k < i \leq n} \bigwedge_{x \in \text{Vars}} \left((X_i = X'_k \wedge \text{Wr}_{ar_i}.x) \implies \bigwedge_{k < j < i} \neg \text{Wr}_{ar_j}.x \right) \qquad (\phi-\text{NOCONFLICT})$$

Theorem 2. *The answer to the verification problem in Definition 3 for a history $H = \langle \text{Vars}, \{T_1, \ldots, T_n\} \rangle$, consistency model cm $\in \{CC, PSI, PC, SI, SER\}$, and program assertion ϕ_{PROG} is YES iff $\Phi \wedge \neg \text{PROGRAM-PROP}$ is not satisfiable.*

Example 1. Figure 4(a) encodes a serializable execution by sequencing the symbolic states in the arbitration order. It feeds the output state of a transaction

T_{ar_i} to the input transaction of $T_{ar_{i+1}}$ where $T_i \xrightarrow{ar} T_{ar_{i+1}}$. In a serializable execution, the prefix state which summarize the effects of first i transactions w.r.t. the arbitration is equal to the output valuation of the ith transaction.

Example 2. Figure 4(b) encodes an execution of transactions under snapshot isolation. In that particular execution, both transactions T_{ar_2} and T_{ar_3} operate on the output snapshot of T_{ar_1} (i.e., $T_{ar_1} \xrightarrow{vis} T_{ar_2}$ and $T_{ar_1} \xrightarrow{vis} T_{ar_3}$) and they are concurrent to each other (i.e., $T_{ar_2} \xrightarrow{vis} \!\!\!\!\!\!/\;\; T_{ar_3}$ and $T_{ar_3} \xrightarrow{vis} \!\!\!\!\!\!/\;\; T_{ar_2}$). This is a valid execution under SI iff T_{ar_2} and T_{ar_3} update a disjoint set of variables. Similar to the serializable case, Y_0 keeps the initial values of the data variables which is read by the transaction with the smallest arbitration, $Y_1 = X[1]$ keeps the updates of T_{ar_1}. The snapshots Y_2 and Y_3 keep the effects up to the second and third transactions in the arbitration respectively. In this example, the symbolic valuations Y and X differ from each other. Consider $T_{ar_2} \xrightarrow{ar} T_{ar_3}$ where T_{ar_2} writes to $x \in$ Vars and T_{ar_3} writes to $y \in$ Vars. Then, the symbolic states X_2 and X_3 would be respectively be aware of only the updates on x and y respectively. On the other hand, Y_3 would summarize the effects of all three transactions, incorporating the updates on both x and y. Consider an alternative execution of the same example in Fig. 4(b) under causal consistency, which allows conflicting updates. In a case where both T_{ar_2} and T_{ar_3} write to the same variable, the value in the snapshot Y_3 would be determined by the conflict resolution policy (denoted with $\odot$ in the figure). For LWW policy, the final value is the value written by the transaction with the highest arbitration among the concurrent transactions (as given in (OUTPUT-STATES) formula), resulting in *lost update* in this example.

4   Experiments

We show the applicability of our approach on a set of benchmarks extracted from the literature related to weakly consistent databases. We encoded our formulas in Boogie language [3] using its support for symbolic variables and symbolically executed the transactions using Symbooglix [26] symbolic execution engine.

We performed our experiments on Auction, an online auction application from [29], Courseware, a course registration service adapted from [20,28,29], FusionTicket, a ticket sales application adapted from [21], and a simple banking system, SimpleBank, extracted from [16], all of which operate on key-value data stores. We implemented these systems in Boogie language and instrumented with the encoding of our formula. Then, we symbolically executed the instrumented transactions using Symbooglix and checked whether concurrent execution of some benchmark set of transactions satisfy the applications' properties.

Table 2 lists the number of transactions (#T) in each benchmark and whether the application properties are satisfied (ϕ) under different consistency models. We also report the number of satisfiability queries solved (#q) and run time in seconds (t) for computing different paths of the symbolic execution of the instrumented transactions. In addition to the consistency model, the number of satisfiability queries and hence the run time depend on the number of transactions, the number of variables read/written by the transactions, and variable accesses of concurrent transactions (i.e., the paths with certain concurrent accesses are infeasible for some consistency models, pruning further exploration of certain paths). We collected the results on a machine with a 2.6 GHz Intel Core i7 processor and 16 GB memory running macOS Catalina.

Auction models an auction system with transactions to start an auction, place a bid, and close an auction. The application requires that when an auction is closed, the declared winner is the bidder with the highest bid. Two different versions of the application are given in [29]. In the first version, the application property can be violated in the concurrent execution of transaction for placing bids, and close of an auction. The second version aims to satisfy the property by introducing tokens to replicas and closing an auction only after all tokens are collected. We implemented and verified both versions. As shown in Table 2, concurrent execution of start/close auction and two bidding transactions may fail to satisfy the application property under consistency models weaker than serializability in the first version (V1), while the second version (V2) satisfies it.

Courseware application provides transactions to add courses, add students, enroll students to courses, and schedule courses to timetable slots. In the first benchmark (B1), we check whether the property of having unique names for each course holds if two transactions concurrently add a course with different ids but the same name. While the property is satisfied under serializability, transactions writing to different keys of the courses table can commit the same course name in the weaker consistency models. In (B2), we check whether the property of assigning each slot to a single course holds if two transactions concurrently schedule a course. As explained in the example in Fig. 1(b), this property holds under weaker consistency models SI and PSI as well as SER. In (B3), we run transactions for adding a student, adding a course and enrolling the newly added student to the newly added course concurrently. We verify that the application property that requires each enrolled student and course exist in students and courses respectively is satisfied in all consistency models.

FusionTicket application provides transactions to add events and purchase tickets. The application updates the price of a ticket based on the sold number of tickets and has an application property on the expected amount to be collected from the tickets. Concurrent execution of multiple purchase transactions (B1) may violate this property under weak consistency models. The application also requires each event to be assigned to a different venue. Concurrent execution of multiple transactions for adding events (B2), does not violate that property under SI and PSI as well as SER. Because, the transactions writing to the same venue cannot commit concurrently under SI and PSI.

SimpleBank is the implementation of the example in Fig. 1(a). Concurrent transactions to withdraw some amount may violate the property of nonnegative balance under consistency models weaker than SER.

Our experiments show that our approach can be used for verifying whether an application's properties hold when a set of transactions are run concurrently on a weakly consistent database. As the method is parametric to the consistency model, it is easy to check for the properties for a spectrum of consistency models.

Table 2. Experimental results for the benchmarks for varying consistency models.

Benchmark		T	SER			SI			PSI			PC			CC		
			#q	t	ϕ	#q	t	ϕ	#q	t	ϕ	#q	t	ϕ	#q	t	ϕ
Auction	V1	4	14000	360	✓	15134	490	✗	14414	418	✗	13982	381	✗	13262	300	✗
	V2	4	17993	1578	✓	18001	1393	✓	18349	1653	✓	17945	1495	✓	17897	1533	✓
Courseware	B1	2	1073	23	✓	833	19	✗	593	13	✗	739	15	✗	499	9	✗
	B2	2	1514	353	✓	949	95	✓	589	62	✓	843	94	✗	483	34	✗
	B3	3	1745	509	✓	1325	298	✓	1257	323	✓	977	160	✓	881	82	✓
FusionTicket	B1	3	1340	35	✓	1329	35	✓	1322	34	✓	1318	35	✗	1311	31	✗
	B2	2	956	31	✓	825	24	✓	753	21	✓	765	22	✗	693	17	✗
SimpleBank	B1	2	446	26	✓	348	16	✗	314	12	✗	280	12	✗	246	8	✗

5 Related Work

A vast amount of work is devoted to relaxing the consistency in the context of both databases and weak memory. Here we limit our focus to the correctness of weakly consistent programs assuming the correctness of the underlying system.

A line of existing work reason about the correctness of weakly consistent programs based on the serializability of the transactions [10,11,15,28,33]. The notion of *robustness* against consisteny models [7] is introduced to characterize whether the program produces the same behavior on a weakly consistent or serializable system. The serializability of weakly consistent transactions is analyzed using both dynamic and static methods. The work in [10] builds a dynamic analyzer which incorporates commutativity and absorption properties of operations, and [11] presents a static analysis tool for detecting non-serializable behaviors. The work in [28] reduces serializability checking to a satisfiability problem for automated detection of serializability violations. Focusing on widely used consistency models, recent work presents algorithms for verifying robustness against SI [4] and CC [5]. The robustness notion is also extended for different consistency models (e.g., robustness against PSI towards SI) [17]. While these definitions relax the serializability requirement, robustness towards a consistency model is still restrictive for checking the correctness of applications.

Some works verify the application properties of the specifications of weakly consistent programs. The work in [20,30] propose a proof system for showing the application invariants hold under some choice of consistency guarantees of distributed operations. While this work requires low level operational reasoning, the work in [22] presents a system for compositional rely-guarantee style proof system for concurrent transactions running on weakly consistent systems. The work in [23] presents a program transformation based technique for verifying transactional programs with relaxed operations. With a motivation of preserving program invariants, *Explicit Consistency* [2] is proposed as a variant of weak consistency that exploits static analysis techniques to infer conflicting operations. In a recent work, [29] presents a proof rule to verify specifications of distributed objects. Differently, our method verifies implementations of transactional programs by modeling the behavior of underlying weakly consistent system.

In the context of exploring program behaviors, Repliss tool [34] exercises executions of an application with randomized invocations. Commander [18] explores the execution of a weakly consistent program using a bounded scheduler parameterized in both the schedule exploration strategy and also the consistency model. Different from execution based approaches which runs the system for different possible executions, we present an encoding which symbolically captures all behaviors of the program implementation under a consistency specification.

6   Conclusion

We presented a satisfiability based method for the verification of transactional programs running on weak consistency models. Our method summarizes the transactions by using symbolic execution, encodes the set of possible program executions under a consistency model into a satisfiability formula and checks the program assertions in the symbolic set of program states satisfying the formula. To the best of our knowledge, our work is the first to utilize symbolic execution techniques for the analysis of weakly consistent transactions.

Acknowledgements. We would like to thank Rupak Majumdar for his feedback and contribution during various stages of this work.

References

1. Ahamad, M., Neiger, G., Burns, J.E., Kohli, P., Hutto, P.W.: Causal memory: definitions, implementation, and programming. Distributed Comput. **9**(1), 37–49 (1995)
2. Balegas, V., et al.: Putting consistency back into eventual consistency. In: The 10th European Conference on Computer Systems, EuroSys, pp. 6:1–6:16. ACM (2015)
3. Barnett, M., Chang, B.-Y.E., DeLine, R., Jacobs, B., Leino, K.R.M.: Boogie: a modular reusable verifier for object-oriented programs. In: de Boer, F.S., Bonsangue, M.M., Graf, S., de Roever, W.-P. (eds.) FMCO 2005. LNCS, vol. 4111, pp. 364–387. Springer, Heidelberg (2006). https://doi.org/10.1007/11804192_17
4. Beillahi, S.M., Bouajjani, A., Enea, C.: Checking robustness against snapshot isolation. In: Dillig, I., Tasiran, S. (eds.) CAV 2019. LNCS, vol. 11562, pp. 286–304. Springer, Cham (2019). https://doi.org/10.1007/978-3-030-25543-5_17
5. Beillahi, S.M., Bouajjani, A., Enea, C.: Robustness against transactional causal consistency. In: 30th International Conference on Concurrency Theory, CONCUR. LIPIcs, vol. 140, pp. 30:1–30:18 (2019)
6. Berenson, H., Bernstein, P.A., Gray, J., Melton, J., O'Neil, E.J., O'Neil, P.E.: A critique of ANSI SQL isolation levels. In: ACM SIGMOD International Conference on Management of Data, pp. 1–10. ACM Press (1995)
7. Bernardi, G., Gotsman, A.: Robustness against consistency models with atomic visibility. In: 27th International Conference on Concurrency Theory, CONCUR. LIPIcs, vol. 59, pp. 7:1–7:15 (2016)

8. Bernstein, P.A., Hadzilacos, V., Goodman, N.: Concurrency Control and Recovery in Database Systems. Addison-Wesley (1987)
9. Brewer, E.A.: Towards robust distributed systems (abstract). In: The 9th Annual ACM Symposium on Principles of Distributed Computing, p. 7. ACM (2000)
10. Brutschy, L., Dimitrov, D., Müller, P., Vechev, M.T.: Serializability for eventual consistency: criterion, analysis, and applications. In: The 44th ACM SIGPLAN Symposium on Principles of Programming Languages, POPL, pp. 458–472. ACM (2017)
11. Brutschy, L., Dimitrov, D., Müller, P., Vechev, M.T.: Static serializability analysis for causal consistency. In: The 39th ACM SIGPLAN Conf. on Programming Language Design and Implementation, PLD, pp. 90–104. ACM (2018)
12. Burckhardt, S.: Principles of eventual consistency. Found. Trends Program. Lang. **1**(1–2), 1–150 (2014)
13. Burckhardt, S., Gotsman, A., Yang, H., Zawirski, M.: Replicated data types: specification, verification, optimality. In: The 41st Annual ACM SIGPLAN-SIGACT Symposium on Principles of Programming Languages, POPL, pp. 271–284. ACM (2014)
14. Burckhardt, S., Leijen, D., Protzenko, J., Fähndrich, M.: Global sequence protocol: a robust abstraction for replicated shared state. In: 29th European Conference on Object-Oriented Programming, ECOOP, LIPIcs, vol. 37, pp. 568–590 (2015)
15. Cahill, M.J., Röhm, U., Fekete, A.D.: Serializable isolation for snapshot databases. ACM Trans. Database Syst. **34**(4), 20:1–20:42 (2009)
16. Cerone, A., Bernardi, G., Gotsman, A.: A framework for transactional consistency models with atomic visibility. In: 26th International Conference on Concurrency Theory, CONCUR. LIPIcs, vol. 42, pp. 58–71 (2015)
17. Cerone, A., Gotsman, A.: Analysing snapshot isolation. J. ACM **65**(2), 11:1–11:41 (2018)
18. Dabaghchian, M., Rakamaric, Z., Kulahcioglu Ozkan, B., Mutlu, E., Tasiran, S.: Consistency-aware scheduling for weakly consistent programs. ACM SIGSOFT Softw. Eng. Notes **42**(4), 1–5 (2017)
19. Fekete, A., Liarokapis, D., O'Neil, E.J., O'Neil, P.E., Shasha, D.E.: Making snapshot isolation serializable. ACM Trans. Database Syst. **30**(2), 492–528 (2005)
20. Gotsman, A., Yang, H., Ferreira, C., Najafzadeh, M., Shapiro, M.: 'cause i'm strong enough: reasoning about consistency choices in distributed systems. In: The 43rd Annual ACM SIGPLAN-SIGACT Symposium on Principles of Programming Languages, POPL, pp. 371–384. ACM (2016)
21. Holt, B., Bornholt, J., Zhang, I., Ports, D.R.K., Oskin, M., Ceze, L.: Disciplined inconsistency with consistency types. In: The 7th ACM Symposium on Cloud Computing, pp. 279–293. ACM (2016)
22. Kaki, G., Nagar, K., Najafzadeh, M., Jagannathan, S.: Alone together: compositional reasoning and inference for weak isolation. In: Proceedings ACM Programming Language, vol. 2(POPL), pp. 27:1–27:34 (2018)
23. Kuru, I., Kulahcioglu Ozkan, B., Mutluergil, S.O., Tasiran, S., Elmas, T., Cohen, E.: Verifying programs under snapshot isolation and similar relaxed consistency models. In: The 9th ACM SIGPLAN Workshop on Transactional Computing (2014)
24. Lakshman, A., Malik, P.: Cassandra: a decentralized structured storage system. Operating Syst. Rev. **44**(2), 35–40 (2010)
25. Lamport, L.: Time, clocks, and the ordering of events in a distributed system. Commun. ACM **21**(7), 558–565 (1978)

26. Liew, D., Cadar, C., Donaldson, A.F.: Symbooglix: a symbolic execution engine for boogie programs. In: 2016 IEEE International Conference on Software Testing, Verification and Validation, ICST, pp. 45–56. IEEE Computer Society (2016)

27. Lloyd, W., Freedman, M.J., Kaminsky, M., Andersen, D.G.: Don't settle for eventual: scalable causal consistency for wide-area storage with COPS. In: The 23rd ACM Symposium on Operating Systems Principles 2011, SOSP, pp. 401–416. ACM (2011)

28. Nagar, K., Jagannathan, S.: Automated detection of serializability violations under weak consistency. In: 29th International Conference on Concurrency Theory, CONCUR. LIPIcs, vol. 118, pp. 41:1–41:18 (2018)

29. Nair, S.S., Petri, G., Shapiro, M.: Proving the safety of highly-available distributed objects. ESOP 2020. LNCS, vol. 12075, pp. 544–571. Springer, Cham (2020). https://doi.org/10.1007/978-3-030-44914-8_20

30. Najafzadeh, M., Gotsman, A., Yang, H., Ferreira, C., Shapiro, M.: The CISE tool: proving weakly-consistent applications correct. In: The 2nd Workshop on the Principles and Practice of Consistency for Distributed Data, pp. 2:1–2:3. ACM (2016)

31. Shapiro, M., Preguiça, N., Baquero, C., Zawirski, M.: Conflict-free replicated data types. In: Défago, X., Petit, F., Villain, V. (eds.) SSS 2011. LNCS, vol. 6976, pp. 386–400. Springer, Heidelberg (2011). https://doi.org/10.1007/978-3-642-24550-3_29

32. Sovran, Y., Power, R., Aguilera, M.K., Li, J.: Transactional storage for geo-replicated systems. In: The 23rd ACM Symposium on Operating System Principles 2011, SOSP, pp. 385–400. ACM (2011)

33. Zellag, K., Kemme, B.: How consistent is your cloud application? In: ACM Symposium on Cloud Computing, SOCC, p. 6 (2012)

34. Zeller, P.: Testing properties of weakly consistent programs with repliss. In: The 3rd International Workshop on Principles and Practice of Consistency for Distributed Data. pp. 3:1–3:5 (2017)

NetSheriff: Sheltering Software-Defined Networks from Rogue Switches

Paolo Laffranchini[1,2]($^{(\boxtimes)}$) (iD), João Miranda[1], Nuno Machado[3], Luís Rodrigues[1], Etienne Rivière[2], and Ramin Sadre[2]

[1] INESC-ID, IST, ULisboa, Portugal
{paolo.laffranchini,joaoshmiranda,ler}@tecnico.ulisboa.pt
[2] ICTEAM, UCLouvain, Belgium
{paolo.laffranchini,etienne.riviere,ramin.sadre}@uclouvain.be
[3] Teradata, San Diego, USA
nuno.machado@teradata.com

Abstract. We present NetSheriff – a system to automatically isolate faulty switches in Software-Defined Networks. To pinpoint the devices responsible for network misbehaviors, NetSheriff performs a differential analysis between expected paths of packets (obtained from a formal model of the network forwarding specification) and the corresponding observed paths taken by flows (obtained through network monitoring). We have built a prototype of NetSheriff supporting both OpenFlow and P4 Programmable devices and evaluated it on different network topologies, simulating real traffic behavior following recent data center studies. Our results show that NetSheriff is able to accurately identify the switch(es) responsible for different types of errors.

1 Introduction

The Software-Defined Networking (SDN) paradigm has emerged as an appealing and powerful approach for simplified network management [23,28] and troubleshooting [11,16], by allowing a logically centralized view of the network, through which network operators can apply fine-grained routing policies to network traffic. It provides a clear separation between the *data plane*, a collection of switches in charge of forwarding packets, and the *control plane*, which defines the actual network behavior by installing routing rules specifying how the packet-handling is performed at each switch. The controller entity communicates these rules using a standard API such as OpenFlow [24]. Recent advances

This work was supported by national funds through Fundação para a Ciência e a Tecnologia (FCT) via projects COSMOS (via the OE with ref. PTDC/EEI-COM/29271/2017 and via the "Programa Operacional Regional de Lisboa na sua componente FEDER" with ref. Lisboa-01-0145-FEDER-029271) and UIDB/50021/2020. Paolo Laffranchini was supported by a fellowship from the Erasmus Mundus Joint Doctorate in Distributed Computing (EMJD-DC) program funded by the European Commission (EACEA) (FPA 2012-0030).

C. Georgiou and R. Majumdar (Eds.): NETYS 2020, LNCS 12129, pp. 279–295, 2021.
https://doi.org/10.1007/978-3-030-67087-0_18

in programmable switching hardware also allow programming custom forwarding behavior and monitoring algorithms via a high-level language such as P4 [6].

The well-defined architecture of SDN along with a clear-cut semantics of the control protocol offers new capabilities for automatic testing and verification of different layers of the SDN stack [12]. A large body of recent work in SDN has been devoted to the development of such tools [1,7,10,15–17,25,26,29]. Despite these advances, debugging SDNs still remains a daunting task. In fact, errors such as forwarding loops, black holes, suboptimal routing, and access control violations can potentially stem from firmware and hardware bugs in the equipment[14,30] that prevent the forwarding devices from operating as expected. The root causes of these errors are not easily identifiable [13,21]. Verification tools are not adequate for this type of situations, because they are based on high-level models, derived from static configuration analysis, and rely on predictable models of the network to detect problems. Due to their nondeterministic nature, errors caused by hardware faults can only be detected at runtime. To help network operators identify misbehaving devices, tools such as OFRewind [29], ndb [10] and EverFlow [33] typically resort to instrumentation, event logging, and replay mechanisms. However, inspecting the event trace in order to isolate the faulty component(s) is usually time-consuming [8,26].

In this paper, we propose NetSheriff, a system that combines features from both verification and debugging tools to automatically isolate faulty switches in SDNs. NetSheriff achieves its goal by comparing the expected path of a flow (computed statically) against the actual route followed in the network (captured dynamically). Concretely, NetSheriff leverages its knowledge of the network model and exploits the forwarding rules issued by the controller to compute the path expected to be followed by the packets as they traverse the network. Then, at runtime, NetSheriff records the actual sequence of switches a packet traverses and performs an analysis between the expected and the observed paths to check whether they match. If a mismatch is detected, NetSheriff searches for the location where the two paths began to diverge and reports the faulty components responsible for the error. Since issues are characterized by peculiar differences between the expected and observed paths, NetSheriff is also able to indicate the nature of the error (e.g., suboptimal routing or black hole). This helps network operators diagnose and fix problems in a more timely manner. We evaluated our prototype of NetSheriff on networks with different topologies and facing different bugs. The results of our experiments show that NetSheriff is able to accurately and efficiently identify faulty switches.

NetSheriff is built upon existing tools and systems, namely VeriFlow [16], NetSight [11], VeriDP [32], and MAFIA [20]. Each of these systems have limitations when used in isolation. VeriFlow cannot detect run-time errors; NetSight and MAFIA can extract debug information from the switches but leave up to the network administrator the work of analyzing the logs to detect the root cause of a bug; VeriDP can only detect a limited number of bugs. The main contribution of our work is to show that, by combining these tools, it is possible to create a system that detects bugs in a more efficient and comprehensive manner than with previous work.

2   Related Work

Over the past few years a number of solutions have been proposed to improve the reliability of Software Defined Networks. In this section, we overview some of the prior efforts on this topic that are most related to our work.

An important line of research is represented by approaches whose goal is to capture and replay sequences of events in order to reproduce an issue. Interesting systems that follow in this category are NetSight [11], OFRewind [29], STS [26] and EverFlow [33]. OFRewind is a debugging tool that allows the record and replay of packets flowing in the network. A network operator can then reproduce the bug multiple times in an attempt to isolate the root cause. NetSight records the packet histories and offers an interactive debugger (*ndb* [10]) that eases the navigation through different states of the network in order to help network operators identify which sequences of events cause the incorrect behavior. Note that both NetSight and OFRewind offer the means to inspect a sequence of packets that lead to a failure, but do not provide any clue about the switch(es) that actually caused the error. As a consequence, network operators still have to progressively inspect these sequences in order to isolate the problem. Ever-Flow permits fine-grained recording of specific packets by marking them with a "debug" flag. EverFlow is then able to inject the recorded packet as an exact copy of the original and trace its behavior in the network. Although the granularity of the recording allows for precise identification of errors, operators still need to detect the issues before being able to trace the behavior of the probe in the network. STS [26], on the contrary, aims at reducing the effort spent on troubleshooting SDN control software by automatically eliminating from buggy traces the events that are not related to the error. This curated trace, denoted *minimal causal sequence*, contains the smallest amount of events responsible for triggering the bug. STS is, however, unable to detect errors outside the control software (for instance, hardware problems in switches).

Several tools focus on verifying the correctness of Software Defined Networks [3,7]. Some follow a *static approach*, usually prior to deployment, performing either symbolic execution of controller and switch implementations or thorough testing against a model of the network. For instance, NICE [7] combines model checking and symbolic execution to automatically discover errors in SDN controller programs, by generating a sequence of carefully crafted packets that triggers the flaw. VeriCon [3] verifies SDN programs at compilation time, validating their correctness not only for any admissible topology but also for all possible sequences of network events. VeriCon has the advantage of guaranteeing that a given SDN program is indeed free of errors. In turn, SOFT [17] is a tool designed to find bugs in OpenFlow implementations or interoperability problems among switches from different vendors. VeriFlow [16] is a real-time approach that intercepts commands issued by the controller and certifies, by building a static model of the forwarding policy, whether the forwarding rules installed do not violate network invariants. VeriFlow is able to detect flawed configurations in real-time but its outcome only highlights issues intrinsic to the policies, as it does not take into account the actual switch runtime behavior.

Conversely to static tools, systems that employ a *dynamic approach* perform verification of the forwarding behavior of the network at runtime. ATPG [30] frequently generates probe packets that verify reachability policies and performance health in the data plane, however, it does not check the trajectory of probes. In contrast, SDN Traceroute [1] is a tool to collect information about the path taken by probes forged with specific header fields that mimick real data packets in the network. However, it does not provide automatic checking for the whole network model, thus not relieving the user from the burden of checking the correctness of the network configuration. Monocle [25] takes similar concepts a step forward and aims at verifying whether the switch actions over the packets are consistent with the ones intended by the set of rules installed. It does so by periodically generating probes whose goal is to test the appropriate matching of all rules installed in each switch. However, the probes may be treated differently from real packets. PathletTracer [31] and CherryPick [27], instead, perform tagging of switch identifiers directly in the packets to be able to reconstruct their paths. However, they do not perform any verification that packets actually respect the routing policy specified from the controller. VeriDP [32] checks if the routing policies are being applied by having the switches tag packets with their identifier (and input/output port) as they flow. The path a packet takes is directly encoded in its header by means of a Bloom filter updated at each hop. When the packet leaves the network, a report is sent to a centralized collector which then verifies the path. However, it may suffer limitations in the presence of a switch hardware fault which prevents a packet from completing the processing pipeline. In this case, the report for the packet may never be generated and the problem might remain indefinitely in the network.

3   Motivation and Fault Scenarios

To motivate our work, we illustrate how hardware and/or software faults can cause forwarding errors in current networks. These bugs are common reasons for network failures according to a survey of network operators [30].

Inconsistent Routing. Due to limited hardware resources (and in particular memory), modern SDN switches typically split forwarding tables between hardware and software [14]. While hardware innovations will eventually enable larger memory capacity, there still exists a fundamental trade-off between the size of the rules table, power consumption, and costs. A hybrid hardware-software implementation of forwarding tables requires, however, the usage of rule eviction policies which may fail to respect dependencies among multiple forwarding rules [14]. Furthermore, some implementations lack features such as rule priority ordering [19,32]. All of these issues may cause a switch to handle a packet using an incorrect forwarding rule, thus causing a mismatch between the routing policy known by the controller and its actual execution in the network.

Connectivity Loss. The process of reliably updating the network data plane is challenging in SDN [18]. Switches might fail in correctly installing or updating forwarding rules [25], causing a mismatch between the routing behavior and the controller's policy. This issue typically stems from an incorrect execution of the acknowledgment protocol between the switch and the controller [19, 32]. An overloaded switch might even indefinitely delay the execution of controller commands [9]. These problems could inevitable cause packet losses or reachability issues, hence degrading performance and the overall quality of service.

4 NetSheriff

NetSheriff is a system that automatically detects incorrect traffic paths and pinpoints the network devices responsible for the network misconfiguration. NetSheriff relies on features from model checking to compute the expected path of a packet, as well as tracing mechanisms to efficiently obtain the respective observed path. NetSheriff supports two different tracing mechanisms. The first, only requiring standard SDN switches, is based on an extension of NetSight [11] and relies on the online generation of *postcards*. The second is designed to work with programmable switches and uses the MAFIA [20] interface to implement a robust P4-based variant of VeriDP [32]. While the first implementation is more general, the second is able to trace paths more efficiently.

NetSheriff comprises four components: (1) the *seer*, (2) the *instrumenter* proxies, (3) the *collector*, and (4) the *checker*. These components, depicted in Fig. 1, are described in the following paragraphs.

Seer. The *seer* component in NetSheriff is responsible for computing in real-time the expected path of a packet. The *seer* is built upon VeriFlow [16], which models the network's behavior as a set of *forwarding graphs*. A forwarding graph is a representation of how packets belonging to the same *equivalence class* should traverse the network. Any two packets $p1$ and $p2$ are said to belong the same equivalence class (EC) if and only if, for any network device R, the forwarding action at R is identical for $p1$ and $p2$. Forwarding graphs indicate, therefore, how the traffic is expected to flow across the network. Vertices in a forwarding graph represent switches, while edges model network links and indicate forwarding decisions between pairs of switches. To maintain the network model consistent, VeriFlow intercepts OpenFlow messages exchanged between the controller and the switches and updates forwarding graphs according to the newly installed rules. Results are then reported to the NetSheriff checker, which will store them to perform the differential analysis between expected and observed packet flows.

Instrumenter. After being processed by the seer, OpenFlow messages are then intercepted by the *instrumenter*. The role of the instrumenter is to setup actions in the switches that allow NetSheriff to trace the actual path followed by packets of a given flow. These actions force switches to create, in certain conditions, a *postcard* for an incoming packet that matches an installed rule. These postcards are forwarded to the NetSheriff's collector for analysis. Currently, NetSheriff supports two different technologies to generate postcards when packets of a target flow are forwarded by a given switch. The first is based on NetSight [11] and works with any SDN compliant switch. The second uses the MAFIA [20] interface and only works with programmable switches.

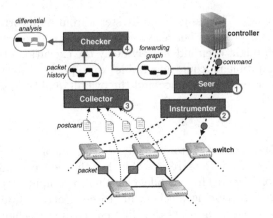

Fig. 1. Overview of NetSheriff building blocks

Collector. The collector component consists of a server (centralized or distributed) that receives the postcards sent from the switches and reorganizes them in order to create multiple distinct collections called *packet histories* [11]. The collector can run on the same host as the SDN controller, assuming it is capable to handle the additional load of processing packet histories. A packet history corresponds to the set of all postcards generated by a packet while traversing the network. The packet history allows to (1) reconstruct the path taken by a given packet, and (2) understand which switches performed any header modifications. The propagation of postcards can be performed in two different modes: *in-band* or *out-of-band*. With the former, postcards share the same network used by normal traffic and therefore consume part of the available bandwidth; with the latter postcards are instead routed via dedicated links that connect each switch to the collector, avoiding bandwidth reservation at the expense of additional hardware dedicated to this purpose.

Checker. The checker component is responsible for comparing the expected and observed graphs of packets and signaling unexpected forwarding decisions, pinpointing the switch that misbehaved. To this end, the checker leverages both the forwarding graphs generated by the seer and the packet histories assembled by the collector to perform a differential analysis. The differential analysis consists in projecting the expected path of a packet (given by the forwarding graph) against its actual path (indicated by the packet history) and in checking for potential divergences. If the projection of the two paths yields a perfect match, then the packet was correctly forwarded across the network and NetSheriff does not report any anomaly. On the other hand, when a mismatch is detected NetSheriff reports the issue indicating the switch where the divergence occurred. This switch is then deemed as responsible for the fault. As an example, consider the scenario in Fig. 2, which depicts a network of five switches: $A, B, C, D,$ and E and assume that a given packet is expected to be routed from A to E via $A \rightarrow D \rightarrow E$ (Fig. 2b). If the actual trajectory of the packet ends to

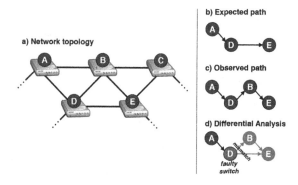

Fig. 2. Differential analysis performed by NetSheriff's checker.

be $A \rightarrow D \rightarrow B \rightarrow E$ (Fig. 2c), the checker would be able to notice the mismatch while performing the differential analysis between the two paths and, as a result, report an error identifying switch D as the source of the problem.

Depending upon the pattern of the mismatch in the path projection, NetSheriff is able to report additional information regarding the type of the error, *e.g.,* a black hole or suboptimal routing. Section 5 further details the algorithm allowing to infer the type of error according to the projection. NetSheriff can also handle scenarios where there are multiple correct paths for a given flow (*e.g.,* when using load balancing); however, in the current implementation, we only assume that a single correct path exists. An extension to cover the use of multiple paths is planned for future work.

5   Implementation

We have built NetSheriff's by leveraging upon the features provided by previous works: VeriFlow [16], NetSight [11], VeriDP [32], and MAFIA [20]. In particular, the seer component is built upon VeriFlow, adding the necessary code to communicate the computed graphs to NetSheriff. One version of the instrumenter is based on NetSight. The other is a variant of VeriDP [32] that uses MAFIA [20][1]. The NetSheriff collector and checker are built on top of NetSight's server. Since both VeriFlow and NetSight have been implemented by introducing a proxy layer between the SDN controller and the switches, our implementation follows this approach and connects the two proxies together. Forwarding rules issued by the controller are thus first intercepted by VeriFlow, which uses them to compute the expected graphs that will then be notified to NetSheriff. Then, the rules are relayed to the instrumenter, that uses NetSight or MAFIA to create the actions required to generate postcards. Only the packet headers are sent to the collector and the payload is stripped. In the current implementation, we

---

[1] Hybrid setups can also be supported by instrumenting P4 compliant switches using MAFIA code, whereas the remaining switches would be configured using NetSight.

install postcard generation rules to track all flows. Clearly, the system is flexible to allow fine-grained monitoring of a selection of flows and reducing network overheads. Postcards generated by switches are sent to the collector which will perform the differential analysis and identify possible forwarding mismatches. In the following, we describe the implementation of these steps.

5.1   NetSight-Based Instrumentation

The first implementation of the instrumenter is an extension of NetSight's *Flow Table State Recorder* [11] and has the goal of enabling the capture of the information required to reconstruct the path that packets follow at runtime. To achieve this, it intercepts forwarding rule modifications sent to the switches and augments them with two new actions. The first action instructs the switch to create a *postcard* for any incoming packet that matches the newly installed rule. The postcard consists of a copy of the original packet extended to carry additional information, namely the identity of the switch, an identifier indicating the version of the switch's flow table, and the input port and then truncated to the minimum network packet size. The second action, in turn, instructs the switch to forward the postcard to the NetSheriff's collector. In this case, postcards are created for every packet of the flow being analyzed, and at every switch. The advantage of this implementation is that it works with any SDN compliant switch, although with a non-negligible signaling overhead (discussed in the evaluation).

5.2   MAFIA-Based Instrumentation

The second implementation of the instrumenter uses the MAFIA [20] interface to implement a robust variant of VeriDP [32]. This method significantly reduces the number of postcards generated, but only works with programmable switches. This implementation requires switches to have the ability to inspect and change packet fields on the fly, something that is supported by P4 [6] compliant switches.

In this implementation, the instrumenter instructs the ingress switch to *sample* packets of the flow. A fraction of these packets are tagged to be processed by other switches in a horizon that is set to a value from 1 to the maximum path length (different sampled packets use different horizons). Packets that have been tagged will be processed by other switches in their path until the horizon is reached. When the horizon is reached, a postcard is generated and sent to the collector. This simple mechanism allows to implement a simplified version of traceroute in the SDN context [1], without requiring much involvement from the SDN controller and generating way less probing traffic.

In order to setup the action in each switch, we leverage the MAFIA [20] language, that has been designed to simplify the development of monitoring solutions for SDN networks. MAFIA, that stands for Measurements As FIrst-class Artifacts, defines a set of reusable primitive building blocks that can be composed to express measurement tasks in a concise way. MAFIA code associated with the NetSheriff instrumentation described above is presented in Figs. 3 and 4. It consists of a brief state declaration and the operations to be executed

```
1    // Code executed at ingress switch
2    flowid = key(ip.src,ip.dest,tcp.src,tcp.dest,ip.proto)
3    // Current horizon values
4    horizons = HashMap(key=flowid, size=1024, type=Counter(width=4));
5    // Per-flow horizon values. Configured by the controller
6    horizons_max = HashMap(key=flowid, size=1024, type=Counter(width=4));
7
8    pkts
9       ≫ tag(pkt.mafia.monitor, 0x1)
10      ≫ match(horizons.read() == horizons_max.read()) ≫ horizons.reset()
11      ≫ horizons.set(horizons.read() + 1)
12      ≫ tag(pkt.mafia.horizon, horizons.read()) )
```

Fig. 3. MAFIA code for ingress switches.

```
1    // Code executed at all switches (including the ingress)
2    location = key(pkt.input_port, switch.id, pkt.output_port)
3    trajectory = BloomFilter(alg="membership", nhash=4, key=location, size=16);
4    horizon = Counter(width=4);
5
6    pkts
7       ≫ match(pkt.mafia.monitor == 0x1)
8       ≫
9            (
10               ≫ trajectory.insert()
11               ≫ tag(pkt.mafia.path_bf, pkt.mafia.path_bf | trajectory.read()))
12               ≫ trajectory.reset() )
13           +
14         ( ≫ horizon.set(pkt.mafia.horizon − 1)
15               ≫ tag(pkt.mafia.horizon, horizon.read())
16               ≫ match(pkt.mafia.horizon == 0) ≫ duplicate(reports) )
17     reports
18        ≫ collect()
```

Fig. 4. MAFIA code to generate the path Bloom filter.

for each incoming packet. The packets that need to be traced are tagged with two control fields: a Bloom filter that captures the path followed by the packet and a *horizon* field that indicates when a postcard needs to be generated.

Figure 3 depicts the relevant code that runs at the ingress switch. Two hashmaps indexed by the flow 5-tuple (Lines 4 and 6) are used as persistent state about the flow horizons. The former will store the latest value used while the latter will hold its max value as configured by the controller (*e.g.*, the expected path length). The switch sets the *monitor* flag to 1 and sets the *horizon* counter to a value in the interval $[1, path\_length]$. The current horizon value is incremented for each packet (Line 11). Each packet is tagged, therefore, with a different horizon in a round-robin manner.

Figure 4 depicts the relevant code to generate the Bloom filter representation of the packet's path. It is executed at all switches, including the ingresses. Persistent state includes a Bloom filter (Line 3) which is constructed on a per-packet basis and a counter (Line 4) to handle the packet's horizon. Only packets that have the *monitor* flag set to 1 are processed (Line 7), by executing the following sequence of actions: first, the trajectory Bloom filter is computed using the switch identifier and the current packet's input and (expected) output port(Line 10); then, its value written back in the packet into the *path_bf* field (Line 11) and finally reset (locally). Afterwards, the *horizon* counter is decremented (Line 14) and, if the horizon has reached the value 0, a postcard is generated (Line 16). Postcards are finally sent to a pre-configured collector (Lines 17–18).

5.3 Postcard Consolidation and Construction of $\mathcal{G}_O$

NetSheriff works by comparing a graph $\mathcal{G}_E$ representing its expected path $\mathcal{P}_E$ and the graph $\mathcal{G}_O$ representing its observed path $\mathcal{P}_O$. The observed path is constructed by consolidating multiple postcards associated with multiple individual packets. Consolidation is mandatory in the MAFIA-based version of NetSheriff because postcards are generated for different packets at different points in the path (depending on the horizon parameter, as described above). Thus multiple postcards need to be combined to create a complete observed path. However, even with the NetSight implementation postcards can be lost in the network and by consolidating postcards generated by multiple individual packets it is possible to obtain a more reliable observation of the actual path.

Postcard consolidation is performed by the collector as follows. First, postcards produced by the MAFIA instrumentation are *unfolded* by creating a separate postcard for every switch included in the Bloom filter, *as if* an individual postcard has been sent by each of these switches. This allows to process MAFIA postcards in the same way as NetSight postcards. Then, postcards associated with the same packet are grouped. The sets of postcards from the same packet are then fed to the algorithm that constructs the observed path. The graph $\mathcal{G}_O$ representing the observed path $\mathcal{P}_O$ is constructed as follows. Let v_i and v_j be two adjacent vertices of the physical network graph (i.e., they represent switches that are directly connected to each other). If in the set of consolidated postcards there is a postcard from v_i *and* one from v_j, such that both postcards belong to the same packet, then both v_i, v_j, and the edge between these vertices are added to $\mathcal{G}_O$. This process is performed for all adjacent vertices.

5.4 Differential Analysis

Depending upon the divergences between the expected and the observed paths, NetSheriff categorizes different forwarding errors. Routing flaws appear as peculiar patterns in the observed graphs when compared to the expected one. Consider, for a packet of a given EC, a graph $\mathcal{G}_E$ representing its expected path $\mathcal{P}_E$ and the graph $\mathcal{G}_O$ representing its observed path $\mathcal{P}_O$. We can distinguish four macro-situations:

1. $\mathcal{G}_E \equiv \mathcal{G}_O$: if the expected and observed graphs match, then the packet traversed the network topology correctly and no error is reported.
2. $\mathcal{G}_E \supset \mathcal{G}_O$: if the observed path is a subgraph of the expected, then packets have been incorrectly dropped at some switch. This typically captures the existence of a black hole in the network.

3. $\mathcal{G}_E \subset \mathcal{G}_O$: if the expected path is a subgraph of the observed, then a switch might have forwarded a packet to a switch it was not expected to. This error may cause an access control violation as packets may reach a protected network segment and/or network congestion since switch and link resources may be used by unexpected flows.

4. $\mathcal{G}_E \not\equiv \mathcal{G}_O$: if the observed path is not equivalent to the expected, meaning that they diverge in some vertex, then the packet traversed the network via switches it was not supposed to use. The packet might however reach its destination, although not along the path that was defined by the rules defined by the controller. This may cause suboptimal routing in the network, possibly affecting its overall performance and efficacy.

6   Evaluation

We evaluated NetSheriff's prototype in terms of its efficacy in identifying faulty switches and differentiate multiple types of errors. The experiments were performed on an Intel i7-720QM with 8GB RAM DDR3, 250 GB SSD and Ubuntu 14.04, using Mininet [22]. To evaluate NetSheriff's efficiency in detecting errors, we randomly injected different faults in switches.

We evaluate the impact of NetSheriff's instrumentation overhead, *i.e.,* how long it takes to compute expected paths and configure the switches tables and actions, in terms of the delay to setup a TCP connection. Finally, we measure the efficiency at which NetSheriff is able to process packet histories to detect forwarding errors. Unless otherwise specified, we employ simple linear topologies for the microbenchmarks since the number of hops in a path is the only factor affecting the experiments. Different topologies variate features such as the number of back-up paths or the average network diameter, but NetSheriff mechanisms are independent of these characteristics.

6.1   Proxy Overhead

When a new path is setup, NetSheriff requires SDN commands to be intercepted by the seer and by the instrumenter, such that the expected graph is extracted and the actions to generate postcards are installed at the switches. In the case of the MAFIA implementation, postcard generation code is embedded in the P4 MAFIA program loaded on the switch but requires initial state (*e.g.,* flow horizons) to be set up by the measurement controller. We measure the delay of performing these steps by establishing a TCP connection between two hosts and monitoring the TCP handshaking phase. Figure 5 depicts the average overhead across ten runs (variance negligible) for the various approaches. As it can be seen, the overhead increases with the number of switches. This happens because, in the current prototype, the deployment of the required rules at each individual switch in the path is done sequentially.

Thus, the longer the path, the larger the impact of both a non-instrumented system and of a system using NetSheriff during routing policy changes (*e.g.,* new

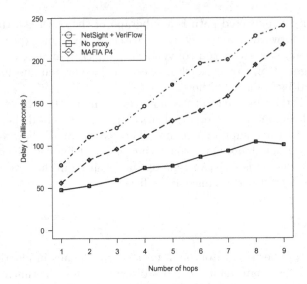

Fig. 5. The impact of NetSight and NetSheriff proxies on TCP handshaking. Both include VeriFlow's graph computation times.

flow setup or steering), because both forwarding graph and switch configuration need to be updated. Note that even in a system without instrumentation, the setup of a path also grows proportionally with the number of hops. In the figure, it is possible to see that the NetSight implementation is slower than the MAFIA implementation, because with NetSight the postcard generation actions are generated and deployed on the fly while the corresponding code is pre-installed in the MAFIA implementation.

6.2 Performance of the Differential Analysis

To evaluate the performance of NetSheriff while processing the postcards it receives, we conducted various experiments recording the time it takes to fully check the history of a packet. We vary the path length up to a maximum of ten switches, which is a fair upper bound for the average diameter of most modern networks, with topologies that can even be optimized down to a diameter of 2–3 [5]. Figure 6 shows the CDF of the processing latency of one million packets injected into the network. The history processing time stays below 6 microseconds for paths up to 5 hops, while it may require up to 10 and 15 microseconds as the length increases to 7 and 10 switches, respectively. For fat trees topologies, which experience an average path length less than 5 hops, hence, the verification throughput stays between $14 \cdot 10^6$ and $16 \cdot 10^6$ histories per second in 90% of the cases. However, as our implementation is still non-optimized and single-threaded, we expect a higher verification throughput in the future.

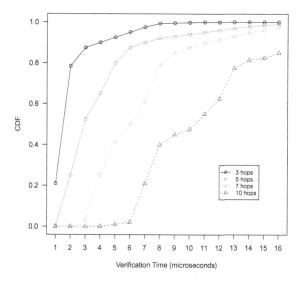

Fig. 6. CDF of the history processing delay in NetSheriff.

6.3   Error Identification

We have run an extensive evaluation of the tool, by manually injecting several types of faults in different configurations of fat-tree network topologies [2], commonly adopted in data centers. Figure 7 illustrates the forwarding errors generated by the faults (using a simplified network view). The faults were injected by modifying directly the forwarding tables in the switches. In all cases, NetSheriff was able to pinpoint the faulty switch responsible for the errors.

Table 1 shows the error detection latency for the various bugs. To detect a routing error, in a NetSight-based instrumentation, we need to wait for a single packet to traverse its path consisting of N hops (NT_d) and for the corresponding postcards to arrive at the collector (T_c). The MAFIA-based instrumentation adds an additional $N\delta$ to the latency, because it needs to collect postcards from N packets, until a complete path is formed (each packet generates a postcard at a different hop). The latency for detecting partial and total drops is dominated by a timeout (which can be configured), since postcard generation is interrupted after the misbehaving hop. If the network gets congested due to a spike in traffic, postcards might get delayed and received after the timeout is expired, causing false positives; this can be easily solved by raising an alarm after multiple, subsequent packet histories indicate the presence of a forwarding error.

6.4   Overhead

Figure 8 shows the traffic increase due to the postcard generation. We use the same metric as in the original NetSight paper [11]. The plot shows the traffic increase in percentage for the two different versions of NetSheriff, namely the

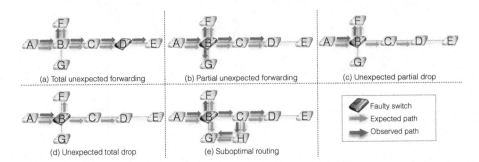

Fig. 7. Forwarding bugs detected by NetSheriff. Green arrows depict the expected paths; red arrows the faulty observed paths. (Color figure online)

Table 1. Error detection latency (N: correct path length; T_d: single hop latency; δ: inter-packet arrival time; T_c: time for a postcard to reach the collector).

Bug	NetSheriff	
	NetSight-based	Mafia-based
Routing errors	$N T_d + T_c$	$N\delta + N T_d + T_c$
Partial/Total drop	$N T_d + T_c + Timeout$	$N\delta + N T_d + T_c + Timeout$

NetSight based implementation (lines tagged as "NS") and the MAFIA based implementation (lines tagged as "M"). Naturally, the overhead is a function of the average packet size in the network and the size of the postcard. Both implementations generate postcards that are truncated to the minimum network packet size, which in this case is 64 Bytes. We have also considered three different average network packet sizes, namely 1,031 Bytes, as reported in the NetSight paper [11], 850 Bytes, a value observed in datacenters [4], and a network with a smaller average packet size of 576 Bytes. In the x-axis we varied the number of hops of the flow path. As expected, with the NetSight implementation, traffic increase is larger for paths with larger number of hops, given that a postcard is generated at every hop for every packet. Conversely, in the MAFIA implementation, a single postcard is generated for each data packet at deterministic points in the path, as deep as the current horizon value for the flow. Thus, the overhead of the MAFIA implementation is below 12%, even in networks with a small average packet size. The overhead for the NetSight implementation is 31% for a network with average packet size of 1,031 Bytes and paths of 5 hops (as detailed by Handigol *et al.* [11]), but can be substantially larger in networks with smaller average packet size.

Table 2 shows the additional switch resources consumed by NetSheriff. If NetSight-based, instrumenting the switch to generate the postcards requires 4 additional OpenFlow actions (3 tagging, 1 sampling); we couldn't characterized the amount of stages required because it varies between OpenFlow implementations. If MAFIA-based, the resource overhead consists of 4 packet manipulations

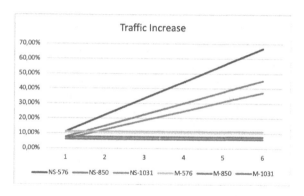

Fig. 8. Traffic increase due to postcards.

Table 2. NetSheriff processing overhead.

Overhead	NetSheriff	
	NetSight-based	MAFIA-based
Stateful computations	4 OpenFlow actions	4 pkt manipulations + 14 mem. read/write
Pipeline stages	NA	7

actions (same as OpenFlow), plus 14 stateful memory read/write associated to the generation of the path bloom filter and horizon updating. These actions are spread across 7 stages of the P4 switch pipeline. The resource overhead for the MAFIA case is low given its capability to drastically reduce postcard traffic.

7 Conclusions

We proposed and evaluated NetSheriff, an automatic debugging tool for SDN. NetSheriff combines formal validation techniques and packet recording mechanisms with the goal of monitoring the consistency between the forwarding behavior and the policies defined by the SDN controller. NetSheriff works with standard SDN switches and with programmable switches, offering different coverage/efficiency trade-offs. We experimentally evaluated NetSheriff with different types of errors, showing that NetSheriff was able to pinpoint the faulty switch and categorize the errors.

Acknowledgments. We thank the anonymous reviewers and Elad Schiller for their constructive feedback, that allowed us to improve this paper.

References

1. Agarwal, K., Rozner, E., Dixon, C., Carter, J.: SDN traceroute: tracing sdn forwarding without changing network behavior. In: HotSDN (2014)

2. Al-Fares, M., Loukissas, A., Vahdat, A.: A scalable, commodity data center network architecture. In: SIGCOMM (2008)
3. Ball, T., et al.: Vericon: towards verifying controller programs in software-defined networks. In: SIGPLAN Not (2014)
4. Benson, T., Anand, A., Akella, A., Zhang, M.: Understanding data center traffic characteristics. SIGCOMM Comput. Commun. Rev. **40**(1), 92–99 (2010)
5. Besta, M., Hoefler, T.: Slim fly: a cost effective low-diameter network topology. In: SC 2014: Proceedings of the International Conference for High Performance Computing, Networking, Storage and Analysis (2014)
6. Bosshart, P., et al.: P4: programming protocol-independent packet processors. SIGCOMM Comput. Commun. Rev. **44**(3), 87–95 (2014)
7. Canini, M., Venzano, D., Perešíni, P., Kostić, D., Rexford, J.: A nice way to test openflow applications. In: NSDI (2012)
8. Cisco Systems Inc.: Spanning tree protocol problems and related design considerations. http://www.cisco.com/c/en/us/support/docs/lan-switching/spanning-tree-protocol/10556-16.html (2005)
9. Curtis, A.R., Mogul, J.C., Tourrilhes, J., Yalagandula, P., Sharma, P., Banerjee, S.: DevoFlow: scaling flow management for high-performance networks. In: SIGCOMM (2011)
10. Handigol, N., Heller, B., Jeyakumar, V., Maziéres, D., McKeown, N.: Where is the debugger for my software-defined network? In: HotSDN (2012)
11. Handigol, N., Heller, B., Jeyakumar, V., Mazières, D., McKeown, N.: I know what your packet did last hop: using packet histories to troubleshoot networks. In: NSDI (2014)
12. Heller, B., et al.: Leveraging SDN layering to systematically troubleshoot networks. In: HotSDN (2013)
13. Hendriks, L., Schmidt, R., Sadre, R., Bezerra, J., Pras, A.: Assessing the quality of flow measurements from openflow devices. In: TMA (2016)
14. Katta, N., Alipourfard, O., Rexford, J., Walker, D.: Cacheflow: dependency-aware rule-caching for software-defined networks. In: SOSR (2016)
15. Kazemian, P., Chang, M., Zeng, H., Varghese, G., McKeown, N., Whyte, S.: Real time network policy checking using header space analysis. In: NSDI (2012)
16. Khurshid, A., Zhou, W., Caesar, M., Godfrey, P.B.: VeriFlow: verifying network-wide invariants in real time. In: HotSDN (2012)
17. Kuzniar, M., Peresini, P., Canini, M., Venzano, D., Kostic, D.: A soft way for openflow switch interoperability testing. In: CoNEXT (2012)
18. Kuzniar, M., Peresini, P., Kostić, D.: Providing reliable fib update acknowledgments in SDN. In: CoNEXT (2014)
19. Kuźniar, M., Perešíni, P., Kostić, D.: What you need to know about SDN flow tables. In: PAM (2015)
20. Laffranchini, P., Rodrigues, L., Canini, M., Krishnamurthy, B.: Measurements as first-class artifacts. In: IEEE InfoCom (2019)
21. di Lallo, R., Gradillo, M., Lospoto, G., Pisa, C., Rimondini, M.: On the practical applicability of SDN research. In: NOMS (2016)
22. Lantz, B., Heller, B., McKeown, N.: A network in a laptop: rapid prototyping for software-defined networks. In: HotNets IX (2010)
23. McKeown, N.: How SDN will shape networking, October 2011. https://www.youtube.com/watch?v=c9-K5O_qYgA
24. McKeown, N., et al.: OpenFlow enabling innovation in campus networks. SIGCOMM Comput. Commun. Rev. **38**(2), 69–74 (2008)

25. Perešíni, P., Kuźniar, M., Kostić, D.: Monocle: dynamic, fine-grained data plane monitoring. In: CoNEXT (2015)
26. Scott, C., et al.: Troubleshooting blackbox SDN control software with minimal causal sequences. In: SIGCOMM (2014)
27. Tammana, P., Agarwal, R., Lee, M.: CherryPick: tracing packet trajectory in software-defined datacenter networks. In: SOSR (2015)
28. Wang, R., Butnariu, D., Rexford, J.: Openflow-based server load balancing gone wild. In: Hot-ICE2011 (2011)
29. Wundsam, A., Levin, D., Seetharaman, S., Feldmann, A.: OFRewind: enabling record and replay troubleshooting for networks. In: ATC (2011)
30. Zeng, H., Kazemian, P., Varghese, G., McKeown, N.: Automatic test packet generation. In: CoNEXT (2012)
31. Zhang, H., Lumezanu, C., Rhee, J., Arora, N., Xu, Q., Jiang, G.: Enabling layer 2 pathlet tracing through context encoding in software-defined networking. In: HotSDN (2014)
32. Zhang, P., et al.: Mind the gap: monitoring the control-data plane consistency in software defined networks. In: CoNEXT (2016)
33. Zhu, Y., et al.: Packet-level telemetry in large datacenter networks. In: SIGCOMM (2015)

Self-stabilizing Uniform Reliable Broadcast

Oskar Lundström[1], Michel Raynal[2], and Elad M. Schiller[1(✉)]

[1] Chalmers University Technology, Gothenburg, Sweden
osklunds@student.chalmers.se, elad@chalmers.se
[2] Institut Universitaire de France IRISA, Rennes, France
michel.raynal@irisa.fr

Abstract. We study a well-known communication abstraction called *Uniform Reliable Broadcast* (URB). URB is central in the design and implementation of fault-tolerant distributed systems, as many non-trivial fault-tolerant distributed applications require communication with provable guarantees on message deliveries. Our study focuses on fault-tolerant implementations for time-free message-passing systems that are prone to node-failures. Moreover, we aim at the design of an even more robust communication abstraction. We do so through the lenses of *self-stabilization*—a very strong notion of fault-tolerance. In addition to node and communication failures, self-stabilizing algorithms can recover after the occurrence of *arbitrary transient faults*; these faults represent any violation of the assumptions according to which the system was designed to operate (as long as the algorithm code stays intact). We propose the first self-stabilizing URB algorithm for asynchronous (time-free) message-passing systems that are prone to node-failures. The algorithm recovers within $\mathcal{O}(\mathsf{bufferUnitSize})$ (in terms of asynchronous cycles) from transient faults, where bufferUnitSize is a predefined constant. Also, the communication costs are similar to the ones of the non-self-stabilizing URB. The main differences are that our proposal considers repeated gossiping of $\mathcal{O}(1)$ bits messages and deals with bounded space (which is a prerequisite for self-stabilization). Moreover, each node stores up to $\mathsf{bufferUnitSize} \cdot n$ records of size $\mathcal{O}(\nu + n \log n)$ bits, where n is the number of nodes and ν is the number of bits needed to encode a single URB instance.

1 Introduction

We propose a self-stabilizing implementation of a communication abstraction called *Uniform Reliable Broadcast* (URB) for time-free message-passing systems whose nodes may fail-stop.

Context and Motivation. Fault-tolerant distributed systems are known to be hard to design and verify. Such complex challenges can be facilitated by high-level communication primitives. These high-level primitives can be based on low-level ones, such as the one that allows nodes to send a message to only one other node at a time. When an algorithm wishes to broadcast message m

© Springer Nature Switzerland AG 2021
C. Georgiou and R. Majumdar (Eds.): NETYS 2020, LNCS 12129, pp. 296–313, 2021.
https://doi.org/10.1007/978-3-030-67087-0_19

to all nodes, it can send m individually to every other node. Note that if the sender fails during this broadcast, it can be the case that only some of the nodes receive m. Even in the presence of network-level support for broadcasting or multicasting, failures can cause similar inconsistencies. To the end of simplifying the design of fault-tolerant distributed algorithms, such inconsistencies need to be avoided.

There are many examples that show how reliable broadcasts significantly simplify the development of fault-tolerant distributed systems, *e.g.*, State Machine Replication [24,30], Atomic Commitment [27], Virtual Synchrony [6] and Set-Constrained Delivery Broadcast [23], to name a few. The weakest variance, named *Reliable Broadcast* (RB), lets all non-failing nodes agree on the set of delivered messages. Stronger RB variants specify additional requirements on the delivery order. Such requirements can simplify the design of fault-tolerant distributed consensus, which allows reaching, despite failures, a common decision based on distributed inputs. Consensus algorithms and RB are closely related problems [22,28], which have been studied for more than three decades.

Task Description. *Uniform Reliable Broadcast* (URB) is a variance of the reliable broadcast problem, which requires that if a node (faulty or not) delivers a message, then all non-failing nodes also deliver this message [22]. The task specifications consider an operation for URB broadcasting of message m and an event of URB delivery of message m. The requirements include URB-validity, *i.e.*, there is no spontaneous creation or alteration of URB messages, URB-integrity, *i.e.*, there is no duplication of URB messages, as well as URB-termination, *i.e.*, if the broadcasting node is non-faulty, or if at least one receiver URB-delivers a message, then all non-failing nodes URB-deliver that message. Note that the URB-termination property considers both faulty and non-faulty receivers. This is the reason why this type of reliable broadcast is named *uniform*. This work considers a URB implementation that is *quiescent* in the sense that every URB operation incurs a finite number of messages. Moreover, our implementation uses a bounded amount of local memory.

Fault Model. We consider a time-free (a.k.a asynchronous) message-passing system that has no guarantees on the communication delay, no notion of global clocks nor does the algorithm can explicitly access the local clock (or timeout mechanisms). Our fault model includes (*i*) detectable fail-stop failures of nodes, and (*ii*) communication failures, such as packet omission, duplication, and reordering. In addition, to the failures captured in our model, we also aim to recover from *arbitrary transient faults*, *i.e.*, any temporary violation of assumptions according to which the system and network were designed to operate, *e.g.*, the corruption of control variables, such as the program counter, packet payload, and operation indices, which are responsible for the correct operation of the studied system. Since the occurrence of these failures can be arbitrarily combined, we assume that these transient faults can alter the system state in unpredictable ways. In particular, when modeling the system, we assume that these violations bring the system to an arbitrary state from which a *self-stabilizing system* should recover.

Related Work. The studied problem can be traced back to Hadzilacos and Toueg [22] who consider asynchronous message-passing systems, where nodes may crash. They solved a number of variants to the studied problem with respect to the delivery order, *e.g.*, FIFO (first in, first out), CO (causal order), and TO (total order). They also showed that TO-URB and consensus have the same computability power in the context above. We offer the basic version of URB (with a FIFO extension in the technical report [26]). To the end of satisfying the quiescent property, we consider a more advanced model, see the remark in [28, Section 4.2.1]. For a detailed presentation of existing non-self-stabilizing URB solutions and their applications, we refer the reader to [1,28] and our summary in Sect. 3. We follow the design criteria of self-stabilization, which was proposed by Dijkstra [10] and detailed in [4,11]. Delaët *et al.* [9] present a self-stabilizing algorithm for propagation of information with feedback (PIF) that can be the basis for implementing a self-stabilizing URB. However, Delaët *et al.* do not consider node failures [9, Section 6]. To the best of our knowledge, there is no self-stabilizing algorithm that solves the studied problem for the studied fault-model. Moreover, set-constraint delivery (SCD) broadcast [28] is an extension to uniform reliable broadcast with FIFO message delivery. The set of applications to SCD broadcast includes snapshot objects and distributed shared counters. We note the existence of self-stabilizing SCD broadcast algorithm and these two application [25], which serve as alternative manners for implementing self-stabilizing snapshot objects [21] and vector-clocks [29]. Furthermore, there are earlier proposals for self-stabilizing high-level communication abstractions [18–20].

Contributions. We present an important module for dependable distributed systems: a self-stabilizing algorithm for Uniform Reliable Broadcast (URB) for time-free message-passing systems that are prone to node failures. To the best of our knowledge, we are the first to provide a broad fault model that includes detectable fail-stop failures, communication failures, such as packet omission, duplication, and reordering as well as arbitrary transient faults. The latter can model any violation of the assumptions according to which the system was designed to operate (as long as the algorithm code stays intact).

The stabilization time of the proposed solution is in $\mathcal{O}(\mathsf{bufferUnitSize})$ (in terms of asynchronous cycles), where $\mathsf{bufferUnitSize}$ is a predefined constant. Our solution uses only a bounded amount of space, which is a prerequisite for self-stabilization. Specifically, each node needs to store up to $\mathsf{bufferUnitSize} \cdot n$ records and each record is of size $\mathcal{O}(\nu + n \log n)$ bits, where n is the number of nodes in the system and ν is the number of bits needed to encode a single URB instance. Moreover, the communication costs of our algorithm are similar to the ones of the non-self-stabilizing state-of-the-art. The main difference is that our proposal considers repeated gossiping of $\mathcal{O}(1)$ bits messages. Our solution uses a novel self-stabilizing deterministic flow control scheme that itself deserves an independent interest when designing, for example, transport layer protocols. We also show a self-stabilizing extension for FIFO order delivery that, due to the page limit, appears in the technical report version of this work [26] along with more proof details, such as the closure proof.

2   System Settings

We consider a time-free message-passing system that has no guarantees on the communication delay. Moreover, there is no notion of global (or universal) clocks and the algorithm cannot explicitly access the local clock (or timeout mechanisms). The system consists of a set, $\mathcal{P}$, of n fail-prone nodes (or processors) with unique identifiers. Any pair of nodes $p_i, p_j \in \mathcal{P}$ have access to a bidirectional communication channel, $channel_{j,i}$, that, at any time, has at most channelCapacity $\in \mathbb{N}$ packets on transit from p_j to p_i (this assumption is due to a well-known impossibility [11, Chapter 3.2]). Note that we do not require the communication channels to be reliable [14,15].

Our analysis considers the *interleaving model* [11], in which the node's program is a sequence of *(atomic) steps*. Each step starts with an internal computation and finishes with a single communication operation, *i.e.*, a message *send* or *receive*. The *state*, s_i, of node $p_i \in \mathcal{P}$ includes all of p_i's variables and $channel_{j,i}$. The term *system state* (or configuration) refers to the tuple $c = (s_1, s_2, \cdots, s_n)$. We define an *execution (or run)* $R = c[0], a[0], c[1], a[1], \ldots$ as an alternating sequence of system states $c[x]$ and steps $a[x]$, such that each $c[x+1]$, except for the starting one, $c[0]$, is obtained from $c[x]$ by $a[x]$'s execution.

Task Specifications. The set of *legal executions* (*LE*) refers to all executions in which the task requirements hold. Let T_{URB} denote the task of Uniform Reliable Broadcast (URB) and LE_{URB} denote the set of executions in which the system fulfills T_{URB}'s requirements, which Definition 1 specifies and considers the operation, urbBroadcast(m), and the event urbDeliver(m). When node $p_i \in \mathcal{P}$ URB-broadcasts message m, it does so by calling urbBroadcast(m). The specifications assume that every broadcasted message is unique, say, by associating a message identity, *i.e.*, the pair (*sender identifier, sequnce number*), where the sequence number is an (integer) index that is locally generated by the sender.

Definition 1 (Uniform Reliable Broadcast [28]). *Let R be a system execution. We say that the system demonstrates in R a URB construction if the validity, integrity and termination requirements are satisfied. (Validity) Suppose that p_i URB-delivers message m in step $a_i \in R$ with p_j as a sender. There is a step $a_j \in R$ that appears in R before a_i in which p_j URB-broadcasts m. (Integrity) Every message can be delivered at most once. I.e., R includes at most one step in which node p_i URB-delivers message m. (Termination) Suppose that a non-faulty p_i takes a step in R that URB-broadcasts or URB-delivers message m. Each non-faulty $p_j \in \mathcal{P}$ URB-delivers m during R.*

The URB implementation considered in this paper also satisfies the quiescent property (in a self-stabilizing manner). Our implementation uses MSG and

	Frequency	
Duration	*Rare*	*Not rare*
Transient	Any violation of the assumptions according to which the system operates (but the code stays intact). This can result in state corruption.	Packet failures: omissions, duplications, reordering (yet fair communications).
Permanent	Detectable fail-stop failures.	

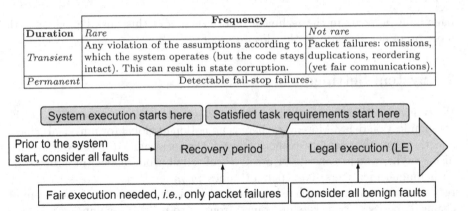

Fig. 1. The table above details our fault model and the chart illustrates when each fault set is relevant. The chart's gray shapes represent the system execution, and the white boxes specify the failures considered to be possible at different execution parts and recovery guarantees of the proposed self-stabilizing algorithm. The set of benign faults includes both packet failures and fail-stop failures.

MSGack messages for conveying data added to the system via urbBroadcast operations. We say that execution R satisfies the *quiescent* property if every URB-broadcast message that was URB-delivered incurs a finite number of MSG and MSGack messages. We note that the quiescent property does not consider all the messages that the proposed solution uses. Specifically, we use GOSSIP messages of constant size that the algorithm sends repeatedly. Note that self-stabilizing systems can never stop sending messages, because if they did, it would not be possible for the system to recover from transient faults [11, Chapter 2.3].

Fault Model. We model failures as environment (rather than algorithm) steps.

Benign Failures. When the occurrence of a failure cannot cause the system execution to lose legality, we refer to that failure as a benign one (Fig. 1).

Node Failure. We consider *fail-stop failures*, in which nodes stop taking steps in a way that can be detected, say, via unreliable failure detectors [8].

Communication Failures and Fairness. We consider time-free message-passing systems that are oblivious to the time in which the packets arrive and departure. We assume that the communication channels are prone to packet failures, such as omission, duplication, reordering. However, if p_i sends a message infinitely often to p_j, node p_j receives that message infinitely often. We refer to the latter as the *fair communication* assumption. For example, the proposed algorithm sends infinitely often GOSSIP messages from any node to any other. Despite the possible loss of messages, the communication fairness assumption implies that every node receives infinitely often GOSSIP messages from any non-failing node.

Arbitrary Transient Faults and Self-stabilization. We consider any violation of the assumptions according to which the system was designed to operate. We refer to these violations and deviations as *arbitrary transient faults* and assume that they can corrupt the system state arbitrarily (while keeping the program code intact). The occurrence of an arbitrary transient fault is rare. Thus, our model assumes that the last arbitrary transient fault occurs before the system execution starts [11]. Moreover, it leaves the system to start in an arbitrary state. An algorithm is *self-stabilizing* with respect to LE's task, when every execution R of the algorithm reaches eventually a suffix $R_{legal} \in LE$ that is legal. That is, Dijkstra [10] requires that $\forall R : \exists R' : R = R' \circ R_{legal} \wedge R_{legal} \in LE \wedge |R'| \in \mathbb{N}$, where the operator $\circ$ denotes that $R = R' \circ R''$ concatenates R' with R''. The main complexity measure of self-stabilizing algorithms, called *stabilization time*, is the time it takes the system to recover after the occurrence of the last transient fault. We say that a system execution is *fair* when every step that is applicable infinitely often is executed infinitely often and fair communication is kept. Since asynchronous systems do not consider the notion of time, we use the term (asynchronous) cycles as an alternative way to measure the period between two system states in a fair execution. The first (asynchronous) cycle (with round-trips) of a fair execution $R = R' \circ R''$ is the shortest prefix R' of R, such that each non-failing node executes at least one complete iteration in R'. The second cycle in execution R is the first cycle in execution R'', and so on. Note that, in the absence of transient faults, no fairness assumptions are required in any practical settings. Also, existing non-self-stabilizing solutions (Sect. 3) do not make any fairness assumption, but they do not consider recovery from arbitrary transient faults regardless of whether the execution eventually becomes fair or not.

Building-Blocks: Self-stabilizing Unreliable Failure Detectors. As in [28], unreliable failure detectors are used for providing the quiescent property. We denote by $Faulty \subseteq \mathcal{P}$ the set of nodes that eventually fail-stop during execution R and $Correct = \mathcal{P} \setminus Faulty(F)$. We assume the availability of self-stabilizing Θ failure detectors [28], which [7] has implemented. *I.e.*, the locally accessible set *trusted* satisfies the Θ-accuracy and Θ-liveness requirements. The former implies that at any time, $trusted_i$ includes at least one non-faulty node, which may change over time, and the latter implies that eventually $trusted_i$ includes only non-faulty processors. We also assume the availability of a class of self-stabilizing HB (heartbeat) failure detectors [28], which has the HB-completeness and HB-liveness properties. The former implies that any faulty node is eventually suspected by every non-failing node and the latter there is a time after which only the faulty nodes are suspected. A self-stabilizing HB failure detector lets $p_i \in \mathcal{P}$ broadcast its heartbeat information on a periodic basis. When $p_j \in \mathcal{P}$ receives a heartbeat message from p_i, it takes the maximum of the locally stored and received entries. Moreover, once any entry reaches the value of the maximum integer, $MAXINT$, a global reset procedure is used (see Sect. 6).

3   Non-self-stabilizing URB Algorithms

For the reader's assistance, we briefly review existing URB solutions. In the absence of failures, one can substitute urbBroadcast(m) with {foreach $p_j \in \mathcal{P}$ send $MSG(m)$ to p_j} and raise urbDeliver(m) upon p_j's reception of m. The following algorithms are from [2,3]. We follow here their description as given in [28]. Algorithm 1 considers undetectable fail-stop failures but with reliable communications. Node p_i broadcasts message m by sending $MSG(m)$ to itself (line 1). Upon the arrival of a fresh message (line 3), the receiver propagates $MSG(m)$ to all other nodes (except itself and the sender) before raising urbDeliver(m) (line 4).

Algorithm 1: URB assuming reliable communications; code for $p_i \in \mathcal{P}$

---

1 **operation** urbBroadcast(m) **do send** $MSG(m)$ **to** p_i;
2 **upon** MSG(m) **arrival from** p_k **begin**
3   **if** *first reception of m* **then**
4   {**foreach** $p_j \in \mathcal{P} \setminus \{p_i, p_k\}$ **do send** MSG(m) **to** p_j}; urbDeliver(m);

Algorithm 2 considers a system in which at most $t < n/2$ nodes may crash undetectability and unreliable communications. Node p_i broadcasts m by sending MSG(m) to itself (line 5) while assuming it has a reliable channel to itself. Upon MSG(m)'s first reception (line 7), p_i creates the set $recBy[m] = \{i, k\}$ to contain the identities of nodes that have received MSG(m), before activating the $Diffuse(m)$ task. In case this is not MSG(m)'s first arrival (line 8), p_i merely adds the sender identity, k, to $recBy[m]$. The task $Diffuse(m)$ is responsible for transmitting (and retransmitting) MSG(m) to at least a majority of the nodes before URB-delivering m (lines 11 to 12).

Algorithm 2: URB for $t < n/2$ undetectable node failures; p_i's code

---

5 **operation** urbBroadcast(m) **do send** $MSG(m)$ **to** p_i;
6 **upon** MSG(m) **arrival from** p_k **begin**
7   **if** *not the first reception of m* **then** $recBy[m] \leftarrow recBy[m] \cup \{k\}$;
8   **else allocate** $recBy[m]$; $recBy[m] \leftarrow \{i, k\}$; **activate** $Diffuse(m)$ **task**;

9 **do forever begin**
10   **foreach active** $Diffuse(m)$ ***task* do**
11   **foreach** $p_j \in \mathcal{P} : j \notin recBy[m]$ **do send** MSG(j, seq) **to** p_j;
12   **if** $(|recBy[m]| \geq t + 1) \wedge (p_i$ *has not URB-delivered* $m)$ **then**
            urbDeliver(m);

Note that the task $Diffuse(m)$ never stops transmitting messages. Using Θ failure detectors (Sect. 2), Algorithm 3 avoids such infinite number of retransmissions by enriching Algorithm 2 as follows. (i) The URB-delivery condition,

---

Algorithm 3: Quiescent URB using Θ-failure detectors; code for $p_i \in \mathcal{P}$

---

13 **operation** urbBroadcast(m) **do send** $MSG(m)$ **to** p_i;
14 **upon** MSG(m) **arrival from** p_k **begin**
15   **if** *not the first reception of m* **then** $recBy[m] \leftarrow recBy[m] \cup \{k\}$;
16   **else allocate** $recBy[m]$; $recBy[m] \leftarrow \{i, k\}$; **activate** $Diffuse(m)$ **task**;
17   **send** MSGack(m) **to** p_k;
18 **upon** MSGack(m) **arrival from** p_k **do** $\{recBy[m] \leftarrow recBy[m] \cup \{k\}\}$
19 **do forever begin**
20   **foreach active** $Diffuse(m)$ **task do**
21   **foreach** $j \in trusted \setminus recBy[m]$ **do send** MSG(m) **to** p_j;
22   **if** $trusted \subseteq recBy[m] \wedge (p_i$ *has not URB-delivered m*) **then**
            urbDeliver(m);

$trusted \subseteq recBy[m]$, (line 22) substitutes the condition $|recBy[m]| \geq t + 1$ (line 12). (ii) Upon MSG(m) reception, p_i replies with MSGack(m). Moreover, when p_i receives MSGack(m) from p_k, it marks the fact that p_k received m by adding k to $recBy[m]$. (iii) Node p_i can eventually avoid sending messages to a faulty node p_j since p_i repeatedly transmits MSG(m) to p_j as long as p_j is trusted and $j \notin recBy[m]$ (line 21). Eventually, either p_j receives MSG(m) and acknowledges it, or in case p_j is faulty, $j \notin trusted_i$ due to the Θ-completeness. Moreover, due to the strong Θ-accuracy, $j \notin trusted_i$ cannot hold before p_j fails (if it is faulty).

Algorithm 4 adds the quiescent property to Algorithm 3 by allowing p_i to transmit MSG(m) to p_j only when $j \in recBy[m]$ (because from p_i's perceptive, p_j has not yet received MSG(m)) and $HB[j]$ has increased since the previous iteration (because from p_i's perspective, p_j is not failing).

4 Unbounded Self-stabilizing Uniform Reliable Broadcast

Algorithm 5 is a self-stabilizing quiescent URB algorithm. This first transient-fault tolerance solution uses bounded space, thus, it is more evolved than Algorithm 4.

Local Variables and their Purpose (lines 36 to 41). Algorithm 5 maintains unique message numbers, *seq*, which is incremented upon urbBroadcast invocations. The *buffer* variable stores all active messages as records with the fields: (i) *msg*, which is a URB message, (ii) *id*, which is the URB-broadcaster identifier, (iii) *seq* is the message number, (iv) *delivered*, which holds True only after message delivery, (v) *recBy*, which is a set of identifiers of nodes that have acknowledged *msg*, and (vi) *prevHB*, which is a failure detector value used for deciding when to re-transmit *msg*. Every node stores at most $n \cdot$ bufferUnitSize records, where bufferUnitSize can be set according to the available memory. When accessing *buffer* records, we use a query-oriented notation,

---

Algorithm 4: Quiescent URB via Θ-&HB-failure detectors; code for p_i

---

23 **operation** urbBroadcast(m) **do send** $MSG(m)$ to p_i;
24 **upon** MSG(m) **arrival from** p_k **begin**
25 | **if** *not the first reception of m* **then** $recBy[m] \leftarrow recBy[m] \cup \{k\}$;
26 | **else allocate** $recBy[m]$;$recBy[m]\leftarrow\{i,k\}$; **activate** *Diffuse*(m, [-1,...,-1]) task;
27 | **send** MSGack(m) to p_k;

28 **upon** MSGack(m) **arrival from** p_k **do** $\{recBy[m] \leftarrow recBy[m] \cup \{k\}\}$
29 **do forever begin**
30 | **foreach active** *Diffuse*(m, *prevHB*) **task do**
31 | | **let** $curHB := HB$;
32 | | **foreach** $j \in trusted \setminus recBy[m] \wedge prevHB[m][j] < curHB[m][j]$ **do**
33 | | | **send** MSG(m) to p_j
34 | | $prevHB[m] \leftarrow curHB[m]$;
35 | | **if** $trusted \subseteq recBy[m] \wedge (p_i$ *has not URB-delivered* $m)$ **then** urbDeliver(m);

---

e.g., ($\bullet$, $id = j$, $seq = s$, $\bullet$) $\in$ *buffer* considers all records that their *id* and *seq* fields hold j and s, respectively.

A Self-stabilizing Flow Control Scheme for Bounding *buffer*. Algorithm 5 bounds *buffer* using a flow control technique. In a nutshell, every sender keeps track of the buffer space at the receiver-side and defer URB broadcasts whenever it does not know that all trusted receivers have the space for new messages. To that end, receivers and senders share, via gossip messages, the message sequence numbers that their buffers store. This allows the nodes to detect inconsistencies. For example, the sender makes sure that it never creates any new sequence number that is not greater than all sequence number stored at the receiver-sides. Also, the sender checks that it stores the entire window of messages so that it could retransmit any messages that the receiver is missing.

On the receiver-side, there is a need to keep track of the highest sequence number that was removed from the buffer. We say a record, with sequence number s, is *obsolete* if it had received acknowledgments from all trusted nodes and then it was URB-delivered. Moreover, since p_i needs to remove obsolete records from its buffer, we also define that any record with sequence number lower than s to be also obsolete. This way, p_i can keep track of all the obsolete records it has deleted using a single counter $rxObsS[k]$, per sender p_k, which stores the highest sequence number of records that p_i considered to be obsolete. The counter array $txObsS_i[]$ facilitates the sender, p_i, control over its sending flow since it can receive $rxObsS_i[k]$ from p_k and store it at $txObsS_k[k]$. (We denote variable X's value at node p_i by X_i.) The flow control mechanism can simply defer the processing a new URB-message when p_k's sequence number minus the minimum value stored in $txObsS[]$ (that arrived from a node that p_k trusts) is smaller than the maximum number of records, bufferUnitSize, that a receiver can buffer.

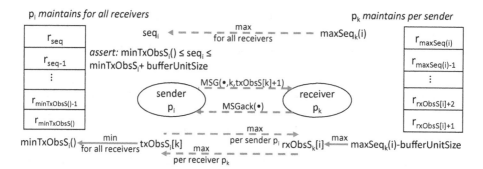

Fig. 2. The self-stabilizing flow control scheme. The arrays on the figure sides represent the portion of peers' *buffer* variables that include records r_s, where s is a sequence number of a message sent from p_i to p_k. The single line arrows (dashed or not) and the text next to them represent a logical update, *e.g.*, $x \xleftarrow{\text{max}} y$ stands for $x \leftarrow \max\{x, y\}$. The text that appears below the arrow clarifies whether a single variable aggregates these update or different entries in the array store the updated values. The dashed arrows refer to updates that require communication between p_i and p_k. Note that all communications occur concurrently.

Figure 2 describes our flow control scheme. The receiver p_k repeatedly sends to the sender, p_i, the maximum p_i's sequence number, $\mathsf{maxSeq}_k(i)$, that it stores in its buffer, see the top dashed left arrow. This allows p_i to make sure that seq_i is greater than any sequence number in the system that is associated with p_i, as shown by Theorem 1's Argument (3). The buffer of p_k cannot store more than $\mathsf{bufferUnitSize}$ with messages from p_i. Therefore, p_k stores only messages that their sequence numbers are between $\mathsf{maxSeq}_k(i)$ and $\mathsf{maxSeq}_k(i) - \mathsf{bufferUnitSize}$ and reports to p_i the highest sequence number, $rxObsS_k[i]$, of its obsolete records that are associated with p_i, see the lowest dashed arrow. The latter stores this value in $rxObsS_i[k]$ and makes sure it has the latest value from p_k by sharing $rxObsS_i[k]$ with it. The sender, p_i, also uses $rxObsS_i[k]$ for bounding $buffer_i$. Specifically, $\mathsf{minTxObsS}_i()$ aggregates the minimum value in $rxObsS_i[k]$ for any trusted receiver p_k (line 44). Using $\mathsf{minTxObsS}_i()$, the sender, p_i, can assert that $\mathsf{minTxObsS}_i() < seq_i \leq \mathsf{minTxObsS}_i() + \mathsf{bufferUnitSize}$ and $buffer_i$ includes all the records that their sequence numbers are between $\mathsf{minTxObsS}_i()$ and seq_i (line 550). Since, due to a transient fault, p_i's state might indicate the reception of acknowledgment for a message that p_k's state shows that it has never received, p_i repeatedly resends the message that has the sequence number s, such that $s = rxObsS_i[k] + 1$ (line 61), cf. double dashed line arrows between p_i and p_k.

Algorithm 5's Description. Upon $\mathsf{urbBroadcast}(m)$'s invocation, Algorithm 5 lets p_i process m without blocking as long as there is available space at all trusted receivers (line 45). If so, then p_i creates a unique operation index, seq and calls $\mathsf{update}(m, j, s, k)$. The latter considers first the case in which $buffer_i$ does not include a record with the identifier (j, s) of message m, which was forwarded from p_k. In this case, p_i adds to $buffer_i$ the record $(m, j, s, \mathsf{False}, \{j, k\}, [-1, \ldots, -1])$

(line 49), which stands for the application message and its unique identifier, as well as stating that it was not yet been delivered but that the identifiers of the sending (j) and forwarding (k) nodes appear in *recBy*. Also, the record holds a vector that is smaller than any value of the *HB* failure detector. If *buffer$_i$* has the record, p_i adds to *recBy* the identifiers of the sending and forwarding nodes (line 50). Algorithm 5's do forever loop performs: (i) removal of stale information (lines 53 to 64), (ii) processing of arriving messages (lines 58 to 62), and (iii) gossiping of information that is needed for flow control and transient fault recovery (line 65).

(i) The removal of stale information includes emptying the buffer whenever there are records for which the *msg* field is $\perp$ or when there are two records with the same message identifier (line 53). Lines 55 to 63 implement recovery strategies that facilitate the bounds on the buffer size. Algorithm 5 tests for the case in which, due to an arbitrary transient fault, the sender does not store all of its messages such that their sequence number is between $mS+1$ and *seq* (line 55), where $mS :=$ minTxObsS() is the smallest obsolete number that p_i had received from a trusted receiver. The recovery here is done by sending up to bufferUnitSize of the newest messages that can flush stale messages on the receiver-side. On the receiver-side, Algorithm 5 makes sure that the gap between the largest obsolete record, $rxObsS[k]$ (of p_k's messages) and the largest buffered sequence number, maxSeq(k), is not larger than bufferUnitSize (line 57). Algorithm 5 updates the receiver-side counter that stores the highest obsolete message number per sender (line 63). To the end of bounding *buffer$_i$*, node p_i keeps any message, m, that it has not yet received an indication from all trusted receivers that they consider m to be obsolete. It also keeps all non-obsolete messages.

(ii) p_i delivers messages that their *recBy* has acknowledgments from all trusted nodes (line 59) and mark them as delivered. Otherwise, it samples the *HB* failure detector (line 60) and decides when a retransmission is needed (line 61) in case acknowledgments are missing or because the message sequence number is greater by one than the largest obsolete message number known to the sender. (The latter information facilitate to recover from arbitrary transient faults.) These messages are received (line 66) and acknowledged to the sender, cf. line 67.

(iii) p_i gossips to p_k control information about the maximum *seq* value that p_i stores in a p_k record as well as p_k's obsolete records (lines 65 and 68). The former allows p_k to maintain the correctness invariant, *i.e.*, seq_k is not smaller than any other *seq* value in the system that is associated with p_k. The latter lets p_k to control the flow of URB broadcasts according to the available space.

5 Correctness

Theorem 1 shows that Algorithm 5 recovers after the occurrence of transient faults. Theorem 2 shows that Algorithm 5 satisfies the task specifications. Definition 2 presents Theorem 1's conditions for bringing the system to a legal execution.

Algorithm 5: Self-stabilizing uniform reliable broadcast; code for p_i

---

36 **global constants:** bufferUnitSize;   /* max records per node in *buffer* */
37 **local variables:** (Initialization is optional in the context of self-stabilization.)
38 $seq := 0$;   /* message index num. */
39 $buffer := \emptyset$;   /* set of $(msg, id, seq, delivered, recBy, prevHB)$ records */
40 $rxObsS[1..n] := [0, \ldots, 0]$;   /* highest receiver's obsolete seq a node */
41 $txObsS[1..n] := [0, \ldots, 0]$;   /* highest sender's obsolete seq a node */
42 **macro** nxtObs$(r) := (rxObsS[r.id] + 1 = r.seq \wedge trusted \subseteq r.recBy \wedge r.delivered)$;
43 **macro** maxSeq$(k) := \max(\{s : (\bullet, id = k, seq = s, \bullet) \in buffer\})$;
44 **macro** minTxObsS$() := \min\{txObsS[k] : k \in trusted\}$;
45 **operation** urbBroadcast(m) **do** {**wait**$(seq < $ minTxObsS$() + $ bufferUnitSize);
     $seq \leftarrow seq + 1$; update(m, i, seq, i);}
46 **procedure** update(m, j, s, k) **begin**
47 | **if** $s \leq rxObsS[j]$ **then return** ;
48 | **if** $(\bullet, id = j, seq = s, \bullet) \notin buffer \wedge m \neq \bot$ **then**
49 | | $buffer \leftarrow buffer \cup \{(m, j, s, $ False, $\{j, k\}, [$-1$, \ldots, -1])\}$;
50 | **else foreach** $(\bullet, id = j, seq = s, \bullet, recBy = r, \bullet) \in buffer$ **do** $r \leftarrow r \cup \{j, k\}$;

51 **do forever begin**
52 | **if** $(\exists r, r' \in buffer : r.msg = \bot \vee (r \neq r' \wedge ((r.id, r.seq) = (r'.id, r'.seq))))$ **then**
53 | | $buffer \leftarrow \emptyset$
54 | **if** $\neg((mS < seq \leq mS + $ bufferUnitSize$) \wedge (\{mS + 1, \ldots, seq\} \subseteq \{s : (\bullet, id = i, seq = s, \bullet) \in buffer\})$ **where** $mS := $ minTxObsS$()$ **then**
55 | | $txObsS[] \leftarrow [seq, \ldots, seq]$
56 | **foreach** $p_k \in \mathcal{P}$ **do**
57 | | $rxObsS[k] \leftarrow \max\{rxObsS[k], $ maxSeq$(k) - $ bufferUnitSize$\}$
58 | **foreach** $(msg = m, id = j, seq = s, delivered = d, recBy = r, prevHB = e) \in buffer$ **do**
59 | | **if** $(trusted \subseteq r) \wedge (\neg d)$ **then** urbDeliver(m); $d \leftarrow $ True;
60 | | **let** $u := HB$;
61 | | **foreach** $p_k \in \mathcal{P} : (k \notin r \vee (i = j \wedge s = txObsS[k] + 1)) \wedge (e[k] < u[k])$ **do**
62 | | | $e[k] \leftarrow u[k]$; **send** $MSG(m, j, s)$ **to** p_k; /* piggyback ll. 62-65 */
63 | **while** $\exists r \in buffer : $ nxtObs(r) **do** $rxObsS[r.id] \leftarrow rxObsS[r.id] + 1$;
64 | $buffer \leftarrow \{(\bullet, id = i, seq = s, \bullet) \in buffer : $ minTxObsS$() < s\} \cup \{(\bullet, id = k, seq = s, \bullet) \in buffer : p_k \in \mathcal{P} \wedge ((rxObsS[k] < s \wedge $ maxSeq$(k) - $ bufferUnitSize $\leq s))\}$;
65 | **foreach** $p_k \in \mathcal{P}$ **do send** GOSSIP(maxSeq(k), $rxObsS[k]$, $txObsS[k]$) **to** p_k;

66 **upon** MSG(m,j,s) arrival from p_k **do** {update(m,j,s,k); **send** MSGack(j,s) **to** p_k;}
67 **upon** MSGack(j, s) arrival from p_k **do** {update$(\bot, j, s, k)$;}
68 **upon** GOSSIP$(seqJ, rxObsSJ, txObsSJ)$ arrival from p_j **do** $(seq, rxObsS[j], txObsS[j]) \leftarrow (\max\{seqJ, seq\}, \max\{rxObsSJ, rxObsS[j]\}, \max\{txObsSJ, txObsS[j]\})$

Definition 2 (Algorithm 5's consistent sequence and buffer values).
Let c be a system state and $p_i \in \mathcal{P}$ a non-faulty node. Suppose that (i) $(\nexists r, r' \in buffer : r.msg = \bot \vee (r \neq r' \wedge ((r.id, r.seq) = (r'.id, r'.seq))))$, $((mS \leq seq_i \leq mS + $ bufferUnitSize$) \wedge (mS + 1, \ldots, seq_i) \subseteq \{s : (\bullet, id = i, seq = s, \bullet) \in buffer_i\})$,

$\forall p_k \in \mathcal{P} : (\mathsf{maxSeq}_i(k) - rxObsS_i[k]) \leq \mathsf{bufferUnitSize}, \nexists r \in \textit{buffer}_i : \mathsf{nxtObs}(r),$
$\forall(\bullet, id = i, seq = s, \bullet) \in \textit{buffer}_i : mS < s, \forall(\bullet, id = k, seq = s, \bullet) \in$
$\textit{buffer}_i : p_k \in \mathcal{P} \wedge rxObsS_i[k] < s \wedge \mathsf{maxSeq}_i(k) \leq (s + \mathsf{bufferUnitSize}),$ where
$mS := \mathsf{minTxObsS}_i()$. Moreover, (ii) seq_i is greater than or equal to any p_i's
sequence values in the variables and fields related to seq (including p_i's records
in $\textit{buffer}_k$, where $p_k \in \mathcal{P}$ is non-failing, and incoming messages to p_k) and
$\forall p_j \in \mathcal{P} : sMj \leq rxObsS_j[i]$, where sMj is either $txObsS_i[j]$ or the value of
the fields $txObsSJ$ and $rxObsSJ$ in a GOSSIP$(\bullet, txObsSJ, \bullet)$ message in transit
from p_j to p_i, and respectively, GOSSIP$(\bullet, rxObsSJ)$ message in transit from p_i
to p_j. Also, (iii) $\forall k \in \textit{trusted}_i : |\{(\bullet, id = i, \bullet) \in \textit{buffer}_k\}| \leq \mathsf{bufferUnitSize}$ and
$seq_i \leq \mathsf{minTxObsS}_i() + \mathsf{bufferUnitSize}$. In this case, we say that p_i's values in the
variables and fields related to seq's values and buffer are consistent in c.

Not any system state that satisfies Definition 2 starts a legal execution. E.g.,
consider a system with $\mathcal{P} = \{p_i, p_j\}$ and an execution R that starts in a state
in which $\textit{buffer}_i = \{(m, i, 1, \bullet)\}$, $\textit{buffer}_j = \{(m', i, 1, \bullet)\}$, and $m \neq m'$. The
deliveries of m and m' violate Definition 1's validity requirement. Theorem 2
circumvents this difficulty using the conditions of Definition 3.

Definition 3 (Complete execution with respect to urbBroadcast). *Let R
be an Algorithm 5's execution. Let $c, c'' \in R$ denote the starting system states
of R, and respectively, R'', for some suffix R'' of R. We say that message m is
completely delivered in c if (i) the channels do not include MSG$(msg = m, \bullet)$
messages (or MSGack messages with a message identifier (id, seq) that refers to
m), and (ii) for any non-failing $p_j \in \mathcal{P}$ and $r = (msg = m, \bullet) \in \textit{buffer}_j$, it holds
that $r.delivered = \mathsf{True}$ and for any non-failing $p_k \in \mathcal{P}$, we have $k \in r.recBy$.
Suppose that $R = R' \circ R''$ has a suffix R'', such that for any urbBroadcast message
m that is not completely delivered in c'', it holds that m either does not appear
in c or it is completely delivered in c. Then, we say that R'' is complete with
respect to R's urbBroadcast invocations.*

Theorems 1 and 2 consider Definition 4 and use Lemma 1.

Definition 4 (The $diffuse()$ predicate). *The predicate $diffuse_i(m) : p_i \in \mathcal{P}$
holds in $c \in R$ if, and only if, $\exists(msg = m, \bullet, delivered = \mathsf{False}, \bullet) \in \textit{buffer}_i$.*

Lemma 1. *Let R be an Algorithm 5's execution and $p_i, p_j \in \mathcal{P}$ be non-failing
processors. Suppose that in any system state $c \in R$, $diffuse_i(m)$ holds, such that
$(msg \neq \bot, \bullet, recBy = r, \bullet) \in \textit{buffer}_i$ is true, but $j \in r$ is not. (i) Node p_i sends,
infinitely often, $MSG(m, j, s)$ messages to p_j and p_j replies, infinitely often,
via $MSGack(j, s)$ messages to p_i. (ii) The reception of such replies guarantees
$j \in r$ eventually. (iii) If R is fair, invariants (i) and (ii) occur within $\mathcal{O}(1)$
asynchronous cycles.*

Proof of Lemma. Since $j \in Correct \wedge j \notin r$ in c, p_i sends $MSG(m, j, s)$ to p_j
infinitely often (lines 58 to 62 and HB-liveness). Also, p_j receives p_i's message
(line 66), and replies, infinitely often, so that p_i receives p_j's replies (line 67),

infinitely often, while making sure that j is included in r (line 50). Invariant (iii) is implied by the fairness assumption and Invariant (ii).   □

Theorem 1 shows that the system reaches a state that satisfies Definition 2.

Theorem 1 (Convergence). *Let R be Algorithm 5's fair execution. Within $\mathcal{O}(\mathsf{bufferUnitSize})$ asynchronous cycles, the system reaches a state, $c \in R$, after which a suffix R' of R starts, such that R' is complete with respect to its* $\mathsf{urbBroadcast}$ *invocations. Also, seq and buffer are consistent in any $c' \in R'$.*

Proof. The proof is implied by arguments (1) to (5).

Argument (1): *The case in which* $\mathsf{MSG}(m, \bullet)$ *(or its correspondent* $\mathsf{MSGack}(\bullet)$*) appears in a communication channel at R's starting system state.* Suppose that in R's starting system state, it holds that $\mathsf{MSG}(m, \bullet)$ appears in an incoming channel to p_k. Since R is fair, within $\mathcal{O}(1)$ asynchronous cycles, $\mathsf{MSG}(m, \bullet)$, or respectively, $\mathsf{MSGack}(\bullet)$ arrives to p_k. For the case of $\mathsf{MSG}(m, \bullet)$, this causes line 66's execution and then line 49 if m's record was not already in $buffer_k$. For the case of $\mathsf{MSGack}(\bullet)$ and $(m, \bullet) \in buffer_k$, line 67 has a similar effect, and the case of $\mathsf{MSGack}(\bullet)$ and $(m, \bullet) \notin buffer_k$ does not change p_k's state. Thus, w.l.o.g., the rest of the proof assumes that $\exists_{p_k \in \mathcal{P}} : (m, \bullet) \in buffer_k$ in R's starting state.

Argument (2): *Definition 2's Invariant (i) holds.* Within $\mathcal{O}(1)$ asynchronous cycles, p_k runs lines 51 to 62. Invariant (i) is implied by lines 53 to 64.

Argument (3): *Definition 2's Invariant (ii) holds in c'.* Within $\mathcal{O}(1)$ asynchronous cycles, any message that was in transit in R's starting system state arrives. Thus, w.l.o.g., the proof focuses on seq_i's value at the non-failing nodes $p_i, p_k \in \mathcal{P}$. Other than in seq_i, every p_i's sequence value can only be stored in $(\bullet, id = i, seq = s', \bullet) \in buffer_k$ records. Suppose that in R's starting system state, it holds that $s' > seq_i$. By lines 65 and 68, within $\mathcal{O}(1)$ asynchronous cycles, p_k gossips $s_k \geq s'$ to p_i and the latter updates seq_i upon reception. The proof is done since only p_i (line 45) can have new seq values for p_i. Thus, the first part of Invariant (ii) holds. Within an asynchronous cycle, all message arrive, and thus, w.l.o.g., we focus on sMj's values at the non-failing node $p_i \in \mathcal{P}$. Suppose that in R's starting system state, $txObsS_i[j] \leq rxObsS_j[i]$ does not hold for $p_j \in \mathcal{P} : j \in trusted_i$. By lines 65 and 68, within $\mathcal{O}(1)$ asynchronous cycles, p_j gossips $rxObsS_j[i]$ to p_i and the latter updates $txObsS_i[j]$ upon reception as well as p_i gossips $txObsS_i[j]$ to p_j and the latter updates $rxObsS_j[i]$ upon reception. Thus, the second part of Invariant (ii) holds is any system state that follows.

The rest of the proof assumes, w.l.o.g., that Definition 2's invariants (i) and (ii) hold throughout R. Generality is not lost due to arguments (1) to (3).

Argument (4): *first part of Definition 2's Invariant (iii).* Let $p_i, p_k \in \mathcal{P}$ be two non-faulty nodes. For the case of p_k's records in $buffer_i$, Definition 2's Invariant (i) says $\forall (\bullet, id = k, seq = s_k, \bullet) \in buffer_i : \max\{s'_k : (\bullet, id = k, seq = s'_k, \bullet) \in buffer_i\} \leq (s_k + \mathsf{bufferUnitSize})$. I.e., the largest sequence number of a p_k's records in $buffer_i$ minus $\mathsf{bufferUnitSize}$ is smaller than s_k of any p_k's records in $buffer_i$.

Argument (5): *second part of Definition 2's Invariant (iii)*. Let $c \in R$ and $x_c = (seq_i - \mathsf{minTxObsS}_i())$. Assume, towards a contradiction, that $x_c \geq \mathsf{bufferUnitSize}$ for at least $\mathcal{O}(\mathsf{bufferUnitSize})$ asynchronous cycles. Let $A_c = \cup_{k \in trusted_i}\{r \in buffer_k : r.id = i \wedge \neg\mathsf{nxtObs}_k(r)\}$ and $B_c = \cup_{k \in trusted_i}\{r \in buffer_i : r.id = i \wedge txObsS_i[k] < r.seq\}$ as well as $rec \in A_c$ and $rec' \in B_c$ be the records with the smallest sequence number (among all the records with $id = i$) that p_k, and respectively, p_i stores in c. We start the proof by showing that, within $\mathcal{O}(1)$ asynchronous cycles, the system reaches $c' \in R$ for which $rec \notin A_{c'}$ and $rec' \notin B_{c'}$ hold. We then show that $x_{c'} < \mathsf{bufferUnitSize}$ holds.

Showing $rec \notin A_{c'}$ since $\mathsf{nxtObs}(rec)$ holds. Let $p_i \in \mathcal{P} : i \in Correct$. Suppose $\exists p_k \in \mathcal{P} : (\bullet, id = i, delivered = d_k, recBy = r_k, \bullet) \in buffer_k \wedge k \in trusted_i \wedge d_k = \mathsf{False}$ holds for some r_k in c. For any $p_j \in \mathcal{P}$ for which $j \in trusted_k$ holds during R's first $\mathcal{O}(1)$ asynchronous cycles, $j \in r_k$ (invariants (i) and (ii) of Lemma 1). Once $\forall j \in trusted_k : j \in r_k$ holds, p_k assigns True to d_k (line 59). Thus, within $\mathcal{O}(1)$ asynchronous cycles, $rec \notin A_{c'}$ and $\mathsf{nxtObs}(rec)$ hold due to rec's choice.

Showing $rec' \notin B_{c'}$. Since $rec' \in B_c$, p_i sends $\mathsf{MSG}(rec'.msg, rec'.id, rec'.seq)$ infinitely often to p_k (line 62). Within an asynchronous cycle, p_k receives it. Lines 66 and 47 to 50 imply that either $(rec'.msg, rec'.id, rec'.seq, \bullet) \in A_{c'}$ or $rec'.seq \leq rxObsS_k[i]$. Then $(rec'.msg, rec'.id, rec'.seq, \bullet) \notin A_{c'}$ and $\mathsf{nxtObs}(rec)$ hold (due to the proof of the $rec \notin A_{c'}$ case), within $\mathcal{O}(1)$ asynchronous cycles and $rxObsS_k[rec'.id] \geq rec'.seq$ (line 63). Also, $rec' \notin B_{c'}$ due to the fact that $txObsS_k[rec'.id] \geq rec'.seq$ and Argument (3).

Showing a contradiction, i.e., $x_{c'} < \mathsf{bufferUnitSize}$. Due to the assumption in the proof start, during R's first $\mathcal{O}(\mathsf{bufferUnitSize})$ asynchronous cycles, p_i does not increment seq_i and call $\mathsf{update}()$ (line 45). Thus, on the one hand, no new p_i's record enters $buffer_k$ during R's first $\mathcal{O}(\mathsf{bufferUnitSize})$ asynchronous cycles, while on the other hand, within $\mathcal{O}(1)$ asynchronous cycles, either p_i stops including p_k in $trusted_i$ or it removes at least one record from A_c and B_c. The latter can repeat itself at most $\mathsf{bufferUnitSize}$ times due to Argument (5). This completes the argument and the theorem proofs.

Theorem 2 considers system executions that reach suffixes, R, that satisfy Definitions 2 and 3. Theorem 2 shows that R satisfies Definition 1. Due to the page limit, the proof of Theorem 2 appears in [26].

Theorem 2 (Closure). *Let R be an Algorithm 5's execution that is complete w.r.t. $\mathsf{urbBroadcast}$ invocations (or R is a suffix of an execution $\mathcal{R} = \mathcal{R}' \circ R$ for which R is complete with respect to $\mathsf{urbBroadcast}$ invocations in $\mathcal{R}$) as well as sequence values and buffers are consistent in $c \in R$. R is a URB construction.*

6   Bounded Self-stabilizing Uniform Reliable Broadcast

In this section, we explain how to transform our unbounded self-stabilizing URB algorithm to a bounded one. We note the existence of several such techniques, *e.g.*, Awerbuch *et al.* [5], Georgiou *et al.* [21], and Dolev *et al.* [17, Section 10]. The ideas presented in these papers are along the same lines. They present a transformation that takes a self-stabilizing algorithm for message passing systems that uses unbounded operation indices and transforms it into an algorithm that uses bounded indices. The transformation uses a predefined maximum index value, say, MAXINT $= 2^{64} - 1$, and it has two phases. (Phase A) As soon as p_i discovers an index that is at least MAXINT, it disables new invocations of operations. (Phase B) Once all non-failing nodes have finished processing their operations, the transformation uses an agreement-based global restart for initializing all system variables. After the end of the global restart, all operations are enabled. For further details, please see [5,17,21]. We note the existence of alternative solutions to the above, such as the ones that uses epoch numbers [13]. Yet, such solutions provide a weaker notion of self-stabilization since they do not guarantee recovery within a bounded time. Another solution worth mentioning is self-stabilizing reconfiguration [12], which can allow dealing with crashes.

7   Conclusions

We showed how non-self-stabilizing algorithms [1,22,28] for (quiescent) uniform reliable broadcast can be transformed into one that can recover after the occurrence of arbitrary transient faults. This requires non-trivial considerations that are imperative for self-stabilizing systems, such as the explicit use of bounded buffers. To that end, we developed a flow control scheme. Since URB is the basis for a number of important applications [28], such as consensus, state-machine replication, set-constraint delivery, to name a few, our bounded URB solution can serve as a basis for explicitly bounding such applications, whether they are self-stabilizing or not. The need to have this new scheme shows that currently there is no "meta" self-stabilizing scheme that transfers all non-self-stabilizing algorithms from the textbooks into self-stabilizing ones.

Acknowledgments. M. Raynal was partially supported by the French ANR project DESCARTES (16-CE40-0023-03) devoted to layered and modular structures in distributed computing. E.M. Schiller was partially supported by the Swedish Vinnova (FFI) project AutoSPADA (reference number 2019-05884) devoted for automotive stream processing and distributed analytics. We thank Oskar Jedvert, Chibin Kou, and Chaiyapruek Muangsiri for helpful discussions.

References

1. Kawazoe Aguilera, M., Chen, W., Toueg, S.: Heartbeat: a timeout-free failure detector for quiescent reliable communication. In: Mavronicolas, M., Tsigas, P. (eds.) WDAG 1997. LNCS, vol. 1320, pp. 126–140. Springer, Heidelberg (1997). https://doi.org/10.1007/BFb0030680
2. Aguilera, M.K., Chen, W., Toueg, S.: On quiescent reliable communication. SIAM J. Comput. **29**(6), 2040–2073 (2000)

3. Kawazoe Aguilera, M., Toueg, S., Deianov, B.: Revisiting the weakest failure detector for uniform reliable broadcast. In: Jayanti, P. (ed.) DISC 1999. LNCS, vol. 1693, pp. 19–34. Springer, Heidelberg (1999). https://doi.org/10.1007/3-540-48169-9_2

4. Altisen, K., Devismes, S., Dubois, S., Petit, F.: Introduction to Distributed Self-Stabilizing Algorithms. Synthesis Lectures on Distributed Computing Theory. Morgan & Claypool Publishers, San Rafael (2019)

5. Awerbuch, B., Patt-Shamir, B., Varghese, G.: Bounding the unbounded. In INFOCOM 1994, pp. 776–783. IEEE Computer Society (1994)

6. Birman, K.P.: A review of experiences with reliable multicast. Softw. Pract. Exper. **29**(9), 741–774 (1999)

7. Blanchard, P., Dolev, S., Beauquier, J., Delaët, S.: Practically self-stabilizing paxos replicated state-machine. In: Noubir, G., Raynal, M. (eds.) NETYS 2014. LNCS, vol. 8593, pp. 99–121. Springer, Cham (2014). https://doi.org/10.1007/978-3-319-09581-3_8

8. Chandra, T.D., Toueg, S.: Unreliable failure detectors for reliable distributed systems. J. ACM **43**(2), 225–267 (1996)

9. Delaët, S., Devismes, S., Nesterenko, M., Tixeuil, S.: Snap-stabilization in message-passing systems. J. Parallel Distrib. Comput. **70**(12), 1220–1230 (2010)

10. Dijkstra, E.W.: Self-stabilizing systems in spite of distributed control. Commun. ACM **17**(11), 643–644 (1974)

11. Dolev, S.: Self-Stabilization. MIT Press, Cambridge (2000)

12. Dolev, S., Georgiou, C., Marcoullis, I., Schiller, E.M.: Self-stabilizing reconfiguration. In: NETYS, pp. 51–68 (2017)

13. Dolev, S., Georgiou, C., Marcoullis, I., Schiller, E.M.: Practically-self-stabilizing virtual synchrony. J. Comput. Syst. Sci. **96**, 50–73 (2018)

14. Dolev, S., Hanemann, A., Schiller, E.M., Sharma, S.: Self-stabilizing end-to-end communication in (bounded capacity, omitting, duplicating and non-fifo) dynamic networks. In: Richa, A.W., Scheideler, C. (eds.) SSS 2012. LNCS, vol. 7596, pp. 133–147. Springer, Heidelberg (2012). https://doi.org/10.1007/978-3-642-33536-5_14

15. Dolev, S., Liba, O., Schiller, E.M.: Self-stabilizing byzantine resilient topology discovery and message delivery. In: Gramoli, V., Guerraoui, R. (eds.) NETYS 2013. LNCS, vol. 7853, pp. 42–57. Springer, Heidelberg (2013). https://doi.org/10.1007/978-3-642-40148-0_4

16. Dolev, S., Gouda, M.G., Schneider, M.: Memory requirements for silent stabilization. Acta Inf. **36**(6), 447–462 (1999)

17. Dolev, S., Petig, T., Schiller, E.M.: Self-stabilizing and private distributed shared atomic memory in seldomly fair message passing networks. CoRR abs, 1806.03498, : http://arxiv.org/abs/1806.03498. An earlier version appeared as Robust and Private Distributed Shared Atomic Memory in Message Passing Networks in PODC **2015**, 311–313 (2018)

18. Dolev, S., Schiller, E.: Communication adaptive self-stabilizing group membership service. IEEE Trans. Parallel Distrib. Syst. **14**(7), 709–720 (2003)

19. Dolev, S., Schiller, E.: Self-stabilizing group communication in directed networks. Acta Inf. **40**(9), 609–636 (2004)

20. Dolev, S., Schiller, E., Welch, J.L.: Random walk for self-stabilizing group communication in ad hoc networks. IEEE Trans. Mob. Comput. **5**(7), 893–905 (2006)

21. Georgiou, C., Lundström, O., Schiller, E.M.: Self-stabilizing snapshot objects for asynchronous failure-prone networked systems. In: Atig, M.F., Schwarzmann, A.A. (eds.) NETYS 2019. LNCS, vol. 11704, pp. 113–130. Springer, Cham (2019). https://doi.org/10.1007/978-3-030-31277-0_8

22. Hadzilacos, V., Toueg, S.: A modular approach to fault-tolerant broadcasts and related problems. Cornell University, Ithaca, NY, USA, Technical report (1994)
23. Imbs, D., Mostéfaoui, A., Perrin, M., Raynal, M.: Set-constrained delivery broadcast: definition, abstraction power, and computability limits. In: 19th Distributed Computing and Networking, ICDCN, pp. 1–10. ACM (2018)
24. Lamport, L.: The implementation of reliable distributed multiprocess systems. Comput. Netw. **2**, 95–114 (1978)
25. Lundström, O., Raynal, M., Schiller, E.M.: Self-stabilizing set-constraint delivery broadcast. In: 40th IEEE International Conference on Distributed Computing Systems, (ICDCS) (2020), to appear
26. Lundström, O., Raynal, M., Schiller, E.M.: Self-stabilizing uniform reliable broadcast. CoRR abs/2001.03244 (2020). https://arxiv.org/abs/2001.03244
27. Raynal, M.: A case study of agreement problems in distributed systems: Non-blocking atomic commitment. In: 2nd High-Assurance Systems Engineering Workshop (HASE '97), pp. 209–214. IEEE Computer Society (1997)
28. Raynal, M.: Fault-Tolerant Message-Passing Distributed Systems - An Algorithmic Approach. Springer, Cham (2018). https://doi.org/10.1007/978-3-319-94141-7
29. Salem, I., Schiller, E.M.: Practically-self-stabilizing vector clocks in the absence of execution fairness. In: 6th Networked Systems, NETYS, pp. 318–333 (2018)
30. Schneider, F.B.: Implementing fault-tolerant services using the state machine approach: a tutorial. ACM Comput. Surv. **22**(4), 299–319 (1990)

Fully Anonymous Consensus and Set Agreement Algorithms

Michel Raynal[1,2] and Gadi Taubenfeld[3(✉)]

[1] Univ Rennes IRISA, Rennes, France
[2] Department of Computing, Polytechnic University, Hong Kong, China
[3] The Interdisciplinary Center, Herzliya, Israel
tgadi@idc.ac.il

Abstract. Process anonymity has been studied for a long time. Memory anonymity is more recent. In an anonymous memory system, there is no a priori agreement among the processes on the names of the shared registers they access. As an example, a shared register named A by a process p and a shared register named B by another process q may correspond to the very same register X, while the same name C may correspond to different shared registers for the processes p and q. This article focuses on solving the consensus and set agreement problems in the *fully anonymous* model, namely a model in which both the processes and the registers are anonymous. It is shown that consensus, and its weak version called set agreement, can be solved despite full anonymity, in the presence of any number of process crashes. As far as we know, this is the first time where non-trivial concurrency-related problems are solved in such a strong anonymity context. A noteworthy property of the proposed algorithms lies in their conceptual simplicity.

Keywords: Anonymity · Anonymous shared memory · Anonymous processes · Asynchrony · Atomic read/write register · Atomic read/modify/write register · Concurrency · Consensus · Crash failure · Process crash · Set agreement · Obstruction-freedom · Wait-freedom

1 Introduction: Computing Model

1.1 On the Process Side

Process Anonymity. The notion of *process anonymity* has been studied for a long time from an algorithmic and computability point of view, both in message-passing systems (e.g., [4,8,32]) and shared memory systems (e.g., [6,9,13]). Process anonymity means that processes have no identity, have the same code and the same initialization of their local variables (otherwise they could be distinguished). Hence, in a process anonymous system, it is impossible to distinguish a process from another process.

A few of the results were mentioned in a brief announcement published in SSS'19 [25].

© Springer Nature Switzerland AG 2021
C. Georgiou and R. Majumdar (Eds.): NETYS 2020, LNCS 12129, pp. 314–328, 2021.
https://doi.org/10.1007/978-3-030-67087-0_20

Process Model. The system is composed of a finite set of $n \geq 2$ asynchronous, anonymous sequential processes denoted $p_1, .., p_n$. Each process p_i knows n, the number of processes, and m, the number of registers. The subscript i in p_i is only a notational convenience, which is not known by the processes. *Sequential* means that a process executes one step (instruction) at a time. *Asynchronous* means that each process proceeds in its own speed, which may vary with time and always remains unknown to the other processes. On the failure side, any number of processes may crash (a crash is a premature stop of a process).

1.2   On the Memory Side

Memory Anonymity. The notion of *memory anonymity* has been recently introduced in [30]. Let us consider a shared memory R made up of m atomic registers. Such a memory can be seen as an array with m entries, namely $R[1..m]$. In a non-anonymous memory system, for each index x, the name $R[x]$ denotes the same register whatever the process that accesses the address $R[x]$. Hence in a non-anonymous memory, there is an a priori agreement on the names of the shared registers. This facilitates the implementation of the coordination rules the processes have to follow to progress without violating the safety properties associated with the application they solve [17,23,29].

The situation is different in an anonymous memory, where there is no a priori agreement on the name of each register. Moreover, all the registers of an anonymous memory are assumed to be initialized to the same value (otherwise, their initial values could provide information allowing processes to distinguish them). In [24], the interested reader may find an introductory survey on models where (1) only processes are anonymous, and (2) only the memory is anonymous. This paper which considers agreement problems, and [26] which considers the mutual problem, are the first to introduce the notion of fully anonymous shared memory systems, where *both* processes and memory are anonymous.

Anonymous Shared Memory. The shared memory is made up of $m \geq 1$ atomic anonymous registers denoted $R[1...m]$. Hence, *all* the registers are anonymous. As already indicated, due to its anonymity, $R[x]$ does not necessarily indicate the same object for different processes. More precisely, a memory-anonymous system is such that:

- For each process p_i an adversary defined a permutation $f_i()$ over the set $\{1, 2, \cdots, m\}$, such that when p_i uses the address $R[x]$, it actually accesses $R[f_i(x)]$,
- No process knows the permutations, and
- All the registers are initialized to the same default value denoted $\perp$.

An example of anonymous memory is presented in Table 1. To make apparent the fact that $R[x]$ can have a different meaning for different processes, we write $R_i[x]$ when p_i invokes $R[x]$.

Table 1. Illustration of an anonymous memory model

Identifiers for an external observer	Local identifiers for process p_i	Local identifiers for process p_j
$R[1]$	$R_i[2]$	$R_j[3]$
$R[2]$	$R_i[3]$	$R_j[1]$
$R[3]$	$R_i[1]$	$R_j[2]$
Permutation	$f_i() : [2, 3, 1]$	$f_j() : [3, 1, 2]$

Anonymous Register Model. We consider three types of anonymous register models.

- RW (read/write) model. In this model, all the registers can be read or written by any process.
- RW/Snapshot (in short RW/Snap) model. In this model, all the registers can be read or written by any process. In addition, each process can apply an atomic *snapshot* operation to obtain the values of all the registers in one atomic step. Thus, for example, assuming that processes communicate through a memory anonymous array $R[1..m]$, the operation $R.\mathsf{snapshot}()$ obtains the values of all the m entries of the array R in one instantaneous step.[1]
- RMW (read/modify/write) model. In this model, each register can be read, written or accessed by an operation that atomically reads the register and (according to the value read) possibly modifies it. More precisely, this operation denoted $\mathsf{compare\&swap}(R[x], old, new)$ has three input parameters, a register $R[x]$ and two values old and new, and returns a Boolean value. It has the following effect: if $R[x] = old$ the value new is assigned to $R[x]$, and the value $\mathtt{true}$ is returned (the $\mathsf{compare\&swap}()$ operation is then successful). If $R[x] \neq old$, $R[x]$ is not modified, and the value $\mathtt{false}$ is returned.

In these models, *atomic* [19] means that the operations on the registers appear as if they have been executed sequentially, each operation appearing between its start event and its end event, and for any $x \in \{1, ...m\}$, each read operation of a register $R[x]$ returns the value v, where v is the last value written in $R[x]$ by a write or a successful $\mathsf{compare\&swap}(R[x], -, -)$ operation (we also say that the execution is *linearizable* [18]). We notice that the RMW model is at least as strong as the RW model.

1.3   Motivation and Content of the Paper

Motivation. This article addresses consensus and set agreement in fully anonymous systems, and has two primary motivations. The first is related to the

---

[1] For a model where the registers are non-anonymous, it is known that the computational power of the RW model and the RW/Snap model are the same despite asynchrony and any number of process crashes [1,3]. For fully anonymous systems, this question is open.

basics of computing, namely, computability and complexity lower/upper bounds. Increasing our knowledge of what can (or cannot) be done in the context of full anonymity (i.e., when both the processes and the memory are anonymous), and providing associated necessary and sufficient conditions, helps us determine the weakest system assumptions under which fundamental problems, such as consensus and set agreement can be solved.

The second motivation is application-oriented. It appears that the concept of an anonymous memory allows epigenetic cell modification to be modeled from a computing point of view [27]. In [27] the authors model histone modifiers (which are a specific type of proteins) as two different types of writer processors and two different types of eraser processors that communicate by accessing an anonymous shared memory array which corresponds to a stretch of DNA, and for such a setting formally define the epigenetic consensus problem. Hence, anonymous shared memories could be useful in biologically inspired distributed systems [21,22]. If this is the case, mastering agreement problems in such an adversarial context could reveal to be important from an application point of view.

Consensus. Consensus is the most important agreement problem of fault-tolerant distributed computing. Let us consider that any number of processes may crash. A crash is a premature halting (hence, until it possibly crashes, a process behaves correctly, i.e., reliably executes its code). The consensus problem consists in building a one-shot operation, denoted propose(), which takes an input parameter (called *proposed* value) and returns a result (called *decided* value). *One-shot* means that a process can invoke the operation at most once. The meaning of this operation is defined as follows:

- Validity: A decided value is a proposed value.
- Agreement: No two processes decide different values.
- Liveness (Wait-freedom): If a process does not crash, it decides a value.

Algorithms solving consensus in different types of non-anonymous shared memory systems are described in several textbooks (e.g.,[17,23,29]). In this paper, we consider the multi-valued version of consensus (i.e., the domain of proposed values is not restricted to be binary). While consensus can be solved from registers in a non-anonymous RMW memory [14], it cannot be solved in a non-anonymous RW memory [12,20]. It is, however, possible to solve a weaker version of consensus in non-anonymous RW system, when the progress condition is weakened as follows [15]:

- Liveness (Obstruction-freedom): If a process does not crash, and executes alone during a long enough period, it decides. I.e., if a process runs alone starting from some point in the execution then it eventually decides.

Set agreement. Set agreement captures a weaker form of consensus in which the agreement property is weakened as follows:

- At most $n-1$ different values are decided upon.

Table 2. Structure of the article

Problem	Section	Crashes possible?	Register model	Progress condition	# of processes n	# of registers m
Set agreement	2	Yes	RW	Obstruction-freedom	$n > 1$	$m \geq 3$
Consensus	3	Yes	RW	Obstruction-freedom	$n = 2$	$m \geq 3$
Consensus	4	Yes	RW/Snap	Obstruction-freedom	$n > 1$	$m \geq 2n - 1$
Consensus	5	Yes	RMW	Wait-freedom	$n > 1$	$m \geq 1$

That is, in any given run, the size of the set of the decision values is at most $n-1$. In particular, in runs in which the n processes propose n different values, instead of forcing the processes to agree on a single value, set agreement forces them to eliminate one of the proposed values. The set agreement problem as defined above is also called the $(n-1)$-set agreement problem [10]. While much weaker than consensus, as consensus, set agreement cannot be solved in crash-prone non-anonymous RW memory systems [7,16,28] (and consequently cannot be solved in a crash-prone anonymous memory systems either), but, as consensus, it can be solved when considering the weaker obstruction-freedom progress condition.

Content of the paper. Table 2 describes the technical content of the paper. As an example, the first line associated with set agreement, states that Sect. 2 presents a set agreement algorithm for an anonymous RW system for any number of $n > 1$ processes and $m \geq 3$ registers.

The paper leaves open the interesting question of whether there exists a fully anonymous obstruction-free consensus algorithm for $n \geq 3$ processes using RW registers.

2 Fully Anonymous Obstruction-Free Set Agreement Using RW Registers

Considering any number $n > 1$ of processes, this section presents an obstruction-free set agreement algorithm for a crash-prone anonymous n-process system, where communication is through $m \geq 3$ anonymous RW registers.

2.1 A Fully Anonymous RW Set Agreement Algorithm

The algorithm is described in Fig. 1. Each anonymous RW register can store the preference of a process. Each participating process p_i scans the m registers trying to write its preference ($mypref_i$) into each one of the m registers.

Before each write, the process scans the shared array (line 3), and operates as follows:

- If its preference appears in all the m registers (line 8), it decides on its preference and terminates.
- Otherwise, if some preference appears in more than half of the registers (line 4), the process adopts this preference as its new preference (line 5).

Afterward, the process finds some arbitrary entry in the shared array that does not contain its preference (line 6) and writes it into that entry (line 7). Once the process finishes writing it repeats the above steps.

2.2   Proof of the Algorithm

Lemma 1 (Set agreement and Termination under Obstruction-freedom). *Any participating process that runs alone for a sufficiently long time, eventually decides. Moreover, the processes that decide, decide on at most $n-1$ different values.*

Proof. Clearly, in all the runs in which less than n processes decide, they decide on at most $n-1$ different values. So, we have to prove that in runs in which all the n processes participate and decide, the n processes decide on at most $n-1$ different values.

Let ρ be an arbitrary run in which all the n processes participate and decide. Each one of the n processes, *before* deciding (line 9), must first read all the m registers (line 3), find out that its preference appears in all the m registers (line 8), decide on its preference and terminate. We call this last reads of the m registers by a specific process a *successful collect* (SC) of that process. We emphasize that from the moment a process starts its successful collect until it decides, it does not write.

Let us denote by p_i and p_j the *last* two processes which start their SC in the run ρ. Clearly, by definition, during these two last SCs, each one of the other processes has either decided and terminated or has already started it SC, and hence does not write during p_i and p_j SCs. We show that p_i and p_j must decide on the same value which implies, as required, that the n processes decide on at most $n-1$ different values in ρ.

From now on we focus only on the processes p_i and p_j. Assume w.l.o.g. that p_i has started its (last and only) SC before process p_j has started its (last and only) SC. Let t_0 and t_1 denote: the last time p_i enters the repeat loop just before reading the m registers (between lines 2–3), and the last time at which p_i exits the repeat loop (between lines 8–9), respectively. At the time interval $[t_0, t_1]$, p_i never writes, and it completes an SC. That is, p_i reads the array once, and finds out that its preference (i.e., $mypref_i$) appears in all the m registers. Let v be the value that p_i reads in its last SC. There are two possible cases.

1. *At time t_0, the values of all the m registers equal v.* After time t_0, and before executing line 3, process p_j might write at most once into one of the m registers possibly overwriting the v value. Thus, when executing line 4, p_j will find that v appears in at least $m-1$ of the entries of $myview_j[1..m]$. Since $m \geq 3$, this means that p_j will find that v appears in more than half

ALGORITHM 1: CODE OF AN ANONYMOUS PROCESS p_i

Constants:
n, m: positive integers   // # of processes and # of shared registers
Anonymous RW registers:
$R[1..m]$: array of $m \geq 3$ registers, initially all $\perp$ // $\perp$ cannot be proposed
Local variables:
$myview_i[1..m]$: array of m variables
$mypref_i$: integer; j: ranges over $\{0, ..., m\}$

---

operation propose(in_i) **is**   // in_i value proposed by p_i
1   $mypref_i \leftarrow in_i$
2   **repeat**
3   **for** $j = 1$ **to** m **do** $myview_i[j] \leftarrow R_i[j]$ **od**   //read the shared array
4   **if** $\exists\, value \neq \perp$ which appears in more than half of the entries of $myview_i[1..m]$
5   **then** $mypref_i \leftarrow value$ **fi**   //update preference
6       $j \leftarrow$ an arbitrary index $k \in \{1, ..., m\}$ such that $myview_i[k] \neq mypref_i$ // search
            or 0 if no such index exists
7   **if** $j \neq 0$ **then** $R_i[j] \leftarrow mypref_i$ **fi**   // write
8   **until** $\forall j \in \{1, ..., m\} : myview_i[j] = mypref_i$ // my $mypref_i$ is everywhere
9   **return**($mypref_i$).   // decide

Fig. 1. Fully anonymous obst.-free set agr. algorithm for $n \geq 2$ proc. and $m \geq 3$ RW registers

of the entries of $myview_j[1..m]$. Thus, p_j will set its preference to v (line 5). From that point on, since p_i does not write anymore, the only possible decision value for p_j is v.

2. *At time t_0, not all the values of the m registers equal v.* Since in the time interval $[t_0, t_1]$, p_i has found that the value of each one of the m registers equals v, it must be that process p_j has written the value v into all the registers with values other than v. Thus, p_j when writing v p_j's preference must be v. Since p_i does not write anymore, the only possible decision value for p_j is v.

As both p_i and p_j decide on the same value v in ρ, it follows that the n processes together decide on at most $n - 1$ different values in ρ.

Let us now show that, under obstruction-freedom (that is, if it runs alone for a sufficiently long time), each process eventually decides (and terminates). When a process, say process p_i, runs alone from some point on in a computation, p_i will read the shared array (line 3) and set its preference to some value v. From that point on, in each iteration of the repeat loop, p_i will set one more entry of the shared array to v. Thus, after at most m iterations the values of all the m entries will equal v, and p_i will be able to exit the repeat loop, decide v and terminate.   □

Lemma 2 (Validity). *The decision value is the input of a participating process.*

Proof. At each point, the current preference of a process is either its initial input or a value (different from $\perp$), it has read from a register. Since a process may only write its preference into a register, the result follows. □

Theorem 1. *Algorithm 1 solves obstruction-free set agreement in a fully anonymous system made up of $n \geq 2$ processes and $m \geq 3$ RW registers.*

Proof. The proof that the algorithm satisfies the Validity, Agreement, and Obstruction-freedom properties (which define set agreement) follows directly from Lemma 1 and Lemma 2. □

3   Fully Anonymous Obstruction-Free Consensus Using RW Registers

As the reader can easily check, instantiating Algorithm 1 with $n = 2$ provides us with 2-process obstruction-free consensus built using $m \geq 3$ RW registers.

Corollary 1. *Algorithm 1 solves consensus in a fully anonymous system made up of two processes and $m \geq 3$ anonymous RW registers. (In the case of binary consensus, the registers are 3-valued registers.)*

It is interesting to note that while it is possible to solve binary consensus for two processes in a fully anonymous system using only 3-valued registers. It is not possible to do so using only 2-valued registers (i.e., bits). It was recently proved in [31] that there is no obstruction-free consensus algorithm for two non-anonymous processes using only anonymous bits. Thus, as was shown in [31], anonymous bits are strictly weaker than anonymous (and hence also non-anonymous) multi-valued registers.

Let us consider a modified version of Algorithm 1, which assumes $n \geq 3$, in which the requirement $m \geq 3$ is strengthened to $m \geq 2n - 1$. It is tempting to think that the resulting algorithm solves obstruction-free consensus for $n \geq 3$ processes.

The (incorrect) supporting argument may go like this. Assume some process p is the first to decide on the value v, after reading that the values of all the $m \geq 2n - 1$ registers equal v. Each of the remaining $n - 1$ processes, before reading the array (line 3), may write at most once into one of the m registers possibly overwriting the v value. Thus, at most $n - 1$ of the values might be overwritten (leaving a majority of v values), before the processes will execute line 3 and find that v appears in more than half of the entries of $myview_i[1..m]$. Each process that finds that v appears in more than half of the entries will set its preference to v (line 5) and must later decide on v.

However, this argument is wrong, and as we prove below the resulting algorithm does not even solve obstruction-free consensus for three processes using five registers.

Theorem 2. *Let $A(n, m)$ be Algorithm 1, in which n is the number of processes and m is the number of anonymous RW registers. Then, for any $n \geq 3$ and any $m \geq 1$, $A(n, m)$ does not solve obstruction-free consensus in a fully anonymous system.*

Proof. The proof is by contradiction. Assume $n = 3$ and $m \geq 1$ registers. Clearly, a result for $n = 3$ implies the result for $n \geq 3$. Let us call the processes p_0, p_1, and p_2. Assume that p_0, p_1, p_2 start with inputs 0,1,0, respectively. Furthermore, we prove the result even under the assumption that, in Algorithm 1, $R[1..m]$ is an array of *non-anonymous* registers. So, below we assume that the registers are non-anonymous.

We first build an infinite run, ρ, which involves p_0 and p_1 only, in which the values of each one of the m registers changes from 0 to 1 and vice versa infinitely many times. To this end, we use the function $\mathsf{dist}(a_1, a_2) = (a_2 - a_1) \bmod m$, defined for $a_1, a_2 \in \{1, ..., m\}$. If we think of the m numbers $1, ..., m$ as being arranged clockwise in a circle, then $\mathsf{dist}(a_1, a_2)$ is the distance one must travel clockwise around the circle starting from a_1 before reaching a_2. In the special case that $a_1 = a_2$, the distance is 0. Thus, $0 \leq \mathsf{dist}(a_1, a_2) \leq m - 1$, and $a_1 + \mathsf{dist}(a_1, a_2) \equiv a_2 \bmod m$.

For $j \in \{1, ..., m\}$ and $v \in \{0, 1\}$, we define the function $\mathsf{next}(j, v)$ to be the value k such that (1) $R[k] \neq v$, and (2) for every $\ell \in \{1, ..., m\}$ where $R[\ell] \neq v$, $d(k, j) \leq d(\ell, j)$. If we think of the m registers $R[1], ..., R[m]$ as being arranged clockwise in a circle, then $\mathsf{next}(j, v)$ is the closest register to $R[j]$ whose value is different than v, where the distance is measured as the number of steps one must travel clockwise around the circle starting from $R[j]$ before reaching $R[k]$. In the special case that $R[j] \neq v$, $\mathsf{next}(j, v) = j$.

The run ρ, which involves processes p_0 and p_1, is constructed as follows:

```
v → 0
repeat forever
    for j = 1 to m do
        ℓ₀ ← next(j, 0); ℓ₁ ← next(j, 1)
        p_v writes v into R[ℓ_v], scans the array and does not change its preference
        p_{1-v} writes 1 − v into R[ℓ_{1-v}], scans the array and does not change its preference
        v ← 1 − v
    end do
end repeat.
```

We notice that until all the m registers are written once, in each iteration of the for loop the two processes write into the same register, and thereafter in each iteration they write into different registers. None of the two processes ever needs to change its preference, and each process writes infinitely many times into each one of the registers. Thus, the above procedure produces the required run ρ.

Since the algorithm is only obstruction-free, the existence of such an infinite run is not yet a problem. To produce the counterexample, consider the run ρ. Now let's interleave read operations of the third process p_2 into the run ρ, such that whenever p_2 reads a register it will see the value 0. Thus, at some point, according to the algorithm, p_2 must decide 0 (without ever writing). At that point, let p_1 continue to run alone and, it will decide on 1. A contradiction. □

We point out that (1) this counterexample will not work if the scan of p_2 (reading the m registers) is done in one atomic step (that is using a snapshot operation), and (2) the counterexample applies for the case where the registers are non-anonymous (and hence also for the case where they are anonymous).

It is known that obstruction-free consensus can be solved for n anonymous processes using $O(n)$ non-anonymous RW registers [9,13]. It is also known that (symmetric) obstruction-free consensus can be solved for n non-anonymous processes using $O(n)$ anonymous RW registers [30]. We leave open the question of whether there exists a *fully anonymous* obstruction-free consensus algorithm for $n \geq 3$ processes using RW registers.

4   Fully Anonymous Obstruction-Free Consensus Using RW/Snapshot Registers

For any number $n > 1$ of processes, we present an obstruction-free consensus algorithm for a crash-prone anonymous n-process system, where communication is through $m \geq 2n - 1$ anonymous RW registers which support snapshot operations.

4.1   A Fully Anonymous Consensus Algorithm

The algorithm is described in Fig. 2. It is similar to that from Fig. 1, where the scan of the array (line 3) is replaced with a snapshot operation. The anonymous memory is made up of $m \geq 2n - 1$ registers. Each anonymous register can store the preference of a process. Each participating process p_i takes a snapshot of the m registers trying to write its preference ($mypref_i$) into each one of the m registers. Before each write, the process takes a snapshot of the shared array (line 4), and operates as follows:

- If its preference appears in all the m registers (line 8), it decides on its preference and terminates.
- Otherwise, if some preference appears in more than half of the registers (line 4), the process adopts this preference as its new preference (line 5).

Afterward, the process finds some arbitrary entry in the shared array that does not contain its preference (line 6) and writes it into that entry (line 7). Once the process finishes writing it repeats the above steps.

4.2   Proof of the Algorithm

Lemma 3 (Consensus and Termination under Obstruction-freedom).
Any participating process that runs alone for a sufficiently long time, eventually decides. Moreover, the processes that decide, decide on the same value and terminate.

ALGORITHM 2: CODE OF AN ANONYMOUS PROCESS p_i

Constants:
  n, m: positive integers   // # of processes and # of shared registers
Anonymous RW/Snapshot registers:
  $R[1..m]$: array of $m \geq 2n - 1$ registers, initially all $\perp$ // $\perp$ cannot be proposed
Local variables:
  $myview_i[1..m]$: array of m variables
  $mypref_i$: integer; j: ranges over $\{0, ..., m\}$

operation propose(in_i) **is**   // in_i value proposed by p_i
1 $mypref_i \leftarrow in_i$
2 **repeat**
3      $\boxed{myview_i[1..m] \leftarrow R.\text{snapshot}()}$ //atomic snapshot of the memory
4   **if** $\exists\, value \neq \perp$ which appears in more than half of the entries of $myview_i[1..m]$
5   **then** $mypref_i \leftarrow value$ **fi**   //update preference
6      $j \leftarrow$ an arbitrary index $k \in \{1, ..., m\}$ such that $myview_i[k] \neq mypref_i$ // search
            or 0 if no such index exists
7   **if** $j \neq 0$ **then** $R_i[j] \leftarrow mypref_i$ **fi**   // write
8 **until** $\forall j \in \{1, ..., m\} : myview_i[j] = mypref_i$ // my $mypref_i$ is everywhere
9 **return**($mypref_i$).   // decide

Fig. 2. Fully anony. obst.-free consensus for $n \geq 2$ proc. and $m \geq 2n-1$ RW/Snapshot re.g.

Proof. Let process p_i be the first process to decide, and denote the value that p_i decides on by v. This means that, before deciding, after taking a snapshot of the anonymous memory, process p_i has found that, *at a certain moment in time*, the value of each one of the m registers equals v. Each one of the other $n - 1$ processes might write into one of the registers overwriting the v value. Since $m \geq 2n - 1$, *all* the other processes, when executing line 7, will find that v appears in more than half of the entries of $R[1..m]$ (i.e., v appears in at least $m - n + 1$ entries), and each one of them will change its preference to v (line 5). From that point on, the only possible decision value is v.

Let us now show that each process eventually decides (and terminates) under the obstruction-freedom assumption. When a process, say process p_i, runs alone from some point on in a computation, p_i will take a snapshot of the shared array (line 3) and set its preference to v (if it is not v already). From that point on, in each iteration of the repeat loop, process p_i will set one additional entry of the shared array to v. Thus, after at most $m \geq 2n - 1$ iterations the values of all the m entries will equal v, and process p_i will be able to exit the repeat loop, decide v and terminate.   □

Lemma 4 (Validity). *The decision value is the input of a participating process.*

Proof. At each point, the current preference of a process is either its initial input or a value (different from $\perp$), it has read from a register. Since a process may only write its preference into a register, the result follows. □

Theorem 3. *Algorithm* 2 *solves obstruction-free consensus in a fully anonymous system made up of* $n \geq 2$ *processes and* $m \geq 2n - 1$ RW/Snapshot *registers.*

Proof. The proof that the algorithm satisfies the Validity, Agreement, and Obstruction-freedom properties (which define set agreement) follows directly from Lemma 3 and Lemma 4. □

Remark. Algorithm 1 and Algorithm 2 are actually two instances of an agreement-oriented generic algorithm suited for the crash-prone fully asynchronous model, which ensures termination under the obstruction-freedom assumption. The genericity dimension resides in line 3, which states the way a process reads the content of the anonymous memory, namely an asynchronous scan (Algorithm 1) or a snapshot (Algorithm 2). When $m \geq 2n - 1$ (condition for Algorithm 2), the atomicity of the snapshot operation is powerful enough to go from set-agreement (Algorithm 1) to consensus (Algorithm 2).

5   Fully Anonymous Wait-Free Consensus Using RMW Registers

When considering a fully anonymous system of size $m = 1$, consensus can be easily solved with the compare&swap() operation: the first process that writes its value in the single register $R[1]$ (initialized to $\perp$) imposes it as the decided value (actually, when $m = 1$ the memory is not really anonymous). When using anonymous objects, the fact that a given problem can be solved using only one object (i.e., $m = 1$) does *not* imply that the problem can also be solved using any finite number of $m \geq 1$ objects [5]. For a fully anonymous system, we prove the following simple result,

Theorem 4. *There is a fully anonymous wait-free consensus algorithm for* n *processes using* m RMW *registers, for any* $n \geq 1$ *and* $m \geq 1$.

Proof. The simple algorithm described in Fig. 3 presents a simple consensus algorithm for any size $m \geq 1$ of the anonymous RMW memory. This algorithm assumes that the set of values that can be proposed is totally ordered. Each process tries to write the value it proposes into each anonymous register. Assuming that at least one process that does not crash invokes propose(), there is a finite time after which, whatever the concurrency/failure pattern, each anonymous register contains a proposed value. Then, using the same deterministic rule the processes decide the same value (let us notice that there is an a priori statically defined agreement on the deterministic rule used to select the decided value). □

ALGORITHM 3: CODE OF AN ANONYMOUS PROCESS p_i

Constants:
  n, m: positive integers   // # of processes and # of shared registers
Anonymous RMW registers:
  $R[1..m]$: array of m RMW registers, initially all $\perp$ // $\perp$ cannot be proposed

operation propose(in_i) **is**   // in_i value proposed by p_i
1 **for each** $j \in \{1, ..., m\}$ **do** compare&swap($R_i[j], \perp, in_i$) **od**   // try to write
2 return(max($R_i[1], ..., R_i[m]$))   // decide the max value in $R[1..m]$.

Fig. 3. Consensus for $n \geq 2$ anonymous processes and $m \geq 1$ anonymous RMW registers

6 Conclusion

This article has several contributions. The first is the introduction, together with [26], of the notion of *fully anonymous* shared memory systems, namely systems where the processes are anonymous, and there is no global agreement on the names of the shared registers (any register can have different names for distinct processes). The article has then addressed the design of agreement algorithms (consensus and set agreement) in specific contexts where the anonymous registers are read/write (RW) registers, RW/snapshot registers, or read/modify/write (RMW) registers. We leave open the interesting question of whether there exists a fully anonymous obstruction-free consensus algorithm for three or more processes using RW registers.

Last but not least, let us notice that, despite the strong adversary context (full anonymity and failures), the proposed algorithms are relatively simple to understand[2]. However, some of their proofs are subtle.

Acknowledgments. M. Raynal was partially supported by the French ANR project DESCARTES (16-CE40-0023-03) devoted to layered and modular structures in distributed computing.

References

1. Afek, Y., Attiya, H., Dolev, D., Gafni, E., Merritt, M., Shavit, N.: Atomic snapshots of shared memory. J. ACM **40**(4), 873–890 (1993)
2. Aigner, M., Ziegler, G.M.: Probability makes counting (sometimes) easy. Proofs from THE BOOK, p. 274. Springer, Heidelberg (2018). https://doi.org/10.1007/978-3-662-57265-8_45. ISBN 978-3-642-00856-6

---

[2] Let us remind that simplicity is a first class property [2,11]. A stated by J. Perlis (the recipient of the first Turing Award) "Simplicity does not precede complexity, but follows it".

3. Anderson, J.H.: Multi-writer composite registers. Distrib. Comput. **7**(4), 175–195 (1994)
4. Angluin D., Local and global properties in networks of processes. In: Proceedings 12th Symposium on Theory of Computing (STOC'80), pp. 82–93. ACM Press (1980)
5. Aghazadeh Z., Imbs D., Raynal M., Taubenfeld G., Woelfel, P.: Optimal memory-anonymous symmetric deadlock-free mutual exclusion. In: Proceedings 38th ACM Symposium on Principles of Distributed Computing (PODC'19), p. 10. ACM Press (2019)
6. Attiya, H., Gorbach, A., Moran, S.: Computing in totally anonymous asynchronous shared-memory systems. Inf. Comput. **173**(2), 162–183 (2002)
7. Borowsky E. and Gafni E., Generalized FLP impossibility results for t-resilient asynchronous computations. In: Proceedings 25th ACM Symposium on Theory of Computing (STOC'93), pp. 91–100 . ACM Press (1993)
8. Bonnet, F., Raynal, M.: Anonymous asynchronous systems: the case of failure detectors. Distrib. Comput. **26**(3), 141–158 (2013)
9. Bouzid, Z., Raynal, M., Sutra, P.: Anonymous obstruction-free (n, k)-set agreement with $(n-k+1)$ atomic read/write registers. Distrib. Comput. **31**(2), 99–117 (2018)
10. Chaudhuri, S.: More choices allow more faults: set consensus problems in totally asynchronous systems. Inf. Comput. **105**(1), 132–158 (1993)
11. Dijkstra, E.W.: Some beautiful arguments using mathematical induction. Algorithmica **13**(1), 1–8 (1980)
12. Fischer, M.J., Lynch, N.A., Paterson, M.S.: Impossibility of distributed consensus with one faulty process. J. ACM **32**(2), 374–382 (1985)
13. Guerraoui, R., Ruppert, E.: Anonymous and fault-tolerant shared-memory computations. Distrib. Comput. **20**, 165–177 (2007)
14. Herlihy, M.P.: Wait-free synchronization. ACM Trans. Programm. Lang. Syst. **13**(1), 124–149 (1991)
15. Herlihy M.P., Luchangco V., Moir M.: Obstruction-free synchronization: double-ended queues as an example. In: Proceedings 23th International IEEE Conference on Distributed Computing Systems (ICDCS 2003), pp. 522–529. IEEE Press (2003)
16. Herlihy, M.P., Shavit, N.: The topological structure of asynchronous computability. J. ACM **46**(6), 858–923 (1999)
17. Herlihy, M., Shavit, N.: The Art of Multiprocessor Programming, p. 508. Morgan Kaufmann, Cambridge (2008). ISBN 978-0-12-370591-4
18. Herlihy, M.P., Wing, J.M.: Linearizability: a correctness condition for concurrent objects. ACM Trans. Programm. Lang. Syst. **12**(3), 463–492 (1990)
19. Lamport, L.: On interprocess communication, part I: basic formalism. Distrib. Comput. **1**(2), 77–85 (1986)
20. Loui, M., Abu-Amara, H.: Memory requirements for agreement among unreliable asynchronous processes. Adv. Comput. Res. **4**, 163–183. JAI Press (1987)
21. Navlakha, S., Bar-Joseph, Z.: Algorithms in nature: the convergence of systems biology and computational thinking. Mol. Syst. Biol. **7**(546), 1–11 (2011)
22. Navlakha, S., Bar-Joseph, Z.: Distributed information processing in biological and computational systems. Communi. ACM **58**(1), 94–102 (2015)
23. Raynal, M.: Concurrent Programming: Algorithms, Principles and Foundations, p. 515. Springer, Dordrecht (2013). https://doi.org/10.1007/978-3-642-32027-9. ISBN 978-3-642-32026-2
24. Raynal, M., Cao, J.: Anonymity in distributed read/write systems: an introductory survey. In: Podelski, A., Taïani, F. (eds.) NETYS 2018. LNCS, vol. 11028, pp. 122–140. Springer, Cham (2019). https://doi.org/10.1007/978-3-030-05529-5_9

M. Raynal and G. Taubenfeld

25. Raynal, M., Taubenfeld, G.: Brief announcement: fully anonymous shared memory algorithms. In: Ghaffari, M., Nesterenko, M., Tixeuil, S., Tucci, S., Yamauchi, Y. (eds.) SSS 2019. LNCS, vol. 11914, pp. 301–306. Springer, Cham (2019). https://doi.org/10.1007/978-3-030-34992-9_24
26. Raynal, M., Taubenfeld, G.: Mutual exclusion in fully anonymous shared memory systems. Inf. Process. Lett. **158**, 105938 (2020)
27. Rashid S., Taubenfeld G., Bar-Joseph, Z.: Genome wide epigenetic modifications as a shared memory consensus problem. In: 6th Workshop on Biological Distributed Algorithms (BDA'18), London (2018)
28. Saks, M., Zaharoglou, F.: Wait-free k-set agreement is impossible: the topology of public knowledge. SIAM J. Comput. **29**(5), 1449–1483 (2000)
29. Taubenfeld, G.: Synchronization algorithms and concurrent programming, p. 423. Prentice Hall, Pearson Education (2006). ISBN 0-131-97259-6
30. Taubenfeld G.: Coordination without prior agreement. In: Proceeding 36th ACM Symposium on Principles of Distributed Computing (PODC 2017), pp. 325–334. ACM Press (2017)
31. Taubenfeld, G.: Set agreement power is not a precise characterization for oblivious deterministic anonymous objects. In: Censor-Hillel, K., Flammini, M. (eds.) SIROCCO 2019. LNCS, vol. 11639, pp. 293–308. Springer, Cham (2019). https://doi.org/10.1007/978-3-030-24922-9_20
32. Yamashita, M., Kameda, T.: Computing on anonymous networks: part I - characterizing the solvable cases. IEEE Trans. Parallel Distrib. Syst. **7**(1), 69–89 (1996)

Cutoffs for Symmetric Point-to-Point Distributed Algorithms

Thanh-Hai Tran[1], Igor Konnov[2(✉)], and Josef Widder[2]

[1] TU Wien, Vienna, Austria
[2] Informal Systems, Vienna, Austria
`igor@informal.systems`

Abstract. Distributed algorithms are typically parameterized in the number of participants. While in general, parameterized verification is undecidable, many distributed algorithms such as mutual exclusion, cache coherence, and distributed consensus enjoy the cutoff property, which reduces the parameterized verification problem to verification of a finite number of instances. Failure detection algorithms do not fall into one of the known classes. While consensus algorithms, for instance, are quorum-based, failure detectors typically rely on point-to-point communication and timeouts. In this paper, we formalize this communication structure and introduce the class of symmetric point-to-point algorithms. We show that the symmetric point-to-point algorithms have a cutoff. As a result, one can verify them by model checking small instances. We demonstrate the feasibility of our approach by specifying the failure detector by Chandra and Toueg in TLA$^+$, and by model checking them with the TLC and the APALACHE model checkers.

Keywords: TLA$^+$ · Parameterized model checking · Failure detectors · Symmetry · Point-to-point communication

1 Introduction

Nowadays, many high-reliability systems are distributed and parameterized in some manner, e.g. the number of participants, or the size of message buffers. Since the number and the cost of failures of these systems increases [2], industry has applied many automated techniques to reason about their correctness at the design and implementation levels, such as model checking [6,17,24,28], and testing [19]. While these methods report positive results in analyzing individual system configurations with fixed parameter values, the real goal is to verify *all* configurations, i.e., with infinitely many vectors of parameter values.

Unfortunately, the parameterized verification problem is typically undecidable, even if every participant follows the same code [1,3,27]. This negative result has led naturally to two approaches of algorithm analyses: (a) semi-automated

Supported by Interchain Foundation (Switzerland) and the Austrian Science Fund (FWF) via the Doctoral College LogiCS W1255.

C. Georgiou and R. Majumdar (Eds.): NETYS 2020, LNCS 12129, pp. 329–346, 2021.
https://doi.org/10.1007/978-3-030-67087-0_21

methods based on user-guided invariants and proof assistants, and (b) automatic techniques for restricted classes of algorithms and properties. A particularly fascinating case is the cutoff property that guarantees that analyzing a few small instances is sufficient to reason about the correctness of all instances [8,15]. In a nutshell, given a property ξ and a system that has a parameter **m**, there exists a number $B \geq 1$ such that whenever all instances that assign a value not greater than B to a parameter **m** satisfy ξ, then all instances which assign an arbitrary number to **m** satisfy ξ. Hence, verification of algorithms that enjoy the cutoff property can be done by model checking of finite instances.

In this paper, we introduce the class of symmetric point-to-point algorithms that enjoys the cutoff property. Informally, an instance in this class contains N processes that follow the same algorithm, and communicate with each other by sending and receiving messages through point-to-point communication channels. At each process, local memory can be partitioned into regions such that one region corresponds one-to-one with a remote process, e.g. the array element *timeout* $[p,q]$ at a process p stores the maximum waiting time for a process q by the process p. The failure detector [5] is one example of this class. Let $1..N$ be a set of indexes. We show two cutoffs for these algorithms:

1. Let i be an index, and $\omega_{\{i\}}$ be an LTL\X (the stuttering-insensitive linear temporal logic) formula in which every predicate takes one of the forms: $P_1(i)$ or $P_2(i,i)$. Properties of the form $\bigwedge_{i \in 1..N} \omega_{\{i\}}$ has a cutoff of 1.
2. Let i and j be different indexes, and $\psi_{\{i,j\}}$ be an LTL\X formula in which every predicate takes one of the (syntactic) forms: $Q_1(i)$, or $Q_2(j)$, or $Q_3(i,j)$, or $Q_4(j,i)$. Properties of the form $\bigwedge_{i,j \in 1..N}^{i \neq j} \psi_{\{i,j\}}$ has a cutoff of 2.

For instance, by the second cutoff result, we can verify the following property called the strong completeness property of the failure detector in [5] by model checking of an instance of size 2.

$$\mathbf{FG}(\forall i,j \in 1..N : (Correct(i) \land \neg Correct(j)) \Rightarrow Suspected(i,j))$$

This formula means that every crashed process is eventually permanently suspected by every correct process. We are writing $\mathbf{F}$ and $\mathbf{G}$ to denote "eventually" and "globally" operators of linear temporal logic (LTL), see [9]. We demonstrate the feasibility of our approach by specifying Chandra and Toueg's failure detectors [5] in the language TLA$^+$ [22], and model checking the specification with two model checkers: TLC [28] and APALACHE [20].

Related work. Our work is inspired by the cutoff results for various models of computation: ring-based message-passing systems [14,15], purely disjunctive guards and conjunctive guards [12,13], token-based communication [8], and quorum-based algorithms [23]. Additionally, there are semi-decision procedures based on invariants, induction, and abstraction that are successful in many interesting cases [4,7,18,21,25]. Interactive verification methods with proof assistants [10,16,26] have produced positive results in proving distributed algorithms.

The paper is organized as follows. Section 2 presents our motivating example - Chandra and Toueg's failure detector [5], and challenges in verification of these algorithms. Section 3 defines the model of computation as a transition system.

Section 4 shows our main contributions: two cutoff results in the class of symmetric point-to-point distributed algorithms. Section 5 presents how we encode the model of computation, and the failure detector of [5] in TLA$^+$, and the model checking results. Section 6 concludes the paper with a discussion of future extensions.

2   Motivating Example

This section starts with a description of our motivating example – Chandra and Toueg's failure detector [5]. Then, we present challenges in verification of the failure detector, and state-of-the-art verification techniques.

Algorithm 1 presents the pseudo-code of the failure detector of [5]. A system instance has N processes that communicate with each other by sending-to-all and receiving messages through N^2 point-to-point communication channels. A process performs local computation based on these messages (we assume that a process also receives the messages that it sends to itself). In one system step, all processes may take up to one step. Some processes may crash, i.e., stop operating. Correct processes follow Algorithm 1 to detect crashes in the system. Initially, every correct process sets a default value for a timeout of each other, i.e. how long it should wait for others and assumes that no processes have crashed (Line 4). Every correct process p has three tasks: (i) repeatedly sends an "alive" message to all (Line 6), and (ii) repeatedly produces predictions about crashes of other processes based on timeouts (Line 8), and (iii) increases a timeout for a process q if p has learned that its suspicion on q is wrong (Line 12). Notice that a process p raises suspicion on the operation of a process q (Line 8) by considering only information related to q: *timeout* $[p, q]$, *suspected* $[p, q]$, and messages that p has received from q recently. In other words, its suspicions about other processes grow independently.

Let *Correct*(p) be a predicate whether a process p is correct. (However, p can crash later. A crashed process p_1 satisfies $\neg Correct(p_1)$.) Let *Suspected*(p, q) be a predicate whether a process p suspects a process q. The failure detector should guarantee the following properties [5]:

- Strong completeness: Every crashed process is eventually permanently suspected by every correct process.

$$\mathbf{FG}(\forall p, q \in 1..N : (Correct(p) \wedge \neg Correct(q)) \Rightarrow Suspected(p, q))$$

- Eventual strong accuracy: There is a time after which correct processes are not suspected by any correct processes.

$$\mathbf{FG}(\forall p, q \in 1..N : (Correct(p) \wedge Correct(q)) \Rightarrow \neg Suspected(p, q))$$

In the asynchronous model, Algorithm 1 does not satisfy eventually strong accuracy since there exists no bound on message delay, and messages sent by correct processes might always arrive after the timeout expires. The correctness of failure detectors is based on two implicit time constraints: (1) the transmission delay of messages and (2) the relative speeds of different processes [5]. Even if these upper bounds exist but are unknown, failure detectors can satisfy both strong completeness and eventual strong accuracy.

Algorithm 1. The eventually perfect failure detector algorithm in [5]

1: *Every process* $p \in \Pi$ *executes the following*:
2: **for all** $q \in \Pi$ **do**   ▷ Initalization step
3:     $timeout\,[p, q]$ = default-value
4:     $suspected\,[p, q] = \bot$ }

5:
6: Send "alive" to all $q \in \Pi$ ▷ Task 1: repeat periodically

7:
8: **for all** $q \in \Pi$ **do**   ▷ Task 2: repeat periodically
9:     **if** $suspected\,[p, q] = \bot$ **and not hear** q during last $timeout\,[p, q]$ ticks **then**
10:        $suspected\,[p, q] = \top$

11:
12: **if** $suspected\,[p, q]$ **then**   ▷ Task 3: when receive "alive" from q
13:     $timeout\,[p, q] \leftarrow timeout\,[p, q] + 1$
14:     $suspected\,[p, q] = \bot$

Note that the symmetry exists in both the failure detectors of [5] and the above correctness properties. First, every process is isomorphic under renaming. A correct process p always sends a message to all and raises suspicion on a process q by considering only information related to q. Second, there are only point-to-point communication channels. Third, the contents of in-transit messages is identical. They are merely "keep-alive" messages that may arrive at different times. Finally, all variables in both properties strong completeness and eventual strong accuracy are variables over process indices, and they are bound by universal quantifiers. The symmetry is captured by our model of computation and is the key point in our proofs of the cutoff results.

As a result, verification of failure detectors faces the following challenges:

1. Algorithms are parameterized by the number of processes. Hence, we need to verify infinitely many instances of algorithms.
2. Its model of computation lies between synchrony and asynchrony since multiple processes can take a step in a global transition.
3. The algorithm relies on a global clock and local clocks. A straightforward encoding of a clock with an integer would produce an infinite state space.
4. The algorithm is parameterized with the upper bounds on transmission time of messages, and the relative speeds of different processes. These upper bounds are called Δ and Φ, respectively.

In this paper, we focus on Challenges 1–2: Our model of computation in Sect. 3 does not restrict the number of processes that simultaneously take a step, and we show cutoffs on the number of processes in Sect. 4. Our cutoff results apply for checking LTL\X formulas of the forms $\bigwedge_{i \in 1..N} \omega_{\{1\}}$ and $\bigwedge_{i,j \in 1..N}^{i \neq j} \psi_{\{1,2\}}$. Hence, we can verify the failure detector of [5] by model checking its few instances. We demonstrate the feasibility of our approach by specifying and model checking the failure detector in the *synchronous* case. Our specification contains optimizations for Challenge 3, which allows us to efficiently encode global and local clocks. In the synchronous case, we can skip Challenge 4, which we leave for furture work.

3   Model of Computation

In this section, we formalize a distributed system as a transition system. This formalization captures the semantics of the theoretical model of [5,11], but does not consider the restrictions on the execution space given by Δ and Φ. A global system is a composition of N processes, N^2 point-to-point outgoing message buffers, and N control components that capture what processes can take a step. Every process is identified with a unique index in $1..N$, and follows the same deterministic algorithm. Moreover, a global system allows: (i) multiple processes to take (at most) one step in one global transition, and (ii) some processes to crash. Every process may execute three kinds of transitions: *internal*, *round*, and stuttering. Notice that in one global transition, some processes may send a message to all, and some may receive messages and do computation. Hence, we need to decide which processes move, and what happens to the message buffers. We introduce four sub-rounds: *Schedule*, *Send*, *Receive*, and *Computation*. The transitions for these sub-rounds are called internal ones. A global round transition is a composition of four internal transitions. We formalize sub-rounds and global transitions later. As a result of modeling, there exists an arbitrary sequence of global configurations which is not accepted in [5,11]. We define so-called *admissible* sequences of global configurations that are accepted in [5,11]. We did encode our formalization in TLA^+, and our specification is presented in Sect. 5.

Since every process follows the same algorithm, we first define a process template that captures the process behavior. This formalization focuses on symmetric point-to-point algorithms parameterized by N. Every process is an instance of the process template. Then, we present the formalization of a global system.

3.1   The Process Template

We fix a set of process indexes as $1..N$. Moreover, we assume that the message content does not have indexes of its receiver and sender. We let Msg denote a set of potential messages, and $\mathrm{Set}(\mathrm{Msg})$ denote a set of sets of messages.

We model a process template as a transition system $\mathcal{U}_N = (Q_N, Tr_N, Rel_N, q_N^0)$ where $Q_N = Loc \times \mathrm{Set}(\mathrm{Msg})^N \times \mathcal{D}^N$ is a set of template states, Tr_N is a set of template transitions, $Rel_N \subseteq Q_N \times Tr_N \times Q_N$ is a template transition relation, and $q_N^0 \in Q_N$ is an initial state. These components of $\mathcal{U}_N$ are defined as follows.

States. A *template state* ρ is a tuple $(\ell, S_1, \ldots, S_N, d_1, \ldots, d_N)$ where:

- $\ell \in Loc$ refers to a location of a program counter, and Loc is a set of locations. We assume that $Loc = Loc_{snd} \cup Loc_{rcv} \cup Loc_{comp} \cup \{\ell_{crash}\}$, and three sets $Loc_{snd}, Loc_{rcv}, Loc_{comp}$ are disjoint, and ℓ_{crash} is a special location of crashes. To access the program counter, we use a function $pc \colon Q_N \to Loc$ that takes a template state at its input, and produces its program counter as the output. Let $\rho(k)$ denote the kth component in a template state ρ. For every $\rho \in Q_N$, we have $pc(\rho) = \rho(1)$.
- $S_i \in \mathrm{Set}(\mathrm{Msg})$ refers to a set of messages. It is to store the messages received from a process p_i for every $i \in 1..N$. To access a set of received messages from

a particular process whose index in $1..N$, we use a function $rcvd\colon Q_N \times 1..N \to$ Set(Msg) that takes a template state ρ and a process index i at its input, and produces the $(i+1)^{th}$ component of ρ at the output, i.e. for every $\rho \in Q_N$, we have $rcvd(\rho, i) = \rho(1+i)$.

- $d_i \in \mathcal{D}$ refers to a local variable related to a process p_i for every $i \in 1..N$. To access a local variable related to a particular process whose index in $1..N$, we use a function $lvar\colon Q_N \times 1..N \to \mathcal{D}$ that takes a template state ρ and a process index i at its input, and produces the $(1+N+i)^{th}$ component of ρ as the output, i.e. $lvar(\rho, i) = \rho(1+N+i)$ for every $\rho \in Q_N$.

Initial State. The initial state q_N^0 is a tuple $q_N^0 = (\ell_0, \emptyset, \ldots, \emptyset, d_0, \ldots, d_0)$ where ℓ_0 is a location, every box for received messages is empty, and every local variable is assigned a constant $d_0 \in \mathcal{D}$.

Transitions. We define $Tr_N = CSnd \cup CRcv \cup \{comp, crash, stutter\}$ where

- $CSnd$ is a set of transitions. Every transition in $CSnd$ refers to a task that does some internal computation, and sends a message to all. For example, in task 1 in Algorithm 1, a process increases its local clock, and performs an instruction to send "alive" to all. We let $csnd(m)$ denote a transition referring to a task with an action to send a message $m \in$ Msg to all.
- $CRcv$ is a set of transitions. Every transition in $CRcv$ refers to a task that receives N sets of messages, and does some internal computation. For example, in task 2 in Algorithm 1, a process increases its local clock, receives messages, and remove false-negative predictions. We let $crcv(S_1, \ldots, S_N)$ denote a transition referring to a task with an action to receive sets $S_1, \ldots, S_N$ of messages. These sets $S_1, \ldots, S_N$ are delivered by the global system.
- $comp$ is a transition which refers to a task with purely local computation. In other words, this task has neither send actions nor receive actions.
- $crash$ is a transition for crashes.
- $stutter$ is a transition for stuttering steps.

Transition Relation. For two states $\rho, \rho' \in Q_N$ and a transition $tr \in Tr_N$, we write $\rho \xrightarrow{tr} \rho'$, instead of $(\rho, \xrightarrow{tr}, \rho')$. In the model of [5,11], each process follows the same deterministic algorithm. Hence, we assume that for every $\rho_0 \xrightarrow{tr_0} \rho'_0$ and $\rho_1 \xrightarrow{tr_1} \rho'_1$, if $\rho_0 = \rho_1$ and $tr_0 = tr_1$, then it follows that $\rho'_0 = \rho'_1$. Moreover, we assume that there exist the following functions which are used to define constraints on the template transition relation:

- A function $nextLoc\colon Loc \to Loc$ takes a location at its input and produces the next location as the output.
- A function $genMsg\colon Loc \to$ Set(Msg) a location at its input, and produces a singleton set that contains the message that is sent to all processes in the current task. The output can be an empty set. For example, if a process is performing a receive task, the output of $genMsg$ is an empty set.
- A function $nextVar\colon Loc \times$ Set(Msg) $\times \mathcal{D} \to \mathcal{D}$ takes a location, a set of messages, and a local variable's value, and produces a new value of a local variable as the output.

Let us fix functions $nextLoc$, $genMsg$ and $nextVar$. We define the template transitions as follows.

1. For every $m \in \mathsf{Msg}$, for every pair of states $\rho, \rho' \in Q_N$, we have $\rho \xrightarrow{csnd(m)} \rho'$ if and only if
   (a) $pc(\rho') = nextLoc(pc(\rho)) \wedge \{m\} = genMsg(pc(\rho))$
   (b) $\forall i \in 1..N : rcvd(\rho, i) = rcvd(\rho', i)$
   (c) $\forall i \in 1..N : lvar(\rho', i) = nextVar(pc(\rho), rcvd(\rho', i), lvar(\rho, i))$
   Constraint (a) implies that the update of a program counter and the construction of a sent message m depend on only the current value of a program counter, and a process wants to send only m to all in this step. Constraint (b) is that no message was delivered. Constraint (c) implies that the value of $lvar(\rho', i)$ depends on only the current location, a set of messages that have been delivered and stored in $rcvd(\rho', i)$, and the value of $lvar(\rho, i)$.

2. For every $S_1, \ldots, S_N \subseteq \mathsf{Msg}$, for every pair of states $\rho, \rho' \in Q_N$, we have $\rho \xrightarrow{crcv(S_1, \ldots, S_N)} \rho'$ if and only if the following constraints hold:
   (a) $pc(\rho') = nextLoc(pc(\rho)) \wedge \emptyset = genMsg(pc(\rho))$
   (b) $\forall i \in 1..N : rcvd(\rho', i) = rcvd(\rho, i) \cup S_i$
   (c) $\forall i \in 1..N : lvar(\rho', i) = nextVar(pc(\rho), rcvd(\rho', i), lvar(\rho, i))$
   Constraint (a) in $crcv$ is similar to constraint (a) in $csnd$, except that no message is sent in this sub-round. Constraint (b) refers that messages in a set S_i are from a process indexed i, and have been delivered in this step. Constraint (c) in $crcv$ is similar to constraint (c) in $csnd$.

3. For every pair of states $\rho, \rho' \in Q_N$, we have $\rho \xrightarrow{comp} \rho'$ if and only if the following constraints hold:
   (a) $pc(\rho') = nextLoc(pc(\rho)) \wedge \emptyset = genMsg(pc(\rho))$
   (b) $\forall i \in 1..N : rcvd(\rho', i) = rcvd(\rho, i)$
   (c) $\forall i \in 1..N : lvar(\rho', i) = nextVar(pc(\rho), rcvd(\rho', i), lvar(\rho, i))$
   Hence, this step has only local computation. No message is sent or delivered.

4. For every pair of states $\rho, \rho' \in Q_N$, we have $\rho \xrightarrow{crash} \rho'$ if and only if the following constraints hold:
   (a) $pc(\rho) \neq \ell_{crash} \wedge pc(\rho') = \ell_{crash}$
   (b) $\forall i \in 1..N : rcvd(\rho, i) = rcvd(\rho', i) \wedge lvar(\rho, i) = lvar(\rho', i)$
   Only the program counter is updated by switching to ℓ_{crash}.

5. For every pair of states $\rho, \rho' \in Q_N$, we have $\rho \xrightarrow{stutter} \rho'$ if and only if $\rho = \rho'$.

3.2   Modeling the Distributed System

Given N processes which are instantiated from the same process template $\mathcal{U}_N = (Q_N, Tr_N, Rel_N, q_N^0)$, the global system is a composition of (i) these processes, and (ii) N^2 point-to-point buffers for in-transit messages, and (iii) N control components that capture what processes can take a step. We formalize the global system as a transition system $\mathcal{G}_N = (\mathcal{C}_N, T_N, R_N, g_N^0)$ where $\mathcal{C}_N = (Q_N)^N \times \mathsf{Set}(\mathsf{Msg})^{N \cdot N} \times \mathsf{Bool}^N$ is a set of global configurations, and T_N is a set of global *internal*, *round*, and stuttering transitions, and $R_N \subseteq \mathcal{C}_N \times T_N \times \mathcal{C}_N$ is a global transition relation, and g_N^0 is an initial configuration. These components are defined as follows.

Configurations. A *global configuration* κ is defined as a following tuple $\kappa = (q_1, \ldots, q_N, S_1^1, S_1^2 \ldots, S_s^r, \ldots S_N^N, act_1, \ldots, act_N)$ where:

- $q_i \in Q_N$: This component is a state of a process p_i for every $i \in 1..N$. To access a local state of a particular process, we use a function $lstate: \mathcal{C}_N \times 1..N \rightarrow Q_N$ that takes input as a global configuration κ and a process index i, and produces output as the ith component of κ which is a state of a process p_i. Let $\kappa(i)$ denote the ith component of a global configuration κ. For every $i \in 1..N$, we have $lstate(\kappa, i) = \kappa(i) = q_i$.
- $S_s^r \in \mathsf{Set}(\mathsf{Msg})$: This component is a set of in-transit messages from a process p_s to a process p_r for every $s, r \in 1..N$. To access a set of in-transit messages between two processes, we use a function $buf: \mathcal{C}_N \times 1..N \times 1..N \rightarrow \mathsf{Set}(\mathsf{Msg})$ that takes input as a global configuration κ, and two process indexes s, r, and produces output as the $(s \cdot N + r)^{th}$ component of κ which is a message buffer from a process p_s (sender) to a process p_r (receiver). Formally, we have $buf(\kappa, s, r) = \kappa(s \cdot N + r) = S_s^r$ for every $s, r \in 1..N$.
- $act_i \in \mathsf{Bool}$: This component says whether a process p_i can take one step in a global transition for every $i \in 1..N$. To access a control component, we use a function $active: \mathcal{C}_N \times 1..N \rightarrow \mathsf{Bool}$ that takes input as a configuration κ and a process index i, and produces output as the $((N+1) \cdot N + i)^{th}$ component of κ which refers to whether a process p_i can take a step. Formally, we have $active(\kappa, i) = \kappa((N+1) \cdot N + i) = b_i$ for every $i \in 1..N$. The environment sets the values of $act_1, \ldots, act_N$ in the sub-round Schedule defined later.

We will write $\kappa \in (Q_N)^N \times \mathsf{Set}(\mathsf{Msg})^{N \cdot N} \times \mathsf{Bool}^N$ or $\kappa \in \mathcal{C}_N$.

Initial Configuration. The global system $\mathcal{G}_N$ has one initial configuration g_N^0, and it must satisfy the following constraints:

1. $\forall i \in 1..N: \neg active(g_N^0, i) \wedge lstate(N, i) = q_N^0$
2. $\forall s, r \in 1..N: buf(g_N^0, s, r) = \emptyset$

Global Round Transitions. Intuitively, every *round* transition is a sequence of a $\xrightarrow{\mathsf{Sched}}$ transition, a $\xrightarrow{\mathsf{Snd}}$ transition, a $\xrightarrow{\mathsf{Rcv}}$ transition, and a $\xrightarrow{\mathsf{Comp}}$ transition defined below. We let $\rightsquigarrow$ denote *round* transitions. The semantics of round transitions is defined as follows: for every pair of global configurations $\kappa_0, \kappa_4 \in \mathcal{C}_N$, we say $\kappa_0 \rightsquigarrow \kappa_4$ if there exist three global configurations $\kappa_1, \kappa_2, \kappa_3 \in \mathcal{C}_N$ such that $\kappa_0 \xrightarrow{\mathsf{Sched}} \kappa_1 \xrightarrow{\mathsf{Snd}} \kappa_2 \xrightarrow{\mathsf{Rcv}} \kappa_3 \xrightarrow{\mathsf{Comp}} \kappa_4$. Notice that every correct process can make at most one global internal transition in every global round transition. Moreover, round transitions allow some processes to crash only in the sub-round *Schedule*. We call these faults *clean-crashes*.

Global Stuttering Transition. In the proof of Lemma 5 presented in Section 4, we do projection. Therefore, we extend the relation $\rightsquigarrow$ with stuttering: for every configuration κ, we allow $\kappa \rightsquigarrow \kappa$.

Admissible Sequences. An infinite sequence $\pi = \kappa_0\kappa_1\ldots$ of global configurations in $\mathcal{G}_N$ is *admissible* if the following constraints hold:

1. κ_0 is the initial state, i.e. $\kappa_0 = g_N^0$, and
2. π is stuttering equivalent with an infinite sequence $\pi' = \kappa_0'\kappa_1'\ldots$ such that
$$\kappa_{4k}' \xrightarrow{\text{Sched}} \kappa_{4k+1}' \xrightarrow{\text{Snd}} \kappa_{4k+2}' \xrightarrow{\text{Rcv}} \kappa_{4k+3}' \xrightarrow{\text{Comp}} \kappa_{4k+4}' \text{ for every } k \geq 0.$$

Notice that it immediately follows by this definition that if $\pi = \kappa_0\kappa_1\ldots$ is an admissible sequence of configurations in $\mathcal{G}_N$, then $\kappa_{4k}' \rightsquigarrow \kappa_{4k+4}'$ for every $k \geq 0$. From now on, we only consider admissible sequences of global configurations.

Global Internal Transitions. In the model of [5], many processes can take a step in a global transition. We assume that a computation of the distributed system is organized in rounds, i.e.global ticks, and every round is organized as four sub-rounds called *Schedule, Send, Receive,* and *Computation.* To model that as a transition system, for every sub-round we define a corresponding transition: $\xrightarrow{\text{Sched}}$ for the sub-round *Schedule,* $\xrightarrow{\text{Snd}}$ for the sub-round *Send,* $\xrightarrow{\text{Rcv}}$ for the sub-round *Receive,* $\xrightarrow{\text{Comp}}$ for the sub-round Comp. These transitions are called global *internal* transitions. We define the semantics of these sub-rounds as follows.

1. Sub-round *Schedule.* The environment starts with a global configuration where every process is inactive, and move to another by non-deterministically deciding what processes become crashed, and what processes take a step in the current global transition. Every correct process takes a stuttering step, and every faulty process is inactive. If a process p is crashed in this sub-round, every incoming message buffer to p is set to the empty set. Formally, for $\kappa, \kappa' \in \mathcal{C}_N$, we have $\kappa \xrightarrow{\text{Sched}} \kappa'$ if the following constraints hold:
   (a) $\forall i \in 1..N : \neg active(\kappa, i)$
   (b) $\forall i \in 1..N : lstate(\kappa, i) \xrightarrow{stutter} lstate(\kappa', i) \vee lstate(\kappa, i) \xrightarrow{crash} lstate(\kappa', i)$
   (c) $\forall i \in 1..N : pc(lstate(\kappa', i)) = \ell_{crash} \Rightarrow \neg active(\kappa', i)$
   (d) $\forall s, r \in 1..N : pc(lstate(\kappa', r)) \neq \ell_{crash} \Rightarrow buf(\kappa, s, r) = buf(\kappa', s, r)$
   (e) $\forall r \in 1..N : pc(lstate(\kappa', r)) = \ell_{crash} \Rightarrow (\forall s \in 1..N : buf(\kappa', s, r) = \emptyset)$
2. Sub-round *Send.* Only processes that perform send actions can take a step in this sub-round. Such processes become inactive at the end of this sub-round. Fresh sent messages are added to corresponding message buffers. To define the semantics of the sub-round Send, we use the following predicates:

$$Enabled(\psi, i, L) \triangleq active(\kappa, i) \wedge pc(lstate(\kappa, i)) \in L$$

$$Frozen_S(\psi_1, \psi_2, i) \triangleq \wedge lstate(\kappa, i) \xrightarrow{stutter} lstate(\kappa', i)$$
$$\wedge active(\kappa, i) = active(\kappa', i)$$
$$\wedge \forall r \in 1..N : buf(\kappa, i, r) = buf(\kappa', i, r)$$

$$Sending(\psi_1, \psi_2, i, m) \triangleq \wedge \forall r \in 1..N : m \notin buf(\kappa, i, r)$$
$$\wedge \forall r \in 1..N : buf(\kappa', i, r) = \{m\} \cup buf(\kappa, i, r)$$
$$\wedge lstate(\kappa, i) \xrightarrow{csnd(m)} lstate(\kappa', i)$$

Formally, for $\kappa, \kappa' \in \mathcal{C}_N$, we have $\kappa \xrightarrow{\text{Snd}} \kappa'$ if the following constraints hold:

(a) $\forall i \in 1..N: \neg Enabled(\kappa, i, Loc_{snd}) \Leftrightarrow Frozen_S(\kappa, \kappa', i)$
(b) $\forall i \in 1..N: Enabled(\kappa, i, Loc_{snd}) \Leftrightarrow \exists m \in \texttt{Msg}: Sending(\kappa, \kappa', i, m)$
(c) $\forall i \in 1..N: Enabled(\kappa, i, Loc_{snd}) \Rightarrow \neg active(\kappa', i)$

3. Sub-round *Receive*. Only processes that perform receive actions can take a step in this sub-round. Such processes become inactive at the end of this sub-round. Delivered messages are removed from corresponding message buffers. To define the semantics of this sub-round, we use the following predicates:

$$Frozen_R(\psi_1, \psi_2, i) \triangleq \wedge \; lstate(\kappa, i) \xrightarrow{stutter} lstate(\kappa', i)$$
$$\wedge \; active(\kappa, i) = active(\kappa', i)$$
$$\wedge \forall s \in 1..N: buf(\kappa, s, i) = buf(\kappa', s, i)$$
$$Receiving(\kappa, \kappa', i, S_1, \ldots, S_N) \triangleq \wedge \forall s \in 1..N: S_s \not\subseteq buf(\kappa', s, i)$$
$$\wedge \forall s \in 1..N: buf(\kappa, s, i) \cup S_s = buf(\kappa', s, i)$$
$$\wedge \; lstate(\kappa, i) \xrightarrow{crcv(S_1,\ldots,S_N)} lstate(\kappa', i)$$

Formally, for $\kappa, \kappa' \in \mathcal{C}_N$, we have $\kappa \xrightarrow{Rcv} \kappa'$ if the following constraints hold:
(a) $\forall i \in 1..N: \neg Enabled(\kappa, i, Loc_{rcv}) \Leftrightarrow Frozen_R(\kappa, \kappa', i)$
(b) $\forall i \in 1..N: Enabled(\kappa, i, Loc_{rcv})$
   $\Leftrightarrow \exists S_1, \ldots, S_N \subseteq \texttt{Msg}: Receiving(\kappa, \kappa', i, S_1, \ldots, S_N)$
(c) $\forall i \in 1..N: Enabled(\kappa, i, Loc_{rcv}) \Rightarrow \neg active(\kappa', i)$

4. Sub-round *Computation*. Only processes that perform internal computation actions can take a step in this sub-round. Such processes become inactive at the end of this sub-round. Every message buffer is unchanged. Formally, for $\kappa, \kappa' \in \mathcal{C}_N$, we have $\kappa \xrightarrow{Comp} \kappa'$ if the following constraints hold:
(a) $\forall i \in 1..N: Enabled(\kappa, i, Loc_{comp}) \Leftrightarrow lstate(\kappa, i) \xrightarrow{comp} lstate(\kappa', i)$
(b) $\forall i \in 1..N: \neg Enabled(\kappa, i, Loc_{comp}) \Leftrightarrow lstate(\kappa, i) \xrightarrow{stutter} lstate(\kappa', i)$
(c) $\forall s, r \in 1..N: buf(\kappa, s, r) = buf(\kappa', s, r)$
(d) $\forall i \in 1..N: Enabled(\kappa, i, Loc_{comp}) \Rightarrow \neg active(\kappa', i)$

Remark 1. Observe that the definitions of $\kappa \xrightarrow{Snd} \kappa'$, and $\kappa \xrightarrow{Rcv} \kappa'$, and $\kappa \xrightarrow{Comp} \kappa'$ allow $\kappa = \kappa'$, that is stuttering. This captures, e.g. global transitions in [5,11] where no process sends a message.

4   Cutoff Results

Let $\mathcal{A}$ be a symmetric point–to–point algorithm. In this section, we show two cutoff results for the number of processes in the algorithm $\mathcal{A}$. With these cutoff results, one can verify the strong completeness and eventually strong accuracy of the failure detector of [5] by model checking two instances of sizes 1 and 2.

Theorem 1. *Let $\mathcal{A}$ be a symmetric point–to–point algorithm. Let $\mathcal{G}_1$ and $\mathcal{G}_N$ be instances of 2 and N processes respectively for some $N \geq 1$. Let $Path_1$ and $Path_N$ be sets of all admissible sequences of configurations in $\mathcal{G}_1$ and in $\mathcal{G}_N$, respectively. Let $\omega_{\{i\}}$ be a LTL\X formula in which every predicate takes one of the forms: $P_1(i)$ or $P_2(i, i)$ where i is an index in $1..N$. Then,*

$$\left(\forall \pi_N \in Path_N \colon \mathcal{G}_N, \pi_N \models \bigwedge_{i \in 1..N} \omega_{\{i\}}\right) \Leftrightarrow \left(\forall \pi_1 \in Path_1 \colon \mathcal{G}_1, \pi_1 \models \omega_{\{1\}}\right).$$

Theorem 2. *Let $\mathcal{A}$ be a symmetric point–to–point algorithm. Let $\mathcal{G}_2$ and $\mathcal{G}_N$ be instances of 2 and N processes respectively for some $N \geq 2$. Let $Path_2$ and $Path_N$ be sets of all admissible sequences of configurations in $\mathcal{G}_2$ and in $\mathcal{G}_N$, respectively. Let $\psi_{\{i,j\}}$ be an LTL\X formula in which every predicate takes one of the forms: $Q_1(i)$, or $Q_2(j)$, or $Q_3(i,j)$, or $Q_4(j,i)$ where i and j are different indexes in 1..N. It follows that:*

$$\left(\forall \pi_N \in Path_N \colon \mathcal{G}_N, \pi_N \models \bigwedge_{i,j \in 1..N}^{i \neq j} \psi_{\{i,j\}}\right) \Leftrightarrow \left(\forall \pi_2 \in Path_2 \colon \mathcal{G}_2, \pi_2 \models \psi_{\{1,2\}}\right).$$

Since the proof of Theorem 1 is similar to the one of Theorem 2, we focus on Theorem 2 here. Its proof is based on the symmetric characteristics in the system model and correctness properties, and on the following lemmas.

– Lemma 1 says that every transposition on a set of process indexes 1..N preserves the structure of the process template $\mathcal{U}_N$.
– Lemma 2 says that every transposition on a set of process indexes 1..N preserves the structure of the global transition system $\mathcal{G}_N$ for every $N \geq 1$.
– Lemma 5 says that $\mathcal{G}_2$ and $\mathcal{G}_N$ are trace equivalent under a set $AP_{\{1,2\}}$ of predicates that take one of the forms: $Q_1(i)$, or $Q_2(j)$, or $Q_3(i,j)$, or $Q_4(j,i)$.

In the following, we present definitions and constructions to prove these lemmas. We end this section with the proof sketch of Theorem 2.

4.1   Index Transpositions And symmetric point–to–point systems

We first recall the definition of transposition. Given a set 1..N of indexes, we call a bijection $\alpha \colon 1..N \to 1..N$ a transposition between two indexes $i, j \in 1..N$ if the following properties hold: $\alpha(i) = j$, and $\alpha(j) = i$, and $\forall k \in 1..N \colon (k \neq i \wedge k \neq j) \Rightarrow \alpha(k) = k$. We let $(i \leftrightarrow j)$ denote a transposition between two indexes i and j.

The application of a transposition to a template state is given in Definition 1. Informally, applying a transposition $\alpha = (i \leftrightarrow j)$ to a template state ρ generates a new template state by switching only the evaluation of *rcvd* and *lvar* at indexes i and j. The application of a transposition to a global configuration is provided in Definition 2. In addition to process configurations, we need to change message buffers and control components. We override notation by writing $\alpha_S(\rho)$ and $\alpha_C(\kappa)$ to refer the application of a transposition α to a state ρ and to a configuration κ, respectively. These functions α_S and α_C are named a local transposition and a global transposition, respectively.

Definition 1 (Local Transposition). *Let $\mathcal{U}_N$ be a process template with process indexes 1..N, and $\rho = (\ell, S_1, \ldots, S_N, d_1, \ldots, d_N)$ be a state in $\mathcal{U}_N$. Let $\alpha = (i \leftrightarrow j)$ be a transposition on 1..N. The application of α to ρ, denoted as $\alpha_S(\rho)$, generates a tuple $(\ell', S_1', \ldots, S_N', d_1', \ldots, d_N')$ such that*

1. *$\ell = \ell'$, and $S_i = S_j'$, and $S_j = S_i'$, and $d_i = d_j'$ and $d_j = d_i'$, and*
2. *$\forall k \in 1..N \colon (k \neq i \wedge k \neq j) \Rightarrow (S_k = S_k' \wedge d_k = d_k')$*

Definition 2 (Global Transposition). *Let $\mathcal{G}_N$ be a global system with process indexes 1..N, and κ be a configuration in $\mathcal{G}_N$. Let $\alpha = (i \leftrightarrow j)$ be a transposition on 1..N. The application of α to κ, denoted as $\alpha_C(\kappa)$, generates a configuration in $\mathcal{G}_N$ which satisfies following properties:*

1. *$\forall i \in 1..N \colon lstate(\alpha_C(\kappa), \alpha(i)) = \alpha_S(lstate(\kappa, i))$.*
2. *$\forall s, r \in 1..N \colon buf(\alpha_C(\kappa), \alpha(s), \alpha(r)) = buf(\kappa, s, r)$*
3. *$\forall i \in 1..N \colon active(\alpha_C(\kappa), \alpha(i)) = active(\kappa, i)$*

Since the content of every message in $\mathtt{Msg}$ does not have indexes of the receiver and sender, no transposition affects the messages. We define the application of a transposition to one of send, compute, crash, and stutter template transitions return the same transition. We extend the application of a transposition to a receive template transition as in Definition 3.

Definition 3 (Receive-transition Transposition). *Let $\mathcal{U}_N$ be a process template with process indexes 1..N, and $\alpha = (i \leftrightarrow j)$ be a transposition on 1..N. Let $crcv(S_1, \ldots, S_N)$ be a transition in $\mathcal{U}_N$ which refers to a task with a receive action. We let $\alpha_R(crcv(S_1, \ldots, S_N))$ denote the application of α to $crcv(S_1, \ldots, S_N)$, and this application returns a new transition $crcv(S_1', \ldots, S_N')$ in $\mathcal{U}_N$ such that:*

1. *$S_i = S_j'$, and $S_j = S_i'$, and*
2. *$\forall k \in 1..N \colon (k \neq i \wedge k \neq j) \Rightarrow (S_k = S_k' \wedge d_k = d_k')$*

We let $\alpha_U(\mathcal{U}_N)$ and $\alpha_G(\mathcal{G}_N)$ denote the application of a transposition α to a process template $\mathcal{U}_N$ and a global transition $\mathcal{G}_N$, respectively. Since these definitions are straightforward, we skip them in this paper. We prove later that $\alpha_S(\mathcal{U}_N) = \mathcal{U}_N$ and $\alpha_C(\mathcal{G}_N) = \mathcal{G}_N$ (see Lemmas 1 and 2).

Lemma 1 (Symmetric Process Template). *Let $\mathcal{U}_N = (Q_N, Tr_N, Rel_N, q_N^0)$ be a process template with indexes 1..N. Let $\alpha = (i \leftrightarrow j)$ be a transposition on 1..N, and α_S be a local transposition based on α (from Definition 1). The following properties hold:*

1. *α_S is a bijection from Q_N to itself.*
2. *The initial state is preserved under α_S, i.e. $\alpha_S(q_N^0) = q_N^0$.*
3. *Let $\rho, \rho' \in \mathcal{U}_N$ be states such that $\rho \xrightarrow{crcv(S_1, \ldots, S_N)} \rho'$ for some sets of messages $S_1, \ldots, S_N \in \mathbf{Set}(\mathtt{Msg})$. It follows $\alpha_S(\rho) \xrightarrow{\alpha_R(crcv(S_1, \ldots, S_N))} \alpha_S(\rho')$.*

4. *Let ρ, ρ' be states in $\mathcal{U}_N$, and $tr \in Tr_N$ be one of send, local computation, crash and stutter transitions such that $\rho \xrightarrow{tr} \rho'$. Then, $\alpha_S(\rho) \xrightarrow{tr} \alpha_S(\rho')$.*

Lemma 2 (Symmetric Global System). *Let $\mathcal{U}_N = (Q_N, Tr_N, Rel_N, q_N^0)$ be a process template, and $\mathcal{G}_N = (\mathcal{C}_N, T_N, R_N, g_N^0)$ be a global transition system such that the process indexes is a set $1..N$, and every process is instantiated with $\mathcal{U}_N$. Let α be a transposition on $1..N$, and α_C be a global transposition based on α (from Definition 2). The following properties hold:*

1. *α_C is a bijection from $\mathcal{C}_N$ to itself.*
2. *The initial configuration is preserved under α_C, i.e. $\alpha_C(g_N^0) = g_N^0$.*
3. *Let κ and κ' be configurations in $\mathcal{G}_N$, and $tr \in T_N$ be either a internal transition such that $\kappa \xrightarrow{tr} \kappa'$. It follows $\alpha_C(\kappa) \xrightarrow{tr} \alpha_C(\kappa')$.*
4. *Let κ and κ' be configurations in $\mathcal{G}_N$. If $\kappa \rightsquigarrow \kappa'$, then $\alpha_C(\kappa) \rightsquigarrow \alpha_C(\kappa')$.*

4.2 Trace Equivalence of $\mathcal{G}_2$ and $\mathcal{G}_N$ Under $AP_{\{1,2\}}$

Let $\mathcal{G}_2$ and $\mathcal{G}_N$ be two global transition systems whose processes follow the same symmetric point–to–point algorithm. In the following, our goal is to prove Lemma 5 that says $\mathcal{G}_2$ and $\mathcal{G}_N$ are trace equivalent under a set $AP_{\{1,2\}}$ of predicates which take one of the forms: $Q_1(1), Q_2(2), Q_3(1,2)$, or $Q_4(2,1)$. To do that, we first present two construction techniques: Construction 1 to construct a state in $\mathcal{U}_2$ from a state in $\mathcal{U}_N$, and Construction 2 to construct a global configuration in $\mathcal{G}_2$ from a given global configuration in $\mathcal{G}_N$. Then, we present two Lemmas 3 and 4. These lemmas are required in the proof of Lemma 5.

To keep the presentation simple, when the context is clear, we simply write $\mathcal{U}_N$, instead of fully $\mathcal{U}_N = (Q_N, Tr_N, Rel_N, q_N^0)$. We also write $\mathcal{G}_N$, instead of fully $\mathcal{G}_N = (\mathcal{C}_N, T_N, R_N, g_N^0)$.

Construction 1 (State Projection). *Let $\mathcal{A}$ be an arbitrary symmetric point–to–point algorithm. Let $\mathcal{U}_N$ be a process template of $\mathcal{A}$ for some $N \geq 2$, and ρ^N be a process configuration of $\mathcal{U}_N$. We construct a tuple $\rho^2 = (pc_1, rcvd_1, rcvd_2, v_1, v_2)$ based on ρ^N and a set $\{1,2\}$ of process indexes in the following way:*

1. *$pc_1 = pc(\rho^N)$.*
2. *For every $i \in \{1,2\}$, it follows $rcvd_i = rcvd(\rho^N, i)$.*
3. *For every $i \in \{1,2\}$, it follows $v_i = lvar(\rho^N, i)$.*

Construction 2 (Configuration Projection). *Let $\mathcal{A}$ be a symmetric point–to–point algorithm. Let $\mathcal{G}_2$ and $\mathcal{G}_N$ be two global transitions of two instances of $\mathcal{A}$ for some $N \geq 2$, and $\kappa^N \in \mathcal{C}_N$ be a global configuration in $\mathcal{G}_N$. We construct a tuple $\kappa^2 = (s_1, s_2, buf_1^1, buf_1^2, buf_2^1, buf_2^2, act_1, act_2)$ based on the configuration κ^N and a set $\{1,2\}$ of indexes in the following way:*

1. *For every $i \in \{1,2\}$, a component s_i is constructed from $lstate(\kappa^N, i)$ with Construction 1 and indexes $\{1,2\}$.*

2. *For every* $s, r \in \{1, 2\}$, *it follows* $buf_s^r = buf(\kappa^N, s, r)$.
3. *For every process* $i \in \{1, 2\}$, *it follows* $act_i = active(\kappa^N, i)$.

Note that a tuple ρ^2 constructed with Construction 1 is a state in $\mathcal{U}_2$, and a tuple κ^2 constructed with Construction 2 is a configuration in $\mathcal{G}_2$. We call ρ^2 (and κ^2) the *index projection* of ρ^N (and κ^N) on indexes $\{1, 2\}$. The following Lemma 3 says that Construction 2 allows us to construct an admissible sequence of global configurations in $\mathcal{G}_2$ based on a given admissible sequence in $\mathcal{G}_N$.

Lemma 3. *Let $\mathcal{A}$ be a symmetric point–to–point algorithm. Let $\mathcal{G}_2$ and $\mathcal{G}_N$ be two transition systems such that all processes in $\mathcal{G}_2$ and $\mathcal{G}_N$ follow $\mathcal{A}$, and $N \geq 2$. Let $\pi^N = \kappa_0^N \kappa_1^N \ldots$ be an admissible sequence of configurations in $\mathcal{G}_N$. Let $\pi^2 = \kappa_0^2 \kappa_1^2 \ldots$ be a sequence of configurations in $\mathcal{G}_2$ such that κ_k^2 is the index projection of κ_k^N on indexes $\{1, 2\}$ for every $k \geq 0$. Then, π^2 is admissible in $\mathcal{G}_2$.*

The proof of Lemma 3 is based on the following observations:

1. The application of Construction 1 to an initial template state of $\mathcal{U}_N$ constructs an initial template state of $\mathcal{U}_2$.
2. Construction 1 preserves the template transition relation.
3. The application of Construction 2 to an initial global configuration of $\mathcal{G}_N$ constructs an initial global configuration of $\mathcal{G}_2$.
4. Construction 2 preserves the global transition relation.

Moreover, Lemma 4 says that given an admissible sequence $\pi^2 = \kappa_0^2 \kappa_1^2 \ldots$ in $\mathcal{G}_2$, there exists an admissible sequence $\pi^N = \kappa_0^N \kappa_1^N \ldots$ in $\mathcal{G}_N$ such that κ_i^2 is the index projection of κ_i^N on indexes $\{1, 2\}$ for every $0 \leq i$.

Lemma 4. *Let $\mathcal{A}$ be an arbitrary symmetric point–to–point algorithm. Let $\mathcal{G}_2$ and $\mathcal{G}_N$ be global transition systems of $\mathcal{A}$ for some $N \geq 2$. Let $\pi^2 = \kappa_0^2 \kappa_1^2 \ldots$ be an admissible sequence of configurations in $\mathcal{G}_2$. There exists an admissible sequence $\pi^N = \kappa_0^N \kappa_1^N \ldots$ of configurations in $\mathcal{G}_N$ such that κ_i^2 is index projection of κ_i^N on indexes $\{1, 2\}$ for every $i \geq 0$.*

Lemma 5. *Let $\mathcal{A}$ be a symmetric point–to–point algorithm. Let $\mathcal{G}_2$ and $\mathcal{G}_N$ be its instances for some $N \geq 2$. Let $AP_{\{1,2\}}$ be a set of predicates that take one of the forms: $Q_1(1)$, $Q_2(2)$, $Q_3(1, 2)$ or $Q_4(2, 1)$. It follows that $\mathcal{G}_2$ and $\mathcal{G}_N$ are trace equivalent under $AP_{\{1,2\}}$.*

4.3   Cutoff Results Of symmetric point–to–point algorithms

In the following, we prove the cutoff result in Theorem 2 (see Page 10). A proof of another cutoff result in Theorem 1 is similar.

Proof sketch of Theorem 2. We have $\left(\forall \pi_N \in Path_N: \mathcal{G}_N, \pi_N \models \bigwedge_{i,j \in 1..N}^{i \neq j} \psi_{\{i,j\}}\right)$
$\Leftrightarrow \left(\bigwedge_{i,j \in 1..N}^{i \neq j}(\forall \pi_N \in Path_N: \mathcal{G}_N, \pi_N \models \psi_{\{i,j\}})\right)$. Let i and j be two process indexes in a set $1..N$ such that $i \neq j$. It follows that $\alpha^1 = (i \leftrightarrow 1)$ and $\alpha^2 = (j \leftrightarrow 2)$ are transpositions on $1..N$ (*). By Lemma 2, we have: (i) $\psi_{\{\alpha^1(i), \alpha^2(j)\}} = \psi_{\{1,2\}}$, and (ii) $\alpha^2((\alpha^1(\mathcal{G}_N))) = \alpha^2(\mathcal{G}_N) = \mathcal{G}_N$, and (iii) $\alpha^2((\alpha^1(g_N^0))) = \alpha^2(g_N^0) = g_N^0$.

Since $\psi_{\{i,j\}}$ is an LTL\X formula, $\mathbf{A}\psi_{\{i,j\}}$ is a CTL*\X formula where $\mathbf{A}$ is a path operator in CTL*\X (see [9]). By the semantics of the operator $\mathbf{A}$, it follows $\forall \pi_N \in Path_N: \mathcal{G}_N, \pi_N \models \psi_{\{i,j\}}$ if and only if $\mathcal{G}_N, g_N^0 \models \mathbf{A}\psi_{\{i,j\}}$. By point (*), it follows $\mathcal{G}_N, g_N^0 \models \mathbf{A}\psi_{\{i,j\}}$ if and only if $\mathcal{G}_N, g_N^0 \models \mathbf{A}\psi_{\{1,2\}}$. We have that $\mathcal{G}_N, g_N^0 \models \bigwedge_{i,j \in 1..N}^{i \neq j} \mathbf{A}\psi(i,j)$ if and only if $\mathcal{G}_N, g_N^0 \models \mathbf{A}\psi(1,2)$, because both i and j are arbitrary and different. By the semantics of the operator $\mathbf{A}$, we have $\mathcal{G}_N, g_N^0 \models \mathbf{A}\psi(1,2)$ if and only if $\forall \pi_N \in Path_N: \mathcal{G}_N, \pi_N \models \psi(1,2)$. It follows $\forall \pi_N \in Path_N: \mathcal{G}_N, \pi_N \models \psi(1,2)$ if and only if $\forall \pi_2 \in Path_2: \mathcal{G}_2, \pi_2 \models \psi(1,2)$ by Lemma 5. Then, Theorem 2 holds. □

5   Experiments

To demonstrate the feasibility of our approach, we specified the failure detector [5] in TLA$^+$ [22] [1]. Our specification follows the model of computation in Section 3. It is close to the pseudo-code in 1, except that these tasks are organized in a loop: task 1, task 2, and task 3. Moreover, our encoding contains the upper bounds on transmission time of messages and on the relative speeds of different processes, called Δ and Φ respectively. The user can verify our specification with different values of Δ and Φ by running model checkers TLC [28] and APALACHE [20]. Our experiments were set up in the synchronous case where $\Delta = 0$ and $\Phi = 1$. To reduce the state space, we apply abstractions to a global clock, local clocks, and received messages. Our abstractions are explained in detail in our TLA$^+$ specification.

We ran the following experiments on a laptop with a core i7-6600U CPU and 16GB DDR4. Table 1 presents the results in model checking the failure detectors [5] in the synchronous model. From the theoretical viewpoint, an instance with $N = 1$ is necessary, but we show only interesting cases with $N \geq 2$ in Table 1. (We did check an instance with $N = 1$, and there are no errors in this instance.) The strong accuracy property is the following safety property: $\mathbf{G}(\forall p, q \in 1..N: (Correct(p) \wedge Correct(q)) \Rightarrow \neg Suspected(p,q))$. The column "depth" shows the maximum execution length used by our tool as well as the maximum depth reached by TLC while running breadth-first search. For the second and forth benchmarks, we used the diameter bound that was reported by TLC, which does exhaustive state exploration. Hence, the verification results with APALACHE are complete. The abbreviation "TO" means timeout of 10 h.

---

[1] Our specification is available at https://github.com/banhday/netys20.git.

Table 1. Checking the failure detector [5] in the synchronous case

#	Property	N	Tool	Runtime	Memory	Depth
1		2	TLC	2 s	112M	36
2		2	APALACHE	1 m	1.12G	37
3	Strong accuracy	4	TLC	17 m	774 M	40
4		4	APALACHE	72 m	2.27G	41
5		6	TLC	TO	943M	2
6		6	APALACHE	TO	3M	31
7		2	TLC	2 s	140M	36
8	Eventually strong accuracy	4	TLC	20 m	683M	40
9		6	TLC	TO	839M	2
10		2	TLC	2 s	134 M	36
11	Strong completeness	4	TLC	23 m	678 M	40
12		6	TLC	TO	789M	3
13		2	TLC	20 s	192M	
14		2	APALACHE	1 m	674M	
15	Inductive invariant	3	TLC	TO	1.1G	
16		3	APALACHE	3 m	798M	
17		4	APALACHE	31 m	1.14G	

The inductive invariant is on the transition $\rightsquigarrow$, and contains type invariants, constraints on the age of in-transit messages, and constraints on when a process executes a task.

6   Conclusion

We have introduced the class of symmetric point-to-point algorithms that capture some well-known algorithms, e.g. failure detectors. The symmetric point-to-point algorithms enjoy the cutoff property. We have shown that checking properties of the form $\omega(i)$ has a cutoff of 1, and checking properties of the form $\psi(i,j)$ has a cutoff of 2 where $\omega(i)$ is an LTL\X formula whose predicates inspect only variables with a process index i, and $\psi(i,j)$ is an LTL\X formula whose predicates inspect only variables with two different process indexes $i \neq j$. We demonstrated the feasibility of our approach by specifying and model checking the failure detector by Chandra and Toueg under synchrony with two model checkers TLC and APALACHE.

We see two directions for future work. The first is to find new cutoffs for checking other properties in symmetry point-to-point algorithms. For example, given a correctness property with k universal quantifiers over process index variables, we conjecture that checking k small instances whose size is less than or equal to k is sufficient to reason about the correctness of all instances. The second is to extend our results to the model of computation under partial synchrony. This model has additional time constraints on message delay Δ and the relative process speed Φ. Algorithms under partial synchrony are parameterized by Δ and Φ. We explore techniques to deal with these parameters.

References

1. Apt, K., Kozen, D.: Limits for automatic verification of finite-state concurrent systems. IPL **15**, 307–309 (1986)
2. Bailis, P., Kingsbury, K.: The network is reliable. Queue **12**(7), 20–32 (2014)
3. Bloem, R., et al.: Decidability of parameterized verification. Syn. Lect. Dist. Comput. Theory **6**(1), 1–170 (2015)
4. Bouajjani, A., Jonsson, B., Nilsson, M., Touili, T.: Regular model checking. In: Emerson, E.A., Sistla, A.P. (eds.) CAV 2000. LNCS, vol. 1855, pp. 403–418. Springer, Heidelberg (2000). https://doi.org/10.1007/10722167_31
5. Chandra, T.D., Toueg, S.: Unreliable failure detectors for reliable distributed systems. J. ACM **43**(2), 225–267 (1996)
6. Cimatti, A., Clarke, E.M., Giunchiglia, E., Giunchiglia, F., Pistore, M., Roveri, M., Sebastiani, R., Tacchella, A.: NuSMV 2: An opensource tool for symbolic model checking. CAV. LNCS **2404**, 359–364 (2002)
7. Clarke, E., Talupur, M., Veith, H.: Proving ptolemy right: the environment abstraction framework for model checking concurrent systems. In: Ramakrishnan, C.R., Rehof, J. (eds.) TACAS 2008. LNCS, vol. 4963, pp. 33–47. Springer, Heidelberg (2008). https://doi.org/10.1007/978-3-540-78800-3_4
8. Clarke, E., Talupur, M., Touili, T., Veith, H.: Verification by network decomposition. In: Gardner, P., Yoshida, N. (eds.) CONCUR 2004. LNCS, vol. 3170, pp. 276–291. Springer, Heidelberg (2004). https://doi.org/10.1007/978-3-540-28644-8_18
9. Clarke Jr, E.M., Grumberg, O., Kroening, D., Peled, D., Veith, H.: Model checking. MIT press (2018)
10. Debrat, H., Merz, S.: Verifying fault-tolerant distributed algorithms in theheard-of model. Archive of Formal Proofs **2012** (2012)
11. Dwork, C., Lynch, N., Stockmeyer, L.: Consensus in the presence of partial synchrony. J. ACM **35**(2), 288–323 (1988)
12. Emerson, E.A., Kahlon, V.: Reducing model checking of the many to the few. In: McAllester, D. (ed.) CADE 2000. LNCS (LNAI), vol. 1831, pp. 236–254. Springer, Heidelberg (2000). https://doi.org/10.1007/10721959_19
13. Emerson, E.A., Kahlon, V.: Exact and efficient verification of parameterized cache coherence protocols. In: Geist, D., Tronci, E. (eds.) CHARME 2003. LNCS, vol. 2860, pp. 247–262. Springer, Heidelberg (2003). https://doi.org/10.1007/978-3-540-39724-3_22
14. Emerson, E.A., Kahlon, V.: Parameterized model checking of ring-based message passing systems. In: Marcinkowski, J., Tarlecki, A. (eds.) CSL 2004. LNCS, vol. 3210, pp. 325–339. Springer, Heidelberg (2004). https://doi.org/10.1007/978-3-540-30124-0_26
15. Emerson, E.A., Namjoshi, K.S.: Reasoning about rings. In: Proceedings of the 22nd ACM SIGPLAN-SIGACT symposium on Principles of programming languages. pp. 85–94 (1995)

16. Hawblitzel, C., Howell, J., Kapritsos, M., Lorch, J.R., Parno, B., Roberts, M.L., Setty, S., Zill, B.: Ironfleet: Proving safety and liveness of practical distributed systems. Commun. ACM **60**(7), 83–92 (2017)
17. Holzmann, G.J.: The model checker spin. IEEE Trans. Software Eng. **23**(5), 279–295 (1997)
18. Kaiser, A., Kroening, D., Wahl, T.: Dynamic cutoff detection in parameterized concurrent programs. In: Touili, T., Cook, B., Jackson, P. (eds.) CAV 2010. LNCS, vol. 6174, pp. 645–659. Springer, Heidelberg (2010). https://doi.org/10.1007/978-3-642-14295-6_55
19. Kingsbury, K.: Jepsen: Testing the partition tolerance of postgresql, redis, mongodb and riak, 2013
20. Konnov, I., Kukovec, J., Tran, T.H.: TLA$^+$ model checking made symbolic. Proceedings of the ACM on Programming Languages 3(OOPSLA), 1–30 (2019)
21. Kurshan, R.P., McMillan, K.: A structural induction theorem for processes. In: Proceedings of the eighth annual ACM Symposium on Principles of distributed computing. pp. 239–247 (1989)
22. Lamport, L.: Specifying systems: The TLA$^+$ language and tools for hardwareand software engineers. Addison-Wesley (2002)
23. Marić, O., Sprenger, C., Basin, D.: Cutoff bounds for consensus algorithms. In: Majumdar, R., Kunčak, V. (eds.) CAV 2017. LNCS, vol. 10427, pp. 217–237. Springer, Cham (2017). https://doi.org/10.1007/978-3-319-63390-9_12
24. Newcombe, C., Rath, T., Zhang, F., Munteanu, B., Brooker, M., Deardeuff, M.: How Amazon Web Services uses formal methods. Comm. ACM **58**(4), 66–73 (2015)
25. Pnueli, A., Ruah, S., Zuck, L.: Automatic deductive verification with invisible invariants. In: Margaria, T., Yi, W. (eds.) TACAS 2001. LNCS, vol. 2031, pp. 82–97. Springer, Heidelberg (2001). https://doi.org/10.1007/3-540-45319-9_7
26. Schiper, N., Rahli, V., Van Renesse, R., Bickford, M., Constable, R.L.: Developing correctly replicated databases using formal tools. In: 2014 44th Annual IEEE/IFIP International Conference on Dependable Systems and Networks. pp. 395–406. IEEE (2014)
27. Suzuki, I.: Proving properties of a ring of finite-state machines. Inf. Process. Lett. **28**(4), 213–214 (1988)
28. Yu, Y., Manolios, P., Lamport, L.: Model checking TLA$^+$ specifications. In: Pierre, L., Kropf, T. (eds.) CHARME 1999. LNCS, vol. 1703, pp. 54–66. Springer, Heidelberg (1999). https://doi.org/10.1007/3-540-48153-2_6

Short Papers

Stateless Distributed Ledgers

François Bonnet[1], Quentin Bramas[2(✉)], and Xavier Défago[1]

[1] School of Computing, Tokyo Institute of Technology, Tokyo, Japan
{bonnet,defago}@c.titech.ac.jp
[2] ICUBE, University of Strasbourg, CNRS, Strasbourg, France
bramas@unistra.fr

Abstract. In public distributed ledger technologies (DLTs), such as Blockchains, nodes can join and leave the network at any time. A major challenge occurs when a new node joining the network wants to retrieve the current state of the ledger. Indeed, that node may receive conflicting information from honest and Byzantine nodes, making it difficult to identify the current state.

In this paper, we are interested in protocols that are *stateless*, i.e., a new joining node should be able to retrieve the current state of the ledger just using a fixed amount of data that characterizes the ledger (such as the genesis block in Bitcoin).

We define three variants of stateless DLTs: weak, strong, and probabilistic. Then, we analyze this property for DLTs using different types of consensus.

Keywords: Distributed ledger technology · Blockchain · Consensus

1 Introduction

Distributed Ledger Technologies (DLTs) are usually partitioned depending on the type of consensus used to order incoming transactions. Here, we consider the three most used classes of technologies: Byzantine agreement, Proof of Work, and Proof of Stake.

Byzantine agreement protocols [7] are used to maintain consistent states replicated over multiple servers. It can tolerate crash or Byzantine faults, up to a number that depends on the synchrony assumption of the communications. Such protocols are executed by known servers in a fixed network environment, a setting called *permissioned*. They can easily be used by nodes to maintain a ledger of transactions. Every insertion in the ledger is the result of a consensus among participating nodes.

Blockchains based on *Proof of Work (PoW)* are the first distributed ledger technologies that work in an environment where nodes can join and leave and any node can participate to the protocol. Nodes are elected randomly proportionally to their computational power, and an elected node can append transactions to the ledger. All current PoW Blockchains, including Bitcoin, work with

This research is partly supported by Japan Science and Technology Agency (JST) OPERA Grant Number JY280149.

C. Georgiou and R. Majumdar (Eds.): NETYS 2020, LNCS 12129, pp. 349–354, 2021.
https://doi.org/10.1007/978-3-030-67087-0_22

synchronous communications, and assume correct nodes to have strictly more computational power than Byzantine nodes.

Blockchains based on *Proof of Stake (PoS)* are similar to the PoW based ones, but nodes are elected proportionally to the amount of tokens they own in the blockchain itself. In protocols based on PoS, a well-known concern is called *long-range* attacks [2], where a group of nodes create an alternative chain extending an old block. This is made possible because block generation is not computationally heavy, and if a node can extend a block at a given time, nothing prevents it from extending the same block in a different way at a later time. This attack becomes even worse when the nodes owning a majority of tokens at a previous time, do not have stake at the current time. Performing such attacks could be appealing as they have nothing to lose. This problem is known as posterior corruption [1].

Existing Proof of Stake based protocols such as SnowWhite [1], Algorand [4], Ouroboros [6], have identified such risks. The main solution proposed is to have some sort of checkpointing mechanism to avoid considering past majorities of stake holders. A variant of this attack is called stake-bleeding attacks [3]. It uses other mechanisms such as block rewards and transaction fees to allow even a past minority of stake holders to execute long-range attacks.

Contributions. In this paper we aim at defining a general model to capture the main difference between various kind of Distributed Ledger Technologies (DLTs). Our model is abstract enough to be independent of the implementation and capture only the main mechanisms of the DLTs. Then, we focus on one property that we call the *Stateless Property*. We define this property in our general DLT model and show whether existing technologies satisfies it or not. In particular the fact that Proof of Stake based DLTs are not Stateless implies the existence of the long-range attack vulnerability.

We believe that our model could be use independently to capture other properties and compare technologies in an abstract way.

2   Model

We consider that time is discrete and at each time $t \in \mathbb{N}$, $\mathcal{N}_t$ represents the set of nodes in the network. We consider that communication is instantaneous and there is a communication link between any two nodes in the network at any given time. We also assume that each node is identified, and is able to securely sign messages.

A distributed ledger is a data structure with an *"append"* function. It is maintained by a set of processing nodes. The network receives events and the nodes react to the events according to the distributed ledger protocol. Each time the ledger is updated, a new time instant begins. Formally, a DLT is characterized by its initial state I and a state transition function σ that takes a current state S_t, the events E_t, and the network $\mathcal{N}_t$ containing all the nodes that are online at least once before the next "append". Then σ returns a new state S_{t+1} when the "append" function is called at time $t + 1$. A state can be seen as a sequence of "append" and we write $S \preccurlyeq S'$ when state S is a prefix of state S', *i.e.*, S' can be obtained from S by appending data. The state S^{-k} denotes the truncated state S where the last k occurrences of "append" of S are omitted.

Given a DLT (I, σ), a sequence of $\mathcal{N} = (\mathcal{N}_t)_{t \in \mathbb{N}}$ of networks and a sequence $E = (E_t)_{t \in \mathbb{N}}$ of events, we can construct the sequence of states $States(I, \sigma, \mathcal{N}, E) = (S_t)_{t \in \mathbb{N}}$ in the following way $S_0 = I$ and $\forall t \in \mathbb{N}, S_{t+1} = \sigma(S_t, \mathcal{N}_t, E_t)$.

Stateless DLT. When a new node joins the network, it obtains the current state from the other nodes in the network. Informally, we say a DLT is stateless if a new joining node is able to deduce what is the current state of the DLT from the information received from the current network and by knowing the initial state.

At a given time t, each node $u \in \mathcal{N}_t$ has a local state $LS(u)$. For a correct node, the local state is exactly the current state S_t (communications are supposed instantaneous so all correct nodes agree on the current state at any time). For Byzantine nodes, the local state is constructed by an adversary. The set of pairs $(u, LS(u))$ for all nodes u in N_t is denoted $\mathbb{S}_t$ *i.e.*, $\mathbb{S}_t = \{(u, LS(u)) \mid u \in \mathcal{N}_t\}$.

Definition 1 (Weakly Stateless DLT). *A DLT is weakly stateless if there exists a function f such that $f(I, \mathbb{S}_t) = S_t$.*

Definition 2 (Strongly Stateless DLT). *A DLT is strongly stateless if there exists a function f such that $f(I, \mathbb{S}_t) = S_t$ and, for any subset $A \subset \mathbb{S}_t$, $f(I, A) = S_t$ or $\bot$.*

Definition 3 (Probabilistically Stateless DLT). *A DLT is probabilistically stateless if there exists a function f such that $\forall k, t, t' \in \mathbb{N}$, with $k \leq t \leq t'$, $f(I, \mathbb{S}_t)^{-k} \preccurlyeq S_{t'}$ with probability greater than $1 - O(e^{-ck})$ for some constant $c > 0$.*

3 Examples of Stateless DLTs

Byzantine Agreement Protocols. It is well-known that, in a fixed network C of known nodes where communication is synchronous, consensus is possible and can tolerate up to $\frac{(|C|-1)}{2}$ Byzantine nodes [7].

We denote by σ_{BA} the transition function of a Byzantine agreement protocol among the nodes in C. σ_{BA} represents the fact that, at time t, the nodes in $C \subset \mathcal{N}_t$ perform a Byzantine agreement to order the transactions received in E_t and update the state S_t accordingly to obtain S_{t+1}. In the Byzantine agreement protocol, we consider that the state contains the information about the set C of nodes participating in the consensus protocol.

Interestingly, when a majority of nodes in C are correct, any node u outside C can ask the nodes in C for the current state. Then, the current state is the one received by a majority of nodes in C, and is guaranteed to be correct. From this we deduce the following theorem:

Theorem 1. *For a set of nodes C and an initial state I (which contains the information of C), if $\forall t \in \mathbb{N}$, $C \subset \mathcal{N}_t$ and at most $\frac{(|C|-1)}{2}$ nodes in C are Byzantine, then the DLT (I, σ_{BA}) is strongly stateless.*

Proof. Assuming at most $\frac{(|C|-1)}{2}$ nodes are Byzantine, for any sequence $\mathcal{N}$ and E, all the correct nodes in C agree on all the state $S_t \in States(I, \sigma_{BA}, \mathcal{N}, E)$ for any $t \in \mathbb{N}$. The function f returns the local state that appears in at least $\frac{|C|+1}{2}$ pairs associated with a node in C. If no such state exists (if the set of local states is only a subset of $\mathbb{S}$), f returns $\bot$. Formally, we have
$f(I, A) = S$ if $|\{u \in C | (u, S) \in A\}| > \frac{|C|}{2}$, and $f(I, A) = \bot$ otherwise.   □

Proof of Work Blockchains. In PoW Blockchains, there are no assumptions about the nodes in the network, except that at any time t, in $\mathcal{N}_t$, the computational power of the correct nodes is strictly greater than the computational power of the Byzantine nodes. Then, the transition function σ_{PoW} applies an ordering on the transactions received in E_t (decided by some node in the network) and appends the block of transactions to state S_t resulting in S_{t+1}. In addition, from state S_t, one can compute the proof of work performed until time t, denoted $PoW(S_t)$. So $PoW(S_{t+1})$ is the sum of $PoW(S_t)$ and the proof of work corresponding to the last "append". For the initial state I, $PoW(I) = 0$.

Theorem 2. *For an initial state I, if for all t the computational power of correct nodes in $\mathcal{N}_t$ is strictly greater than the computational power of Byzantine nodes in $\mathcal{N}_t$, then the DLT (I, σ_{PoW}) is probabilistically stateless.*

Proof. Let f be the function returning the local state that maximizes the Proof of Work, $f(I, \mathbb{S}_t) = \mathbf{argmax}_S(\{PoW(S) | \exists u, (u, S) \in \mathbb{S}_t\})$. Such a local state could have been generated by an adversary. If k denotes the number of blocks we have to truncate to obtain a prefix of the correct state S_t, then the probability decreases exponentially fast when k tends to infinity. Indeed, let p_t, resp. q_t, be the computational power of the correct nodes, resp. of the adversary, at time t. By assumption, $\forall t, p_t > q_t$. Let $\lambda_t = \max_{t' \leq t}(p_{t'} q_{t'})$.
From [5] (Th.2), we deduce that, at a given time t, the probability that an adversary rewrites the last k blocks is in $O(e^{-cz})$ with $c = \log(1/(4\lambda_t)) > 0$.   □

4   Impossibility of Stateless Proof of Stake Blockchains

In PoS Blockchains, the consensus at a given time t is possible assuming the nodes owning a majority of the tokens are correct. So we can assume that the state transition function σ_{PoS} is performed by those correct nodes, owning a majority of the tokens, creating a new state S_{t+1} from state S_t and incoming events E_t. However nothing prevents the nodes in $\mathcal{N}_0$ to create an alternative state after time 0.

Theorem 3. *Even if, at each time, all the nodes owning tokens are correct, the PoS DLT is not weakly stateless.*

Proof. To simplify, assume that, at some time $t > 0$, all nodes in $\mathcal{N}_0$ are owned by the adversary. Indeed, there is no assumption on the correctness of $\mathcal{N}_0$ after time 0. Then, the adversary can simulate an execution of the DLT in a sequence of networks $\mathcal{N}'_t$ where each node in $\mathcal{N}'_t$ is owned by the adversary and such that there is a bijection m mapping any nodes in $u \in \mathcal{N}_t$ to a malicious node $m(u) \in \mathcal{N}'_t$, for all $t \in \mathbb{N}$ ($m(u) = u$ if u is already malicious). Hence, the sequences of networks $(\mathcal{N}'_t)_t$ and $(\mathcal{N}_t)_t$ differ only in the addresses that identify nodes. The adversary can execute the same DLT using the same sequence of events $(E_t)_t$ but in the malicious sequence of networks $\mathcal{N}' = (\mathcal{N}'_t)_t$, which gives a different sequence of states $States(I, \sigma_{PoS}, \mathcal{N}', E) \neq States(I, \sigma_{PoS}, \mathcal{N}, E)$.

At time t, the adversary can connect all nodes $\mathcal{N}'_t$ to the network so that the set of local states is $\mathbb{S}_t = \{(u, LS(u)) | u \in \mathcal{N}_t\} \cup \{(u, LS(u)) | u \in \mathcal{N}'_t\}$. The set is symmetric as half of the local states contain S_t and the other half contain S'_t and both states differ only in the addresses used to identify nodes.

$States(I, \sigma_{PoS}, \mathcal{N}', E)$ is a valid sequence of states if the sequence of networks was $\mathcal{N}'$ and if the adversary creates symmetrically the state S_t using the sequence of networks $\mathcal{N}_t$. A function f should answer S_t in the first case and S'_t in the second case, with exactly the same input, which is a contradiction. $\qquad\square$

One way to make the PoS DLT stateless is to assume that any set of nodes owning a majority of the token at a given time t are correct at any time $t' > t$. This is a very strong assumption as for instance, it gives the same kind of trust in the initial set of nodes as in the Byzantine agreement protocol. Indeed, if the nodes in $\mathcal{N}_0$ are still connected at time t then, they act as a trusted committee. We could even remove the proof of stake entirely and only rely on standard Byzantine agreement between nodes in $\mathcal{N}_0$. In the case where nodes in $\mathcal{N}_0$ go offline, they can select replacement nodes (using any method including election or simply one-to-one replacement), and include a signed message that define their choice in the state so that any joining node could identify the current set of trusted nodes. In future work, we plan to identify other sufficient conditions for the existence of Stateless DLTs.

References

1. Bentov, I., Pass, R., Shi, E.: Snow white: Provably secure proofs of stake. IACR Cryptology ePrint Archive **2016**, 919 (2016)
2. Deirmentzoglou, E., Papakyriakopoulos, G., Patsakis, C.: A survey on long-range attacks for proof of stake protocols. IEEE Access **7**, 28712–28725 (2019)
3. Gaži, P., Kiayias, A., Russell, A.: Stake-bleeding attacks on proof-of-stake blockchains. In: 2018 Crypto Valley Conference on Blockchain Technology (CVCBT), pp. 85–92. IEEE (2018)
4. Yossi, G., Rotem, H., Silvio, M., Georgios, V., Nickolai, Z.: Algorand: Scaling byzantine agreements for cryptocurrencies. In: Proceedings of the 26th Symposium on Operating Systems Principles, pp. 51–68 (2017)
5. Grunspan, C., Pérez-Marco, R.: Double spend races. Int. J. Theor. Appl. Finance **21**(08), 1850053 (2018)

6. Kiayias, A., Russell, A., David, B., Oliynykov, R.: Ouroboros: a provably secure proof-of-stake blockchain protocol. In: Katz, J., Shacham, H. (eds.) CRYPTO 2017. LNCS, vol. 10401, pp. 357–388. Springer, Cham (2017). https://doi.org/10.1007/978-3-319-63688-7_12
7. Michel, R.: Distributed algorithms for message-passing systems. Springer, Heidelberg (2013)

Stability Under Adversarial Injection of Dependent Tasks (Extended Abstract)

Vicent Cholvi[1]($\boxtimes$), Juan Echagüe[1], Antonio Fernández Anta[2], and Christopher Thraves Caro[3]

[1] Universitat Jaume I, Castellón de la Plana, Spain
{vcholvi,echague}@uji.es
[2] IMDEA Networks Institute, Madrid, Spain
antonio.fernandez@imdea.org
[3] Departamento de Ingeniería Matemática, Facultad de Ciencias Físicas y Matemáticas, Universidad de Concepción, Concepción, Chile
cthraves@ing-mat.udec.cl

Abstract. In this work, we consider a computational model of a distributed system formed by a set of servers in which jobs, that are continuously arriving, have to be executed. Every job is formed by a set of dependent tasks (i. e., each task may have to wait for others to be completed before it can be started), each of which has to be executed in one of the servers. The arrival and properties of jobs are assumed to be controlled by a bounded adversary, whose only restriction is that it cannot overload any server. This model is a non-trivial generalization of the Adversarial Queuing Theory model of Borodin et al. and, like that model, focuses on the stability of the system: whether the number of jobs pending to be completed is bounded at all times. We show multiple results of stability and instability for this adversarial model under different combinations of the scheduling policy used at the servers, the arrival rate, and the dependence between tasks in the jobs.

Keywords: Tasks scheduling · Task queuing · Dependent tasks · Adversarial queuing models · Stability

1 Introduction

In this work, we consider a model of jobs formed by dependent tasks that have to be executed in a set of servers. The dependencies among the tasks of a job restrict the order and time of their execution. For instance, a task q may need some information from another task p, so that the latter must complete before

---

This submission is a short paper. This work was partially funded by the Spanish grant PID2019-109805RB-I00 (ECID), the Region of Madrid EdgeData-CM program (P2018/TCS-4499), and the NSF of China grant 61520106005.

C. Georgiou and R. Majumdar (Eds.): NETYS 2020, LNCS 12129, pp. 355–360, 2021.
https://doi.org/10.1007/978-3-030-67087-0_23

q can be executed. This model embodies, for instance, the dynamics of Network Function Virtualization (NFV) systems [2,5] or Osmotic Computing (OC) [4]. In a NFV system, network services (which are job types) are specified as service chains, obtained by the concatenation of network functions. These network functions are dependent computational tasks to be executed in the NFV Infrastructure (e.g., servers distributed over the network). In an OC system, an application is divided into microservices that are distributed and deployed on an edge/cloud server infrastructure. The user requests (jobs) involve processing (tasks) in several of these microservices, as defined by an orchestrator that takes into account the dependencies between the microservices. In that line, it also encompasses a number of features of Orchestration Languages (see, for instance, [3]), which propose a way to relate concurrent tasks to each other in a controlled fashion: the invocation of tasks to achieve a goal, the synchronization between tasks, managing priorities, etc.

In our model, we consider a dynamic system in which job requests (or jobs for short) are continuously arriving. Each job contains the whole specification of its dependent tasks: the collection of tasks to be executed, the server that must execute each task, the time the execution incurs, the dependencies among tasks, etc. In our model we assume the existence of an adversary that has full control of the job requests arrivals, and the specification of their tasks. The only restriction on the adversary is that no server can be overloaded in the long run (while some burstiness in the load is allowed). In this adversarial framework, the objective is to achieve stability in the system. This means that the system is able to cope with the adversarial arrivals, maintaining the number of pending job requests in the system bounded at all times. (This usually also implies that all the job requests are eventually completed.)

The study of the quality of service that can be provided under worst-case assumptions in a given system (NFV or OC, for instance) is important in order to be able to honor Service Level Agreements (SLA). The positive results we obtain in this paper show that it is possible to guarantee a certain level of service even under pessimistic assumptions. These results can also be used to separate resource allocation and scheduling as long as the resource allocation guarantees that servers are not overloaded, since we prove that it is possible to guarantee stability in this case.

2   Model

In this section, we define the *Adversarial Job Queueing* (AJQ) model. The AJQ model is designed to analyze systems of queueing jobs. The three main components of an AJQ system $(S, P, \mathcal{A})$ are:

- a set $S = \{s_1, s_2, \ldots, s_n\}$ of n servers,
- an *adversary* $\mathcal{A}$ who injects jobs in the system, and
- a scheduling *policy* P, which is the criteria used by servers to decide which task to serve next among the tasks waiting in their queues.

The system evolves over time continuously. In each moment, the adversary may inject jobs to the system while the servers process those jobs. In each moment as well, some tasks may be waiting to be executed, others may be in process, and others may be completed. A job is considered *completed* when all its tasks are completed. When a job is completed, all its tasks disappear from the system.

Each job $\langle K, f^K \rangle$ consists of a finite set K of tasks and a function f^K that determines dependencies among the tasks. (For simplicity we will denote the job $\langle K, f^K \rangle$ by its task set K.) Let $K = \{k_1, k_2, k_3, \ldots, k_{l_K}\}$ be a job, where each k_i is a task of K. The integer l_K denotes the number of tasks of K. Each task k_i is defined by three parameters $\langle s_i^K, d_i^K, t_i^K \rangle$. The parameter $s_i^K \in S$ is the server in which k_i must be executed. The parameter $d_i^K \geq 0$ is the *activation delay* of k_i. The parameter $t_i^K > 0$ is the *processing time* of k_i, i. e., the time server s_i^K takes to execute task k_i.

Let $(S, P, \mathcal{A})$ be an AJQ system. Let $T_{max} := \max_{i,K}\{t_i^K\}$, $T_{min} := \min_{i,K}\{t_i^K\}$, $D_{min} := \min_{i,K}\{d_i^K\} \geq 0$, and $D_{max} := \max_{i,K}\{d_i^K\}$, be the maximum and minimum time required to complete a task, and minimum and maximum activation delay, respectively, among all tasks of any job injected in the system. We assume that all these quantities are bounded and do not depend on the time.

Feasibility. Let $\mathcal{P}(K)$ be the *power set* of K, i. e., the set of all subsets of K. Furthermore, let $\mathcal{P}^2(K)$ be the *second power set* of K, i. e., the set of all subsets of $\mathcal{P}(K)$. Given a job K, a *feasibility function* $f^K : K \to \mathcal{P}^2(K)$ determines which tasks of K are *feasible*, which means that they are ready to be executed, once the activation delay has passed. Let $f^K(k_i)$ be equal to $\{A_1, A_2, \ldots, A_{\ell_i}\}$. The sets A_x for $1 \leq x \leq \ell_i$ are called *feasibility sets* for k_i. Then, the task k_i is *feasible* at a time t if there exists a feasibility set A_x for k_i such that all tasks in A_x have been completed by time t. Otherwise, k_i is *blocked*, and still has to wait for some other tasks of K to complete before becoming feasible.

The activation delay d_i^k of a task k_i represents a setup cost, expressed in time, that k_i must incur once it becomes feasible and before it can start to be processed. If t is the time instant at which k_i becomes feasible, then k_i will incur its activation delay during time interval $[t, t + d_i^k]$. Hence, it cannot be executed during such interval, in which we say that task k_i is a *delayed* feasible task (or only *delayed task*). When k_i completes its activation delay at time $t + d_i^k$, it can be served, and since that moment will be referred to as an *active* feasible task, or simply *active task*. Equivalently, a feasible task is active if it has been feasible for at least d_i^k time. A job with at least one feasible (resp., active) task will be referred to as a *feasible* (resp., *active*) job.

The feasibility function provides the AJQ model with a high level of flexibility at the time of forcing the execution sequence of the tasks of a job. For instance, it allows the coexistence of AND dependencies and OR dependencies.

Doability. Let K be a job and k_i be a task of K. We say that k_i is an *initial* task of K if $\emptyset \in f^K(k_i)$. Observe that all initial tasks k_i are automatically feasible at the time the job K is injected, and they become active d_i^K time later.

We assign a *layer* $\lambda(K, i)$ to the tasks k_i of a job K as follows. All initial tasks have layer $\lambda(K, i) = 1$. For any $j > 1$, a task k_i is assigned layer $\lambda(K, i) = j$ if it is not feasible when all tasks of layers $1, ..., j - 2$ are completed, but it becomes feasible when additionally the tasks of layer $j - 1$ are completed. Let $\lambda_K \leq l_K$ denote the number of layers of job K. If a task k_i has layer $\lambda(K, i) = \ell$, then there is a feasibility set $A_x \in f^K(k_i)$ for k_i such that $A_x \subseteq \{k_j \in K : \lambda(K, j) < \ell\}$.

Observe that the above definition does not guarantee that all tasks of a job will be assigned a layer. In fact, it is not hard to create jobs that have tasks dependencies (e.g., cyclic dependencies) that prevent some tasks from being assigned a layer. This will prevent a job to complete. We want every job to be potentially completed. Therefore, we impose some restrictions over every feasibility function.

Definition 1. *Let K be a job and $f^K : K \to \mathcal{P}^2(K)$ be its feasibility function. We say that K is* doable *if every task k_i of K can be assigned a layer.*

It is worth mentioning that, deciding whether a job is doable or not as defined can be computed in polynomial time with respect to the size of the job (that takes into account the number of tasks and the size of the feasibility function). Indeed, layer 1 can be computed by checking which tasks have the empty set as a feasibility set. Then, a simple recursive algorithm computes all tasks in layer i using all the tasks in layers $1, 2, \ldots, i - 1$.

The next proposition says that the doable condition is necessary for a job to be completed, and that it is also sufficient if it is the only job injected in a system and the scheduling policy is work conserving.

Proposition 1. *Let $(S, P, \mathcal{A})$ be a system where the adversary $\mathcal{A}$ injects only one job K and P is work conserving. Then, K can be completed if and only if K is doable.*

Topologies. Let K be a job, and tasks $k_i, k_j \in K$. We say that k_i *depends* on k_j if there exists a feasibility set $A_x \in f^K(k_i)$ for k_i such that $k_j \in A_x$. The *skeleton* of a job K is the directed graph $H_K = (V, E)$, where $V(H_K) := \{k_1, k_2, \ldots, k_{l_K}\}$ and $E(H_K) := \{(k_j, k_i) : k_i \text{ depends on } k_j\}$. It is worthwhile to mention that a skeleton does not define the feasibility function of a job.

The *topology of a job* K is the directed graph obtained by mapping the skeleton of K into the set of servers, where each task k_i is mapped into its corresponding server s_i^K. Given a system $(S, P, \mathcal{A})$, the *topology of the system* is the directed graph obtained by overlapping the topology of all jobs injected by $\mathcal{A}$ in the system.

Scheduling policy. We assume that each server has an infinite buffer to store its own queue of tasks. Every active task waits in the queue of its corresponding server. In each server, a scheduling policy P specifies which task of all active tasks in its queue to serve next. We assume that scheduling policies are greedy/work conserving (i. e., a server always decides to serve if there is at least one active task in its queue). Examples of policies are *First-In-First-Out (FIFO)* which gives priority to the task that first came in the queue, or *Last-In-First-Out (LIFO)* which gives priority to the task that came last in the queue.

Adversary. We assume that there is an adversary $\mathcal{A}$ who injects *doable* jobs into the system. In order to avoid trivial overloads, the adversary is bounded in the following way. Let $N_s(I)$ be the total load injected by the adversary during time interval I in server s (i. e., $N_s(I) = \sum t_i^K$ over all jobs K injected during I and tasks k_i such that $s_i^K = s$). Then, for every server s and interval I the adversary is bounded as

$$N_s(I) \leq r|I| + b, \tag{1}$$

where $0 < r \leq 1$ is called the *injection rate*, and $b > 1$ is called the *burstiness* allowed to the adversary. Observe that (1) implies $\max_{i,K}\{t_i^K\} \leq b$, since jobs are injected instantaneously. An adversary that satisfies (1) is called a *bounded (r,b)-adversary*, or simply an *(r,b)-adversary*.

    The system formed by an (r,b)-adversary $\mathcal{A}$ injecting doable jobs in the set of servers S using the scheduling policy P is called an AJQ system $(S, P, \mathcal{A})$. The number of active tasks in the queue of server s at time t is denoted $Q_s(t)$.

Definition 2. *An AJQ system $(S, P, \mathcal{A})$ is* stable *if there exists a value M such that $Q_s(t) \leq M$ for all t and for all $s \in S$, where M may depend on the system parameters (adversary, servers, and jobs characteristics) but not on the time.*

Definition 3. *A policy P is* universally stable, *if any system $(S, P, \mathcal{A})$ is stable against any (r,b)-adversary $\mathcal{A}$ with rate $r < 1$.*

3   Our Results

Finally, we present our results. Due to lack of space, we omit the proofs. The proofs and complementary figures are shown in [1].

Theorem 1. *Let LIS (Longest-In-System) be the scheduling policy that gives priority to the task (and hence the job) that has been in the system for the longest time. Then an AJQ system $(S, LIS, \mathcal{A})$, where $\mathcal{A}$ is an (r,b)-adversary with $r < T_{min}/(T_{max} + D_{max})$, is stable.*

Theorem 2. *FIFO and LIFO are unstable for every $r > 0$.*

    These two theorems prove for AJQ systems that the scheduling policy used has an important impact on performance. In particular, they show that popular policies like *FIFO* and *LIFO* may not be the best choice. These were facts known for packet scheduling in networks, but it was not obvious they would also hold in AJQ systems. In the following theorem, we show that a feed-forward topology (i.e., a topology where there are no cycles) is a sufficient condition for stability in a system.

Theorem 3. *Let $(S, P, \mathcal{A})$ be an AJQ system with feed-forward topology. Then, for any (greedy) policy P and any (r,b)-adversary $\mathcal{A}$ with injection rate $r \leq 1$, the system $(S, P, \mathcal{A})$ is stable.*

This result has implications in the design of distributed systems. For instance, it implies that, if an order is defined among servers, and jobs order their tasks always respecting this order, then the system is stable using any scheduling policy, even at full load.

References

1. Cholvi, V., Echagüe, J., Fernández Anta, A., Caro, C.T.: System stability under adversarial injection of dependent tasks. arXiv:1910.01869v1 (2019)
2. Herrera, J.G., Botero, J.F.: Resource allocation in nfv: a comprehensive survey. IEEE Trans. Netw. Serv. Manage. **13**(3), 518–532 (2016)
3. Kitchin, D., Quark, A., Cook, W., Misra, J.: The Orc programming language. In: Lee, D., Lopes, A., Poetzsch-Heffter, A. (eds.) FMOODS/FORTE -2009. LNCS, vol. 5522, pp. 1–25. Springer, Heidelberg (2009). https://doi.org/10.1007/978-3-642-02138-1_1
4. Villari, M., Fazio, M., Dustdar, S., Rana, O., Ranjan, R.: Osmotic computing: a new paradigm for edge/cloud integration. IEEE Cloud Comput. **3**(6), 76–83 (2016)
5. Yi, B., Wang, X., Li, K., Huang, M., et al.: A comprehensive survey of network function virtualization. Comput. Netw. **133**, 212–262 (2018)

Collaborative Filtering: Comparative Study Between Matrix Factorization and Neural Network Method

Driss El Alaoui[1]([✉]), Jamal Riffi[1], Badraddine Aghoutane[2], Abdelouahed Sabri[1], Ali Yahyaouy[1], and Hamid Tairi[1]

[1] LISAC Laboratory, Department of Informatics, Faculty of Sciences Dhar El Mahraz, Sidi Mohamed Ben Abdellah University, Fez-Atlas, 1796 Fez, Morocco
El-Alaoui-Driss@hotmail.com
[2] Team of Processing and Transformation of Information, Polydisciplinary Faculty of Errachidia, Moulay Ismaïl University, Zitoune, 11201 Meknes, Morocco
http://fsdmfes.ac.ma/, http://www.fpe.umi.ac.ma/

Abstract. With the rise of the Web and technological developments, the amount of data to use or analyse has become very large. It has therefore become difficult to know what data to look for and where to find it. This problem has contributed to the establishment of recommendation systems that allow users to access relevant resources as quickly as possible according to their preferences. Collaborative Filtering (CF) is the most well-known technique for recommendation. CF technique uses the user' behaviour in form of user-item ratings, as their information source for prediction. This article presents a comparison study between two methods of collaborative filtering: the Singular Value Decomposition (which is considered as the most powerful matrix factorization technique to reduce dimensionality) and deep multilayer perceptron (is a class of feedforward artificial neural network, it can add the non-linear transformation to existing recommendation system approaches and interpret them into neural extensions). Both systems are evaluated on a dataset with metrics: recall at top k, NDCG@k.

Keywords: Recommender systems · Collaborative filtering · Model-based · Matrix factorization · Singular value decomposition · Neural networks method · Multilayer perceptron

1 Introduction

Collaborative filtering (CF) is a technique used by recommender systems, this term [1] was first coined by David Goldberg et al. [2] in 1992 to describe an email filtering system called "Tapestry". These kinds of systems utilize user interactions to filter for items of interest. We can visualize the set of interactions with a matrix, where each entry (i, j) represents the interaction between user i and item j. Collaborative systems is classified based on the way in which the collective preferences are aggregated; as Memory-based or model based approaches (Fig. 1).

© Springer Nature Switzerland AG 2021
C. Georgiou and R. Majumdar (Eds.): NETYS 2020, LNCS 12129, pp. 361–367, 2021.
https://doi.org/10.1007/978-3-030-67087-0_24

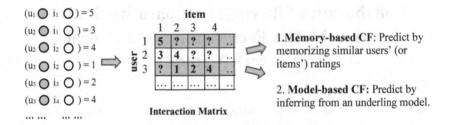

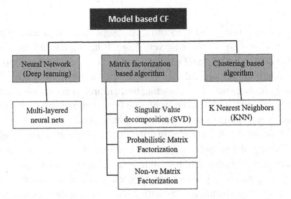

Fig. 1. Collaborative filtering (CF)

It should be noted that we have used model-based CF method to set up a collaborative filtering recommendation system. The algorithms of this method can be broken down into several sub-types [3] (Fig. 2):

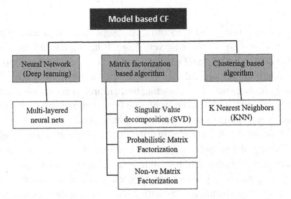

Fig. 2. Types of models based on collaborative filtering

This document is organized as follows: Sect. 2 is devoted to discuss about two methods used in collaborative filtering model-based: Singular Value decomposition (SVD) and neural collaborative filtering by deep Multilayer perceptron (MLP). Section 3 explains the evaluation metrics applied to the models. The description of the dataset used in this study, the results obtained from these experiments, their interpretations and analyses are the subject of Sect. 4. While the last section focuses on conclusions and future work.

2 Matrix Factorization vs Neural Network

2.1 Singular Value Decomposition (SVD)

The singular value decomposition [4] is a factorization of a real or complex matrix [5] that generalizes the Eigen decomposition of a square normal matrix to any m × n matrix via an extension of the polar decomposition. This technique first reduces the dimensionality of a matrix, before using the result of this process to approximate the original scores. SVD decomposes a matrix (m × n) into three matrices, U, S and V:

$$Y = U S V^T \tag{1}$$

Where U and V are m × m and n × n orthogonal matrices respectively, S is the m × n singular orthogonal matrix with non-negative elements and contains all the singular values of Y.

As the decomposition is only partial; the solution is not exact, but it would be for k = rank (Y) (i.e. we have to find k which constitutes the low rank approximation of the matrix Y). Once we have obtained $U_k \in R^{m \times k}$ and $V_k \in R^{n \times k}$ for the first k factors of the decomposition corresponding to the k largest singular values, we reconstruct the matrix Y as follows:

$$Y_k = U_k S_k V_k^T \tag{2}$$

With S_k is the k × k principle diagonal sub-matrix of S, U_k and V_k are m × k and n × k the matrices containing the singular vectors associated with the singular values of Y respectively.

Once the transformation is completed, user and items can be thought off as points in the k-dimensional space, which saves space and computing power in addition to suppressing the noise data of Y [6].

2.2 Neural Collaborative Filtering

Despite the effectiveness of matrix factorization for collaborative filtering, its performance is hindered by the simple multiplication of latent features (inner product), and that may not be sufficient to capture the complex structure of user interaction data, for this reason it is necessary to design a better interaction function for modeling the latent feature interaction between users and items. Neural Collaborative Filtering (NCF) aims to solve this through neural network architecture. It utilizes a Multi-Layer Perceptron (MLP) to learn user-item interactions. This is an upgrade over MF as MLP can (theoretically) learn any continuous function and has high level of nonlinearities (due to multiple layers) making it well-endowed to learn user-item interaction function.

We can explain this model adopted by (Xue et al. 2017) [7], which is based on MLP in this way: They use feed-forward neural networks to model a (user, item) interaction $\hat{y}_{ui}$, as shown in Fig. 3. This model consists of three layers, the bottom embedding layer, the middle hidden layers and the output prediction layer.

1) *Embedding Layer:* The goal of this layer is to transform both users and items into some shared low-dimensional latent feature space. After embedding, we acquire a dense vector representation for each user and item.
2) *Hidden Layers:* Those layers are a stack of fully connected layers built above the embedding layer. The obtained dense vectors from embedding layer are concatenated together, resulting in a dense vector jointly encoding user preference and item attribute. Then the concatenated vector is fed into the hidden layers. Hidden layers are the key to endow our model with the capacity to learn highly nonlinear interactions between latent features.

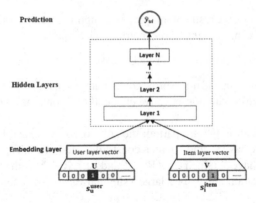

Fig. 3. Neural collaborative filtering

3) *Prediction Layer:* Or output layer, it maps previous layers' output to the prediction score $\hat{y}_{ui}$, which expresses the extent user u prefers item i. The prediction score given by this network neural can be formulated as follows:

$$\hat{y}_{ui} = f\left(U^T s_u^{user}, V^T s_i^{item} | U, V, \theta\right) \tag{3}$$

Where: $U \in R^{mxk}$ and $V \in R^{nxk}$, denoting the latent factor matrix for users and items, respectively; s_u^{user}, One-hot identifier of user u, (u = 1,...,M); s_i^{item}, One-hot identifier of item i, (i = 1,...,N), f(·): multilayer perceptron, θ: the model parameters of the interaction function f.

The function f can be formulated as:

$$f\left(U^T s_u^{user}, V^T s_i^{item}\right) = \varphi_{out}\left(\varphi_X\left(\cdots\varphi_2\left(\varphi_1\left(U^T s_u^{user}, V^T s_i^{item}\right)\right)\cdots\right)\right) \tag{4}$$

Where φ_{out} and φ_X respectively denote the mapping function for the output layer and x-th neural collaborative filtering (NCF) layer, and there are X neural CF layers in total.

3 Experiments

3.1 Evaluation Metrics

In this study, we use the recall at k where k is integer that match the number of items that we consider most relevant for a user. It must be remembered that the Recall at k [8] is the proportion of relevant items found in the top-k recommendations. Mathematically Recall@k is defined as follows:

$$Recall@k = \frac{(Recommended\ items@k\ that\ are\ relevant)}{(Total\ number\ of\ relevant\ items)} \tag{5}$$

Our recommendation system returns a result as a classified list of items; it is desirable to also take into account the order in which the returned items are presented. Normalized

Cumulative Discounted Gain (NDCG) [9] is popular method for measuring the quality of a set of search results. NDCG at position n is defined as:

$$NDCG@n = \frac{1}{IDCG} \times \sum_{i=1}^{n} \frac{2^{r_i}-1}{\log_2(i+1)} \tag{6}$$

Where r_i is the relevance rating of document at position i. IDCG is set so that the perfect ranking has a NDCG value of 1. In our problem, r_i is 1 if the document is recommended correctly.

3.2 Dataset

In this work, we used two datasets that are shared on Kaggle Datasets: Articles Sharing and Reading from CI&T Deskdrop:

The first file contains information about articles shared between the employees in an internal communications platform of a company. Each article has its sharing date (timestamp), the original url, title, content in plain text, and information about the user who shared the article (author). There are two possible event types at a given timestamp:

– CONTENT SHARED: The article was shared in the platform and is available for users.
– CONTENT REMOVED: The article was removed from the platform and not available for further recommendation. The second file contains logs of user interactions on shared articles. It can be joined to articles_shared.csv by contentId column.

The eventType values are:

– VIEW: The user has opened the article.
– LIKE: The user has liked the article.
– COMMENT CREATED: The user created a comment in the article.
– FOLLOW: The user chose to be notified on any new comment in the article.
– BOOKMARK: The user has bookmarked the article for easy return in the future.

3.3 Comparing the Methods

In our experiments, we have 1139 users processed and 3047 articles.

Through the Figure (Fig. 4): we see that the Neural Collaborative Filtering has a better performance: (recall@5 = 44% and recall@10 = 62,4%), compared to Collaborative Filtering approach by SVD: (recall@5 = 33,4% and recall@10 = 46,8%). In addition, we can see some increase in the recall value, for both models when the value of k goes from 5 to 10.

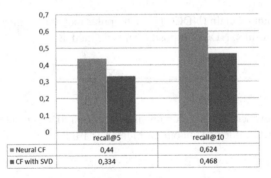

Fig. 4. Recall@k for each model

The Fig. 5 represents a graph that reveals the difference between the two models (collaborative filtering based on SVD, Neural collaborative filtering). Each point on the NDCG@k curves corresponds to the first k items that interests a user, with k ∈ [1; 80]. We note that the value of NDCG varies for the two models, depending on the value of k. Sometimes we record superiority of the SVD-based system if k < 40. Whereas if k ≥ 40 the curves intersect and the collaborative neural filtering system begins to give better results than the other model. Depending on the performance results obtained, we can deduce that Neural collaborative filtering is the most accurate system, on the other hand if we take into account the order of the relevant items returned; we find that the CF system based on SVD is the most effective when given a few ranks, but around k = 40 it levels off. Neural collaborative filtering approach gains an upper hand when provided with more ranks. However, since the users care more about recommendations at low ranks, we can say that the SVD method gives better results.

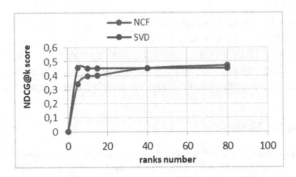

Fig. 5. NDCG@k according to the number of items

4 Conclusion and Future Work

In this paper, our goal was to make a comparative study between two types of model-based collaborative filtering approaches, both of which are considered the most powerful and the most used in the recommendation systems of this kind.

We showed that: despite the priority of the neural collaborative filtering system (NCF) in terms of recall, we can't reduce the value of a recommendation system to a good recall score, which has pushed us to measure the NDCG@k to take into account the order in the search for information and we found in this case that the model CF based on SVD generally gives better results. Finally, it should be mentioned that this field is constantly evolving and that it is impossible to conduct an exhaustive study of recommendation algorithms. The work presented here is only an overview of some existing methods in this area of recommendation and information retrieval, but this does not preclude further improvements and more testing on other algorithms and to use other deep networks like (CNN, LSTM) for sequential recommender systems, so that you can perform a more complete analysis, comprehensive and reliable study possible, to combine the algorithms giving the best results and to find a more efficient hybrid solution.

References

1. Konstan, J.A., et al.: GroupLens: applying collaborative filtering to Usenet news. Commun. ACM 40(3), 77–87 (1997)
2. Goldberg, D., Nichols, D., Oki, B.M., Terry, D.: Using collaborative filtering to weave an information tapestry. Commun. ACM 35(12), 61–70 (1992)
3. Su, X., Khoshgoftaar, T.M.: A survey of collaborative filtering techniques. Advances in Artificial Intelligence archive (2009)
4. Karypis, G., Konstan, J., Riedl, J., Sarwar, B.: Incremental singular value decomposition algorithms for highly scalable recommender systems. GroupLens Research Group (2000)
5. Koren, Y.: Matrix factorization techniques for recommender systems. IEEE Comput. Soc. 42(8), 30–37 (2009)
6. Girase, S., Mukhopadhyay, D., Bokde, D.: Role of matrix factorization model in collaborative filtering algorithm: a survey. In: IJAFRC (2014)
7. Xinyu, D., Jianbing, Z., Shujian, H., Jiajun, C., Hong-Jian, X.: Deep matrix factorization models for recommender systems. In: IJCAI, pp. 3203–3209 (2017)
8. Manning, C.D., Raghavan, P., Schütze, H.: Introduction to Information Retrieval. Cambridge university press (2008)
9. Järvelin, K., Kekäläinen, J.: Cumulated gain-based evaluation of IR techniques. ACM Trans. Inf. Syst. (TOIS) 20(4), 422–446 (2002)

Routing in Generalized Geometric Inhomogeneous Random Graphs
(Extended Abstract)

Andrés Sevilla[1]([⊠])[ID] and Antonio Fernández Anta[2][ID]

[1] Dpto. de Sistemas Informáticos, Technical University of Madrid, Madrid, Spain
andres.sevilla@upm.es
[2] IMDEA Networks Institute, Madrid, Spain
antonio.fernandez@imdea.org

Abstract. In this paper we study a new random graph model that we denote (κ, π)-KG and new greedy routing algorithms (of deterministic and probabilistic nature). The (κ, π)-KG graphs have power-law degree distribution and small-world properties. (κ, π)-KG roots on the Geometric Inhomogeneous Random Graph (GIRG) model, and hence they both preserve the properties of the hyperbolic graphs and avoid the problems of using hyperbolic cosines. In order to construct (κ, π)-KG graphs, we introduce two parameters κ and π in the process of building a (κ, π)-KG graph. With these parameters we can generate Kleinberg and power-law networks as especial cases of (κ, π)-KG. Also, we propose two new greedy routing algorithms to reduce the fail ratio and maintaining a good routing performance. The first algorithm is deterministic and the second is, in essence, a weighted random walk. We use simulation techniques to test our network model, and evaluate the new routing algorithms on the two graph models (GIRG and (κ, π)-KG). In our simulations, we evaluate the number of hops to reach a destination from a source and the routing fail ratio, and measure the impact of the parameters (κ and π) on the performance of the new routing algorithms. We observe that our graph model (κ, π)-KG is more flexible than GIRG, and the new routing algorithms have better performance than the routing algorithms previously proposed.

1 Introduction

In the latest years, geometric approaches have been used to build scale-free networks for modeling complex/large networks [1,7,9]. In particular, hyperbolic geometric models have been used to construct these networks [9]. In these models, each node is assigned a virtual coordinate in the hyperbolic space, and nodes are linked using a probability distribution based on a distance function. For instance, Boguñá et al. [1] proposed a method to embed Internet in a hyperbolic disc of radius R, where the node density grows exponentially with the distance from the disk center. The nodes are linked with a

This submission is a short paper. This work was partially funded by the Spanish grant TIN2017-88749-R (DiscoEdge), the Region of Madrid EdgeData-CM program (P2018/TCS-4499), and the NSF of China grant 61520106005.

C. Georgiou and R. Majumdar (Eds.): NETYS 2020, LNCS 12129, pp. 368–373, 2021.
https://doi.org/10.1007/978-3-030-67087-0_25

probability according to the product of their expected degrees (drawn from a power-law distribution) and re-scaled by their distance. Using this embedding, the authors claim a 97% of path success with a geographic greedy routing algorithm[1].

Graphs embedded in hyperbolic spaces are also frequently used to propose new routing algorithms. For instance, Kleinberg [8] uses the hyperbolic coordinates to implement a geographic routing algorithm for ad-hoc wireless networks with guarantee of successfully reach a destination from a source. On their hand, Cassagnes et al. [4] propose a dynamic P2P overlay embedded in a hyperbolic space in which a node computes its coordinates without global knowledge of the graph topology.

The GIRG Model. Brigmann et al. [2] proposed an alternative model of hyperbolic graphs called Geometric Inhomogeneous Random Graphs (GIRG). It is inspired in the Chung-Lu [5,6] random graphs and basically is a model for scale-free networks with an underlying geometry. The GIRG model assigns to each node a weight which is used by a probabilistic process to link the nodes.

More formally, a GIRG is a graph $G = (V, E)$ where each node $v \in V$ has an uniform random position (x_v) in a geometric space T^δ and a weight $w_v \in R^+$. The weights are drawn from a power-law distribution. The links E are also random, so that two nodes are linked with a probability that increases with the node weight (power-law factor) and decreases with the distance between nodes (Kleinberg [7] factor). Concretely, two nodes u and v are linked with probability

$$P_{uv} = \left(\frac{1}{d_{uv}}\right)^{\delta\alpha} \left(\frac{w_u w_v}{W}\right)^\alpha, \tag{1}$$

where d_{uv} is the distance between node u and v, $\alpha > 1$ is a decay parameter, δ is the dimension of the geometric space, and W is the aggregated weight of all nodes. In particular, the nodes are placed in a δ-dimensional torus $(T^\delta = R^\delta/Z^\delta)$, and as distance metric the ∞-norm on T^δ is used (the authors claim that other metrics can be used). The GIRG model avoids the use of cosines and preserves the properties of a hyperbolic random graphs.

With the graph model, Brigmann et al. [3] proposed a new greedy routing algorithm with constant probability of success, that we denote GIRG-Φ. The GIRG greedy routing algorithm [3] is used to send a message from a source node to a destination node. In addition to the position of the destination (which is part of the message), it only uses local information at the current node holding the message (i.e., the weights and coordinates of its neighbors). The routing algorithm works in rounds. In each round, an objective function Φ (Eq. 2) is evaluated to obtain the objective value for the current node and each of its neighbors. If no neighbor has larger objective value than the current node, the routing fails, and the message is dropped. Otherwise the message is sent to the neighbor with largest objective value.

The objective function proposed in [3] is

$$\Phi(v, t) = \frac{w_v}{N \cdot w_{\min} \cdot d_{ut}^\delta}, \tag{2}$$

---

[1] A geographic algorithm routes a message to the neighbor closest to the destination.

where t is the destination node, $w_{\min} = \min_{v \in V}\{w_v\}$ is the minimum weight drawn from the weight power-law distribution, N is the number of nodes of the graph, and δ is the dimension of the geometric space ($\delta = 2$ by default).

Contributions. In this paper we present a new model, denoted (κ, π)-KG, to build graphs with power-law and small-world properties, inspired on the Kleinberg [7] and GIRG [3] models. As in the former, our model uses an underlying complete torus T^δ, in which (unlike GIRG) all torus links are preserved (short links). One long link is added per node (like in Kleinberg model), using a probability expression similar GIRG's (Eq. 1). In this new probability expression, we have introduced two parameters, κ and π, in order to tune and evaluate separately the role and impact of Kleinberg and power-law factors. For example, this modification allows giving more influence to the Kleinberg (resp., power-law) factor in order to study its influence in the topology, the degree distribution, or the performance of routing algorithms.

Then, we propose greedy routing algorithms that could be used in both GIRG and (κ, π)-KG graphs. The routing algorithms proposed are inspired in GIRG's. They are fully distributed, and try to find a tradeoff between a low stretch factor (the maximum ratio between the length of the paths obtained by the routing algorithm and the distance between the source and the destination) and a small fail ratio.

The first algorithm is deterministic, guided by an objective function that has to be increased in each step until reaching the destination. The algorithm is based on GIRG's [3], but adapted so that the route never fails if the message gets close enough to the destination node. This reduces significantly the fail ratio without increasing the stretch. Additionally, we propose a second probabilistic routing algorithm. This algorithm uses the objective function as a weight for a probabilistic decision, in a similar way to a traditional random walk. This algorithm never fails, and shows by simulation route lengths very close to the lengths obtained with the deterministic routing algorithm.

2 (κ, π)-KG Model

In the (κ, π)-KG model, the nodes of a graph $G = (V, E)$ are those of a complete torus T^δ, as Kleinberg [7] used in his model. For simplicity, we assume $\delta = 2$ in the rest of the presentation. Hence, each node $u \in V$ has a pair of coordinates (x_u, y_u) and four local neighbors[2], so that there is always a route for all pair of nodes (which is not guaranteed in GIRG). The weight $w_u \geq 0$ of a node $u \in V$ is drawn from a power-law probability distribution with parameter $\beta \in (2, 3)$, with maximum and minimum weights w_{max} and $w_{min} > 0$, respectively. Then, each node $u \in V$ chooses an extra neighbor $v \neq u$ independently with probability

$$P_{uv} = \left(\frac{1}{d_{uv}}\right)^{\delta\kappa} \left(\frac{w_v}{W}\right)^\pi. \tag{3}$$

As can be observed, this probability has two factors (as in Eq. 1): the Kleinberg factor is a function of the distance d_{uv} between nodes[3], while the power-law factor

---

[2] All links are considered bidirectional.

[3] The distance can be Euclidean, Manhattan, or based on the $\infty - norm$.

depends on the node weights (w_u and w_v). (κ, π)-KG introduces the parameters $\pi \geq 0$ and $\kappa \geq 0$ in the probability expression (3) in order to modulate the two factors independently. Given different values to these parameters it is possible to build networks with different properties and test on them the behavior of greedy routing algorithms.

3 Routing Algorithms

We present in this section two routing algorithms for GIRG and (κ, π)-KG graphs.

Deterministic Routing. We propose first a new greedy routing algorithm denoted τ-Det, where τ is a parameter of the algorithm. τ-Det works as GIRGS's greedy routing with a new objective function

$$\Phi_1(u,t) = w_u/d_{ut}^k, \qquad (4)$$

where $k = \tau \ln(w_{\max}/w_{\min})$ and $d_{ut} \in \mathbb{N}$ is the distance from u to the destination t. Function Φ_1 uses the parameter τ (via k) to ensure greedy routing success. It makes sure a message reaches the destination when it is at a distance no higher than a threshold τ, as the following lemma shows.

Lemma 1 *Let $u, t \in V$ be nodes such that $d_{ut} \leq \tau$, then for any $v \in V$ such that $d_{vt} < d_{ut}$ it holds that $\Phi_1(v,t) > \Phi_1(u,t)$.*

Proof. We want to prove that $\Phi_1(v,t) = w_v/d_{vt}^k > \Phi_1(u,t) = w_u/d_{ut}^k$. In the extreme case, $w_v = w_{\min}$ and $w_u = w_{\max}$. Hence, it is enough to prove that $w_{\min}/w_{\max} > (d_{vt}/d_{ut})^k$. We have that $d_{vt} \leq d_{ut} - 1$, $d_{ut} \leq \tau$, and $\frac{x-1}{x}$ is strictly increasing for $x > 0$. Hence, it is enough to prove that $w_{\min}/w_{\max} > \left(\frac{\tau-1}{\tau}\right)^k = (1 - 1/\tau)^k$. Now, since $1 - x < e^{-x}$ for $x \neq 0$, it is enough that $w_{\min}/w_{\max} \geq e^{k/\tau}$, which holds since $k = \tau \ln(w_{\max}/w_{\min})$. □

The value of k in Eq. 4 is a function of the maximum and minimum weights, and the threshold value. The successful ratio of the greedy routing increases with τ (and k), making this ratio tunable. Unfortunately, we have observe that the route length increases with τ as well.

Probabilistic Routing. We present now a second distributed routing algorithm for GIRG and (κ, π)-KG denoted τ-RW. With the new algorithm a message follows a random walk. When the message is at a node $u \in V$, the next hop is selected among its neighbors with probabilities proportional to their value of the objective function Φ_1 (Eq. 4).

In can be proven that with this new algorithm all messages eventually reach their destinations, since the graph is connected. This is the main difference with the deterministic algorithm (and GIRG's algorithm), with which the routing process can fail. We will study the route length with this new algorithm by simulation, and compare it with the route length with the deterministic algorithms. We observe that the removal of failed routing comes as a very low cost in route length.

Table 1. Comparing the best average hops and fail ratio on GIRG and (κ, π)-KG graphs using deterministic and probabilistic routing algorithms. In a table entry h/f means h hops and f fail ratio. Values in bold represent the best result of the routing algorithms.

		GIRG ($\alpha = 1.5$)	($\kappa = 1, \pi = 2$)-KG
Deterministic	Geo	12.82 / 0.00	8.92 / 0.00
	GIRG-Φ	12.03 / 0.90	**5.88** / 0.50
	τ-Det ($\tau = 1$)	**10.36** / 0.39	6.51 / 0.19
	τ-Det ($\tau = 2$)	10.71 / 0.26	7.24 / 0.16
	τ-Det ($\tau = 3$)	10.97 / 0.19	7.59 / 0.13
	τ-Det ($\tau = 4$)	11.15 / **0.13**	7.79 / **0.11**
Random Walk	Geo	131.79 / 0.00	60.32 / 0.00
	GIRG-Φ	71.68 / 0.00	17.19 / 0.00
	τ-RW ($\tau = 1$)	11.33 / 0.00	**6.68** / 0.00
	τ-RW ($\tau = 2$)	**11.02** / 0.00	7.24 / 0.00
	τ-RW ($\tau = 3$)	11.11 / 0.00	7.56 / 0.00
	τ-RW ($\tau = 4$)	11.25 / 0.00	7.77 / 0.00

4   Experimental Evaluation

We have developed a tool for creating multiple GIRG and (κ, π)-KG graphs, and simulating the routing of messages in them with the described algorithms. In all the graphs created, we have simulated the following routing algorithms.

- Deterministic algorithms: GIRG-Φ, τ-Det, and geographic.
- Probabilistic algorithms: GIRG-Φ, τ-RW, and geographic random walks[4].

We have introduced a little change in the algorithm GIRG-Φ. As describe above, in the original algorithm when the objective function (Eq. 2) reaches a local minimum, the message is dropped. In our version, geographic routing is used to continue the routing to the destination node.

Simulation Parameters. We run the simulations on graphs obtained from a 2-dimensional torus 101×101. The node weights are drawn from a power-law distribution $p(w) \sim w^{-}\beta$ with $\beta = 2.1$, $w_{min} = 1$ and $w_{max} = 10^5$. The distance threshold τ of the Φ_1 objective function will take the following value $3, 10, 30, 100$ (100 is largest distance for the Manhattan and the ∞-norm metrics, and it is larger than the Euclidean maximum distance). Note that this parameter is only relevant for the τ-Det and τ-RW routing algorithms. Each simulation includes the routing of 50.000 messages. Every message is routed from a source to a destination chosen uniformly at random.

---

[4] The next hop is chosen with probability inversely proportional to the distance to the destination.

Simulation Results. Table 1 shows the average results using Manhattan distance of the routing algorithms on GIRG (with $\alpha = 1.5$) and (κ, π)-KG (with $\kappa = 1$ and $\pi = 2$) graphs. These graphs yield the best routing algorithm results among the collection of values of α, κ and π explored (not shown due to space limit). Comparing the graphs, (κ, π)-KG presents better performance than GIRG both in hops and fail ratio. Regarding routing algorithms, while deterministic routing algorithms have the best performance in hops, they have a positive fail ratio. Among them, the algorithm τ-Det outperforms the other deterministic algorithms, both in hops and fail ratio (excluding Geo). Probabilistic algorithms never fail at the cost of longer routes. However, the τ-Det and τ-RW algorithms show almost identical results in number of hops.

References

1. Boguná, M., Papadopoulos, F., Krioukov, D.: Sustaining the internet with hyperbolic mapping. Nat. Commun. **1**(62), 1–8 (2010)
2. Bringmann, K., Keusch, R., Lengler, J.: Geometric inhomogeneous random graphs. Theor. Comput. Sci. **760**, 35–54 (2019)
3. Bringmann, K., Keusch, R., Lengler, J., Maus, Y., Molla, A.R.: Greedy routing and the algorithmic small-world phenomenon. In: Proceedings of the ACM Symposium on Principles of Distributed Computing, PODC 2017, New York, NY, USA, pp. 371–380. ACM (2017)
4. Cassagnes, C., Tiendrebeogo, T., Bromberg, D., Magoni, D.: Overlay addressing and routing system based on hyperbolic geometry. In: IEEE Symposium on Computers and Communications (ISCC), pp. 294–301 (2011)
5. Chung, F., Linyuan, L.: The average distances in random graphs with given expected degrees. Proc. Natl. Acad. Sci. **99**(25), 15879–15882 (2002)
6. Chung, F., Linyuan, L.: Connected components in random graphs with given expected degree sequences. Ann. Comb. **6**(2), 125–145 (2002)
7. Kleinberg, J.M.: Navigation in a small world. Nature **406**(6798), 845 (2000)
8. Kleinberg, R.: Geographic routing using hyperbolic space. In: IEEE INFOCOM 2007–26th IEEE International Conference on Computer Communications, pp. 1902–1909 (2007)
9. Krioukov, D., Papadopoulos, F., Kitsak, M., Vahdat, A., Boguñá, M.: Hyperbolic geometry of complex networks. Phys. Rev. E **82**, 036106 (2010)

Author Index

Printed in the United States
By Bookmasters